Handbook of Research on Computational Intelligence Applications in Bioinformatics

Sujata Dash
North Orissa University, India

Bidyadhar Subudhi
National Institute of Technology, India

A volume in the Advances in Bioinformatics and
Biomedical Engineering (ABBE) Book Series
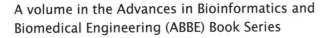

Medical Information Science
REFERENCE
An Imprint of IGI Global

Published in the United States of America by
   Medical Information Science Reference (an imprint of IGI Global)
   701 E. Chocolate Avenue
   Hershey PA, USA 17033
   Tel: 717-533-8845
   Fax: 717-533-8661
   E-mail: cust@igi-global.com
   Web site: http://www.igi-global.com

                 Library of Congress Cataloging-in-Publication Data

Names: Dash, Sujata, 1969- editor. | Subudhi, Bidyadhar, 1963- editor.
Title: Handbook of research on computational intelligence applications in
   bioinformatics / Sujata Dash and Bidyadhar Subudhi, editors.
Description: Hershey, PA : Medical Information Science Reference, 2016. |
   Includes bibliographical references and index.
Identifiers: LCCN 2016010985| ISBN 9781522504276 (hardcover) | ISBN
   9781522504283 (ebook)
Subjects: LCSH: Bioinformatics. | Computational biology--Research.
Classification: LCC QH324.2 H35763 2016 | DDC 570.285--dc23 LC record available at https://lccn.loc.gov/2016010985

This book is published in the IGI Global book series Advances in Bioinformatics and Biomedical Engineering (ABBE) (ISSN: 2327-7033; eISSN: 2327-7041)

British Cataloguing in Publication Data
A Cataloguing in Publication record for this book is available from the British Library.

For electronic access to this publication, please contact: eresources@igi-global.com.

Advances in Bioinformatics and Biomedical Engineering (ABBE) Book Series

Ahmad Taher Azar
Benha University, Egypt

ISSN: 2327-7033
EISSN: 2327-7041

MISSION

The fields of biology and medicine are constantly changing as research evolves and novel engineering applications and methods of data analysis are developed. Continued research in the areas of bioinformatics and biomedical engineering is essential to continuing to advance the available knowledge and tools available to medical and healthcare professionals.

The **Advances in Bioinformatics and Biomedical Engineering (ABBE) Book Series** publishes research on all areas of bioinformatics and bioengineering including the development and testing of new computational methods, the management and analysis of biological data, and the implementation of novel engineering applications in all areas of medicine and biology. Through showcasing the latest in bioinformatics and biomedical engineering research, ABBE aims to be an essential resource for healthcare and medical professionals.

COVERAGE

- Biomedical Sensors
- Drug Design
- Biomechanical Engineering
- Prosthetic Limbs
- Nucleic Acids
- DNA Structure
- Biostatistics
- Robotics and Medicine
- DNA Sequencing
- Chemical Structures

IGI Global is currently accepting manuscripts for publication within this series. To submit a proposal for a volume in this series, please contact our Acquisition Editors at Acquisitions@igi-global.com or visit: http://www.igi-global.com/publish/.

Titles in this Series

For a list of additional titles in this series, please visit: www.igi-global.com

Applying Business Intelligence to Clinical and Healthcare Organizations
José Machado (University of Minho, Portugal) and António Abelha (University of Minho, Portugal)
Medical Information Science Reference • copyright 2016 • 347pp • H/C (ISBN: 9781466698826) • US $165.00 (our price)

Biomedical Image Analysis and Mining Techniques for Improved Health Outcomes
Wahiba Ben Abdessalem Karâa (Taif University, Saudi Arabia & RIADI-GDL Laboratory, ENSI, Tunisia) and Nilanjan Dey (Department of Information Technology, Techno India College of Technology, Kolkata, India)
Medical Information Science Reference • copyright 2016 • 414pp • H/C (ISBN: 9781466688117) • US $225.00 (our price)

Big Data Analytics in Bioinformatics and Healthcare
Baoying Wang (Waynesburg University, USA) Ruowang Li (Pennsylvania State University, USA) and William Perrizo (North Dakota State University, USA)
Medical Information Science Reference • copyright 2015 • 528pp • H/C (ISBN: 9781466666115) • US $255.00 (our price)

Emerging Theory and Practice in Neuroprosthetics
Ganesh R. Naik (University of Technology Sydney (UTS), Australia) and Yina Guo (Taiyuan University of Science and Technology, China)
Medical Information Science Reference • copyright 2014 • 377pp • H/C (ISBN: 9781466660946) • US $265.00 (our price)

Technological Advancements in Biomedicine for Healthcare Applications
Jinglong Wu (Okayama University, Japan)
Medical Information Science Reference • copyright 2013 • 382pp • H/C (ISBN: 9781466621961) • US $245.00 (our price)

Biomedical Engineering and Cognitive Neuroscience for Healthcare Interdisciplinary Applications
Jinglong Wu (Okayama University, Japan)
Medical Information Science Reference • copyright 2013 • 472pp • H/C (ISBN: 9781466621138) • US $245.00 (our price)

Pharmacoinformatics and Drug Discovery Technologies Theories and Applications
Tagelsir Mohamed Gasmelseid (King Faisal University, Kingdom of Saudi Arabia)
Medical Information Science Reference • copyright 2012 • 442pp • H/C (ISBN: 9781466603097) • US $245.00 (our price)

www.igi-global.com

701 E. Chocolate Ave., Hershey, PA 17033
Order online at www.igi-global.com or call 717-533-8845 x100
To place a standing order for titles released in this series, contact: cust@igi-global.com
Mon-Fri 8:00 am - 5:00 pm (est) or fax 24 hours a day 717-533-8661

Dash Nilamadhab, *C V Raman College of Engineering, India*
Thukral Nitin, *Delhi Technological University, India*
Acarya D. P., *VIT University, India*
Mondal Sankar Prasad, *National Institute of Technology, India*
Mishra Rachita, *C V Raman College of Engineering, India*
R. Rathipriya, *Periyar University, India*
Khalid Raza, *Jamia Millia Islamia Central University, India*
Priyadarshini Rojalina, *C V Raman College of Engineering, India*
Mahanty Rupa, *Tata Consultancy Services, Australia*
Behera H. S., *VSSUT, India*
Mohanty Sachidananda, *KIIT, India*
P. Selvakumar, *National Institute of Technology, India*
P. Sivashanmugam, *National institute of Technology, India*
Rai Sneha, *Netaji Subhas Institute of Technology, India*
Bhatnagar Sonika, *Netaji Subhas Institute of Technology, India*
T. R. Sooraj, *VIT University, India*
Padhy Sudarshan, *Institute of Mathematics, India*
Ekka Sushmita, *National Institute of Technology, India*
Hasija Yasha, *Delhi Technological University, India*

Table of Contents

Section 1
Big Data Mining and Pattern Discovery

Section 2
Computational Intelligence in Bioinformatics

Section 3
Nature-Inspired Computing for Analysis of DNA and Protein Microarray Data

Detailed Table of Contents

Section 1
Big Data Mining and Pattern Discovery

Section 1 embodies four chapters which primarily focus on the data-mining techniques to deal with enormous amount of data. Methods to address the problem inherent to micro-array datasets i.e., curse of dimensionality are presented in this section. Advance feature selection and classification techniques to handle high dimensional data are also discussed. Spatial data-mining and its challenges are also addressed here. Different knowledge representation techniques and an extensive review of use of artificial intelligence in pattern mining are presented in this section.

We live in an ocean of data. Big Data is characterized by vast amounts of data sized in the order of petabytes or even exabytes. Though Big Data has great potential, Big data by itself has no value unless one can derive meaningful results from it. That is where Artificial Intelligence pitches in. Artificial Intelligence's most common application is about finding patterns in enormous quantities of data. The confluence of Big Data and Artificial Intelligence allows companies to automate and improve complex descriptive, predictive and prescriptive analytical tasks. In other words, Big Data can offer great insights with the help of Artificial Intelligence (AI). Artificial Intelligence can act as a catalyst to derive tangible value from Big data and serve as key to unlocking Big data. This review article focuses on applications of artificial intelligence to Big Data, its Limitations and issues.

Efficient classification and feature extraction techniques pave an effective way for diagnosing cancers from microarray datasets. It has been observed that the conventional classification techniques have major limitations in discriminating the genes accurately. However, such kind of problems can be addressed by an ensemble technique to a great extent. In this paper, a hybrid RotBagg ensemble framework has been proposed to address the problem specified above. This technique is an integration of Rotation Forest and Bagging ensemble which in turn preserves the basic characteristics of ensemble architecture i.e., diversity and accuracy. Three different feature selection techniques are employed to select subsets of genes to improve the effectiveness and generalization of the RotBagg ensemble. The efficiency is validated through five microarray datasets and also compared with the results of base learners. The experimental results show that the correlation based FRFR with PCA-based RotBagg ensemble form a highly efficient classification model.

Anuradha Jagadeesan, VIT University, India
Prathik A, VIT University, India
Tripathy B K, VIT University, India

With tremendous development in the field of science and technology, there is vast amount of data which are used in analytics for decision making. Considering its spatial characteristics for mining will enhance the accuracy of decision. So, obtaining knowledge from spatial data becomes very essential and meaningful. The spatial database contains very numerous amounts of spatial and non-spatial data of different forms. Interpretation and analyzing of vast data is far beyond human ability. In order to acquire knowledge on such scenario we need spatial data mining. The challenges involved in spatial mining are to deal with different objects that represent the spatial characteristics. This makes spatial data mining a dominant research field. This chapter briefs about the characteristics of spatial data mining and the methods of spatial data mining in recent years.

Atta ur Rahman, Barani Institute of Information Technology, Pakistan

Knowledge Representation (KR) is an emerging field of research in AI and Data Mining. Knowledge represented in an effective way guarantees a good retrieval. In this regard, a number of effective approaches have been proposed in the literature and Semantic Networks (SN) are one of them. In SN knowledge is represented in the form of directed graph, where concepts and relationships are appeared at vertices and edges respectively. 'is a' is one of the most frequently used relationship in SN. 'is a' expresses the exact relationship between any pair of objects. But there exists a huge amount of knowledge that cannot be represented by just 'is a', like the knowledge where approximations are involved. To overcome this issue, fuzzy semantic networks (FSN) are proposed in this chapter. In FSN 'is a' is replaced by a fuzzy membership function 'μ' having value between [0,1]. So the relationship between a pair of concepts can be expressed as a certain degree of membership. This chapter focuses on applications of FSN and its significance over the traditional SN.

Section 2
Computational Intelligence in Bioinformatics

This section explains the development various intelligent computational models for predicting complex biological problems. A complex novel hybrid model using radial basis function neural network and multi-objective algorithm based classifier is introduced to predict protein structural class. This section proposes the use of rough sets in conjunction with techniques like Fuzzy sets and Granular (Neighborhood Approximation) computing for the classic problem of data representation, dimensionality reduction, generation and harvest of minimal rules. The challenges faced by conventional computing methods in dealing with real world problems by natural systems are also addressed here. An efficient Rough set theory model to capture uncertainty in data and the processing of data using rough set techniques is discussed. The last chapter presents some general ideas for the time line of different uncertainty models to handle uncertain information and their applications in the various fields of biology.

Chapter 5

Protein folding has played a vital role in rational drug design, pharmacology and many other applications. The knowledge of protein structural class provides useful information towards the determination of protein structure. The exponential growth of newly discovered protein sequences by different scientific communities has made a large gap between the number of sequence-known and the number of structure-known proteins. Accurate determination of protein structural class using a suitable computational method has been a challenging problem in protein science. This chapter is based on the concept of Chou's pseudo amino acid composition feature representation method. Thus the sample of a protein is represented by a set of discrete components which incorporate both the sequence order and the length effect. On the basis of such a statistical framework a low complexity functional link artificial neural network and a complex novel hybrid model using radial basis function neural network and multi-objective algorithm based classifier are introduced to predict protein structural class.

Chapter 6

Modern epidemiological studies involve understanding individual and social level inferences and their role in the transmission and distribution of disease instances. The geographic relevance in epidemiology has been analysed in concurrence with these inferences. The substantial amount of data involved in an epidemiological study is usually very large and intuitively involves missing values and uncertainty. Rough Set Theory (RST) has been used in medical informatics for 'outcome prediction' and 'feature selection'. It can be used to construct the decision system involving spatial, medical and demographic data effectively. This chapter proposes the use of rough sets in conjunction with parallel techniques like Fuzzy sets, Intuitionistic systems and Granular (Neighborhood Approximation) computing for the classic problem of data representation, dimensionality reduction, generation and harvest of minimal rules. RST handles missing values and uncertainty more specific to spatial and medical features of data.

Chapter 7

Conventional computing methods face challenges dealing with real world problems, which are characterised by noisy or incomplete data. To find solutions for such problems, natural systems have evolved over the years and on analysis it has been found these contain many simple elements when working together to solve real life complex problems. Swarm Intelligence (SI) is one of the techniques which is inspired by nature and is a population based algorithm motivated by the collective behaviour of a group of social insects. Particle swarm optimization (PSO) is one of the techniques belonging to this group, used to solve some optimization problems. This chapter will discuss some of the problems existing in computational biology, their contemporary solution methods followed by the use of PSO to address those problems. Along with this several applications of PSO are discussed in few of the relevant fields are discussed having some future research directions on this field.

Chapter 8

Modeling intelligent system in the field of medical diagnosis is still a challenging work. Intelligent systems in medical diagnosis can be utilized as a supporting tool to the medical practitioner, mainly country like India with vast rural areas and absolute shortage of physicians. Intelligent systems in the field of medical diagnosis can also able to reduce cost and problems for the diagnosis like dynamic perturbations, shortage of physicians, etc. An intelligent system may be considered as an information system that provides answer to queries relating to the information stored in the Knowledge Base (KB), which is a repository of human knowledge. Rough set theory is an efficient model to capture uncertainty in data and the processing of data using rough set techniques is easy and convincing. Rule generation is an inherent component in rough set analysis. So, medical systems which have uncertainty inherent can be handled in a better way using rough sets and its variants. The objective of this chapter is to discuss on several such applications of rough set theory in medical diagnosis.

Chapter 9

This chapter provides the information related to the researches enhanced using uncertainty models in life sciences and biomedical Informatics. The main emphasis of this chapter is to present the general ideas for the time line of different uncertainty models to handle uncertain information and their applications in the various fields of biology. There are many mathematical models to handle vague data and uncertain information such as theory of probability, fuzzy set theory, rough set theory, soft set theory. Literatures from the life sciences and bioinformatics have been reviewed and provided the different experimental & theoretical results to understand the applications of uncertain models in the field of bioinformatics.

Section 3
Nature-Inspired Computing for Analysis of DNA and Protein Microarray Data

In this section many nature inspired computing algorithms are discussed for analyzing and predicting protein and micro-array data. Five chapters are included in this section. Various computational approaches for predicting protein-protein interactions are discussed. Many nature inspired algorithms are discussed in this section to analyze micro-array gene expression dataset. Nature inspired algorithms like PSO K-Means clustering and bi-clustering approaches are discussed to extract the motif information from protein microarray data. Protein microarray data is mainly used to identify the interactions and activities of proteins with other molecules, and to determine their function for a system at normal state and stressed state. This section also classifies individuals that differ in their susceptibility to a particular disease or response to a particular treatment into subpopulations based on individual's unique genetic and clinical information along with environmental factors.

Chapter 10

Sneha Rai, Netaji Subhas Institute of Technology, India
Sonika Bhatnagar, Netaji Subhas Institute of Technology, India

The key signaling pathways in cellular processes involve protein-protein interactions (PPIs). A perturbation in the balance of PPIs occurs in various pathophysiological processes. There are a large numbers of experimental methods for detection of PPIs. However, experimental PPI determination is time consuming, expensive, error prone and does not effectively cover transient interactions. Therefore, overlaying and integration of predictive methods with experimental results provides statistical robustness and biological significance to the PPI data. In this chapter, the authors describe PPIs in terms of types, importance, and biological consequences. This chapter also provides a comprehensive description on various computational approaches for PPI prediction. Prediction of PPI can be done through: 1) Genomic information based methods 2) Structure based methods 3) Network topology based methods: 4) Literature and data mining based methods 5) Machine learning methods. For ease of use and convenience, a summary of various databases and software for PPI prediction has been provided.

Chapter 11

Khalid Raza, Jamia Millia Islamia, India

Microarray is one of the essential technologies used by the biologists to measure genome-wide expression levels of genes in a particular organism under some particular conditions or stimuli. As microarrays technologies have become more prevalent, the challenges of analyzing these data for getting better insight about biological processes have essentially increased. Due to availability of artificial intelligence based sophisticated computational techniques, such as artificial neural networks, fuzzy logic, genetic algorithms, and many other nature-inspired algorithms, it is possible to analyse microarray gene expression data in a better way. In this chapter, we present artificial intelligence based techniques for the analysis of microarray gene expression data. Further, challenges in the field and future work direction have also been suggested.

Chapter 12

Gowri Rajasekaran, Periyar University, India
Rathipriya R, Periyar University, India

Nowadays there are many people affected by the genetic disorder, hereditary diseases, etc. The protein complexes and their functions are detected, in order to find the irregularity in the gene expression. In a group of related proteins, there exist some conserved sequence patterns (motifs) either functionally or structurally similar. The main objective of this work is to find the motif information from the given protein sequence dataset. The functionalities of the proteins are ideally found from their motif information. Clustering approach is a main data mining technique. Besides the clustering approach, the biclustering is also used in many Bioinformatics related research works. The PSO K-Means clustering and biclustering approach is proposed in this work to extract the motif information. The Motif is extracted based on the structure homogeneity of the protein sequence. In this work, the clusters and biclusters are compared based on homogeneity and motif information extracted. This study shows that biclustering approach yields better result than the clustering approach.

Chapter 13

    P. Sivashanmugam, National Institute of Technology, India
    Arun C., National Institute of Technology, India
    Selvakumar P., National Institute of Technology, India

The physical and biological activity of any organisms is mainly depended on the genetic information which stored in DNA. A process at which a gene gives rise to a phenotype is called as gene expression. Analysis of gene expression can be used to interpret the changes that occur at biological level of a stressed cell or tissue. Hybridization technology helps to study the gene expression of multiple cell at a same time. Among them microarray technology is a high- throughput technology to study the gene expression at transcription level (DNA) or translation level (Protein). Analysis the protein only can predict the accurate changes that happens in a tissue, when they are infected by a disease causing organisms. Protein microarray mainly used to identify the interactions and activities of proteins with other molecules, and to determine their function for a system at normal state and stressed state. The scope of this chapter is to outline a detail description on the fabrication, types, data analysis, and application of protein microarray technology towards gene expression profiling.

Chapter 14

    Navneet Kaur Soni, Delhi Technological University, India
    Nitin Thukral, Delhi Technological University, India
    Yasha Hasija, Delhi Technological University, India

Personalized medicine is a model that aims at customizing healthcare and tailoring medicine according to an individual`s genetic makeup. It classifies individuals that differ in their susceptibility to a particular disease or response to a particular treatment into subpopulations based on individual's unique genetic and clinical information along with environmental factors. The completion of Human Genome Project and the advent of high-throughput genome analysis tools has helped in building and strengthening this model. There lies a huge potential in the implementation of personalized medicine to significantly improve the clinical outcomes; however, its implementation into clinical practice remains slow and is a matter of concern. This chapter aims at acquainting readers with the underlying concepts and components of personalized medicine supplemented with some disease-based case studies, discussing challenges and recent advancements in the implementation of the model of personalized medicine.

Section 4
Bio-Inspired Algorithms and Engineering Applications

This section gives in-depth information about bio-inspired algorithms and its application in finding optimized solutions for engineering problems. Different evolutionary computing techniques are discussed to identify complex systems effectively in engineering applications. A popular technique like Bacteria Foraging Algorithm is quite faster in optimization such that there is reduction in the computational burden and also minimal use of computer resource utilization is discussed. Solution of some Differential Equation in Fuzzy Environment by Extension Principle method and its application in Biomathematics problems are explained here. Last chapter discusses application of computational intelligence techniques in wireless sensor networks on the coverage problem in general and area coverage in particular.

Chapter 15

In this chapter, we describe an important class of engineering problem called system identification which is an essential requirement for obtaining models of system of concern that would be necessary for controlling, analyzing the systems. The system identification problem is essentially to pick up the best model out of the several candidate models. Thus, the problem of system identification or modeling building turns out to be an optimization problem. The chapter explain what are different evolutionary computing techniques used in the past and the state- of the art technologies on evolutionary computation. Then, some case studies have been included how the system identification of a number of complex systems effectively achieved by employing these evolutionary computing techniques.

Chapter 16

This chapter presents an analysis on operation of Automatic Load Frequency Control (ALFC) by developing models in SIMULINK which helps us to understand the principle behind ALFC including the challenges. The three area system is being taken into account considering several important parameters of ALFC like integral controller gains (KIi), governor speed regulation parameters (Ri), and frequency bias parameters (Bi), which are being optimized by using Bacteria Foraging Optimization Algorithm (BFOA). Simultaneous optimization of certain parameters like KIi, Ri and Bi has been done which provides not only the best dynamic response for the system but also allows us to use much higher values of Ri than used in practice. This will help the power industries for easier and cheaper realization of the governor. The performance of BFOA is also investigated through the convergence characteristics which reveal that that the Bacteria Foraging Algorithm is quite faster in optimization such that there is reduction in the computational burden and also minimal use of computer resource utilization.

Chapter 17

Sankar Prasad Mondal, National Institute of Technology, India

The concept of fuzzy differential equations is very important for new developments of model in various fields of science and engineering problems in uncertain environments because this theory represent a natural way to modeling dynamical system under uncertain environment. In this way we can modeled mathematical biology problem associated with differential equation in fuzzy environment and solved them. In this chapter we solve two mathematical biology models which are taken in fuzzy environment. A one species prey predator model is considered with fuzzy initial data. Whereas an insect population model are described with fuzzy initial value. The solution procedures of the fuzzy differential equation are taken as extension principle method.

Chapter 18

Subhendu Kumar Pani, Biju Patnaik University of Technology, India

A wireless sensor network may contain hundreds or even tens of thousands of inexpensive sensor devices that can communicate with their neighbors within a limited radio range. By relaying information on each other, they transmit signals to a command post anywhere within the network. Worldwide market for wireless sensor networks is rapidly growing due to a huge variety of applications it offers. In this chapter, we discuss application of computational intelligence techniques in wireless sensor networks on the coverage problem in general and area coverage in particular. After providing different types of coverage encountered in WSN, we present a possible classification of coverage algorithms. Then we dwell on area coverage which is widely studied due to its importance. We provide a survey of literature on area coverage and give an account of its state-of-the art and research directions.

Preface

Computational Intelligence has been an active area of research from which a great potential has emerged over the past decade. There are numerous successful applications of Computational Intelligence in various subfields of biology, including bioinformatics, computational genomics, protein structure prediction, biochemical pathways, microarray data analysis and neuronal systems modeling and analysis. However, there are several open problems in biology which require advanced and efficient computational methodologies. The major issue is the voluminous data that constitute the above mentioned problems that can be reduced and analyzed with the help of automated tools. There is lots of information hidden inside this voluminous data so it is essential for a new generation of computational theories and tools to assist humans in extracting knowledge from big data. Unfortunately, researchers in the field of biology are often unaware of the abundance of computational techniques that they can be used to analyze and understand the data underlying their research interest/inquiries. On the other hand, computational intelligence or big data practitioners are often unfamiliar with the particular problems that their new, state-of-the-art algorithms can be applied to.

Computational intelligence is an established paradigm, where new theories with an adequate biological understanding have been evolving. Current experimental systems have many characteristics of biological computers and are being built to perform a variety of tasks that are difficult or impossible to do with conventional computers. Computational intelligence methods are now being applied to problems in bioinformatics and big data analytics. This area is highly heterogeneous with a combination of technologies such as neural networks, fuzzy systems, rough sets, evolutionary computing, swarm intelligence, probabilistic reasoning, multi agent systems etc. The recent trend is to integrate different components to take advantage of complimentary features and to develop a synergistic system. Bioinformatics involves the creation and advancement of algorithms using techniques including computational intelligence, applied mathematics, statistics, biochemistry and informatics to solve biological problems at molecular level.

The transformation of data into usable knowledge is by no means an easy task even for high-performance large-scale data processing, including exploiting parallelism of current and upcoming computer architectures for data mining. Moreover, this data may involve uncertainty in many different forms. Many different models, like fuzzy sets, rough sets, soft sets, neural networks, their generalizations and hybrid models obtained by combining two or more of these models have been found to be fruitful in representing data. These models are also quite useful for analysis. More often than not, big data are reduced to include only the important characteristics necessary from a particular study point of view or depending upon the application area. So, reduction techniques have been developed. Often the collected data have missing values. These values need to be generated or the tuples with missing values are eliminated from the data set before analysis. More importantly, these new challenges may compromise; sometimes even deteriorate the performance, efficiency and scalability of the dedicated data intensive computing systems. The later approach sometimes leads to loss of information and hence is not preferred. This brings up many research issues in biomedical and healthcare research community in the form of capturing and accessing data effectively. In addition, fast processing while achieving high performance and high throughput, and storing it efficiently for future use is another issue.

Bioinformatics, computational intelligence, knowledge discovery in databases, cloud computing, parallel and distributed computing, network security, data mining, knowledge representation are the fields that have evolved into an importance and active area of research because of theoretical challenges associated with the problems of discovering intelligent solutions for voluminous data/ Big data.

The bioinformatics fields are in a stage of new breakthroughs in dealing with dramatically increased information in terms of number, size and complexity. A new term "Big Data" is used to refer to such large and often diverse, complex, longitudinal and distributed datasets. Big data is usually too large and complex to be processed using traditional data processing applications. It is not so much that the data cannot be processed using traditional tools, but it cannot be processed in reasonable time without newer and faster processing tools. There is and will continue to be an increasing amount of research in this area. As (Shah N. H., 2012) stated, "Data centric approaches that compute on massive amounts of data often referred "Big Data", to discover patterns and to make clinically relevant predictions will gain adoption. Major research efforts in the field include sequence alignment, gene finding, genome assembly, protein structure alignment, protein structure prediction, prediction of gene expression and protein-protein interactions, and the modeling of evolution. Hence, in other words, bioinformatics can be described as the application of computational methods to make biological discoveries (Baldi, P., Brunak, S., 1998). The ultimate goal of the field is to develop new insights into the science of life as well as creating a global perspective, from which the unifying principles of biology can be derived (Baldi, P., Brunak, S., 1998). There are at least 26 billion base pairs (bp) representing the various genomes available on the server of the National Center for Biotechnology Information (NCBI) (Ezziane, Z., 2006). Besides the human genome with about 3 billion bp, many other species have their complete genome available there. Cohen (2004) explained the needs of biologists to utilize and help interpret the vast amounts of data that are constantly being gathered in genomic research. He also pointed out the basic concepts in molecular cell biology, and outlined the nature of the existing data, and illustrated the algorithms needed to understand cell behavior.

Bioinformatics and computational biology are concerned with the use of computation to understand biological phenomena and to acquire and exploit biological data, increasingly large-scale data. Methods from bioinformatics and computational biology are increasingly used to augment or leverage traditional laboratory and observation-based biology. This transformation from a data-poor to a data-rich field began with DNA sequence data, but is now occurring in many other areas of biology (Cohen, 2004). Computational intelligence methods are now being applied to problems in molecular biology and bioinformatics (Baldi, P., Brunak, S., 1998). To name a few, (Tasoulis et al., 2008) present an application of neural networks, evolutionary algorithms, and clustering algorithms to DNA microarray experimental data analysis; Liang and Kelemen (2008) propose a time lagged recurrent neural network with trajectory learning for identifying and classifying gene functional patterns from the heterogeneous nonlinear time series microarray experiments. In a nutshell, which becomes quite apparent in light of the current research pursuits, the area is heterogeneous with a combination of such technologies as neural networks, fuzzy systems, evolutionary computation, swarm intelligence, and probabilistic reasoning. The recent trend is to integrate different components to take advantage of complementary features and to develop a synergistic system. Hybrid architectures like neuro-fuzzy systems, evolutionary-fuzzy systems, evolutionary neural networks, evolutionary neuro-fuzzy systems, rough-neural, rough-fuzzy, etc. are widely applied for real world problem solving.

COMPUTATIONAL INTELLIGENCE TECHNIQUES

Progress in machine learning technology provided various advanced tools for predictions of complex biological problems. Among the many machine learning approaches, artificial neural networks, fuzzy sets, particle swarm optimization, genetic algorithms, and rough sets are the most recently applied computational intelligent tools in the structure prediction.

Artificial Neural Networks: Artificial neural networks have been developed as generalizations of mathematical models of biological nervous systems. In a simplified mathematical model of the neuron, synapses are represented by connection weights that modulate the effect of the associated input signals, and the nonlinear characteristic exhibited by neurons is represented by a transfer function. The neuron impulse is computed as the weighted sum of the input signals, transformed by the transfer function (Bishop, C.M., 1995). The learning capability of an artificial neuron is achieved by adjusting the weights in accordance to the chosen learning algorithm. The basic architecture consists of three types of neuron layers: input, hidden, and output layers. In feed-forward networks the signal flow is from input to output units strictly in a feed-forward direction. The data processing can extend over multiple (layers of) units, but no feedback connections are present, that is, connections extending from outputs of units to inputs of units in the same layer or previous layers. Recurrent networks contain feedback connections. Contrary to feed-forward networks, the dynamical properties of such networks are important.

There are several other neural network architectures (Elman network, adaptive resonance theory maps, competitive networks etc.) depending on the properties and requirement of the application. The learning of the network may be classified into three distinct types. These are supervised learning, unsupervised learning, and reinforcement learning. In supervised learning, an input vector is presented at the input layer together with a set of desired responses, one for each node, at the output layer. A forward pass is done and the errors or discrepancies, between the desired and actual response for each node in the output layer, are found. These are then used to determine weight changes in the network according to the prevailing learning rule. The best-known examples of this technique occur in the back-propagation algorithm, the delta rule, and perceptron rule. In unsupervised learning (or self-organization) an output unit is trained to respond to clusters of patterns within the input. In this paradigm the system is supposed to discover statistically salient features of the input population. Reinforcement learning is learning what to do–how to map situations to actions–so as to maximize a numerical reward signal. These two characteristics, trial-and-error search and delayed reward are the two most important distinguishing features of reinforcement learning.

Rough Sets: Rough set theory is a methodology fairly new to the medical domain capable of dealing with uncertainty in data. It is used to discover data dependencies, evaluate the importance of attributes, discover the patterns of data, reduce redundant objects and attributes, seek the minimum subset of attributes, recognize and classify objects. Moreover, it is being used for extraction of rules from databases. Rough sets have proven useful for representation of vague regions in spatial data. One advantage of rough sets is the creation of readable if-then rules. Such rules have a potential to reveal new patterns in the data material. Furthermore, they also collectively function as a classifier for unseen data. Unlike other computational intelligence techniques, rough set analysis requires no external parameters and uses only the information presented in the given data.

In rough sets theory, the data is collected in a table, called decision table. Rows of the decision table correspond to objects, and columns correspond to attributes. In the data set, we assume that class labels to indicate the class to which each example belongs are given. We call the class label the decision attribute and the rest of the attributes the condition attributes. Rough sets theory defines three regions based on the equivalent classes induced by the attribute values Lower approximation, upper approximation, and the boundary. Lower approximation contains all the objects which are classified surely based on the data collected, and upper approximation contains all the objects which can be classified probably, while the boundary is the difference between the upper approximation and the lower approximation (Pawlak, Z., Grzymala-Busse, J., Slowinski, R., Ziarko, W., 1995). An indiscernibility relation partitions the set of cases or objects into a number of equivalence classes. An equivalence class of a particular object is simply the collection of objects that are indiscernible to the object in question (Pawlak, Z., 1982, 1991).

Fuzzy Logic (FL) and Fuzzy Sets (FS): (Zadeh, L.A., 1965) introduced the concept of fuzzy logic to present vagueness in linguistics, and further implement and express human knowledge and inference capability in a natural way. Fuzzy logic starts with the concept of a fuzzy set. An FS set is a set without a crisp, clearly defined boundary. It can contain elements with only a partial degree of membership. A Membership Function (MF) is a curve that defines how each point in the input space is mapped to a membership value (or degree of membership) between 0 and 1. The input space is sometimes referred to as the universe of discourse. Let X be the universe of discourse and x be a generic element of X. A classical set A is defined as a collection of elements or objects $x \in X$, such that each x can either belong to or not belong to the set A, $A \subseteq X$. By defining a characteristic function (or membership function) on each element x in X, a classical set A can be represented by a set of ordered pairs (x, 0) or (x, 1), where 1 indicates membership and 0 non-membership. Unlike conventional set mentioned above, fuzzy set expresses the degree to which an element belongs to a set. Hence the characteristic function of a fuzzy set is allowed to have value between 0 and 1, denoting the degree of membership of an element in a given set.

Evolutionary Algorithms: Evolutionary Algorithms are adaptive methods, which may be used to solve search and optimization problems, based on the genetic processes of biological organisms. Over many generations, natural populations evolve according to the principles of natural selection and "survival of the fittest," first clearly stated by Charles Darwin in The Origin of Species. By mimicking this process, evolutionary algorithms are able to 'evolve' solutions to real world problems, if they have been suitably encoded. Usually grouped under the term Evolutionary Algorithms (EA) or Evolutionary Computation (EC), we find the domains of genetic algorithms, evolution strategies, evolutionary programming, genetic programming, and learning classifier systems (Goldberg, D.E., 1989). They all share a common conceptual base of simulating the evolution of individual structures via processes of selection, mutation, and reproduction. The processes depend on the perceived performance of the individual structures as defined by the environment.

Particle Swarm Optimization: Swarm intelligence (Kennedy, J. et al., 2001) is a collective behavior of intelligent agents in decentralized systems. Although there is typically no centralized control dictating the behavior of the agents, local interactions among them often cause a global pattern to emerge. Most of the basic ideas are derived from real swarms in the nature including ant colonies, bird flocking, honeybees, bacteria and microorganisms, etc. Ant Colony Optimization (ACO), have already been applied successfully to solve several engineering optimization problems. Swarm models are population based and the population is initialized with a set of potential solutions. These individuals are then manipulated (optimized) over much iteration using several heuristics inspired from the social behavior of insects in an effort to find the optimal solution. The concept of particle swarms, although initially introduced for simulating human social behaviors, has become very popular these days as an efficient search and optimization technique.

The objective of this volume is to disseminate inspiring research results and exemplary computational tools of data mining approaches to cross disciplinary researchers and practitioners from bioinformatics, data mining disciplines, the life sciences and healthcare domains. The book will cover fundamentals of data mining techniques designed to tackle data analysis challenges mentioned above, applications of computational intelligent tools to find optimal generalized solutions for biological problems, and demonstrate with real applications how bio-inspired algorithms can enable biologists, engineers and healthcare scientists to make insightful observations and invaluable discoveries from their data.

ORGANIZATION OF THE BOOK

This book is organized into 4 major parts, covering the following topics: Data Mining and Pattern Discovery (Section 1), Computational Intelligence in Bioinformatics (Section 2), Nature-inspired computing for analysis of DNA and Protein Microarray Data (Section 3), and Bio-Inspired Algorithms and Engineering Applications (Section 4).

Section 1: Data Mining and Pattern Discovery

Chapter 1, entitled "Unleashing Artificial Intelligence onto Big Data - A Review", discusses mining of vast amounts of data in the order of petabytes or even exabytes using artificial intelligent tools, deriving meaningful results. Application of artificial intelligence for finding patterns in enormous quantities of data and confluence of Big Data and Artificial Intelligence allows companies to automate and improve complex descriptive, predictive and prescriptive analytical tasks. This review article focuses on applications of artificial intelligence to Big Data, its Limitations and issues. Chapter 2, entitled "Hybrid Ensemble Learning Methods for Classification of Microarray Data", addresses the major problems of discrimination of potential genes from microarray datasets using hybrid ensemble framework. In this chapter, a hybrid RotBagg ensemble framework has been proposed to address the problem specified above. This technique is an integration of Rotation Forest and Bagging ensemble which in turn preserves the basic characteristics of ensemble architecture i.e., diversity and accuracy. Three different feature selection techniques are employed to select subsets of genes to improve the effectiveness and generalization of the RotBagg ensemble. Chapter 3, entitled "Recent trends in spatial data mining and its challenges", discusses spatial data mining to analyze the spatial characteristics of vast amount of data used in analytics for decision making. Understanding of spatial characteristics of data will enhance the accuracy of decision. The spatial database contains numerous amounts of spatial and non-spatial data of different forms. Interpretation and analysis of vast data is far beyond human ability. This chapter briefs about the characteristics of spatial data mining and the methods of spatial data mining in recent years. Chapter 4, entitled "Knowledge Representation: A Semantic Network Approach", introduces semantic network approach as one of the potential knowledge representation (KR) technique which is one of the hottest areas of research in data mining, AI and big data analysis. Knowledge represented in an effective way, helps in easy traversal, search, reasoning and inference. Limitations of semantic network are also described. To overcome these limitations a modified version is proposed in this chapter that is named as Semantic Fuzzy Networks (SFN) in which the relationship between two concepts was more realistically provided by fuzzy membership function.

Section 2: Computational Intelligence in Bioinformatics

In Chapter 5, entitled "Development of Novel Multi-Objective based Model for Protein Structural Class Prediction", concept of Chou's pseudo amino acid feature representation method has been used to represent protein samples. Protein folding has played a vital role in rational drug design, pharmacology and many other applications. On the basis of a statistical framework a low complexity functional link artificial neural network and a complex novel hybrid model using radial basis function neural network and multi-objective algorithm based classifier are introduced to predict protein structural class. Chapter 6, entitled "Rough Fuzzy Set Theory and Neighborhood Approximation Based Modeling for Spatial Epidemiology", introduces modern epidemiological studies to understand individual and social level inferences and their role in the transmission and distribution of disease instances. The geographic relevance in epidemiology has been analysed in concurrence with these inferences. The substantial amount of data involved in an epidemiological study is usually very large and intuitively involves missing values and uncertainty. Rough Set Theory (RST) has been used in medical informatics for 'outcome prediction' and 'feature selection'. This chapter proposes the use of rough sets in conjunction with techniques like Fuzzy sets and Granular (Neighborhood Approximation) computing for the classic problem of data representation, dimensionality reduction, generation and harvest of minimal rules. Chapter 7, entitled "Applying CI in Biology through PSO", addresses the challenges faced by conventional computing methods in dealing with real world problems by natural systems. This chapter will discuss some of the problems existing in computational biology, their contemporary solution methods followed by the use of PSO to address those problems. Along with this several applications of PSO, some relevant fields are discussed having some future research directions on this field. Chapter 8, entitled "Application of Rough Set Based Models in Medical Diagnosis", discusses several applications of rough set theory in diagnosing medical data. An efficient Rough set theory model to capture uncertainty in data and the processing of data using rough set techniques is discussed. Rule generation is an inherent component in rough set analysis. So, medical systems which have uncertainty inherent can be handled in a better way using rough sets and its variants. In Chapter 9, entitled "Application of Uncertainty Models in Bioinformatics", information related to the researches enhanced using uncertainty models in life sciences and biomedical Informatics is discussed. The main emphasis of this paper is to present the general ideas for the time line of different uncertainty models to handle uncertain information and their applications in the various fields of biology.

Section 3: Nature-Inspired Computing for Analysis of DNA and Protein Microarray Data

In Chapter 10, entitled "Computational Methods for Prediction of Protein-Protein Interactions: PPI Prediction Methods", various computational approaches for predicting protein-protein interactions are discussed. Methods like 1) Genomic information based methods 2) Structure based methods 3) Network topology based methods: 4) Literature and data mining based methods 5) Machine learning methods are employed in this chapter to predict the PPI. For ease of use and convenience, a summary of various databases and software for PPI prediction has been provided. Chapter 11, entitled "Analysis of Microarray Data using Artificial Intelligence Based Techniques", discusses artificial intelligence based techniques for the analysis of microarray gene expression data. Artificial neural networks, fuzzy logic, genetic algorithms, and many other nature-inspired algorithms are described for this purpose. In this chapter, we present artificial intelligence based techniques for the analysis of microarray gene expression data. Further, challenges in the field and future work direction have also been suggested. Chapter 12, entitled "Extraction of Protein Sequence Motif Information using Bio-Inspired Computing" introduces PSO K-Means clustering and bi-clustering approaches to extract the motif information. The Motif is extracted based on the structure homogeneity of the protein sequence. In this work, the clusters and bi-clusters are compared based on homogeneity and motif information extracted. Chapter 13, entitled "Study of basic concepts on the development of protein microarray - gene expression profiling: Protein microarray", introduces detail description on the fabrication, types, data analysis, and application of protein microarray technology towards gene expression profiling. The physical and biological activity of any organisms is mainly depended on the genetic information which stored in DNA. A process at which a gene gives rise to a phenotype is called as gene expression. Protein microarray mainly used to identify the interactions and activities of proteins with other molecules, and to determine their function for a system at normal state and stressed state. Chapter 14, entitled "Personalized Medicine in the Era of Genomics", introduces a model that aims at customizing healthcare and tailoring medicine according to an individual`s genetic makeup. It classifies individuals that differ in their susceptibility to a particular disease or response to a particular treatment into subpopulations based on individual's unique genetic and clinical information along with environmental factors. This chapter aims at acquainting readers with the underlying concepts and components of personalized medicine supplemented with some disease-based case studies, discussing challenges and recent advancements in the implementation of the model of personalized medicine.

Section 4: Bio-Inspired Algorithms and Engineering Applications

In Chapter 15, entitled "Evolutionary Computing Approaches to System Identification", discusses an important class of engineering problem called system identification which is an essential requirement for obtaining models of system of concern that would be necessary for controlling, analyzing the systems. The chapter explain what are different evolutionary computing techniques used in the past and the state- of the art technologies on evolutionary computation. Then, some case studies have been included how the system identification of a number of complex systems effectively achieved by employing these evolutionary computing techniques. Chapter 16, entitled "BFO Optimized automatic load frequency control of a multi area power system", presents an analysis on operation of Automatic Load Frequency Control (ALFC) by developing models in SIMULINK which helps us to understand the principle behind ALFC including the challenges. The three area system is being taken into account considering several important parameters of ALFC like integral controller gains (KIi), governor speed regulation parameters (Ri), and frequency bias parameters (Bi), which are being optimized by using Bacteria Foraging Optimization Algorithm (BFOA). This will help the power industries for easier and cheaper realization of the governor. The performance of BFOA is also investigated through the convergence characteristics which reveal that that the Bacteria Foraging Algorithm is quite faster in optimization such that there is reduction in the computational burden and also minimal use of computer resource utilization. Chapter

17, entitled "Solution of some Differential Equation in Fuzzy Environment by Extension Principle method and its application in Biomathematics", solves two mathematical biological models in fuzzy environment. One species prey predator model is considered with fuzzy initial data. The solution procedures of the fuzzy differential equation are taken as extension principle method. Chapter 18, entitled "Application of Computational Intelligence Techniques in Wireless Sensor Networks: The State of the Art", discusses application of computational intelligence techniques in wireless sensor networks on the coverage problem in general and area coverage in particular. After providing different types of coverage encountered in WSN, we present a possible classification of coverage algorithms. Then we dwell on area coverage which is widely studied due to its importance.

REFERENCES

Altman, R. B., Valencia, A., Miyano, S., & Ranganathan, S. (2001). Challenges for intelligent systems in biology. *IEEE Intelligent Systems, 16*(6), 14–20. doi:10.1109/5254.972065

Baldi, P., & Brunak, S. (1998). *Bioinformatics: The Machine Learning Approach.* Cambridge: MIT Press.

Bishop, C. M. (1995). *Neural Networks for Pattern Recognition.* Oxford: Oxford University Press.

Cohen, J. (2004). Bioinformatics: An introduction for computer scientists. *ACM Computing Surveys, 36*(2), 122–158. doi:10.1145/1031120.1031122

Ezziane, Z. (2006). Applications of artificial intelligence in bioinformatics: A review. *Expert Systems with Applications, 30*(1), 2–10. doi:10.1016/j.eswa.2005.09.042

Goldberg, D. E. (1989). *Genetic Algorithms in Search, Optimization, and Machine Learning.* Reading: Addison-Wesley Publishing.

Gusfield, D. (2004). Introduction to the IEEE/ACM transactions on Computational Biology and Bioinformatics. *IEEE/ACM Transactions on Computational Biology and Bioinformatics, 1*(1), 2–3. doi:10.1109/TCBB.2004.9

Kennedy, J., Eberhart, R., & Shi, Y. (2001). *Swarm Intelligence.* San Francisco: Morgan Kaufmann Academic Press.

Liang, Y., & Kelemen, A. (2008). Time course gene expression classification with time lagged recurrent neural network. *Computational Intelligence in Bioinformatics. Studies in Computational Intelligence, 94,* 149–163. doi:10.1007/978-3-540-76803-6_5

Mitra, S., & Hayashi, Y. (2006). Bioinformatics with soft computing. *IEEE Transactions on Systems, Man and Cybernetics. Part C, Applications and Reviews, 36*(5), 616–635. doi:10.1109/TSMCC.2006.879384

Pawlak, Z. (1982). Rough sets. *Intl. J. Comp. Inform. Science, 11*(5), 341–356. doi:10.1007/BF01001956

Pawlak, Z. (1991). *Rough Sets – Theoretical Aspects of Reasoning About Data.* Dordrecht: Kluwer.

Pawlak, Z., Grzymala-Busse, J., Slowinski, R., & Ziarko, W. (1995). Rough sets. *Communications of the ACM, 38*(11), 88–95. doi:10.1145/219717.219791

Shah, N. H. (2012). Translational bioinformatics embraces big data. *Yearbook of Medical Informatics*, *7*(1), 130–134.

Tasoulis, D. K., Plagianakos, V. P., & Vrahatis, M. N. (2008). Computational intelligence algorithms and DNA microarrays. *Computational Intelligence in Bioinformatics. Studies in Computational Intelligence*, *94*, 1–31. doi:10.1007/978-3-540-76803-6_1

Zadeh, L. A. (1965). Fuzzy sets. *Information and Control*, *8*(3), 338–353. doi:10.1016/S0019-9958(65)90241-X

Acknowledgment

The editors would like to acknowledge the help of all the people involved in this project and, more specifically, to the authors and reviewers that took part in the review process. Without their support, this book would not have become a reality.

First, the editors would like to thank each one of the authors for their contributions. Our sincere gratitude goes to the chapter's authors who contributed their time and expertise to this book.

Second, the editors wish to acknowledge the valuable contributions of the reviewers regarding the improvement of quality, coherence, and content presentation of chapters. Most of the authors also served as referees; we highly appreciate their double task.

Sujata Dash
North Orissa University, India

Bidyadhar Subudhi
National Institute of Technology, India

Section 1
Big Data Mining and Pattern Discovery

Section 1 embodies four chapters which primarily focus on the data-mining techniques to deal with enormous amount of data. Methods to address the problem inherent to micro-array datasets i.e., curse of dimensionality are presented in this section. Advance feature selection and classification techniques to handle high dimensional data are also discussed. Spatial data-mining and its challenges are also addressed here. Different knowledge representation techniques and an extensive review of use of artificial intelligence in pattern mining are presented in this section.

Chapter 1
Unleashing Artificial Intelligence onto Big Data: A Review

Rupa Mahanty
Tata Consultancy Services, Australia

Prabhat Kumar Mahanti
University of New Brunswick, Canada

ABSTRACT

We live in an ocean of data. Big Data is characterized by vast amounts of data sized in the order of petabytes or even exabytes. Though Big Data has great potential, Big data by itself has no value unless one can derive meaningful results from it. That is where Artificial Intelligence pitches in. Artificial Intelligence's most common application is about finding patterns in enormous quantities of data. The confluence of Big Data and Artificial Intelligence allows companies to automate and improve complex descriptive, predictive and prescriptive analytical tasks. In other words, Big Data can offer great insights with the help of Artificial Intelligence (AI). Artificial Intelligence can act as a catalyst to derive tangible value from Big data and serve as key to unlocking Big data. This review article focuses on applications of artificial intelligence to Big Data, its Limitations and issues.

INTRODUCTION

In today's digital world, data has grown 'big' – steering in the era of the petabytes and exabytes. Big Data is characterized by astronomical amounts of data being generated continuously by interconnected systems of people, transactions, media, devices (sensors, smartphones, smart meters, cameras and tablet computers) -- click data, audio/speech data, natural language text (in multiple languages), images/video data. The growth of Big data is a result of the wide variety of data and growing channels in today's world. The internet way of things has a significant contribution in the growth of Big data. By 2015, research firm IDC predicts there will be more than 5,300 exabytes of unstructured digital consumer data stored in databases, and we expect a large share of that to be generated by social networks. Facebook ingests approximately 500 times more data each day than the New York Stock Exchange (NYSE). Twitter stores at least 12 times more data each day than the NYSE [Smith, 2014]. The challenge is to analyze the infor-

DOI: 10.4018/978-1-5225-0427-6.ch001

mation content in these vast, continuous data streams, use them for descriptive and predictive analytics in various domains and build more robust and intelligent learning systems. With big data benefitting from improved and increased storage capabilities at extremely reasonable prices - the cost of a gigabyte of storage has dropped from approximately $16 in February

2000 to less than $0.07 today [SAS, 2012], and with processing technologies specifically designed to handle huge data volumes, thinking moves away from what data/records to keep and store, to muse over the problem of how to make sense and derive logic from these increasing large volumes of data Yvonne Hofstetter, managing director of Teramark Technologies GmbH, a Germany-based provider of big data technologies and artificial intelligence for the industrial Internet states that the core of big data is the analysis of big data and the inference, which is provided by artificial intelligence (AI) and not storage or retrieval of raw data [O'Dwyer, 2014]. Big Data can offer great insights with the help of Artificial Intelligence (AI).

Artificial Intelligence deals with the study and development of software and machines that can imitate human-like intelligence and it is a branch of computer science that is extremely technical. Artificial intelligence is used in a variety of ways and can be found across a large number of industry sectors-manufacturing, life sciences and healthcare, transportation, and healthcare, finance to name a few. Some examples of its usage are in assembly line robots, advanced toys, online search engines, speech recognition systems, medical research, and marketing. Artificial Intelligence's most common application is about finding patterns in enormous quantities of data. Smaller more homogenous fixed data sets will not serve the purpose as the patterns may not be evident in them. This allows companies to automate and improve complex descriptive, predictive and prescriptive analytical tasks, which would be tremendously labor intensive and time consuming if carried out by humans beings.

The aim of this paper is to explore the opportunities of Big Data focusing on applications of artificial intelligence to Big Data problems. The paper begins with a brief overview of Big data and the characteristics of Big data followed by a sections discussing the application of Artificial Intelligence to Big data and limitations and issues of Big data and Artificial Intelligence.

BIG DATA: AN OVERVIEW

Big Data: Definition

The use of the term "big data" can be traced back to discussions of handling huge groups of datasets in both academia and industry during the 1980s [Yan, 2013]. Michael Cox and David Ellsworth were among the first to use the term big data literally, referring to using larger volumes of scientific data for visualization (the term large data also has been used) [Cox and Ellsworth, 1997].

The first formal, academic definition appears in a paper submitted in July 2000 by Francis Diebold of University of Pennsylvania in his work of econometrics and statistics (2000):

Big Data refers to the explosion in the quantity (and sometimes, quality) of available and potentially relevant data, largely the result of recent and unprecedented advancements in data recording and storage technology. In this new and exciting world, sample sizes are no longer fruitfully measured in "number of observations," but rather in, say, megabytes. Even data accruing at the rate of several gigabytes per day are not uncommon.

Wikipedia defines big data as a collection of data sets so enormous and complex that it becomes challenging to process using on-hand database management tools or traditional data processing applications [Press, 2014].

Gartner defines big data as follows:

Big data is high-volume, high-velocity and high-variety information assets that demand cost-effective, innovative forms of information processing for enhanced insight and decision making. ["Gartner IT Glossary," n. d.; Lapkin 2012]

SAS defines big data as follows:

Big data is a relative term describing a situation where the volume, velocity and variety of data surpass an organization's storage or compute capacity for accurate and timely decision making. [SAS, 2012]

Tech-America Foundation defines big data as follows:

Big data is a term that describes large volumes of high velocity, complex and variable data that require advanced techniques and technologies to enable the capture, storage, distribution, management, and analysis of the information. [Tech-America Foundation's Federal Big Data Commission, 2012]

Big Data Characteristics

IBM suggested that big data could be characterized by any or all of three "V" words to investigate situations, events, and so on: volume, variety, and velocity (Zikopoulous et al., 2013).

Perhaps it is best to think of Big Data in multidimensional terms, in which five dimensions or characteristics relate to the primary aspects of Big Data. Figure 1 depicts the characteristics, that is, five V's of Big Data.

The big data characteristics can be elaborated as follows:

1. **Volume:** This characteristic defines the quantity or magnitude or amount of data. The magnitude of available data has been rising at an increasing rate. This applies to both companies and to individuals. A text file is a few kilobytes, a sound file is a few megabytes while a full length movie is a few gigabytes. New data sources are added on nonstop basis. For companies, in the olden days- before the advent of the digitization, all data was created internally by employees. Traditionally, the data volume requirements for analytic and transactional applications were in the order of sub-terabytes [ISO/IEC 2015]. Presently, the data is spawned exponentially by employees, suppliers, partners, customers, machines, sensors, and devices. More sources of data with a larger size of data combine to increase the volume of data that has to be analyzed. This is a major issue for those looking to put that data to use instead of letting it just disappear. Peta byte data sets are common these days and exabyte is not far away. Big Data is characterized by large volumes of data generated from diverse sources. Enterprises are flooded with data, easily accruing terabytes or petabytes or even exabytes of information. One exabyte equals 1 million terabytes. Facebook's databases ingest approximately 500 terabytes of data each day [Smith, 2014]. The volume of data may approach 8 zettabytes by 2015 [Gens, 2011].

Figure 1. Big data characteristics

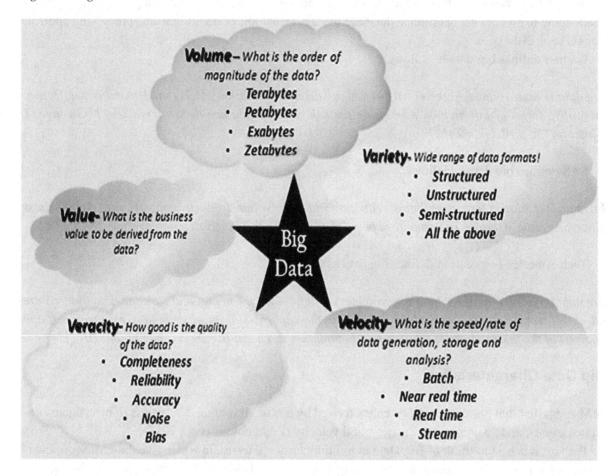

Definitions of big data volumes are relative and fluctuate by factors, such as time and the type of data. What may be considered big data today may not meet the threshold in the future because storage capacities will increase, allowing even bigger data sets to be captured and stored. In addition, the type of data, discussed under variety, delineates what is meant by 'big'. Two datasets of the same size may necessitate different data management technologies based on their type, e.g., tabular versus video data [Gandomi & Haider, 2015].

2. **Variety:** Traditionally, enterprise data implementations for analytics and transactions worked on a single structured, row-based, relational domain of data [ISO/IEC 2015]. Variety refers to the wide range of formats in which the data are being generated and or stored. Big Data extends beyond structured data to include semi-structured data and unstructured data of all varieties. Different applications, processes and systems generate and store data in varied formats. These include text, audio, video, emails, social media text messages, video, still images, graphs, click streams, log files, output from all types of machine-generated data from sensors, devices, weather satellites, set-top boxes, surveillance/CCTV cameras, traffic cameras, radio-frequency identification (RFID) readers, ATMs, smart phones, smart meters, GPS signals, DNA analysis devices, wearable devices and more. These different formats of data cannot be stored in structured relational database systems.

a. **Structured Data**: Data that is located in a fixed field within a record or file is called structured data. Structured data constitutes only 5% of all existing data [Cukier, 2010]. Structured data refers to the data which has a pre-defined data model/schema/structure and is often either relational in nature or is closely resembling a relational model. Structured data can be managed by means of the traditional tools/techniques and stored in relational databases. Structured data is often managed by means of Structured Query Language (SQL) – a programming language made for handling and querying data in relational database management systems. Structured data includes data in the relational databases, data from CRM systems, data warehouses, etc.

b. **Unstructured Data:** Unstructured data is the data that does not have a well-defined data model or does not fit well into the relational world. If the data element to be stored does not have tags (metadata about the data) and has no conventional schema, ontology, glossary, or consistent organization, it is unstructured. Unstructured data includes flat files, spreadsheets, word documents, streaming instrument data, photos, PowerPoint presentations, images, audio files, video files, feeds, PDF files, scanned documents, blog entries, etc.

c. **Semi-Structured Data**: Semi-structured data lies between unstructured and structured data. Semi-structured data do not have a defined structure like a relational database with tables and relationships does not conform to the formal structure of data models linked with relational databases. However, unlike unstructured data, semi-structured data have tags (like XML extensible markup language used for documents on the web) or other markers to isolate the elements and provide a hierarchy of records and fields, which define the data. XML, other markup languages, email, and electronic data interchange (EDI) messages are all forms of semi-structured data. In object-oriented databases, one often finds semi-structured data.

3. **Veracity:** The enormous amounts of data can lead to inconsistencies, duplication, inaccuracies, statistical errors and misinterpretation of the collected information. Pureness of the data is vital for value. Veracity relates to the accuracy, reliability/trustworthiness, applicability, noise, bias, abnormality, completeness and other quality aspects of Big data. Veracity is crucial to the value associated with or developed from the data for a particular business case, problem or application.

4. **Velocity:** Velocity refers to the speed/rate at which the data are created/generated, transmitted, stored, processed, analyzed, accessed and visualized. Initially, companies analyzed data by means of a batch process. Each batch feed contained a huge volume of data, a job runs on the server to process the batch feed and delivers the result once the job run, which may last from few minutes to few hours, is done. This works when the incoming data rate/speed is slower than the batch processing rate and when the result is useful despite the delay. With the new sources of data such as sensors, social and mobile applications, the batch process breaks down. The data is now streaming into the server in real time, in a continuous manner and the result is only beneficial if the delay is very short [Soubra, 2012]. More and more data are produced and must be collected in shorter time frames. High speed internet produces data at a very high speed, with every click of a mouse data is generated. Even conventional retailers are generating high-frequency data [Gandomi & Haider, 2015]. Wal-Mart, for instance, processes more than one million transactions per hour (Cukier, 2010). Velocity is used to refer to data-in-motion, in contract to data-in-rest. Examples of data-in-motion are stream of readings recorded from a sensor or the log history of web page visits, or messages posted on a social network (like tweets on Twitter or messages and status updates/likes/shares on Facebook) and clicks by each and every visitor to a web site. Every minute 100 hours of video are uploaded on YouTube. In addition, every minute over 200 million emails are sent, around 20 mil-

lion photos are viewed and 30,000 photos are uploaded on Flickr, almost 300,000 tweets are sent and almost 2.5 million queries on Google are performed [Holland, 2015].

Often time sensitive, Big Data must be used as it is streaming into the enterprise in order to maximize its value to the business, but it must also still be available from the archival sources as well [Ohlhorst, 2012]. For example, there are more than 250 million tweets per day [Pingdom, 2012]. Tweets lead to decisions about other Tweets, intensifying the velocity [O'Leary, 2013].

5. **Value:** Value refers to the business value to be derived from Big data. The business value of different data varies considerably. Usually, there is a mine of valuable information hidden in a larger bulk of non-traditional data; the challenge, however, is determining and isolating what is valuable and then extracting and transforming that data for analysis and decision making and /or reporting purposes. Based on Oracle's definition, big data are frequently characterized by relatively "low value density". That is, the data received in the original form generally has a low value relative to its volume. However, a high value can be obtained by analyzing large volumes of such data [Gandomi & Haider, 2015]. In other words, most big data has low value until rolled up and analyzed, at which point it becomes valuable; in addition, the availability of low-cost open-source solutions and commodity infrastructure (including cloud computing) is making systems that were previously only available to government agencies and large corporations, cost-effective for a broader market [Dumbill 2012; Mitchell & Wilson 2012].

McKinsey (2011) projected in an industry report that five new kinds of value might come from big data (McKinsey Global Institute, 2011):

1. Creating transparency in organizational activities which can be used to increase efficiency;
2. Enabling more comprehensive analysis of employee and system performance in ways that allow experiments and feedback;
3. Segmenting populations in order to customize actions;
4. Replacing/supporting human decision making with automated algorithms;
5. Innovating new business models, products, and services.

A data environment can become extreme [SAS, 2012] along any of the dimensions/characteristics or with a combination of two or more of them at the same time. Also, the relativity of big data volumes discussed formerly applies to all dimensions. Thus, universal benchmarks do not exist for volume, variety, and velocity that describe big data. The defining limits are influenced by the size, sector, and location of the firm and these limits evolve over time [Gandomi & Haider, 2015].

Also, the dimensions are not independent of one another. As one dimension changes, the probability increases that another dimension will also change as a result. However, a 'three-V tipping point' exists for every organization beyond which traditional data management and analysis technologies are no longer for deriving timely intelligence. The Three-V tipping point is the threshold beyond which organizations start dealing with big data. The organizations should then trade-off the future value expected from big data technologies against their implementation costs [Gandomi & Haider, 2015].

Applying Artificial Intelligence (AI) to Big Data

Unleashing AI on big data can have a noteworthy influence on the role data plays in conducting business, analytics and decision making. Big data is not component of Artificial intelligence [Umbler Corp., 2015]. However, the two are entwined: AI provides the large-scale analytics necessary to extract meaning and value from big data, while big data provides the knowledge required for AI to continue to learn and evolve — or to become more intelligent [Umbler Corp., 2015]. In other words, AI offers the technology and methodology for better understanding of the ever-growing amounts of data. Artificial intelligence solutions are by nature multi-disciplinary, encompassing computer science, mathematics, statistics, philosophical thinking and the industry sector the problem corresponds to. Some of the applications of artificial intelligence have origins in academia, while others have their origins in the research divisions of private companies or even individuals that managed to market their products.

The big data market has been maturing for years now. There is a plethora of technology that can crunch the numbers and spit them out in a spreadsheet or chart. Now, entrepreneurs are beginning to fill this gap with technology that not only synthesizes the data, but interprets it, too [Lapowsky, 2014]. Some of them are as follows [Lapowsky, 2014, Rijmenam, 2014]:

- Chicago-based Narrative Science, has developed a program called Quill provides users with a written report of the data in story form. This artificial intelligence engine generates, evaluates and gives voice to ideas as it discovers them in the data.
- Rocket Fuel, uses AI to deliver a programmatic media-buying platform to improve marketing ROI in digital media across web, mobile, video, and social channels.
- Expertmaker uses AI to transform search, discovery and recommendation, and enable broad deployment of intelligent solutions.
- Path Intelligence maps 3D visitor journeys to generate data-driven insights into visitor and customer behaviour using Artificial Intelligence.
- The Grid has announced an AI-based software that will speed and simplify web development. The Grid harnesses the power of artificial intelligence and big data The AI based software to take everything you throw at it – videos, images, text, urls and more – and automatically shape them into a custom website unique to you. The Grid will automatically make all the design, development, content and A/B test decisions a web agency generally does [Mongardi, 2015].
- Persado has developed a Marketing Language Engineering technology platform that uses AI to apply analytics to the information in content such as emails, ads and landing and determine the most effective wording to use in them. [Umbel Corp., 2015, Levine, 2015]
- Sumo Logic applies machine learning to data center operations, using data analysis to isolate anomalies, predict and uncover potentially disruptive events, and detect vulnerabilities. Sumo Logic uses pattern-recognition technology to distill hundreds of thousands of log messages into a page or two of patterns, radically reducing the time it takes to discover the root cause of an operational or security issue. Customers include Netflix, McGraw-Hill, Orange, Pagerduty, and Medallia [Fortuna's Corner, 2014].

- Ayasdi applies big-data analysis to resolve complex problems, including finding clues for cancers and other diseases, exploring new energy sources, and preventing terrorism and financial fraud. Ayasdi believes that observing at the shape of the data, rather asking questions and writing queries, is far more useful. Ayasdi claims that the large data sets have a distinct shape, or topology, and that shape has significant meaning. Ayasdi claims to help companies determine that shape within minutes, so they can automatically discern insights from their data, without ever having to articulate questions, formulate queries, or write code. Customers include: GE, Citi, Merck, USDA, Mt. Sinai Hospital, the Miami Heat, and the CDC [Fortuna's Corner, 2014].

Like Big Data, AI is about exploding volumes, velocities and variety of data. Under situations of astronomical volumes of data, AI permits delegation of difficult pattern recognition, learning, and other tasks to computer-based approaches. Effective machine language translation is statistics-based, benefitting from the availability of huge data sets. For example, more than one-half of the world's stock trades are done using AI-based systems. In addition, AI lends to the velocity of data, by assisting rapid computerized decisions that lead to other decisions. For example, since so many stock trades are made by AI-based systems rather than people, the velocity of the trades can increase, and one trade could lead to others. Finally, variety issues aren't solved simply by parallelizing and distributing the problem. Instead, variety is mitigated by capturing, structuring, and understanding unstructured data using AI and other analytics [O'Leary, 2013].

Social media big data has a huge potential locked in unstructured data, which comprises of the billions of user-generated written posts, pictures, and videos that circulate on social media. However, only a small fraction of its potential is currently being realized. Artificial intelligence is quickly changing the way social big data is mined for insights and used in emerging marketing applications. Keeping up with the massive volume of messages, photos, and videos that consumers upload and share on social networks every day is a task that only automated intelligent machines can deal with. The task would simply be beyond scope and capacity of human-directed, manual systems. Artificial intelligence, and in particular, a subset of AI known as "deep learning," is key to social media's future as an industry and as a force in society. AI systems are capable of not just computing, but actually learning — machine learning, along with a subset of machine learning called deep learning. Machine learning is aspect of AI and refers to the capability of machines to learn and progress through exposure to new data [Umbel Corp., 2015]. With deep learning, machines themselves figure out which rules to follow based on data researchers feed them. Deep learning is only possible with big data, because an enormous quantity of data is needed to "teach" AI systems. The other component necessary for deep learning is the algorithmic power to make sense of all that data [Umbel Corp., 2015]. The ability of Deep Learning to extract high-level, complicated abstractions and data representations from large sizes of data, specifically unsupervised data, makes it attractive as a valuable tool for Big Data Analytics. More specifically, Big Data problems such as semantic indexing, data tagging, fast information retrieval and discriminative modeling can be better addressed with the help of Deep Learning. More traditional machine learning and feature engineering algorithms are not competent enough to extract the complex and non-linear patterns normally witnessed in Big Data. By extracting such features, Deep Learning facilitates the use of comparatively simpler linear models for Big Data analysis tasks, such as classification and prediction, which is significant when developing models to deal with the scale of Big Data [Najafabadi et al., 2015].

Machine-learning algorithms can be applied to streaming data. High volume data streams (high speed continuous flow of data) arise in numerous settings, like IT operations, sensors, and social media to name a few. Medical domains include many settings where data is produced in a streaming fashion, such as anatomical and physiological sensors, or incidence records and health information systems. Xmp from Argyle Data consist of algorithms for online learning and real time pattern detection. Feature Stream is a new web service for applying machine-learning to data streams. Yahoo! recently released SAMOA—a distributed streaming machine-learning framework. SAMOA lets developers code algorithms once and execute them in multiple stream processing environments [O'Reilly, 2015].

Consumer Internet companies are in a hurry to build out their AI talent and acquire the most advanced machine-learning systems. Some of the major acquisitions from the AI field that occurred in recent months [Cooper, 2014]:

- Facebook launched a new research lab dedicated entirely to advancing the field of AI so that they can predict what consumers will do in the future.
- Google acquired DeepMind, a company that built learning algorithms for e-commerce, simulations, and games, for $US400 million.
- LinkedIn acquired Bright, a company that focused on data- and algorithm-driven job matches, for $US120 million — its largest acquisition to date.
- Pinterest acquired Visual Graph, a company that specialized in image recognition and visual search. Visual Graph helped build Google's first machine vision application to improve image search.

Artificial Intelligence and Big data can be used for fraud management. Neural networks are analytics that learn to distinguish complex patterns of behavior (in customer transactions, network activity, etc.). This analytic technique imitates how neurons in the brain store knowledge in their connections to other neurons and how the strengths of those synapses change with different kinds of mental activity. Neural networks have been widely deployed in fraud management because they excel at swiftly spotting abnormal data patterns within large amounts of transaction data. Features can be thought of as super-variables, as they are variables which have been engineered (selected, combined, calculated) by an analytics expert to make them highly predictive. In fraud detection, a feature might be the number of card transactions in the last hour, or the number of transactions over a specific amount during the last 12 hours between the hours of 3am and 6am compared to overall dollar volume [Najafabadi et al., 2015].

In development, a neural network undergoes supervised training, in which it evaluates enormous volumes of historical data labeled with an outcome. By analyzing months of cardholder transaction data, for example, a fraud model's hidden layer incrementally learns the sometimes complex and understated feature relationships connected with the outcome of a fraudulent transaction. It changes the "weights" (relative strengths) of these connections to recognize the weighted feature relationships that best foresees that outcome. A deployed neural network model trained this way can instantaneously detect predictive patterns in new data as huge volumes of it stream in (e.g., from cardholder transactions, network activity and sensor readings). When deployed with dynamic profiles, an associated analytic technique, the model also learns the typical patterns for individual entities (e.g., a specific cardholder, merchant or ATM), and so can spot suspicious deviations [Najafabadi et al., 2015].

At Griffith's School of ICT, Australia, interdisciplinary research using Artificial Intelligence technology in the area of Coastal management has generated camera-based technology for analyzing enormous amounts of digital video images of beach scenes to count and comprehend the behavior of persons on the shore along Australia's coast. This technology is accurate to 80-90% and can discover, from very low-resolution video, whether a person is walking or running along the beach or entering the ocean. The application of this work can help in beach safety and support the work of lifeguards to detect swimmers in danger. Another research work being undertaken involves merging the fields of IT and Engineering for forecasting the deterioration of bridges in Queensland (10,000 in total) using Artificial Neural Network (ANN) technology. This research work, undertaken in collaboration between the City of Gold Coast and the Queensland State Government, has created predictive models trained using historical bridge data to guarantee the safety and effective maintenance of important State assets. The research in this area has generated effective models to forecast the deterioration of bridges up to 20-30 years into the future with the capability to save millions of dollars through prioritization of asset maintenance regimes. Another interdisciplinary research, which intersects information technology and the environment, has fashioned accurate and sophisticated AI models for the prediction of flood events on the Gold Coast. Using a assortment of data from sensors located at several catchments around the Gold Coast, rainfall data and other complementary information, ANNs have been trained to understand historical trends and are able to perform predictive analytics for forecasting flood events up to three hours ahead, which provides adequate time for undertaking effective disaster management. This work being undertaken at Griffith's School of ICT is scalable and can be extended across the State and indeed the Nation [Griffith Sciences].

Social networking experiences are becoming increasingly centered around photos and video [Cooper, 2014].

- Facebook users upload 350 million photos each day [Cooper, 2014].
- Snapchat users share 400 million "snaps" (Snapchat's term for photos and videos shared over the network) each day [Cooper, 2014].
- Instagram users upload 55 million photos each day [Cooper, 2014].
- 30,000 are uploaded on Flickr every minute [Holland, 2015].

However, it is extremely difficult to extract information from visual content. Because of this, image and video recognition are two of the more exciting disciplines being worked on in the field of AI and deep learning. Advances in "deep learning," cutting-edge AI research that tries to program machines to perform high-level thought and abstractions, are enabling marketers to extract information from the billions of photos, videos, and messages uploaded and shared on social networks each day. Image recognition technology is now advanced enough to identify brand logos in photos. Web giants such as Google and Baidu (a China-based search engine) are using a deep learning-derived technique known as "back-propagation," in order to classify images in user photo collections. Back-propagation is a method for training computer systems to match images with labels or tags that were pre-defined by users. For example, if enough people upload photos tagged "cat," then a system has a large enough sample size that it can reference to identify new photos of cats, and tag them appropriately. This is one of the reasons why services such as Facebook and Instagram encourage users to tag objects and people in photos. However, there is very little user-generated data identifying the contents of online video, which so far means that back-propagation is a poor method for video recognition [Smith, 2014].

Speech recognition is another field where machine learning can be applied to big data. Speech recognition is the transformation of spoken words into text. At Baidu, the Chinese-based search giant, the objective is to have mobile phone software accurately transcribe words in languages such as English or Mandarin and understand the request. With its Deep Speech system, which first came out in December 2014, Baidu trained it on more than 100,000 hours of voice recordings, first getting people to read to the machine and then adding synthesized noise over the top to make it sound like they are talking in a noisy room, cafeteria, or car. Then it let the system learn to recognize speech even amid all that noise. Baidu's Deep Speech system uses deep learning algorithms that are trained on a recurrent neural network, or simulation of connected neurons [Hof, 2014; Merrett, 2015]

Text mining is another field that is quickly evolving. A team of Belgian computer science researchers developed an opinion mining algorithm that can identify positive, negative, and neutral sentiment in Web content with 83% accuracy for English text. Accuracy vacillates depending on the language of the text because of the diversity of linguistic expressions. The more complex a language is, the more training a machine-learning system needs [Smith, 2014].

Particle Swarm Optimization (PSO) is a computational procedure used in data mining to competently harvest useful information from big data, by repetitively improving candidate solutions to optimize a given problem. These candidate solutions (also called particles) can be moved around a search space through simple mathematical formula. These particles follow flocking rules to form swarms, moving the swarm towards solutions, in due course allowing a particle to find a position that surpasses minimal requirements given to a solution [Dervojeda, 2013].

Agent-based computational economics studies dynamic systems of interacting agents and can be used to model economic processes and even entire economies, through agent-based models. In these models, the interaction of agents is modelled according to rules that model behaviour and social interactions, which permits for behavioural forecasting and price movements. This methodology necessitates involvement of experts in order for the rules and models to correctly reflect reality, which then could tap into big data to cater for dynamic, real time analysis and forecasting [Dervojeda, 2013].

From digital advertisements to landing pages, marketing content has become progressively more challenging to create, fine-tune and manage so customers receive the most appealing and effective messages. What makes content creation and management challenging is the increasing number of channels and the volume of content that companies must deal with today. AI-based solutions are available to help the creation and deployment of the most effective, targeted content possible, often in near real time [Umbel Corp., 2015]. Some examples are:

- A Top 100 online US retailer used marketing language engineering to improve its AdWords advertising, appealing more successfully to audiences and resulting in 358% order rate improvement. The company worked with Persado to identify and apply the most effective wording for its advertisements [Umbel Corp., 2015].
- Lord & Taylor, the clothing retailer/e-tailer worked with advertising optimization company Rocket Fuel to recognize the audience for its message and adjust its advertising accordingly to increase online women's fashion sales. Rocket Fuel's AI-driven Direct Response Booster solution, part of its Advertising That Learns platform, is credited with empowering Lord & Taylor to boost customer acquisition by improving customer targeting [Umbel Corp., 2015].

Artificial Intelligence systems are helping marketers and advertisers garner insights from the vast ocean of unstructured consumer data collected by the world's largest social networks. Audience targeting and personalized predictive marketing using social data are expected to be some of the business areas that benefit the most from mining big data. IBM Watson Engagement Advisor, a cognitive computing assistant, can help a business to better serve its consumers. IBM Watson Engagement Advisor permits brands to crunch big data and transform the fashion that they engage clients in key functions, such as customer service, marketing, and sales. IBM Watson Engagement Advisor can learn, adapt, and gain an understanding of a company's data, enabling customer-facing personnel to assist consumers with deeper insights faster than previously possible [Takeda & Onodera, 2013]. Watson uses natural language processing to comprehend words and their relationships. It also depends on cognitive computing techniques to sift through more than 200 million-plus pages of structured and unstructured data that consume approximately 4 terabytes of disk space. Among other things, Watson can mine posts on Twitter to better recognize market trends and brand sentiment [Greengard, 2014]. According to Booz & Company, 61% of data professionals say big data will renovate marketing for the better. However, although machine-learning systems are being tasked with analyzing users on an individual basis, the value to marketers is grouping like-minded consumers together, so that they can target people at scale [Smith, 2014].

Systems based on Artificial Intelligence have an ability to evaluate massive and growing stores of customer data and apply the results to enhance customer experiences. The ability to suggest a product that specifically fits a customer's need right at the moment of decision is the holy grail of marketing for businesses ranging from fashion and beauty companies to media and entertainment providers — and from retailers to etailers. To achieve this ability, necessitates moving away from traditional systems that filter products based on previous purchases [Umbel Corp., 2015]. Using data from multiple sources, AI can construct a store of knowledge that will in due course of time, enable accurate predictions about you as a customer which are based not just on what you purchase, but on how much time you spend in a specific part of an site or store, what you look at while you are there, what you do purchase compared with what you don't — and a multitude of other bits of data that AI can synthesize and add to, ultimately getting to know you and what you want extremely well [Umbel Corp., 2015]. For instance, if a woman accesses a retailer's Web site and looks at a dress, the Web site might record the length of time she spent at the page, what color options she eyed, and compare the clicks to other Web surfing activity--as well as other variables ranging from her overall purchase patterns to past purchases--to identify exactly what triggers a purchase. If she leaves an item in her shopping cart, she might receive a promotion a couple of days later with a free shipping coupon or a certain percentage off coupon code or, perhaps, a gift-with-purchase offer. Moreover, the data might be used to customize pricing in the future and adjust promotions so that she is more likely to close the purchase immediately. Of course, different customers would receive diverse experiences and offers based on their exclusive data fingerprints [Greengard, 2014]. All of this is done by AI software. In short, companies are using AI based recommendation engines that make suggestions based on everything they know about a shopper, not just what they bought before. Companies that are already using AI and big data for product recommendations include [Umbel Corp., 2015]:

- **eBay**: eBay has a solution, eBay explorer that uses interactive Q&A to recommend gift ideas from among eBay's many thousands of products. The solution applies optimization algorithms, text classification and other AI algorithms to the data assimilated from shoppers to propose suitable gifts. The company behind the technology, Expertmaker, which offers AI-powered optimizing solutions that actually leverage the potential of big data.
- **Netflix**: Netflix uses a recommendation engine which is based on deep learning for recommending movies. To "train" the software to provide recommendations, Netflix provides it with enormous volumes of information which the recommendation engine can use to ascertain patterns. The goal is make suggestions based on what you actually like about your favorite shows and movies instead of stop recommending movies based on what you have seen.

- **Yahoo**: Yahoo has a product named 'Yahoo Recommends' that works at mass scale to produce personalized content recommendations and convey native advertising to users. This product syndicates a rich collection of input signals with machine-based learning, including adaptive learning, to characterize content relevance.
- **Birchbox**: Birchbox takes Artificial Intelligence beyond etailing and behind the storefront, through an in-store touchscreen and iPads which gather insights from customers to personalize product recommendations. The new instore recommendation engine uses the same AI and machine learning technology which characterize the company's extremely successful online platform. The iPad apps in the store endorse personal care products based on skin tone, hair color and other explicit individual attributes.

Limitations and Issues of Big Data and Artificial Intelligence

Irrespective of how powerful and how much value big data brings, it has its limitations. Big data has its distinctive characteristics that can provide decision-makers with more timely, rich information, but without the specific context, data on its own can never tell the whole story. Like any data, big data is not a panacea to solve all questions for all organizations. An organization should consider at least the "Three V's" of its data and its practical capacities before implementing big data technologies. Also big data cannot replace traditional analytics. With its complexity and its requirements for technology and talent, big data is more appropriate to organizations with large-scale, multi-structured datasets [Yan, 2013].

With big data there will also be dirty data, with potential errors, incompleteness, or differential precision. AI can be used to identify and clean dirty data or use dirty data as a means of establishing context knowledge for the data. For example, "consistent" dirty data might indicate a different context than the one assumed—for example, data in a different language [O'Leary 2013]. In short, the adage Garbage in, garbage out (GIGO) applies when AI is applied to dirty data.

Current AI algorithm sets are often non-standard and primarily research-based. Algorithms might lack documentation, support, and clear examples. Further, historically the focus of AI has largely been on single-machine implementations. With big data, we now need AI that's scalable to clusters of machines or that can be logically set on a MapReduce structure such as Hadoop. MapReduce allows the development of approaches that can handle larger volumes of data using larger numbers of processors. As a result, some of the issues caused by increasing volumes and velocities of data can be addressed using parallel-based approaches. As a result, effectively using current AI algorithms in big data enterprise settings might be limited. First, unfortunately, the nature of some machine-learning algorithms—for example, iterative approaches such as genetic algorithms—can make their use in a MapReduce environment more difficult. However, recently, MapReduce has been used to develop parallel processing approaches to AI algorithms. Hadoop (http://hadoop.apache.org), named after a boy's toy elephant, is an open source version of MapReduce [O'Leary 2013].

CONCLUSION

Artificial Intelligence and Big data mesh well. Artificial Intelligence and Big data when put together opens up innumerable opportunities for resolving the problems faced in modern society in 21st century and beyond. Big data is about the stunningly increasing growth of data, and companies can gain competitive advantage by better understanding the ever-growing amounts of data. Artificial intelligence offers the technology and methodology to do so. The combination of Artificial Intelligence based analytics and Big Data is stimulating because it increases the likelihood of better and faster information extraction from large-scale data [FICO, 2014].

Since big data are noisy, greatly interrelated, and unreliable, it will likely lead to the development of statistical techniques more readily apt for mining big data while remaining sensitive to the unique characteristics [Gandomi & Haider, 2015]. The quality issues in the data, needs to be either tackled at the data pre-processing stage or by the learning algorithm [Zhou, 2014]. Going beyond samples, additional valuable insights could be obtained from the colossal volumes of less 'trustworthy' data [Gandomi & Haider, 2015].

Continued innovations in AI are certainly promising and merit renewed interest in the discipline. While none of these techniques are a "silver bullet"—and human analytic and business domain expertise remain indispensable—they can improve the return on Big Data analytic investments in numerous important ways [FICO, 2014]. To make the best out of AI and big data, big data needs to be aligned with a specific business goal or a well-defined problem statement. Gains from Big Data and AI will be governed by right analytic practices, clear understanding of business requirements that is- what is AI aiming to achieve from the data, relevant data and active involvement and collaboration amongst stakeholders - data scientist, domain/subject matter experts, business and data analysts) and top management support for the endeavor.

REFERENCES

Cox, M., & Ellsworth, D. (1997). Managing Big Data for Scientific Visualization.*Proc. of ACM Siggraph* (pp. 5-1–5-17).

Cukier, K. (2010). Data, data everywhere: A special report on managing information. *The Economist*. Retrieved from http://www.economist.com/node/15557443

Dervojeda, K., Verzijl, D., Nagtegaal, F., Lengton, M., & Rouwmaat, E. (2013, September). Big Data Artificial Intelligence, Business Innovation Observatory Contract No 190/PP/ENT/CIP/12/C/N03C01. *European Union*. Retrieved from http://ec.europa.eu/enterprise/policies/innovation/policy/business-innovation-observatory/files/case-studies/09-bid-artificial-intelligence_en.pdf

Diebold, F.X. (2000, August). Big data dynamic factor models for macroeconomic measurement and forecasting. *Presented at the 8th World Congress of the Econometric Society*, Seattle. Retrieved from http://www.upenn.edu/~fdiebold/papers107/ABCD_HOED.pdf

Dumbill, E. (2012, January 11). What is big data? An introduction to the big data landscape. O'Reilly Radar.

FICO. (2014). Does AI + Big Data = Business Gain? *Insights White Paper*. Retrieved from http://www.fico.com/en/latest-thinking/white-papers/insightsdoes-ai--big-data--business-gain

Fortuna's Corner. (2014). Ten Big Data Start-Ups To Watch. Retrieved from http://fortunascorner.com/2014/04/17/ten-big-data-start-ups-to-watch/

Gandomi, A., & Murtaza, H. (2015). Beyond the hype: Big data concepts, methods, and analytics *International Journal of Information Management, 35*(2), 137–144. doi:10.1016/j.ijinfomgt.2014.10.007

Big Data. (n. d.). Gartner IT Glossary. Retrieved from http://www.gartner.com/it-glossary/big-data/

Gens, F. (2011). IDC 2012 Predictions: Competing for 2020. Retrieved from http://cdn.idc.com/research/Predictions12/Main/downloads/IDCTOP10Predictions2012.pdf

Greengard, S. (2014). Artificial Intelligence: Ready To Live Up To Its Hype? *Insight/ Market Research, CMO by Adobe*. Retrieved from http://www.cmo.com/articles/2014/11/5/artifical_intelligence.html

Sciences, G. (n. d.). Deep Learning from Big data. *Impact @ Griffith Sciences*. Retrieved from http://app.griffith.edu.au/sciencesimpact/deep-learning-big-data/

Hof, R. (2014). Baidu Announces Breakthrough In Speech Recognition, Claiming To Top Google And Apple. *Forbes*. Retrieved from http://www.forbes.com/sites/roberthof/2014/12/18/baidu-announces-breakthrough-in-speech-recognition-claiming-to-top-google-and-apple/2/

Holland, P. (2015). Characteristics of Big Data – Part One. Retrieved from http://makingdatameaningful.com/2015/05/26/characteristics-of-big-data-part-one/

IS0/IEC 2015 ISO/IEC JTC 1. (n. d.). Information technology 2015, Big Data Preliminary Report 2014. Retrieved from http://www.iso.org/iso/big_data_report-jtc1.pdf

Lapowsky, I. (2014). 4 Big Opportunities in Artificial Intelligence. *Inc.com*. Retrieved from http://www.inc.com/issie-lapowsky/4-big-opportunities-artificial-intelligence.html

Lapkin, A. (2012). *Hype Cycle for Big Data*. Gartner.

Levine, B. (2015). Persado scores $21M to become the Moneyball of marketing. VB News. Retrieved from http://venturebeat.com/2015/01/22/persado-scores-21m-to-become-the-moneyball-of-marketing/

McKinsey Global Institute. (2011, May). Big data: The next frontier for innovation, competition, and productivity.

Merrett, R. (2015). Intelligent machines part 1: Big data, machine learning and the future. CIO. Retrieved from http://www.cio.com.au/article/576664/intelligent-machines-part-1-big-data-machine-learning-future/

Mitchell, I., & Wilson, M. (2012). Linked data Connecting and exploiting big data (White paper). Retrieved from from www.fujitsu.com/.../Linked-data-connecting-and-exploiting-big-data-(v1.0). pdf

Mongardi, S. (2015). 'What is the Grid and why it's a revolution. *The Web Mate*. Retrieved from http://www.thewebmate.com/2015/05/18/what-is-the-grid-and-why-its-a-revolution/

Najafabadi, M., Villanustre, F., Khoshgoftaar, T. M., Seliya, N., Wald, R., & Muharemagic, E. (2015). Deep learning applications and challenges in big data analytics. *Journal of Big Data*. Retrieved from http://www.journalofbigdata.com/content/2/1/1

O'Dwyer, M. (2014). How companies can make the most of big data. *Dell.com*. Retrieved from http://techpageone.dell.com/technology/companies-can-make-big-data/

Ohlhorst, F. J. (2012). *Big Data Analytics: Turning Big Data into Big Money*. Cary, North Carolina, USA: SAS Institute Inc. doi:10.1002/9781119205005

Big Data Now: 2014 Edition. (2015). O'Reilly Media, Inc. United States of America.

Pingdom. (2012). Internet 2011 in Numbers. *Pingdom.com*. Retrieved from http://royal. pingdom. com/2012/01/17/internet-2011-in-numbers

Press, G. (2014). 12 Big Data Definitions: What's Yours?" Forbes.com. Retrieved from http://www. forbes.com/sites/gilpress/2014/09/03/12-big-data-definitions-whats-yours/

van Rijmenam, M. (2014). Is Artificial Intelligence About To Change Doing Business Forever? Retrieved from http://www.bigdata-startups.com/artificial-intelligence-change-business-forever/

SAS. (2012). Big Data Meets Big Data Analytics (White Paper). SAS.com. Retrieved from http://www. sas.com/content/dam/SAS/en_us/doc/whitepaper1/big-data-meets-big-data-analytics-105777.pdf

Smith, C. (2014). Social Media's New Big Data Frontiers -- Artificial Intelligence, Deep Learning, And Predictive *Marketing. Business Insider.com*. Retrieved from: http://www.businessinsider.com.au/social-medias-new-big-data-frontiers-artificial-intelligence-deep-learning-and-predictive-marketing-2014-2

Soubra, D. (2012). The 3Vs that define Big Data. *Data Science Central.com*.http://www.datascience-central.com/forum/topics/the-3vs-that-define-big-data

Takeda, K., & Onodera, T. (2013). Artificial Intelligence: Learning Through Interactions and Big Data. IBM Redbooks Point-of-View publication. Retrieved from http://www.redbooks.ibm.com/abstracts/ redp4974.html?Open

Demystifying big data: A practical guide to transforming the business of Government. (2012). TechAmerica. Retrieved from http://www.techamerica.org/Docs/fileManager.cfm?f=techamerica-bigdatareport-final.pdf

Corp, U. (2015). AI meets Big Data (White paper). Retrieved from http://etailwest.wbresearch.com/ ai-meets-big-data-ml

Yan, J. (2013). Big Data, Bigger Opportunities. *Meritalk*. Retrieved from http://www.meritalk.com/pdfs/ bdx/bdx-whitepaper-090413.pdf

Zhou, Z.-H., Chawla, N. V., Jin, Y., & Williams, G. J. (2014). *Big Data Opportunities and Challenges: Discussions from Data Analytics Perspectives*. IEEE Computational Intelligence Magazine, 9(4). 62-74.

Zikopoulous, P., Deroos, D., Parasuraman, K., Deutsch, T., Corrigan, D., & Giles, J. (2013). *Harness the Power of Big Data*. McGraw-Hill.

Chapter 2

Hybrid Ensemble Learning Methods for Classification of Microarray Data:
RotBagg Ensemble Based Classification

Sujata Dash
North Orissa University, India

ABSTRACT

Efficient classification and feature extraction techniques pave an effective way for diagnosing cancers from microarray datasets. It has been observed that the conventional classification techniques have major limitations in discriminating the genes accurately. However, such kind of problems can be addressed by an ensemble technique to a great extent. In this paper, a hybrid RotBagg ensemble framework has been proposed to address the problem specified above. This technique is an integration of Rotation Forest and Bagging ensemble which in turn preserves the basic characteristics of ensemble architecture i.e., diversity and accuracy. Three different feature selection techniques are employed to select subsets of genes to improve the effectiveness and generalization of the RotBagg ensemble. The efficiency is validated through five microarray datasets and also compared with the results of base learners. The experimental results show that the correlation based FRFR with PCA-based RotBagg ensemble form a highly efficient classification model.

INTRODUCTION

Cancer is caused due to the changes or mutation in the expression profiles of certain genes which elevates the importance of feature selection techniques to find relevant genes for classification of the disease. The most significant genes selected from the process are useful in clinical diagnosis for identifying disease profiles (Yang et al., 2006). The discriminative genes are selected through feature selection techniques that aim to select an optimal subset of genes. But, high dimension and small sample size characteristics of microarray dataset creates lot of computational challenges for selecting optimal subsets of genes

DOI: 10.4018/978-1-5225-0427-6.ch002

such as the problem of "curse of dimensionality" and over-fitting of training dataset. Feature selection is often used as a preprocessing step in machine learning. Only non-redundant and relevant features are sufficient enough to provide effective and efficient learning. However, selecting an optimal subset is very difficult (Kohavi & John, 1997) as the possible number of subsets grows exponentially when the dimension of the dataset increases.

The feature selection techniques can be broadly classified into filter (Hall, 2000; Liu, Motoda & Yu, 2002; Yu & Liu, 2003) and wrapper model (Hsu et al., 2011; Dash, Patra & Tripathy, 2012). The filter model uses specific evaluation criterion which is independent of learning algorithm to select feature subset from the dataset. It depends on various evaluation measures which are employed on the general characteristics of the training data such as information, distance, consistency and dependency. The wrapper method measures the goodness of the selected subsets using the predictive accuracy of the learning algorithm. But these methods require intensive computation for high dimensional dataset. Apart from this another key factor in feature selection is search strategy. The trade-off between optimal solution and computational efficiency is attained by adopting an appropriate search strategy such as random, exhaustive and heuristic search (Dash & Liu, 2003).

There are feature selection methods available for supervised (Yu & Liu, 2003; Dash & Liu, 1997) and unsupervised (Dash, Choi, Scheuermann & Liu., 2002) learning methods and it has been applied in several applications like genomic microarray data analysis, image retrieval, text categorization, intrusion detection etc. But, the theoretical and empirical analysis has demonstrated that the presence of irrelevant and redundant features (Kohavi & John, 1997; Hall, 2000) in the dataset reduces the speed and accuracy of the learning algorithms, thus need to be removed from the dataset. Most of the feature selection techniques employed so far has considered individual feature evaluation and feature subset evaluation (Guyon & Elisseeff, 2003; Abraham, 2004). Individual feature evaluation method ranks the features with respect to their capability of differentiating instances of different classes and eliminates the irrelevant and redundant features likely to have the same rankings. The feature subset evaluation method finds a subset of minimum features satisfying measure of goodness removes irrelevant and redundant features. It is observed that the advance search strategies like heuristic search and greedy search used for subset evaluation even after reducing the search space from $O\ (2^{\,N})$ to $O\ (N^{\,2})$ prove to be inefficient for high-dimensional dataset. This shortcoming encourages exploring different techniques for feature selection which will address both feature relevance and redundancy for high-dimensional microarray dataset.

There are various uncertainties associated with fabrication of microarray data such as the gathering of data, hybridization and image processing. They introduce lot of noises which need to be addressed by a robust and reliable classification model (Piao, Piao, Park & Ryu, 2012). On the other hand, conventional machine learning algorithms encounter many challenges to develop an effective and reliable classification model. The generalization capability of such kind of classifier algorithm based on a few significant genes and small number of training samples cannot be dependable. Therefore, it is essential to devise generalized robust classification methods which could overcome the constraints of small sample size and uncertainties associated with the datasets. This study motivates to develop ensemble classifier which is not very sensitive to the above specified constraints.

Ensemble learning technique is an advanced mechanism to combine multiple number of learning techniques to achieve better prediction accuracy (Liu et al., 2010; Dietterich, 2000; Yang, Yang, Zhou & Zomaya, 2010). It has the advantage of ignoring the constraint of sample size and the potential threat of overfitting by averaging and incorporating over multiple learning models (Hansen & Salamon, 1990). That is how the dataset is being used in an effective way, which was highly difficult for many bioinformatics applications to handle. The research findings of ensemble learning have shown a promising improvement in the classification accuracy while dealing with data under uncertainties (Dietterich, 2000; Hansen & Salamon, 1990). However, the ensemble classifier only can outperform its own individual base learners if and only if its base learners are accurate and diverse (Dietterich, 2000). The base learners are considered as accurate, if the classification error rate of new samples is better than the randomly guessing classes. Similarly, two base learners can be regarded as diverse if their decisions on the same sample are different and always they do not converge to a single decision.

The ensemble methods employ a base learning algorithm to the training sets permutated differently. The popular examples of these techniques include Bagging (Dietterich, 2000; DeBock, Coussement & Vanden Poel, 2010), AdaBoost (Zhang & Zhang, 2010), Rotation Forest (Liu & Huang, 2008), Random Subspace (Breiman, 1996) and Random Forest (Zhang & Zhang, 2008). In bagging, bootstrap method is used to construct each base classifier from the original training set T i.e., a random sample is derived with replacement from the original dataset. Then majority voting is used to find the classification accuracy of the ensemble classifier where the new test data is being assigned with a class having highest number of votes obtained from the base learners (DeBock, Coussement & Vanden Poel, 2010).

Another ensemble method which is very popular in terms of simplicity and adaptability is AdaBoost (Zhang & Zhang, 2010). It builds an ensemble of classifiers by using a specified learning algorithm as base learner for the datasets that are obtained from the original training set either using resampling or reweighting (Zhang & Zhang, 2010). However, AdaBoost attempts to produce new "strong" classifiers that are able to better predict the hard instances of the training set.

Rotation Forest (Liu & Huang, 2008) is a variant of bagging ensemble method. But this ensemble classifier is built with a set of decision trees as the base learners. The bootstrap method is used to extract samples from the original training set to construct a new training set for each base learner. Subsequently, the features of the new training dataset are split randomly into some subsets, which are then transformed individually using some transformation techniques. As we know, a small perturbation may build a complete different tree but transformation techniques only can guarantee the diversity of the ensemble system (Liu & Huang, 2008; Dash, 2015). Moreover, at the same time Rotation Forest (Liu & Huang, 2008) enhances the generalization capability of the base learners as well as the diversity in the ensemble classifiers when compared with other ensemble classifiers, such as Bagging (Breiman, 1996), AdaBoost (Freund & Schapire, 1997), and Random Forest (Breiman, 2001).

C. Zhang and J. Zhang (2008) have developed a novel ensemble classifier "RotBoost" by combining two different ensemble techniques i.e., Rotation Forest and AdaBoost. They have replaced the base classifier of Rotation Forest with AdaBoost and established that the RotBoost performs better than the individual ensembles integrated together in this model. The performance of the model is also validated with gene related datasets from UCI repository.

In this paper, a hybrid ensemble learning methodology is proposed by combining a correlation based feature relevancy and redundancy (CO-FRFR) (Dash & Dash, 2014) feature selection method and PCA-based RotBagg ensemble classification technique. The efficiency of the model has been verified through publicly available microarray datasets and also compared with the experimental results of ICA-based-RotBoost (Osareh & Shadgar, 2013) technique. In addition to this, the efficiency of CO-FRFR-PCA- RotBagg has also been compared with the ensemble techniques used as base learners in the proposed model. To fix the values of the parameters of the base learners and of the ensemble model, a comparison among two variants of the RotBagg model such as PCA-based RotBagg and RP (Random Projection)-based RotBagg has been made. The integrated PCA-based RotBagg ensemble with CO-FRFR exhibited superior average performance in terms of achieving generalization accuracy in comparison to other ensemble classifiers. Therefore, this model needs to be recommended as the most effective and efficient classification technique for predicting microarray datasets. The rest of the paper encompasses section 2 explaining feature relevance and redundancy concept and section 3 proposing the framework of RotBagg ensemble technique and feature selection method. In section 4 an empirical study of the proposed method in terms of efficiency and effectiveness comparing with other approaches are discussed. Section 5 provides a conclusion with future directions.

RELEVANCE AND REDUNDANCY OF FEATURES

It is observed that, a considerable number of features are not informative because of their irrelevance or redundancy (Abeel et al., 2010) to the class concept in high-dimensional dataset. Redundant and irrelevant features reduce classification accuracy and run-time of the system (Hall, 2000; Dash, Choi, Scheuermann & Liu., 2002). Conventional approaches of feature selection have given more emphasis on relevant data but very little attention to feature redundancy (Kohavi & John, 1997; Liu et al., 2010). The features of the dataset can be broadly classified into three categories considering feature relevance characteristic namely strongly relevant, weakly relevant and irrelevant (Kohavi & John, 1997). These three concepts of feature relevance cannot handle redundancy all alone. The formal definition can be stated as: Let F be a full set of features and for a feature F_i, $S_i = F - \{F_i\}$

Definition 1 (Strong relevance) *A feature Fi is strongly relevant iff*

$$P(C \setminus Fi, Si) \neq P(C \setminus Si)$$

Definition 2 (Weak relevance) *A feature Fi is weakly relevant iff*

$$P\big(C \,|\, Fi, Si\big) = P\big(C \,|\, Si\big), \text{and}$$

$$\exists S_i' \subset S_i, \text{ such that } P\,(C \mid F_i, S_i') \neq P\,(C \mid S_i')$$

Definition 3 (Irrelevance) *A feature Fi is irrelevant iff for all* $S_i' \subseteq S_i$, $P\,(C \mid F_i, S_i') = P\,(C \mid S_i')$

An optimal subset contains strong relevant features and the removal of which always affects the conditional class distribution. In case of weak relevance, the feature may not always require for an optimal subset but at certain conditions it may be required. Irrelevance suggests that the feature is not required. An optimal subset should contain all strongly relevant features, none of the irrelevant features, and a subset of weakly relevant features. Unfortunately, the definitions do not explain which of the weakly relevant features need to be selected for the optimal subset and which are not. Therefore, at this stage feature redundancy need to be investigated among relevant features. It is observed that, two features are redundant to each other if they are correlated completely. But, when a feature is partially correlated with a set of features, it may not be so easy to determine the feature redundancy existing in the dataset.

Correlation Measures

In feature selection process, we deal with mainly two types of correlation measures namely, linear and non-linear which exist between genes or between target class and genes. In the proposed method, non-linear correlation measures which are based on the information –theoretical concept of *entropy,* a measure of the uncertainty of a random variable is applied. The entropy of a variable X is defined as:

$$H(X) = -\sum i P(x_i) \log_2 (P(X_i))$$

and the entropy of *X* after observing values of another variable *Y* is defined as

$$H(X \,/\, Y) = -\sum j P(y_j) \sum i P(x_i \,/\, y_j) \log_2 (P(x_i \,/\, y_j))$$

where the prior probability is $P(x_i)$ for all X_i and the posterior probability for all X given the values of Y is $P(x_i/y_i)$. The additional information given by Y to X is called *information gain,*

$$IG(X \,/\, Y) = H(X) - H(X \,/\, Y)$$

In this article, symmetrical uncertainty has been used to make up for information gain's bias towards high valued features and confines the values in the range of [0, 1]. Value 1 informs that if we know the value of either of the features we can completely predict the value of the other and value 0 indicates both are independent of each other. It can be expressed as:

$$SU(X, Y) = 2 \left[\frac{IG(X \,/\, Y)}{H(X) + H(Y)} \right]$$

ENSEMBLE FRAMEWORK AND FEATURE SLECTION METHOD

RotBagg Ensemble Framework

The proposed ensemble method, RotBagg, is a hybrid intelligent classifier developed by combining the concept of Rotation Forest and Bagging ensemble classifier techniques with the objective of achieving higher accuracy than either of the individual techniques. Rotation Forest is a robust multiple classifier system which employs base classifiers which are accurate and the diversity among them is low. The framework of this method requires a linear transformation technique to project the dataset of each classifier or base learner into a new feature space and then is described as follows. In the framework of Rotation Forest, a linear transformation method is required to project data into new feature space for each classifier, and then the base classifiers are trained in different spaces so as to increase the accuracies of base classifiers and reduce the diversity in the ensemble system. Principal component analysis

(PCA), non-parametric discriminant analysis (NDA) and random projections (RP) are used as feature transformation techniques in Rotation Forest.

Rotation Forest is a multiple classifier system which extracts different set of features to train independently all the L decision trees (base learners) (Breiman, (2001)). Let X be the training set, ω be the labels of each training sample and F *is* the feature set. Assuming that there are N *t*raining samples with n *f*eatures in a microarray dataset, then X *is* an N×*n* *m*atrix. Let ω be the set of class labels $\{\omega 1, \omega_2.$. ω m} ass,gned to each training sample. The training of base classifiers Ci requ,res a mapping to be established between the input sample spaces and the class labels. If the feature set F is s*p*lit randomly into k subs*e*ts of approximate size, then there may be L base classifiers required for the Rotation Forest which can be denoted by D1, . . ., D*L. There*fore, L and *k* are *t*wo important parameters which need to be determined carefully.

Now the following steps need to be followed to process the training dataset of an individual classifier Di.

Step 1: Randomly split F into k disjoint subsets and assume that the size of each subset be M = *n/k* .

Step 2: Consider Fij *be* the j *th* subset of features for training classifier Di, *a*nd Xij *be* the dataset X *for* the features in Fij.

Step 3: Select randomly a nonempty subset of classes from Xi*j f*or each subset. Then apply bootstrap technique to extract 75% of data from the original dataset to form a new training dataset, which is denoted by Xi*j'*.

Step 4: Apply a linear transformation technique on Xi*j'* and generate coefficients in matrix Qi*j*. Denote the coefficients by $a_i j1,\ldots a_i j^{mj}$. This indicates the size of Xi*j'* is $M^x 1$.

Step 5: At the end, construct a sparse rotation matrix Ri usi*ng* the coefficients generated in matrix Qij (C.-*X*. Zhang and J.-S. Zhang, 2010).

$$
R_i = \begin{pmatrix} a_{i1}^{(1)},...,a_{i1}^{(M_1)} & \{0\} & \{0\} \\ \{0\} & a_{i2}^{(1)},.....,a_{i2}^{(M_2)} & \{0\} \\ \{0\} & \{0\} & a_{ik}^{(1)},......,a_{ik}^{(M_k)} \end{pmatrix}
$$

Now the columns of sparse rotation matrix are rearranged as per the original feature sequence and it is denoted by Rai. Then the transformed training dataset for the corresponding classifier Di would be represented by XRai. The above process shows all the classifiers will be trained in a parallel manner.

During the validation phase of the classification process, for a test sample x, the classifier Di will have the probability dij (XRai) for the hypothesis that x belongs to the class ω j . The confidence of a class can be computed by using average combination method which is shown below:

$$
\varphi_j(x) = \frac{1}{L}\sum_i^L =d_{ij}(xR_i^a), \text{j} = 1,....,\text{m}
$$

In the proposed RotBagg ensemble classifier, the base classifiers D1, . . ., DL of Rotation Forest are replaced by Bagging classifiers. Bagging (Bootstrap aggregating) was introduced by Breimen (Breiman L., 1996) and it randomly replaces the original training dataset by N items. The replaced training sets are known as bootstrap replicates wherein some instances may not appear but others may appear more than once. The ensemble classifier is constructed by aggregating the base classifiers where all of them have equal vote.

The integration of bagging with rotation forest enhances the computational ability in terms of accuracy and diversity of the integrated RotBagg ensemble classifier. RotBagg is more advantageous than bagging because it has the ability of parallel execution.

The pseudocode 1 explains how each sub-ensemble created by bagging learns without depending on other ensembles. The learning principle is explained through pseudocode 1. Some of the important parameters of RotBagg ensemble classifier need to be decided beforehand i.e., the values of S and T which specify the number of iterations performed by rotation forest and bagging respectively. Similarly, the values of another two parameters such as k and M which specify the number of subsets and the size of each subset respectively need to be fixed. After fixing the above parameters, the RotBagg ensemble algorithm can be implemented. However, the fast decision tree learners (REP Tree) are being employed as the base learners of the proposed RotBagg ensemble algorithm.

Transformation Techniques

As it is known that decision trees are used as the base learners to construct rotation forest and RotBagg, they need to satisfy the two characteristics of ensemble system i.e., accuracy and diversity. A bootstrap mechanism is used to form a new training set from the original for each base classifier of the ensemble. Then the new training set is randomly split into disjoint subsets which are then transformed individually by a linear transformation technique. The transformed features of each tree, subsequently reconstruct the full feature set of the ensemble. Since a small rotation in the axis creates a different tree, the transformation technique can guarantee the quality of diversity of the ensemble system. As a matter of fact, all the outputs are fused by the average rule. Mostly, there have been three types of transformation techniques adopted by different researchers (Kuncheva & Rodriguez, 2007) such as non-parametric discriminant analysis (NDA), principal component analysis (PCA) and random projections (RP). It has been found that PCA -based rotation forest performs better than the other two. Indeed, the principal components use to preserve all the discriminatory information of the dataset after transformation and the rotation of axes primarily generate diversity among the base classifiers instead of weakening the individual classifiers. In addition to this, an efficient sparse random projection (RP) method has been mentioned (Kuncheva & Rodriguez, 2007) with effective performance. Therefore, in this paper PCA and RP method has also been considered for comparison in the microarray dataset classification experiment.

Pseudocode-1 of RotBagg Ensemble Classifier

Input

1. **L:** a training set, L= $\{(x_i, y_i)\}_{i=1}^{N}$ = [XY]
   where X is an N × n matrix containing the input values and y is an N –dimensional column vector containing the class labels.
2. **K:** number of attributes subsets (or M: number of input attributes contained in each subset).
3. **C:** a base learner.
4. **S:** number of iteration for Rotation Forest.

5. **T**: No of iteration for Bagging.
6. **x**: a data point to be classified.

Training Phase

For s = 1, 2, ..., S

1. Use the steps similar to those in Rotation Forest to compute the Rotation matrix, say, R_s^a and let $L^a = [XR_t^aY]$ be the training set for classifier C_S .
2. Initialize the weight distribution over L^a as $D_1(i) = 1/N (i = 1, 2, ..., N)$
3. For t = 1, ..., T
    a. According to distribution D_t perform N extractions randomly from L^a with replacement to compose a new set L_t^a
    b. Apply ω to L_t^a to train a classifier C_t^a and then compute the error of C_t^a as
    $$\varepsilon_t = Pr_{i \sim D_t}(C_t^a(x_i) \neq y_i) = \sum_{i=1}^{N}(C_t^a(x_i) \neq y_i))D_t(i)$$
    c. If $\varepsilon_t > 0.5$ then set D_t (i) = 1/N (i = 1, 2, ..., N) and go to step(a); if $\varepsilon_t = 0$, then set $\varepsilon_t = 10^{-10}$ to continue the following iterations
    d. Choose $\alpha_t = 1/2 \mathrm{In}((1-\varepsilon_t)/\varepsilon_t)$
    e. Update the distribution D_t over L^a as: $D_{t+1}(i) = \dfrac{D_t(i)}{Z_t} \times \begin{cases} e^{-\alpha_t}, if C_t^a(x_i)=y_i \\ e^{\alpha_t}, if\ C_t^a(x_i)=y_i \end{cases}$

    Where Z_t is a normalization factor being chosen so that D_{t+1} is a probability distribution over L^a .
    End for
4. Let $C_s(x) = \mathrm{argma}\ x_{y \in 0} \sum_{t=1}^{T} \alpha_t I(C_t^a(x) = y)$
    End for

Output
    The class label for x predicted by the final ensemble C^* as

$$C^*(x) = \mathrm{argma}\ x_{y \in 0} \sum_{s=1}^{s} I(C_s(x) = y)$$

where I (.) is an indicator function.

Feature Selection

The sample size of microarray datasets available in public database is very small compared to the number of attributes involved and this ratio problem is referred to as curse of dimensionality. This problem becomes a challenge for many classification techniques. As a matter of fact, only a small subset of attributes of microarray dataset is responsible for causing cancer. This necessitates the development of a data reduction technique to remove irrelevant, redundant and noisy data to find an effective solution to increase the classification accuracy. On the other hand, if RotBagg ensemble is applied directly to the dataset without reduction then a rotation matrix with thousands of dimensions is required for each tree which increases the computational complexity to a large extent. There are two major categories of feature selection algorithms (Dash & Dash, 2014) such as filter and wrapper algorithm used to find the predictive genes. The filter model finds the significant attributes using only the general characteristics of the dataset without the learning algorithm involvement whereas the wrapper model uses incremental approach involving an evaluation function to validate the subsets of features generated. Although, this method finds subset of features which provides a superior learning performance, still they are computationally expensive than filter model (Dash, Patra & Tripathy, 2012). In this paper, a correlation based feature relevance and feature redundant (CO-FRFR) technique which is already applied in (Dash & Dash, 2014) and suggest that CO-FRFR identifies the redundancy among relevant features. The advantage of this model is it uses interdependence of features along with the dependence to the class and identifies predominant features by reducing the dimension to a greater extent. Thus, it improves the classification accuracy in return. It has been explained in pseudocode-2.

Pseudocode-2 of Correlation Based Feature Relevancy and Redundancy Algorithm (CO-FEFR)

Relevance Analysis

1. Rank the features according to the decreasing values of $SU_{i,c} > Rel\text{-}parameter$
2. Redundancy analysis
3. Initialize F_i with the value of first feature in the list
4. Compare and eliminate features for which F_i forms an approximate redundant cover
5. Set F_i as the predominant feature in the list
6. Repeat step 3 until the end of the list
7. Evaluate the predictive significance of the predominant feature list using RotBagg ensemble

EXPERIMENTAL STUDY

Microarray Dataset

The efficiency of the proposed method is measured through three publicly available multi-category and two binary microarray datasets. The datasets include MLL Leukemia, Lung cancer, ovarian cancer, CNS and SRBCT. Table 1 summarizes the characteristics of the microarray datasets. The out-liars of the datasets are removed through preprocessing which is an important step for handling gene expression data. This includes two steps: filling missing values and standardization. The missing values of the datasets are filled using the average value of the corresponding gene. Standardization is performed so that every gene expression has mean 0 and standard deviation 1.

Experimental Design and Analysis

In this work, we have used open source tool WEKA to implement the proposed RotBagg ensemble classifier and the feature selection / reduction techniques. The efficiency of the proposed feature reduction

Table 1. Microarray Data sets used in this experiment

DATA SET	No. of Features	No. of Samples	No. of Classes	References
MLL Leukemia	12534	72	03	Armstrong et al., 2002
Ovarian Cancer	15154	253	02	Emanuel F Petricoin III, et al, 2002
Lung Tumour	12601	203	05	Arindam Bhattacharjee, et al., 2001
SRBCT	2308	83	04	Khan J et al., 2001
CNS	7129	60	02	Scott L. Pomeroy, et al. 2002

technique (CO-FRFR) has been compared with two representative feature reduction methods such as correlation-based feature selection (CFS) and ReliefF in this experiment. The dataset is cleaned removing all missing values and converting it to mean 0 and standard deviation 1.

ReliefF (Dash & Dash, 2014; Ambroise & McLachlan, 2002) has the ability to deal with multiclass problems and more robust towards noisy and incomplete data. It evaluates the worth of an attribute by repeatedly sampling an instance and considering the value of the given attribute for the nearest instance of the same and different class. The CFS method (Hall, 2000) depends on a set of heuristics to assess the adequacy of the subsets. The heuristics used in this method take in to consideration both the correlation among the features and the dependency of features to the class.

To select the most informative features and reduce the computational complexity of the problem, all the feature selection method such as CFS, ReliefF and CO-FRFR are used to derive the features for each method. The selected features are shown in Table 2 for each datasets and it is evident from the table that the selection of features is different for each dataset and largely depends on the feature selection algorithms. It is quite apparent from Table 2 that CO-FRFR selects least number of predictive features while achieving highest reduction in dimension of the datasets. Therefore, it conforms to the theoretical concept of CO-FRFR to recognize and ignore redundant features.

The classification accuracy of the selected features is evaluated using RotBagg ensemble using a fast decision tree (REP tree) as the base learner and compared with the performance of integrated ensembles RotBagg and also with the base learner performance which is shown in the Tables 3 to 14. This learner is applied to the reduced datasets obtained from the feature selection algorithms and the overall classification accuracy is recorded using stratified 10-fold cross validation method to achieve statistically reliable predictive measurements (Dash & Liu, 2003; Dash & Liu, 1997). It is observed from the table that, CO-FRFR outperforms the other two feature selection algorithms in terms of achieving least

Table 2. No. of selected genes for each gene selection algorithms

Dataset	Initial Attribute/ Sample nos	Co-FRFR	ReliefF	CFS
MLL	12533/72	23	34	150
Ovarian cancer	15154/253	30	42	36
Lung	12600/203	15	28	550
SRBCT	2308/83	14	38	119
CNS	7130/60	14	29	40

Table 3. Stratified 10-fold-CV learning performance of CO-FRFR based RotBagg ensemble using PCA/ RP transformation methods for all 5 datasets

Datasets	% of Accuracy	Precision	F-score	MCC	ROC Area	Kappa Statistic	FP Rate
MLL	97.22/ 95.833	0.975/ 0.959	0.972/ 0.958	0.960/ 0.938	**0.999/ 0.996**	0.9581/ 0.9371	0.011/ 0.020
Ovarian	*99.2095/ 98.8142*	0.992/ 0.988	0.992/ 0.988	0.983/ 0.974	**1.0/ 0.999**	0.9828 /0.9741	0.014/ 0.021
Lung	93. 1034 / 92.1182	0.932 / 0.924	0.927/ 0.914	0.849/ 0.832	**0.986/ 0.975**	0.8544/ 0.8304	0.129/ 0.151
SRBCT	**100 / 97. 5904**	1.0 / 0.976	1.0 / 0.976	1.0 / 0.967	**1.0 / 0.998**	1.0 / 0.9665	0.0 / 0.012
CNS	85.00/ 83.333	0.853 / 0.849	0.844 / 0.821	0.664 / 0.632	**0.912 / 0.897**	0.6512/ 0.5912	0,235/ 0.288

number of features. The classification accuracy, precision, F-score, MCC, ROC area of all the datasets are significantly better for the CO-FRFR based hybrid ensemble RotBagg when compared with other combination of feature selection methods. Two types of transformation techniques such as PCA and RP are used along with the hybrid ensemble classification. It is observed from the experiment that PCA based transformation outperforms RP transformation in hybrid RotBagg as well as in single Rotation Forest ensemble. To compare the classification performance of the classifiers, 10-fold cross validation has been used for all the experiments. In this method, each dataset is divided into 10 disjoint sets, each having roughly same distribution. But, the single classifier such as a decision tree does not provide results like an accurate classifier when it is applied to microarray gene classification problem which suffers lot of limitations like uncertainties, noises and curse of dimensionality. The results obtained from Table 6 to Table 14 conforms the findings of (Osareh & Shadgar, 2013).

The challenges encountered by a single decision tree algorithm have been overcome by a robust and accurate ensemble algorithm "RotBagg". This ensemble classifier operates on the discriminative features obtained from the feature selection method CO-FRFR, ReliefF and CFS. Along with the RotBagg, another two ensemble classifiers namely rotation forest and bagging are also developed and trained using the reduced data in this experiment. All the ensembles have used a decision tree as a base learner (Yang, Yang, Zhou & Zomaya, 2010) because it is more sensitive to the changes made in the dataset. A first decision tree learner (REP tree) was used by all the methods as the base learners without pruning. Now each of the ensemble methods will train a large number of base classifiers nearly 100 in numbers to construct the ensemble classifiers. The total number of iterations for both rotation forest and bagging can be balanced by setting $S = T = 10$ which is similar to (Osareh & Shadgar, 2013). As per the concept, a moderate value needs to be set for the parameter M according to the size of the feature set F. Therefore, the performance of RotBagg will vary for different size of the features contained in each subset M. But, when compared the performance of the classification results varying M from 1 to 20, it is observed that the variation is insignificant. This shows there is no consistent relationship exists between M and the learning accuracy (Ambroise & McLachlan, 2002). In this experiment an optimum value is set for M i.e., $M = 3$ to established a consistent relationship between the diversity and classification accuracy of the base learners.

To find the most effective transformation technique to maintain the diversity and accuracy of the base classifiers, two well-known transformation techniques i.e., PCA and RP have been used in this experiment. After the transformation of the datasets, the principal components preserve the discriminatory information. Then the axes are rotated optimally which primarily develops the diversity among the classifiers rather than weakening the individual classifiers. As a result, a trade-off between diversity and accuracy can be maintained.

The small number of instances in the microarray dataset led to unreliable solutions. To counter this problem, 10-fold cross validation method (Peng, 2006) was suggested to split the datasets into 10 equal fold to validate the solution. However, in this work, a 10-fold cross validation is deployed to evaluate the performance of the feature selection algorithm.

Table 3 shows CO-FRFR based RotBagg classification accuracy, precision, F-score, MCC, ROC area and FP rate for all the five datasets when both the transformation matrix are applied. The classifier is trained 10 times such that in each iteration a different set is kept for testing. The AUROC (Area under the Receiver Operating Characteristic) value and MCC are computed as the average of each of these iterations. Many statistical techniques have been applied to compare the performance of classifier across multiple datasets. Again the performance of the classifiers can be ranked (Kuncheva & Whitaker, 2003) using average AUROC values with 1 being the best. Similarly, Friedman and Bonferroni-Dunn tests (Kuncheva & Whitaker, 2003) are performed to determine whether or not the newly introduced methods are statistically better than the existing methods. It is quite apparent from Table 3 that PCA-based RotBagg performs significantly better than RP-based RotBagg for all the datasets and achieves full rank for ovarian cancer and SRBCT. It can also be noted from Table 3 that PCA–based RotBagg ensembles outperform RP-based counterparts in terms of accuracy of classification. Also it is important to record that all these experiments have been performed on the features selected by CO-FRFR algorithm.

After choosing the transformation method, a comparative study on the performance of PCA/RP-based RotBagg using ReliefF and CFS feature selection methods to reduce the feature space is made. Table 4 and 5 demonstrates the classification accuracy of each classification method on the selected datasets. CO-FRFR based PCA-RotBagg ensemble performs significantly better than bagging and rotation forest invariably for all the datasets.

Table 4. Stratified 10-fold-CV learning performance of ReliefF based RotBagg ensemble using PCA/RP Transformation methods for all 5 datasets

Datasets	% of Accuracy	Precision	F-score	MCC	ROC Area	Kappa Statistic	FP Rate
MLL	97.22/ 95.833	0.975/ 0.959	0.972/ 0.958	0.960/ 0.938	**0.996/ 0.998**	0.9581/ 0.9371	0.011/ 0.020
Ovarian	99.2095/ 98.8142	0.992/ 0.988	0.992/ 0.988	0.983/ 0.974	**1.0/ 0.999**	0.9828 /0.9741	0.014/ 0.021
Lung	93. 1034 / 92.1182	0.932 / 0.924	0.927/ 0.914	0.849/ 0.832	**0.986/ 0.975**	0.8544/ 0.8304	0.129/ 0.151
SRBCT	100 / 97. 5904	1.0 / 0.976	1.0 / 0.976	1.0 / 0.967	**1.0 / 0.998**	1.0 / 0.9665	0.0 / 0.012
CNS	85.00/ 83.333	0.853 / 0.849	0.844 / 0.821	0.664 / 0.632	**0.912 / 0.897**	0.6512/ 0.5912	0.235/ 0.288

Table 5. Stratified 10-fold-CV learning performance of Correlation Feature Selection (CFS) based RotBagg ensemble using PCA/RP Transformation methods for all 5 datasets

Datasets	% of Accuracy	Precision	F-score	MCC	ROC Area	Kappa Statistic	FP Rate
MLL	100/ 98.6111	1.0/ 0.987	1.0/ 986	1.0/ 0.979	**1.0/ 1.0**	1.0/ 0.9789	0.0/ 0.009
Ovarian	99.6047/ 97.6285	0.996/ 0.976	0.996/ 0.976	0.991/ 0.948	**1.0/ 0.999**	0.9914/ 0.9483	0.007/ 0.033
Lung	93. 1034/ 91.133	0.936/ 0.918	0.916/ 0.898	0.839/ 0.814	**0.978/ 0.976**	0.8466/ 0.8382	0.110/ 0.120
SRBCT	98.7952/ 97.5904	0.988/ 0.977	0.988/ 0.976	0.982/ 0.966	**1.0 / 1.0**	0.9833/ 0.9667	0.005/ 0.009
CNS	81.6667/ 81.6667	0.816/ 0.823	0.810/ 0.806	0.585/ 0.587	**0.895/ 0.889**	0.5736/ 0.5635	0.275/ 0.297

The most important issue of ensemble learning technique is the balance between diversity and accuracy of the classifiers involved in the ensemble as base learners. The base learners in an ensemble should have high accuracy and should avoid making misclassification errors. Thus, the accuracy of fused outputs will be more than that of the individual classifier (Ambroise & McLachlan, 2002). However, the diversity conflict with accuracy of base learners, i.e., the more accurate the base learners are, the lower the diversity is. So, it is difficult to define a single measure of diversity that measures the performance of ensemble. In this experiment, pair wise diversity measure has been utilized to measure the ability of the proposed PCA-based RotBagg which can build accurate and diverse base learners effectively.

Comparing the performance of Table 3, 4 and 5 with 6, 7 and 8, it is understood that the performance of hybrid ensemble is more significant when paired with CO-FRFR. But it is also apparent from the table that irrespective of the feature selection method chosen the performance of the hybrid RotBagg is most effective than the performance of the individual ensembles and the decision tree learner.

Table 6. Stratified 10-fold-CV learning performance of CO-FRFR based Rotation Forest ensemble using PCA/RP Transformation methods for all 5 datasets

Datasets	% of Accuracy	Precision	F-score	MCC	ROC Area	Kappa Statistic	FP Rate
MLL	95.333/ 94.444	0.959/ 0.948	0.958/ 0.945	0.937/ 0.919	**0.999/ 0.993**	0.9368/ 0.9162	0.023/ 0.025
Ovarian	98.8142/ 97.6285	0.988/ 0.976	0.988/ 0.976	0.974/ 0.948	**0.999/ 0.998**	0.9741/ 0.9483	0.021/ 0.033
Lung	90.6404/ 90.6404	0.909/ 0.904	0.899/ 0.896	0.798/ 0.987	**0.984/ 0.983**	0.7997/ 0.7972	0.173/ 0.163
SRBCT	97.5904/ 96.3855	0.976/ 0.965	0.976/ 0.964	0.966/ 0.948	**0.998/ 0.995**	0.9666/ 0.9499	0.012/ 0.017
CNS	86.6667/ 83.3333	0.868/ 0.849	0.863/ 0.821	0.702/ 0.632	**0.920/ 0.910**	0.6935/ 0.5984	0.204/ 0.288

Table 7. Stratified 10-fold-CV learning performance of CO-FRFR based Bagging ensemble for all 5 datasets

Datasets	% of Accuracy	Precision	F-score	MCC	ROC Area	Kappa Statistic	FP Rate
MLL	91.6667	0.916	0.916	0.875	**0.984**	0.874	0.041
Ovarian	97.2332	0.972	0.972	0.940	**0.993**	0.9395	0.040
Lung	93.5961	0.937	0.933	0.871	**0.987**	0.8656	0.108
SRBCT	97.5904	0.976	0.976	0.976	**0.998**	0.9665	0.012
CNS	80.00	0.808	0.786	0.547	**0.897**	0.5181	0.327

Table 8. Stratified 10-fold-CV learning performance of CO-FRFR based first decision tree (REP Tree) learner for all 5 datasets

Datasets	% of Accuracy	Precision	F-score	MCC	ROC Area	Kappa Statistic	FP Rate
MLL	91.6667	0.920	0.917	0.876	**0.929**	0.8744	0.039
Ovarian	97.2332	0.972	0.972	0.940	**0.965**	0.9398	0.035
Lung	91.133	0.914	0.912	0.821	**0.916**	0.8216	0.100
SRBCT	80.7229	0.826	0.810	0.739	**0.896**	0.7332	0.077
CNS	75.00	0.743	0.741	0.427	**0.696**	0.4186	0.354

Table 9. Stratified 10-fold-CV learning performance of ReliefF based Rotation Forest ensemble using PCA/RP Transformation methods for all 5 datasets

Datasets	% of Accuracy	Precision	F-score	MCC	ROC Area	Kappa Statistic	FP Rate
MLL	94.4444/ 93.0556	0.946/ 0.932	0.945/ 0.930	0.916/ 0.896	**0.990/ 0.986**	0.9156/ 0.8944	0.032/ 0.039
Ovarian	99.6047/ 98.8142	0.996/ 0.998	0.996/ 0.988	0.991/ 0.974	**1.0/ 0.994**	0.9914/ 0.9742	0.007/ 0.016
Lung	91.1333/ 90.6404	0.911/ 0.907	0.908/ 0.899	0.812/ 0.798	**0.970/ 0.958**	0.818/ 0.7996	0.121/ 0.163
SRBCT	97.5904/ 95.1807	0.976/ 0.952	0.976/ 0.952	0.976/ 0.952	**0.998/ 0.996**	0.9667/ 0.9332	0.010/ 0.025
CNS	80.00/ 75.00	0.822/ 0.761	0.780/ 0.721	0.555/ 0.422	**0.806/ 0.772**	0.5062/ 0.375	0.349/ 0.420

The classification performance of the RotBagg ensemble obtained for the reduced dataset derived from ReliefF and CFS is compared with the performance of individual ensemble and observed that RotBagg performs better than others can be observed from Table 9, 10, 11, 12, 13 and 14.

In order to measure the level of agreement between a pair of base learners, a k-metric or kappa statistic (Pomeroy et al, 2002) is used while correcting the chance. For c- class labels, k is defined on $c \times c$

Table 10. Stratified 10-fold-CV learning performance of ReliefF based Bagging ensemble methods for all 5 datasets

Datasets	% of Accuracy	Precision	F-score	MCC	ROC Area	Kappa Statistic	FP Rate
MLL	91.6667	0.916	0.916	0.875	**0.984**	0.875	0.041
Ovarian	97. 2332	0.976	0.976	0.948	**0.995**	0.9483	0.033
Lung	91.6256	0.916	0.915	0.818	**0.963**	0.8284	0.121
SRBCT	92.7711	0.932	0.929	0.903	**0.993**	0.9005	0.024
CNS	73.33	0.725	0.726	0.392	**0.802**	0.387	0.363

Table 11. Stratified 10-fold-CV learning performance of ReliefF based first decision tree (REP Tree) learner for all 5 datasets

Datasets	% of Accuracy	Precision	F-score	MCC	ROC Area	Kappa Statistic	FP Rate
MLL	91.6667	0.917	0.915	0.877	**0.960**	0.8734	0.042
Ovarian	96.8379	0.968	0.968	0.931	**0.950**	0.931	0.042
Lung	85.2217	0.852	0.853	0.716	**0.890**	0.7116	0.126
SRBCT	85.5422	0.858	0.855	0.857	**0.924**	0.8006	0.051
CNS	70.00	0.694	0.700	0.696	**0.700**	0.3258	0.381

Table 12. Stratified 10-fold-CV learning performance of CFS based Rotation Forest ensemble using PCA/RP Transformation methods for all 5 datasets

Datasets	% of Accuracy	Precision	F-score	MCC	ROC Area	Kappa Statistic	FP Rate
MLL	98.6111/ 95.8333	0.987/ 0.959	0.986/ 0.958	0.986/ 0.958	**0.999/ 0.995**	0.9789/ 0.9371	0.009/ 0.020
Ovarian	99.6047/ 97.2332	0.996/ 0.972	0.996/ 0.972	0.991/ 0.940	**1.0/ 0.999**	0.9914/ 0.9395	0.002/ 0.040
Lung	91.6256/ 91.133	0.916/ 0.911	0.906/ 0.895	0.830/ 0.810	**0.989/ 0.989**	0.8227/ 0.8086	0.131/ 0.152
SRBCT	97.5904/ 96.3855	0.976/ 0.964	0.976/ 0.964	0.966/ 0.948	**0.999/ 0.995**	0.9667/ 0.9499	0.010/ 0.017
CNS	80.00/ 75.00	0.808/ 0.781	0.800/ 0.750	0.786/ 0.712	**0.906/ 0.870**	0.5181/ 0.359	0.327/ 0.442

coincidence matrix M of the two classifiers. The entry $m\,k_s$ of M is the proportion of the data set, which Di labels as wk and Dj labels as ws. Now, the agreement between Di and Dj is given by

$$K_{i,j} = \frac{\sum Km_{k,k} - \text{ABC}}{1 - \text{ABC}}$$

Table 13. Stratified 10-fold-CV learning performance of CFS based Bagtging ensemble methods for all 5 datasets

Datasets	% of Accuracy	Precision	F-score	MCC	ROC Area	Kappa Statistic	FP Rate
MLL	91.6667	0.917	0.914	0.878	**0.983**	0.8726	0.020
Ovarian	97.6285	0.976	0.976	0.948	**0.989**	0.9483	0.033
Lung	91.133	0.911	0.897	0.813	**0.984**	0.8087	0.151
SRBCT	95.1807	0.952	0.952	0.934	**0.995**	0.9336	0.016
CNS	78.3333	0.783	0.758	0.516	**0.794**	0.4583	0.380

Table 14. Stratified 10-fold-CV learning performance of CFS based first decision tree (REP Tree) learner for all 5 datasets

Datasets	% of Accuracy	Precision	F-score	MCC	ROC Area	Kappa Statistic	FP Rate
MLL	80.5556	0.807	0.806	0.708	**0.896**	0.7053	0.099
Ovarian	96.4427	0.964	0.964	0.923	**0.958**	0.9226	0.044
Lung	87.6847	0.884	0.887	0.871	**0.920**	0.7542	0.105
SRBCT	80.7229	0.818	0.807	0.807	**0.879**	0.7333	0.076
CNS	61.6667	0.596	0.617	0.602	**0.582**	0.1085	0.514

If the value of $k = 1$ then the classifiers decisions are the same otherwise $k = 0$, which represent the case when the classifiers are entirely independent, and the agreement of the two classifiers equals that expected by chance (Cohen, 1960). Table 3 shows the value of kappa statistic k for both *PCA-based-RotBagg* and RP-based- RotBagg ensemble classifiers. It is observed from the table that for ovarian cancer and SRBCT the value of k is 1 i.e., the classifiers decisions are same whereas the value of k for CNS is 0.65 in PCA-based RotBagg. In Table 3, 4 and 5, the value of kappa statistic is very close to 1 for RotBagg ensemble for all the three feature selection methods whereas it is significantly less for all the individual ensembles shown in remaining tables.

CONCLUSION

In this study, we proposed a novel concept of correlation based feature relevancy and redundancy (CO-FRFR) selection algorithm and a hybrid robust ensemble classifier, "RotBagg". This ensemble technique preserves the most essential characteristic of an ensemble framework, i.e., accuracy and diversity. In order to overcome the limitation of curse of dimensionality, uncertainties and noises, a small subset of most informative features were selected using 3 representative feature selection techniques namely, CFS, CO-FRFR and ReliefF. Then the ensemble classifier RotBagg was employed on the selected datasets. The experiment was conducted using two types of transformation matrices, i.e., PCA and RP method to implement RotBagg ensemble.

The efficiency of the proposed ensemble was assessed with different ensemble algorithms including rotation forest and bagging. The experimental results showed that the combination of CO-FRFR feature selection and PCA-based RotBagg ensemble with decision tree as base learners construct a robust classifier for the microarray datasets. The proposed method has achieved the highest generalization ability in comparison to its counterparts. It has also established a trade-off between the diversity and accuracy of the base learners involved.

REFERENCES

Abraham, A. (2004). Meta-Learning Evolutionary Artificial Neural Networks. N*eurocomputing, 56,* 1–38. doi:10.1016/S0925-2312(03)00369-2

Ambroise, C., & McLachlan, G. J. (2002). Selection bias in gene extraction on the basis of microarray gene-expression data. *Proceedings of the National Academy of Sciences of the United States of America, 99*(10), 6562–6566. doi:10.1073/pnas.102102699 PMID:11983868

Armstrong, S. A., Staunton, J. E., Silverman, L. B., Pieters, R., den Boer, M. L., Minden, M. D., & Korsmeyer, S. J. et al. (2002). MLL translocations specify a distinct gene expression profile that distinguishes a unique leukemia. *Nature Genetics, 30*(1), 41–47. doi:10.1038/ng765 PMID:11731795

Bhattacharjee, A., Richards, W. G., Staunton, J., Li, C., Monti, S., Vasa, P., & Meyerson, M. et al. (2001). Classification of human lung carcinomas by mRNA expression profiling reveals distinct adenocarcinoma subclasses. *PNAS. The National Academy of Sciences, USA, 98*(24), 13790–13795. doi:10.1073/pnas.191502998 PMID:11707567

Breiman, L. (1996). Bagging predictors. *Machine Learning, 24*(2), 123–140. doi:10.1007/BF00058655

Breiman, L. (2001). Random forests. *Machine Learning, 45*(1), 5–32. doi:10.1023/A:1010933404324

Cohen, J. (1960). A coefficient of agreement for nominal scales. *Educational and Psychological Measurement, 20*(1), 37–46. doi:10.1177/001316446002000104

Dash, M., Choi, K., Scheuermann, P., & Liu, H. (2002). Feature selection for clustering – a filter solution. *Proc.of theSecond International Conference on Data Mining* (pp. 115–122).

Dash, M., & Liu, H. (1997). Feature selection for classification, *Intelligent Data Analysis. International Journal (Toronto, Ont.), 1*(3), 131–156.

Dash, M., & Liu, H. (2003). Consistency-based search in feature selection. *Artificial Intelligence, 151*(1-2), 155–176. doi:10.1016/S0004-3702(03)00079-1

Dash, S. (2015). A Diverse Meta learning ensemble technique to handle imbalanced microarray dataset. *Proceedings of Seventh World Congress on Nature and Biologically Inspired Computing (NaBIC2015), Advances in Nature and Biologically Inspired Computing, Advances in Intelligent Systems and Computing.* DOI: doi:10.1007/978-3-319-27400-3_1

Dash, S., & Dash, A. (2014). A correlation based multilayer perception algorithm for cancer classification with gene-expression dataset. *Proceedings of theInternational conference on Hybrid Intelligent Systems (HIS)*. doi:10.1109/HIS.2014.7086190

Dash, S., Patra, B., & Tripathy, B. K. (2012). A hybrid Data Mining Technique for Improving the Classification accuracy of Microarray Dataset. *I.J. Information engineering and electronics Business*, 2, 43-50.

DeBock, K. W., Coussement, K., & VandenPoel, D. (2010). Ensemble classification based on generalized additive models. *Computational Statistics & Data Analysis*, *54*(6), 1535–1546. doi:10.1016/j.csda.2009.12.013

Dietterich, T. (2000). Ensemble methods in machine learning. *Proceedings of the Multiple Classifier System Conference* (pp. 1– 15). doi:10.1007/3-540-45014-9_1

Dietterich, T. G. (2000). An experimental comparison of three methods for constructing ensembles of decision trees: Bagging, boosting, and randomization. *Machine Learning*, *40*(2), 139–157. doi:10.1023/A:1007607513941

Freund, Y., & Schapire, R. E. (1997). A decision-theoretic generalization of on-line learning and an application to boosting. *Journal of Computer and System Sciences*, *55*(1), 119–139. doi:10.1006/jcss.1997.1504

Guyon, I., & Elisseeff, A. (2003). An introduction to variable and feature selection. *Journal of Machine Learning Research*, *3*, 1157–1182.

Hall, M. A. (2000). Correlation-based feature selection for discrete and numeric class machine learning. *Proc.Seventeenth International Conference on Machine Learning* (pp. 359–366).

Hansen, L. K., & Salamon, P. (1990). Neural network ensembles. *IEEE Transactions on Pattern Analysis and Machine Intelligence*, *12*(10), 993–1001. doi:10.1109/34.58871

Hsu, H.-H., Hsieh, C.-W., & Lu, M.-D. (2011). Hybrid feature selection by combining filters and wrappers. *Expert Systems with Applications*, *38*(7), 8144–8150. doi:10.1016/j.eswa.2010.12.156

Khan, J., Wei, J. S., Ringner, M., Saal, L. H., Ladanyi, M., Westermann, F., & Meltzer, P. S. et al. (2001). Classification and diagnostic of cancers using gene expression profiling and Artificial neural networks. *NCBI*, *7*(6), 673–679. PMID:11385503

Kohavi, R., & John, G. H. (1997). Wrappers for feature subset selection. *Artificial Intelligence*, *97*(1-2), 273–324. doi:10.1016/S0004-3702(97)00043-X

Kuncheva, L. I., & Rodriguez, J. J. (2007). An experimental study on Rotation Forest ensembles. Proceedings of MCS 2007, LNCS (Vol. 4472, pp. 459–468). Berlin: Springer. doi:10.1007/978-3-540-72523-7_46

Kuncheva, L. I., & Whitaker, C. J. (2003). Measures of diversity in classifier ensembles. *Machine Learning*, *51*(2), 181–207. doi:10.1023/A:1022859003006

Liu, H., Liu, L., & Zhang, H. (2010). Ensemble gene selection for cancer classification. *Pattern Recognition*, *43*(8), 2763–2772. doi:10.1016/j.patcog.2010.02.008

Liu, H., Motoda, H., & Yu, L. (2002). Feature selection with selective sampling. *Proc. Nineteenth International Conference on Machine Learning* (pp. 395–402).

Liu, K.-H., & Huang, D.-S. (2008). Cancer classification using Rotation Forest. *Computers in Biology and Medicine*, *38*(5), 601–610. doi:10.1016/j.compbiomed.2008.02.007 PMID:18394595

Osareh, A., & Shadgar, B. (2013). An efficient ensemble learning method for gene microarray classification. Biomed Research International, 2013.

Peng, Y. (2006). A novel ensemble machine learning for robust microarray data classification. *Computers in Biology and Medicine*, *6*(36), 553–573. doi:10.1016/j.compbiomed.2005.04.001 PMID:15978569

Petricoin, E. F. III, Ardekani, A. M., Hitt, B. A., Levine, P. J., Fusaro, V. A., Steinberg, S. M., & Liotta, L. A. et al. (2002). Use of Proteomic Patterns in Serum to Identify Ovarian Cancer. *Lancet*, *359*(9306), 572–577. doi:10.1016/S0140-6736(02)07746-2 PMID:11867112

Pomeroy, S. L., Tamayo, P., Gaasenbeek, M., Sturla, L. M., Angelo, M., McLaughlin, M. E., & Golub, T. R. et al. (2002). Prediction of central nervous system embryonal tumor outcome based on gene expression. *Nature*, *415*(6870), 436–442. doi:10.1038/415436a PMID:11807556

Thomas, A., & Thibault, H. (2010). Robust biomarker identification for cancer diagnosis with ensemble feature selection methods. *Bioinformatics (Oxford, England)*, *26*(3), 392–398. doi:10.1093/bioinformatics/btp630 PMID:19942583

Yang, K., Cai, Z., Li, J., & Lin, G. (2006). A stable gene selection in microarray data analysis. *BMC Bioinformatics*, *7*(1), 228. doi:10.1186/1471-2105-7-228 PMID:16643657

Yang, P., Yang, Y. H., Zhou, B. B., & Zomaya, A. Y. (2010). A review of ensemble methods in bioinformatics. *Current Bioinformatics*, *5*(4), 296–308. doi:10.2174/157489310794072508

Yongjun, P., Minghao, P., Kiejung, P., & Keun, H. R. (2012). An ensemble correlation-based gene selection algorithm for cancer classification with gene expression data, *Data and Text Mining*. *Bioinformatics (Oxford, England)*, *28*(24), 3306–3315. doi:10.1093/bioinformatics/bts602 PMID:23060613

Yu, L., & Liu, H. (2003). Feature selection for high-dimensional data: a fast correlation- based filter solution, Proc. *Proceedings of theTwentieth International Conference on Machine Learning* (pp. 856–863).

Zhang, C.-X., & Zhang, J.-S. (2008). RotBoost: A technique for combining rotation forest and Adaboost. *Pattern Recognition Letters*, *29*(10), 1524–1536. doi:10.1016/j.patrec.2008.03.006

Zhang, C.-X., & Zhang, J.-S. (2010). A variant of rotation forest for constructing ensemble classifiers. *Pattern Analysis & Applications*, *13*(1), 59–77. doi:10.1007/s10044-009-0168-8

KEY TERMS AND DEFINITIONS

Base Learners: The component / individual learner of the ensemble which are combined together strategically is referred to as base learners. Base (weak) learner must focus on correctly classifying the most highly weighted examples while strongly avoiding over-fitting.

Correlation-Based: Fluctuation of one variable reliably predicts a similar fluctuation in another variable i.e., change in one causes the change in other.

Diversity: The relation that holds between two entities / objects when and only when they are not identical; the property of being numerically distinct.

Ensemble Learning: It is the process by which multiple models, such as classifiers or experts are strategically generated and combined using a particular rule to solve complex computational intelligence problem.

Feature Redundancy (FR): Duplicated features or information, that adds as a precaution against failure or error.

Hybrid Ensemble: Combining two different ensemble models to enhance the prediction/ generalization capability of the ensemble model.

Principal Component Analysis: It's a method of analysis which involves finding the linear combination of a set of variables that has maximum variance and removing its effect and repeating this successively.

Random Projection: In mathematics and statistics, random projection is a technique used to reduce the dimensionality of a set of points which lie in Euclidean space.

Chapter 3
Recent Trends in Spatial Data Mining and Its Challenges

Anuradha Jagadeesan
VIT University, India

Prathik A
VIT University, India

Tripathy B K
VIT University, India

ABSTRACT

With tremendous development in the field of science and technology, there is vast amount of data which are used in analytics for decision making. Considering its spatial characteristics for mining will enhance the accuracy of decision. So, obtaining knowledge from spatial data becomes very essential and meaningful. The spatial database contains very numerous amounts of spatial and non-spatial data of different forms. Interpretation and analyzing of vast data is far beyond human ability. In order to acquire knowledge on such scenario we need spatial data mining. The challenges involved in spatial mining are to deal with different objects that represent the spatial characteristics. This makes spatial data mining a dominant research field. This chapter briefs about the characteristics of spatial data mining and the methods of spatial data mining in recent years.

INTRODUCTION

Spatial data mining refers to discovering hidden and interesting patterns or rules from large amount of spatial database. Large amount of space related data is stored in spatial database which has relational database with different characteristics that contains information about distance and geology.

Data are organized in multi-structural spatial index dimension and often needs mathematical calculations and geographic reasoning and complicated operations. Spatial characteristic involves mining of information that faces many challenging issues. Because spatial data is different from other data such

DOI: 10.4018/978-1-5225-0427-6.ch003

as numbers, points, polygons, classification and symbols which is traditionally treated by data mining techniques.

Data mining is about pattern extraction from larger database, there is strong spatial component which exists in that larger database, for example, satellite observing earth which maps the entire earth surface systematically collects about terabyte of spatial data every day. A Larger database includes weather, climate and U.S Census. The mining classical relational database is different from those of mining spatial database. Compare to common dataset, spatial data mining is more complex, different and larger. Spatial extent refers to each data item that has a spatial reference where occurrence of each entity will take on a continuous surface or where the two nearby entities have a spatial-relationship existing between them.

Spatial data does not only include location data and attribute data but also the spatial entities relationship. Moreover, data structure is complex in spatial database than the table's in common relational database. In spatial database there are vector and raster graphical data along with numerical data. Storing the features of graphical data is not clear and at the same time, only basic analytical functionalities are given by contemporary GIS. Raster data model in spatial data mining is represented by Single Square of for the land cover and corresponding to land cover each cell has its value as shown in *Figure 1*.

Raster data is better for representing:

- Data are continuous (e.g. slope, elevation etc.).
- Data with multiple feature types (e.g. lines, polygons) and also has single feature types(cell)
- Data with rapid calculation ("map algebra") in which mathematical expression of raster layers are treated as elements.
- Data with multi-variant analysis (e.g. satellite image processing)
- Disk space hogging.

Vector data model in spatial data mining is represented by points, lines, polygons and the TIN's (Triangulated irregular networks) is shown in *Figure 2*. Vectors data are good at:

- Accurately representing true shape and size.
- Representing non-continuous data (e.g., rivers, political boundaries, road lines, mountain peaks).
- Creating aesthetically pleasing maps.
- Conserving disk space.

Spatial mining has its application in the field of Geographic Information System (GIS), remote sensing, medical imaging, exploration of image database and other areas where spatial data is used. Knowledge

Figure 1. Raster image

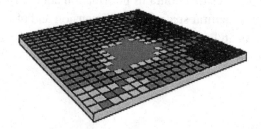

Figure 2. Vector image

Discovery is an interesting field of study that applied in various ways in spatial data such as characteristic and discriminate rule, prominent structure description and extraction or clusters and spatial association.

Spatial Data Mining Structure

Spatial data mining is used in locating the relation between space and the non-space data. Knowledge base is setup for spatial data, data query should be excelled and reorganize spatial database and obtain short total characteristic etc.

As shown in *Figure 3*, the spatial data mining structure can be divided as user face, mine and the data resource. User face layer is important for input and output of data or information, managing data is done by mine layer and select algorithm, storage of mined data and in original data of spatial data mining includes spatial database and related database

Figure 3. Spatial data mining structure

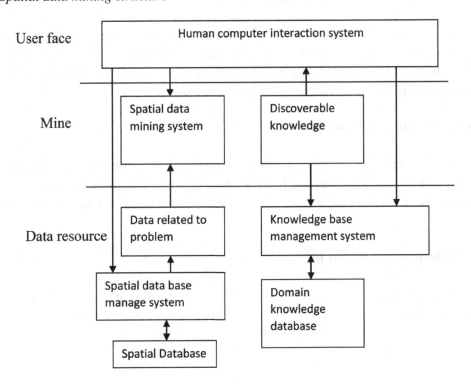

CHARACTERISTIC OF SPATIAL DATA

Spatial objects have distance and location properties. The relationship between spatial data is more complex as there exists certain interaction between adjacent objects. Spatial data are characterized based on the indefinite form and large quantities. Spatial data are said to be indefinite because depending on the type of data, each spatial objects content and structure are represented. Further, two objects which are of same type may differ with number of points; sub-objects etc. spatial data may be voluminous which may exceed the size of DBMS.

Massive Data

Data collected from spatial objects occupies large space, which makes the algorithms difficult to implement on large amount of data and therefore the main task of spatial data mining is to create new strategy for computing these types of data and identify an efficient algorithm to overcome the difficulties created by massive data.

Non-Linear Relationship between Attribute in Spatial Data

It is important sign of the complication of space system, where systems internal functions mechanism is reflected. The spatial attribute data may be character (value like places, location etc.) numerical data like longitude and latitude etc. The main difficult faced by spatial data mining is to correlate this type of attribute.

Scale Characteristic of Spatial Data

To measure the spatial and non-spatial feature, a standardized scaling is needed. Unlike location and distance, measurement of earth's surface location attribute is not having. Scaling the spatial data is another manifestation of complexity and can be used to expose the law of gradual change of characteristic in the process of refinement of information and generalization.

Spatial Dimension Increasing

There is a rapid increase in the spatial data objects properties, as in remote sensing field, due to numerous development of sensor technology, the band size increases in tens of even thousands. So, mining on huge data and discovering knowledge from dimensional space becomes another difficult task of spatial data mining.

The Ambivalence of Spatial Information

There exists the uncertainty in almost all type of spatial information, such as the spatial location, the ambivalence of spatial correlation, as well as in data attribute value of fuzzy etc.

Lack of Spatial Data

In some cases, there exists an irresistible additional forces like numerous data has been lost and cannot be acquired. However, to estimate the parameters distribution of data and to recover the lost data is difficult.

MAIN METHODS OF SPATIAL DATA MINING

Spatial data mining has collected the results from different categories such as recognition of pattern, machine learning, databases, artificial intelligence and information management system (Li et al, 1994). In general, spatial data mining methods are put into four categories: spatial classification, spatial clustering, spatial association rules, spatial co-location and spatial trend analysis.

Spatial Classification Methods

Spatial classification refers to as deriving classification model based on the analysis of spatial objects related to its spatial characteristics, such as areas of region, roads, and ponds or rives. Finding spatial classification rules between spatial and non-spatial attribute in a spatial database is the main aim of spatial classification, and is more predominant direction in the field of spatial data mining in recent years. Ester et al (1997) using ID3 algorithm proposed a first spatial classification method. The algorithm apart from spatial properties, considers non-spatial properties of adjacent objects. Adjacent object is the one which satisfies the adjacent relation. Moreover, the algorithm does not have ability to analyse the aggregated value of adjacent objects and relevant analysis cannot be carried, and the relationship between attributes of spatial and non-spatial objects. Koperski et al (1998) suggested a two-step strategy of spatial data classification. Initial step, through appropriate low cost spatial calculation to obtain the spatial predicate and find the correlation analysis between them, in the final step, refine a more accurate decision tree through further calculation.

Classification can be made number of ways, notably in two ways. First, is to correlate the classification based on the spatial objects image and the second one is the classification based on the location of the object. Correlated geographical data set would assume if that the point (a, b) has a classification of X, then it is likely that point $(a+1, b)$ has a classification of X as well.

Supervised Classification

In supervised classification, based on the samples created from the domain knowledge, the approach of classifier is created. In this method, for creating the classifier for the image, pre-loaded image for the object is required. In dealing with large data set such as spatial data, it has significant limitations.

In supervised classification shown in above *Figure 4*, the classes beforehand are known only to the interpreter is present and within the scene each one or more location occur. Image and areas where these are located contains examples of classes are circumscribed (making them training sites) for each such class statistical analysis on multiband is performed with the class discriminant. All pixels in the image lying outside training sites are then compared with each being assigned to the class it is closest to (with usually for pixels remaining unknown) which can be reasonably accurate.

Figure 4. Supervised classifications

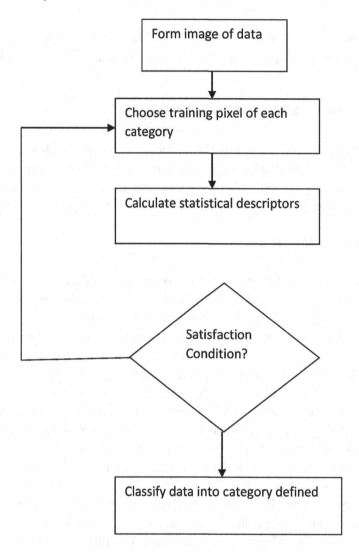

Unsupervised Classification

In unsupervised classification, to observe which one is closest, any individual pixel is compared to each discrete cluster. To determine which cluster each pixel belongs to is done through classification, is produced more commonly assigned to each cluster. In this classification to produce data set classifier cluster data points are used. Identification of classifiers must be done by the domain scientist in order to label the groups. Grouping of data based on the particular area is determined by the domain scientist and cluster should be combined that has not been separated.

In addition to the problem of classification, its disadvantage is that it requires the knowledge of the subject to determine the method for particular data sets. One advantage of this type of method is that it the domain scientist only needs to group the subject not the individual sample points.

Figure 5. Unsupervised classifications

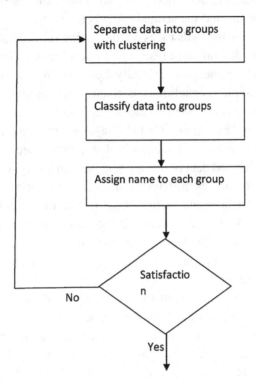

Due to very large amount of data points in the large data set, this type of method is beneficiary, but classification of large amount would be much expansive. Creating a classifier is inefficient in large data set, as computation time is lengthy.

Semi-Supervised Classification

This method is obtained from the use of non-label sample to support the supervised learning. This notation leads to unsupervised method which able to deal with numerous amount of large data points. Unsupervised method may lack in accuracy due to missing of class label, but the goal of semi-supervised method is to focus on process as well as accuracy.

There are numerous methods that can determine the classifier of a data sets in traditional semi-supervised classification. These methods include Expectation Maximization (EM), co-training, Transductive SVM, self- training. Of these methods, EM method is most popular implemented method. Many of these methods have not been applied for current spatial data mining, other approaches is for semi-supervised learning.

The motivation of this method is to benefit unlabeled random data which are extensively available. The cost of improving the classification will decrease, when near unlimited unlabeled points are combined with limited labelled data points. This works because, once the random sampling data distribution will provide statistically significant cross section of data, when creating small samples of labelled data points, which can reduce the domain scientist and computation time and will assists in creating represented clusters.

Semi-supervised classification is classified into two stages. First stage, is the collection of both unlabeled and labelled data points and the second stage is to create classifier initially which are to be used in the third stage. Most of the methods focus on integrating the second and the third stage together.

Fair assumption has been made from most research that deriving labelled of data samples are done by domain scientist which should examine the and classify the data samples manually. The basic assumption of the use of unlabeled data sample is beneficiary is given by this assumption.

Bias into the feature selection is provided by the labelled data, when scientists try to typically label interesting features. As suggested by Jennifer G et al (2004), normalizing the bias is assisted by the use of unlabeled data samples that is introduced due to labelled samples. Second assumption is that from the completed data set, a set of unlabeled data points are selected randomly. This assumption is widespread in literature, but should not be treated as the trivial task. Identification of unlabeled data points must be done with in the set of labelled data points. Actual classification of unlabeled data points should match the known labelled data points. As identification of classification is possible, it is not a problem in many data sets that may not be the possibly in case of classification of image. Solution to this problem is to allow ignore the improper data by random sampling of data. This method however lacks in efficiency as it requires continues computation.

One problem of unsupervised method is that guessing of initial parameters has to be done for classification, which may lead to slow and indifferent classification solution if condition in the model is appropriate. Due to this number of problem may be created. One solution for this is that, as an initial estimates use labelled sample distribution in semi-supervised learning. This can be done by Bayesian classifier, probability distribution function is used to represent the mixture model. The resulting function produces the model

$$P(X_1) | \big(P(Y_1 | X_1) * P(X_1) + P(Y_1 | Y_2) * P(X_2)\big) P(X_1 | Y_1) = P(Y_1 | X_1) * P(X_2) \tag{3.1}$$

Where area 1 is X_1 area 2 is X_2 classification 1 is Y_1. For measuring the appropriate model from the given data set, we can use the inverse of this and can create a function.

The third part is based on the initial classifier given by the estimates is to actually find the classifier, as well as the use of both labelled and unlabeled sets of data. The most popular method to use within the spatial context is the EM (Expectation maximization). Determining of classifier is done in two steps.

First, is for each sample in E step calculates the classifier and determine the likelihood of a given distribution instep M. Repeat the step if newly calculated likelihood is better than the previous step. Repetition is done until the maximum is found.

SPATIAL CLUSTERING METHODS

In the field of data mining, clustering is an important research topic. As discussed by Gomez-chova et al (2003), grouping of data objects based on the similarity, discovering the distribution characteristic of spatial data, data which are having same similarity is formed under one cluster and data of different forms different clustering as much as possible. According to some characteristics, spatial clustering analysis is to divide the objects of spatial database into subclasses meaningfully, the same subclass objects have high similarity and objects in different subclass have obvious difference.

Clustering analysis advantages are: clusters or a structure, grouping of data does not require any background knowledge. In spatial database, clustering is predominantly used. For example, creating thematic map can be done by grouping feature vectors as clusters.

Types of Clustering

1. **Segmentation-Based Method:** This method involves an iterative repositioning technology, which increases clustering effect and objects movement among divisions. Cluster with similar size can be generated with these methods that are in application such as facility location.
2. **Hierarchical-Based Method:** Collected objects are decomposed with this kind of methods. According to hierarchical mode of decomposition, this method is subdivided into two kinds: cohesion and division. BIRCH algorithm and CURE algorithm is a popularly known hierarchical-based clustering method.
3. **Density-Based Method:** For each data points with class label and scope in an area should cross the threshold limit to form a cluster, irrespective of arbitrary shape and noisy data. Most common algorithms in this method are OPTICS and DBRS.
4. **Grid-Based Method:** This method divides the space into limited number of units or a multi-resolution grid structure is used. Clustering operations are carried within the units. Processing time is independent to speed of processing and number of objects. The well-known algorithm of this method are STING algorithm, CLIQUE algorithm etc.

Clustering Methods of Spatial Data Mining

1. **PAM (Partitioning Around Medoids):** Assuming that there are 'n' objects, by finding each clusters representative objects, PAM finds k clusters. In this algorithm representative of each cluster called medoids are centrally located. Once k medoid is selected, the algorithm analysis all possible pair of objects and makes a better choice of medoids, such that one is medoid and other is not. Quality of cluster measured based on the compactness of the cluster.
   By choosing the Medoids for next iteration, the best choice of point in one iteration is chosen. Single iteration cost is $O(k(n-k)^2)$. Therefore, computation for large values of n & k is quite inefficient.
   Let 'v_i' be a cluster and object is 'x_j'. Therefore, 'x_j' is assigned to the cluster that is closer to its medoids 'v_i' nearer to the medoid.
   $d(x_j, v_j) \leq d(x_j, v_p)$ for all p=1, ..., k. The object function should be minimized by 'k' representation of their nearest medoid. This is the sum of dissimilarities of all objects.
   The algorithm processes into two steps:
   a. **BUILD Step:** In this step, 'k' centrally located objects are sequentially selected which is used as an initial medoids.
   b. **SWAP Step:** Unselected and selected objects should be swapped. This is done, to decrease the object function.
2. **Clustering LARge Application (CLARA):** CLARA can deal with larger data sets compared to PAM. Centrally located clusters are found in CLARA like PAM, dissimilarity matrix at a time is found entirely, is the main problem in PAM, so PAM space complexity becomes O(n^2). But CLARA avoids this problem; actual measurement is accepted in CLARA (i.e., data matrix).

CLARA assigns objects to clusters in the following way

a.   **BUILD Step:** A centrally located 'k' objects are selected, to be used as initial medoids, now the least possible average distance between object to their medoids are selected that forms clusters.

b.   **SWAP Step:** Try to reduce the average distance between medoids and the objects. This is done by replacing representative objects. An object which is assigned to the nearest medoids is the one which does not belong to the sample.

3.   **Clustering Large Application Based upon RANdomized Search (CLARANS):** CLARANS algorithm said by Kaufman et al (1990) is the combination of PAM and CLARA, which identify only by subsets of the datasets and it does not enclose itself to any sample at any given time. Neighbour of the node is examined by the former and is the key between CLARAS and PAM. In this, method each sample is drawn forcible in the sense that no nodes correlating to particular objects are eliminated outside. In each step of CLARANS search sample of neighbour is drawn. The localized area search is not confined.

CLARANS Algorithm

a.   **Step 1:** Create parameter max neighbour and numlocal; initialize p to 1, and large number to mincost.

b.   **Step 2:** Arbitrary node is set from current node in $G_n : K$

c.   **Step 3:** Set q to 1

d.   **Step 4:** Neighbour s of current is randomly considered and based on s, cost difference of two nodes are calculated.

e.   **Step 5:** If lowest cost is s, set s as current, and go to step 3

f.   **Step 6:** Otherwise, increase q by 1, if p is maxneighbor then go to step 4

g.   **Step 7:** Otherwise when q>maxneighbor, mincost is compared with cost of current,
     If current< mincost, mincost = cost of current and current = best node.

h.   **Step 8:** Increase p by 1 and if p> numlocal, output the best node and halt, otherwise go to step.

With progressively low cost, above step 3 to 6 search for nodes, for declaring a current node as local minimum it still be the lowest cost, when compared with max number of neighbour node. Then in step 7 lowest cost obtained is correlated with local minimum cost. Until the numlocal is found, the search of CLARANS algorithm is repeated for other local minimum.

4.   **Spatial dominant approach SD (CLARNS):** In this algorithm, spatial component of data are gathered, after that clustering is used depending on CLARANS most natural number k_o of cluster is found by using CLARANS.

SDCLARANS Algorithm

a.   **Step 1:** Using SQL queries, find the initial set of similar tuples from the given data, for a given learning request.

     Step 2: In order to find the cluster most natural number k_o, we should apply CLARANS to the spatial attribute.

b.   **Step 3:** Cluster obtained for above for each of k.

     i.   Gather the tuples non-spatial component included in the current cluster

     ii.   Non-spatial components collection should be applied with DBLEARN.

5. **Non Spatial Dominant Approach NSD (CLARANS):** This method is a non-spatial dominant approach, involving non- spatial generalization and then the spatial clustering. For performing attribute oriented generalization on attribute of non-spatial objects, DBLEARN is used. Number of generalization tuples is produced.

    To find k_o cluster for each and every generalized tuples using CLARANS method all the spatial components are collected and clustered, overlapping of clusters is checked with cluster in the final step. If the cluster overlaps, then cluster are combined and combining of corresponding tuples is also done.

    NSD CLARANS Algorithm

    a. **Step 1:** Relevant tuples set is found initially SQL queries, for a given learning request.
    b. **Step 2:** Until the number of final generalize tuples comes below a certain threshold, apply DBLEARN method to non-spatial attributes.
    c. **Step 3:** For, each obtained generalized tuples above

    Spatial components are gathered from tuples representing by current generalized tuple.

    Clusters k_o, the most natural number is found by applying the heuristic and CLARANS.

    i. **Step 3:** If cluster overlap or inserted from all cluster obtained from above, then that cluster should be combined.

SPATIAL CO-LOCATION MINING

Co-location pattern is a subset of different features $f_{1,......}, f_s$ having spatial co-location within a distance Q_d, Q_d is the neighborhood distance. Features of a group are said to have spatial co-location features, if each possible pairs are neighbor to each other. If the Euclidian distance of two feature instances is not more than the neighbourhood distance Q_d, they are neighbour to each other.

Let A= { $f_1, f_2, ..., f_s$} be a co-location pattern. In an instance of C cluster, one instance from each of the s features will be present for all these feature instances are neighbour to each other.

When image is taken as input, with the use of colour identification, the instance is identified and the instance coordinates are obtained which are stored in a text file. From the obtained coordinates item sets are generated. As discussed by Priya et al (2011) co-location is implemented, the coordinates are mapped in a grid map. The distances between instances are calculated.

Set of 2 items are considered for comparing neighbourhood grid in places. If minimum participating index is missing, then they are discarded. By using non pruned items, 3 item sets are calculated. Interesting patterns are recognized depending upon the participation index. The above mentioned architecture is feasible for co-location pattern mining.

In close geographical proximity, co-location pattern represent subsets of Boolean spatial features which locate the instances. For examples, E-services are developing in rapid speed along with mobile computing infrastructure such as cellular phones and PDAs.

Among Boolean spatial features, finding co-occurrence frequently is of interest for scientists in ecology. E.g. EI Nino, drought, considerable increase and drop is vegetation, very high precipitation etc. As suggested by Estivill-castro et al (2001), these organizations are scattered across many domains including management of environment and ecology, safety of public, public heath transportation, business and tourism.

Figure 6. General Architecture of Co-Location Mining

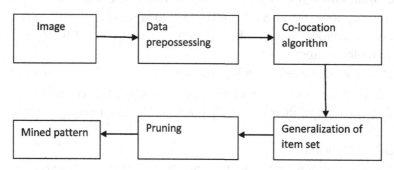

In the real world, gathering of instances of Boolean spatial features are included in spatial datasets (eg, leaf vegetation, drought). Fig 7 shows the persistent co-occurrence of some spatial feature, types represented by different objects. It can be seen from the spatial features of instances in sets {'+','×'} and {'O','*'} and are located together.

Figure 7. Spatial co-location pattern illustrations

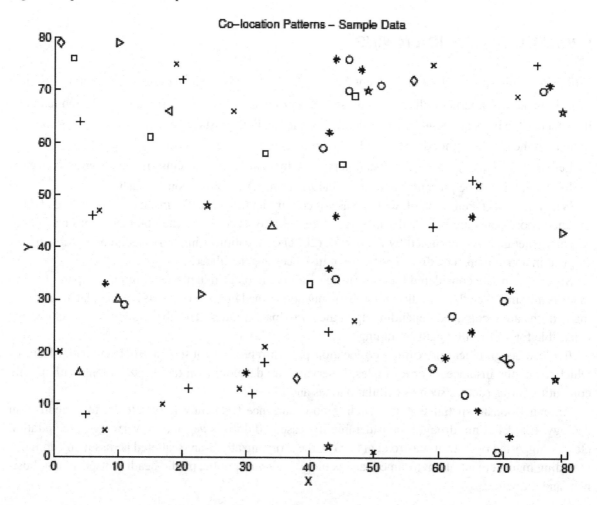

Figure 8. Illustrate collocation pattern

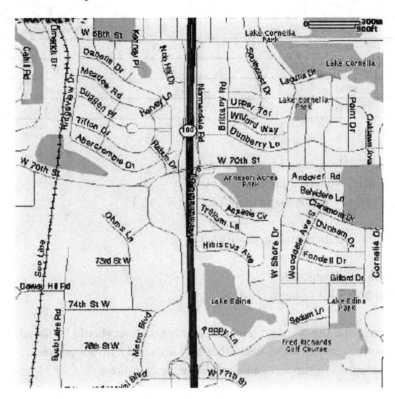

Collocation pattern is illustrated in Fig 8, which shows instances among elaborated spatial features namely road types, on an urban roadmap. Frontage roads are nearby in large metropolitan area highway. As discussed by Koperski et al (1996), recognition of such co-location is useful in, selected test sites for calculating in vehicles navigation tech. As item type, Boolean spatial features can be thought. Because of continuing underlying space, there may not be any explicit finite set of transaction. So, applying classic association rule mining directly to spatial contexts is difficult.

SPATIAL ASSOCIATION RULE

The elaboration of association rule of traditional data mining is spatial association rule. Association rule is of form X→Y [a%, b%], X represents the collection of spatial predicates, and Y indicates the collection of predicates which are non-spatial. Support degree is indicated by a% and, rules credibility is indicated by c%.

Spatial relationship should be calculated among lot of spatial objects due to mining of spatial association rule. So, optimization of stepwise refinement is done in large number of spatial association mining. First, initial spatial database should be mined with fast algorithm, and secondly, we should carry mining of trimmed database derived from the previous step.

Examples:

Table 1. Example transaction for support and confidence

Transaction ID	Item Bought
2000	A,B,C
1000	A,C
4000	A,D
5000	B,E,F

- Rule form: Body→ Head[support, confidence]
- Buys (A, chocolate)→buys(A, juice)[0.5%,60%]
- Major (A,'CS') takes (A,'DB')→ grade (A,'X') [1%,75%].

Basic concepts of association rules is given by,

- Details of transaction{database}
- Every transaction is a list of items.

The rule that correspond the one data sets with another data set should be found. For example, 98% of people get automotive services done, when they buy tires and auto accessories.

Interestingness measures of support and confidence are as follows

- Find all rules A and B=>C with minimum confidence and support.
- Support s, transaction problem is that it contains {P=>Q=>R}
- Confidence c, transaction conditional problem is that, having {P=>Q} also contains R.

Let us have the minimum support and minimum confidence be 50%, we have

- A=>C (50%, 66.6%).
- C=>A (50%, 100%).

UNCERTAINITY IN SPATIAL DATA MINING

The need to manage indefinite and large information concerning spatial data has been widely managed (Goodchild et al, 1990) concisely in geographic information system (GIS). To analyse the reliability of information which is based on decision is dependent on decision makers ability and the value of GIS as a decision making tool. The mistakes in nature and degree in spatial data base must be accessed by GIS users.

GIS operation can be tracked for errors and can estimate the output in a tabular format. An only interesting aspect to model errors in GIS is by fuzzy set technique. Considering the features, attribute and value, many operations is applied to spatial data mining. There exists a inexactness in features and attribute value. From language processing, information concept, non-monotonic logic and fuzzy sets. Uncertainty model have been suggested for spatial information.

Any one of the integer value {0, 1} defines the fuzzy set membership. Real number of value of range value between [0, 1] defines the fuzzy sets membership. For identification of sets membership is by the terminal value and intermediate degree of sets belonging is defined by intervening value, for example, a membership of 0.5 reflects the higher degree of belongings to the set then a membership of 0.25. The object illustrated is lower like that of central concept of the set.

Identification of fuzzy membership is commonly done by one of two methods:

1. **The Similarity Relation Model:** Like traditional clustering and the classification method, that search for pattern with in a dataset. Fuzzy neural networks and fuzzy C means algorithm are most widely used methods.
2. **The Semantic Import Model:** In this method as mentioned by user or another export, it is derived from a formula or formulae.

Large number of studies involving geographical information has applied with fuzzy set. In geographical data probability, there are numerous applications to the fuzzy sets. Fuzzy set theory which is in high number of soft set theories.

SPATIAL TREND ANALYSIS

As discussed by Ester et al (1997), spatial trend refer to the difference of non-spatial attributes for away given spare objects for exam the different trend in situation of economy, when getting farther and farther far from the city centre, the analysis results may be of positive, negative or no trend. Moreover, spatial data structure and spatial access methods analysis need to be done by using regression and related analysis methods.

Since, own particularity of space objects, the traditional regression method may not be a appropriate method. With conventional database technology in addition, the data mining method need to be integrated fully. Accuracy of result will increase when greater technology is used.

SPATIAL DATA MINING PROBLEMS

1. Most algorithms in spatial data mining is relocation from general algorithm in data mining, and storage, processing of spatial data characteristic is not considered. Spatial data mining is dissimilar from other relational database, spatial event and spatial objects are not analysed in traditional data mining techniques.
2. Finding the pattern of spatial data by algorithm is not cleared and efficiency of algorithm in spatial data mining is not high. In spatial data mining uncertainty appears, error pattern is high and there is a large possibility of problem dimension. By that, the search space of algorithm increases and the blind search possibility increase.
3. For spatial data mining, there is no agreed standardized query language. Data base technology is rapidly development due to improvement in database query language. Therefore, spatial data mining query language should be developed in order to increase the efficiency of spatial data mining.

4. Knowledge discovery interaction method of spatial data mining is not stronger. Use of domain expert's knowledge, fully and efficiency is very different.
5. Spatial data mining concentrate on the spatial task. So, the knowledge is limited.
6. Combination of spatial data mining with other system is not enough and avoiding the role of GIS in spatial knowledge discovery. Due to the method and function of spatial data mining is single, there may be large restrictions. Knowledge extraction is difficult in spatial data base than traditional relational database from these problems described above. There are many theories and methods in-depth for development of spatial data mining.

APPLICATION OF SPATIAL DATA MINING

1. In business prospecting, spatial data mining finds the collocation of a business with another franchise, which may improve its sales (ex; collocation of blockbuster video store with restaurant).
2. Spatial data mining can be applied in determining the good store location within 50 mile of major city, within the state with no tax.
3. Based on the population of patient, who live in each neighbourhood can be used to determine the best location to open as hospital with the help of spatial data mining.
4. Another important application of spatial data mining is automobile insurance, in which based on the customer area of leaving; determine the area with low or high rate of accident claim or auto thefts.
5. Identifying fire hot spots in forests is done by employing frequency theory and incremental spatial data mining.
6. Spatial data mining techniques can be used in making a Railway Geographic Information System (RGIS) which can be used for spatial data presentation and statistical analysis besides helping in making well informed decisions.
7. Spatial data mining can be used to analyse many social aspects through geographical data.

CONCLUSION

Spatial data mining can observe important and meaningful knowledge from a vast spatial data or database. Mining in spatial data helps to dig out interesting relationship between object spread across geographically. These relationship or patterns will enhance the decision making of many applications. The most challenging task in spatial mining is to deal with spatial objects, which may also be of geometry patterns like lines, polygon etc. This leads to an interesting field called computational geometry. The data in every field grows exponentially that leads to Big Data. Hence parallel processing and distributed computing plays a major role in mining these data. Spatial data is not exceptional for high dimensional data or big data and has a large scope for improvement in big data analytics under spatial mining. In past few years, the development of spatial data mining technique is rapidly increasing and lot of methods and theories in spatial data mining has been studied much closer. Parallel to the improvement and development of own method and theories, spatial data mining has yet to be explored fully. Results obtained using spatial data mining are much useful in many fields. Spatial data mining not only contributes for science and technology but also helps in transforming the world. Thus, human society is served better.

REFERENCES

Dy, J. G., & Brodley, C. E. (2004). Feature Selection for Unsupervised Learning. *Journal of Machine Learning Research, 5*, 845–889.

Ester, M., Kriegel, H. P., & Sander, J. (1997). Spatial data mining: A database approach. In *Advances in spatial databases* (pp. 47–66). Springer Berlin Heidelberg. doi:10.1007/3-540-63238-7_24

Ester, M., Kriegel, H. P., Sander, J., & Xu, X. (1996) A density-based algorithm for Discovering cluster in large database with noise.*Proc of 2nd KDD, Portland* (pp 226-231).

Estivill-Castro, V., & Houle, M. E. (2001). Robust distance-based clustering with applications to spatial data mining. *Algorithmica, 30*(2), 216–242. doi:10.1007/s00453-001-0010-1

Gomez-Chova, L., Calpe, J., Camps-Valls, G., Martin, J. D., Soria, E., Vila, J., & Moreno, J. (2003, September). Semi-supervised classification method for hyperspectral remote sensing images. Proceedings of the International Geoscience and Remote Sensing Symposium (Vol. 3, pp. III-1776). doi:10.1109/IGARSS.2003.1294247

Goodchild, M. F., & Gopal, S. (Eds.). (1989). *The accuracy of spatial databases*. CRC Press.

Kaufman, L & Rousseeuw, P.J. (2009). *Finding groups in data: an introduction to cluster analysis*. John Wiley & Sons.

Koperski, K., Adhikary, J., & Han, J. (1996). Spatial data mining: progress and challenges survey paper. *Proc. ACM SIGMOD Workshop on Research Issues on Data Mining and Knowledge Discovery*, Montreal, Canada (pp. 1-10).

Koperski, K., Han, J., & Nebojsa, S. (1998). An efficient two-step method for classification of spatial data. *Proceedings of International Symposium on Spatial Data Handling* (SDH'98) (pp. 45-54).

Lee, A. J., Hong, R. W., Ko, W. M., Tsao, W. K., & Lin, H. H. (2007). Mining spatial association rules in image databases. *Information Sciences, 177*(7), 1593–1608. doi:10.1016/j.ins.2006.09.018

Li, D. R., & Cheng, T. (1994), KDG-Knowledge Discovery from GIS.*Proceedings of the Canadian Conference on GIS, Ottawa* (pp. 123-145).

Lu, W., Han, J., & Ooi, B. C. (1993) Discovery of general knowledge in large spatial databases. *In proceedings FarRast Workshop on Geographic Information System*, pp 275-289.

Miller, H.J., & Han, J. (2001). *Geographic datamining and knowledge discovery*. London.

Priya. G., Jaisankar, N., & Venkatesan, M. (2011). Mining Colocation patterns from Spatial Data using Rulebased Approach. *Journal of Global Research in Computer Science, 2*(7), 58-61.

Xiong, H., Tan, P., & Kumar, V. (2003). mining strong affinity association pattern in datasets with skewed support distribution. *Proceedings of international third Conference on Data Mining*, pp. 387-394. doi:10.1109/ICDM.2003.1250944

Zhang, T., Ramakrishnan, R., & Livny, M. (1996). *BIRCH: An efficient data clustering method for very large database. Proceedings of ASM-SIGMOD international conference on management of data* (pp. 103–114). New York: ACM. doi:10.1145/233269.233324

KEY TERMS AND DEFINITIONS

Association Rule Mining: It is a method of discovering interesting relationship among a set of items or objects in a relational database, transactional database and other information repositories.

Clustering: It's a process in which a group of objects which are similar to each other are grouped together.

Co-Location Mining: Discovers the subsets of features whose events are frequently located together in geographic space.

Computational Geometry: It's the field of computer science dedicated to the study of algorithm which can be expressed in terms of geometry.

Delaunay Triangulation: A Delaunay triangulation for a set P of points in a plane is a triangulation DT (P) such that no point in P is inside the circumcircle of any triangle in DT (P).

Hierarchical: It's the process of arranging the objects based on the nature of hierarchy.

Image Segmentation: It's the process of partitioning the digital image into multiple segments otherwise, set of pixels.

Mediods: Medoids are the pattern representatives of a data set or a cluster containing patterns whose average dissimilarity to all the objects in cluster is least.

Spatial Classification: Classification based on the analysis of spatial objects related to its spatial characteristics, such as areas of region, roads, and ponds or rives.

Spatial Data Mining: It is the method of revealing interesting and previously unknown pattern from spatial databases.

Chapter 4
Knowledge Representation: A Semantic Network Approach

Atta ur Rahman
Barani Institute of Information Technology, Pakistan

ABSTRACT

Knowledge Representation (KR) is an emerging field of research in AI and Data Mining. Knowledge represented in an effective way guarantees a good retrieval. In this regard, a number of effective approaches have been proposed in the literature and Semantic Networks (SN) are one of them. In SN knowledge is represented in the form of directed graph, where concepts and relationships are appeared at vertices and edges respectively. 'is a' is one of the most frequently used relationship in SN. 'is a' expresses the exact relationship between any pair of objects. But there exists a huge amount of knowledge that cannot be represented by just 'is a', like the knowledge where approximations are involved. To overcome this issue, fuzzy semantic networks (FSN) are proposed in this chapter. In FSN 'is a' is replaced by a fuzzy membership function 'μ' having value between [0,1]. So the relationship between a pair of concepts can be expressed as a certain degree of membership. This chapter focuses on applications of FSN and its significance over the traditional SN.

INTRODUCTION

Knowledge Representation (KR) is one of the hottest areas of research in data mining, AI and big data analytics etc. Knowledge represented in an effective way, helps in easy traversal, searching, reasoning, prediction and inferencing. In this regard, a number of approaches, algorithms, techniques and methods have been proposed in the literature and implemented with their own pros and cons.

KR, though not a new concept, however, its usefulness was not felt as necessary as present. KR is becoming a root of almost every Decision Support System (DSS), Expert Systems (ES) and many other intelligent systems. Moreover, it is one of the prominent component of AI paradigm. A number of techniques for KR are proposed in the literature, Semantic Networks are one of the prominent technique among them. Semantic networks were originally proposed by (Quinlin, 1969). In this technique knowledge is represented by directed graph structure, where vertices (nodes) represent the objects (concepts) and

DOI: 10.4018/978-1-5225-0427-6.ch004

the edges represent the relationship between them. 'is a' is one of the most useful relationship between any pair of objects. However, it does not cover the range of relationship between 'is a' and 'is not a'. To overcome this limitation, Semantic Fuzzy Networks (SFN) are proposed in this chapter. Also their applications and implementation details are provided.

This chapter is organized as follows:

- Basic concepts and definitions are presented in first section
- Section two contains a brief introduction of semantic networks
- Section three contains the introduction of fuzzy semantic network concept
- Section four contains the applications of fuzzy semantic network in general
- Section five contains the application of fuzzy semantic network in various domains

BACKGROUND

Semantic Networks

Semantic Networks are one of the oldest and effective-most techniques for KR. A semantic network or net is a graph structure for representing knowledge in patterns of interconnected nodes and arcs. Computer implementations of semantic networks were first developed for artificial intelligence and machine translation, but earlier versions have long been used in philosophy, psychology, and linguistics. The Giant Global Graph of the Semantic Web is a large Semantic Network (Berners-Lee et al. 2001; Hendler & van Harmelen, 2008).

Semantic Networks were initially invented for computers by Richard H. R. et al in 1956 of the Cambridge Language Research Unit (CLRU), for sake of machine translation of natural languages. Semantic Networks were further developed by Klien & Robert in 1963. In subsequent years, remarkable work on semantic nets was done by Allan M. et al., (1969-1970). From 1960 to 1980 the idea of semantic network was related to hyperlink in hypertext. Also many software tools have been developed to implement the semantic networks in that era.

About six most common types of Semantic Network are given in literature by Sowa et al. (1991). Following is their short description:

1. **Definitional Networks:** This is a kind of network in which "is a" relationship is used to create the subtypes. The resulting network, also called a *generalization* or *subsumption* hierarchy, supports the rule of *inheritance* for copying properties defined for a super-type to all of its subtypes. For example, super-type is "Prophet" then its subtypes are "Mohammad," "Mosa," etc. moreover, the information in such networks is assumed to be necessarily true.
2. **Assertional Networks:** These are designed to assert propositions. Unlike definitional networks, the information in an assertional network is assumed to be contingently true, unless it is explicitly marked with a modal operator. Some assertional networks have been proposed as models of the *conceptual structures* underlying natural language semantics.
3. **Implicational Networks:** These networks use implication operator as the primary relation for connecting nodes. They may be used to represent patterns of beliefs, causality, or inferences. These networks are intensively used in deductive learning.

4. **Executable Networks:** These networks include some mechanism, such as marker passing or attached procedures, which can perform inferences, pass messages, or search for patterns and associations

5. **Learning Networks:** These networks are built or extend their representations by acquiring knowledge from examples. The new knowledge may change the old network by adding and deleting nodes and arcs or by modifying numerical values, called weights, associated with the nodes and arcs. Systems that use network representations can modify the networks in three ways:

    a. **Rote Memory:** The simplest form of learning is to convert the new information to a network and add it without any further changes to the current network.

    b. **Changing Weights:** Some networks have numbers, called weights, associated with the nodes and arcs. In an implicational network, for example, those weights might represent probabilities, and each occurrence of the same type of network would increase the estimated probability of its recurrence.

    c. **Restructuring:** The most complex form of learning makes fundamental changes to the structure of the network itself. Since the number and kinds of structural changes are unlimited, the study and classification of restructuring methods is the most difficult, but potentially the most rewarding if good methods can be found.

    Systems that learn by rote or by changing weights can be used by themselves, but systems that learn by restructuring the network typically use one or both of the other methods as aids to restructuring commercially, rote memory is of enormous importance, since the world economy depends on exact record keeping. For such applications, information is sometimes stored in tables, as in relational databases, but networks are also used. Either representation could be converted to the other. For better efficiency and usability, most database systems add indexes to speed up the search, and they support query languages, such as SQL, which perform transformations to extract and combine the information necessary to answer a request. Since a learning system must be able to distinguish common features and exceptions among similar examples, another feature is essential: the ability to measure *similarity* and to search the database for networks that are similar, but not identical to any given example.

    Neural networks are a widely-used technique for learning by changing the weights assigned to the nodes or arcs of a network. Their name, however, is a misnomer, since they bear little resemblance to actual neural mechanisms. Figure 1 shows a typical neural network, whose input is a sequence of numbers that indicate the relative proportion of some selected features and whose output is another sequence of numbers that indicate the most likely concept characterized by that combination of features. In an application such as optical character recognition, the features might represent lines, curves, and angles, and the concepts might represent the letters that have those features.

6. **Hybrid Networks**: These networks combine two or more of the previous techniques, either in a single network or in separate, but closely interacting networks.

From the discussion above, it can be concluded that Semantic Network is a fancy data structure which lot depends on program that maintains it. In order to understand this concept further, few more examples of Semantic Network are given below.

In Figure 2, a semantic network is given that represents relationship from a specific dog breed to general. This can be deduced that by simple rules about 'is a' arcs that would let program retrieve deduction that "Guss is an animal" etc.

Figure 1. Example of a neural network
(Sowa et al. 1991)

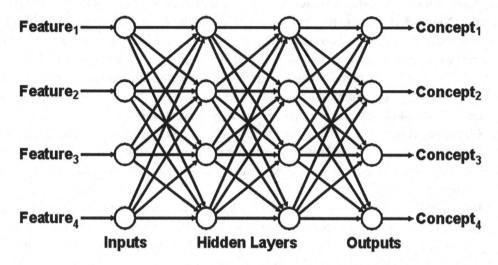

Figure 3 shows an example of semantic network in which property list is introduced. A property list is also represented by the 'is a' link. Like Beryl owning a nest from March to September becomes complicated this involves: Ownership, thing, start time, end time i.e. a predicate with four arguments. Whereas conventional arcs have two arguments need a "case frame" with a set of outgoing arcs --- forming a template. Here in this example it is apparent that 'is a' can easily be used to represent the object's properties like ownership etc. in this example.

Types of Semantic Relationships:

1. *Set-membership relation....* $\in$

It can be read as 'member of'. It refers to typical crisp set membership with membership value exactly '1'. In this way it can be shown that a concept or object fully or wholly belongs to a class or another concept. It is depicted in Figure 4. *John* belongs to class of *Employee*.

2. *Subset relationship .... IsA*

It can also be read as 'is a' or 'is an'. It is depicted in Figure 5. Like Employee is a person.

Figure 2. A typical semantic network

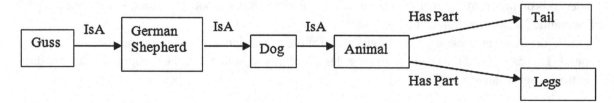

Figure 3. A Semantic Network with property list

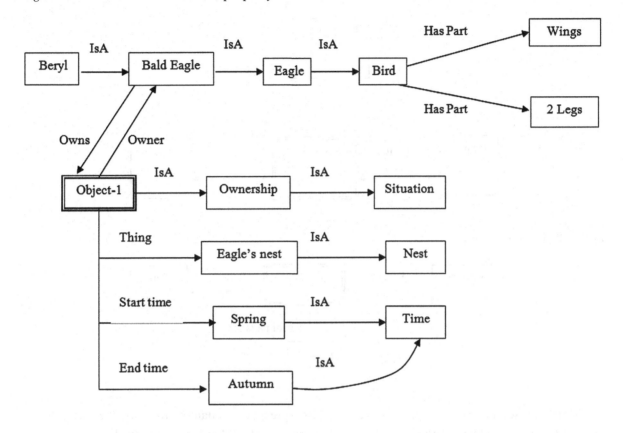

Figure 4. Set membership relation

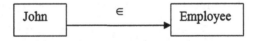

Figure 5. Subset relationship

3.   *Events by "Case Frames".*

Events can also be represented as a concept or a class. However, just to distinguish it from other concepts it is written in doube square. It is depicted in Figure 6. Like John (agent) is punching (event) tom (object).

4.   *N-arg relations (with n>2)*

Figure 6. Events by "case frames"

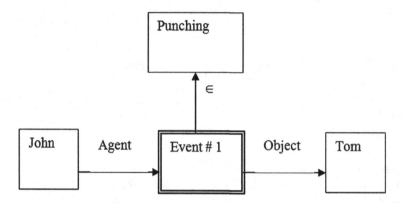

Figure 7. N-arg relations

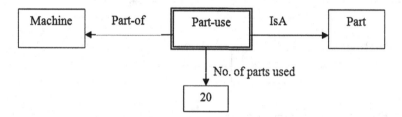

While representing the concepts, one may need to express some quantity, then N-arg relationship is used. It is represented by creating an entity or case frame to stand for N-arg relationship e.g. machine uses 20 Parts. It is depicted in Figure 7.

In order to depict all of the above mentioned relationships in one semantic network Figure 8 can be viewed as an example.

MAIN FOCUS OF THE CHAPTER

Issues, Controversies, Problems

This chapter focuses on a comprehensive overview of Semantic Network as paradigm for knowledge representation. Through examples, it is shown that how a semantic network can be used to represent knowledge so that it can be retrieved consequently. The types of semantic relationships that appear on the edges of the semantic network graph, are explained with examples.

It is observed that these relationships can be used for representing the knowledge or facts that are in an exact form without any doubt or approximation. However, it is necessary that all the knowledge in a particular field can always be in the exact form, it can rather be in approximation or a wage valued relationship. Traditional semantic network does not incorporate such kind of knowledge.

In order to overcome this issue, fuzzy logic and fuzzy set theory is proposed in conjunction with traditional semantic networks. The new semantic network is named as Fuzzy Semantic Networks. Tra-

Figure 8. Semantic network with more than one relations

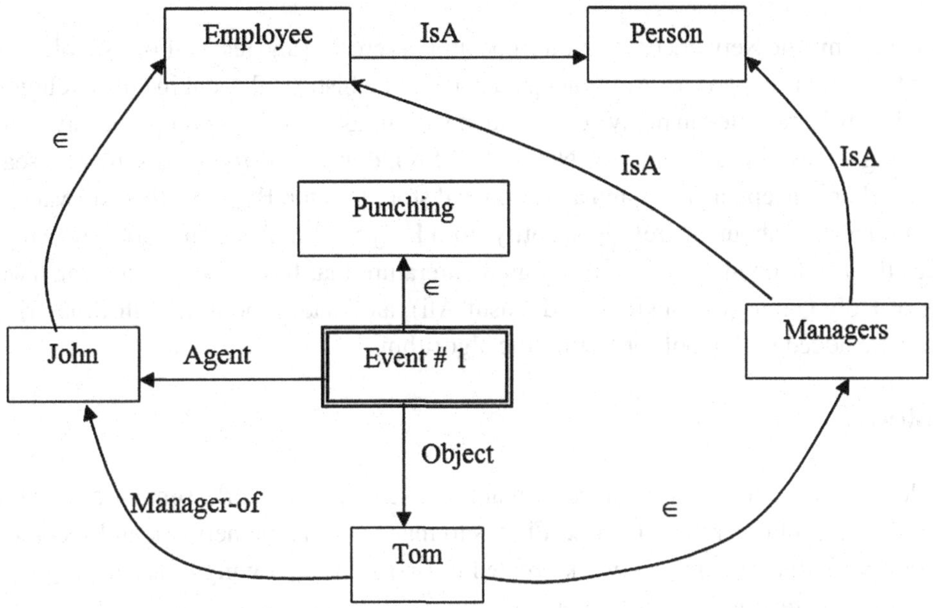

ditional relationships are replaced by fuzzy relationships and membership functions. So it is possible to express any type of relationship through the proposed approach. Not only representation, it guarantees the relevant most search and effective traversal.

Limitations of Basic Semantic Network

In the above discussion, it can easily be deduced that a major part of the basic semantic network is based on the relationship 'is a'. 'is a' is the relationship that shows the object's relationship with a membership value one, which can be zero otherwise. This discrete nature is actually a property of crisp sets where the membership value is exactly one. In a real world scenario 'is a' may not be able to represent the actual/exact knowledge about the objects and their relationships especially when the objects' properties are being represented. This is the case where relationship is not clear, rather wage and approximate. For example, the facts like:

- Machine takes about 20 seconds to boot.
- This cloth is dirty.
- Ali is a tall boy.
- Jinnah is a famous person.

Now the facts that 'about 20 seconds', dirtiness, being tall and being famous are relative properties, in which the relationship is not exact but approximate and that cannot be exactly expressed in terms of 'is a'.

SEMANTIC NETWORK BASED SEARCH (AN EXAMPLE)

In this example, Semantic Network of religious repository is created and tested. For a scholar, this is really hard to get information about a specific concept, a person or a historical event in entire religious domain at once since it may be repeated in many verses and in various aspects. This comprehensive software tool helps in creating a Customized Semantic Network (CSN), doing a customized semantic search (CSS) against any word or concept, a parser and a customized story builder. By using this software one can get all relevant information about any religious entity from Holy Quran, Ahadith, Bible etc. Moreover, this tool provides the mechanism to add more religious literature that has a specific format. Two different translations of Holy Quran (by Pickthall and Yusuf Ali), an Ahadith book (Sahih Bukhari) and Bible (King James) are added in the tool for testing the algorithm.

System Model

System model describes the steps involved in making a semantic network, semantic search etc. There are two major aspects of this research work. First is to make a semantic network and second is search a word or phrase using the semantic network created in first step. Following diagram (Figure 9) depicts the steps involved in creating a semantic network.

Figure 9. Steps to create a semantic network

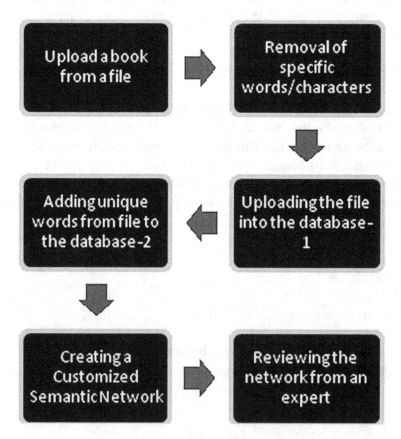

Following is given the brief description of each step:

1. **Upload a Book from File:** Many translations of the Holy Quran are available by different authors, electronically. Most of them are given in MS-Word or text document format. The verses from different Sura"h are given in following style.
    [Sura"h#:Verse# Verse translation]
    So in this phase one can add a book translation of any religious book in above format by browsing option in the software.
2. **Removal of Unused Characters**: In this step the extra characters like dots, commas, semi-colons etc are erased from the uploaded file.
3. **Uploading File into Database-1**: In this step file with erased characters in uploaded in database-1. This database contains all the sura'h and verses in a chronological order as it appears originally in the source file.
4. **Adding Unique Words to Database-2**: In this step unique (distinct) words are picked from source file and added into a word database. Since multiple files may be incorporated in the database at the same time and there are a number of repeated words so this step just unify them.
5. **Creating a Semantic network**: User is given a facility to create his/her own customized semantic network. For example, in many translations there used word "Allah" while in another "God", similarly, "mosa" and "moses" etc. So through semantic network we can associate them using a link "alias of" etc. Similarly, "is a" is very useful link since most of the relationships can be described by using this. In this way, one can create semantic network of any dimension using his/her own link descriptions and way to connect the concepts. Following is shown (Figure 10) a semantic network view.
6. **Expert Review**: Though there is given a customized approach in creation of semantic network, yet this is a religious semantic network, scholar has to consult an expert or a teacher to verify the semantic network. This is because when this tool will become operational then religious institutions can use it for research etc so authentication aspects are provided.

Figure 10. Semantic network example

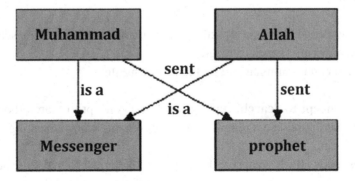

Figure 11. Searching algorithm flowchart

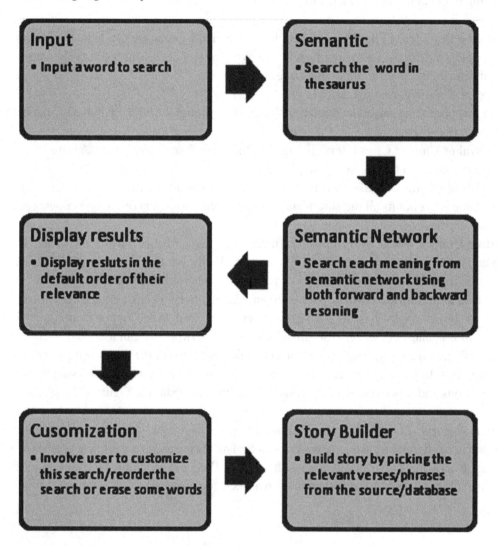

ALGORITHM USED

In this section we demonstrate the basic algorithm for searching a word using a semantic network. The algorithm is given in following flowchart (Figure 11).

The above flowchart can be summarized by the following steps:

1. **Input a Word/Concept to Search:** Input a word or a concept to search though the religious repository. Word could purely be a religious concept or name whose meaning may not be available in ordinary thesaurus.

2. **Search in Thesaurus (Basic Search):** This option is kept just to make the search wider. If there are meanings available in the thesaurus, then a list will be populated if not then same word will be returned.

3. **Search through Semantic Network (Advanced Search):** Word/s in the previous steps will be searched through semantic network using backward and forward reasoning techniques. Each related concept will be populated in a new list in order of occurrence in the network. That is words appearing in immediate nodes will be enlisted first and so on.
4. **Customization:** The searched list will be given to user if he/she wants to change the order or even wants to erase a meaning from list.
5. **Story Builder:** This tool will pick all the related verses from the database which is consisted of all books" material, and display them in form of a report (Crystal Report).

So all search results that may be consisted of many pages will be displayed. User can order them in terms of the books where those verses taken from. Default order is as under, first verses from Holy Quran, then from Ahadith, then from Bible or any other book.

6. **Generate Book:** In this step user can simply export that report in form of MS Word or PDF document. Now this document contains the most relevant search results order by books and the meaning in Semantic Network as well as thesaurus.

RESULTS AND DISCUSSION

In our examples Quanic translations contains a dot (.) separator while in King James Bible colon (:) is used as a common separator. Parser (Figure 12) will trim off these separators and show aya't in next grid by clicking on "Show Grid" button. After that "Distinct Words" button will become active by clicking it, all distinct words in the uploaded file will be enlisted in left side pane. Also the noise words and characters will be eliminated like "is", "in", "a" etc. Then lastly upon clicking the save button these unique words will be saved in the database.

Figure 13 shows relationship toolkit that helps in creating new dimensions of semantic network of any depth. New links can be created also old links can be repeated. Like in above example, "Muhammad is a messenger" and "Muhammad is a Prophet". Similarly, new links can be added like "Yaseen is an alias of Muhammad" etc. This can go arbitrarily long. In fact, as the customized semantic network (CSN)

Figure 12. File parser and concept picker

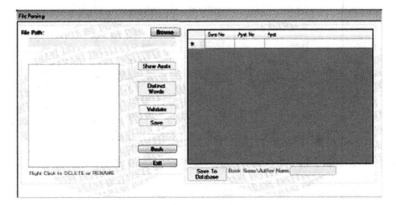

Figure 13. Semantic network toolkit

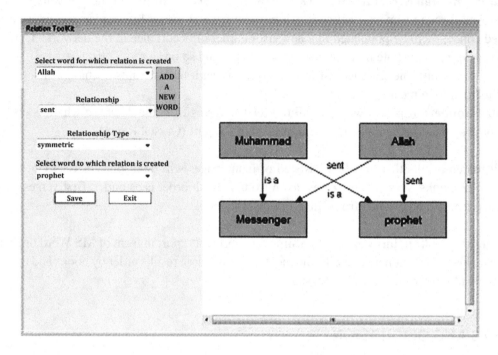

Figure 14. Expert verification

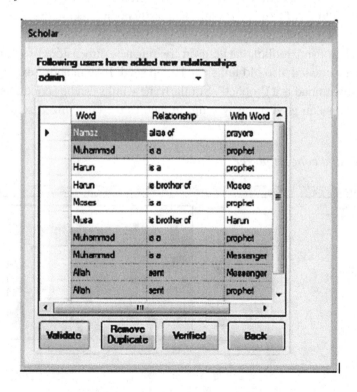

Figure 15. Semantic search results

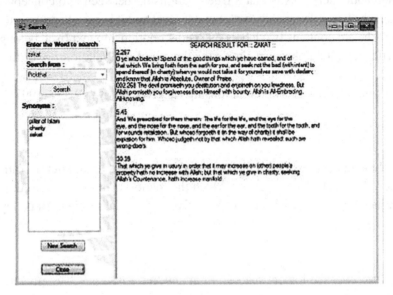

will grow our customized semantic search (CSS) will be even efficient, so this application provides an evolutionary mechanism to build a rich semantic network of the religious literature we mentioned above.

Figure 14 shows the verification process of new links added by the user. Duplicate links will be eliminated by "Remove Duplicate" button. Upon validation this process will be completed.

Figure 15 show interface of the semantic search engine (SSE). In this interface first text box takes the word to be searched. Next drop down control asks for whether to search from a specific book like there is shown "Pickthall" or entire database. After clicking "Search" button synonyms will be populated in the next window and in right side pane all verses that contains anyone of those synonyms will be populated along with their references. For example, top most ayat (verse) is (2:267) that means two-hundred-sixty-seventh ayat of Sura"h Baqarah, as it is second Sura"h of the Holy Quran. Similarly, next two results are (5:45) and (30:39) that shows forty-fifth verse of fifth Sura'h and thirty-ninth verse of thirtieth Sura'h respectively.

If we add Bible too in our search area then there may not be a word like "zakat" instead there may be word "charity", that so search engine will search for word "charity" in Bible domain. In this all the occurrences of searched word can be found on a single click which manually may take weeks to search. After finalizing the search results there is a facility to export this search pane as MS Word or PDF document so that one can use it later or as reference in some religious discussion.

FUZZY SEMANTIC NETWORK

Fuzzy Semantic Networks (FSN) are a blend of basic Semantic Network and the Fuzzy Logic. In this concept a fuzzy membership function (FMF) is introduced that can express the true/exact relationship between any pair of facts. The semantic relationship "is a" between two facts is considered as a special case of this fuzzy membership function with a fuzzy membership value 1. The name of this membership value is coined as "similarity index" whose value may vary between 0 and 1. The benefit of adding this FMF to the Semantic Networks is that a true relationship between two concepts can be provided since fuzzy provides the best relationship to a granular level and it is easy to represent the relationships in this way. In FSN, the arc contains two labels one is the relationship text (is a, belongs to, part of, has and certain properties) and a number that shows the degree of that relationship or the similarity index between two objects.

A brief introduction to Fuzzy sets and relationships is given below. (Wang, 1997)

Fuzzy Logic

Fuzzy logic is a technique in computing which is based on "degrees or amount of truth" rather than the usual "true or false" (1 or 0) Boolean logic on which the modern computer is based. The idea of fuzzy logic was first advanced by Dr. Lotfi Zadeh of the University of California at Berkeley in the 1960s.

Fuzzy Sets

Fuzzy sets are used to cover the logical spaces. So in any fuzzy rule base system sufficient number of fuzzy sets must be chosen so that they can cover input output spaces. For example, we have to model temperature of some element as an input then one thing that comes in mind is like hot and cold. If we are talking about crisp sets then this information seems enough like either it would be member of hot or cold. But in fuzzy set theory we can have other possibilities as well so it can be even more quantified. Like it can be very hot, hot, warm, normal, cool, cold, and very cold. Now there are seven fuzzy sets for modeling temperature as an input.

Also there are certain properties of these sets like they can be overlapping. Mean there might be some temperature that falls in the two fuzzy sets at the same time. Also they must be complete; means there must not leftover space between the sets. Same phenomenon is for all input and output fuzzy sets. So the choice of appropriate number of fuzzy sets for input output space is a critical task.

Different operations on fuzzy sets are also defined like those defined for the crisp sets like:

- Union
- Intersection
- Complement

Union

In Union of two fuzzy sets the membership of relevant elements are compared and the maximum of the two is kept in the union set. Suppose there are two fuzzy sets Fame and Intelligence described as below.

Fame = {Ali/0.8, John/0.2, Naveed/0.5, Arsal/0.9}

Intelligence = {Ali/0.4,John/0.6,Naveed/0.7,Arsal/0.6}

Then the union of two set, say 'Famous Intelligent'.

Fame U Intelligence = {Ali/max(0.8,0.4),John/max(0.2,0.6),Naveed/max(0.5,0.7),Arsal/max(0.9,0.6)}

Which turns out to be,

Fame U Intelligence = {Ali/0.8,John/0.6,Naveed/0.7,Arsal/0.9}

So element 'Ali' with membership 0.8 in set 'Fame' written Ali/0.8 in fuzzy set notion. In another set 'Intelligence' is Ali/0.4, when union of these two sets is taken the value of Ali in the new set 'Fame U Intelligence' will be Ali/max (0.8, 0.4) which results in Ali/0.8.

Intersection

Fame ∩ Intelligence = {Ali/min(0.8,0.4),John/min(0.2,0.6),Naveed/min(0.5,0.7),Arsal/min(0.9,0.6)}

Which turns out to be,

Fame ∩ Intelligence = {Ali/0.4, John/0.2,Naveed/0.5, Arsal/0.6}

Similarly, in Intersection of two fuzzy sets the membership of relevant elements are compared and the minimum of the two is kept. Let say there is a variable Ali with membership 0.8 in set 'Fame' written Ali/0.8 in fuzzy set notion. In another set 'Intelligence' is Ali/0.4, when intersection of these two sets is taken the value of Ali in the new set 'Fame ∩ Intelligence' will be Ali/min (0.8, 0.4) which results in Ali/0.4.

Complement

Complement of the set 'Fame' can be written as,

Complement (Fame) = {Ali/(1-0.8), John/(1-0.2), Naveed/(1-0.5), Arsal/(1-0.9)}

Which turns out to be,

Complement (Fame) = {Ali/0.2, John/0.8, Naveed/0.5, Arsal/0.1}

Now in the complement operation the membership of an element in the new set will (1-old membership). For example say there is a variable Ali with membership 0.8 in set 'Famous'. Then in the complemented set 'Non-famous' its membership will be Ali/ (1-0.8) that would result in Ali/0.2.

Figure 16. Set membership relation

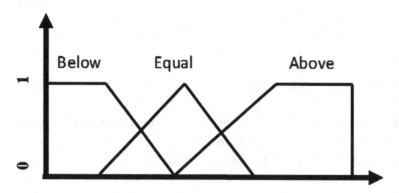

Membership Function

A membership function can be defined as a function through which membership of an input or output variable can be assign. They must be continued and finite functions so that every variable should have a finite value between [0, 1].

There are some famous and standard membership functions like triangular, trapezoidal, Gaussian memberships etc. Once plotted these functions their x-axis represents the range of value in real world while the y-axis is usually high from 0 to 1. So when some value is given in x-axis, it's appropriate and according value can be obtained from the y-axis. Some functions are demonstrated in Figure 16.

Label

It is a name that is given to a membership function so that it can represent more realistic concept, e.g., Low, Medium, High etc. A similar example is shown in Figure 16, in which three labels are shown.

Scope

Entire input space is divided among different membership functions. This division is mostly equally likely but even it may be the other way round. This is the area where a function is mapped.

Type of Fuzzy Semantic Relationships:

1. Fuzzy Set-membership relation.... ∈. It can be read as 'member of set with degree of membership μ'. Where $0 \leq \mu \leq 1$, 0 means no membership and 1 means full member. It is depicted in Figure 17.
2. Fuzzy Subset relationship .... IsA. It can also be read as 'an object belongs to a class with degree of membership μ'. Where $0 \leq \mu \leq 1$. It is depicted in Figure 18.

Figure 17. Set membership relation

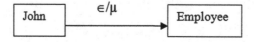

Figure 18. Set membership relation

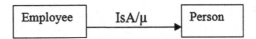

Fuzzy Semantic Network Construction

There could be various approaches for construction of FSN. The one we found the most appropriate is given below.

As the Fuzzy Semantic Network being constructed strictly belongs to particular domain or it comprehends a specific area of research for which the network is being constructed, so initially, a sufficient information regarding that domain must be obtained. This information can be in the form of a data dictionary, thesaurus, database or even text documents. For each form different approaches can be used for data preparation. In practice following steps are followed for data preparation. Naseem et al (2011):

1. Collection of material in the form of different formats
2. Unifying the formats by converting them into a common format
3. Data cleaning/cleansing (what to keep, what to discard?)
4. Uploading the unique words into a database

Once the data (words) are inserted in the database it is easy to construct the semantic network as well as fuzzy semantic network. That can be done in following manner. Naseem et al (2012)

1. Enlist all the distinct words as the rows (records) in a database table
2. Explore the thesaurus for each word and add the synonyms in the field next to the words already added
3. Take the semantic similarity (degree of membership/similarity index) in the next column of the database table
4. Exhaust the whole list of words in the thesaurus in this way
5. If some expert knowledge is available that is a plus point, add such knowledge in the another column of the table

In this fashion a true realization of FSN can be expressed in a database table and can be queried by using the Structured Query Language (SQL). In practice people have expressed the semantic networks especially semantic web in form of xml databases and RDF graphs rather than conventional relational databases for easy incorporation in the web. Similarly, to query such semantic web contents a query language is also devised named SPARCLE.

General Applications of Fuzzy Semantic Network

There are a number of areas where Fuzzy Semantic Networks can be used. In fact, all those areas where semantic networks are used, FSN can also be used with a better accuracy in knowledge representation. Few of these areas are given below.

1. Classification
2. Natural Language Processing
3. Semantic web
4. Data mining

Classification

Classification is one of the most important areas of many domains in computer science and engineering. In this field the data or objects are to be classified into a number of predefined classes based on some characteristics or attributes. Few examples of such areas are;

- Text classification/categorization
- Document classification
- Disease classification
- Behaviour classification

Working Model

In order to use FSN for sake of classification. It is important to construct the FSN of the domain in which classification is being done. Network construction could be automated or manual. As network is consisted of nodes (objects, concepts, relation) and arcs/vertices (fuzzy relationships between any two objects), proper selection of objects and the relationships with appropriate fuzzy likelihood value should be incorporated.

Once the network is constructed, the next important task is information retrieval. For this purpose, following steps should be followed.

Word or Sentence Classification

For sake of word of sentence classification, following algorithm can be used effectively.

Algorithm

1. Take the input which is a word, combination of words or even a sentence to be classified
2. In case the input is a sentence:
    a. Remove the noise words like 'in,' 'a,' 'the,' etc. from the sentence
    b. Find the distinct words among the remaining words
    c. Find the synonyms of these words in the FSN
    d. Match each word in the class captions
    e. Find frequency of each word
    f. Declare the class with the word of highest frequency

Document Classification

It is also one of the most important areas of research especially the search engines use this technique while crawling through the websites. There are a number of documents on the web in form of PDF, doc and other such formats, that are still unclassified and unstructured. In order to classify these documents FSN can be a good approach. For this purpose, following algorithm may be used.

Algorithm

1. Input the document in the form of text
2. Scan the whole document and remove the noise words (automatic/custom)
3. Find the frequency of each word in the cleaned document
4. Sort the words in descending order with respect to their frequencies
5. Once sorted pick the highest frequency words (keywords)
6. Find the relevant words of the keywords in FSN
7. If any word is repeated discard it
8. Remaining words describe the type/class or category of the document

SOLUTIONS AND RECOMMENDATIONS

The algorithms presented in the chapter can be implemented in any programming language like Java and C# with a database connection like Microsoft SQL Server.

FUTURE RESEARCH DIRECTIONS

This chapter presents a theoretical framework for implementation of Fuzzy Semantic Networks. However, in future its detail implementation may be investigated. Fuzzy rule based system may be used to make traversals even better. There is a lot of room to play around with the fuzzy sets, membership functions and inference engines. Together these components can make the proposed scheme even better.

CONCLUSION

This chapter presents a brief description of Semantic networks their limitations and proposes Fuzzy Semantic Network (FSN) for knowledge representation. A framework to use the FSN for knowledge representation in different fields of study and retrieval is described.

REFERENCES

Allan, M., Collins, A., & Quillian, M. R. (1969). Retrieval time from semantic memory. *Journal of Verbal Learning and Verbal Behavior, 8*(2), 240–248. doi:10.1016/S0022-5371(69)80069-1

Allan, M., Collins, A., & Quillian, M. R. (1970). Does category size affect categorization time? *Journal of Verbal Learning and Verbal Behavior, 9*(4), 432–438. doi:10.1016/S0022-5371(70)80084-6

Allen, J., & Frisch, A. (1982). What's in a Semantic Network. *Proceedings of the 20th. annual meeting of ACL*, Toronto (pp. 19-27). doi:10.3115/981251.981256

Bates, M. (1995, October24). Models of natural language understanding. *Proceedings of the National Academy of Sciences of the United States of America, 92*(22), 9977–9982. doi:10.1073/pnas.92.22.9977 PMID:7479812

Berners-Lee, T., Hendler, J., & Lassila, O. (2001). The Semantic Web. *Scientific American*, (May), 2001. PMID:11323639

Grigoris, A., & van Harmelen, F. (2008). *A Semantic Web* (2nd ed.). The MIT Press.

Hendler, J. A., & van Harmelen, F. (2008). The Semantic Web: webizing knowledge representation, In Hendler, J., & van Harmelen, F. (Eds.), Foundations of Artificial Intelligence (pp. 821-839). Springer.

Klein, S., & Simmons, R.F. (1963). Syntactic dependence and the computer generation of coherent discourse. *Mechanical Translation, 7*.

Richens, R. H. (1956). Preprogramming for mechanical translation. *Machine Translation, 3*(1), 20–25.

Sebastiani, F. (2002). Machine learning in automated text categorization. *ACM Computing Surveys, 34*(1), 1–47. doi:10.1145/505282.505283

Shahzadi, N., Atta-ur-Rahman & A. Shaheen. (2011). Semantic Network based Semantic Search of Religious Repository. *International Journal of Computer Applications, 36*(9), pp. 1-5.

Shahzadi, N., Atta-ur-rahman, A.-, & Jamil Sawar, M. (2012). Semantic Network based Classifier of Holy Quran. *International Journal of Computers and Applications, 39*(5), 43–47. doi:10.5120/4820-7069

Sowa, J.F., & Borgida, A. (1991). Principles of Semantic Networks: Explorations in the Representation of Knowledge.

Wang, L. X. (1997). *A Course in Fuzzy Systems and Controls*. Prentice Hall Publications.

Section 2
Computational Intelligence in Bioinformatics

This section explains the development various intelligent computational models for predicting complex biological problems. A complex novel hybrid model using radial basis function neural network and multi-objective algorithm based classifier is introduced to predict protein structural class. This section proposes the use of rough sets in conjunction with techniques like Fuzzy sets and Granular (Neighborhood Approximation) computing for the classic problem of data representation, dimensionality reduction, generation and harvest of minimal rules. The challenges faced by conventional computing methods in dealing with real world problems by natural systems are also addressed here. An efficient Rough set theory model to capture uncertainty in data and the processing of data using rough set techniques is discussed. The last chapter presents some general ideas for the time line of different uncertainty models to handle uncertain information and their applications in the various fields of biology.

Chapter 5
Development of Novel Multi–Objective Based Model for Protein Structural Class Prediction

Bishnupriya Panda
Siksha O Anusandhan University, India

Babita Majhi
G.G Viswavidyalaya, India

ABSTRACT

Protein folding has played a vital role in rational drug design, pharmacology and many other applications. The knowledge of protein structural class provides useful information towards the determination of protein structure. The exponential growth of newly discovered protein sequences by different scientific communities has made a large gap between the number of sequence-known and the number of structure-known proteins. Accurate determination of protein structural class using a suitable computational method has been a challenging problem in protein science. This chapter is based on the concept of Chou's pseudo amino acid composition feature representation method. Thus the sample of a protein is represented by a set of discrete components which incorporate both the sequence order and the length effect. On the basis of such a statistical framework a low complexity functional link artificial neural network and a complex novel hybrid model using radial basis function neural network and multi-objective algorithm based classifier are introduced to predict protein structural class.

INTRODUCTION

Proteins play a significant role in every biological process. Proteins are large molecules consisting of amino acids which the cells need to function properly. The human body is made up of approximately 100 trillion cells - each one has a specific function. Each cell has thousands of different proteins, which together make the cell do its job - the proteins are tiny machines within the cell.

DOI: 10.4018/978-1-5225-0427-6.ch005

Amino acids are the basic building block of all proteins. All amino acids have the same basic structure an amino group, a carboxyl group and a hydrogen atom but differ due to the presence of a side-chain. This side-chain varies dramatically between amino acids, from a simple hydrogen atom in the amino acid glycine to a complex structure found in tryptophan. Hydrophilicity or Hydrophobicity is determined by the side chain.

The function of a protein is based on its structure. Knowledge of protein structure plays a significant role in molecular biology, cell biology, pharmacology and medical science. However, despite years of both experimental and theoretical study, protein structure determination remains one of the most difficult tasks in proteomics. With exponential growth of protein database, experimental determination of structure is not cost effective. Therefore, development of a robust computational model is highly significant.

Accurate determination of protein structural class is a two-step process: Effective representation of protein sequence and then developing a prediction model. Many in-sillico structural class prediction algorithm and methods have been proposed earlier. Amino Acid Composition (AAC) is highly related to protein structural class (Chou, 1995). Several classification methods such as distance classifier, principal component analysis (Du & Jiang, 2006), Bayesian classifier, fuzzy clustering (Ding & Zhang, 2007), support vector machine (Cai, Liu, Xu &Zhou, 2001) and multilayer artificial neural network (Cai & Zhou, 2000) have been proposed in the literature. Though many promising results have been achieved, AAC of protein lacks sequence order and sequence length information. Sequence order and sequence length information also play a significant role in predicting protein structural class because amino acid composition do not differentiate between protein molecules of different sequence order and sequence length. This chapter along with pseudo amino acid composition, amphiphillic correlation factors of protein molecule (Panda, Mishra, Majhi &Rout, 2013) and the spectral characteristics of the protein (Sahu & Panda, 2010) have been used to capture the sequence order information.

Classification is a supervised method where the class label is known and we train the model by using that class label. Classification has two steps. The first one is model construction and the second process is model usage. Model construction describes a set of predetermined classes. Model usage is for classifying future or unknown objects.

Many authors have proposed neural network as a good candidate for classification of protein structural class. But how to choose the number of layers and number of neurons in each layer to enhance the classification accuracy is highly complex problem.

SIGNIFICANCE OF PROTEIN SECONDARY STRUCTURE

The function of a protein is based on its structure. Knowledge of protein structure plays a significant role in molecular biology, cell biology, pharmacology and medical science. However, despite years of both experimental and theoretical study, the determination of protein structure remains one of the most difficult problems.

Protein secondary structure prediction plays a vital role due to following reasons:

1. Experimental determination of structure is not cost effective.
2. It helps in predicting the 3D structure.

Also Protein database is growing everyday so it's not feasible to conduct experiment to find structure for every protein molecule. Moreover, homologous proteins can be predicted more easily if a computationally stable model could be designed.

Levitt and Chothia (1976) reported 10 structural class, 4 principal and 6 small classes in a data set of 31 globular proteins (Levit & Chothia, 1976). However biological community recognizes 4 principal classes depending on percentage of alpha helices and beta strand. These are:

1. α class: mainly contains alpha helices.
2. β class: mainly contains beta strands.
3. α + β class: contains both alpha helices and beta strands but beta strands are anti- parallel.
4. α/β class: contains both alpha helices and beta strands but beta strands are parallel.

Representation of Protein Data Set

In developing a method for predicting protein structural class location, the first problem we face is how to represent the sample of a protein. Two kinds of representations were generally used in this regard:

1. **Sequential Representation (Pseudo Amino Acid Composition):** The most typical sequential representation for a protein sample is its entire amino acid sequence, which can contain the most complete information of the protein. However, it loses both protein sequence order information and sequence length information.
2. **Non-Sequential Representation:** Rather than a series of successive amino acid codes according a certain order, the non-sequential representation for a protein sample is expressed by a set of discrete numbers and, hence, is also called the discrete representation. Various discrete models for this kind of representation were developed such as:
    a. Amphiphillic Pseudo Amino Acid Composition
    b. DCT-Amphiphillic Pseudo AAC.

Pseudo Amino Acid Composition (PseAAC) Feature of Protein

This is a sequential representation of protein in which a protein molecule is defined by a 20-dimensional feature vector in Euclidean space. The protein corresponds to a point whose co-ordinates are given by the occurrence frequencies of the 20 constituent amino acids.

For a query protein x, let f_i represents the occurrence frequencies of its 20 constituent amino acids. Hence the composition of the amino acids (p_k) in the query protein is given by:

$$P_k(x) = \frac{f_k(x)}{\sum_{i=1}^{20} f_i(x)} \quad i, k = 1, 2 \dots 20 \tag{1}$$

The protein x in the composition space is then defined as:

$$P(x) = \left[p_1(x), p_2(x), \dots p_{20}(x) \right] \tag{2}$$

Thus a protein sample is represented as:

$$P = \begin{bmatrix} P_1 \\ P_2 \\ \cdot \\ \cdot \\ \cdot \\ \cdot \\ \cdot \\ P_{20} \end{bmatrix} \tag{3}$$

where

$$P_u = \begin{cases} \dfrac{f_u}{\sum\limits_{i=1}^{20} f_i}, 1 \leq u \leq 20 \end{cases} \tag{4}$$

In this type of representation, the protein sequence order and length information are completely lost which in turn affect the prediction accuracy.

Amphiphillic Pseudo Amino Acid Composition (AmPseAAC) Feature of Protein

This is a non-sequential representation of protein which in which all the details of its sequence order and length is preserved. Unfortunately, it is not feasible to establish a predictor with such a requirement, as it requires huge experiments. Further, protein sequence lengths vary widely, which pose an additional difficulty for admitting the sequence-order information in the feature extraction of protein (Chou, 2005). Hence Chou in 2001 has proposed an effective way of representation of protein known as pseudo amino acid composition (PseAAC) in his seminal study. In this representation the protein character sequence is coded by some of its physicochemical properties. The hydrophobicity and hydrophilicity of the constituent amino acids in a protein play very important role on its folding, its interaction with the environment and other molecules, as well as its catalytic mechanism (Zhan, Zing & Chou, 2008). Thus these two indices may be used to effectively reflect the sequence order effects. Actually, different types of proteins have different amphiphillic features, corresponding to different hydrophobic and hydrophilic order patterns. In view of this, the sequence-order information is indirectly, partially but quite effectively governed by the following equations. Suppose a protein P with a sequence of L amino acid residues is defined as $P_1P_2P_3....P_L$ where P_1 represents the residue at position 1 along the sequence and P_2 the residue at position 2 and so forth. The sequence order effect along a protein chain is approximately reflected by a set of sequence order correlation factors defined as:

$$\theta_\tau = \frac{1}{L-\tau} \sum_{i=1}^{L-\tau} \theta\left(P_i, P_{i+\tau}\right), \left(\tau = 1, 2, 3 ...... \lambda \, and \, \lambda < L\right) \tag{5}$$

In Equation-5, L and θ_τ denote the length of the protein and the τth rank of coupling factor that harbors the τth sequence order correlation factor respectively. The correlation function θ(Pi; Pj) may assume different forms of representation.

θ(Pi; Pj) term is defined as:

$$\theta\left(P_i, P_j\right) = H\left(P_i\right) \times H\left(P_j\right) \tag{6}$$

where H(P$_i$) and H(P$_j$) represent hydrophobicity values of the amino acids P$_i$ and P$_j$ respectively. Similarly, the correlation factors for hydrophilicity values are also calculated. But before substituting the values of hydrophobicity and hydrophilicity into equation 6 they are all subjected to a standard conversion as described the following equation:

$$H^1(R_i) = \frac{H_0^1(R_i) - \sum_{k=1}^{20} H_0^1(R_k)/20}{\sqrt{\sum_{u=1}^{20}\left[H_0^1(R_u) - \sum_{k=1}^{20} H_0^1(R_k)/20\right]^2 / 20}} \tag{7}$$

$$H^2(R_i) = \frac{H_0^2(R_i) - \sum_{k=1}^{20} H_0^2(R_k)/20}{\sqrt{\sum_{u=1}^{20}\left[H_0^2(R_u) - \sum_{k=1}^{20} H_0^2(R_k)/20\right]^2 / 20}} \tag{8}$$

where we use the R_i (i = 1, 2, . . ., 20) to represent the 20 native amino acids according to the alphabetical order of their single-letter codes: A, C, D, E, F, G, H, I, K, L, M, N, P, Q, R, S, T, V, W and Y. The symbols H_0^1 and H_0^2 represent the original hydrophobicity and hydrophilicity values of the amino acid in the brackets right after the symbols, and their values are taken from (Tanford,1962) and (Hopp &Woods,1981), respectively. The converted hydrophobicity and hydrophilicity values obtained using Equations-6 and 7 will have a zero mean value over the 20 native amino acids, and will remain unchanged if going through the same conversion procedure again. Figure 1 shows a schematic diagram of first rank(Tier1),and second rank(Tier-2) sequence order coupling mode along a protein sequence through a hydrophobicity and hydrophilicity correlation function. These two types of correlation factors form the basis of amphiphillic pseudo AAC(AmPseAAC) feature vector of a protein.

Thus a protein sample is represented in a AmPseAAC form as:

Figure 1. Different tier correlations of amino acids

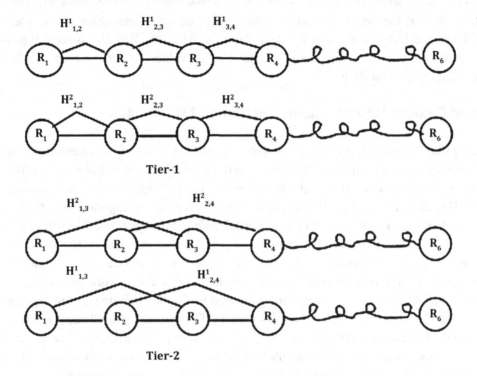

$$
P = \begin{bmatrix}
P_1 \\
P_2 \\
\cdot \\
\cdot \\
P_{20} \\
P_{20+1} \\
\cdot \\
\cdot \\
P_{20+\lambda} \\
P_{20+\lambda+1} \\
\cdot \\
\cdot \\
\cdot \\
P_{20+2\lambda}
\end{bmatrix}
\tag{9}
$$

where p_u as:

$$
P_u = \begin{cases}
\dfrac{f_u}{\displaystyle\sum_{i=1}^{20} f_i + w \sum_{j=1}^{2\lambda} \theta_j} & (1 \le u \le 20) \\[4mm]
\dfrac{w\theta_{u-20}}{\displaystyle\sum_{i=1}^{20} f_i + w \sum_{j=1}^{2\lambda} \theta_j} & (20+1 \le u \le 20+2\lambda)
\end{cases}
\tag{10}
$$

where f_i, i = 1,2,3... 20 are the normalized occurrence frequencies corresponding to 20 native amino acids in the protein P, the symbol j represents the jth tier sequence correlation factor. The symbol w represents the weight factor which is judiciously chosen as 0.01. The first 20 values in Equation-9 represent the classic amino acid composition and the next 2λ values reflect the amphiphillic sequence correlation along the protein chain.

DCT Based Feature Representation Scheme of the Protein

A Discrete Cosine Transform (Ahmed, Natarajan & Rao1974) expresses a sequence of finitely many data points in terms of a sum of cosine functions oscillating at different frequencies. DCTs are important to numerous applications(Ahmed,2009) in science and engineering from lossy compression of audio(e.g.MP3) and images (e.g.JPEG) (where small high-frequency components can be discarded), to spectral methods for the numerical solution of partial differential equations. The use of cosine rather than sine functions is critical in these applications: for compression, it turns out that cosine functions are much more efficient (as explained below, fewer are needed to approximate a typical signal), whereas for differential equations the cosines express a particular choice of boundary conditions.

In particular, a DCT is a Fourier-related transform similar to the Discrete Fourier Transform (DFT), but using only real numbers. DCTs are equivalent to DFTs (Liu, Meng & Chou, 2005; Liu, 2005) of roughly twice the length, operating on real data with even symmetry (since the Fourier transform of a real and even function is real and even), where in some variants the input and/or output data are shifted by half a sample. There are eight standard DCT variants, of which four are common.

The DCT is a real valued and quasi orthogonal transformation that preserves the norms and angles of the vectors. Therefore, it involves lower computational complexities than the DFT. Further as in DFT the time signal is truncated and is assumed periodic, hence discontinuity is introduced in time domain and some corresponding artefacts are introduced in frequency domain. But in DCT as even symmetry is assumed while truncating the time signal, no discontinuity and related artefacts are introduced. The DCT also exhibits more compact representation. Due to these useful properties, the DCT is chosen to be a better substitute of DFT in the context of feature extraction of protein sequences.

The discrete cosine transform (DCT) of the coded protein sequence (P) is defined as:

$$G(K) = \alpha(k) \sum_{n=0}^{L-1} H(p_n) \cos\left[\frac{(2n+1)k\Pi}{2L}\right], k = 0,1,2,...,L-1 \qquad (11)$$

where $\alpha(k)$

$$\alpha(k) = \begin{cases} \sqrt{\dfrac{1}{L}}, k = 0 \\ \sqrt{\dfrac{2}{L}}, k \neq 0 \end{cases} \qquad (12)$$

where G(0) represents the average value of the signal and is called the DC or constant component and the remaining are called time varying or harmonic of the sequence. The low-frequency components of DCT represent the global information of the coded sequence. The type of protein is represented by the curve of the hydrophobic values of the residues whose global shape represented by the low frequency components of the DCT is more important (Zhan & Ding, 2007) in determining the type of structural class. Hence some low frequency DCT coefficients are taken to represent the spectral characteristics of the protein.

In this chapter the AAC, the 2λ correlation factors of both hydrophobic and hydrophilic sequence and the δ low frequency DCT coefficients are taken to form the new pseudo amino acid composition vector. Accordingly, a protein sample is:

$$P = \begin{bmatrix} P_1 \\ P_2 \\ \cdot \\ \cdot \\ \cdot \\ P_{20} \\ P_{20+1} \\ \cdot \\ \cdot \\ \cdot \\ P_{20+\lambda} \\ P_{20+\lambda+1} \\ \cdot \\ \cdot \\ \cdot \\ P_{20+2\lambda} \\ P_{20+2\lambda+1} \\ \cdot \\ \cdot \\ P_{20+2\lambda+\delta} \end{bmatrix} \tag{13}$$

$$P_u = \begin{cases} \dfrac{f_u}{\sum\limits_{i=1}^{20} f_i + w\sum\limits_{j=1}^{2\lambda} \theta_j + w\sum\limits_{k=1}^{\delta} \gamma_k} & (1 \le u \le 20) \\[3ex] \dfrac{w\theta_{u-20}}{\sum\limits_{i=1}^{20} f_i + w\sum\limits_{j=1}^{2\lambda} \theta_j + w\sum\limits_{k=1}^{\delta} \gamma_k} & (21 \le u \le 20+2\lambda) \\[3ex] \dfrac{w\gamma_{u-(20+2\lambda)}}{\sum\limits_{i=1}^{20} f_i + w\sum\limits_{j=1}^{2\lambda} \theta_j + w\sum\limits_{k=1}^{\delta} \gamma_k} & (20+2\lambda+1) \le u \le (20+2\lambda+\delta) \end{cases} \tag{14}$$

where f_i $i = 1, 2,\dots 20$ are the normalized occurrence frequencies corresponding to 20 native amino acids in the protein P, the symbol θ_j represents the j-tier sequence correlation factor. The low frequency DCT coefficients of the protein are denoted by k and the symbol w represents the weight factor which governs the degree of the sequence order effect to be incorporated. In essence the first 20 values in Equation-14 represent the classic amino acid composition, the next 2λ values reflect the amphiphillic sequence correlation along the protein chain and the remaining δ discrete values contain the low frequency global information of the protein.

Classification of Protein Structural Class using Different Computational Model

- Classification using Functionally Linked Artificial Neural Network [FLANN]
- Classification using RBF network
- Classification using RBF with NSGA-II

Classification Protein Structural Class using FLANN

The Functional-Link Neural Network has been developed as an alternative architecture to the well-known Multi-Layer Perceptron (MLP) network with application to both function approximation and pattern recognition (Patra, Pal, Chatterji & Panda, 1999). The FLANN proposed by (Pao,1989), is a single layer artificial neural network structure and is a nonlinear network with simple operations and provides comparable performance as that of multi-layer ANN.

Below figure shows an adaptive FLANN architecture with one neuron and nonlinear inputs. The nonlinearity in the input is introduced by a functional expansionof input values. According to Covers theorem (Haykin,2009), a complex pattern-classification problem cast in a high-dimensional space nonlinearly is more likely to be linearly separable than in a low-dimensional space. The functional expansion block makes use of a functional model comprising of a subset of orthogonal sine and cosine basic functions and the original pattern along with its outer products. There are three types of functional expansions used in FLANN

Figure 2. Adaptive FLANN architecture

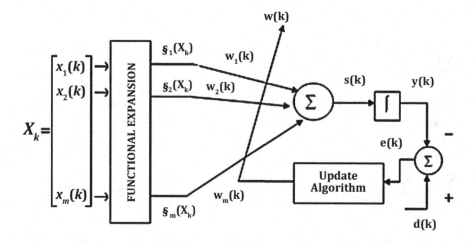

These are:

1. **Trigonometric Expansion:** The input pattern consisting of jxi; x_j, j can be expanded using Trigonometric expansion as: $\phi(x) = \left[x_1, \sin \pi(x_1), \cos \pi(x_1), \ldots, x_2, \sin \pi(x_2), \cos \pi(x_2),\right]$ (15)

2. **Legendre Polynomial:** Similarly the enhanced pattern of using Legendre polynomial is formed as $L_0(x) = 1, L_1(x) = x, L_2(x) = \frac{1}{2}\left[3x^2 - 1\right]$ (16)

3. **The Chebyshev Polynomials:** Also a set of orthogonal polynomials and for $1 < x < 1$ these are generated using a recursive formula $C_{n+1} = 2xC_n(x) - C_{n-1}(x)$ (17)

The first few Chebyshev polynomials are obtained as: $C_0(x) = 1, C_1(x) = x, C_2(x) = 2x^2 - 1, C_3(x) = 4x^3 - 3x$ (18)

After nonlinear mapping of the input features simple linear combiner is used to obtain the output which is then passed through a nonlinear function. The weights of the FLANN are updated using simple LMS algorithm.

A generalized FLANN classifier structure is introduced and shown in figure where only trigonometric expansion is considered as others are giving very poor results for this particular protein structural class prediction. The protein data is represented as DCTAmPseAAC and is then normalized as:

$$norm(x) = \frac{(x_k - x_{min})}{(x_{max} - x_{min})}$$ (19)

Figure 3. FLANN classification model for 4 classes

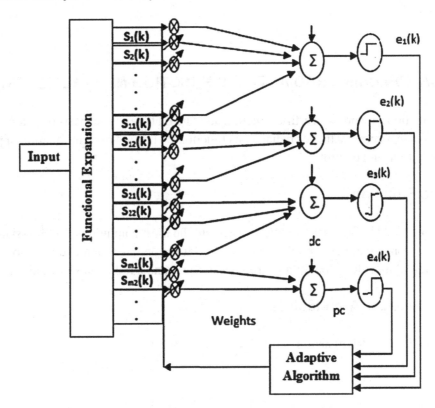

where x_k is k^{th} sample value x_{min} is minimum value of the data set x_{max} is maximum value of the data set. On the normalized data, 80 percent isused for training the classifier and the remaining is used for validating the model. The design of the classifier proceeds as follows:

Step 1: Each input data is applied sequentially.

Step 2: Trigonometric functional expansion of input data is carried out.

Step 3: The weights are initialized as random values between 0 and 1.

Step 4: The features with the corresponding weights of the model are multiplied.

Step 5: The weighted sum is passed through the activation function which results in Weights of the network are updated using LMS rule.

Step 7: The entire process is repeated till mean squared error(MSE) is reduced to the largest possible level where network output.

where

$$MSE = \frac{1}{p} \sum_{k=1}^{p} e^2(k) \tag{20}$$

where

$$e = output_{expected} - output_{actual} \tag{21}$$

and

$$w_{k+1} = w_k + \eta e_k x_k \tag{22}$$

CLASSIFICATION USING RADIAL BASIS FUNCTION NEURAL NETWORK (RBF)

A radial basis function network is an artificial neural network that uses radial basis functions as activation functions. It is a linear combination of radial basis functions. They are used in function approximation, time series prediction, and control.

Radial Basis Function

Different types of radial basis functions can be used, but the most common is the Gaussian function: If there is more than one predictor variable, then the RBF function has as many dimensions as there are variables. The radial basis function for a neuron has a center and a radius (also called a spread).

RBF Neural Network Architecture

A Radial Basis Function (RBF) neural network has three layers:

Figure 4. RBF neural network model for 4 classes

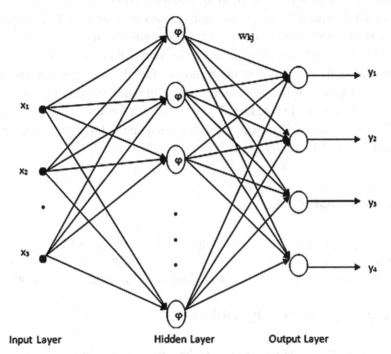

1. **Input Layer:** The Input patterns enter on this layer and is subjected to a direct transfer function i.e. the output of the node equals to its input. The input neurons feed the values to each of the neurons in the hidden layer.

2. **Hidden Layer:** This layer has a variable number of neurons (the optimal number is determined by the training process). Each neuron consists of a radial basis function centered on a point with as many dimensions as there are predictor variables. The spread (radius) of the RBF function may be different for each dimension. The centers and spreads are determined by the training process. When presented with the x vector of input values from the input layer, a hidden neuron computes the Euclidean distance of the test case from the neurons center point and then applies the RBF kernel function to this distance using the spread values. The resulting value is passed to the summation layer also known as output layer.

3. **Output Layer:** The value coming out of a neuron in the hidden layer is multiplied by a weight associated with the neuron (W1, W2, ..., Wn in this figure) and passed to the summation which adds up the weighted values and presents this sum as the output of the network.

Training of RBF Networks

The following parameters are determined by the training process:

1. The number of neurons in the hidden layer.
2. The coordinates of the center of each hidden-layer RBF function.

3. The radius (spread) of each RBF function in each dimension.
4. The weights applied to the RBF function outputs as they are passed to the summation layer. Various methods have been used to train RBF networks. One approach first uses K-means clustering to find cluster centres which are then used as the centres for the RBF functions. However, K-means clustering is a computationally intensive procedure, and it often does not generate the optimal number of centers. Another approach is to use a random subset of the training points as the centers. It is also very difficult to choose random values. In this chapter a multi-objective optimization technique i.e. NSGA-II (Deb, Pratap & Agarwal, 2002) has been applied to optimize the structure and error square of the RBF model as two objectives.

WHAT IS OPTIMIZATION?

Optimization refers to finding one or more feasible solutions which corresponds to extreme values of one or more objectives. Its need comes mostly from the extreme purpose of either designing a solution for minimum possible cost of fabrication or for maximum possible reliability or others.

Single and Multi-Objective Optimization

When an optimization problem involves only one objective function in the task of finding the optimal solution it is called single objective optimization. When an optimization problem involves more than one objective function for the task of finding one or more optimal solutions it is called multi-objective optimization. Since most real world optimization problems exist with multiple objectives, equal importance to each objective has to be given when the optimal solution to a problem is required.

Fundamental Differences

Single objective optimization optimizes only one objective function, gets a Single optimal solution and Maximum/Minimum fitness value is selected as the best solution where multi-objective optimization (Srinivas & Deb, 1995) optimizes two or more than two objective functions, gets a set of optimal solutions and the solutions can be compared by

*   Domination
*   Non-Domination

    Two Approaches to Multi-Objective Optimization

1. Classical Techniques
2. Evolutionary Methods

Classical Methods

These methods formulate as a single objective with weighted sum of all objective functions.

It may guarantee optimal solution but results in single point solution.

Limitation:

1. In real world, Decision makers often need different alternatives.
2. Result depends on weights.
3. Difficult to select proper combination of weights.
4. Multiple runs of algorithm required to get the whole range of solutions.

WHY EVOLUTIONARY ALGORITHM (EA)?

The classical way to solve multi-objective optimization problems is to follow the preference based approach, where a relative preference vector is used to scalarize multiple objectives. Since classical search of optimization methods use a point by-point approach, where one solution in each iteration is modified to a different solution, the outcome of using a classical optimization method is a single optimized solution. Since only a single optimized solution could be found, it is necessary to convert the task of finding multiple trade of solutions in a multi-objective optimization to one of finding a single solution of a transformed single objective optimization problem. However, the field of search and optimization has changed over the last few years by the introduction of a number of non-classical, unorthodox and stochastic search and optimization algorithms. Of these, the evolutionary algorithm mimics nature's evolutionary principles to drive its search towards an optimal solution. One of the most obvious differences to classical search and optimization algorithms is that EA uses a population of solutions in each iteration, instead of a single solution. Since a population of solutions are processed in each iteration, the outcome of an EA is also a population of solutions. If an optimization has a single optimization, all EA population members can be expected to converge to that optimum solution. Evolutionary optimization principles are different from classical optimization methodologies in the following main ways

1. An Evolutionary Optimization (EO) procedure does not usually use gradient information in its search process. Thus, EO methodologies are direct search procedures, allowing them to be applied to a wide variety of optimization problems.
2. An EO procedure uses more than one solution (a population approach) in an iteration, unlike in most classical optimization algorithms which updates one solution in each iteration (a point approach). The use of a population has a number of advantages:
   a. It provides an EO with a parallel processing power achieving a computationally quick overall search.
   b. It allows an EO to find multiple optimal solutions, thereby facilitating the solution of multi-modal and multi-objective optimization problems.
   c. It provides an EO with the ability to normalize decision variables (as well as objective and constraint functions) within an evolving population using the population best minimum and maximum values.

3. An EO procedure uses stochastic operators, unlike deterministic operators used in most classical optimization methods. The operators tend to achieve a desired effect by using higher probabilities towards desirable outcomes, as opposed to using predetermined and fixed transition rules. This allows an EO algorithm to negotiate multiple optima and other complexities better and provide them with a global perspective in their search. An EO begins its search with a population of solutions usually created at random within a specified lower and upper bound on each variable. Thereafter, the EO procedure enters into an iterative operation of updating the current population to create a new population by the use of four main operators: selection, crossover, mutation and elite-preservation. The operation stops when one or more pre-specified termination criteria are met.

Principles of Multi-Objective Optimization

A multi-objective optimization problem involves a number of objective functions which are to be either minimized or maximized. As in a single-objective optimization problem, the multi-objective optimization problem may contain a number of constraints which any feasible solution (including all optimal solutions) must satisfy. Since objectives can be either minimized or maximized, we state the multi objective optimization problem in its general form:

$$
\begin{aligned}
& \textit{Minimize / Maximize } f_m(x), \ m = 1, 2, \ldots\ldots M \\
& \textit{subject } \text{to } g_j(x) \geq= 0, \ j = 1, 2 \ldots\ldots\ldots J \\
& \qquad\qquad h_k(x) = 0, \ k = 1, 2, \ldots\ldots\ldots K
\end{aligned}
\tag{23}
$$

Objectives of Multi-Objective Optimization

It is clear that the search space in the context of multi objectives can be divided into two non-overlapping regions, namely one which is optimal and one which is non-optimal. In the case of conflicting objectives, usually the set of optimal solutions contains more than one solution. In the presence of multiple pareto-optimal solutions, it is difficult to prefer one solution over the other without any further information about the problem. There are two goals in a multi- objective optimization.

1. To find a set of solutions as close as possible to the Pareto-optimal front. (Horn, Nafplotis & Goldberg, 1994)
2. To find a set of solutions as diverse as possible.

The first goal is common to any optimization problem. Converging a set of solutions which are not close to the true optimal set of solutions is not desirable. On the other hand, the second goal is entirely specific to multi objective optimization. In addition to being converged close to the pareto-optimal front, they must also be sparsely spaced in the Pareto-optimal region.

Non-Conflicting Objectives

Many real-world problems involve multiple Conflicting objectives. A solution that is extreme with respect to one objective requires a compromise in other objectives. A sacrifice in one objective is related to the gain in other objective(s). Example: Buying a car either we have to sacrifice cost or comfort level.

Figure 5. A set of points and the list non-domination front are shown

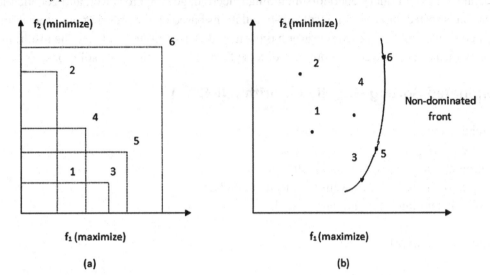

(a)   (b)

DOMINANCE AND NON-DOMINANCE

A solution x_1 is said to dominate the other solution x_2; if both the following conditions are true:

1. The solution x_1 is no worse than x_2 in all objectives. Thus, the solutions are compared based on their objective function values (or location of the corresponding points (z_1 and z_2) on the objective space).
2. The solution x_1 is strictly better than x_2 in at least one objective.

Concept of Dominance

For a given set of solutions (or corresponding points on the objective space, for example, those shown in Figure 5), a pair-wise comparison can be made using the above definition and whether one point dominates the other can be established. All points which are not dominated by any other member of the set are called the non-dominated points of class one, or simply the non-dominated points. For the set of six solutions shown in the figure, they are points 3, 5, and 6. One property of any two such points is that a gain in an objective from one point to the other happens only due to a sacrifice in at least one other objective. This trade-off of property between the non-dominated points makes the practitioners interested in finding a wide variety of them before making a final choice. These points make up a front when viewed them together on the objective space; hence the non-dominated points are often visualized to represent a non-domination front.

NON-ELITIST MULTI-OBJECTIVE GENETIC ALGORITHM (NSGA)

The objective of the NSGA algorithm is to improve the adaptive fit of a population of candidate solutions to a Pareto front constrained by a set of objective functions. The algorithm uses an evolutionary process with surrogates for evolutionary operators including selection, genetic crossover, and genetic mutation. The population is sorted into a hierarchy of sub-populations based on the ordering of Pareto dominance. Similarity between members of each sub-group is evaluated on the Pareto front, and the resulting groups and similarity measures are used to promote a diverse front of non-dominated solutions.

Non-Dominated Sorting Genetic Algorithm (NSGA)

Common features with the standard GA:

1. Variation operators crossover and mutation,
2. Selection method Stochastic Reminder Roulette-Wheel,
3. Standard generational evolutionary model.

   Algorithm 1 (NSGA Algorithm):

1. Initialize population of solutions
2. Repeat
   a. Calculate objective values and assign fitness values
   b. Generate new population until stopping condition is full-filled.

Advantages

The main advantages of an NSGA is the assignment of fitness according to non-dominated sets. Since better non-dominated sets are emphasized systematically, an NSGA progresses towards the pareto-optimal region front-wise. Moreover, performing sharing in the parameter space allows phenotypically diverse solutions to emerge when using NSGAs. If desired, the sharing can also be performed in the objective space.

Disdvantages

It has been observed that the performance of NSGA is sensitive to the sharing method parameter. However, if it is chosen according to the suggestion equation, a reasonable good spread of solutions can be obtained.

NON-DOMINATED SORTING GENETIC ALGORITHM (NSGA-II)

NSGA II is an elitist non-dominated sorting Genetic Algorithm to solve multi objective optimization problem. It has been reported that NSGA II can converge to the global Pareto-optimal front and can maintain the diversity of population on the Pareto-optimal front. The computational complexity of NSGA II is also lesser that other multi-objective evolutionary algorithms. The main concept of this algorithm lies on the concept of non-domination between two solutions. For unconstrained optimization problem, a solution x will dominate another solution y, if (a) the solution x is no worse than solution y in all objectives, and (b) the x is strictly better than y in at least one objective. If any one of (a) and (b) is violated, the solution x does not dominate solution y. The dominating concept is illustrated using the Figure 6.

Figure 6. Un-constrained non-domination

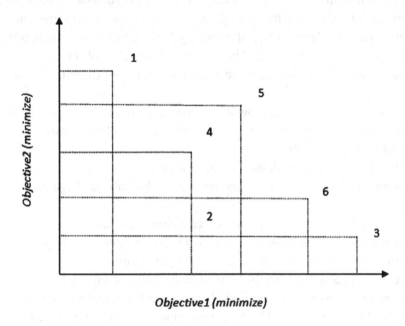

Objective1 (minimize)

Here, solution 1, 2, and 3 are the non-dominating solutions. But solution 4 is dominated by solution 2 as the solution 2 is better in one objective and is equal in other objective. On the other hand, solution 6 is also dominated by solution 2. In this case, solution 6 is not worse than solution 2 with respect to the second objective, but the solution 2 is strictly better than solution 6 with respect to the first objective. Solution 5 is dominated by solution 2 and 4 as 2 and 4 are better than solution 5 in both the objectives.

For constrained optimization problem, a solution p will dominate a solution q, if (a) p is feasible, and q is infeasible solution, (b) solution p and q are both infeasible, but the constrained violation of p is less than q, and (c) solution p, and q are both feasible, and solution p dominate solution q.

The solutions 1, 2, and 3 are in the feasible region, and the solutions 4 and 5 are on the infeasible region. If 4 and 5 are compared, then 5 is dominated by 4 as constrain violation of solution 4 is lesser than the solution 5. For 2 and 5, though 5 is better than 2 in respect to all the objectives, but 5 is dominated by 2 as 5 is in the infeasible region. Similarly, if solution 2 is compared with solution 3, solution 3 is dominated by solution 2 as per unconstrained domination rules. Similarly, the solutions 1 and 2 are non-dominating as per the unconstrained domination rules.

The steps involved in the NSGA II algorithm are shown in Figure-7. These steps are described below.

NSGA-II Algorithm

1. Initialize the population. The initial population may be generated using uniformly distributed random numbers.
2. Calculate all the objective functions values, separately.
3. Rank the population using the constrained non-dominating criteria. The first non-dominating front is generally assigned a rank of one. Similarly, the second non dominating front has a rank of two and so on. The solutions having lesser rank are the better candidates to be selected for the next generation.

4. Calculate the crowding distance of each solution. The crowding distance is measured as the distance of the biggest cuboids containing the two neighbouring solutions of the same non-dominating front in the objective space. Higher the value of crowding distance better is the probability of the solution to be selected for the next generation. The solutions at the ends of the non-dominating front are assigned a large value of crowding distance so as to incorporate extremities of the non-dominating front.

5. Selection is done according to the crowding distance operator. The crowding distance operator function as follows: for a minimization type optimization problem, a solution x wins the tournament with another solution y if:

   a. The solution x has better rank than solution y, or,

   b. If the solutions x and y have the same rank, but solution x has large crowding distance than solution y.

6. Apply crossover and mutation operator to generate children solutions.

7. The children and parent population are combined together in order to implement elitism and the non-dominating sorting is applied on the combined population.

8. Replace the old parent population by the better members of the combined population. The solutions of the lower ranking fronts are selected initially to replace the parent population. If all the solutions of a front cannot be accommodated in the parent population, the solutions having large crowding distance will get preference to replace the parent solutions.

These steps are repeated till the termination criteria are satisfied.

DIFFERENT GENETIC OPERATORS OF NSGA-II ALGORITHM

1. Tournament Selection Operator
2. Simulated Binary Crossover
3. Polynomial mutation
4. Selection

All the genetic operators are discussed briefly below.

Tournament Selection Operator

During the tournament selection, two individuals are chosen at random from the population and the winner (the one with the best fitness) for crossover is selected (based on Rank and the Crowding Operator). A problem with Pareto Domination Tournament Selection, is that two individuals can be non-dominated/dominated. Crowding Distance is a method of tie-break between two such individuals and ensures a good spread of solutions.

$$if\ i_{rank} < j_{rank}$$

or

Figure 7. NSGA-II algorithm

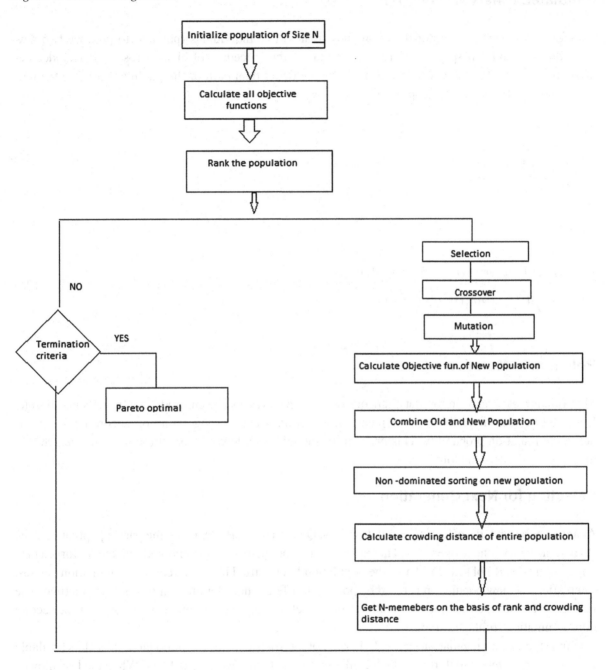

$$if \ i_{rank} = j_{rank} \ and \ i_{CD} > j_{CD}$$

then solution *i* is selected.

Simulated Binary Cross Over

Crossover is a genetic operator that combines (mates) two individuals (parents) to produce two new individuals (Childs/off springs). Here it is simulating the procedure of binary crossover. The idea behind crossover is that the new chromosome may be better than both of the parents if it takes the best characteristics from each of the parents.

$$
b = \begin{cases} (2*r)^{\frac{1}{\mu+1}}, & \text{if } r \le 0.5 \\ \dfrac{1}{2*(1-r)}^{\frac{1}{\mu+1}}, & \text{if } r > 0.5 \end{cases}
\tag{24}
$$

where

$$
child_1(j) = \frac{1}{2}\big((1+b)*parent_1(j)+(1-b)*parent_2(j)\big)
$$
$$
child_2(j) = \frac{1}{2}\big((1-b)*parent_1(j)+(1+b)*parent_2(j)\big)
\tag{25}
$$

Polynomial Mutation

Mutation is a genetic operator that alters one or more gene values in a chromosome from its initial state. It is used to keep diversity in the population. Mutation occurs during evolution according to a user-definable mutation probability. This probability should be set low. If it is set too high, the search will turn into a primitive random search.

Selection for Next Generation

At any generation t, the offspring population (say, Q_t) is first created by using the parent population (say, Pt) and the usual genetic operators. Thereafter, the two populations are combined together to form a new population (say, R_t) of size 2N. Then, the population R_t classified into different non-domination classes. Thereafter, the new population is filled by points of different non-domination fronts, one at a time. The filling starts with the first non-domination front (of class one) and continues with points of the second non-domination front, and so on.

Since the overall population size of R_t is 2N, not all fronts can be accommodated in N slots available for the new population. All fronts which could not be accommodated are deleted. When the last allowed front is being considered, there may exist more points in the front than the remaining slots in the new population. This scenario is illustrated in Figure 8. Instead of arbitrarily discarding some members from the last front, the points which will make the diversity of the selected points the highest are chosen.

Simulation Results of Classification

The flow graph of the proposed model can be visualized as:

Figure 8. NSGA-II mechanism

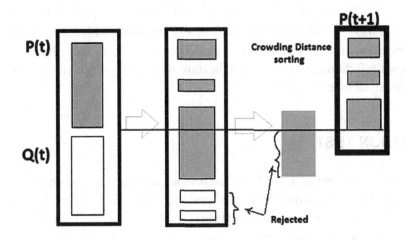

Figure 9. The flow graph of the classification schemes

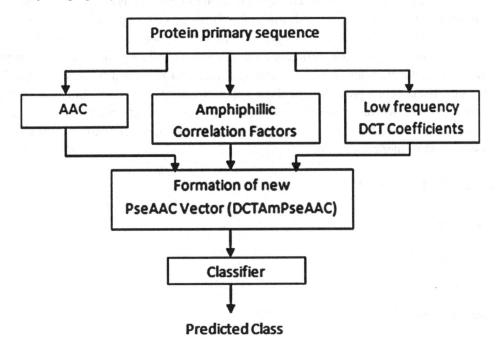

Initially for each of the standard protein data set the Amino acid composition (AAC), Amphiphillic Pseudo amino acid (AmPseAAC) composition and the spectral characteristics features are extracted.

Conventionally in statistical prediction and classification problems, cross validation tests are often used to assess the performance of the predictor or classifier. There are three commonly used cross validation tests such as:

1.   Re-substitution Test
2.   Independent data sets Test

3.   Jackknife Test

Re-substitution is used for the self-consistency of the algorithm whereas the rest two are used for testing the result by cross-validation. However, as elucidated in (Chou & Shen, 2007), among these cross validation methods, the jackknife test is deemed the most objective that can always yield a unique result for a given benchmark dataset.

RE-SUBSTITUTION TEST

This is also called Self-consistency Test. When the resubstitution test is performed, the structural class for each of the domains in a given data set is predicted using the rules derived from the same data set, the so-called development data set or training data set. in other words, the parameters derived from the training data set include the information of a domain later it is plugged back in the test. This will certainly give an optimistic error estimate because of the memorization effect i.e. the same domains are used to derive the prediction rule and to test them. The resubstitution examination is essential because it reflects the self-consistency of a prediction method, especially for its algorithm part. A prediction algorithm certainly cannot be deemed a good one if its self-consistency is poor. In other words, the resubstitution examination is necessary but not sufficient for evaluating a prediction method. As a complement, a cross-validation examination for an independent testing dataset is needed because it can reflect the extrapolating effectiveness of a prediction method. This is important especially for checking the validity of a training database: whether it contains sufficient information to reflect all the important features concerned so as to yield a high success rate in application. However, how to carry out cross-validation properly is worthy of further clarification.

Independent Dataset Test

This is of two types:

1.   Singe-test-set analysis
2.   Sub-sampling Test

Singe-Test-Set Analysis

Here, the prediction rules are derived from the training dataset and are examined by observing the predicted results for the domains in an independent testing dataset. However, the selection of a testing dataset is arbitrary, and the accuracy thus obtained lacks an objective criterion unless the testing dataset is sufficiently large. On the other hand, even if a domain in the testing set is incorrectly predicted by an algorithm, this does not necessarily mean that anything is wrong with the algorithm because that domain might be just outside the frame of the classification defined by the limited number of domains in the current training dataset. A problem caused by these two factors cannot be avoided unless:

1.   The testing dataset is sufficiently large and

2. The training database has become an ideal one, i.e. a statistically complete one that is able to represent all the domains in the testing dataset.

In view of this, the single-test set examination is not a very good approach for cross-validation.

Sub-Sampling Test

Another approach for cross-validation is sub-sampling analysis, according to which a given data set is divided into a training set and a testing set. However, a serious problem arises as to how to divide the whole dataset into a training set and a testing set. As shown below, the number of possible divisions might be extremely large. Suppose there are N domains in a given dataset, which is divided into a training dataset (with N1 domains) and a testing dataset (with N2 domains). The number of such divisions is given by

$$(N_1 + N_2)! / N_1! N_2! = N! / [(N - N_2)! N_2!\}$$ (26)

Therefore, analysis can be carried out for only a very small subset of the possible divisions selected randomly or arbitrarily.

Jackknife Test (Leave-One-Out Test)

In comparison with the single-set-test examination and the sub-sampling analysis, the jackknife test seems to be most effective. In the jackknife test, each domain in the dataset is singled out in turn as a test domain and all the rule-parameters are determined from the remaining N-1 domains. Hence the memorization effects that are included in the resubstitution tests can be completely removed. During the process of jackknife analysis, both the training and testing datasets are actually open, and a domain will in turn move from each to the other.

SIMULATION RESULTS OF CLASSIFICATION USING FLANN

Each of the feature patterns is expanded using the trigonometric expansion. The nonlinearly mapped input pattern is weighted, added together and passed through the activation function, *tanh()* to give the final value, y(k). The output of FLANN is compared with the target value to produce the error. Then the simple LMS based algorithm is used to update the weights of the classifier and process continues until the error square is minimum. The value of the error square corresponding to each iteration is stored and plotted below to show the convergence characteristics for 204, 277 and 498 domain protein data set respectively.

It is observed that the $\alpha+\beta$ class is more difficult to predict as it contains more variability of helices. The classification accuracy of the model is compared using AAC, AmPseAAC and DCTAmPseAAC in all the three data sets. The following tables show the comparison result of prediction accuracy for 204, 277 and 498 protein domain data sets with AAC, AmPseAAC and DCTAmPseAAC features. The same is also represented in histograms. It is evident that DCTAmPseAAC feature representation of the protein data gives better accurate classification result than AmPseAAC and AAC.

Figure 10. Comparison of convergence characteristics of FLANN based classifier for the 204 protein domain using AAC, AmPseAAC and DCTAmPseAAC features

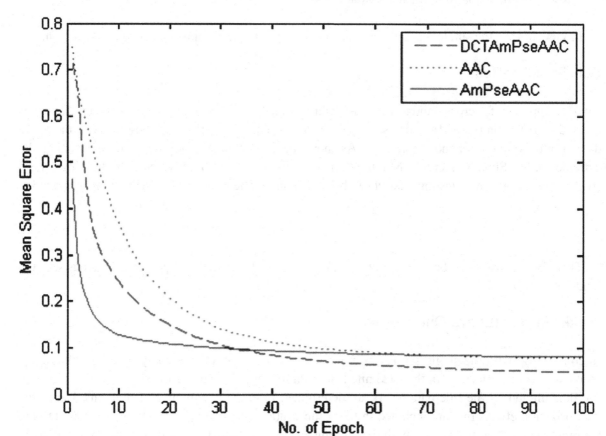

Table 1. Comparison of classification accuracy of 204 protein domain data set with AAC, AmPseAAC and DCTAmPseAAC features

Features	All α	All β	α+β	α/β	Overall Accuracy
AAC	53.8	45	46.6	100	56.81
AmPseAAC	90	17.6	30	68	63.63
DCTAmPseAAC	94.2	94.2	70.2	86.79	87.25

SIMULATION RESULTS OF CLASSIFICATION USING RBFNN AND NSGA-II

This table shows both the self-consistency and jacknife test of RBFNN model for DCTAmPseAAC feature representation of Protein.

Figure 11. Comparison of convergence characteristics of FLANN based classifier for the 277 protein domain using AAC, AmPseAAC and DCTAmPseAAC features

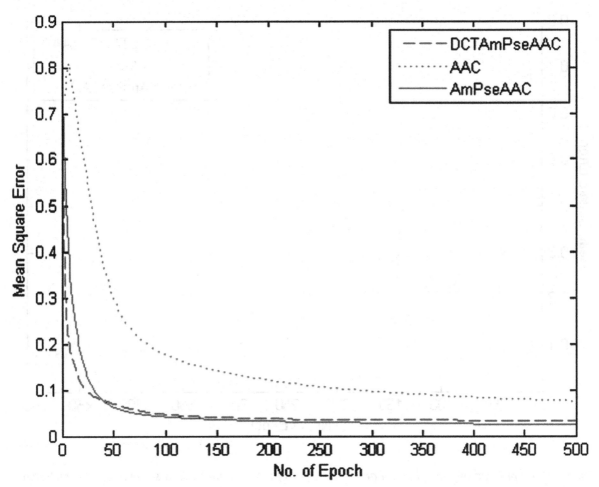

Table 2. Comparison of classification accuracy of 277 protein domain data set with AAC, AmPseAAC and DCTAmPseAAC features

Features	All α	All β	α+β	α/β	Overall Accuracy
AAC	22.7	71.5	74.1	76.9	57.97
AmPseAAC	100	52.1	66.7	72.3	71.05
DCTAmPseAAC	92.6	86.7	91.1	95.31	89.59

Comparison between FLANN and RBF Classifiers

The following table shows the comparison of Jackknife accuracy of three different protein domain datasets with FLANN and RBF Classifiers.

Figure 12. Comparison of convergence characteristics of FLANN based classifier for the 498 protein domain using AAC, AmPseAAC and DCTAmPseAAC features

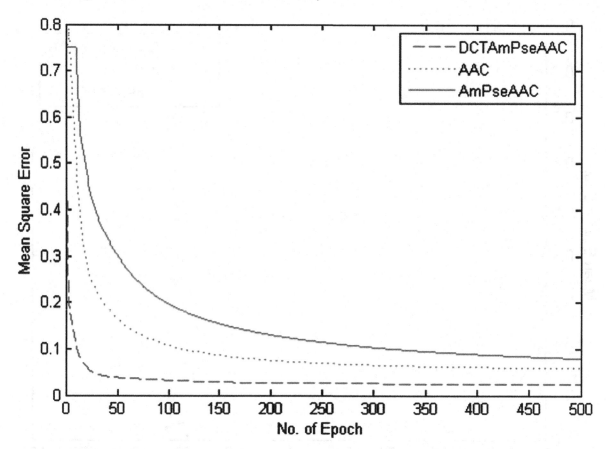

Table 3. Comparison of classification accuracy of 498 protein domain data set with AAC, AmPseAAC and DCTAmPseAAC features

Features	All α	All β	α+β	α/β	Overall Accuracy
AAC	75	60	50	62.9	58.89
AmPseAAC	63	92	52.9	88.5	74.72
DCTAmPseAAC	93.8	95	94.8	95.68	94.12

CONCLUSION

Classification of protein structural class prediction is a challenging task. The size of the protein data base is growing exponentially every day. Many classification strategies have been proposed in this area. This chapter uses two classification strategies i.e. FLANN and RBF with NSGA-II. These classification schemes are based on the concept of Chou's pseudo amino acid composition feature representation method which is composed of the amino acid composition information, the amphiphillic correlation factors and the spectral characteristics of the protein. Thus the sample of a protein is represented by a set of discrete components which incorporate both the sequence order and the length effect. This representation

Figure 13. Comparison of overall classification accuracy of 204 protein data set using AAC, AmPseAAC and DCTAmPseAAC features

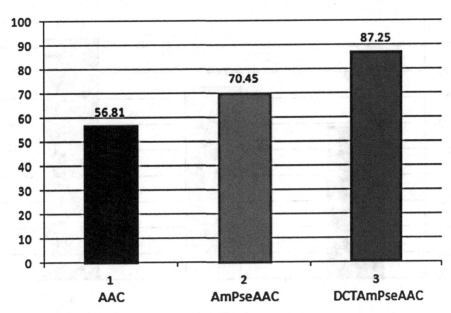

Figure 14. Comparison of overall classification accuracy of 277 protein data set using AAC, AmPseAAC and DCTAmPseAAC features

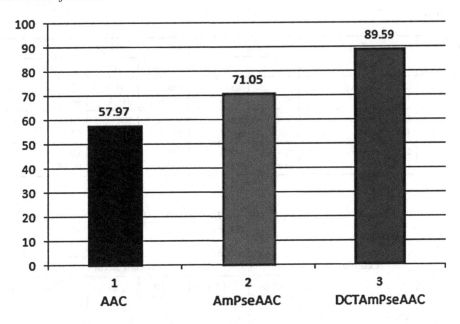

of protein data is known as Discrete co-sine transformation amphiphillic pseudo amino acid composition (DCTAmPseAAC). Here DCT has been used for feature extraction which helps in preserving the spectral characteristic of protein. In this chapter, trigonometric functional expansion has been used in FLANN. The purpose of using FLANN is that it is a low complexity network and it requires less number

Figure 15. Comparison of overall classification accuracy of 498 protein data set using AAC, AmPseAAC and DCTAmPseAAC features

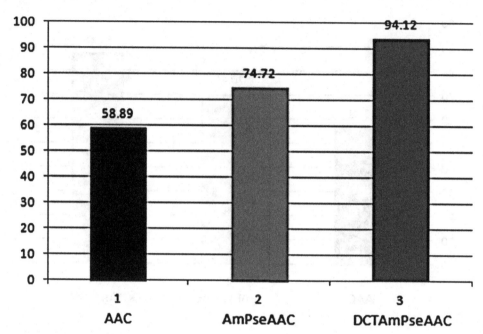

Table 4. Classification accuracy of the proposed (DCTAmPseAAC + RBFNN) method for self-consistency and Jackknife tests

Dataset	Test	Accuracy				
		All α	ALL β	A+β	A/β	Overall Accuracy
204 domain	Self-consistency	100	100	100	100	100
	Jackknife test	94.23	92.30	95.75	94.34	94.11
277 domain	Self-consistency	100	100	100	100	100
	Jackknife test	97.01	96.67	92.31	92.19	94.42
498 domain	Self-consistency	100	100	100	100	100
	Jackknife test	91.83	95	96.32	100	96.14

Table 5. Comparison of Jackknife accuracy of three different protein domain datasets with FLANN and RBF Classifiers

Dataset	Classifier	Jackknife Accuracy				
		All α	ALL β	A+β	A/β	Overall Accuracy
204 domain	FLANN	94.2	94.2	70.2	86.79	87.25
	RBF	94.23	92.30	95.75	94.34	94.11
277 domain	FLANN	92.6	86.7	91.1	95.31	89.59
	RBF	97.01	96.67	92.31	92.19	94.42
498 domain	FLANN	93.8	95	94.8	95.68	94.12
	RBF	91.83	95	96.32	100	96.14

Figure 16. Comparison of Jackknife accuracy of three different protein domain datasets with FLANN and RBF Classifiers

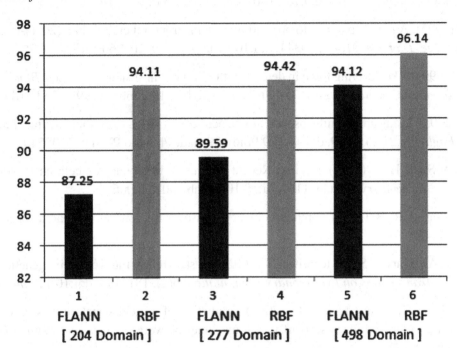

of parameter optimization. However this results in less accuracy in prediction. In this chapter RBFNN has been used for higher prediction accuracy and NSGA-II has been used for parameter optimization of the network. A set of exhaustive simulation studies demonstrates high success rate of classification using the self-consistency and jackknife test on the benchmark datasets.

REFERENCES

Ahmad, M. S. (2009). Iris recognition using the discrete cosine transform and artificial neural networks. *J. Computer Science, 5*(4), 369373.

Ahmed, N., Natarajan, T., & Rao, K. R. (1974). Discrete cosine transforms. *IEEE Transactions on Computers, C-32*, 9093.

Andreeva, A., Howorth, D., Chandonia, J.M., Brenner, S.R., Hubbard, T.J., Clothia, C. & Murzin, A.G. (2008). Data growth and its impact on the SCOP database: New developments. *Nucleic Acids Research, 36*(Database issue), D419-D425.

Cai, Y., & Zhou, G. (2000). Prediction of protein structural classes by neural network. *Biochimie, 82*(8), 783785. doi:10.1016/S0300-9084(00)01161-5 PMID:11018296

Cai, Y., & Zhou, G. (2000). Prediction of protein structural classes by neural network. *Biochimie, 82*(8), 783785. doi:10.1016/S0300-9084(00)01161-5 PMID:11018296

Cai, Y. D., Liu, X. J., Xu, X., & Zhou, P. (2001). Support vector machines for predicting protein structural class. *BMC Bioinformatics*, *2*(1), 3. doi:10.1186/1471-2105-2-3 PMID:11483157

Chou, K. C. (1995). A novel approach to predicting protein structural classes in a (20-1)-D amino acid composition space. *Proteins*, *21*(4), 319344. doi:10.1002/prot.340210406 PMID:7567954

Chou, K. C. (1999). A key driving force in determination of protein structural classes. *Biochemical and Biophysical Research Communications*, *264*(1), 216224. doi:10.1006/bbrc.1999.1325 PMID:10527868

Chou, K. C. (2005). Using amphiphilic pseudo amino acid composition to predict enzyme. *Bioinformatics (Oxford, England)*, *21*(1), 1019. doi:10.1093/bioinformatics/bth466 PMID:15308540

Chou, K. C., & Shen, H. B. (2007). Review: Recent progresses in protein sub cellular location prediction. *Analytical Biochemistry*, *370*(1), 116. doi:10.1016/j.ab.2007.07.006

Deb, K., & Agrawal, R. B. (1995). Simulated binary crossover for continuous search space. *Complex Systems*, *9*, 115148.

Deb, K., Pratap, A., Agarwal, S., & Meyarivan, T. (2002). A fast and elitist multi objective genetic algorithm: NSGA-II. *IEEE Transactions on Evolutionary Computation*, *6*(2), 181–197. doi:10.1109/4235.996017

Ding, Y. S., Zhang, T. L., & Chou, K. C. (2007). Prediction of protein structure classes with pseudo amino acid composition and fuzzy support vector machines network. *Protein and Peptide Letters*, *14*, 811815. PMID:17979824

Du, Q. S., Jiang, Z. Q., He, W. Z., Li, D. P., & Chou, K. C. (2006). Amino acid principal component analysis (AAPCA) and its applications in protein structural class prediction. *Journal of Biomolecular Structure & Dynamics*, *23*(6), 635640. doi:10.1080/07391102.2006.10507088 PMID:16615809

Haykin, S. (2009). *Neural Network*. Prentice Hall.

Horn, J., Nafploitis, N., & Goldberg, D. E. (1994). *A niched Pareto genetic algorithm for multi objective optimization* (p. 8287). IEEE Press.

Levitt. & Chothia. (1976). Structural patterns in globular proteins. *Nature,* 261(5561), 52558.

Liu, H., Meng, W., & Chou, K. C. (2005a). Low-frequency Fourier spectrum for predicting membrane protein types. *Biochemical and Biophysical Research Communications*, *336*(3), 737739. doi:10.1016/j.bbrc.2005.08.160 PMID:16140260

Liu, H., Yang, J., Wang, M., Xue, L., & Chou, K. C. (2005b). Using Fourier spectrum analysis and pseudo amino acid composition for prediction of membrane protein types. *The Protein Journal*, *24*(6), 385–389. doi:10.1007/s10930-005-7592-4 PMID:16323044

Majhi, R., Panda, G., & Sahoo, G. (2009). Development and performance evaluation of FLANN based model for forecasting of stock markets. *Expert Systems with Applications*, *36*(3), 6800–6808. doi:10.1016/j.eswa.2008.08.008

Panda, B., Mishra, A. P, Majhi, B. & Rout, M. (2013). Performance evaluation of FLANN based model for Protein Structural Class Prediction. *International journal of Artificial Intelligence and Neural Networks*, 3(4).

Pao, Y. H. (1989). *Adaptive pattern recognition and neural networks*. Reading, MA: Addison Wesley.

Patra, J. C., Pal, R. N., Chatterji, B. N., & Panda, G. (1999). Identification of Nonlinear Dynamic Systems Using Functional-Link Artificial Neural Networks. *IEEE Trans. on Systems, Man, and Cybernetics-part B. Cybernetics*, *29*(2), 254–262. PMID:18252296

Sahu, S. S., & Panda, G. (2010). A novel feature representation method based on Chou's pseudo amino acid composition for protein structural class prediction. *Computational Biology and Chemistry*, *34*(5-6), 320327. doi:10.1016/j.compbiolchem.2010.09.002 PMID:21106461

Srinivas, N., & Deb, K. (1995). Multi objective function optimization using non dominated sorting genetic algorithms. *Evolutionary Computation*, *2*(3), 221248.

Tanford, C. (1962). Contribution of hydrophobic interactions to the stability of the globular conformation of proteins. *Journal of the American Chemical Society*, *84*(22), 42404274. doi:10.1021/ja00881a009

Zhang, T. L., & Ding, Y. S. (2007). Using pseudo amino acid composition and binary tree support vector machines to predict protein structural classes. *Amino Acids*, *33*(4), 623629. doi:10.1007/s00726-007-0496-1 PMID:17308864

Zhang, T.L, Ding, Y.S & Chou, K.C (2008). Prediction protein structural classes with pseudo-amino acid composition: approximate entropy and hydrophobicity pattern. *J. Theoretical Biology*, *250*, 186-193.

Zhou, G. (1998). An intriguing controversy over protein structural class prediction. *Journal of Protein Chemistry*, *17*(8), 729738. doi:10.1023/A:1020713915365 PMID:9988519

KEY TERMS AND DEFINITIONS

Amino Acid: Basic building block of protein molecules.

Amphiphilicity: Molecules having both water loving and repelling property.

Crossover: Genetic procedure for generation of new population.

Elitism: Taking the best attributes of previous generation to next generation without applying any genetic operators.

Hydrophobicity: Water repelling property of molecules.

Hydrophilicity: Water loving property of molecules.

Selection: Genetic procedure to select chromosomes from gene pool.

Chapter 6
Rough Fuzzy Set Theory and Neighbourhood Approximation Based Modelling for Spatial Epidemiology

Balakrushna Tripathy
VIT University, India

Sharmila Banu K.
VIT University, India

ABSTRACT

Modern epidemiological studies involve understanding individual and social level inferences and their role in the transmission and distribution of disease instances. The geographic relevance in epidemiology has been analysed in concurrence with these inferences. The substantial amount of data involved in an epidemiological study is usually very large and intuitively involves missing values and uncertainty. Rough Set Theory (RST) has been used in medical informatics for 'outcome prediction' and 'feature selection'. It can be used to construct the decision system involving spatial, medical and demographic data effectively. This chapter proposes the use of rough sets in conjunction with parallel techniques like Fuzzy sets, Intuitionistic systems and Granular (Neighborhood Approximation) computing for the classic problem of data representation, dimensionality reduction, generation and harvest of minimal rules. RST handles missing values and uncertainty more specific to spatial and medical features of data.

BACKGROUND

Recent and past literatures have documented the relationship between locations, individuals and diseases. Geographic Information Systems (GIS) have been widely used to study problems involving public health. Spatial analysis with respect to epidemiology has been addressed in recent researches. Transmission and distribution of SARS - severe acute respiratory syndrome was studied and analysed by Meng et al. (2002), Wang (2006) documented risk exposure pattern, Ulegtekin et al. (2007) analysed

DOI: 10.4018/978-1-5225-0427-6.ch006

distribution of measles in Turkey, Slowinski et al. (1996) predicted *pancreatitis* using Rough Set Theory, Rowland et al. (1998) predicted ambulation after spinal cord injuries, Vinterbo and Øhrn (1999) built a rough set based predictor for myocardial infarction, Bai et al. (2010) used RST to uncover spatial decision rules in neural-tube birth defect. Spatial analysis employing statistical models and spatial regression methods to study population dynamics is reported in Chi and Zhu (2008) and the use of weighted centroid method to predict outbreak of *Escherichia Coli* in Buscema et al (2013). The results have depended on specific features of dataset like configuration, distribution, spatial heterogeneity and autocorrelation. Bai et al. (2010) substantiate that being discernibility based, ability to handle inconsistent data, applicability to any number of outcomes, dimensionality reduction, suitability for spatial data are some of the features that make Rough Sets very conducive to epidemiological study.

To better express the multifaceted nature of the real world and address the limitation of knowledge and uncertainty of factual data, *fuzziness* can be used to represent some attributes of data. It has been used to represent the classification of land-cover types in Shi (2005) and effect of environmental factors on birth defects in Bai et al. (2010). A geographic phenomenon may tend to be closely related and distant related entities based on the distance. This is spatial auto correlation and upheld by Tobler's *law of geography* as in Miller (2004). In RST, an object tends to have *roughness* where the object is a subset of universe with some property states Pawlak (1984). Lower and Upper approximations are used to define an object. The roughness of an object can be précised upon collecting more attributes about the object. Bai et al. (2014) affirm that *roughness* is not a *fuzzy* concept by nature and so fuzzy sets cannot be used to represent roughness *Rough Fuzzy Sets* which is an extension of rough sets can be used to construct the decision system for spatial analytics. Combining *Intuitionistic* approach along with rough fuzzy sets will tend to better accuracy of results leading to crisp conditions and probability based fuzzy decisions.

Dimensionality reduction which is also addressed by RST needs an extra step on dealing with spatial and non-spatial attributes of the decision system. Spatial attributes which are *continuous* in nature will have to be discretised for RST to construct equivalence classes. Jensen and Shen (2004) approve that the discretization may sometimes lead to loss of information. Liao (2012) substantiated the use of *Neighborhood Rough Set approximation* to work with continuous attributes without discretising them.

Neighbourhoods are defined using nearest neighbour methods or by distance from central point to boundary. Using the this method, for a given set of continuous attributes in space, a neighbourhood is defined for every object in U, as $\delta\left(x\right) = \{x \mid x \in U, d(x, x1 \leq \delta)$ where $\delta > 0$ and $\delta\left(x\right)$ is δ neighbourhood information granule of x. Neighborhood approximation is applied to identify the positive and boundary region. The set of objects in the positive region are identified into decision classes without ambiguity. Non-spatial attributes can be reduced using RST reducts. The minimal reduct induced can be combined with the attributes determined using Neighbourhood Rough Sets from which the rules can be inferred. Treating the spatial and non-spatial attributes separately and integrating them later will uphold the inherent spatial features critical to the semantics of rules.

This chapter will discuss Rough Fuzzy Intuitionistic Decision System for identifying the Spatial Distribution of Disease Instances involving demographic, medical, continuous and auto correlated spatial attributes for spatial data based on Neighborhood Rough Sets. However, the temporal nature of medical data is to be accounted for. Any errors due to missing or inconsistent data should be addressed with the construction of error matrix. The rules generated should be verified for being minimal, correctness and accuracy.

EPIDEMIOLOGY

Epidemiological studies have been instrumental in analysing public health. The forerunners of this field, Hippocrates, Caprasto, Sir Edwin, John Snow and others have laid out the principles on which modern epidemiology is built. They used statistics, demographics and maps to understand the relationship between diseases, people and environment. Understanding prevalent and incident diseases, their root causes, potential treatment and medical prescription for the same are the directions along which diseases are studied. Elaborate studies on transmission models and intervention methods have been carried out. With the advent of GIS (Geographical Information Systems) where data are referred geographically, studying environment has become more sophisticated.

As an important science of public health, ecological studies of epidemiology are persuaded by scientists and administrators. This is relevant as climatic conditions, exposure to natural and man-induced environmental factors and prevalence of social imbalance are posing serious challenges to public health. A strategic way of comprehending public health issues is the need of the hour in developing countries and exploiting geographic feature of data is just striking the right chord. Epidemics and endemics have wiped out millions of lives in the past centuries. And exhaustive studies on transmission models, distribution of disease clusters and impact of globalization have helped scientists to come up with effective interventions and authorities to make informed decisions.

Boulos (2004) emphasizes that including geographical information leads to evidence based spatio-temporal approach in analysing public health. This work recalls the need for exploring spatial patterns in disease outcomes. Song and Kulldorff (2003) discusses the indices used to identify spatial distribution of disease clusters. Moran's Index, Spatial scan statistic, k-nearest neighbour etc., are discussed. Spatial auto correlation is also measured using these statistics.

Dunn (1995) studied the effects of environmental pollutants and its association with asthma incidences in North East England. Briggs (2000) discusses environmental threats to human health and classifies them as risk, health and hazard indicators. The effect of pollutants from industries on public health can be a decisive study contributing to the welfare of people at large and social cause. Cities that have capitalized from Industries are marked by humongous outlet of effluents and air pollutants. Eventually people living in the affected area are prone to a spectrum of infections and diseases. Data Mining based on soft computing techniques like Rough Set Theory can be used to explore spatial conclusive rules on predominant diseases caused by pollution and look for spatial associations related to the diseases.

Conventionally, scientists have used maps to study relationships between places, surroundings and diseases. Later researchers focused on GIS based spatial analysis combined with visual capabilities. Epidemiologists are also working at the spatial analysis based spread of infectious diseases like the transmission of SARS in Beijing Meng et al. (2002). Studies to find the next most likely to be affected areas based on pollution characteristics are thus possible. Spatial data inherits the core and peripheral nature which can be potentially captured using Rough Set theory. The explicit location and extension of spatial instances define implicit relations of spatial neighborhood (such as topological, distance, and direction relations), which can be used by the rough set based clustering algorithm. New techniques are required for effective and efficient data mining with spatial patterns.

In most of the research efforts where the associations between location, environment and disease are analyzed in epidemiology, researchers have traditionally used maps. The Geographic Information system is well fit for studying these associations because of its spatial analysis and display capacity. Rough set theory has been used to identify the NTD birth defect spatial pattern with respect to geographic locations in China and to explore the spatial rules Bai et al. (2010). Determining the spatial characteristics of the disease distribution will help in identifying the worst affected population and respective demographics. It can further help to build and test theories, plan and evaluate epidemiological surveys, forecast trends and test control measures. The proposed approach is first of its kind and would serve as an important tool for public health researchers and practitioners.

Rough set theory is an extension of standard set theory. The central objective of Rough Set Analysis is to synthesize an approximation of concepts and has been successfully applied in pattern recognition, machine learning and automated knowledge acquisition. As such problems involve identifying spatial correlations, it would be augmentative to quote that Rough interpretations can be simplified and standardized.

Data mining models will generate conclusive information on how to identify the potential infected areas and associated statistics. Additionally, spatial relevance will enable the authorities to have an insight into the situation of proposal looks at how data mining can be applied for early detection and management of pandemics. Techniques combining data modeling and spatial data mining to find interesting characteristics of disease spread are used. This will help the authorities in taking informed decisions and thus make provision for healthier living of our citizens. This model can be used to carry out evaluations (impact estimate on the health of population in the specific space) in a given location before setting up any industry based on expected the pollutant output. The model can also be extended to predict the increase in the level of pollutants over a period of time and its impact on the population in that space. Such studies will empower the authorities with a broader understanding of geographic locations and its impeding relationship with the cause and spread of diseases caused by pollution. The results can be validated on test data based on training data like any other data mining validation. The studies will not only enlighten the authorities but also support them to make informed decisions at the time of crisis.

Carrying out ecological studies to analyse population demographics and health outcomes may incur *ecological fallacy* where a population level inference may be assumed to be individual level inference. Time variance may reflect myriad changes in studies conducted. Hence modeling for the study should consider this *demographic shift.*

The *health outcome* oriented data will include sensitive information of individuals. Ensuring privacy to sensitive data is becoming an important criterion in the data access policies of governments and corporations. Providing security to data using non-cryptographic based techniques has been in use for a long time. They are used to provide security to Health data, finance data and the like. Data are distorted using various approaches to hide sensitive information and provide privacy. A whole line of methods from statistical disclosure control to distortion based techniques are in use. The scale of geographic area studied for disease instances bears significance on the quality of results obtained. Pixel dimensions are carefully based on the type of problems studied like predicting bird nesting on coastal regions, colocation pattern mining, urban, resource planning etc.,

SPATIAL RELATIONSHIPS

According to Tobler's Law of Geography, spatial attributes tend to have spatial correlation and instinctively exhibit spatial neighbourhoods. Spatial relationships like distances, directions and topology are studied extensively only in novel applications. Addressing topological relationships like intersections, adjacency and overlaps are discussed in Randell and Cohn (1992) using Region connected Calculus. Spatial data is a real world representation model and therefore encompasses uncertainty. Murgante

(2007) used rough sets for identifying periurban fringes in a province. This work recalls Burrough and Frank (1996) where periurban fringes are said to be the spatial regions with uncertain boundaries. On comparison with Map Algebra, Rough Sets based approach was found to better classify the regions. Beaubouef and Petry (2002) profoundly discuss uncertain nature of spatial data with respect to topology. They have proposed a rough set based approach to the RCC-8 algorithm put forth by Randall & Cohn (1992). The work discusses eight possible relations that hold between vague regions – *partially overlapping, tangential proper par and its inverse, non-tangential proper part and its inverse, equal, externally connected and disconnected.* Further, they have discussed representation of these relations in rough sets by giving a mathematical model for uncertain regions.

DECISION SYSTEMS

The rough set method has been used to find out land control knowledge, with a case study indicating its feasibility in Wang et al. (2001). And, the rough set method has been applied for spatial classification and uncertainty analysis in Ahlqvist et al. (2003). Rough set theory was used in preprocessing and the classification of remotely sensed imagery and attributes analysis in GIS by Li D R et al. (2006). But it did not explicitly study the mining of rules for the classification of spatial data as said in Leung et al. (2007). So they proposed a novel rough set approach for discovering classification rules in spatial data was proposed. The Spatial patterns of risk exposure were identified and mapped using geographical techniques and mathematical modeling to represent the spatio-temporal spread of SARS by Wang J F et al. (2006).

The advantages of discernibility-based methods for data mining are highlighted in the health sciences, and demonstrated that these ideas are applicable by formulating pertinent and innovative medical applications. Rough set theory has been used to extract most relevant clinical attributes and generate rules for arriving at decisions using the concept of 'Core' and 'reduct'. Rough Set theory has been used to select relevant attributes from data set for predicting Diabetes in Su C.T et al. (2006). And several other work show that a number of medical reasoning models observe the core (reduct) ideas of Rough Set theory in diagnostic models. Bai et al (2010) used Rough set approaches are exclusively applied for identifying birth defects in China involving spatial reference and correlations.

A decision system with a set of objects, conditional and decision attributes is constructed. It is defined as (U, CA ∩ DA) where U is the universe of non-empty objects, CA are the conditional attributes and DA the decision attributes. Construction of the decision requires understanding of the nature of objects we deal which involve spatial, demographical and medical data. The attributes may involve fuzzy nature. When we construct decision system based on rough sets, equivalence classes based on equivalence relation are found and an associated indiscernibility is defined. The objects that belong in an indiscernibility relation are similar to each other with respect to the attributes based on which equivalence relation is defined. For any subset $X \subseteq U$ and any $F \subseteq CA$, is an associated equivalence relation $INDs = \{(x, x') \subseteq U^2 \mid \forall a \in Fa(x) = a(x')\}$ called F-indiscernibility relation. The equivalence class of this is specified as $[x]_F$. Lower and upper approximations of X with respect to F are defined as $\underline{F}X$ and $\overline{F}X$ where $\underline{F}X = \{x \mid [x]_F \subseteq X\}$ and $\overline{F}X = \{x \mid [x]_F \cap X \neq \varnothing\}$. The difference of these two sets is the boundary set. A set is rough if the boundary region is not empty.

The number of attributes to be considered for an ecological study may include temperature, rainfall, humidity, wind pattern, soil type, slope, rock types, rivers, road connectivity, proximity to basic services; demographic data – male-female population, educational background, work nature, per capita income, GDP to represent industrialization, density – distribution -type of industries; medical data-disease instances, anonymised patient details etc., The attributes that preserve indiscernibility relation are retained. This is achieved by identifying reduct and core in RST. Thangavel and Pethalakshmi (2006) proposed Reduct algorithm for feature selection, also other variants, genetic algorithm based reducts etc., are available to identify reducts. This ensures that classificatory performance of reduced set of attributes is same as the original set. After identifying the reducts, decision rules are extracted. Decision rules generated should be minimal and complete. Error analysis should be conducted by constructing error matrix and other methods to conclude the work. The rules generated should be verified with data and domain experts for validation.

Neighborhood Rough Sets and Spatial Data

Spatial data involves attributes like temperature, rainfall, slope, humidity and generally are continuous and involve real numbers. Discretising them may lead to loss of information. In the context of Spatial Decision System, the continuous values of attributes are to be preserved. Neighborhood systems use similarity metric to relate data and reduce the chances of information loss. Lin .T. Y (1989) used neighborhood system for approximation in numerical analysis for which a neighborhood of tolerance has to be identified even before the approximation commences. Neighborhood Rough Sets can be used for continuous attributes represented in the decision system. It involves distance measures can be used for handling continuous spatial data.

Neighborhood Granulation

Definition 1: Given a N dimension real number space U, two objects $x_i, x_j \in U$, the distance metric δ between the two data objects, then following properties are satisfied in the neighborhood model.

(1) $\delta\left(x_i, x_j\right) \geq 0, iff\, i = j, \delta\left(x_i, x_j\right) = 0$

(2) $\delta\left(x_i, x_j\right) = \delta\left(x_j, x_i\right)$

(3) $\delta\left(x_i, x_j\right) + \delta\left(x_j, x_k\right) \geq \delta\left(x_i, x_k\right)$

Then we called (U, δ) is a real number space. The above three properties are reflexivity, symmetry and non-transitive properties of neighborhood relation.

Definition 2: Given a finite set of objects $U\{x_1, x_2, x_3, .., x_n\}$ in real number space, for every object x_i in U, then the δ-neighborhood definition is as follows:

(4) $\delta\left(x_i\right) = \left\{x | x \in U, d\left(x, x_i\right) \leq \delta\right\}$

where $\delta > 0, \delta(x_i)$ is δ neighborhood information granulation from x_i and called as x_i neighborhood granulation.

Neighborhood relations are a kind of similarity relations, which satisfy reflexivity and symmetry properties. The data objects are drawn together for similarity in terms of distances and the samples in the same neighborhood granule are close to each other. Considering two x_i, x_j objects in a

M-dimensional space with attribute set $A = \left\{A_1, A_2, ..., A_M\right\}$, $f\left(x, A_i\right)$ represents the value of object x in attribute A_i, a Minkowsky distance defined by

$$(5) \quad \delta_p\left(x_i, x_j\right) = \left(\sum_{i=1}^{M}\left|f\left(x_i, A_i\right) - f\left(x_j, A_j\right)\right|^p\right)^{1/p}$$

$\delta_p\left(x_i, x_j\right)$ is Manhattan distance if $p=1$, Euclidean distance if $p=2$ and Chebychev distance if $p = \infty$. Distance functions are discussed by Wilson & Martinez (1997) in detail. $\delta_A\left(x_i\right)$ is the neighborhood of data object x_i and its size is based on the threshold δ.

Q. Hu et al. (2008) discuss neighbourhoods involving numerical and categorical attributes.

Definition 3: Let $N \subseteq A$ and $C \subseteq A$ be numerical and categorical attributes respectively. The neighborhood for a for a subset x, effected by N and C and N $\cup$ C are defined by Q. Hu et al. (2008) as

$$(6) \quad \delta_N\left(x\right) = \left\{x_i | \Delta_N\left(x, x_i\right) \leq \delta, x_i \epsilon U\right\};$$

$$(7) \quad \delta_C\left(x\right) = \left\{x_i | \Delta_C\left(x, x_i\right) = 0, x_i \epsilon U\right\};$$

$$(8) \quad \delta_{N \mid C}\left(x\right) = \left\{x_i | \Delta_N\left(x, x_i\right) \leq \delta \Delta_C\left(x, x_i\right) = 0, x_i \epsilon U\right\};$$

where $\wedge$ is the *AND* operator. Other distance measures for attributes involving numerical and categorical attributes are *heterogeneous overlap metric function, value difference metric, heterogeneous value difference metric and interpolated value difference metric* proposed by Randall and Tony (2007) and Wang (2006).

Neighborhood Approximation

Considering a set of objects $U = \left\{x_1, x_2, .., x_n\right\}$ a neighborhood relation R, then the neighborhood approximation space $S = \{U, R\}$ and for any $X \subseteq U$, lower and upper approximations are defined as follows and *opr* is the approximation operator:

$$\left\{\begin{array}{l} \underline{R}_{opr}(X) = \left\{x_i \in U | \delta\left(x_i\right) \ X, \ x_i \in U\right\} \\ \overline{R}_{opr}(X) = \left\{x_i \in U | \delta\left(x_i\right) \cap X, \ x_i \in U\right\} \end{array}\right.$$

The positive, negative and boundary region are as follows:

$$\left\{\begin{array}{l} POS\left(X\right) = \underline{R}_{opr}\left(X\right) \\ NEG\left(X\right) = \sim \overline{R}_{opr}\left(X\right) \\ BND\left(X\right) = \overline{R}_{n}\left(X\right) - \underline{R}_{opr}\left(X\right) \end{array}\right.$$

A data object will fall in positive or boundary region. Also, roughness of subset X in the approximation space is inferred from the size of boundary region. The set of objects in positive region can be classified with certainty while the objects in boundary region will have indeterminate classification. Yao (1998) has defined the properties of neighborhood operators and has established a framework for it.

Approximations are based on the neighborhood operator *opr*. It is based on the rough set algebra defined by $\left(2^{U}, \cap, \cup, \sim, \underline{R}_{opr}, \overline{R}_{opr}\right)$. Further Yao (1998) has defined the pair approximations for a random neighborhood operator.

1. $\underline{R}_{opr}\left(X\right) = \sim \overline{R}_{opr}\left(\sim X\right))$
2. $\overline{R}_{opr}\left(X\right) = \sim \left(\underline{R}_{opr}\left(\sim X\right)\right)$
3. $\underline{R}_{opr}\left(U\right) = U$
4. $\overline{R}_{opr}\left(\varnothing\right) = \varnothing$
5. $\underline{R}_{opr}\left(X \cap Y\right) = \underline{R}_{opr}\left(X\right) \cap \underline{R}_{opr}\left(Y\right)$
6. $\overline{R}_{opr}\left(X \cup Y\right) = \overline{R}_{opr}\left(X\right) \cup \overline{R}_{opr}\left(Y\right)$

Yao (1998) states more properties derived from the above set.

Q.Hu et al. (2008) has documented that the lower and upper approximations defined require further adequacy. His work has recalled Variable Precision Rough Sets by Ziarko (1993) which uses an inclusion degree. Considering two sets X and Y from a universal set of objects U, inclusion of X in Y is represented as,

$$Inc\left(X\right) = \frac{cardinality\left(X \cap Y\right)}{cardinality\left(X\right)}$$

assuming X is a not-null set.

Definition 4: The lower and upper approximation from approximation space (U, X, R) as in definition 3, only for a variable precision rough set which considers partial inclusion is defined by

$$\left[\begin{array}{l} \underline{R}^{k} X = \left\{x_{i} \in U | Inc\left(\delta\left(x_{i}\right), X\right) \geq k, \ x_{i} \in U\right\} \\ \overline{R^{k}} X = \left\{x_{i} \in U | Inc\left(\delta\left(x_{i}\right), X\right) \geq 1 - k, x_{i} \in U\right\} \end{array}\right.$$

and *k* falls between 0.5 and 1.

FUZZY FLAIR TO DECISION SYSTEMS

Decision systems may involve decision attributes of fuzzy nature. If $d_{1}, d_{2}, ..d_{n}$ the decision values are a fuzzy set of the Universe, they will result in fuzzy decision system. The membership of a decision value v, is $\mu_{v} = U \rightarrow \left[0,1\right]$. Dubois and Prade (1990) introduced rough fuzzy theory and defined lower and upper approximations as

$$\mu_{\bar{B}(S)}\left(x\right) = \max\left\{\mu_S\left(y\right), y \in \left[x\right]_B\right\}$$

$$\mu_{\underline{B}(S)}\left(x\right) = \min\left\{\mu_S\left(y\right), y \in \left[x\right]_B\right\}$$

respectively where U, $AT \cup D$ is an information system $B \subseteq AT$ (conditional attributes) and S $\in D$ (Decision attribute of fuzzy nature). This kind of decision system will be useful in representing spatial data and has to deal with its uncertainty, spatial correlation, roughness and fuzziness. Approximations of such systems were initiated by Xu et al. (2003), Li et al. (2008) and others. Bai et al. (2014) have used fuzzy decision information system to deal with decision attributes which are fuzzy and mined spatial rules. Dimensionality reduction and rule generation for fuzzy based decision systems were put forth by Xu et al. (2003). Spatial layers of data may be represented as attributes and hybrid soft computing techniques can be used to represent and model them.

CONCLUSION AND FUTURE DIRECTIONS

Epidemiology involves studies whose solutions have a greater societal impact. It involves number difficult parameters that require exclusive considerations and hence pose a challenging area. The interdisciplinary work among Medicine and Computer Science has created remarkable development in the last few decades and has affected the practice of Medicine and Health Care services, but it still needs major collaborative efforts, exploring of new dimensions and enhancements.

Spatio-temporal patterns in disease occurrence and spread in a population is deemed as evidence-based and calls for a lot of studies in this area. Exploiting soft computing techniques that call for hybrid approaches and working with domain experts, statisticians, computer science engineers and administrators is the need of the hour. For further work, construction of robust Decision Systems based on granulation and approximation strategies with different similarity measures and topological properties can be carried out.

REFERENCES

Ahlqvist, O., Keukelaar, J., & Oukbir, K. (2003). Rough and fuzzy geographical data integration. *International Journal of Geographical Information Science*, *17*(3), 223–234. doi:10.1080/13658810210157750

Bai, H., Ge, Y., Wang, J., & Liao, Y. L. (2010). Using Rough Set Theory to identify villages affected by birth defects: The example of Heshun, Shanxi, China. *International Journal of Geographical Information Science*, *24*(4), 559–576. doi:10.1080/13658810902960079

Bai, H., Ge, Y., Wangm, J., Li, D., Liao, Y., & Zheng, X. (2014). A method for extracting spatial rules from spatial data based on rough fuzzy sets. *Knowledge-Based Systems*, *57*, 28–50. doi:10.1016/j.knosys.2013.12.008

Beaubouef, T., & Petry, F. (2002), A Rough Set Foundation for Spatial Data Mining Involving Vague Regions. *Proc. of IEEE Intl. Conference on Fuzzy Systems* (pp. 761–772). doi:10.1109/FUZZ.2002.1005090

Boulos, M. N. K. (2004). Towards evidence-based, GIS driven national spatial health information infrastructure and surveillance services in the United Kingdom. *International Journal of Health Geographics*, *3*(1), 1. doi:10.1186/1476-072X-3-1 PMID:14748927

Briggs, D. (2000). *Environmental Health Hazard Mapping for Africa*. World Health Organization – Regional Office for Africa.

Burrough, P. A., & Frank, A. U. (1996). *Geographic objects with indeterminate boundaries*. Taylor & Francis.

Buscema, M., Grossi, E., Bronstein, A., Lodwick, W., Asadi-Zeydabadi, M., Benzi, R., & Newman, F. (2013). A new algorithm for possible epidemic sources with application to the German *E. coli* outbreak. *International Journal of Geographical Information Science*, *2*(1), 155–200.

Chi, G., & Zhu, J. (2008). Spatial regression models for demographic models. *Population Research and Policy Review*, *27*(1), 17–42. doi:10.1007/s11113-007-9051-8

Dunn, C. E., Woodhouse, J., Bhopal, R. S., & Acquilla, S. D. (1995). Asthma and factory emissions in northern England: Addressing public concern by combining geographical and epidemiological methods. *Journal of Epidemiology and Community Health*, *49*(4), 395–400. doi:10.1136/jech.49.4.395 PMID:7650463

Jensen, R., & Shen, Q. (2004). Semantics-preserving dimensionality reduction: Rough and fuzzy-rough based approaches. *IEEE Transactions on Knowledge and Data Engineering*, *16*(12), 1457–1471. doi:10.1109/TKDE.2004.96

Leung, Y., Fung, T., Mi, J., & Wu, W. (2007). A rough set approach to the discovery of classification rules in spatial data. *International Journal of Geographical Information Science*, *21*(9), 1033–1058. doi:10.1080/13658810601169915

Li, D.R., Wang, S.L., & Li, D.Y. (2006). *Spatial data mining theories and applications*. Beijing: Science Press.

Liao, W. (2012). The rough method for spatial data subzone similarity measurement. *Journal of Geographic Information System*, *4*(01), 37–45. doi:10.4236/jgis.2012.41006

Meng, B., Wang, J., Liu, L., Wu, J., & Zhong, E. (2002). Understanding spatial diffusion process of severe acute respiratory syndrome in Beijing. *Public Health*, *119*(12), 1080–1087. doi:10.1016/j.puhe.2005.02.003 PMID:16214187

Miller, H. J. (2004). Tobler's first law and spatial analysis. *Annual Association – America,* *94*(2), pp. 284-289.

Murgante, B., Las Casas, G., & Sansone, A. (2007). *A spatial rough set for locating the periurban fringe*. SAGEO.

Pawlak, Z. (1982). Rough Sets. *International Journal of Man-Machine Studies*, *21*(2), 127–134. doi:10.1016/S0020-7373(84)80062-0

Randell, D., Cui, Z., & Cohn, A. (1992), A spatial logic based on regions and connection. *Proc. of 3rd Intl. Conference on Knowledge Representation and Reasoning* (pp. 165-176).

Rowland, T., Ohrn, A., & Ohno-Machado, L. (1998). Building manageable rough set classifiers. *Proceedings AMIA 1998 Annual Symposium*, Orlando, FL.

Shi, W. (2005). *Principles of modeling uncertainties in spatial data and analysis, Science. CRC Press.* Taylor & Francis.

Slowinski, K., Slowinski, R., & Stefanowski, J. (1988). Rough sets approach to analysis of data from peritoneal lavage in acute pancreatic. *International Journal of Medical Informatics*. PMID:3054367

Song, C., & Kulldorff, M. (2003). Power evaluation of disease clustering tests. *International Journal of Health Geographics*, 2(1), 9. doi:10.1186/1476-072X-2-9 PMID:14687424

Su, C. T., Yang, C., Hsu, K., & Chiu, W. (2006). Data mining for the diagnosis of type II diabetes from three-dimensional body surface anthropometrical scanning data. *Computers & Mathematics with Applications (Oxford, England)*, 51(6–7), 1075–1092. doi:10.1016/j.camwa.2005.08.034

Thangavel, K., & Pethalakshmi, A. (2006). Feature selection for medical database using rough system. *International Journal of Artificial Intelligence and Machine Learning*, 6(1), 11–17.

Ulegtekin, N., Alkoy, S., Seker, D. Z., & Goksel, C. (2007). Use of GIS in Epidemiology: A case study in Istanbul. *International Journal of Environmental Science & Health*, 41(9), 2013–2026.

Vinterbo, S., & Øhrn, A. (2000). Minimal Approximate Hitting Sets and Rule Templates. *International Journal of Approximate Reasoning*, 25(2), 123–143. doi:10.1016/S0888-613X(00)00051-7

Wang, J. F. (2006). Spatial Dynamics of an epidemic of severe acute respiratory syndrome in an urban area. *Bulletin of the World Health Organization*, 84(12), 965–968. doi:10.2471/BLT.06.030247 PMID:17242832

Wang, S. L., Wang, X. Z., & Shi, W. Z. (2001). Developing and Testing Geo-Spatial. *Information Science*, 4(1), 68–76.

Yao, Y. Y. (1998). Relational Interpretations of Neighborhood Operators and Rough Set Approximation Operators. *Information Science*, 111(1-4), 239–259. doi:10.1016/S0020-0255(98)10006-3

KEY TERMS AND DEFINITIONS

Granulation: It is using groups or clusters of data objects formed on the basis of similarity in an incomplete information system.

Neighborhood Systems: They provide granulation structure for each element of a universe.

Spatial Correlation: The values of a spatial attribute tend to be close to each other and vary gradually from core to periphery of a geographic region.

Spatial Data Mining: Mining patterns or rules from spatial data with respect to a geographic reference.

Chapter 7
Applying CI in Biology through PSO

Rojalina Priyadarshini
C. V. Raman College of Engineering, India

Nilamadhab Dash
C. V. Raman College of Engineering, India

Brojo Kishore Mishra
C. V. Raman College of Engineering, India

Rachita Misra
C. V. Raman College of Engineering, India

ABSTRACT

Conventional computing methods face challenges dealing with real world problems, which are characterised by noisy or incomplete data. To find solutions for such problems, natural systems have evolved over the years and on analysis it has been found these contain many simple elements when working together to solve real life complex problems. Swarm Intelligence (SI) is one of the techniques which is inspired by nature and is a population based algorithm motivated by the collective behaviour of a group of social insects. Particle swarm optimization (PSO) is one of the techniques belonging to this group, used to solve some optimization problems. This chapter will discuss some of the problems existing in computational biology, their contemporary solution methods followed by the use of PSO to address those problems. Along with this several applications of PSO are discussed in few of the relevant fields are discussed having some future research directions on this field.

INTRODUCTION

A massive growth is seen in gathering biological information by scientific communities in these years. This information comes in the form of genomes, protein sequences and gene expression data and so on which causes a need for and efficient computational tools to store, analyze and construe these data. The term bioinformatics and CB always used interchangeably in the field of computer science, which liter-

DOI: 10.4018/978-1-5225-0427-6.ch007

ally means the science of informatics as applied to biological research. Informatics on the other hand is the management and analysis of data using various advanced computing techniques. Hence, in other words, bioinformatics can be described as the application of computational methods to make biological discoveries and explorations (Clote & Backofen, 2000). It can also be defined as the appliance of computer technology to the management of biological information, encircling a study of the inherent genetic information, underlying molecular structure, resulting biochemical functions, and the exhibited phenotypic properties (Sushmita Mitra, Yoichi Hayashi,(2006)). The final goal and attempt of this area is to create new insights into the science of life as well as developing a global perspective (Das, Abraham & Konar, 2008). Three major objectives of bioinformatics can be put forward as to develop:

- Algorithms and mathematical models for searching the relationships among the members of huge biological dataset.
- Analyze and interpret the variety of heterogeneous data including nucleotide and amino acid sequences, protein domains and protein structures.
- Tools that enable proficient and effective storage, retrieval and management of high-volume biological databases.

In recent times, large number of biologically motivated algorithms have been developed and are being used for handling many complex problems. For instance, neural computing (Haykin, 1999) attempts to imitate the biological nervous systems of the living creatures inspired by the amount of parallel and distributed processing done inside the brain of a human. Genetic algorithm (GA) is inspired by the Darwinian evolutionary process through cross-over and mutation of biological chromosomes. They have successfully been used in many bioinformatics tasks that need intelligent search, optimization and machine learning approaches. Sushmita Mitra and Yoichi Hayashi, (2006) provide a comprehensive survey of the research in this direction. For the past few years there has been a slow but steady increase of research papers reporting the success Computational Intelligence (CI) based searching, classification and clustering techniques applied to the field of **CB** (Das, Panigrahi & Pattnaik, 2009). CI is constituted with the study of a set of nature-inspired computational methodologies, techniques and approaches to address complex real-world problems to which traditional approaches are ineffective or infeasible. While traditional models often fail to handle uncertainty, noise and the presence of an ever-changing context, CI provides solutions for complicated real problems. It primarily includes artificial neural networks (ANN), evolutionary computation (EC) and fuzzy logic (FL). In addition, CI also embraces biologically inspired algorithms such as SI, artificial immune systems, which can be seen as a part of EC.

This chapter presents some fundamental problems present in CB, the existing and traditional solution methods to answer these problems, the issues and challenges associated with these. Some of the contemporary problems solving approaches based on CI are then discussed.

BACKGROUND

To understand bioinformatics in any meaningful way, it is necessary for a computer scientist to understand some basic biology. In this chapter a short and basic introduction to the fundamentals and relevant to computational thing is given which are illustrated below.

Genetic Material: An Overview

Biology at the microscopic level began in 1665 when, Robert Hooke discovered that organisms are composed of individual compartments called cells. A cell's traits were inherent in its genetic information, which was passed to its offspring, and the same was organized into genes that resided on chromosomes. Later on proteins and DNA (Dioxyribo Nucleic Acids) were discovered in 1869 by Johann Friedrich Miescher which consist of four types of bases: Adenine (A), Thymine (T), Guanine (G), and Cytosine (C). Later biologists discovered that not all Ribo Nucleic Acids (RNAs) are destined to serve as templates for building proteins. Some RNAs (like transfer RNA described below) play a different role.

DNA: TAC CGC GGC TAT TAC TGC CAG GAA GGA ACT

RNA: AUG GCG CCG AUA AUG ACG UC CUU CCU UGA

Protein: Met Ala Pro Ile Met Thr Val Leu Pro Stop

The process of turning an mRNA into a protein is called translation, since it translates information from the RNA (written in a four-letter alphabet) into the protein (written in 20-letter alphabet). All proteins, including the ones necessary for this process, are produced by this process. This flow of information is emphatically referred to as the central dogma in molecular biology.

DNA → transcription → RNA → translation → protein,

Figure 1 describes the analysis of DNA.

Figure 1. DNA analysis

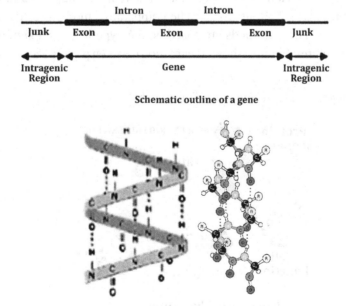

Schematic outline of a gene

MAIN FOCUS OF THE CHAPTER

In this section, we provide a basic understanding of the fundamentals problems of computational biology like protein structure, folding, DNA microarray data interpretation, inferring the gene regulatory networks that are relevant to this article.

Protein Structure Prediction

Proteins are built up by polypeptide chains of amino acids, which consist of DNA as the building block. An amino acid is an organic molecule made up of an amine (NH) and a carboxylic (CO) acid group (backbone), collectively bonded with a side-chain (hydrogen atom and residue R) that creates separation between them. Proteins are polypeptides, created in cells as a linear chain of amino acids. Chemical properties that differentiate the 20 individually different amino acids cause the protein chains to fold up into specific3-D structures that define their particular functions in the cell. Given the primary structure of a protein, in terms of a linear sequence of amino acids, folding tries to predict its stable 3-D structure. All these interactions governed by the laws of physics and chemistry to predict 3-D positions of different atoms in the protein molecule. Protein folding is a reaction involving other interacting amino acids and water molecules. The two-dimensional (2-D) secondary structure can involve an α-helix (with the CO group of the ith residue hydrogen (H) bonded to the NH group of the (i +4) th one) or a β-sheet (corrugated or hairpin structure) formed by the H-bonds between the amino acids. The parts of the protein that are not characterized by any regular H-bonding patterns are called random coils or turns. The tertiary structure refers to the 3-D conformation of the protein.

The total number of experimentally determined structure is less compare to actually known protein sequences (Schulze-Kremer, 2000). The difficult determination of these structures, using experimental methods such as X-ray or nuclear magnetic resonance (NMR), contributes to increase this gap between sequence and protein structures. Therefore, it is necessary the use of computational methods which predict 3D protein structures in a cheaper and faster way. According to biological approximation the methods for PSP falls into three groups: (1). Homology based Comparative modeling, (2) *ab* initio methods and (3). Threading (Priyadarshini, Dash, & Rout, 2012). The comparative model uses the predicted structures from the Protein data bank. These methods are based on the hypothesis that similar protein sequences determine similar 3D structures. Figure 2 shows the relation between protein sequence and their structure.

Figure 2. Protein Sequence-Structure-Function Relationship

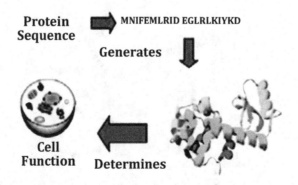

Structure of the protein

The problem of protein structure prediction has two dimensions:

1. **Secondary Structure:** A step on the way to a prediction of the full 3-D structure of protein is predicting the local conformation of the polypeptide chain, called the secondary structure. The whole framework was pioneered by Chou and Fasmann. They used a statistical method, with the likelihood of each amino acid being one of the three (alpha, beta, coil) secondary structures estimated from known proteins. The data consist of proteins obtained from the PDB. A fixed size window constitutes the input to the machine learning model. The machine classifier predicts the secondary structure corresponding to the centrally located amino-acid of the sequence within the window. The contextual information about the rest of the sequence in the window is also considered according to the model of the machine.

2. **Tertiary Structure and Folding:** Protein structure comparison is often used to identify set of residue equivalencies between proteins based on their 3-D coordinates, and has a wide impact on the understanding of protein sequence, structure, function, and evolution. The determination of an optimal 3-D conformation of a protein corresponds to folding, and has manifold implications to drug design. An active site structure determines the functionality of a protein. A ligand (enzyme or drug) docks into an active site of a protein. Many automated docking approaches have been developed, and can be categorized as: 1) rigid docking: both ligand and protein are rigid; 2) flexible-ligand docking: ligand flexible and protein rigid; and 3) flexible-protein docking: both ligand and protein are flexible (only a limited model of protein variation allowed, such as side-chain flexibility or small motions of loops in the binding site).

Primary Genome Sequence Analysis

The nucleus of a cell carries chromosomes that are built upon the double helical DNA molecules. In the human case the DNA genome is arranged into 24 dissimilar chromosomes. Each chromosome contains a number of genes, which are the fundamental physical and functional units of heredity. But, genes encompass only about 2% of the human genome; the remainder consists of non-coding regions, whose functions may embrace providing chromosomal structural integrity and regulating where, when, and in what amount and quantity proteins are built. DNA is transcribed to generate messenger (m)-RNA, which is then translated to make protein. The m-RNA is single stranded and has a ribose sugar molecule. A gene contains "Promoter" and "Termination" sites, which are responsible for the initiation and termination of transcription. Translation consists of mapping from triplets (codons) of four bases to the 20 amino acids building block of proteins. Genes are typically organized as exons (coding regions) and introns (noncoding regions). Hence, the main task of gene identification, from the primary genomic sequence, involves coding region recognition and splice junction4 detection. Sequence data are typically dynamic and order-dependent. A protein sequence motif is a signature or consensus pattern that is embedded within sequences of the same protein family. Identification of the motif leads to classification of an unknown sequence into a protein family for further biological analysis. Available protein motif databases include PROSITE5 and PFAM.

Microarrays Data Analysis

A microarray is a glass slide on to which DNA molecules are statically set in an orderly manner at precise and definite positions called spots (or features). A microarray may contain thousands of spots and each spot may contain a few million copies of identical DNA molecules that uniquely correspond to a gene. This measures the relative m-RNA profusion between two samples, which are labelled with different flourescent dyes, viz., red and green. The m-RNA binds (hybridizes) with the Codon DNA(cDNA) probes on the array. The relative abundance of a spot or gene is measured as the logarithmic ratio between the intensities of the dyes, and constitutes the gene expression data. Gene expression levels can be determined for samples taken:

1. At multiple time instants of a biological process (different phases of cell division) or
2. Under various conditions (e.g., tumor samples with different histopathological diagnosis).

Each gene corresponds to a high-dimensional vector of its expression profile. The data contain a high level of noise due to experimental procedures. Moreover, the expression values of single genes demonstrate large biological variance within tissue samples from the same class. A major cause of co-expression of genes is their sharing of the regulation mechanism (coregulation) at the sequence level. Clustering of coexpressed genes, into biologically meaningful groups, helps in inferring the biological role of an unknown gene that is coexpressed with a known gene(s). Cluster validation is essential, from both the biological and statistical perspectives, in order to biologically validate and objectively compare the results generated by different clustering algorithms.

In Figure 3, a microarray may contain thousands of spots. Each spot contains many copies of the same DNA sequence that uniquely represents a gene from an organism. Spots are arranged in an orderly fashion into Pen groups. Figure 4 represents schematic of the experimental protocol to study differential expression of genes. The organism is grown in two different conditions (a reference condition and a test condition). RNA is extracted from the two cells, and is labelled with different dyes (red and green) during the synthesis of cDNA by reverse transcriptase. Following this step, cDNA is hybridized onto the microarray slide, where each cDNA molecule representing a gene will bind to the spot containing its complementary DNA sequence. The microarray slide is then excited with a laser at suitable wavelengths to detect the red and green dyes (Das et al. 2006).

Understanding Gene Regulatory Network

A gene regulatory network or genetic regulatory network (GRN) is a group of related regulators intermingle with each other and with other external substances in the cell which are responsible to manage the gene expression levels of mRNA and proteins. The regulator can be RNA, protein and their complex. The interaction can be direct or indirect (through their transcribed RNA or translated protein). In this processes they may generate mass, energy, information transfer, and cell-fate specification. The whole process of a cell during this is integrated through a complex network of cellular constituents and reactions. Such a metabolic network consists of nodes, i.e., substrates (genes or proteins), that are interconnected through links. The degree of interconnectivity of the network may be characterized by its diameter, which is the shortest biochemical pathway averaged over all pairs of substrates. The topology of a network reflects a long evolutionary process molded for a robust response toward internal defects

Figure 3. Microarray expressions

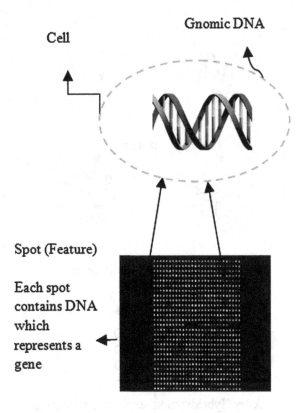

Cell

Gnomic DNA

Spot (Feature)

Each spot contains DNA which represents a gene

and environmental fluctuations. Despite significant variation of individual constituents and pathways, metabolic networks have the same topological scaling properties and exhibit striking similarities to the inherent organization of complex, robust non-biological systems. It is a knowledge base for systematic analysis of gene functions in terms of the networks of genes and molecules. The data objects are represented as graphs, and various computational methods are developed to detect graph features that can be related to biological functions. For example, it can: 1) reconstruct biochemical pathways from the complete genome sequence; 2) predict gene regulatory networks from gene expression profiles, obtained by microarray experiments; and 3) Single-stranded DNA that is complementary to mRNA or DNA that has been synthesized from messenger RNA by the enzyme reverse transcriptase. Predicting the gene expression levels is a main task associated with these networks. Along with the conventional approaches like directed graph, Boolean network, Bayesian network etc. some machine learning approaches is used to model these networks (Chan, Havukkala, Jain, Hu, & Kasabov, 2008). So that they can be interpreted well, this in turn predicts the expression level more accurately. If the level of accuracy percentage is more, then it provides a better way to explore how drugs affect a system of genes as well as for finding which genes are interrelated in a particular process.

Sequence Alignment

It is the way of arranging biological sequences such as DNA, RNA, or protein sequence to identify regions of similarity that may be a consequence of functional, structural, or evolutionary relationships between

Figure 4. Experimental gene expression data

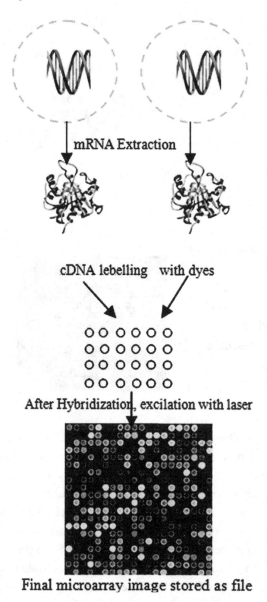

mRNA Extraction

cDNA lebelling   with dyes

After Hybridization, excilation with laser

Final microarray image stored as file

the sequences. Aligned sequences of nucleotide or amino acid residues are typically represented as rows within a matrix. Gaps are inserted between the residues so that identical or similar characters are aligned in successive columns. These techniques are grouped into two categories a) pair-wise sequence alignment b) Multiple sequence alignment. If alignment is done on two sequences, it is said to be pair wise else it is said to be multiple alignment. Either the whole input sequence is aligned from the beginning to the end of the sequence; otherwise some of the conserved regions are only aligned with the given sequence. In the first case it is said to be the global alignment and the latter case is said to be local alignment.

CI METHODS FOR SOLVING COMPUTATIONAL BIOLOGY PROBLEMS

Several CI methods like ANN, fuzzy logic, GA, SVM are being used for solving different kinds of bioinformatics problems, which are discussed in this section.

Methods for Solving Protein Structure Prediction

The main SC paradigms for the application of PSP are ANN, EC and SVMs (Márquez-Chamorroa, Asencio-Cortes, Santiesteban-Toca & Aguilar-Ruiz, 2015).

Neural Network Methods

The authors in Casadio, Compiani, Fariselli, and Vivarelli (1995) present a feed-forward neural network which is trained with matching sets of amino acid sequences and two different types of structural information. The corresponding secondary structure and the contact map of known proteins. The input of the network consists of a window of 61 residues. The hidden layer has 300 neurons and the output layer 30 neurons used to predict contacts between the amino acid that occupies the central positions in the window and the rest of the residues of the window. Three additional neurons are used to predict the tertiary motifs. The method proposed in Cho and Ryu (2002) is based on two input neurons which use input vectors with information about the residue–residue contact and its environment, the number of amino acids and the separation between amino acids. In addition, several variables are added, such as the hydrophobicity of the environment, as well as evolutionary information.

A supervised feed-forward network which is Radial basis function (RBF) network, is being used (Casadio, Compiani, Fariselli & Vivarelli, 1995) to optimally predict the free energy contributions of proteins due to hydrogen bonds, hydrophobic interactions, and the unfolded state, with simple input measures.

Support Vector Machines

SVM techniques performs classification tasks building a hyper-plane in a multidimensional space, trying to maximize the margin between each different classes. The function that performs the transformation of the space is called kernel function. SVMs are used as a machine learning tool to predict tertiary structure from the primary sequence. The input to the classifier are the result of multiple sequence alignment (MSA) (Cheng & Baldi, 2007) data of similar proteins after transformation to a specific input domain, amino acid physic chemical properties or contact potentials, local window features of the sequences.

As limitations of these types of methods, it can be cited that the kernel models over fits the model selection criterion, the difficulty in the selection of the optimal kernel function parameters and the algorithmic complexity and extensive memory requirements in large-scale tasks.

Evolutionary Computation (EC)

Methods based on EC may use various possible representations of a protein structure: dihedral or torsion angles and lattice models. According to the representation models the evolutionary models may differ. Some methods use dihedral or torsion angles some use 3- torsion angles without using the mutation operator (Cui, Chen & Hung, 1998; Schulze-Kremer, 2000). The fitness function consists of hydrophobic interactions and Vander Waals contact measures. A force field model, that represents chemical reactions and physical forces that occur in a protein is developed for GA. Mainly the fitness function used here are for minimizing the potential energy of the hydrogen bonds of the amino acids which makes a 3D structure of a protein as stable.

Methods for Genome Sequence Analysis

Neural Networks

ANN is used for predicting both types of genes, that is, protein coding and RNA coding (Goel, Singh & Aseri, 2013). One of the earliest attempts to ANN network for gene prediction is made in 1991, GRAIL (gene recognition and analysis internet link). A multilayer feed-forward neural network is applied in GRAIL-I, that accepts input from seven statistical measures taken on a 99-base window. A similar system to GRAIL came in 1993. A program named Gene Parser, which is employed to predict protein genes in genomic DNA sequences. This program uses the content statistics as well as site statistics to predict exons, introns, and their boundaries. Both single and multilayer neural networks are used here to unite information from these statistics and database search information. Here a recursive optimization procedure based on dynamic programming is used to find the most probable combinations of exon and introns. Many gene prediction techniques utilize homology information, which helps in improving the prediction results. In the latest version of Grail, homology information has been incorporated. The new system resulted in improved performance and named as GrailExp (Vimaladevi & Kalaavathi, 2014). A computational gene prediction system GIN (gene identification using neural nets and homology information) was developed in 1998 to avoid false positive predictions. The technique combines homology information from protein and expressed sequence tag databases into back-propagation neural network (Márquez-Chamorroa et al. 2015). The program can recognize multiple genes within genomic DNA. GIN performs better than other methods (e.g., GeneID or GeneParser3) that make use of homology information to predict genes. The performance of the system is better than GENSCAN in gene level accuracy. This technique does not work well in the absence of homology information.

Methods for Microarray Data Analysis

Microarray data analysis domain is the management of complicated experimental data for application of computational methods in biology. Complicated experimental data causes two types of problems. The first one is data need to be pre-processed. Pre-processing is the process by which the data needs to be modified which would be suitably used by computational intelligence methods. The second is the analysis of the specific data which depends on what we intend to search for. Most microarray data analysis packages implement five distinct steps in microarray data analysis (Dembele & Kastner, 2003; Babu, 2004):

1. Data pre-processing (intra-chip and inter-chip normalisation).
2. Gene Selection (identifying differentially expressed genes).
3. Clustering (identifying common expression patterns – co-expression analysis).
4. Functional Enrichment/Biological Pathway analysis (identifying the biological significance of the selected genes).
5. Classification (developing a classification system for unclassified samples).

Fuzzy Systems

Fuzzy c-means is a popular fuzzy based algorithm used for clustering microarray overlapping data. Different features of the functions regulations can be explored by fuzzy clustering which enables genes to belong to multiple groups at the same time. Fuzzy c-means algorithm has been applied to cluster microarray data (Sarhan, 2009). The value of the fuzzifier is appropriately chosen and fine-tuned for selection of genes, based on resultant distribution of distances between them. The clusters are formed by tight association and coupling among the genes.

ANNs

The two major mining tasks, modelled here, are clustering and classification. While unsupervised learning is self-organized, supervised learning helps incorporate known biological functions of genes into the knowledge discovery process of gene expression pattern analysis for gene discovery and prediction:

1. **Clustering:** Kohonen's Self Organising Maps (SOM) are used to make clusters of gene expression data (Dembele &. Kastner, 2003). It provides a good visualization as well as generates a robust and accurate clustering of large and noisy data. SOMs require a selected node in the gene expression space (along with its neighbours) to be rotated in the direction of a selected gene expression profile (pattern). However, the pre definition of a 2-D topology of nodes can often be a problem considering its biological relevance.
2. **Classification:** A wide range of supervised learning algorithms have been applied to microarray data for sample classification. Techniques ranging from ANN to SVM, from K Nearest Neighbour (KNN) to Naïve Bayesian Classifiers (NBC) have been applied to microarray data classification and their adequacy assessed.

Classification of acute leukemia has been made by combining a pair of classifiers trained with mutually exclusive features (Cho & Ryu, 2002). A neural network combines the outputs of the multiple classifiers. Feature selection with non-overlapping correlation encourages the classifier ensemble to learn different aspects of the training data in a wide solution space. Ahmad M. Sarhan (2009) has presented a stomach cancer detection system based on ANN, and the Discrete Cosine Transform (DCT). DCT has been used to extract classification features from stomach micro arrays in this system. The extracted features from the DCT coefficients are being applied to an ANN for classification (tumor or non-tumor). The micro array images used in this study have been obtained from the Stanford Medical Database (SMD). Bharathi and Natarajan (2010) have tried to fetch the minimum set of genes that can ensure accurate classification of cancer to a higher rate from micro array data. They used supervised machine learning algorithms. Bo Li, Chun-Hou Zheng, De-Shuang Huang, Lei Zhang and Kyungsook Han (2010) have discussed that the gene expression data collected from DNA micro array are characterized by a large amount of genes but with only a small amount of observations (experiments). They have proposed a manifold learning method which can map the gene expression data to a low dimensional space, and then tried to discover the internal structure of the features which could classify the micro array data with more accuracy. The proposed algorithm could able to bring the gene expression data into a subspace with high intra-class compactness and inter-class separability. Their experimental results on six DNA micro array datasets have shown that the used method is effective for discriminant feature extraction and gene expression data classification (Vaishali & vinayababu, 2011).

SOLUTIONS AND RECOMMENDATIONS

SI is a discipline which deals with natural and artificial systems composed of many individual components which coordinate among themselves using decentralized control and self-organization (Blum & Merkle, 2008). This discipline focuses on the collective behaviour of individual objects with local interactions of the individuals with each other and with their environment which comprises of Particle Swarm Optimization (PSO), Artificial Bee Colony (ABC), and Ant Colony Optimization (ACO).

A swarm is a cluster of same type of, simple agents which interacts among themselves locally, and their environment. They do not have central control over themselves. Swarm-based algorithms have recently emerged as a new class of nature-inspired, population-based algorithms that are capable of providing low cost, fast, and robust solutions to several complex real life problems. SI can be defined as a relatively new branch of Artificial Intelligence that is used to model the collective behaviour of social swarms in nature, such as ant colonies, honey bees, and bird flocks. Although these agents (insects or swarm individuals) are having limited capabilities on their own, they are interacting together with certain behavioural patterns to cooperatively achieve the goal towards the tasks necessary for their survival (Belal, Gaber, El-Sayed & Almojel, 2006; Dorigo, Bonabeau & Theraulaz, 2000). There can be direct or indirect social interactions among swarm objects. The pheromone trail secretion can be taken as the example of indirect contact where on a change by the individual in the present environment, other objects respond to this. The indirect interaction which involves the environment is referred to as stigmergy, means communication with the help of the environment.

Characteristic of a Swarm Intelligence System

The typical swarm intelligence system has the following characteristics:

- It is composed of more than one individual objects, each called as an agent or a particle;
- The particles or agents are relatively homogeneous (i.e., they are either all identical or they belong to a particular and specific category);
- The rules through which the interactions among the individuals happens are based on local information that the individuals exchange either directly or indirectly through the surroundings (stigmergy);
- The interactions of individuals with each other and with their environment is represented as the overall collective behaviour or group behaviour of the system results from their interaction, which is termed as, the group behaviour self-organizes. (Dorigo, 1992; Karaboga, 2005; Karaboga & Basturk, 2007).

The collective and social behaviour of living creatures inspired researchers to commence the study of SI (Lim, Jain, & Dehuri, 2009). The phrase Swarm Intelligence was coined by Beny and Wang in late 1980s (Couzin ID, Krause, James, Ruxton & Franks, 2002) in the context of cellular robotics. In spite of having no centralized control to guard how individual agents should behave, they are controlled globally by local interactions between themselves which lead to the emergence of global behavior (Das, Panigrahi & Pattnaik; Panigrahi, Shi & Lim, 2011). These examples are found in our surrounding such as fish-schools and bird flocks. may change shape and direction, they come into sight to move as a single coherent entity. The main properties of collective behavior are shown in Figure 5:

Figure 5. Different models of collective behavior (adapted from 8)

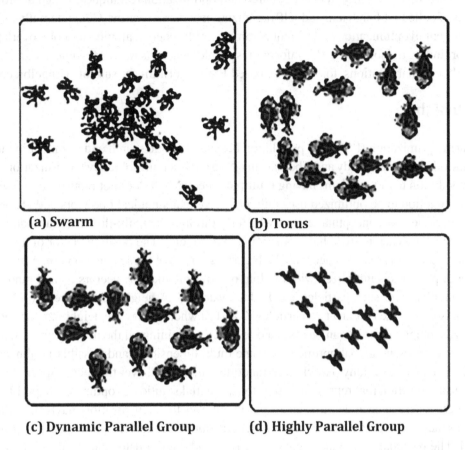

(a) Swarm   **(b) Torus**

(c) Dynamic Parallel Group   **(d) Highly Parallel Group**

- **Homogeneity**: Every bird in flock has the same behavioural model. Without any specific leader flock moves, even though momentary leaders seem to emerge.
- **Locality**: Its nearest flock-mates are only influenced by the motion of each bird. Vision is considered to be the most important senses for flock organization.
- **Collision Avoidance**: They avoid colliding with nearby flock mates.
- **Velocity Matching**: They try to match with the velocity of nearby flock mates.
- **Flock Centering**: All of them in the cluster attempt to reside in close proximity with the nearby flock mates. Each of them attempts to maintain a minimum distance between them sat all times. (Couzin ID et.al, 2002) identified four collective dynamical behaviors as illustrated in Figure 4.
- **Swarm**: An aggregate with cohesion, but a low level of polarization (parallel alignment) among members.
- **Torus**: Individuals perpetually rotate around an empty core (milling). The direction of rotation is random.
- **Dynamic Parallel Group**: The individuals are polarized and move as a coherent group, but individuals can move throughout the group and density and group form can fluctuate.
- **Highly Parallel Group**: Much more static in terms of exchange of spatial positions within the group than the dynamic parallel group and the variation in density and form is minimal (Panigrahi & Pattnaik, 2009).

The SI algorithms are mainly stochastic search and optimization techniques, which are followed by the principles of collective behaviour and self-organization of insect swarms. Coincidentally many jobs in bioinformatics entail optimization of different parameters (like energy, alignment score, overlap strength and so on. For finding the solutions of bioinformatics problems always we go for some in-exact but robust, fast and nearly optimal solutions, for which SI based PSO algorithm are suitable (Engelbrecht, 2002).

PSO: An Insight

Particle swarm optimization (PSO) is a population based stochastic search and optimization technique, which was introduced by Kennedy and Eberhart in (1995). It is a multi-objective optimization method to find optimal solution to the problems having multiple objectives. It does not require any gradient information of the function to be optimized uses only primitive mathematical operators and is conceptually very simple. Particles are conceptual entities which fly through the multi-dimensional search space. At any particular instant, each particle has a position and a velocity. The position vector of a particle with respect to the origin of the search space represents a trial solution of the search problem. At the beginning a population of particles is initialized with random positions marked by vectors Xi and random velocities V_i. The population of such particles is called a 'swarm' S. A neighbourhood relation N is defined in the swarm. N determines for any two particles Zi and Zj whether they are neighbours or not. Thus for any particle Z, a neighbourhood can be assigned as N(Z), containing all the neighbours of that particle. The goal is to reach to the global optimum of some multidimensional and possibly nonlinear function or system (Hsieh, 2014). Initially particles are randomly distributed over the search space. So each particle gets a virtual position that represents a possible potential solution to optimization problem. It is an iterative process where in each iteration every particle moves to a new position, navigating through the entire search space. Each particle keeps track of its position in the search space and its best solution so far achieved. The personal best value is called as pBest and the ultimate goal is to find the global best called as gBest. The standard PSO algorithm broadly consists of the following computational steps

Initialize particles with random positions and velocities;
For each value of k [where 'k' represents the number of particles]
do
Evaluate fitness of each particle's position (p)
If fitness(p) better than fitness(pbest) then pbest= p
Set best of pBests as gBest
Update particles velocity and position
End of for
Stop: giving gBest, optimal solution. (www.swarmintelligence.org(retrived on 20-07-02015))
Here, a particle refers to a potential solution to a problem in d- dimensional design space with k particles.
    Each particle is characterized by
Position vector….. xi(t) and Velocity vector…...vi(t)

Each particle has individual knowledge pbest, its own best-so-far position, Social knowledge gbest, pbest of its best neighbour
    The equations for velocity and position updates are given below

$$v(t+1)=(w * v(t))+(c1 * r1 *(p(t) - x(t))+(c2*r2*(g(t) - x(t)) \tag{1}$$

$$x(t+1) = x(t) + v(t+1) \tag{2}$$

The first equation updates a particle's velocity. The term v (t+1) is the velocity at time t+1. The new velocity depends on three terms. The first term is w * v (t). The w factor is called the inertia weight and is just a constant between 0 to 1. Here the value of w is taken as 0.73, and v (t) is the current velocity at time t.

The second term is c1 * r1 * (p (t) – x (t)). The c1 factor is a constant called the cognitive (or personal or local) weight. The r1 factor is a random variable in the range [0, 1) which is greater than or equal to 0 and strictly less than 1. The p (t) vector value is the particle's best position found so far. The x(t) vector value is the particle's current position.

The third term in the velocity update equation is (c2 * r2 * (g (t) – x (t)). The c2 factor is a constant called the social, or global, weight. The r2 factor is a random variable in the range [0, 1). The g (t) vector value is the best known position found by any particle in the swarm so far. Once the new velocity, v (t+1) has been determined, it is used to compute the new particle position x (t+1).

The updates in PSO can be either synchronous or asynchronous (Aziz, Mubin, Saberi Mohamad & Aziz2, 2014).

Types of PSO

Binary PSO

PSO was originally developed to optimize continuous valued parameters. Kennedy and Eberhart proposed a binary PSO to optimize binary-valued parameters. Here position vectors are binary vectors, and the velocity vectors are still floating-point vectors.

However, velocities are used to determine the probability that an element of the position vector is bit 0 or bit 1.

Angle Modulated PSO

It is developed by Pampara, Engelbrecht and Franken to optimize binary valued parameters by evolving a bit string generating function,

g(x)=sin (2 π (x-a)×b×cos(2 π (x-a)×c))+d

The task is then to find values for a,b,c and d, where these values are floating-points.
Some Advantages of the basic PSO are:

- It can be applied into both scientific research and engineering use.
- PSO have no overlapping and mutation calculation. The search can be carried out by the speed of the particle.

- PSO adopts the real number code, and it is decided directly by the solution. The number of the dimension is equal to the constant of the solution (Qinghai Bai (2010.)

Disadvantages of the basic particle swarm optimization algorithm:

- The method easily suffers from the partial optimism, which causes the less exact at the regulation of its speed and the direction.
- The method cannot work out the problems of scattering and optimization (Yonggang, Fengjie & Jigui, 2006 (In Chinese).
- The method cannot work out the problems of non-coordinate system, such as the solution to the energy field and the moving rules of the particles in the energy field (Bai, 2010).

Use of PSO in Computational Biology Problems

In this section the solutions of the some of the problems in computational biology are discussed using PSO for some of the reason.

PSO for Clustering Gene Expression Data

The standard clustering algorithms such as hierarchical clustering, principle component analysis (PCA), GA and ANNs have been used to cluster gene expression data. But in 2003, Xiao et al. used a new approach based on the hybridization of PSO and the Self Organizing Maps (SOM) for making clusters on them. Authors achieved good and encouraging results by using hybrid SOM-PSO algorithm over the gene expression data of Yeast and Rat Hepatocytes (Xiao, Dow, Eberhart, Miled & Oppelt, 2003).

Jun Sun et al. in 2012 has used the quantum behaved-PSO for gene expression data analysis with clustering methods. The problem of clustering gene expression data consists of N genes and their corresponding N patterns. Each pattern is a D-dimensional vector storing the expression levels of the genes at each of the D time points. The objective of applying MEQPSO clustering algorithm is to divide a gene expression data set into user-defined K groups by taking Euclidean distance as similarity measure, such that this partition minimizes the Total Within-Cluster Variation.

PSO for Protein Structure Prediction

Nashat Mansur et al. in 2012 present a particle swarm optimization (PSO) based algorithm for predicting protein structures in the 3D hydrophobic polar model. Starting from a small set of candidate solutions, their algorithm claimed to efficiently explore the search space and returns 3D protein structures with minimal energy. A particle is a candidate solution given by an array of length n (with index 0, 1, . . ., n-1), where n is the number of amino acids in the respective protein. Each element in the array represents the position X_d of the corresponding amino acid 'd' with respect to the preceding one and its value can be one of six characters {b, f, u, d, l, r} indicating six directions {backward, forward, up, down, left, right}. Initially, the swarm is populated with a set of N candidate solutions which are randomly generated. All the velocities are initially set to 0. A particle is invalid if it experiences collision. Collision occurs if two or more amino acids lie at the same point on the cubic 3D lattice. Invalid particles are not accepted in their algorithm and are repaired using a backtracking repair function, which takes as input the invalid particle and returns as output the repaired one. At last the repaired output is returned. It explores the search space of possible solutions and returns the 3D structure with low energy. It starts with a set of randomly created potential solutions or particles gathered in a swarm. These particles are evaluated against their energy function values. At each iteration this swarm is updated using a function which updates the velocity of the particle. This operator's work is to discover new places of the search space to get the optimal solutions.

PSO for Identifying Gene Regulatory Networks

PSO can be utilized very effectively to solve the GRN identification problem. Each particle may represent the real valued expression levels of all the genes. Each gene has a specific expression level for another gene; thus a total of N genes correspond to N2 expression levels. Fitness of the particles may be computed from the absolute error with generated expression pattern (sum of all expressions) from the target expression pattern.

Role of PSO in Some Other Problems Relevant to Computational Biology

PSO for Feature Selection Using Gene Expression Data

Gene expression data represents the state of a cell at a molecular level, play an important role in medical diagnosis. One of the characteristics of gene expression data there are higher number of genes but comparatively smaller sample size. For which many researchers are presently learning how to select genes effectively before using a classification method to decrease the predictive error rate. In general, gene selection is based on two aspects: one is to find a group of genes having same functions and a close relationship, the other finds the smallest set of genes that can provide meaningful diagnostic information for disease prediction without compromising accuracy. Feature selection uses relatively fewer features since only selective features need to be used which in turn improve predictive error rate. The available training data are less in cancer classification, which is a challenge for some classification methodologies. So a PSO can be used here for doing the work of feature selection from a large number of features. An Improved binary particle swarm optimization (IBPSO) can be used in this case to do feature selection (4. In a binary PSO the individual particles can be represented as binary (0/1) forms which shows the straightforward "yes/no" choice of whether a feature needs to be selected or not. The changes in particle velocity can be interpreted as a change in the probability of finding the particle in one state or another. Since this change is a probability which is limited to a range of {0.0–1.0} (Chuang, Chang, Tu & Yang, 2008).

PSO for Rule Extraction in Medical Diagnosis

While applying conventional neural networks to the medical field it is very difficult to interpret appropriately, in a physically meaningful way, because the learned knowledge is numerically encoded in the trained synaptic weights. So some authors tried to generate if- then rules for transforming the synaptic weights in a neural network into a set of crisp rules. But after training, it is found that some if-then rules are present which are ineffective for classifying the positive instances. In this case a PSO can be used to reduce the rules which are mostly effective for classifying the positive data samples generated by a trained Neural Network, while the recognition performance will not be degraded, rather be improved. The membership function here chosen which measures the degree with which a data pattern, x, belongs to an input space. Initially the crisp rules generated are used as the particles, than the fitness function is evaluated to choose the best out of them (Hsieh, Chun & Wang, 2014).

PSO for Heating System Planning (HSP)

The whole world today faces serious energy and environment problems, with the increase of greenhouse gas emissions in the atmosphere the environments have already reached concerning levels in terms of their potential to cause climate change. Air pollution, acid precipitation, and stratospheric ozone depletion are other serious environmental concerns. An important action to address energy and environmental challenges lies in the intelligent and efficient use of energy, including reducing energy waste and using low- carbon fuels. Sustainable development of heating system requires application of planning procedures, which includes optimization of both demand and supply sides of heating. Here PSO algorithm can be used to design models for owners in making sustainable heating system investment decisions and to improve their decision-bases for administration. The objective function in HSP is the total heat production coast, which has to be minimized, for which PSO can be applied (Ma, Yu, & Hu, 2013).

Cancer Classification by BPNN-PSO

In medical field cancer is one of the major researches. Accurate prediction of various tumour types has huge value in offering better treatment possibilities and toxicity minimization on the patients. DNA microarrays performs biologist to calculate the expression of thousands of genes continuously on a small chip. These microarrays perform the large amount of data and proposed methods are needed to analyze them. The large amount of data needs more time for training when they are passed through a classifier. So to speed up the training time PSO is used. Searching process is started from initializing a group of random inputs. First, all the particles are updated, until a new generation set of particles are generated, and then those new particles are used to search the global best position in the solution space (Vimaladevi & Kalaavathi, 2014; Cho & Ryu, 2002).

FUTURE RESEARCH DIRECTION

One of the foremost important problems associated with all population-based search algorithms is that they provide satisfactory results but there is no heuristic algorithm that could provide a superior performance than others in solving all kind of optimizing problems. In other words, an algorithm may solve some problems better and some problems worse than others (Rashedi, Nezamabadi-pour & Saryazdi, 2009). Hence, proposing new high performance heuristic algorithms are helpful. Recently some emerged techniques like gravitational search algorithms (GSA) can be used in place of PSO. This technique is different from PSO in many ways. In both GSA and PSO the optimization is obtained by agents' movement in the search space, but the strategy of movement is different. Some important differences are:

1. In PSO the direction of an agent is calculated using only two best positions, $pbest_i$ and gbest. But in GSA, the agent direction is calculated based on the overall force obtained by all other agents.
2. PSO uses a kind of memory for updating the velocity (due to $pbest_i$ and gbest). However, GSA is memory-less and only the current position of the agents plays a role in the updating procedure.
3. These advantages of GSA on PSO can be best experimented with the biological problems discussed in this chapter. Recently, an explosive growth is seen in the genomic sequences, proteins in available form, so, managing and manipulating these data and deriving the information accurately in a stipulated time bound has emerged as a challenging and fascinating field of science. So always there is a need to find suitable method and technology to handle big amount of data and the algorithms to process this information in an effective way. This may possibly be handled with suitable parallelization of algorithms. Hybridizing the intelligent soft computing tools with the heuristic swarm intelligence techniques in a parallel environment can be thought of as the future directions to find better solutions to address the above cited problems.

CONCLUSION

SI algorithms have recently gained wide popularity among the researchers, for their remarkable ability in obtaining nearly optimal solutions to a number of NP hard, real world search problems. A survey of the bioinformatics literature discloses the fact that the field has a surplus of problems that needs fast and vigorous search mechanisms. Problems coming under this group include (but are not limited to) the multiple sequence alignment (MSA), protein secondary and tertiary structure prediction, protein ligand docking, promoter identification and the reconstruction of evolutionary trees. Classical deterministic search algorithms and the derivative based optimization techniques are of no use for them as the search space may be massively large and discontinuous at certain parts. SI presents a collection of multi-agent parallel search techniques that can be effectively used for solving bioinformatics related problems of this sort. In this chapter we have tried to address some of the bioinformatics problems and their solutions using the computational intelligence. Then one of the popular and simple swarm intelligence based technique, the PSO has been discussed in various computational biology problems. But this field is not limited to the above. There is always a scope to innovate and renovate a better algorithm to produce a superior performance which will be suitable for answering the problems belonging to this domain.

REFERENCES

Aziz, N. A. A., Mubin, M., Mohamad, M. S., & Aziz, K. A. (2014). Scientific World Journal, 2014.

Babu, M. M. (2004). *An Introduction to Microarray Data Analysis.* Retrieved from www.mrc-lmb.cam. ac.uk/genomes/madanm/microarray

Bai, Q. (2010). Analysis of Particle Swarm Optimization Algorithm. *Computer and information science, 3.*

Belal, M., Gaber, J., El-Sayed, H., & Almojel, A. (2006). Swarm Intelligence. In Chapman & Hall (Eds.), Handbook of Bioinspired Algorithms and Applications (Vol. 7).

Bharathi & Natarajan. (2010). Cancer Classification of Bioinformatics data using ANOVA. *International Journal of Computer Theory and Engineering*, *2*(3), 369–373.

Blum, C., & Merkle, D. (2008). *Swarm Intelligence – Introduction and Applications. Natural Computing*. Berlin: Springer.

Casadio, R., Compiani, M., Fariselli, P. & Vivarelli, F. (1995). Predicting free energy contributions to the conformational stability of folded proteins. *Journal of Intelligent System Molecular Biology*, *3*, 81–88.

Chan, Z. S. H., Havukkala, I., Jain, V., Hu, Y., & Kasabov, N. (2008). Soft computing methods to predict gene regulatory networks: An integrative approach on time-series gene expression data. *Journalof Applied Soft Computing*, *8*(3), 1189–1199. doi:10.1016/j.asoc.2007.02.023

Cheng, J. & Baldi, P. (2007) Improved residue contact prediction using support vector machines and a large feature set. *BMC Bioinform*, *8*, 113.

Cho, S. B., & Ryu, J. (2002). Classifying gene expression data of cancer using classifier ensemble with mutually exclusive features *Proceedings of the IEEE*, *90*(11), 1744–1753. doi:10.1109/JPROC.2002.804682

Chuang, L. Y., Chang, H. W., Tu, C. J., & Yang, C. H. (2008). Improved binary PSO for feature selection using gene expression data. *Computational Biology and Chemistry*, *32*(1), 29–38. doi:10.1016/j.compbiolchem.2007.09.005 PMID:18023261

Chuang, L. Y., Chang, H. W., Tu, C. J., & Yang, C. H. (2008). Improved binary PSO for feature selection using gene expression data. *Computational Biology and Chemistry*, *3*(1), 29–38. doi:10.1016/j.compbiolchem.2007.09.005 PMID:18023261

Clote, P., & Backofen, R. (2000). *Computational Molecular Biology*. John Wiley & Sons Ltd.

Couzin, I. D., Krause, J., James, R., Ruxton, G. D., & Franks, N. R. (2002). Collective Memory and Spatial Sorting in Animal Groups. *Journal of Theoretical Biology*, *218*(1), 1–11. doi:10.1006/jtbi.2002.3065 PMID:12297066

Cui, Y., Chen, R. S., & Hung, W. (1998). Protein folding simulation with genetic algorithm and supersecondary structure constraints. *Proteins*, *31*(3), 247–257. doi:10.1002/(SICI)1097-0134(19980515)31:3<247::AID-PROT2>3.0.CO;2-G PMID:9593196

Das, S., Abraham, A., & Konar, A. (2008). Swarm Intelligence Algorithms in Bioinformatics, *Springer*[SCI]. *Studies in Computational Intelligence*, *94*, 113–147. doi:10.1007/978-3-540-76803-6_4

Das, S., Panigrahi, B. K., & Pattnaik, S. S. (2009). Nature-Inspired Algorithms for Multi-objective Optimization. In Handbook of Research on Machine Learning Applications and Trends: Algorithms Methods and Techniques (Vol. 1, pp. 95–108). Hershey, PA, USA: IGI Global.

Dash, N., Priyadarshini, R., & Misra, R. (2015). An Artificial Neural Network Model to Classify Multinomial Datasets with Optimized Target Using Particle Swarm Optimization Technique, *Springer-Smart Innovation. Systems and Technologies*, *31*, 355–364.

Dembele, D., & Kastner, P. (2003). Fuzzy c-means method for clustering microarray data. *Bioinformatics (Oxford, England)*, *19*(8), 973–980. doi:10.1093/bioinformatics/btg119 PMID:12761060

Dorigo, M. (1992). Optimization, learning and natural algorithms (in Italian) [Ph.D. Thesis]. Dipartimento diElettronica, Politecnico di Milano, Italy.

Dorigo, M., Bonabeau, E., & Theraulaz, G. (2000). Ant algorithms and stigmergy. *Future Generation Computer Systems, 16*(8), 851–871. doi:10.1016/S0167-739X(00)00042-X

Dorigo, M., Maniezzo, V., & Colorni, A. (1991). Positive feedback as a search strategy (Tech. Report 91-016). Dipartimento di Elettronica, Politecnico di Milano, Italy.

Engelbrecht, A. P. (2002). *Computational Intelligence: An Introduction*. England: John Wiley & Sons.

Goel, N., Singh, S., & Aseri, T. C. (2013).A Review of Soft Computing Techniques for Gene Prediction. Hindawi Publishing Corporation.

Haykin, S. (1999). *Neural networks—a comprehensive foundation*. Englewood Cliffs: Prentice Hall.

Hsieh, Y.-Z., Su, M.-C., & Wang, P.-C. (2014). A PSO-based rule extractor for medical diagnosis. *Journal of Biomedical Informatics, 49*, 53–60. doi:10.1016/j.jbi.2014.05.001 PMID:24835617

Karaboga & Basturk, B. (2007). A Powerful and Efficient Algorithm For Numerical Function Optimization: Artificial Bee Colony (ABC) Algorithm. *Journal of Global Optimization, Springer Netherlands, 39*(3), 459471.

Karaboga, (2005) An Idea Based On Honey Bee Swarm for Numerical Optimization (Technical Report-TR06). Erciyes University.

Kennedy, J. & Eberhart, R. (1995). An Introduction Particle Swarm Optimization. *IEEE Transaction*.

Li, B., Zheng, C. H., Huang, D. S., Zhang, L., & Han, K. (2010). Gene expression data classification using locally linear discriminant embedding. *Computers in Biology and Medicine, 40*(10), 802–810. doi:10.1016/j.compbiomed.2010.08.003 PMID:20864095

Lim, C. P., Jain, L. C., & Dehuri, S. (2009). *Innovations in Swarm Intelligence: Studies in Computational Intelligence* (Vol. 248). Springer. doi:10.1007/978-3-642-04225-6_1

Ma, R.J., Yu, N.Y., & Hu, J.Y. (2013). Application of Particle swarm Optimization Algorithm in the Heating System Planning Problem. *The Scientific World Journal*.

Ma, R. J., Yu, N. Y., & Hu, J. Y. (2013). Application of Particle Swarm Optimization Algorithm in the Heating System Planning Problem. The Scientific World Journal.

Mansour, N., Kanj, F., & Khachfe, H. (2012). *Particle Swarm Optimization Approach for Protein Structure Prediction in the 3D HP Model*. Interdisciplinary Science Compute Life Science.

Marquez-Chamorroa, A. E. (2015). Soft computing methods for the prediction of protein tertiary structures: A survey. *Journal of Applied Soft Computing, 35*, 398–410. doi:10.1016/j.asoc.2015.06.024

Mitra, S., & Hayashi, Y. (2006). Bioinformatics with Soft Computing. *IEEE Transactions on Systems, Man and Cybernetics. Part C, Applications and Reviews, 36*(5), 616–635. doi:10.1109/TSMCC.2006.879384

Panigrahi, K., Shi, Y., & Lim, M.-H. (2011). *Handbook of Swarm Intelligence. Series: Adaptation, Learning, and Optimization* (Vol. 7). Springer-Verlag Berlin Heidelberg. doi:10.1007/978-3-642-17390-5

Perez-Rodriguez, J., & Garcia-Pedrajas, N. (2011). An evolutionary algorithm for gene structure prediction. *Journal of Industrial Engineering and Other Applications.*

Priyadarshini, R., Dash, N. & Rout, S. (2012). A Novel Approach for Protein Structure Prediction using Back Propagation Neural Network. *International Journal of Computer Science & Technology, 3*(2).

Rashedi, Nezamabadi-pour & Saryazdi. (2009). GSA: a Grviational Search Algorithm. *Information Sciences, 6,* 2232-2248.

Sarhan, A. M. (2009). Cancer Classification Based on Micro array Gene Expression Data Using DCT and ANN. *Journal of Theoretical and Applied Information Technology, 6*(2), 208–216.

Schulze-Kremer, S. (2000). *Genetic algorithms and protein folding, Protein Struct* (pp. 75–222). Predict.

Vaishali, P.K. & Vinayababu, A. (2011). Application of Microarray Technology and Soft-computing in Cancer Biology: A Review. *International Journal of Biometrics and Bioinformatics, 5*(4).

Vimaladevi, M. & Kalaavathi, B. (2014). Cancer Classification using Hybrid Fast Particle Swarm Optimization with Back-propagation Neural Network, *International Journal of computer and communication technology, 3*(11).

Xiao, X., Dow, E. R., Eberhart, R. C., Miled, Z. B., & Oppelt, R. J. (2003). Gene Clustering Using Self-Organizing Maps and Particle Swarm Optimization. *Proc. of the 17th International Symposium on Parallel and Distributed Processing (PDPS'03)*, Washington DC. doi:10.1109/IPDPS.2003.1213290

KEY TERMS AND DEFINITIONS

Agent: An agent is something that acts in an environment.

Bioinformatics: Bio-informatics can be described as the application of computational methods to make biological discoveries and explorations.

Bio-Inspired Computing: It is field which helps to tackle complex real problems using computational methods based on biology.

Collective Behaviour: Behaviour of a group of social insects.

Fuzzy System: It is a component machine learning techniques which takes membership values within 0 to 1 unlike crisp sets.

Gene: It is a portion of DNA molecule which serves as the basic unit of heredity.

Heuristic: Rule or method based on trial and method that helps us to solve problems quicker.

Neural Network: Neural network is a soft computing paradigm inspired by the working of human brain to inculcate intelligence in machines.

Optimization: A mathematical method to find the solution of a problem towards achieving better performance either in form of minimum or maximum under one or more given constraint.

Protein: Organic macro molecules composed of one or more amino acids.

Swarm Intelligence (SI): SI is one of the techniques which is inspired by nature and is a population based algorithm motivated by the collective behaviour of a group of social insects.

APPENDIX: PSO FOR DATA CLASSIFICATION: A CASE STUDY

Problem Definition: Here we are considering a simple classification problem or we can say a prediction problem, where we are given with an input dataset sample having some instances and their predefined class. The main task in this problem is to partition the group of input objects to their corresponding classes.

In this work the bench mark datasets taken from UCI learning repository for verification and validation of the PSO based model is chosen (Marquez-Chamorroa, Asencio-Cortes, Santiesteban Toca & Aguilar-Ruiz, 2015) A brief of the datasets are as follows

Dataset Description:

The dataset consists of 150 samples which consists of a set of Iris flowers, where the goal is to predict three classes based on sepal (green covering) length and width, and petal (the flower part) length and width. This is the most popular and the simplest of the classification data containing three predictable attributes such as setosa, versicolor and virginica.

```
Input: iris dataset
Output: The instance and its corresponding class
Fitness function chosen is the minimum distance among the features.
Matlab Code:
 clc;
clear all;
irisdata;        % loading iris data into the work space
x=iris(:,1:4); % assigning instances to variable x
v=rand(1,4)-.5;
n1=1;n2=1;n3=1;
r1=.4;              %assigning constant value
r2=.5;
c2 =1.4;          % PSO parameter C1
c1 = 1.4;         % PSO parameter C2
w =0.73;          % PSO momentum or inertia
cd1=x(5,:);       %Randomly assigning data to one calss
cd2=x(65,:);
cd3=x(105,:);
n=1
while n<=5
for i=1:40
    t1=x(i,:);
    for j=1:40
        d1(j)=sqrt((sum(x(i,:)-cd1)).^2);
    end
    [m ind]=min(d1);
    g=x(ind,:);
```

```
        v = w *v + c1*r1*(t1-cd1) + c2*r2*(g-cd1);                    % ve-
locity updation
        cd1=cd1+v;
end
n=n+1;
cd1
end
n=1;
while n<=5
for i=51:90
    t1=x(i,:);
    for j=51:90
        d2(j)=sqrt((sum(x(i,:)-cd2)).^2);
    end
    [m ind]=min(d2);
    g=x(ind,:);
        v = w *v + c1*r1*(t1-cd2) + c2*r2*(g-cd2);
        cd2=cd2+v;
end
n=n+1;
cd2
end
n=1;
while n<=5
for i=101:140
    t1=x(i,:);
    for j=101:140
        d3(j)=sqrt((sum(x(i,:)-cd3)).^2);
    end
    [m ind]=min(d3);
    g=x(ind,:);
        v = w *v + c1*r1*(t1-cd3) + c2*r2*(g-cd3);
        cd3=cd3+v;
end
n=n+1;
cd3
end
 cd1
cd2
 cd3
```

Note: At first the data set will be divided into two sets. The first set will contain 2/3rd of the data which will be treated as training data and rest of the 1/3rd of the data will be treated as the test data. The output of this program will give the value of cd1, cd2 and cd3 which belong to class-1, 2 and 3 respectively for the training dataset. For the testing purpose any classifier can be used .Suppose an artificial neural network will be used as a classifier, the network will be trained by the calculated optimized features using PSO and the test data can be simulated by the classifier.

The Table 1 given below shows the simulated output of iris dataset. The results are compared by accuracy percentage and accuracy up to number of decimal places. Here 120 samples are taken as training and rest 30 are taken as test set.

Table 1. Simulation Accuracy of Iris Dataset

Number of classes	Number of Simulation Result Accurate up to				Total no of test samples
	4 decimal places	3 decimal places	2 decimal places	1 decimal places	
Class 1	10	10	10	10	10
Class 2	10	10	10	10	10
Class 3	09	09	09	09	10
Percentage of Accuracy	98%	98%	98%	98%	Total=30

Chapter 8
Application of Rough Set Based Models in Medical Diagnosis

Balakrushna Tripathy
VIT University, India

ABSTRACT

Modeling intelligent system in the field of medical diagnosis is still a challenging work. Intelligent systems in medical diagnosis can be utilized as a supporting tool to the medical practitioner, mainly country like India with vast rural areas and absolute shortage of physicians. Intelligent systems in the field of medical diagnosis can also able to reduce cost and problems for the diagnosis like dynamic perturbations, shortage of physicians, etc. An intelligent system may be considered as an information system that provides answer to queries relating to the information stored in the Knowledge Base (KB), which is a repository of human knowledge. Rough set theory is an efficient model to capture uncertainty in data and the processing of data using rough set techniques is easy and convincing. Rule generation is an inherent component in rough set analysis. So, medical systems which have uncertainty inherent can be handled in a better way using rough sets and its variants. The objective of this chapter is to discuss on several such applications of rough set theory in medical diagnosis.

INTRODUCTION

Medical diagnosis is still considered an art, despite all standardization efforts. Medical diagnosis is the art of determining a patient's pathological status from an available set of symptoms (findings). It is defined an art, because it is a complicated problem with many and manifold factors, and its solution comprises literally all of a human's abilities including intuition and the subconscious The process of medical diagnosis is composed of, evaluation of a given set of symptoms (findings) performing relevant pathological tests (patient's test data), and ultimately identifying the diseases validating the particular findings. The functioning of the human body is characterized by the complex and extremely interactive chemistry of its organs and the psyche. This concerted effort results homeostasis and the equilibrium of all physiological quantities. This balance is maintained in a level within physiological bounds that varies from individual to individual. Due to internal or of external cause, deviations from it are indica-

DOI: 10.4018/978-1-5225-0427-6.ch008

tive of some kind of perturbation. The identification of the cause of these perturbations is the goal of medical diagnosis. Reaching a foolproof diagnosis is never an easy job for medical practitioner. Today in medical diagnosis it is often impossible to look inside a patient to determine the primary cause that led to the series of effects and reactions the patient complains about. Thus the diagnosis is based on indirect evidence, symptoms and the knowledge of the medical mechanisms that relate presumed causes to observed effects. The problems of diagnosis not only arises due to the incompleteness of knowledge, but also most immediate limitations of the theoretical and practical knowledge implications that lead from an initial cause to its observable effects.

DEFINITIONS AND NOTATIONS

In this section we provide some definitions and notations to be followed in this chapter. Imprecision in data has become a common feature and hence to handle them imprecise models have been developed in literature. In this sequel we have fuzzy sets, rough sets, intuitionistic fuzzy sets and soft sets along with their generalisations and modifications can be found. Our basic aim in this chapter is to deal with only rough sets. So, we start with the definition of rough sets and related concepts.

Let U be a universe of discourse and R be an equivalence relation over U. By U/R we denote the family of all equivalence classes of R, referred to as categories or concepts of R and the equivalence class of an element $x \in U$ is denoted by $[x]_R$. By a knowledge base, we understand a relational system $K = (U, P)$, where U is as above and P is a family of equivalence relations over U. For any subset Q ($\neq \phi) \subseteq$ P, the intersection of all equivalence relations in Q is denoted by IND(Q) and is called the indiscernibility relation over Q.

Definition 1: Given any $X \subseteq U$ and R $\in$ IND (K), we associate two subsets $\underline{R}X$ and $\overline{R}X$ called the R-lower and R-upper approximations of X respectively and are defined as:

1. $\underline{R}X = \bigcup\{Y \in U / R : Y \subseteq X\}$ and
2. $\overline{R}X = \bigcup\{Y \in U / R : Y \cap X \neq \phi\}$.

The R-boundary of X is denoted by $BN_R(X)$ and is given by $BN_R(X) = \overline{R}X - \underline{R}X$.

The elements of $\underline{R}X$ are those elements of U, which can certainly be classified as elements of X, and the elements of $\overline{R}X$ are those elements of U, which can possibly be classified as elements of X, employing knowledge of R. We say that X is rough with respect to R if and only if $\underline{R}X \neq \overline{R}X$, equivalently $BN_R(X) \neq \phi$. X is said to be R-definable if and only if $\underline{R}X = \overline{R}X$, or $BN_R(X) = \phi$.

Definition 2: An information system I is a four tuple <U, A, V, F>, where $U = \{x_1, x_2, ...x_n\}$ is a finite, non-empty set of objects, A = $\{A_1, A_2, ...A_m\}$ is a set of attributes. $V = \bigcup_{i=1}^{m} V_{A_i}$, where V_{A_i} is the domain of the attribute A_i, i = 1, 2...m. $F : U \times A \rightarrow V$ is the total decision function called the information function such that $F(x, A_i) \in V_{A_i}, x \in U \ and \ A_i \in A.$.

If further the attribute set A is decomposed into two sets C and D such that $A = C \cup D$, where C is called the set of condition attributes and D is called the set of decision attributes then the information system is called a decision system.

Definition 3: Let P and Q be two equivalence relations on U. Then the positive region of Q with respect to P is denoted by $POS_P(Q)$ is defined as

$$(3) \quad POS_P(Q) = \bigcup_{X \in U/Q} \underline{P}(X)$$

In fact, the positive region of Q with respect to P contains all those elements of U those can be classified to classes of U/Q using the information in attribute P.

Definition 4: Let **R** be a family of equivalence relations. Suppose R $\in$ **R** be such that IND(**R** \{R})= IND (**R**). Then we say that R is dispensable. Otherwise, R is said to be dispensable.

Definition 5: A family of equivalence relations R is said to be independent if each R $\in$ **R** is indispensable. Otherwise, **R** is said to be dependent.

Definition 6: Let **P** $\subseteq$ **R**. Any subset **Q** $\subseteq$ **P** is said to be a reduct of **P** if **Q** is independent and IND(**P**) = IND(**Q**).

From the definition it follows that **P** can have many reducts.

Definition 7: The set of all indispensible relations in **P** is called the core of **P**.

The relationship between the core and the reducts of **P** is given by

$$(4) \quad \text{core}(\mathbf{P}) = \bigcap_{Q = \mathrm{Re}\,duct(P)} Q$$

LITERATURE REVIEW

Broadly speaking, applications of rough sets in medicine can be classified into two categories, diagnosis and outcome prediction and feature selection, with an overwhelming majority of papers falling into the former. The by far most common application of rough sets in medicine is for diagnosis or prediction of outcomes. This is usually accomplished by synthesizing if-then rules. Based on rough set theory it is possible to construct a set of simple if-then rules from information tables. Often, these rules can reveal previously undiscovered patterns in sample data. Rough set methods can also be used to classify unknown data based on already gained knowledge. Unlike many other techniques, rough set analysis requires no external parameters and uses only the information present in the input data. Rough set theory can be utilised to determine whether sufficient data for a task is available respectively to extract a minimal sufficient set of features for classification which in turn effectively performs feature space dimensionality reduction. Although, compared to other methods, a relatively recent technique, these characteristics have prompted various rough set approaches in the general domain of medical informatics.

Rough Sets in Medical Image Segmentation

One of the most important tasks in medical imaging is segmentation as it is often a pre-cursor to subsequent analysis, whether manual or automated. The basic idea behind segmentation-based rough sets is that while some cases may be clearly labeled as being in a set X (called positive region in rough sets theory), and some cases may be clearly labeled as not being in X (called negative region), limited information prevents us from labeling all possible cases clearly. The remaining cases cannot be distinguished and lie in what is known as the boundary region. Kobashi *et al.* (2004) introduced rough sets to treat nominal data based on concepts of categorization and approximation for medical image segmentation. The proposed clustering method extracts features of each pixel by using thresholding and labeling algorithms. Thus, the features are given by nominal data. The ability of the proposed method was evaluated by applying it to human brain MRI images. Peters *et al.* (2001) presented a new form of indiscernibility relation based on k-means clustering of pixel values. The end result is a partitioning of a set of pixel values into bins that represent equivalence classes. The proposed approach allows introducing a form of upper and lower approximation specialised relative to sets of pixel values. An improved clustering algorithm based on rough sets and entropy theory was presented by Chena and Wang (2006). The method avoids the need to pre-specify the number of clusters which is a common problem in clustering based segmentation approaches. Clustering can be performed in both numerical and nominal feature spaces with a similarity introduced to replace the distance index. At the same time, rough sets are used to enhance the algorithm with the capability to deal with vagueness and uncertainty in data analysis. Shannon's entropy was used to refine the clustering results by assigning relative weights to the set of features according to the mutual entropy values. A novel measure of clustering quality was also presented to evaluate the clusters. The experimental results confirm that both efficiency and clustering quality of this algorithm are improved.

An interesting strategy for colour image segmentation using rough sets has been presented by Mohabey *et al.* (2000). They introduced a concept of encrustation of the histogram, called histon, for the visualisation of multi-dimensional colour information in an integrated fashion and study its applicability in boundary region analysis. The histon correlates with the upper approximation of a set such that all elements belonging to this set are classified as possibly belonging to the same segment or segments showing similar colour value. The proposed encrustation provides a direct means of separating a pool of inhomogeneous regions into its components. This approach can then be extended to build a hybrid rough set theoretic approximations with fuzzy c-means based colour image segmentation. The technique extracts colour information regarding the number of segments and the segment centers of the image through rough set theoretic approximations which then serve as the input to a fuzzy c-means algorithm.

Widz *et al.* (2004) introduced an automated multi-spectral MRI segmentation technique based on approximate reducts derived from the theory of rough sets. They utilised T1, T2 and PD MRI images from a simulated brain database as a gold standard to train and test their segmentation algorithm. The results suggest that approximate reducts, used alone or in combination with other classification methods, may provide a novel and efficient approach to the segmentation of volumetric MRI data sets. Segmentation accuracy reaches 96% for the highest resolution images and 89% for the noisiest image volume. They tested the resultant classifier on real clinical data, which yielded an accuracy of approximately 84%.

Rough Sets in Medical Classification

The computation of the core and reducts from a rough set decision table is a way of selecting relevant features (Pawlak, 1982). It is a global method in the sense that the resultant reducts represent the minimal sets of features which are necessary to maintain the same classification power given by the original and complete set of features. A more direct manner for selecting relevant features is to assign a measure of relevance to each feature and choose the features with higher values. Based on the reduct system, we can generate the list of rules that will be used for building the classifier model for the new objects. Reduct is an important concept in rough set theory and data reduction is a main application of rough set theory in pattern recognition and data mining.

Wojcik (1987) approached the nature of a feature recognition process through the description of image features in terms of rough sets. Since the basic condition for representing images must be satisfied by any recognition result, elementary features are defined as equivalence classes of possible occurrences of specific fragments existing in images. The names of the equivalence classes (defined through specific numbers of objects and numbers of background parts covered by a window) constitute the best lower approximation of the window contents (i.e., names of recognized features). The best upper approximation is formed by the best lower approximation, its features, and parameters, all referenced to the object fragments located within the window. The rough approximation of shapes is robust with respect to accidental changes in the width of contours and lines and to small discontinuities and, in general, to possible positions or changes in shape of the same feature. Rough sets are also used for noiseless image quantization. Swiniarski and Skowron (2003) presented applications of rough set methods for feature selection in pattern recognition. They emphasize the role of basic constructs of rough set approaches in feature selection, namely reducts and their approximations, including dynamic reducts. Their algorithm for feature selection is based on the application of a rough set method to the result of principal component analysis (PCA) used for feature projection and reduction. In their study, mammogram images were evaluated for recognition experiments. The database contains three types of images: normal, benign, and malignant. For each abnormal image the co-ordinates of centre of abnormality and proximate radius (in pixels) of a circle enclosing the abnormality have been given. For classification the centre locations and radii apply to clusters rather than to the individual classifications. From the original mammograms, 64 x 64 pixel sub-images were extracted around the center of abnormality (or at the average co-ordinate for normal cases). They concluded that the rough set methods have shown ability to significantly reduce the pattern dimensionality and have proven to be viable image mining techniques as a front end of neural network classifiers.

Cyran and Mrzek (2001) showed how rough sets can be applied to improve the classification ability of a hybrid pattern recognition system. Their system consists of a feature extractor based on a computer-generated hologram (CGH) where the extracted features are shift, rotation, and scale invariant. An original method of optimizing the feature extraction abilities of a CGH was introduced which uses rough set concepts to measure the amount of essential information contained in the feature vector. This measure is used to define an objective function in the optimisation process. Since rough set based factors are not differentiable, they use a no gradient approach for a search in the space of possible solutions. Finally, rough sets are used to determine decision rules for the classification of feature vectors.

Rough Sets in Medical Data Mining

With increasing sizes of the amount of data stored in medical databases, efficient and effective techniques for medical data mining are highly sought after. Applications of rough sets in this domain include inducing propositional rules from databases using rough sets prior to using these rules in an expert system. (Tsumoto, 1999) presented a knowledge discovery system based on rough sets and feature-oriented generalisation and its application to medicine. Diagnostic rules and information on features are extracted from clinical databases on diseases of congenital anomaly. Experimental results showed that the proposed method extracts expert knowledge correctly and also discovers that symptoms observed in six positions (eyes, noses, ears, lips, fingers, and feet) play important roles in differential diagnosis. (Hassanien el al., 2009) presented a rough set approach to feature reduction and generation of classification rules from a set of medical datasets. They introduced a rough set reduction technique to find all reducts of the data that contain the minimal subset of features associated with a class label for classification. To evaluate the validity of the rules based on the approximation quality of the features, a statistical test to evaluate the significance of the rules was introduced. A set of data samples of patients with suspected breast cancer were used. The rough set classification accuracy was shown to compare favourably with the well-known ID3 classifier algorithm. (Huang & Zhang, 2001) presented a new application of rough sets to ECG recognition. First, the recognition rules for characteristic points in ECG are reduced using rough set theory. Then the reduced rules are used as restriction conditions of eigenvalue determination arithmetic to recognize characteristic points in ECG. Several aspects of correlative arithmetic such as sizer method, difference method and how to choose difference parameters are discussed. They also adopted MIT-BIH data to verify R wave recognition and it is shown that the resulting detection rate is higher than those of conventional recognition methods.

Recently, Independent Component Analysis (ICA)(Swiniarski et al, 2006) has gained popularity as an effective method for discovering statistically independent variables (sources) for blind source separation, as well as for feature extraction. (Swiniarski et al., 2006) studied several hybrid methods for feature extraction/reduction, feature selection, and classifier design for breast cancer recognition in mammograms. The methods included independent component analysis, principal component analysis (PCA) and rough set theory. Three classifiers were designed and tested: a rough sets rule-based classifier, an error back propagation neural network, and a Learning Vector Quantization neural network. Based on a comparative study on two different data sets of mammograms, rough sets rule-based classifier performed with a significantly better level of accuracy than the other classifiers. Therefore, the use of ICA or PCA as a feature extraction technique in combination with rough sets for feature selection and rule-based classification offers an improved solution for mammogram recognition in the detection of breast cancer.

Rough Sets in Medical Decision Support Systems

The medical diagnosis process can be interpreted as a decision-making process, during which the physician induces the diagnosis of a new and unknown case from an available set of clinical data and from clinical experience. This process can be computerized in order to present medical diagnostic procedures in a rational, objective, accurate and fast way. In fact, during the last two or three decades, diagnostic decision support systems have become a well-established component of medical technology. (Podraza et. Al, 2003) presented an idea of complex data analysis and decision support system for medical staff based on rough set theory. The main aim of their system is to provide an easy to use, commonly available tool for efficiently diagnosing diseases, suggesting possible further treatment and deriving unknown dependencies between different data coming from various patients' examinations. A blueprint of a possible architecture of such a system is presented including some example algorithms and suggested solutions, which may be applied during implementation.

The unique feature of the system relies on removing some data through rough set decisions to enhance the quality of the generated rules. Usually such data is discarded, because it does not contribute to the knowledge acquisition task or even hinder it. In their approach, improper data (excluded from the data used for drawing conclusions) is carefully taken into considerations. This methodology can be very important in medical applications as a case not fitting to the general classification cannot be neglected, but should be examined with special care.

(Mitra et al., 2006) implemented a rule-based rough-set decision system for the development of a disease inference engine for ECG classification. ECG signals may be corrupted by various types of noise. Therefore, at first, the extracted signals are undergoing a noise removal stage. A QRS detector is also developed for the detection of R-R interval of ECG waves. After the detection of this R-R interval, the P and T waves are detected based on a syntactic approach. Isoelectric-level detection and base-line corrections are also implemented for accurate computation of different features of P, QRS, and T waves. A knowledge base is developed from medical literature and feedback of reputed cardiologists regarding ECG interpretation and essential time-domain features of the ECG signal. Finally, a rule-based rough-set decision system is generated for the development of an inference engine for disease identification from these time-domain features.

Wakulicz-Deja and Paszek (2003) implemented an application of rough set theory to decision making for diagnosing mitochondrial encephalomyopathies in children. The resulting decision support system maximally limits the indications for invasive diagnostic methods (puncture, muscle and/or nerve specimens). Moreover, it shortens the time necessary for making diagnosis. The system has been developed on the basis of data obtained from the Clinic Department of Pediatrics of the Silesian Academy of Medicine.

APPLICATIONS

Several applications of rough sets and its hybrid models in medical diagnosis are found in the literature. We produce some of this in this chapter. These are

Rough sets in Diabetic Diagnosis (Ali et al, 2015; Anouncia et al, 2013; Choubey et al, 2014)

The less production of a hormone called insulin in a human body causes Diabetes. Insulin helps in transporting the sugar/energy produced from our food into cells. Less insulin leads to accumulation of too much sugar in blood. This causes diabetes. It is primarily of two types. Type-1 diabetes occurs mostly in children and it is occurred due to no production of insulin by the pancreas. But, Type 2 diabetes occurs when pancreas does not produce enough insulin. This is prevalent mostly in people above the age of 45. However, it is now occurring in people of lesser age also.

An attempt is made in (Anouncia et al, 2013) to design and develop a diagnosis system, using a rough set. The system developed is evaluated using a simple set of symptoms that is added to clinical data in determining diabetes and its severity. The system is implemented to diagnose the type of diabetes with the input symptoms given by the user. The system proves to be advantageous in aspects, such as accuracy and time consumption due to the rough set based knowledge representation. The system is adaptable for any number of symptoms and is evaluated with respect to the rule based system containing the symptoms in terms of rules. The results obtained through the rough set based system are comparatively better than the rule-based system. A similar attempt was also made in (Ali et al, 2015) but by taking a hybrid rough set model rather than a pure rough set model.

Rough sets in Intelligent Medical Diagnosis (Ghosh, 2012)

An intelligent system may be considered as an information system that provides answer to queries relating to the information stored in the Knowledge Base (KB), which is a repository of human knowledge. Modeling an intelligent system in medical domain increasingly recognized the importance of explanation capabilities of the system. One survey within potential users of medical diagnostic systems suggested that explanation facility is the most important capability to accept clinical decision tool. In (Ghosh, 2012) a prototype model of an Interactive Intelligent System for Medical Diagnosis (IISMD) proposed for diagnosis of diseases, in a particular domain like the diseases in infancy. Earlier also some models of IISMD were developed using fuzzy logic for knowledge representation and used Generalized Modus Ponens (GMP) for inferencing. The proposed Interactive Intelligent System can be able to directly assist physicians and other health professionals for diagnosis of diseases, in any particular domain, say convulsion in infancy has been considered as a case study in (Ghosh, 2012). In this work attempts have been made for modeling an intelligent system in medical diagnosis by acquiring knowledge from domain experts in form of a set of interconnected rules lacking of efficiency and reliability rather to construct rules from observation and clinically tested data set. Also, a framework of rough-fuzzy intelligent system is proposed, that is a hybridization of rough set and fuzzy set, incorporating the rough-fuzzy rules in a domain of diseases, like diabetes mellitus. Further, a rough-fuzzy-neural network intelligent system, which is a hybridization of rough set and fuzzy set and neural network, in a domain of diseases is proposed. The major concern in this work is to develop tools for modeling intelligent system in medical diagnosis.

Rough sets in Breast Cancer Diagnosis (Arafat et al, 2012; Revett et al, 2005; Sridevi et al 2012)

Breast cancer occurs when cells become abnormal and divide without control or order that can be considered as cancerous growth that begins in the tissues of the breast. Breast cancer has become the most common cancer disease among women. The most effective way to reduce breast cancer deaths is detecting it earlier. Early detection is the best form of cure and accurate diagnosis of the tumor which is extremely vital. Early detection allows physicians to differentiate between benign breast tumors from malignant ones without going for surgical biopsy. It also offers accurate, timely analysis of patient's particular type of cancer and the available treatment options. Extensive research has been carried out on automating the critical diagnosis procedure as various machine learning algorithms have been developed to aid physicians in optimizing the decision task effectively. Rough set theory offers a novel approach to manage uncertainty that has been used for the discovery of data dependencies, importance of features, patterns in sample data, feature space dimensionality reduction and the classification of objects. While rough set on their own provide a powerful technique, it is often combined with other computational intelligence techniques such as

Neural networks, fuzzy sets, genetic algorithms, Bayesian approaches, swarm optimization and support vector machines. Particle Swarm Optimization as a new evolutionary computation technique, in which each potential solution is seen as a particle with a certain velocity flying through the problem space. The Particle Swarms find optimal regions of the complex search space through the interaction of individuals in the population. PSO is attractive for feature selection in that particle

Swarms will discover best feature combinations as they fly within the subset space. Compared with other evolutionary techniques, PSO requires only primitive and simple mathematical operators. In this research, rough set is applied to improve feature selection and data reduction. Particle Swarm Optimization (PSO) is used to optimize the rough set feature reduction to effectively classify breast cancer tumors, either malignant or benign. Attribute reduction is an important issue in rough set theory. It is necessary to investigate fast and effective approximate algorithms to generate a set of

Discriminatory features. In (Arafat et al, 2012) a strategy based on Rough Set Theory (RST) with Particle Swarm Optimization (PSO) is proposed. Particle Swarm Optimization is widely used and rapidly developed for its easy implementation and few particles required to be tuned. This hybrid approach embodies an adaptive feature selection procedure which dynamically accounts for the relevance and dependence of the features. The relevance selected feature subsets are used to generate decision rules for the breast cancer classification task to differentiate the benign cases from the malignant cases by assigning classes to objects. The proposed hybrid approach is supposed to help in improving classification accuracy and also in finding more robust features to improve classifier performance.

In (Revett et al, 2005) a hybrid decision support system was proposed, combining the reductionist approach of rough sets in combination with a probabilistic neural network. With the dataset reduced to essential attributes and then it is applied a probabilistic neural network (PNN) for the final classification task. The result of this hybrid approach is established to be an extremely accurate classifier (with respect to sensitivity and specificity) that is also computationally efficient.

In (Sridevi et al, 2012) attempt is made to reduce the lengthy processes proposed to determine the cause and prevention in an effective manner with lesser number of attributes. In order to improve the accuracy of diagnosis with limited attributes, they used in their paper a rough set based relative reduct algorithm is used to reduce the number of attributes using equivalence relation. The effectiveness of proposed Rough Set Reduction algorithm is analyzed on Wisconsin Breast Cancer Dataset (WBCD) and presented as a part of the paper. The experimental results show that the relative reduct performs better attribute reduction.

Rough Set Based Rule Induction Algorithms (Srimani et al, 2014)

Rule generation is one of the most important features of Data mining and rough sets are frequently used to achieve this. The reason for using rough sets is the reduction of attributes which can be achieved through rough set techniques by removing the redundant attributes from a given set of attributes. This reduces the size of the database and also the rules generated using them. Medical databases in the form of patient details are huge in size and also contain many redundant attributes. So, precise rules and sometimes minimal rules can be generated which will help the naïve as well as the practitioners in dealing with patients, determining their diseases and suggesting remedies. With this idea in view in (Srimani et al, 2014) the authors used Pima data set for their study, which has been widely used in machine learning experiments and is currently available through the UCI repository of standard data sets. To study the positive as well as the negative aspects of the diabetes disease, Pima data set is utilized, which contains

768 data samples. Each sample contains 8 attributes which are considered as high risk factors for the occurrence of diabetes, like Plasma glucose concentration, Diastolic blood pressure (mm Hg), Triceps skin fold thickness (mm), 2-hour serum insulin (mu U/ms), Body mass index (weight in kg/(height in m)) Diabetes pedigrees function and Age (years). All the 768 examples were randomly separated into a training set of 576 cases (378, non-diabetic and 198, diabetic) and a test set of 192 cases (122 non-diabetic and 70 diabetic cases). The whole idea is to generate rules which may help the practitioners.

Rough Sets Post-Hepatitic Cirrhosis (Zhang et al, 2013)

Owing to the typical vagueness of treatment processes in traditional Chinese medicine (TCM), determining the final diagnosis result is very difficult. In (Zhang et al, 2013), a novel hierarchical diagnosis model (HDM) for syndrome prediction problems in TCM is constructed, incorporating rough set theory, expert judgment, and an attribute hierarchical model (AHM). Firstly, using the concept of the attribute hierarchical model, a hierarchical model with three levels – patient level, symptom level and diagnosis level – is built to predict the syndrome of a new case. Secondly, by integrating the positive region, support degree in rough set theory and expert experience, the subjective and objective parts of each attribute on the three levels are acquired. Thirdly, the synthetic attribute-weights at diagnosis level are obtained to predict the syndrome. Finally, an example is studied to illustrate the detailed implementation process of the HDM approach, and a real post-Hepatitic cirrhosis dataset is also diagnosed to evaluate the performance of the model. The encouraging results show the effectiveness of the presented method.

Rough Sets in CT Image Mining (Xu et al, 2010)

There are many reasons of cancer; there IS no way to prevent cancer, so the early diagnosis of cancer for cancer therapy is a very important factor. Through the study, we found that the early diagnosis of hepatic fibrosis to prevent liver cirrhosis, liver cancer has important significance. CT examination is a kind of reliable to early detection methods of lesions. But because of doctor to read

every hospital CT slices, a rate will be dropped, although if a CT slices are two doctors diagnose, then read and diagnosis accuracy will be greatly improved, but it costs too much. So we need computer-aided diagnosis, hoping to achieve higher efficiency and better accuracy. In (Xu et al, 2010), a kind of association rules is proposed based on rough sets and combination of mining method, and describes the whole process of medical CT image mining in this paper. They used the CT image mining processes extracts CT image features and preprocesses the data, and then changes the data into CT image mining database. Also, Mining the CT image mining database with rough sets and association rules technique is done. It is expected here that the result rules we can help doctors to classify the CT image into two classes: normal and abnormal.

Rough Sets in Automated Disease Diagnosis and Drug Design (Mandal et al, 2013)

Incomplete databases are many times natural and occur due to several reasons. Such databases are treated in various ways. In some cases the tuples having incomplete information are deleted from the databases which lead to information loss. In other cases the non-available entries are filled with most frequently occurring values or minimum value in the domain or the maximum value in the domain. But all these attempts are just not enough to ensure the validity of the new entries. Moreover the sizes of the databases are keeping on increasing. Several computational intelligence and soft computing methods are used to extract knowledge from these databases. Medical databases have accumulated large quantities of information about patients and their medical conditions supporting clinical, pathological, radiological and microbiological aspect in term of genetic expression. Identifying hidden relationships and patterns within this data could provide new medical knowledge about the patient. Analysis of medical data can often serve as tool for diagnosis and treatment of a patient with incomplete knowledge. This can be done with management of inconsistent pieces of information and with manipulation of various levels of representation of data using various soft computing tools. The intelligent techniques of data analysis are mainly based on quite strong assumptions and as a result are unable to derive conclusions from incomplete knowledge, or cannot manage inconsistent pieces of information.

In (Mandal et al, 2013) Rough Set Theory is used to develop a process of automated disease diagnosis. The theory of rough sets helps in extracting knowledge from uncertain and incomplete data based information within noisy and missing data environment. The theory assumes that we first have necessary information or knowledge of all the objects in the universe with which the objects can be divided into different groups. If we have exactly the same information of two objects then we say that they are indiscernible (similar), i.e., we cannot distinguish them with known knowledge. As we have discussed earlier, the theory of Rough Set can be used to find dependence relationship among data, evaluate the importance of attributes, discover the patterns of data, learn common decision-making rules, reduce all redundant objects and attributes and seek the minimum subset of attributes so as to attain satisfactory classification. Moreover, the rough set reduction algorithms help to approximate the decision classes using possibly large and simplified patterns.

Lung Aden carcinoma often begins in the outer parts of the lungs and as such well-known symptoms of Lung Cancer such as a chronic cough and coughing up blood may be less common until later stages in the disease. Early symptoms of Aden carcinoma that may be overlooked may include fatigue, mild shortness of breath, or achiness in our back, shoulder, or chest.

In this paper, Rough Set Theory has been introduced for the automated diagnosis of Lung Aden carcinoma using the microarray dataset of Aden carcinoma. For analyzing microarray data, it is required to analyze and interpret the vast amount of data that are available, involving the decoding of around 24000–30,000 human genes. High-dimensional feature selection is important for characterizing gene expression data involving many attributes. Data mining methodologies hold promising opportunity in this direction. Microarray experiments produce gene expression patterns that provide dynamic information about cell function. This information is useful while investigating complex interactions which take place within a cell. Therefore, a normal and a cancerous person have different gene expression levels as genes are responsible for each characteristic or disease as the set of genes responding to a certain level of stress in an organism from its microarray data. So if the sets of responsible genes which have the different value of cancerous & normal persons can be identified on the basis of their dependency, then diagnosis can be easily done with high accuracy.

For this purpose the microarray dataset have been taken that contains data related to those who have been diagnosed with cancer and without cancer. Classification Rule Sets have been generated for the dataset using different techniques. If these decision rule set tally with any of the unknown data set, he can be predicted exactly.

This paper discusses how Rough Set theory can be used to analysis microarray data and for generating classification rules from a set of observed data samples of the Aden carcinoma. The Rough Set reduction technique is applied to find all possible reducts of the data which contains the minimal subset of attributes that are associated with a class label for classification.

Rough Sets in Suspected Acute Appendicitis (Carlin et al, 1998)

Acute appendicitis is one of the most common problems in clinical surgery in the western world, and the diagnosis is sometimes difficult even for experienced surgeons. In the decision making process it is likely that two types of diagnostic errors may occur. The first type of error is predicting unnecessary operations and the second one being the delay in diagnosis which may lead to perforations of the appendix. Since perforation of the appendix leads to morbidity and occasionally death, a high rate of unnecessary surgical interventions is usually accepted. Analysis of collected data with the objective of improving various aspects of the diagnosis is therefore potentially valuable. In (Carlin et al, 1998) a synthesis of low level data has been made which leads to describing patients with suspected acute appendicitis. Rough set theory is used here to develop rules that could predict either the presence or absence of acute appendicitis on the basis of observed patient attributes. The same dataset was studied earlier by other researchers using logistic regression. A comparison between both methods of analysis is done and different aspects of their respective strengths and weaknesses are discussed.

Rough Sets in Cost Effective Feature Selection (Srimani et al, 2011)

Generally, people expect an optimal approach for the diagnosis of any disease. Feature selection is a technique that reduces or lessens the number of features. In medical world, for any disease to be diagnosed there are some tests to be performed and each and every test can be considered as a feature. By the process of feature selection, the performance of tests that are highly expensive and irrelevant could be avoided, which in turn reduces the cost associated with the diagnosis and helps the patients and the doctors to a great extent. In processing the medical data, choosing the optimal subset of features is important, not only to reduce the processing cost but also to improve the classification performance of the model built from the selected data. Rough Set method has been recognized to be one of the powerful tools in the medical feature selection. However, the high storage space and the time-consuming computation restrict its application. In Srimani et al (2011) an investigation is made, which certainly helps in cost reduction associated with the diagnosis, which in turn facilitates the patients and doctors considerably.

Optimal Rule Generation in Medical Data (Srimani et al, 2014)

The diseases caused in lung are described in (Srimani et al, 2014) and we quote the details as follows. The features taken into account when discussing the lung abnormalities are; Structure, Intensity, Surrounding tissues, Evolution, Lung, Position and Age. The structure of lungs may be homogeneous, inhomogeneous or reticular. Another important characteristic of lung cancer is the opacity. In radiographs, lung cancer may appear as a solid nodule, a partly solid nodule, or as a non-solid nodule. Many studies have suggested that these non-solid or partly solid nodules represent precursors to an early den carcinoma. Despite their potential clinical significance, nodules in this category may not be detected by radiographs, and most CAD schemes for detecting lung nodules are designed and optimized for the detection of solid nodules. The difference between diseases is determined by the evolve time of opacities. The benign tumors do not change in time, whereas the malignant tumors grow in years or even months. Also, any lung may be affected by pulmonary diseases, but some of them are preponderant in the right lung. Others, such as pulmonary edema appear in both lungs in the same time. The specific parts of the lung being affected are determined by the origin area. However, most pulmonary diseases may be located anywhere in the lung field. On the other hand, the pulmonary edema starts from the lower lobe of the lung and grows up in time. Pneumococcal pneumonia and secondary tuberculosis are located in the upper part of the lung, and the primary tuberculosis generates opacities in the lower lobe as well as around the hilum. To define the positions of the opacities, the lung is divided into smaller regions. As a first step, each lung is divided into 4 parts: supra-clavicular, infraclavicular, median and basal. This is done for a hypothetical chest image with the lung fields of the training images at their mean location, by computing horizontal lines that divide the lung fields in four parts of approximately area. Some ages are bent for specific pulmonary diseases; other illnesses may appear at any age. Pneumococcal pneumonia appears after 1 year of age; bronchopneumonia is more frequent to children and old men; malignant tumors appear at older ages.

The work in (Srimani et al, 2014) opens new avenues for medical decision-making. The proposed idea of combining different decision modes is novel and offers a viable concept for many applications. The primary decision-making and confirmation algorithms when combined generate decisions of high accuracy. The diagnosis by the two algorithms was of perfect accuracy for the clinical data reported in the paper. Additional developments of the algorithms and large scale testing will be the ultimate proof of diagnostic accuracy for lung cancer and other diseases. The help of rough sets is taken here to reduce the number of features which has led to high-accuracy autonomous diagnosis and lower cost. By using data from noninvasive tests for diagnosis, patients' mortality and morbidity risks is significantly reduced.

Rough Sets in Hepatitis Disease Diagnosis (Tomasz, 2012)

The origin of Hepatitis is the Greek word 'hepat' means liver and the suffix 'it is' denotes inflammation and so meaning inflammation of the liver. It can occur due to infectious or non-infectious causes. The five types of hepatitis viruses are common infectious causes of liver inflammation, and some like hepatitis A (HAV), B (HBV) and C (HCV) are more frequently seen infectious agents. Inflammation may leads to death of the liver cells (hepatocytes) which severely compromises normal liver function. Acute HBV Infection (less than 6 months) may resemble the fever, flu, muscle aches, joint pains and general being unwell. Symptoms specifying that states are: dark urine, loss of appetite, nausea, vomiting, jaundice, pain up the liver. Chronic hepatitis B is infection persisting more than 6 months, the clinical features of that state correspond to liver dysfunction, so signs like this may be noticed: enlarged liver, splenomegaly, hepatosplenomegaly, jaundice, weakness, abdominal pain, confusion and abdominal swelling.

In (Tomasz, 2012) prediction system is proposed using rough set techniques to reduce attributes so as to predict hepatitis disease in people based on real biometric data.

Intuitionistic Fuzzy Rough Relation in Some Medical Applications (Gangwal et al, 2012)

The models of uncertainty other than rough sets which have been widely used in medical diagnosis are the fuzzy sets introduced by L.A.Zadeh in 1965 and its extension Intuitionistic fuzzy sets introduced by K.T. Atanassov in 1986. Many expert systems have been developed by using these models and theories. As established by Dubois and Prade in 1990, the hybrid models of rough and fuzzy sets are more efficient than the individual ones and they complement each other. During this process they introduced the hybrid models of rough fuzzy sets and the Fuzzy rough sets. These models have been further extended to put forth Intuitionistic fuzzy rough sets and rough Intuitionistic fuzzy rough sets. These models have been established to be more efficient than the corresponding fuzzy based models.

An application of intuitionistic fuzzy sets in medical diagnosis was made by De et al. 2001, which was extended to the context of intuitionistic fuzzy soft sets by Saikia et al. in 2003. In (Gangwal et al, 2012) a method to study Sanchez's approach of medical diagnosis through max-min-max and min-max-min composition of intuitionistic fuzzy rough relations was proposed. In fact, an algorithm for medical diagnosis using compositions of intuitionistic fuzzy rough relations is presented. A case study has been taken to exhibit the simplicity of the technique.

Rough Sets in Medical Image Segmentation (Hassanien et al, 2001; Senthilkumaran et al, 2009)

Image segmentation is one of the most challenging tasks in image processing and is a very important preprocessing step in the problems in the area of image analysis, computer vision, and pattern recognition. Medical image segmentation is a complex and challenging task due to the intrinsic nature of the images. The brain has a particularly complicated structure and its precise segmentation is very important for detecting tumors, edema, and necrotic tissues, in order to prescribe appropriate therapy. The majority of research in medical image segmentation pertains to its use for MR images, especially in brain imaging. Because of its ability to derive contrast from a number of tissue parameters, many different pulse sequences exist for acquiring MR images. Determining the optimal pulse sequence for obtaining accurate segmentations is therefore an important problem that requires knowledge of the underlying tissue properties of the anatomy to be segmented. Magnetic resonance imaging (MRI) is an important diagnostic imaging technique for the early detection of abnormal changes in tissues and organs. Many methods have been proposed in the literature for Medical image segmentation. Rough Set Theory proposed by Pawlak is a mathematical tool to analyze vagueness and uncertainty inherent in making decision. It does not rely on accessional information out of data set, and it analyses and discovers reliable relation among data just from the point of view of data's discreditable attribute, just based on the concept of an upper and lower approximation of a set, as well as approximation space and models of sets. Based on analysis mentioned above, in (Senthilkumaran et al, 2009) a study is performed on rough set theory in to brain image segmentation. Experimental results demonstrate the superiority of the rough set method in brain image segmentation. The analysis used in this paper seems to be elementary and has not been compared with other available methods. We shall have a better comparison and analysis of various rough set based and their hybrid models in a later section.

Medical Expert System Rules from Clinical Databases Based on Rough Sets (Tsumoto, 1996)

Automated knowledge acquisition is an important research issue to solve the bottleneck problem in developing expert systems. Although many inductive learning methods have been proposed for this purpose, most of the approaches focus only on inducing classification rules. However, medical experts also learn other information important for diagnosis from clinical cases one of the most important problems in developing expert systems is knowledge acquisition from experts. In order to automate this problem, many inductive learning methods, such as induction of decision trees rule induction methods and rough set theory, are introduced and applied to extract knowledge from databases, which shows that these methods are appropriate. However, most of the approaches focus only on inducing classification rules, although medical experts also learn other information important for medical diagnostic procedures. Focusing on their learning procedures, Matsumura et al. propose a diagnostic model, which consists of three reasoning processes, and develop an expert system, called RHINOS (Rule-based Headache and facial pain Information Organizing System). Since RHINOS diagnostic processes are found to be based on the concepts of set theory, it is expected that a set-theoretic approach can describe this diagnostic model and knowledge acquisition procedures. In order to characterize these procedures, the concepts of rough set theory, which clarifies set-theoretic characteristics of the classes over combinatorial patterns of the attributes, precisely discussed. Based on this theory, we develop a program, called PRIMEROSE-REX (Probabilistic Rule Induction Method based on Rough Sets and Resampling methods for Expert systems), which extracts rules for an expert system from clinical databases, and applies resampling methods to the estimation certainty factors of derived rules.r This system is evaluated on the datasets of RHINOS domain. The results obtained show that the proposed method induces RHINOS diagnostic rules correctly from databases and that resampling methods can estimate the performance of these rules and their certainty factors. The RHINOS is an expert system which diagnoses clinical cases on headache or facial pain from manifestations. In this system, a diagnostic model proposed by Matsumura consists of the following three kinds of reasoning processes: exclusive reasoning, inclusive reasoning, and reasoning about complications. First, exclusive reasoning excludes a disease from candidates when a patient does not have a symptom which is necessary to diagnose. Secondly, inclusive reasoning suspects a disease in the output of the exclusive process when a patient has symptoms specific to a disease. Finally, reasoning about complications suspects complications of other diseases when some symptoms which cannot be explained by the diagnostic conclusion are obtained. In (Tsumoto, 1996), a rule induction method is introduced, which extracts not only classification rules but also other medical knowledge needed for diagnosis. This system is evaluated on a clinical database of headache whose experimental results show that the proposed method correctly induces diagnostic rules and estimates the statistical measures of rules.

Rough Sets in Determination of Life Expectancy for Terminally Ill Patients (Herrera et al, 2011)

According to Medicare regulations, a patient should be referred to hospice if his/her life expectancy is less than 6 months. However, despite the well-documented advantages of hospice services, terminally ill patients do not reap the maximum benefits of hospice care with the majority of them being referred to hospice either prematurely or too late. In general, premature hospice referral is translated to patients losing the opportunity to receive potentially effective treatment, which may have prolonged their lives. Conversely, late hospice referral reduces the quality of life for patients and their families. It is apparent that accurate prognostication of life expectancy is of vital importance for all parties involved in the hospice referral process (e.g. patients, their families, and their physicians). In (Herrera et al,2011) a novel knowledge discovery methodology is developed to identify terminally ill patients with life expectancy less than 6 months. The core of the proposed methodology is Rough Set Theory. This methodology provides a classifier that properly discriminates patients into two groups, those who survive at least 180 days after evaluation for hospice referral and those who do not. The rough set tool ROSETTA is used to perform the analysis.

The dataset used in this study consists of the 9105 cases from the SUPPORT (Study to Understand Prognoses and Preferences for Outcomes and Risks of Treatments) prognostic model dataset (http://biostat.mc.vanderbilt.edu/wiki/Main/DataSets). All the variables in the SUPPORT prognostic model are considered as condition attributes, i.e. the physiologic variables along with the diagnosis groups, age, number of days in the hospital before entering the study, presence of cancer, and neurologic function. The SUPPORT model is the "gold standard" model for prognostication of terminally ill patients. The AUC for prediction of survival for 180 days in the SUPPORT study is 0.79, and 0.82 when SUPPORT model is combined with physician's estimates. This initial exercise in applying knowledge discovery methodologies based on rough set theory shows promise in developing a reliable methodology to predict life expectancy.

Rough Set Approach in Dengue Diagnosis (Rissino et al, 2009; Seethalakshmi, 2014)

Dengue is a debilitating viral disease of the tropics, transmitted by mosquitoes, and causing sudden fever and acute pains in the joints. It is a disease caused by a family of viruses that are transmitted by mosquitoes. Dengue is prevalent throughout the tropics and subtropics. Because dengue fever is caused by a virus, there is no specific medicine or antibiotic to treat it. For typical dengue fever, the treatment is directed toward relief of the symptoms (symptomatic treatment).

Dengue virus was first isolated in India in the year 1945; it is endemic in both urban and semi- urban areas. In recent years, Dengue fever is being the most important arthropod borne viral disease due to its potential to outbreak many existing life threatening diseases. The disease manifests as a sudden onset of severe headache, muscle and joint pains (myalgias and arthralgias), fever, and rash. Dengue poses a serious threat in Tropics, because of the year-round presence of Aedes mosquito vectors. As there is no specific treatment for this fever and only pacification of the symptoms is done as treatment, prevention of this disease is of utmost importance. In (Rissino et al, 2009) an attempt in this direction is made in order to increase the effectiveness of disease prevention and control activities of dengue by proposing the development of a predictive model for detecting epidemics. A rough set approach is used for the extraction of rules from data sets which can be used for the purpose. The vagueness and uncertainty in data could be efficiently handled along with the potential reduction of data collected. The selection of significant attributes using rough set technique is very important.

A similar kind of study is made in (Seethalakshmi et al, 2014), where several rules have been deduced for diagnosing the presence or absence of dengue fever from the symptoms.

Drug Side Effects in Clinical Databases based on Rough Set Model (Tsumoto, 1999)

The rules induced from databases can broadly be classified into two categories; namely the deterministic ones and the probabilistic ones. Deterministic rules are certain in character and are supported by positive examples. On the other hand rules are non-deterministic by nature and are supported by both positive and negative samples. That is, both kinds of rules select positively one decision if a case satisfies their conditional parts. However, domain experts do not use only positive reasoning but also negative reasoning, since a domain is not always deterministic. As an example of negative reasoning we may cite the case that when a patient does not have a headache, migraine should not be suspected.

Therefore, negative rules should be induced from databases in order to induce rules which will be easier for domain experts to interpret. Induction of plausible rules will be important for an interaction between domain experts and rule induction methods. In (Tsumoto, 1999) the characteristics of medical reasoning are focused and two kinds of rules, positive rules and negative rules are defined as a model of medical reasoning. Both rules, for which supporting sets correspond to the lower and upper approximation in rough sets, are defined as deterministic rules with two measures, classification accuracy and coverage. Then, algorithms for induction of positive and negative rules are introduced, which are defined as search procedures using accuracy and coverage as evaluation functions. The proposed method was evaluated on medical databases, the experimental results of which show that induced rules correctly represented experts' knowledge and several interesting patterns were discovered (Tsumoto, 1999).

Kidney Failure Data Set using Rough Sets (Tripathy et al, 2013)

Kidneys are the organs that help filter waste products from the blood. They are also involved in regulating blood pressure, electrolyte balance, and red blood cell production in the body.

Symptoms of kidney failure are due to the build-up of waste products in the body that may cause weakness, shortness of breath, lethargy, and confusion. Inability to remove potassium from the bloodstream may lead to abnormal and sudden death. Initially kidney failure may cause no symptoms.

There are numerous causes of kidney failure, and treatment of the underlying disease may be the first step in correcting the kidney abnormality. Some causes of kidney failure are treatable and the kidney function may return to normal. Unfortunately, kidney failure may be progressive in other situations and may be irreversible. Kidney failure is one of the most dangerous diseases throughout the world. Lot of research is being carried out to find out the various absolute reasons of kidney failures. Unknown viruses are the main reason of kidney failure even after kidney transplantation. The paper (Tripathy et al, 2013) provides the basic idea of rough set theory in the knowledge discovery process for medical dataset as a data mining technique. The aim is to apply rough set concepts as the reduction algorithm to search for patterns specific to kidney failure disease. The applications of rough set theory in the field of medicine with respect to kidney failures are initiated and some failure problems are pointed out.

Diagnosing the kidney failure disease at the early stages is a difficult task due to lack of awareness problem with the common man. Many parameters/problems are there which may cause the kidney failure. Blood pressure, diabetic, Sodium, Potassium, Urea, Serum Creatinine, etc. One of the data mining techniques is rough set theory. Rough set theory has been proved to be very useful in real life applications especially in the field of medicine and this is another example such an application in determining the kidney failure in patients from some symptoms. Again, from several symptoms only a few are used in determining the rules selected by attribute reduction.

Hybrid Models in Medical Diagnosis (Tripathy et al, 2014a; Tripathy et al, 2014b; Tripathy et al, 2015a; Tripathy et al 2015b)

We have discussed earlier in this chapter regarding the origin and development of hybrid models. We shall discuss on only two types of hybrid models and their applications in medical diagnosis. These are the rough fuzzy set and the rough intuitionistic fuzzy set. We see that several clustering algorithms have been developed using these concepts and these algorithms are used for image segmentation. These images are of any type including medical images. From the segmented images the information about the diseases can be obtained. First the definitions of these two hybrid models are provided below.

Definition 8: Let (U, R) be an approximation space and $U/R = \{X_1, X_2, \ldots X_n\}$. Then for any $X \in F(U)$, $\underline{R}X$ and $\overline{R}X$, the lower and upper approximations of X with respect to R are fuzzy sets in U/R as defined in (5) and (6). That is, $\underline{R}X, \overline{R}X : U / R \to [0,1]$ such that for all j = 1, 2...n;

(5) $\quad \underline{R}X(X_j) = \inf_{y \in X_j} \mu_X(y)$ and

(6) $\quad \overline{R}X(X_j) = \sup_{y \in X_j} \mu_X(y)$

If $\overline{R}X \neq \underline{R}X$ then the pair $(\underline{R}X, \overline{R}X)$ is called the rough fuzzy set associated with X with respect to R.

We have discussed in earlier that in the intuitionistic fuzzy set approach every member x of a set $X \subseteq U$ is associated with a grade of membership and a grade of non-membership, which we denote by $\mu_X(x)$ and $\nu_X(x)$ respectively. For all x $\in$ U, both $\mu_X(x)$ and $\nu_X(x)$ are real numbers lying in [0, 1], such that $0 \leq \mu_X(x) + \nu_X(x) \leq 1$. The set of all functions from U to J, where J = {(m, n) | m, n $\in$ [0, 1] and $0 \leq m + n \leq 1$}, is called the intuitionistic fuzzy power set of U and is denoted by IF(U). Basically this is the set of all intuitionistic fuzzy subsets defined over U. Similarly, denoting the set of all fuzzy sets over U by F(U), we note that $P(U) \subseteq F(U) \subseteq IF(U)$.

The function $h_X(x) = 1 - \mu_X(x) - \nu_X(x)$ for all $x \in U$ is called the hesitation function for X. It is easy to see that for a fuzzy set X, $\nu_X(x) = 1 - \mu_X(x)$ and $h_X(x) = 0$, for all x $\in$ U. For X, Y $\in$ U,

Extending the notion of rough fuzzy sets introduced by Dubois and Prade, rough intuitionistic fuzzy sets can be defined as follows.

Definition 9: Let (U, R) be an approximation space and $U/R = \{X_1, X_2, \ldots X_n\}$. Then for any $X \in IF(U)$, $\underline{R}X$ and $\overline{R}X$ the lower and upper approximations of X with respect to R are intuitionistic fuzzy sets in U. That is, $\underline{R}X, \overline{R}X : U / R \to [0,1]$, such that for all i=1, 2...n (7) and (8) hold true.

(7) $\quad \mu_{\underline{R}X}(X_i) = \inf_{y \in X_i} \mu_X(y)$ and $\nu_{\underline{R}X}(X_i) = \sup_{y \in X_i} \nu_X(y)$

(8) $\quad \mu_{\overline{R}X}(X_i) = \sup_{y \in X_i} \mu_X(y)$ and $\nu_{\overline{R}X}(X_i) = \inf_{y \in X_i} \nu_X(y)$

We define $\underline{R}X = (\mu_{\underline{R}X}, \nu_{\underline{R}X})$ and $\overline{R}X = (\mu_{\overline{R}X}, \nu_{\overline{R}X})$. The pair $(\underline{R}X, \overline{R}X)$ is called a rough intuitionistic fuzzy set associated with X.

Clustering is the process of putting similar objects into groups called clusters and putting dissimilar objects into different clusters. In contrast to classification where labeling of a large set of training tuples patterns is necessary to model the groups, clustering starts with partitioning the objects into groups first and then labeling the small number of groups. The large amount of data collected across multiple sources makes it practically impossible to manually analyze them and select the data that is required to perform a particular task. Hence, a mechanism that can classify the data according to some criteria in which only the classes of interest are selected and rests are rejected is essential. Clustering techniques are applied in the analysis of statistical data used in fields such as machine learning, pattern recognition, image analysis, information retrieval, and bioinformatics and is a major task in exploratory data

Figure 1.

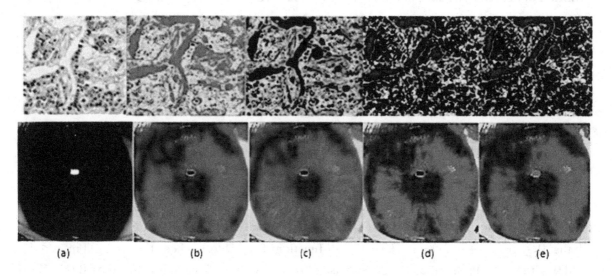

mining. A wide number of clustering algorithms have been proposed to suit the requirements in each field of its application.

Clustering of real life data for analysis has gained popularity and imprecise methods or their hybrid approaches has attracted many researchers of late. In 2013, rough intuitionistic fuzzy c-means algorithm was introduced and studied by Tripathy et al and it was found to be superior to all other algorithms in this family. Replacing the Euclidean distance used in the above algorithms for computing the distance by kernel functions some algorithms have been put forth like the kernel based fuzzy c-means (KFCM) and the kernel based rough c-means (KRCM)] were introduced. Very recently, the kernel based rough fuzzy c-means was introduced and studied by Bhargav and Tripathy. In 2014 kernel based rough fuzzy algorithm was put forth by (Bhargav et al, 2013). A comparative analysis over standard datasets and images has established the superiority of this algorithm over its corresponding standard algorithm. In (Tripathy et al 2013) a kernel based rough intuitionistic fuzzy c-means algorithm was introduced and it was shown that it is superior to all the algorithms in the sequel; i.e. both normal and the kernel based algorithms. Kernel based clustering helps in rectifying the problem of nonlinear separating surfaces among clusters. It has been observed that KRIFCM has the best performance among all these methods.

The following figures show the effect of different clustering algorithms in image segmentation for cancer blood cells and iris infection.

There are several types of kernels available in literature. These are the Gaussian kernel, the RBF kernel and the hyper tangent kernel. The effect of these kernels when combined with the basic clustering algorithms instead of the Euclidean distance in image segmentation in general and medical images in particular was studied in (Tripathy et al, 2015b). It has been established there that the hyper tangent kernel works better than the other kernels for images in general.

CONCLUSION

Rough sets represent models of uncertainty and as medical systems are having inherent impreciseness it is a suitable model to represent, analyze and deduce conclusions through studies of such systems. There is a wide repository of research in this direction with numerous real life applications in addition to the development of general theory. In this chapter we presented both. Rough sets have been extended in many directions to extend its modeling power and make it more useful. One such step is its hybridization with other models of uncertainty like the fuzzy sets and intuitionistic fuzzy sets. These hybrid models have been established to be more efficient than the individual models. We also discussed some of these applications of these models in the field of medical diagnosis mostly through image segmentation and pattern recognition. We have collected the work done, analysed them and presented here.

FUTURE WORKS

- It would be a great interest to extend the two algorithms proposed in (Oliviu, 2008) to larger databases of radiographs, involving more data mining techniques. On the other hand, a combination of rough set theory and k-NN algorithm may lead to interesting results.
- As mentioned in (Tomasz, 2012) further work is necessary for increasing overall procedure accuracy and deeper data analysis as well in hepatitis prediction, may be through a deeper look at application of rough set theory which may be required at more number of stages of the procedure.
- The baseline model using dynamic reducts used in (Herrera, 2011) presents several opportunities for improvement. The use of ROSETTA software constraints the size of the training set. So alternative approaches which do not need to use this software can be thought of.
- Instead of weighing all the conditions equally a careful weighting of the attributes by consulting an expert may greatly improve the classification accuracy of the approach. Also, it is important to remember that regardless of the accuracy of any classifier, medical decisions must take into account the individual patient preferences towards alternative forms of treatments. Therefore, a patient-centric decision support system to facilitate the hospice referral process can be incorporated.
- The notions of extended positive and extended negative rules were introduced in (Tsumoto, 1999). It is proposed there to check whether the combination of extended positive and negative rules will outperform that of positive and negative deterministic rules.
- The result analysis done in (Tripathy et al, 2013) is an elementary one and considers only a small dataset. A more exhaustive study is necessary in this direction by taking large datasets with more attributes and tuples.

REFERENCES

Ahmed, Z., Salama, M. A., Hefny, H., & Hassanien, A. E. (2012). A Hepatitis C Virus Data Sets, Rough Sets-Based Rules Generation Approach. *Proceedings of AMLTA 2012, CCIS*, (Vol. *322*, pp. 52–59).

Ahn, J. Y., Han, K. S., Oh, S. Y., & Lee, C. D. (2011). An Application of Interval-Valued Intuitionistic Fuzzy Sets for Medical Diagnosis of Headache. *International Journal of Innovative Computing, Information, & Control, 7*(5B), 2755–2762.

Ali, R., Hussain, J., Siddiqi, M. H., & Lee, S. (2015). H2RM: A Hybrid Rough Set Reasoning Model for Prediction and Management of Diabetes Mellitus. *Sensors (Basel, Switzerland), 15*(7), 15921–15951. doi:10.3390/s150715921 PMID:26151207

Anouncia, S. M., Clara Madonna, L. J., & Jeevitha, P. & Nandhini. (2013). Design of a Diabetic Diagnosis System Using Rough Sets. *Cybernetics and Information Technologies, 13*(3), 124–139.

Arafat, H., Barakat, S., & Goweda, A. F. (2012). Using Intelligent Techniques for Breast Cancer Classification. *International Journal of Emerging Trends & Technology in Computer Science, 1*(3), 26–36.

Atanassov, K. T. (1986). Intuitionistic Fuzzy Sets. *Fuzzy Sets and Systems, 20*(1), 87–96. doi:10.1016/S0165-0114(86)80034-3

Carlin, U. S., Komoroski, J., & Ohrn, A. (1998): Rough set analysis of medical datasets and a case of patients with suspected acute Appendicitis. *Proceedings of theWorkshop on Intelligent Data Analysis in medicine and pharmacologyECAI 98* (pp. 1 -11).

Chena, C. B., & Wang, L. Y. (2006). Rough set-based clustering with refinement using Shannon's entropy theory. *Computers & Mathematics with Applications (Oxford, England), 52*(10–11), 1563–1576. doi:10.1016/j.camwa.2006.03.033

Choubey, D. K., Paul, S., & Bhattachrjee, J. (2014). Soft Computing Approaches for Diabetes Disease Diagnosis: A Survey. *International Journal of Applied Engineering Research, 9*(21), 11715–11726.

Cyran, K. A., & Mrzek, A. (2001). Rough sets in hybrid methods for pattern recognition. *International Journal of Intelligent Systems, 16*(2), 149–168. doi:10.1002/1098-111X(200102)16:2<149::AID-INT10>3.0.CO;2-S

Deja, W. A., & Paszek, P. (2003). Applying rough set theory to multi stage medical diagnosing. *Fundamenta Informaticae, 54*(4), 387–408.

Dubois, D., & Prade, H. (1990). Rough fuzzy sets and fuzzy rough sets. *International Journal of General Systems, 17*(2–3), 191–208. doi:10.1080/03081079008935107

Duch, W., Krzysztof Gr, ., Adamczak, R., Grudzinski, K., & Hippe, Z. S. (2001). Rules for Melanoma Skin Cancer Diagnosis. *KOSYR, 2001*, 59–68.

Gangwal, C., & Bhaumik, R. N. (2012). Intuitionistic Fuzzy Rough Relation in Some Medical Applications. *International Journal of Advanced Research in Computer Engineering & Technology, 1*(6), 28–32.

Ghosh, J. (2012): Modeling Intelligent System for Medical Diagnosis, Ph. D Thesis, The University of Burdwan, West Bengal, India.

Hassanien, A. E., Abraham, A., Peters, J. F. & Kacprzyk, J. (2001). Rough Sets in Medical Imaging: Foundations and Trends.

Hassanien, A. E., Abraham, A., Peters, J. F. & Kacprzyk, J. (2009). Rough Sets in Medical Informatics Applications, Application of Soft Computing. Advances in intelligent and soft computing, 58, 23-30.

Hassanien, A. E., Ali, J. M., & Hajime, N. (2004): Detection of spiculated masses in mammograms based on fuzzy image processing. *Proceedings of the7th Int. Conference on Artificial Intelligence and Soft Computing*, LNAI (Vol. *3070, pp.* 1002–1007). doi:10.1007/978-3-540-24844-6_156

Herrera, E. G., Ali, Y., Athanasius, T., Barnes, L. E., & Benjamin, D. (2011, August 30 - September 3). Rough Set Theory based Prognostication of Life Expectancy for Terminally Ill Patients. *Proceedings of the 33rd Annual International Conference of the IEEE EMBS*, Boston, Massachusetts USA (pp. 6438-6441).

Hung, X. M., & Zhang, Y. H. (2003). A new application of rough set to ECG recognition. *Proceeding of theInternational Conference on Machine Learning and Cybernetics* (Vol. 3, pp. 1729–1734).

Hyvarinen, A., & Oja, E. (1999). *Independent component analysis: A tutorial (Technical report)*. Laboratory of Computer and Information Science, Helsinki University of Technology.

Kobashi, S., Kondo, K., & Hata, Y. (2004): Rough sets based medical image segmentation with connectedness. *Proceedings of the 5th Int. Forum on Multimedia and Image processing* (pp. 197-202).

Mandal, S. & Saha, G. (2013): Rough Set Theory based Automated Disease Diagnosis using Lung Aden carcinoma as a Test Case. *The SIJ Transactions on Computer Science Engineering & its Applications (CSEA)*, 1(3), 75-82.

Mandal, S., Saha, G., & Pal, R. K. (2013). An Approach towards Automated Disease Diagnosis & Drug Design Using Hybrid Rough-Decision Tree from Microarray Dataset. *J. Comput Sci Syst Biol*, 6(6), 337–343. doi:10.4172/0974-7230.1000130

Mitra, S., Mitra, M., & Chaudhuri, B. B. (2006). A rough set based inference engine for ECG classification. *IEEE Transactions on Instrumentation and Measurement*, 55(6), 2198–2206. doi:10.1109/TIM.2006.884279

Mohabey, A., & Ray, A. K. (2000): Fusion of rough set theoretic approximations and FCM for color image segmentation. *Proceedings of theIEEE Int. Conference on Systems, Man, and Cybernetics* (Vol. 2, pp. 1529–1534). doi:10.1109/ICSMC.2000.886073

Ohrn, A. (1999). Discernibility and Rough Sets in Medicine: Tools and Applications. Norwegian University of Science and Technology, Trondheim, Norway.

Oliviu, M. (2008). Applying Rough Sets Algorithm for Radiography Diagnosis. *Proceedings of the9th International Conference on Development and Application Systems*, Suceava, Romania (pp. 272-277).

Pawlak, Z. (1982). Rough Sets. *International Journal of Computer and Information Sciences*, *11*(5), 341–356. doi:10.1007/BF01001956

Podraza, R., Dominik, A. and Walkiewicz, M. (2003). Decision support system for medical applications. In *Applied Simulation and Modeling*.

Radwan, E., & Assiri, A. M. A. (2013). Thyroid Diagnosis based Technique on Rough Sets with Modified Similarity Relation. *International Journal of Advanced Computer Science and Applications*, *4*(10), 120–126. doi:10.14569/IJACSA.2013.041019

Revett, K., Gorunescu, F., Gorunescu, M., & E-Darzi, E. (2005, November 21-24). A breast cancer diagnosis system: a combined approach using rough sets and probabilistic neural networks. Proceedings of Marius Ene2, EUROCON 2005, Serbia & Montenegro, Belgrade (pp. 1124-1127).

Rissino, S., Martins, H. G., & Torres, G. L. (2009). Applying Rough Set Classification in Dengue Diagnosis. *Proceedings of the First International workshop on rough sets theory (RST09)*, Milano, Italy (pp. 25-27).

Saleha, R., Haider, J. N., & Danish, N. (2002, March 9–12). Rough Intuitionistic Fuzzy Set. *Proc. of 8th Int. conf. on Fuzzy Theory and Technology*, Durham, North Carolina, USA.

Seethalakshmi, P., & Vengataasalam, S. (2014). Application of Rough Set Approach in Dengue Diagnosis. *Applied Mathematical Sciences*, *8*(127), 6313–6324.

Senthilkumaran, N., & Rajesh, R. (2009). A Study on Rough Set Theory for Medical Image Segmentation. *International Journal of Recent Trends in Engineering*, *2*(2), 236–238.

Slezak, D. (2000). Various approaches to reasoning with frequency-based decision reducts: a survey. In L. Polkowski, S. Tsumoto, & T. Y. Lin (Eds.), *Rough Sets in Soft Computing and Knowledge Discovery: New Developments*. Physica Verlag.

Sridevi T. & Murugan A. (2012): Rough set theory based attribute reduction for breast cancer Diagnosis. Indian J. Innovations Dev., 1(5), 309 – 313.

Srimani, P. K. a& Manjula, S. K. (2014). Knowledge Discovery in Medical Data by using Rough Set Rule Induction Algorithms. *Indian Journal of Science and Technology*, *7*(7), 905–915.

Srimani, P. K., & Koti, M. S. (2011). The Impact of Rough Set Approach on Medical Diagnosis for Cost Effective Feature Selection. *International Journal of Current Research*, *3*(12), 175–178.

Srimani, P. K., & Koti, M. S. (2014). Rough set (RS) approach for optimal rule generation in medical data. *International Journal of Conceptions on Computing and Information Technology*, *2*(2), 9–13.

Swiniarski, R., & Skowron, A. (2003). Rough set methods in feature selection and recognition. *Pattern Recognition Letters*, *24*(6), 833–849. doi:10.1016/S0167-8655(02)00196-4

Swiniarski, R. W., Lim, H. J., Shin, Y. H., & Skowron, A. (2006). Independent component analysis, principal component analysis and rough set in hybrid mammogram classification. *Proceedings of theInternational Conference on Image Processing, Computer Vision, and Pattern Recognition* (pp. 640–645).

Tomasz, K. (2012). Hepatitis disease diagnosis using Rough Set- modification of the preprocessing algorithm. Proceedings of the*ICTIC 12* (pp. 47–50).

Tripathy, B. K., Acharjya, D. P., & Cynthia, V. (2011). A Framework for Intelligent Medical Diagnosis Using Rough Set With Formal Concept Analysis. *International Journal of Artificial Intelligence & Applications*, *2*(2), 45–66. doi:10.5121/ijaia.2011.2204

Tripathy, B. K., & Govindarajulu, K. (2013). Data mining a kidney failure data set using Rough Sets. *International Journal of Electronics and Computer Science Engineering, 2*(3), 949–954.

Tripathy, B. K., & Mittal, D. (2015b): Efficiency Analysis of Kernel Functions in Uncertainty Based C-Means Algorithms. *Presentation at the International Conference on Advances in Computing, Communications and Informatics*, Kochi.

Tripathy, B.K., Tripathy, A. & Govindarajulu, K. (2014b). Possibilistic rough fuzzy C-means algorithm in data clustering and image segmentation. *Proceedings of the IEEE ICCIC2014* (pp. 981-986).

Tripathy, B. K., Tripathy, A., & Govindarajulu, K. (2015a). On PRIFCM Algorithm for Data Clustering, Image Segmentation and Comparative Analysis. *Presentation at the IACC conference*, Bangalore (pp. 12 -13).

Tripathy, B.K., Tripathy, A., Govindarajulu, K. & Bhargav, R. (2014a). On kernel Based rough Intuitionistic Fuzzy C-means algorithm and a comparative analysis. *Smart innovation systems and technologies, 27*, 349-359.

Tsumoto, S. (1999). Discovery of Knowledge about Drug Side Effects in Clinical Databases based on Rough Set Model. AAAI Technical Report SS-99-01. Retrieved from www.aaai.org

Tsumoto, S. (2004). Mining diagnostic rules from clinical databases using rough sets and medical diagnostic model. *Information Sciences, 162*(2), 65–80. doi:10.1016/j.ins.2004.03.002

Tsumoto, S. & Tanaka, H. (1996). Automated Discovery of Medical Expert System Rules from Clinical Databases based on Rough Sets. *Data Mining Applications*, 1996, 63-69.

Wei, M. H., Cheng, C. H., Huang, C. S., & Chiang, P. C. (2001). Discovering medical quality of total hip arthroplasty by rough set classifier with imbalanced class, Quality & Quantity. *International Journal of Methodology, 47*(3), 1761–1779.

Widz, S., Revett, K., & Slezak, D. (2004): Application of rough set based dynamic parameter optimization to MRI segmentation. *Proceedings of the23rd International Conference of the North American Fuzzy Information Processing Society* (pp. 440–445). doi:10.1109/NAFIPS.2004.1336323

Wojcik, Z. (1987). Rough approximation of shapes in pattern recognition. *Computer Vision Graphics and Image Processing, 40*(2), 228–249. doi:10.1016/S0734-189X(87)80117-2

Xu, D., & Li, F. (2010). Research and Application of CT Image Mining based on Rough Sets Theory and Association Rules. Proceedings of the 2010 3rd IEEE International Conference on Computer Science and Information Technology (ICCSIT) (pp. 392-394).

Zadeh, L. A. (1965). Fuzzy sets. *Information and Control, 8*(3), 338–353. doi:10.1016/S0019-9958(65)90241-X

Zhang, H., Wang, Y., Wang, L., Lin, Y., & Liu, P. (2013). A Hierarchical Diagnosis Model for Syndrome Prediction in TCM of Post-Hepatitic Cirrhosis. *International Journal of Integrative Medicine, 1*(24), 1–7.

KEY TERMS AND DEFINITIONS

Attribute: An attribute defines a characteristic feature of elements in a dataset. These can be numerical or categorical.

Core: This is the minimum knowledge in a dataset. In factfact, it is the intersection of all the reducts in a dataset.

Decision Table: A decision table is an information table in which the set of attributes is divided into two categories called the condition attributes and the decision attributes.

Fuzzy Set: This is yet another imprecise model introduced by L.A. Zadeh in 1965, where the concept of membership function was introduced. Unlike crisp sets here the belongingness of elements to a fuzzy set are graded in the sense that these values can lie in the interval [0, 1].

Reduct: A reduct is a group of attributes which form a subset of a given set of attributes such that the elements in it cannot be further reduced without losing the representational power of the set. In the rough set terminologyterminology, we say that it is a minimum knowledge under the context.

Rough Set: It is an imprecise model introduced by Z. Pawlak in 1982, where sets are approximated by two crisp sets with respect to equivalence relations. A set is rough with respect to an equivalence relation or not depending upon whether the lower and upper approximations are not equal or otherwise. Several extensions of this basic model also exist.

Rule: A rule is basically an "and...or" rule in the sense that it is an implication where the antecedent part is the conjunction of attributes where aswhereas the consequent part is the disjunction of attributes. They provide some values of the attributes in the antecedent which leads to specific values of the attributes in the consequent part.

Chapter 9
Application of Uncertainty Models in Bioinformatics

B.K. Tripathy
VIT University, India

R.K. Mohanty
VIT University, India

Sooraj T.R.
VIT University, India

ABSTRACT

This chapter provides the information related to the researches enhanced using uncertainty models in life sciences and biomedical Informatics. The main emphasis of this chapter is to present the general ideas for the time line of different uncertainty models to handle uncertain information and their applications in the various fields of biology. There are many mathematical models to handle vague data and uncertain information such as theory of probability, fuzzy set theory, rough set theory, soft set theory. Literatures from the life sciences and bioinformatics have been reviewed and provided the different experimental & theoretical results to understand the applications of uncertain models in the field of bioinformatics.

INTRODUCTION

Bioinformatics is the application of computer technology to the management of biological information. Computers are used to gather, store, analyze and integrate biological and genetic information which can then be applied to gene-based drug discovery and development. The need for Bioinformatics capabilities has been precipitated by the explosion of publicly available genomic information resulting from the Human Genome Project.

The goal of this project – determination of the sequence of the entire human genome (approximately three billion base pairs) – will be reached by the year 2002. The science of Bioinformatics, which is the melding of molecular biology with computer science, is essential to the use of genomic information in understanding human diseases and in the identification of new molecular targets for drug discovery.

DOI: 10.4018/978-1-5225-0427-6.ch009

Figure 1. The cost of sequencing has fallen from $100,000,000/genome in 2001 to $10,000/genome in 2011. The cost of genomics is estimated to fall to $2,000 a genome within the next few years.
Courtesy of the National Human Genome Research Institute

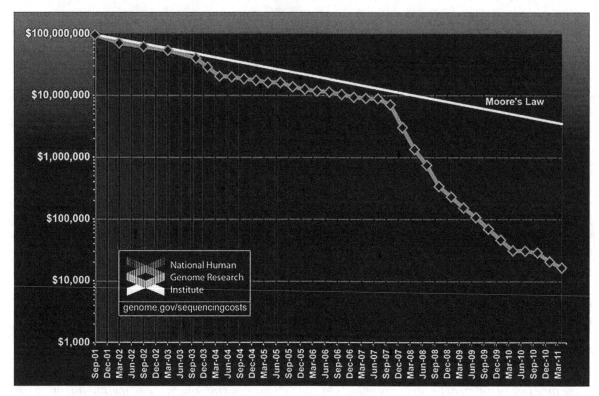

Many times biotechnology and bioinformatics are taken as synonymous. But, bioinformatics combines molecular biology, computer science, mathematics, statistics and engineering to store, maintain, organize, process and analyze biological and chemical data in order to advance medicine and healthcare whereas biotechnology brings together biological sciences with engineering technologies to manipulate living organisms and biological systems to produce products that advances healthcare, medicine, agriculture, food, pharmaceuticals and environmental control.

This analytical branch of genomic research mines large sets of data to answer new research questions and throw light on older ones. Bioinformatics analysis will support the next revolution in genomic science to address fundamental areas of natural history research (Schuh, 2005) including:

- Basic investigations of the phylogenetic relatedness of all life.
- Tracing the geographic distribution of biodiversity across varied environments and regions.
- Unravelling the developmental history of organisms from initial embryonic cellular stages of life to the functional complexity of mature multi-cellular individuals.
- Defining population-level processes of natural selection.
- Initiating landscape-based environmental comparisons of varied habitats around the world.
- Speeding-up species discovery.

Figure 2. DNA barcodes

Bioinformatics involves the manipulation, searching and data mining of DNA sequence data. The development of techniques to store and search DNA sequences (Moein et.al, 2008) have led to widely applied advances in computer science, especially string searching algorithms, machine learning and database theory. In other applications such as text editors, even simple algorithms for this problem usually suffice, but DNA sequences because these algorithms to exhibit near-worst case behaviour due to their small number of distinct characters. Data sets representing entire genomes' worth of DNA sequences, such as those produced by the Human Genome Project (Park et.al, 2008), are difficult to use without annotations, which label the locations of genes and regulatory elements on each chromosome. Regions of DNA sequence that have the characteristic patterns associated with protein or RNA coding genes can be identified by gene finding algorithms (Samatsu et.al, 2008), which allow researchers to predict the presence of particular gene products in an organism even before they have been isolated experimentally.

DNA barcodes (Figure 2) consist of a standardized short sequence of DNA (400-800 bp) that in principle should be easily generated and characterized for all species on the planet. The Blue and Yellow Macaw's barcode is reflected above with greens, reds, and blues representing the nucleotide bases, Image of Ara ararauna, the Blue and Yellow Macaw by Luc Viatour and courtesy of EOL. Image of Blue and Yellow Macaw barcode is courtesy of CBOL.

Bioinformatics combines the multi-disciplinary area such as computer science, biology, physical and chemical principles, designing of tools utilized for the analysis and modelling of large biological data sets, chronic diseases management, learning of molecular computing and cloning etc. (Aversa et.al, 2002). The field of bioinformatics is intensifying for research and development of new technology (Cui & Blockley, 1990). Now fuzzy inference technologies are repeatedly applied in bioinformatics. For example, increase the suppleness of protein motifs and learn about the distinction among polynucleotide, utilizing the fuzzy adaptive resonance theory for the analysis of experimental expression data, applying the dynamic programming algorithm for the alignment of the sequences based on fuzzy recast, fuzzy k-nearest neighbours algorithm used to identify the proteins sub-cellular locations from their dipeptide composition, applying fuzzy c-means and partitioning method for characteristic cluster relationship values of genes, analysis of gene appearance data, functional and ancestral relationships between amino acids with the help of fuzzy alignment method, fuzzy classification rules generated by neural network architecture for the analysis of affairs between genes and decipher of a genetic set-up to process microarray images, use of fuzzy vector filtering framework in the classification of amino acid sequences in to different super families etc.

The latest biotechnology ensures pristine genome preservation for sequencing, and barcode identification. As advances in technology have greatly lowered the cost and accelerated the pace of genomic research, demands on museums for specimens with intact genomes have soared.

We are at a new junction where the tree of life—the biosphere with evolutionary structure–can be collected and preserved at the level of the genome. This global seed bank for all life will prove invaluable to our deeper understanding of life and the potential applications for human health. Biotechnology will assure that these genomic samples are preserved and not degraded from field to freezer to sequencing to safeguard this critical investment in the future of biodiversity research.

Molecular biology represents a fascinating and important application area for machine learning techniques in general and rough set-based methods in particular. Although biology traditionally has been a reductionistic discipline focusing on breaking living systems into increasingly smaller parts, and on studying these parts separately, the discovery of the remarkable order and structure of these systems at the molecular level has suggested the possibility of studying their holistic molecular operation. However, it is only in the last 10 years that technological breakthroughs have made it possible to obtain large scale data that can facilitate such research. The first complete genome was sequenced in 1995 (the bacteria Haemophilus influenzae Rd] and has been followed by many others (including the human genome, see http://www.genomesonline.org). Although important, sequence information only gives us the static code inherited from individual to individual. Other insights such as identifying the functional elements (i.e. genes) of the genomic sequence, understanding how and under which conditions genes are transcribed and translated into protein(s) (i.e. gene regulation) and determining the tasks/interactions carried out by each protein (i.e. protein function) require data on the dynamic operation of biological systems under different conditions. One example of a technology that provides this type of data is DNA microarrays that can measure the transcription levels of thousands of genes in parallel (Duggan et.al, 1999). Moreover, developing technology will soon be able to directly perform similar large-scale measurements of proteins i.e.proteomics (Hvidsten & Komorowski, 2007).

High-throughput experimental technologies have created the need for computer programs and techniques to analyse the resulting data. The field of bioinformatics has thus developed from being a discipline mainly associated with sequence databases and sequence analysis to a computational science that uses different types of data to describe biology (Aversa et.al, 2002). The ultimate goal of this research is to allow computational simulations of complex living systems. This will presumable require that we determine the function of all sequenced proteins (functional genomics) and that we understand the general principles orchestrating protein regulation and interaction (systems biology).

FUZZY SET

The concept of fuzzy logic starts with the fuzzy set. Fuzzy set elements can have partial memberships in a set. which is used in processing of information from the field of molecular biology (for analysing various properties of the transcriptome and proteome of several organism), clinical practice guidelines, automobile and other vehicle subsystems (automatic transmission), pattern recognition, image processing, remote sensing, language filters etc. Fuzzy inference is an effective tool for the expression of guideline recommendations, and that it can be useful for the management of imprecision and uncertainty, fuzzy logic (FL) as an approach of logic-based modelling with the easy interpretability of Boolean models but significant advantages including the ability to encode intermediate values for inputs and outputs. This review will help the researchers to work on new ideas after knowing the old & current themes.

Since Zadeh (1965) introduced fuzzy sets in 1965, many approaches (Hsu & Wu 2010, Pei et.al 2010, Samatsu et.al 2008) and theories (Atanassov, 1986; Atanassov & Gargov, 1989; Pawlak, 1991; Molodtsov, 1999; Buckley, 2006) treating imprecision and uncertainty have been proposed. Some of these theories, such as intuitionistic fuzzy sets, interval-valued fuzzy sets, and interval-valued intuitionistic fuzzy sets are extensions of fuzzy set theory and the others try to handle imprecision and uncertainty in different ways (Park et.al 2008). The concept of intuitionistic fuzzy set has been introduced by Atanassov (1986) as a generalization concept of fuzzy set. Since the first public statement of this notion was made in 1983, intuitionistic fuzzy set has become a popular topic of investigation in the Fuzzy Set community (Buckley 2006, Pei et.al 2010). Later, Turksen introduced the concept of interval valued fuzzy set and Atanassov and Gargov (1989) introduced the concept of interval valued intuitionistic fuzzy set as a generalization of the notion of intuitionistic fuzzy set. The fundamental characteristic of the interval valued fuzzy set and interval valued intuitionistic fuzzy set is that the values of its membership and non-membership function are intervals rather than exact numbers. Let us review the basic concepts of fuzzy set.

Fuzzy Logic and Control of Inspired Oxygen in Ventilated New-Born Infants

Development of chronic lung disease in new born infant due to the toxicity in the oxygen, at this stage mechanical ventilation is required. Insufficient repairs of tissue oxygenation in premature infants are concerned with the development of retinopathy of prematurity (Ahn et.al 2008). For the control delivery of oxygen, ventilated newborns has kept in neonatal intensive care to avoid the effects of too much or too little oxygen. The procedure to provide the control oxygen to mechanically ventilated newborn infants is quite intensive but it must balance sufficient tissue oxygenation against possible toxic effects of oxygen exposure. Many researches in the area of computational programming increase our ability to control the mechanical ventilation, while a very small number of studies are in continuation related to the newborn infants. Fuzzy controller system can be executed to adjust the inspired oxygen concentration in the ventilated newborn. The rules generated by neonatologists are utilized by the controller, which functions in real-time. To check the efficacy of this controller, currently setup a clinical trial at Children's Hospital, Boston, MA, in the neonatal intensive care unit (NICU).

Fuzzy Logic and Anaesthetics

The aesthetic experts manage the consciousness and unconsciousness, pain and its relief, movement of muscles and relaxation during prescribed time range. In the operation theatre anesthetized patient is part of a 'feedback circuit' for the period of an operation. During examine the consistency of the patients, if any change occurs in blood pressure and respiratory rate then regulate the ventilation and modify the drug dosages. In this process anaesthetist will play the role of decision-maker and controller, who will make his own decision to perform best. In a series of ventilated patients Schaublin and co-workers tested a fuzzy logic program that monitored CO_2 and end tidal CO_2 and altered ventilator frequency and tidal volume to keep end-tidal CO_2 at a desired level. The performance of system was not less well than the anaesthetist usual practice under similar conditions. Fuzzy logic have been applied to measure the heart rate, tidal volume, breathing frequency and oxygen saturation, to establish the requirement for pressure support ventilation in intensive care.

Fuzzy Logic in Medicine

In the field of medicine fuzzy logic play an imperative role (Sanchez 1979, Schuh 2005) some examples in which fuzzy logic have been implemented are as follows: Detection of diabetic retinopathy in the early hours and analyse diabetic neuropathy, to decide the suitable lithium dosage, brain tissue volume have been calculated from magnetic resonance imaging (MRI) and to analyse functional MRI data. To identify breast cancer, prostate cancer, or lung cancer, to support the diagnosis of tumours in central nervous systems (astrocytic tumours), to distinguish benign skin gashes from malignant melanomas, to visualize nerve fibres in the human brain, to signify the quantitative estimation of drug use, to study the auditory P50 component in schizophrenia, to learn fuzzy epidemics, to formulate decisions in nursing.

APPLICATION OF FUZZY SETS IN MEDICAL DIAGNOSIS

Now a day uncertainty models like fuzzy sets, rough sets, soft sets are used in medical diagnostic process. In this section, we discuss an application of IFS. In (1979) Sanchez represented physicians medical knowledge as a fuzzy relation between symptoms and diseases. Let $S = \{S_1 \dots S_m\}$, $D = \{D_1 \dots D_n\}$ and $P = \{P_1 \dots P_q\}$ denote the sets of symptoms, diseases and patients respectively. Two fuzzy relations are defined as

$$Q = \left\{ \left\langle (p,s), \mu_Q(p,s), v_Q(p,s) \right\rangle \mid (p,s) \in P \times S \right\}$$

$$R = \left\{ \left\langle (s,d), \mu_R(s,d), v_R(s,d) \right\rangle \mid (s,d) \in S \times D \right\}$$

where $\mu_Q(p,s)$ and $v_Q(p,s)$ indicate the degrees for patient's symptoms. i.e, the degrees are the relationship between patient and symptoms. In other words, $\mu_Q(p,s)$ indicates the degree to which the symptom s appears in patient p and $v_Q(p,s)$ indicates the degree to which the symptom s does not appear in patient p. Similarly, $\mu_R(s,d)$ indicates the degree to which the symptom s confirms the presence of disease d and $v_R(s,d)$ the degree to which the symptom s does not confirm the presence of disease d. The composition of R and Q ($T = R \circ Q$)for disease describes the state of patients in terms of disease as a fuzzy relation from P to D given by the membership function and non-membership function as follows.

$$\mu_T(p,d) = \max_s \left\{ \min \left[\mu_Q(p,s), \mu_Q(s,d) \right] \right\}$$

$$v_T(p,d) = \max_s \left\{ \min \left[v_Q(p,s), v_Q(s,d) \right] \right\} \text{ for all } p \in P \text{ and } d \in D$$

The terms used in algorithms are:

1. Interview chart
2. Aggregate operator
3. Distance Measure.

Approach

The approach is divided into four stages:

Stage 1: Collect the patient's degrees and confirmability degrees (The relationship between symptoms and diseases) for patient's symptoms. Confirmability degrees are shown in the interview chart. Patient degrees (Relationship between patient and symptoms) are assigned by the physician.

Stage 2: Calculate the interval-valued intuitionistic fuzzy weighted arithmetic average operator of the patient's degrees and confirmability degrees respectively using aggregate operator.

Stage 3: Calculate the distance using interval-valued intuitionistic fuzzy weighted arithmetic average operator calculated in stage 2.

Stage 4: Determine the disease of patient based on the distance.

Interview Chart: A diagnosis procedure usually starts off with an interview of patient and doctor (Moein et.al). Therefore, the screening method using questionnaire is helpful in diagnosis of headache and interview chart is a leading part. In our earlier work, we developed an interview chart for preliminary diagnosis of headache, where the qualitative data from the interview chart were obtained and then quantified by dual scaling. However, the method has some problems such as loss of information and insufficient use of physician's knowledge. In the next study, an extended version of our previous interview chart has been implemented. In the chart, we reformed the fuzzy degrees and added some composite symptoms. The chart consisted of 22, 17 and 14 items (symptoms) for the three types of headache (migraine, tension and cluster), respectively. The chart was investigated by 5 physicians. We estimated headache labels of patients using the information obtained from the chart. Two interview charts above had an exact number in [0; 1] as the membership/non-membership degrees. In this study, we developed an improved interview chart, an interval-valued version of the interview chart developed in our previous studies, based on physician's knowledge. The chart consists of $23(M_1 \sim M_{23})$; $17(T_1 \sim T_{17})$ and $15(C_1 \sim C_{15})$ items for the three types of headache, respectively. Table 1 is the interview chart for migraine type. Each item has confirmability degrees with the relation among symptoms and the three types of headache, and has an interval-value in [0; 1] as the degrees. In the chart, 7 items $(M_{21} \sim M_{23}, T_{16} \sim T_{17}, C_{14} \sim C_{15})$ are composite symptoms. Composite symptom is a meaningful item for diagnosis of headache. For example, if a patient simultaneously has symptoms M_5, M_8 and M_{15}, he/she has a composite symptom and the symptoms are displayed in the composite item M_{22}. In the improved chart, two composite items $(M_{23}$ and $C_{15})$ are added in the items of previous version.

An Aggregate Operator

The chart developed has 23 symptoms for the migraine type of headache and the symptoms significantly associated with the type. Likewise, the symptoms for tension and cluster significantly associated with their types, respectively. Therefore, it is general that some symptoms appear simultaneously and compositely from a patient. For example, a patient might have the symptoms $M_3 \_ M_6$, $C_1 \sim C_3$, simultaneously.

Table 1. Interview chart for migraine items

No	Items(Symptoms)	IF degree					
		Migraine		Tension		Cluster	
		μR_c	νR_c	μR_c	νR_c	μR_c	νR_c
M_1	Positive family history...	[0.5,0.6]	[0.2,0.3]	[0.2,0.3]	[0.4,0.6]	[0.2,0.3]	[0.5,0.6]
M_2	At least five attacks ...	[0.7,0.8]	[0.1,0.2]	[0.1,0.2]	[0.6,0.7]	[0.1.0.2]	[0.6,0.7]
M_3	Headache lasting...	[0.5,0.6]	[0.2,0.3	[0.3,0.4]	[0.4,0.6]	[0.1,0.3]	[0.3,0.5]
.	.	.	.	.	.	.	.
.	.	.	.	.	.	.	.
M_{23}	Concurrent with...	[0.6,0.8]	[0.2,0.8]	[0.1,0.2]	[0.6,0.7]	[0.2,0.3]	[0.6,0.7]

In this case, we need to aggregate the interval-valued intuitionistic fuzzy information corresponding to the degrees for patient's symptoms and confirmability degrees. Up to now, many operators have been proposed for aggregating information [8, 30, 31]. Two of the most common operators for aggregating arguments are the weighted averaging operator and the ordered weighted averaging operators.

In this chapter, we utilize the interval-valued intuitionistic fuzzy weighted arithmetic average (IIFWAA) operator developed by Xu to aggregate fuzzy information from the symptoms. It is defined as follows.

Definition: Let $A = \left\{ \left(x_i, M_A(x_i) \right) \right\}$, $I = 1, 2 \ldots$ n be a collection of interval-valued intuitionistic fuzzy values. Then interval-valued intuitionistic fuzzy weighted arithmetic average operator (IIFWAA) is defined as

$$IIFWAA(A) = \left(\left[1 - \prod_{i=1}^{n} \left(1 - M_{AL}(x_i)\right)^{w_i}, 1 - \prod_{i=1}^{n} \left(1 - M_{AU}(x_i)\right)^{w_i} \right] \right),$$
$$\left[\prod_{i=1}^{n} \left(N_{AL}(x_i)\right)^{w_i}, \prod_{i=1}^{n} \left(N_{AU}(x_i)\right)^{w_i} \right]$$

where $w = (w_1, w_2, \ldots, w_n)^T$ be the weight vectors of A. In addition, $w_i > 0$ and $\sum_{i=1}^{n} w_i = 1$.

A distance measure: In diagnosis with IFS data, we generally determine the diagnostic labels of patient p for any disease d such that both inequalities $0.5 < \mu_T(p,d)$ and $0.5 < \nu_T(p,d)$ are satisfied. However, as mentioned above, the max-min-max composition rule is affected by only extreme values. As a result, the diagnosis approaches using the measures, $\mu_T(p,d)$ and $\nu_T(p,d)$ leads to quite conservative results. For example, let use the confirmability membership degrees $(\mu_R(s,d))$ for a patient are 0.7, 0.4 and 0.7. Then the diagnosis measure $\mu_T(p,d)$ based on max-min-max composition is 0.4. However, if the symptoms are significantly associated with a disease, it is reasonable that the diagnosis measure has a value above 0.4. As an alternative to the max-min-max composition, other measurements such as similarity and distance between IFS have attracted many researchers. Szmidt and Kacprzyk proposed the distance measures between IFS for medical diagnosis. Park *et al.* (2008) proposed new distance measures between IVFS. In this study, we propose a measure based on distance between IVIFS. In the measure, we consider the hesitate part to modify Park's distances. The measure, the normalized Hamming distance considering the hesitate part, is defined as follows.

Definition: For any two IVIFS $A = \{(x_i, M_A(x_i), N_A(x_i))\}$ and $B = \{(x_i, M_B(x_i), N_B(x_i))\}$, the normalized hamming distance considering the hesitate part is defined as

$$l(A,B) = (1/4n)\sum \begin{bmatrix} |M_{AL}(x_i) - M_{BL}(x_i)| + |M_{AU}(x_i) - M_{BU}(x_i)| \\ + |N_{AL}(x_i) - N_{BL}(x_i)| + |N_{AU}(x_i) - N_{BU}(x_i)| \\ + |H_{AL}(x_i) - H_{BL}(x_i)| + |H_{AU}(x_i) - H_{BU}(x_i)| \end{bmatrix}$$

where H is the hesitate part.

Illustrative Example: In this section, we present an example to illustrate medical diagnosis process. For medical diagnosis of headache, the example uses the patient's degrees $\langle M_Q(p,s), N_Q(p,s) \rangle$ assigned by a physician, and confirmability degree $\langle M_R(s,d), N_R(s,d) \rangle$ indicated in the interview chart. Let us consider patient P_1. P_1's symptoms are (M_5, M_8, M_{12}, M_{15}, M_{18}, M_{19}) of migraine, (T_3, T_6, T_{10}) of tension headache, and (C_4, C_{11}) of cluster headache. P_1 simultaneously has symptoms M_5, M_8 and M_{15} (the symptoms are displayed in the composite symptom M_{22}), therefore, the symptoms of migraine are represented in (M_{12}, M_{18}, M_{19}, M_{22}). The stages for medical diagnosis of the proposed approach are as follows:

Stage 1: Table 2 is the degrees for P_1's symptoms assigned by a physician, and Table 3 is the confirmability degrees indicated in the interview chart.

Stage 2: Based on Table 2 and Table 3, Table 4 and Table 5 are calculated by applying IIFWAA operator Equation (9). For example, [0.61, 0.71], an IIFWAA M_R of Table 5, is calculated as follows: The confirmability membership degrees of the symptoms (M_{12}, M_{18}, M_{19}, M_{22}) are ([0.6, 0.7], [0.6, 0.7], [0.5, 0.6], [0.7, 0.8]) and w = (1/4; 1/4; 1/4; 1/4). Then,

$$0.61 = 1 - \{(1-0.6)\}^{1/4} * \{(1-0.6)\}^{1/4} * \{(1-0.5)\}^{1/4} * \{(1-0.7)^{1/4}\}$$

$$0.71 = 1 - \{(1-0.7)\}^{1/4} * \{(1-0.7)\}^{1/4} * \{(1-0.6)\}^{1/4} * \{(1-0.8)^{1/4}\}$$

An IIFWAA N_R of Table 5, [0.12, 0.22], is calculated as follows: From the confirmability non-membership degrees ([0.1, 0.2], [0.2, 0.3], [0.1, 0.2], [0.1, 0.2]) of the symptoms (M_5, M_8, M_{18}, M_{19}),

$$0.12 = \{0.1\}^{1/4} * \{0.2\}^{1/4} * \{0.1\}^{1/4} * \{0.1^{1/4}\}$$

$$0.22 = \{0.2\}^{1/4} * \{0.3\}^{1/4} * \{0.2\}^{1/4} * \{0.2^{1/4}\}$$

Stage 3: Table 6 is calculated by applying Equation (10) in Table 4 and Table 5. For example, 0.16, the distance for migraine of Table 6, is calculated as follows:

$$0.16 = (1/12)[(|0.54 - 0.61| + ... + |0.34 - 0.27|) + ... + (|0.50 - 0.37| + ... + |0.36 - 0.39|)]$$

Table 2. Patient P_1's degrees: $\langle M_Q(P_1,s), N_Q(P_1,s) \rangle$

Symptom	M_{12}	M_{18}	M_{19}	M_{22}	T_3	T_6	T_{10}	C_4	C_{11}
M_Q	[0.5,0.6]	[0.5,0.6]	[0.4,0.6]	[0.7,0.8]	[0.6,0.7]	[0.5,0.7]	[0.4,0.6]	[0.5,0.6]	[0.5,0.7]
N_Q	[0.2,0.3]	[0.1,0.3]	[0.1,0.2]	[0.1,0.2]	[0.1,0.2]	[0.2,0.3]	[0.2,0.4]	[0.1,0.2]	[0.2,0.3]

Table 3. Confirmability degrees: $\langle M_R(s,d), N_R(s,d) \rangle$

Symptom	Migraine		Tension		Cluster	
	M_R	N_R	M_R	N_R	M_R	N_R
M_{12}	[0.6,0.7]	[0.1,0.2]	[0.2,0.3]	[0.5,0.6]	[0.1,0.3]	[0.4,0.6]
M_{18}	[0.6,0.7]	[0.2,0.3]	[0.2,0.4]	[0.4,0.6]	[0.4,0.6]	[0.1,0.2]
M_{19}	[0.5,0.6]	[0.1,0.2]	[0.1,0.2]	[0.6,0.7]	[0.3,0.4]	[0.3,0.5]
M_{22}	[0.7,0.8]	[0.1,0.2]	[0.1,0.2]	[0.6,0.8]	[0.1,0.2]	[0.7,0.8]
T_3	[0.3,0.4]	[0.4,0.5]	[0.6,0.7]	[0.1,0.2]	[0.2,0.3]	[0.5,0.6]
T_6	[0.2,0.4]	[0.4,0.6]	[0.6,0.7]	[0.1,0.3]	[0.1,0.3]	[0.5,0.6]
T_{10}	[0.2,0.3]	[0.4,0.5]	[0.5,0.6]	[0.2,0.3]	[0.1,0.2]	[0.4,0.6]
C_4	[0.5,0.6]	[0.2,0.3]	[0.1,0.2]	[0.6,0.7]	[0.6,0.7]	[0.1,0.2]
C_{11}	[0.2,0.4]	[0.3,0.5]	[0.3,0.4]	[0.2,0.3]	[0.5,0.7]	[0.1,0.3]

Table 4. Patient's degrees: (IIFWAA M_Q, IIFWA N_Q)

Q	Symptom M	Symptom T	Symptom C
P_1	([0.54,0.66], [0.12,0.24])	([0.51,0.67],[0.16,0.29])	([0.5,0.65],[0.14,0.24])

Table 5. Confirmability degrees

R	Migraine	Tension	Cluster
Symptom M	([0.61,0.71],[0.12,0.22])	([0.15,0.28],[0.52,0.67])	([0.24,0.40],[0.30,0.47])
Symptom T	([0.23,0.37], [0.40,0.53])	([0.57,0.67],[0.13,0.26])	([0.13,0.27]),[0.46,0.60])
Symptom C	([0.37,0.51], [0.24,0.39])	([0.21,0.31],[0.35,0.46])	([0.55,0.70],[0.10,0.24])

Table 6. Distance for P_1's symptoms: l_h

T	Migraine	Tension	Cluster
P1	0.16	0.26	0.24

Stage 4: The lowest distance points out a proper diagnosis. As a result, we can diagnose that patient P_1 suffers preferentially from migraine.

SOFT SET IN BIOINFORMATICS

Soft set theory is a new mathematical approach to vagueness introduced by Molodtsov [2]. This is a parameterised family of subsets defined over a universal set using a set of parameters. In this chapter, we are redefining the notion of fuzzy soft set and its basic operations concisely; several concepts associated with it efficiently and make the proofs of properties more elegant. Like the soft sets, fuzzy soft set is a notion which allows fuzziness over a soft set model. So far, more than one attempt has been made to define this concept. R. Roy defined fuzzy soft sets and followed by that definition many other operations also defined. Some applications of soft set in bioinformatics have already done. (Tripathy et.al 2015) provides an application of interval valued intuitionistic fuzzy soft set in medical diagnosis for decision making.

Rough Set in Bioinformatics

Rough set-based rule induction allows easily interpretable descriptions of complex biological systems. Molecular biology represents a fascinating and important application area for machine learning techniques in general and rough set-based methods in particular (Hvidsten 2007).

Rough set theory (Pawlak, 1991) is founded on the concept of discernibility, i.e. that data may be described only in terms of what differentiates relevant classes of observations. From the concept of discernibility, decision rules are constructed by extracting minimal information needed to uphold the discernibility structure in the data set. The fact that the framework does not attempt to discern objects that are equal or objects that are from the same class (e.g. have the same function) makes it possible to describe incomplete and conflicting data in terms of easily interpretable decision rules. In this article, we will review some of the successful studies in which rough set-based rule induction has been used to describe biological systems at the molecular level. These studies include:

- Cancer classification using gene expression data,
- Prediction of the participation of genes in biological processes based on temporal gene expression profiles,
- modelling of the combinatorial regulation of gene expression,
- Prediction of molecular function from protein structure,
- Prediction of protein-ligand interactions in drug discovery, and
- modelling of drug resistance in HIV-1

and are modelled using rules such as:

- **IF** Gene A is up-regulated AND Gene D is down-regulated
  - **THEN** Tissue is healthy
- **IF** Transcription factor F binds AND Transcription factor V binds
  - **THEN** Gene is co-regulated with Gene H

- **IF** Protein contains motif J
  - ○ **THEN** Function is magnesium ion binding OR copper ion binding
- **IF** Protein contain motif D AND Ligand water-octanol coeff. $> c1$
  - ○ **THEN** Binding affinity is high
- **IF** Change in frequency of alpha-helix at position X $> c3$
  - ○ **THEN** Resistant to drug W

CONCLUSION

This chapter provides a brief description of uncertainty models and their applications in bioinformatics using uncertainty model. This chapter provides some of the basic notions and definitions of uncertainty based mathematical models.

REFERENCES

Adlassnig, K. P. (1986). Fuzzy set theory in medical diagnosis. *IEEE Transactions on Systems, Man, and Cybernetics*, *16*(2), 260–265. doi:10.1109/TSMC.1986.4308946

Ahn, J. Y., Kim, Y. H., & Kim, S. K. (2003). A fuzzy differential diagnosis of headache applying linear regression method and fuzzy classification. *IEICE Transactions on Information and Systems*, *E86-D*(12), 2790–2793.

Ahn, J. Y., Mum, K. S., Kim, Y. H., Oh, S. Y., & Han, B. S. (2008). A fuzzy method for medical diagnosis of headache. *IEICE Transactions on Information and Systems*, *E91-D*(4), 1215–1217. doi:10.1093/ietisy/e91-d.4.1215

Atanassov, K. (1986). Intuitionistic fuzzy sets. *Fuzzy Sets and Systems*, *20*(1), 87–96. doi:10.1016/S0165-0114(86)80034-3

Atanassov, K., & Gargov, K. (1989). Interval-valued intuitionistic fuzzy sets. *Fuzzy Sets and Systems*, *31*(3), 343–349. doi:10.1016/0165-0114(89)90205-4

Aversa, F., Gronda, E., Pizzuti, S., & Aragno, C. (2002). A fuzzy logic approach to decision support in medicine. *Proc. of the Conf. on Systemics, Cybernetics and Informatics*.

Bergeron, B. (2003). *Bioinformatics Computing*. New Delhi: Pearson Education.

Buckley, J. J. (2006). *Fuzzy Probability and Statistics*. Springer.

Calvo, T., Mayor, G., & Mesiar, R. (2002). *Aggregation Operators: New Trends and Applications*. Physica-Verlag. doi:10.1007/978-3-7908-1787-4

Chaira, T., & Chaira, T. (2008). Intuitionistic fuzzy sets: Application to medical image segmentation. *Studies in Computational Intelligence*, *85*, 51–68. doi:10.1007/978-3-540-75767-2_3

Cui, W., & Blockley, D. I. (1990). Interval provability theory for evidential support. *International Journal of Intelligent Systems*, *5*(2), 183–192. doi:10.1002/int.4550050204

De, S. K., Biswas, R., & Roy, A. R. (2001). An application of intuitionistic fuzzy sets in medical diagnosis. *Fuzzy Sets and Systems*, *117*(2), 209–213. doi:10.1016/S0165-0114(98)00235-8

Duggan, D. J., Bittner, M., Chen, Y., Meltzer, P., & Trent, J. M. (1999). Expression profiling using cDNA microarrays. *Nature Genetics*, *21*, 10–14. doi:10.1038/4434 PMID:9915494

Guo, X., Zhang, H., & Chang, Z. (2010). Image thresholding algorithm based on image gradient and fuzzy set distance. *ICIC Express Letters*, 4(3B), 1059-1064.

Hsu, H. L., & Wu, B. (2010). An innovative approach on fuzzy correlation coefficient with interval data. *International Journal of Innovative Computing, Information, & Control*, *6*(3), 1049–1058.

Hvidsten, T. R., & Komorowski, J. (2007). Rough sets in Bioinformatics. In Transactions on Rough Sets VII, *LNCS* (Vol. *4400*, pp. 225–243).

Innocent, P. R., & John, R. I. (2004). Computer aided fuzzy medical diagnosis. *Information Sciences*, *162*(2), 81–104. doi:10.1016/j.ins.2004.03.003

Lee, C. D., Oh, S. Y., Choi, H. M., & Ahn, J. Y. (2009). (Manuscript submitted for publication). A medical diagnosis based on interval-valued fuzzy sets. *Biomedical Engineering: Applications. Basis and Communications*.

Li, D., & Cheng, C. (2002). New similarity measures of intuitionistic fuzzy sets and application to pattern recognitions. *Pattern Recognition Letters*, *23*(1-3), 221–225. doi:10.1016/S0167-8655(01)00110-6

Liang, Z., & Shi, P. (2003). Similarity measures on intuitionistic fuzzy sets. *Pattern Recognition Letters*, *24*(15), 2687–2693. doi:10.1016/S0167-8655(03)00111-9

Luscombe, N. M., Greenbaum, D., & Gerstein, M. (2001). What is Bioinformatics? A Proposed Definition and Overview of the Field. *Methods of Information in Medicine*, *40*(4), 346–358. PMID:11552348

Moein, S., Monadjemi, S. A., & Moallem, P. (2008). A novel fuzzy-neural based medical diagnosis system, *World Academy of Science. Engineering and Technology*, *37*, 157–161.

Molodtsov, D.A. (1999) Soft Sets. *First Results, Computers and mathematics with applications*, 37, 19-31.

Park, J. H., Lim, K. M., Park, J. S., & Kwun, Y. C. (2008). Distances between interval-valued intuitionistic fuzzy sets. *Journal of Physics: Conference Series*, *96*, 012089. doi:10.1088/1742-6596/96/1/012089

Patterson, S. D., & Aebersold, R. H. (2003). Proteomics: The first decade and beyond. *Nature Genetics*, *33*(Suppl. 3), 311–323. doi:10.1038/ng1106 PMID:12610541

Pawlak, Z. (1991). *Rough Sets: Theoretical Aspects of Reasoning About Data*. Kluwer Academic Publishing. doi:10.1007/978-94-011-3534-4

Pei, Z., Liu, X., & Zou, L. (2010). Extracting association rules based on intuitionistic fuzzy sets. *International Journal of Innovative Computing, Information, & Control*, *6*(6), 2567–2580.

Samatsu, T., Tachikawa, K., & Shi, Y. (2008). GUI form for car retrieval systems using fuzzy theory. *ICIC Express Letters*, *2*(3), 245–249.

Sanchez, E. (1979). *Medical diagnosis and composite fuzzy relations. In Advances in Fuzzy Set Theory and Applications* (M. M. Gupta, R. K. Ragade, & R. R. Yager, Eds.). Elsevier Science Ltd.

Schena, M., Shalon, D., Davis, R., & Brown, P. O. (1995). Quantitative monitoring of gene expression patterns with a complementary DNA microarray. *Science, 270*(5235), 467–470. doi:10.1126/science.270.5235.467 PMID:7569999

Schuh, C. (2005). *Fuzzy sets and their application in medicine. Proc. of the North American Fuzzy Information Society*(pp. 86–91). doi:10.1109/NAFIPS.2005.1548513

Seising, R. (2004). A history of medical diagnosis using fuzzy relations. *Proc. of the Conf. on Fuzziness.* Retrieved from http://www.mnh.si.edu

Shah, S.C., & Kusiak, A.(2004). Data Mining and Genetic Algorithm Based Gene Selection. *Artificial Intelligence in Medicine, 31*, 183-196.

Zadeh, L. A. (1965). Fuzzy Sets. *Information and Control, 8*(3), 338–353. doi:10.1016/S0019-9958(65)90241-X

KEY TERMS AND DEFINITIONS

Bio Informatics: It is the application of computer technology to the management of biological information. Computers are used to gather, store, analyse and integrate biological and genetic information which can then be applied to gene-based drug discovery and development.

Fuzzy Logic: Precise definition of this logic does not exist. It is supposed to be the embedded version of fuzzy sets in infinite valued logic. In another sense, according to Zadeh it is equivalent to computing with words.

Fuzzy Set: It is an extension of the concept of fuzzy set, introduced by Atanassov in 1986. It is more general than fuzzy set. In fuzzy set the non-membership of an element in a set is one's complement of its membership. However, this may not be the same in many real life situations because of the hesitation component. In order to model this in intuitionistic fuzzy sets the sum of membership and non-membership values of an element is not restricted to be one.

Fuzzy Set: It is one of the most popular models of uncertainty introduced by Zadeh in 1965 where each element has a grade of belongingness to the set instead of the dichotomous belongingness in case of crisp sets.

Logic: It is a systematic approach to the art of reasoning. Greek philosopher Aristotle is known to be the father of logic.

Rough Set: This is another model of uncertainty which was introduced by Pawlak in 1982 and it follows the concept of Frege on the boundary region model of uncertainty. Here, a set is approximated by a pair of crisp sets called the lower and upper approximation of the set.

Soft Set: This notion was introduced by Molodtsov in the year 1999 which makes up for lack of parametrization in fuzzy set and rough set. It bases upon the concept of topology. It has been observed by Molodtsov that all fuzzy sets are soft sets.

Section 3
Nature–Inspired Computing for Analysis of DNA and Protein Microarray Data

In this section many nature inspired computing algorithms are discussed for analyzing and predicting protein and micro-array data. Five chapters are included in this section. Various computational approaches for predicting protein-protein interactions are discussed. Many nature inspired algorithms are discussed in this section to analyze micro-array gene expression dataset. Nature inspired algorithms like PSO K-Means clustering and bi-clustering approaches are discussed to extract the motif information from protein microarray data. Protein microarray data is mainly used to identify the interactions and activities of proteins with other molecules, and to determine their function for a system at normal state and stressed state. This section also classifies individuals that differ in their susceptibility to a particular disease or response to a particular treatment into subpopulations based on individual's unique genetic and clinical information along with environmental factors.

Chapter 10
Computational Methods for Prediction of Protein–Protein Interactions:
PPI Prediction Methods

Sneha Rai
Netaji Subhas Institute of Technology, India

Sonika Bhatnagar
Netaji Subhas Institute of Technology, India

ABSTRACT

The key signaling pathways in cellular processes involve protein-protein interactions (PPIs). A perturbation in the balance of PPIs occurs in various pathophysiological processes. There are a large numbers of experimental methods for detection of PPIs. However, experimental PPI determination is time consuming, expensive, error prone and does not effectively cover transient interactions. Therefore, overlaying and integration of predictive methods with experimental results provides statistical robustness and biological significance to the PPI data. In this chapter, the authors describe PPIs in terms of types, importance, and biological consequences. This chapter also provides a comprehensive description on various computational approaches for PPI prediction. Prediction of PPI can be done through: 1) Genomic information based methods 2) Structure based methods 3) Network topology based methods: 4) Literature and data mining based methods 5) Machine learning methods. For ease of use and convenience, a summary of various databases and software for PPI prediction has been provided.

INTRODUCTION

Proteins are essential macromolecules that perform diverse functions in association with other macro and small molecules. Biological processes involve interplay between protein-protein interactions (PPIs) as cell to cell interactions, metabolic and developmental processes are governed by PPIs. A perturbation in the balance of PPIs occurs in various pathophysiological processes due to varying expression

DOI: 10.4018/978-1-5225-0427-6.ch010

levels of disease related proteins. Specifically, PPIs also modulate the host-pathogen interactions in the initial stages and host response in later stages of infection. Modeling PPIs at a large scale for study of topological parameters and essentiality leads to identification of crucial players and pathways in the disease condition. Since proteins may have different interacting partners under diseased and normal state respectively, identification of drug targets from PPI networks is also carried out. Targeting PPIs presents a novel approach for developing therapeutics with high specificity and fewer side effects. Moreover, PPIs aid in forecasting the function of a target protein and drugability of a molecule. There are a large numbers of experimental methods for detection of PPIs that have led to the accumulation of PPI data in publicly available databases. However, experimental PPI determination is time consuming, expensive, error prone and do not effectively cover transient interactions. Therefore, prediction of PPIs by computational methods represents an important development. Overlaying and integration of predictive methods with experimental results provides statistical robustness and biological significance to the PPI data.

The chapter provides an overview on PPIs, its types, importance, biological consequences and factors affecting PPIs. The authors have also provided a comprehensive description on various computational approaches for PPI prediction. Computational methods for PPI prediction are based on sequence, structure, evolution and genomic data. Prediction of PPI can be done through:

1. Genomic information based methods,
2. Structure based methods,
3. Network topology based methods,
4. Machine learning methods and
5. Literature and data mining based methods.

Increment in genetic information obtained through complete genome sequencing methods, had laid down the foundation for PPI prediction at genetic level. These methods are based on the concept that genes that functionally interact are often located in close proximity in the genome. Proteins that interact they co-adapt to the evolutionary forces in order to preserve the interactions. Genomic context based methods apply the concept of genetic linkage, gene fusion, phylogenetic profiles and *in silico* two hybrid systems for PPI prediction. Some computational methods utilize three dimensional information of the protein to predict PPI. The fact behind these methods is that interactions between two proteins can be predicted if interactions between their homologous proteins are known. In fact, interactions between analogous proteins can also be predicted by fold recognition or threading based methods. Protein-protein docking methods are also employed for forecasting interactions between proteins as these resolve the native structure of the protein complexes. Prior knowledge about the interacting residues often reduces the search space for the most optimal complex. Most of the docking methods consider proteins as rigid bodies and consider shape complementarities between interacting surfaces as the main guide. Only a few approaches take protein flexibility in consideration where the interacting proteins are allowed to adopt the active bound conformation. These methods are limited to structural information of a protein but give a more accurate view to PPIs. Biological networks, where nodes represent proteins and edge represents interaction between them, possesses certain characteristics that differentiate them from random networks. In network based methods for PPI prediction, a confidence score is assigned to each edge of the network that facilitate distinction between protein pairs that actually interact from protein pairs that exist by chance. Usually, the confidence score for a particular interaction is calculated by comparing original networks with random networks which are formed based on graph and probability theory. PPI networks also assist in studying network parameters such as degree, degree distribution, clustering coefficient and centralities which are briefly described in the chapter. PPIs can also be predicted on basis of co-occurrence data of proteins in Pubmed abstract and this methodology is employed by literature and data mining based methods. Now days, machine learning based methods are widely used for predicting PPIs. These methods consist of construction of an algorithm that learns from training set and then takes decision or make predictions. A set of conditions with known outputs and a set of parameters that control the system are needed for training. In biology, machine learning algorithm learns from information gathered from gene expression data, codon usage, physiochemical characteristics of amino acids and various other high-throughput experiments. Further, these models can be used to accurately predict PPIs. Various machine learning approaches such as support vector machine, artificial neural networks, K-nearest neighbors, decision tree, random forest and naïve bayes are used for PPI prediction. With high-throughput technologies there has been a substantial increase in known PPIs. To make these data publically available, multitude of databases have been established. There are six main databases for retrieval of PPI's. The databases, namely: BioGRID (Biological General Repository for Interaction Datasets), IntAct (IntAct molecular interaction database), BIND (Biomolecular Interaction Network Database), MINT (Molecular INTeraction database), DIP (Database of Interacting Proteins) and HPRD (Human Protein Reference Database) vary with respect to content and scope. After construction of Protein-Protein Interaction network, visualization and analysis of PPI network is needed. A large number of tools have been developed for this purpose. Some well known software for network visualization and analysis are Cytoscape, Medusa, Navigator and Pajek. Finally, the chapter summarizes various databases and softwares for PPI prediction.

BACKGROUND

With advancement in high-throughput technologies more and more data regarding the function and molecular properties of a protein has been accumulated. Number of protein databases such as Uniprot ("UniProt: a hub for protein information," 2015) accumulate, maintain and manually curate these data (De Las Rivas & Fontanillo, 2010). However, proteins do not work in isolation but in complex with other biological macromolecules. Lines of evidences have shown that almost 80% of the proteins work in complexes (Berggard, Linse, & James, 2007). Large numbers of non-covalent interactions are involved in protein folding, protein assembly and PPIs (Rao, Srinivas, Sujini, & Kumar, 2014). Today, PPIs have also become main focus of systems biology. Proteins do not work in isolation but in complex with other biological macromolecules. Therefore, it is important to know and predict their interaction (Lehne & Schlitt, 2009). Protein-Protein Interactions (PPI's) have an essential role in many cellular processes such as signal transduction, enzyme inhibition, cell growth, proliferation, antigen-antibody detection, DNA transcription, replication, translation, splicing, assemblage of multi-domain proteins, etc (Fernandez-Recio, Totrov, & Abagyan, 2004; Keskin, Ma, Rogale, Gunasekaran, & Nussinov, 2005; Zahiri, Bozorgmehr, & Masoudi-Nejad, 2013) . Thus, to understand molecular basis of a biological process identification and characterization of PPIs is important (Lehne & Schlitt, 2009). Significant classical objectives to be achieved from protein-protein interaction studies are (Golemis, 2002):

1. Detecting motifs involved in protein functions through protein sequence and structure.
2. Identifying key regulatory residues by analyzing evolutionary history and conserved sequences.

3.   Protein function can also be elucidated by knowing the function of interacting partner.

4.   *Drug Design against PPIs:* PPIs are challenging new drug targets that may open up new opportunities for manipulating cellular processes like proliferation, growth, differentiation and apoptosis for therapeutic intervention (Roche P). Development of this exciting new field has helped in development of small inhibitors against IL-2/ IL-2R (Wilson & Arkin, 2011). Beside this, protein-protein interfaces have been targeted in other cases also like Recombinase RAD51 and BRCA2, Bcr and Abl etc (Surade & Blundell, 2012).

5.   *Network Biology Studies:* This new field applies the principles of Network and control theory to biological systems to elucidate their working in disease and pathological conditions, to mine for novel drug targets and to elucidate the mechanism of action of drugs.

6.   Predicting PPIs facilitate recognizing drug targets (Pedamallu & Posfai, 2010). Highly connected protein called hubs mostly contains enzyme families, transcription factors, disordered proteins etc (Dunker, Cortese, Romero, Iakoucheva, & Uversky, 2005; Sarmady, Dampier, & Tozeren, 2011). A variety of interactions and associations can occur between proteins and based on their structural and functional properties PPIs can be classified into in many ways.

Types of Protein-Protein Interaction

Protein interactions can be differentiated on the basis of strength (stable or transient), specificity (specific or non-specific), position of interacting partners on one or on two polypeptide chain and similarity between the interacting sub-units (homo-oligomeric or hetero-oligomeric) (Shoemaker & Panchenko, 2007). Stable or transient interactions can further be classified as either strong or weak based on the strength of the association. Stable interactions are found in proteins that are purified as multi-subunit complexes. The subunit of the complexes can be either identical or different. As an example, Hemoglobin and core RNA-polymerase display stable multi-subunit complex interaction that is critical for their biological function. On the other hand, transient interactions are temporary in nature. However, transient PPIs participate in and are key driving factors for a large number of cellular processes. Many biological processes like signaling cascade, protein modification, folding, transport, cell cycling cell growth involve transient interactions. A specific range of conditions like temperature, salt concentration, presence of other ions, ligands and proteins etc is needed for transient interactions to come into force (Phizicky & Fields, 1995).

Biological Consequences of Protein-Protein Interactions

Two or more interacting proteins have certain measurable effects on each other like (Phizicky & Fields, 1995):

1.   Due to substrate binding or allosteric effects, kinetic properties of enzymes changes.

2.   Interacting proteins enable substrate channeling between subunits or domains, producing an end product.

3.   New binding sites may get created, especially for small effector molecules.

4.   A protein may get destroyed or inactivated (or existing protein may get activated).

5.   Alteration in specificity of protein towards its substrate due to interaction with other proteins.

6.   Regulatory effects on either upstream or downstream processes.

Factors Affecting PPIs

As stated above, PPIs are key factors involved in mediating biological processes and may be of different types. Within any biological system, PPIs are dynamically and finely regulated by a series of coordinated local and global processes. The multitude of factors affecting the existence, nature and strength of PPIs includes:

1. Expression and degradation level of protein that determines its concentration.
2. Affinity of protein towards other partner proteins or ligands.
3. Concentration of ligands, substrate or ions that may facilitate, prevent or modulate the interaction.
4. Covalent modifications (post translational modifications).
5. Compartmentalization within the cell

Need of Computational Method for PPI Prediction

Detection of Protein-protein interaction can be done experimentally (Fernandez-Recio, et al., 2004). Identification of residues or region involved in interaction and recognition of interacting partners are studied using biophysical & biochemical methods such as co-immunoprecipitation, pull-down assays, yeast two hybrid, phage display, cross-linking, chromatographic isolation of complexes etc (Valencia & Pazos, 2003). A full description of the experimental methods for PPI detection lies beyond the scope of this chapter. However, a brief description to some experimental methods has been provided in Table 1 and authoritative treatment of the subject can be found in references (Phizicky & Fields, 1995; Shoe-maker & Panchenko, 2007). These experimental methods possess certain drawbacks, namely; they are expensive, time consuming and labor intensive, prone to experimental errors. Moreover, they may often fail to capture the transient PPIs (Szilagyi, Grimm, Arakaki, & Skolnick, 2005; Zahiri, et al., 2013). Development of bioinformatics approaches for PPI prediction has led to computational methods that can be used to predict interactions that are not detected by high throughput experimental methods. These predictive approaches are based on sequence, structure, evolution, and genomic data. These predicted interactions can help predict PPIs and further be validated by the labor intensive experimental methods.

The new paradigm that involves computational prediction of PPI's uses genomic, structural and biological information of genes and protein to predict functional relationship between proteins. These approaches complement high throughput techniques of experimental detection of PPIs and aid in constructing their interaction networks. PPI networks consist of large number proteins (represented as nodes) joined by interactions (represented by edges). PPI networks have an important role in proteomics and help in functional annotation of unclassified proteins. Analysis of PPI network yields a variety of results such as proteins connected by an edge share same functionality. In addition to this, proteins involved in densely connected subgraphs tend to form biological complexes to carry out a specific function. Functional annotation of human proteins reveals the role of PPI's in physiological and pathophysiological processes and may help in developing PPI based new therapeutics (Surade & Blundell, 2012).

Table 1. Methods for detection of PPIs

Methods	Description
Protein affinity chromatography	The protein of interest is covalently attached to a matrix such as sepharose (stationary phase). A mixture of ligand proteins is passed through the column. Most of the proteins get washed away while the proteins that have specific binding remain bound to immobilized proteins. Bound proteins are eluted by adding excess of ligand and then analyzed (Ratner, 1974).
Immunoprecipitation	The technique involves precipitation of protein antigen from a solution, with help of an antibody that is specific for the antigen. The antigen-antibody complexes are precipitated and analyzed (Phizicky & Fields, 1995).
Cross linking	A cross linking reagent is employed to capture PPIs between two proteins as they interact. Some of the common cross linkers used in PPI study are formaldehyde, imidoesters and N-Hydroxysuccinimide-esters (Traut, Casiano, & Zecherle, 1989).
Protein probing	The method is based on using a labeled protein probe to screen an expression library to recognize protein encoding genes interacting with the probe (Young & Davis, 1983).
Phage display	Phage display method consists of insertion of gene of protein of interest into phase coat protein gene enabling expression protein of interest on the surface. These phages can thus be screened to detect interacting proteins or peptides (Smith, 1985).
Two-hybrid system	The method utilizes transcriptional activity as a measure to detect PPI. Transcription factors consist of a DNA binding domain that leads to expression of specific gene and a transcription activator domain enables other proteins involved in transcription machinery to initiate transcription. The two domains are not covalently bound and are brought together by binding of two proteins. In this method two hybrids are made, DNA binding domain fused to protein X and transcription activator domain fused to protein Y. The two proteins are expressed in a cell having one or more reporter gene. If X and Y interact, it leads to expression of reporter gene (Chien, Bartel, Sternglanz, & Fields, 1991; Fields & Sternglanz, 1994).
Synthetic lethal effects	This method is based on concept that mutations in two genes may lead to death or defects in phenotypes. This phenomenon, called synthetic lethality occurs due to physical interaction between two proteins that perform the same essential function. If protein X and Y interact and form a dimer that performs an important function, then mutation in either X and Y causes partial binding and mutation in both causes no binding, resulting in some defective phenotype (Dobzhansky, 1946).

MAIN FOCUS OF THE CHAPTER

Main focus of the chapter is prediction of PPI. This chapter provides an overview on PPIs and describes various computational approaches for PPI prediction. Through this chapter user shall be able to:

- Know the importance of PPI's, objectives achieved through PPI's studies, biological consequences of PPI's.
- Learn experimental methods for PPI detection and their drawbacks, needs for computational methods for PPI prediction, different computational methods for PPI prediction.
- Identify databases for extracting high confidence protein-protein interactions, tools for predicting first interactors of certain proteins (both macromolecule and small molecules).
- Evaluate whether the PPI network fits the power law and is a typical biological network.
- Analyze the PPI network for its topological properties like nodes with high degree, high Betweenness Centrality and drug targets.

Issues, Controversies, Problems

- Experimental methods for PPI detection are expensive, error-prone and time consuming.
- Transient nature of interactions within complexes is hard to cover.

- A protein may contain number of subunits, which subunits interact with each other is hard to predict.
- When predicting PPI, it is important to distinguish between false-positives and true-positives.
- Structure based methods for PPI prediction can only work for protein whose three dimensional structure are available.
- Machine learning methods that are based on sequence information fails at cross validation step.

Computational Methods for PPI Prediction

Earlier, prediction of Protein-protein interactions was limited to proteins for which three dimensional structure were available. With the increase in genomic information gathered through complete genome sequencing projects, genomic context of genes in complete genome have been laid down. Genes that interact are co-expressed both temporally and spatially. Thus, the proteins they encode are also produced at same time and in same tissue and are supposed to interact with each other to carry out some specific function. Therefore, the protein-protein interactions can be predicted at genomic level also. Further, in absence of sequence or structure information, evolutionary relationships based on genomic context can be detected to predict PPI's (Skrabanek, Saini, Bader, & Enright, 2008). The computational methods for PPI's prediction can be broadly divided into following types (Zahiri, et al., 2013):

1. Methods based on Genomic context.
2. Methods based on Structural information.
3. Methods that employ Network topology to predict PPI's.
4. Literature and text mining based methods.
5. Machine learning methods.

Methods based on Genomic Context

The conserved genomic information extracted from comparison of genomes can be used to predict interactions between gene products. *Table 2* lists tools based on genomic context. Structure independent methods are based on *a priori* biological information and are classified as (Skrabanek, et al., 2008; Szilagyi, et al., 2005):

Co-Localization in Genome (Genetic linkage)

Gene co-localization or gene neighborhood method is based on the fact that genes that functionally interact are often located in close proximity in the genome (Figure 1). The conservation of neighborhood relationship across genomes can be studied by gene order and gene cluster analysis. This method is mostly applied on bacterial and aracheal systems where genes are organized in operons and genes that are functionally related are transcribed on the same polycistronic mRNA.

Scope and Usage: It was found that about 63% of proteins encoded by conserved gene pairs interact physically either directly or indirectly (Huynen, Snel, Lathe, & Bork, 2000).The main drawback of this method is that it works for prokaryotic systems as they contain many operons. However, it can be applied to eukaryotic systems if homology is established with prokaryotic organisms (Valencia & Pazos, 2003). The main requirement for the use of this method is the availability of genomic sequences and

Table 2. Tools, servers and databases for PPI prediction

Genomic Context Based		
Name	**URL**	**Reference**
STRING	http://www.bork.embl-heidelberg.de/STRING/	(Snel, Lehmann, Bork, & Huynen, 2000)
Predictome	http://predictome.bu.edu/	(Mellor, Yanai, Clodfelter, Mintseris, & DeLisi, 2002)
COGs	http://www.ncbi.nlm.nih.gov/COG/_	(Tatusov, Koonin, & Lipman, 1997)
Structure Based		
Name	URL	Reference
Protein-Protein Interaction server	http://www.biochem.ucl.ac.uk/bsm/PP/server/_	(Jones & Thornton, 1996)
InterPreTS	http://www.russell.embl.de/interprets/	(Aloy & Russell, 2003)
PDB	http://www.rcsb.org/pdb/home/home.do_	(Berman et al., 2000)
Modbase	http://modbase.compbio.ucsf.edu/modbase-cgi/index.cgi_	(Pieper et al., 2011)
SCOWLP	http://www.scowlp.org/scowlp/_	(Teyra, Doms, Schroeder, & Pisabarro, 2006; Teyra, Paszkowski-Rogacz, Anders, & Pisabarro, 2008; Teyra, Samsonov, Schreiber, & Pisabarro, 2011)
3DID	http://3did.irbbarcelona.org/_	(Mosca, Ceol, Stein, Olivella, & Aloy, 2014)
EMdatabank	http://www.emdatabank.org/_	(Lawson et al., 2011)
PRISM	http://cosbi.ku.edu.tr/prism/_	(Baspinar, Cukuroglu, Nussinov, Keskin, & Gursoy, 2014; Tuncbag, Gursoy, Nussinov, & Keskin, 2011)
SCOPPI	http://scoppi.biotec.tu-dresden.de/scoppi/_	(Kim, Henschel, Winter, & Schroeder, 2006; Kim & Ison, 2005; Winter, Henschel, Kim, & Schroeder, 2006)

Figure 1. Two genes (in green and red) are in close proximity and are conserved in six genomes

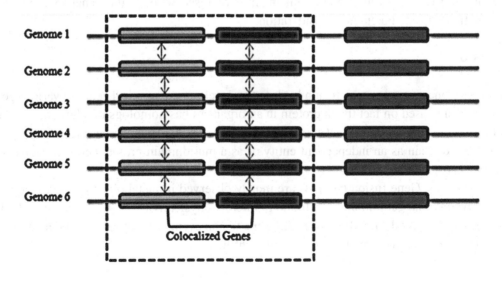

order of the genes concerned. Additional confidence in the prediction of interaction can be gained from co-occurrence of the homologs of the genes in other genomes. The co-localization method is mostly used in case of prokaryotes as compared to eukaryotes. This method has been employed to identify clusters of functionally related genes that are conserved in two bacterial genomes; *Haemophilus influenzae* and *Escherichia coli,* and the genes involved in important cellular function were grouped in nine clusters (Tamames, Casari, Ouzounis, & Valencia, 1997). A statistical method was applied on neighboring gene pairs to study gene order relationship and genome organization. Significant values came for genes that were functionally related and were co-localized. Another method utilizing the concept of co-localization, consisted of detecting potential operons to identify functional coupling between genes (Overbeek, Fonstein, D'Souza, Pusch, & Maltsev, 1999)

Phylogenetic Profiles

Phylogenetic profiling method is based on the concept that interacting proteins co-evolve in order to conserve the interactions and the function for e.g., insulin and its receptors, dockerins and cohexins. Thus, homologs of genes encoding interacting proteins should be conserved across species suggesting their functional relationship. In practice, however, it is the protein domains that represent the independent evolutionary units of the protein. Therefore, phylogenetic profiling is often done with interacting domains.

Scope and Usage: About 34% of proteins in *Mycoplasma genitalium* were found to physically interact directly through phylogenetic profile method (Huynen, et al., 2000). Phylogenetic profiles are simply represented in binary format indicating presence or absence of homologs across mulitple species (Figure 2). Libraries of phylogenetic profiles can then be scanned to find interacting proteins because proteins that interact tend to have similar phylogenetic profiles than non-interacting proteins. The main disadvantage of the phylogenetic profiling method is that it requires the complete genome as input and some stringent threshold to predict presence or absence of homologs (Szilagyi, et al., 2005). The potency of these methods is highly dependent on the number and distribution of genomes used to construct profiles. Also, processes like horizontal gene transfer, non-orthologous gene displacement, gene loss; eukaryotic gene family expansion could make detection of orthologs a difficult task (Skrabanek, et al., 2008). Phylogenetic profiles constitute a strong predictive indication for physical interaction. However, the fact that specific interacting protein domains may be fused with another, changed, inactivated or deleted evolution must be taken into consideration.

Gene Fusion

An evolutionary phenomenon, gene fusion leads to the development of fused genes in various genomes. These methods are based on fact that a protein in an organism has homologs in other organism formed by fusion of two or more independent proteins (Figure 3). Thus, PPI's can be inferred by occurrence of same protein domain as an independent entity or as a mutidomain protein across various genomes (Valencia & Pazos, 2002).

Scope and usage: Gene fusion methods are mostly observed in metabolic enzymes. About 55% of proteins in *Mycoplasma genitalium* were found to interact physically by gene fusion method (Huynen, et al., 2000). These methods have limitation that gene fusion events are not very frequent and vary from gene to gene. Therefore, these methods have limited utility.

Figure 2. Phylogenetic profile which is constructed by assigning presence (1) or absence (0) of a protein in a set of genomes and two interacting proteins have same phylogenetic profiles

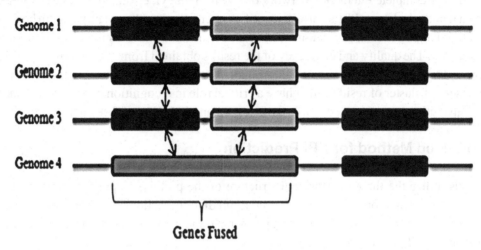

Figure 3. Gene fusion event between two genes resulting into a single gene

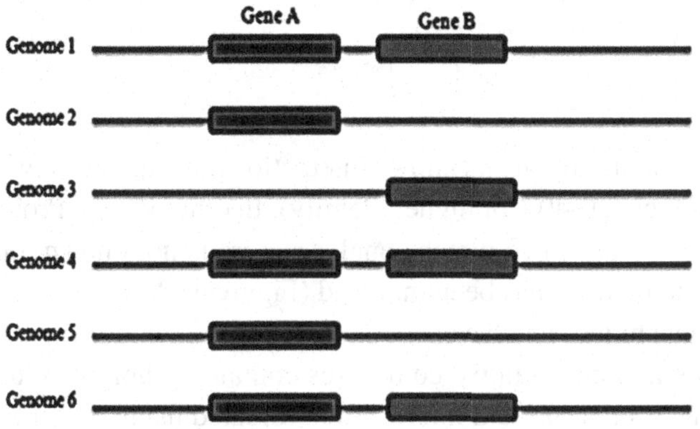

Genome	Gene A	Gene B
1	1	1
2	1	0
3	0	1
4	1	1
5	1	0
6	1	1

In-Silico Two-Hybrid

This approach is based on the notion that proteins that interact co-adapt to the evolutionary forces. Thus, mutations in one protein are reflected by similar mutations in partner proteins in order to conserve the interactions. The *in-silico* two hybrid systems predict PPI's by detecting such mutations across species. In *in-silico* two hybrid systems, pairs of protein families are aligned and are then combined into a single cross-family alignment. The position specific matrix formed from the alignment is then subjected to a co-relation function to identify co-related residues in both within and across protein families. A protein family is group of evolutionary related proteins that have descended from common ancestor. Protein families are further assembled into higher orders like super family based on similarities in sequence and structure and related function. Few examples of protein families are globins, neural globins, SH3, SH2, C2 etc.

Scope and usage: A large number of significant results have been obtained using this approach including construction of complete interaction network of *E.coli* (Szilagyi, et al., 2005). The advantage of this method is that it not only detects PPI's but also identifies interacting residues. The program however needs large computational power to built alignment and number of false positives increases if alignments are not of good quality. The quality and efficiency of the results obtained from *in-silico* two-hybrid methods can be improved by recognizing the significance of hotspots at the protein interaction surfaces. Hotspots are small conserved cluster of residues that have a critical role in recognition at protein interfaces due to their high contribution to surface accessible surface area and lowering of free energy.

Structure Based Method for PPI Prediction

These methods utilize the three dimensional structure of the proteins to predict interactions between them. Further, the information gained can be used to predict interactions between proteins that are homologous to previously determined interacting partners. Table 2 represents tools, servers and databases for structure based PPI prediction.

Scope and usage: The method is limited to proteins whose three dimensional structure has been solved hence can't be applied to large number of proteins. However, much more details can be obtained from structure based methods like residue involved in interactions and biophysical characteristics of the interactions.

PPI Prediction by Homology

Homology based approaches work on the assumption that known interaction information between protein pairs can be extrapolated to their homologs (30-40% or higher identity). In other words, Protein-Protein interaction can be modeled for proteins whose three dimensional structure is not known, on the basis of other homologous proteins whose interactions has been modeled (Figure 4). Few techniques (which are extension of homology modeling technique) involve examination of structure of protein complexes to predict interaction between subunits in some putative complexes containing homologous subunits. Inclination of residue pairs towards the protein-protein interface is evaluated using a scoring function (Szilagyi, et al., 2005).

Scope and usage: A method known as "interaction prediction through tertiary structure" considers 3D structure of complex and alignment of homologues of interacting proteins. Further, it evaluates the fit of interacting pairs of residues in the complex using an empirical function. While being accurate for prediction, methods based on sequence similarity/ structural complementarities must consider the co-expression and co-localization of proteins.

PPI Prediction through Threading Based Methods

In order to predict PPI's among distant or analogous proteins, threading or fold recognition method are used. In dimeric threading process, the sequence of two proteins (potential interaction pair) is threaded on to each structure in the non-redundant fold library. The template structures that have Z-score greater than the threshold are collected in two sets. Each of the templates from two sets is then analyzed to ascertain whether they make complexes. The target sequences are then threaded on the template structures that form a dimer. Optimization of the structure-sequence alignment is then done using a knowledge based

Figure 4. PPI Prediction based homology between protein three dimensional structures.

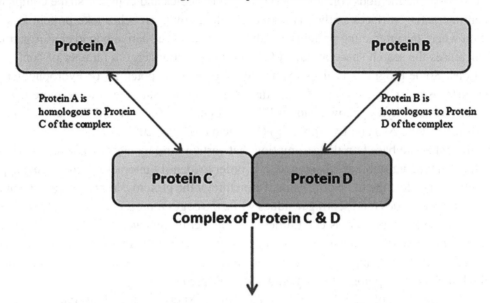

Interactions between Protein C & Protein D in the complex can be extrapolated to predict interaction between their respective homologs A & B.

interfacial potential (Szilagyi, et al., 2005). The template pairs with highest Z-score and lowest interfacial energy are further subjected to filtering. If no other monomeric structure is obtained for either of the sequences with highest Z-score, the interfacial energy is smaller than threshold and Z-score is greater than 5, then this pair of sequences is predicted to form a dimer.

Scope and usage: Multiprospector, is an algorithm based on multimeric threading and was tested on 2457 known interactions of yeast proteome out of which 144 were identified correctly (ref of multiprocessor). Beside this, the method was also applied on *Saccharomyces cerevisiae* proteins and predicted 7321 interactions out of which only 374 interactions were experimentally proved. As protein interface recognition may sometimes depend on the existence of specific recognition motifs instead of entire fold, threading based methods based on distant similarity are likely to yield erroneous results when used without sufficient knowledge of mode of recognition between proteins. Standalone use of these methods is unsuitable for predicting PPIs on a large scale.

Protein-Protein Docking

Given the three dimensional structure of two proteins, docking studies can help in determining the native structure of protein complexes. Prior knowledge about the interacting residues often reduces the search space for the most optimal complex. Residues that are involved in binding are called hot-spot residues and they are usually more conserved than other residues. Prior knowledge of hot-spot residues also smoothens the progress of the search. Beside this, NMR restraints and known coordinates of homologous complexes can aid in the search (Szilagyi, et al., 2005).

Most of the docking methods consider proteins as rigid bodies and consider shape complementarities between interacting surfaces as the main guide. Only a few approaches take protein flexibility in consideration where the interacting proteins are allowed to adopt the active bound conformation. However, this increases the search space as each of the proteins can undergo a number of conformational transformations. Some programs utilizes feature like electrostatic potential or hydrophobicity of the interacting surfaces utilizing the principle that the interacting interfaces tend to be more hydrophobic with large proportion of hydrophobic residues like Val, Leu, Ile, Met, Tyr and Phe and low proportion of polar residues as Glu, Asp and Lys (not Arg) (Valencia & Pazos, 2003).

Other approaches are based on the assumption that certain binding sites or interfaces are energetically unstable and binding stabilizes their energy. In order to identify interacting sites, some approaches employ graph theory. Here the three dimensional structure of the protein is represented as an undirected graph with vertices or nodes representing residues while the edges represent the contacts between them. Based on certain parameters such as centralities, the interacting residues are detected. Centrality is a function that assigns a value to each node present in network. Centrality analysis is done to rank network elements and thus to identify important elements in network. There are various kinds of centralities and are described in Network topology based methods for PPI prediction.

Scope and usage: Combined information gained from experiments and structural insights aid in identification of interacting motifs or patterns. Moreover, methods based on structural alignment have also been developed for identification of interacting sites (Valencia & Pazos, 2003). Again, despite being very accurate, methods based only on structural complementarities may fail as they do not consider co-expression and co-localization.

NETWORK TOPOLOGY BASED METHODS

Biological PPI networks (Figure 5) share similar topological properties in various organisms, this differentiates them from random networks. Analysis of specific topological properties like neighborhood cohesiveness can be used to provides confidence scores to each and every edge in the network, and therefore assist in making a distinction between true positives and true negatives i.e., distinguish protein pairs that actually interact from protein pairs that interact by chance (Goldberg & Roth, 2003). PPI study using network topology also gives insights into evolutionary forces that effect interactions and network dynamics that model the dynamic properties of network. Usually, the confidence score for a particular interaction is calculated by comparing original networks with random networks which are formed based on graph and probability theory (Zahiri, et al., 2013). In random networks, the number of edges and vertices are kept same as that in original network so that the significant properties that remain unchanged can be detected.

Scope and usage: Network topology based methods are still under development due to the evolving use of network methods in biology. Development of new and accurate algorithms as well as data integration will help make these techniques more efficient and sensitive.

Biological networks follow power law that states the presence of a few nodes with large connectivity (called hub nodes) while most of the nodes have few interaction partners. The hub proteins are important in biological processes and deletion of these hub proteins disrupts the protein-protein interaction network. It affects biological processes also; these disruptions are therefore lethal to the organism. This is known as the centrality-lethality rule. For pathogenic organisms, detecting and targeting hub proteins

Figure 5. A biological network with 10 nodes and 25 edges

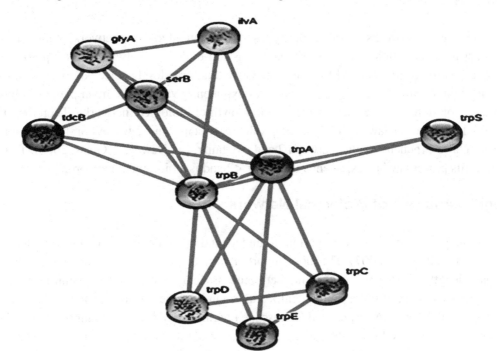

lead to development of new therapeutic strategies for curing the disease but in human system, hub proteins are not used as drug targets as they have major biological roles. Salient topological properties that are evaluated in a protein-protein interaction network can be summarized as follows (Koike & Takagi, 2004; Pavlopoulos, Wegener, & Schneider, 2008; Zahiri, et al., 2013):

- **Degree:** represents number of interactions for a give node.
- **Degree Distribution:** It is the probability distribution of the degrees over the whole network.
- **Hub:** The vertex that has the largest number of interactions and thus has an important role in biological processes.
- **Clustering Coefficient**: It determines network cohesiveness and evaluates the number of triangles passing through a particular node.
- **Shortest Path Length:** It is the path between two nodes that covers the smallest number of links.
- **Average Path Length**: It is a measure of overall navigability of network and is average of all shortest path lengths between all couples of nodes in a network.
- **Degree Centrality:** It is a measure of number of edges or links from or to a node. It is a local measure of centrality as nodes that are in direct contact with a node (whose centrality is to be calculated) are considered.
- **Closeness Centrality (CC):** It uses shortest path lengths within the network and is reciprocal of sum of minimum distances of a node to all other nodes.
- **Betweenness Centrality (BC):** It determines the ability of a node to pass information between a pair of nodes. Nodes that are positioned in shortest path between two selected nodes aid in information flow between the two.

Biological Networks

Large scale biological networks are of various types like protein interaction network, metabolic network and regulatory networks. Biological networks as well as non-biological networks follow power law; $P(k) \sim k^{-\gamma}$, where k is the degree and P(k) is the probability that a randomly selected node has a degree k (X. Zhu, Gerstein, & Snyder, 2007) but the value of exponent γ varies. The main players in biological networks are evolutionary forces that influence the growth of biological networks. Therefore, biological networks follow power law with exponent γ value between 1 and 2 while non-biological network (like internet) have exponent γ value between 2 and 4 (Chung, Lu, Dewey, & Galas, 2003). Thus, a PPI network that fits power law has exponent value $1 < \gamma < 2$ and is a biological network.

Topological Analysis of Biological Network

Topological analysis of a network is important to understand overall network architecture, features and performance (X. Zhu, et al., 2007). The most important topological features of the network are degree, shortest path length, clustering coefficient, betweenness centrality, closeness centrality (discussed above). The measurement of these topological features can be done through various softwares; one of the most popular is NetworkAnalyzer and Centiscape plugins in Cytoscape (Shannon et al., 2003).The PPI network can be analyzed for nodes having highest degree; these nodes are usually termed hubs and take part in various biological processes. In a biological network, essential proteins/ genes are present at the core and they have high degree, betweenness centrality and closeness centrality. The PPI network can also be analyzed for overrepresented pathways through functional annotation software and Gene Ontology. Network biology has become one the popular technique for identification of drug target. In human systems, proteins/genes at core of the network are essential and usually are not targeted, owing to possible side effects. For drug target identification, sub-network, functional cluster, disease gene prioritization analysis can be performed.

DATA MINING BASED METHOD FOR PPI PREDICTION

Some of the PPI prediction methods use literature and text mining algorithms and use of co-occurrence data of proteins in pubmed abstracts. Basically, a literature mining based PPI prediction methods consist of three steps:

1. **Named Entity Recognition:** This step identifies the protein names for further study.
2. **Zoning Step:** This step divides text into blocks and retrieves sentences from text.
3. *Protein-Protein Interaction Step*: It uses number of algorithms to deduce PPI's.
4. Currently, data mining approaches are divided into three categories:
5. Computational Natural language processing and linguistics based methods that describe a grammar and utilize parsers to identify PPI's.
6. Rule based methods, which use some context based rule or pattern to detect PPI's.
7. Machine based methods that use classifiers for PPI prediction.

Various literature sources for identifying proteins associated with a particular biological condition include Pubmed, OMIM, KEGG etc. Pubmed contains 24 million citations from MEDLINE (biomedical literature), life science journal and books. It is a free resource developed and maintained by NCBI, at NLM located NIH. Pubmed comprises of abstract and citations from areas of biomedicine, health, covering life science, bioengineering chemical science behavioral science. Online Mendelian Inheritance in Man (OMIM) is a freely available database of human genes and genetic phenotype, containing information on all human disease and their genetic component. It basically focuses on genotype and phenotype relationship. Kyoto Encyclopedia of Gene and Genome (KEGG) is a database that catalogues pathways, orthology, genes, genomes, modules, disease, compounds ad drugs. Additionally proteins associated with a condition may be identified from Gene Ontology classifications, the Gene expression databases (e.g. Gene Expression Omnibus, ArrayExpress, etc.), Genome wide Association studies (GWAS) database and SNP databases (e.g. dbSNP).

Scope and usage: Data mining can be used to predict novel complex PPIs in an intelligent way by combining multiple parameters. However, due to the enormity and inexactness of data or its representation, large errors may creep in. The use of these methods at a large scale should therefore be undertaken with care.

MACHINE LEARNING BASED METHODS FOR PPI PREDICTION

Machine learning is a field that combines both computer science and statistics. It consists of study and construction of algorithms that learns from a data (training set) and based on knowledge acquired (artificial intelligence) takes decisions or make predictions. Typically, a machine learning algorithm requires a set of conditions with known output and a set of parameters that control the system. The known outputs are used as a training set. In biological systems machine learning based methods integrate information from various sources like gene expression data, codon usage, physiochemical characteristics of amino acids and various other high-throughput experiments to train a model. Further, these models can be used to accurately predict PPIs. Learning can be supervised or unsupervised. In supervised learning, model describes how one set of observation (input) affects another set of observation (output). Input and output are at opposite ends of a causal chain and the model utilizes variables that mediate between input and output. In unsupervised learning, all the observations are caused by a latent set of variable and model tries to find hidden structure within the data. Unsupervised learning can be used for more larger and complex systems than supervised learning. Basically, machine learning algorithms use a collection of descriptors derived from interacting and non-interacting proteins as a training set to classify new pairs of protein as interacting or non-interacting. The different types of machine learning methods used for prediction of PPIs are:

Support Vector Machine

SVM are powerful algorithm for classification and regression analysis. SVM has strong binary decision making tendency and has been widely implemented for prediction of PPI's, subcellular location of protein, protein fold recognition, and functional classification of proteins (Koike & Takagi, 2004).

SVM methods for PPI prediction coalesce all the values (such as amino acid content, localization and usage) into a single a feature vector. The SVM is first trained using a training set consisting of elements of the two (interacting and non-interacting) sets. SVM then classifies a new pair of proteins into one of the two category based on the value of the parameters obtained from the training set. Basically, SVM builds a hyperplane in a infinite dimensional space and performs classification based on the distance of the hyperplane from nearby training data set points.

Scope and usage: Despite being a powerful analytical tool, SVMs do not always succeed with biological data due to ill-defined parameters and fuzzy boundaries between datasets.

Artificial Neural Network (ANN)

Neural Networks is an information processing unit that processes information in same way as the human central nervous system (CNS). Neural networks consist of highly connected components like that of neurons of human CNS and solves a particular problem particularly pattern recognition or classification by learning from examples (training dataset in case of neural network). ANNs are representation of human central nervous system as a mathematical model. Multilayer perceptron (MLP) is a most popular NN model for PPI modeling. MLP is a feedforward ANN and consist of multiple layers. There are basically three layers namely; inner, hidden (or intermediate) and outer layer. Weighted edges fully connect one layer to another. Each of the node is associated with a activation function which regulate the output. Patterns are given as input through the input layer, processing is done in one or more hidden layer and outputs are presented by outer layer. MLP uses backpropagation algorithm where weights are optimized and adjusted according to the training dataset for error minimization.

Scope and usage: ANNs represent some of the most powerful tools for PPI prediction due to their ability to use multiple parameters and weights for decision making. During training, the known cases may be used to successfully tweak the parameter weights for optimum performance. However, the larger, more complex ANNs are difficult to program, train and use.

K-Nearest Neighbors (KNN)

KNN is a non-parametric and simple machine learning algorithm, employed mainly for classification and regression. For computation, KNN needs an integer K, a training data set and a function to calculate closeness between the data items. The choice of K is very critical, as lower k-value generates noise in result and a higher K-value increases computational cost. In this method, objects are assigned a label in feature space according to a majority vote based on K-nearest objects (where K is user defined constant).

Scope and usage: While KNN is one of the simplest of all machine learning methods, the computational cost, complexity and memory requirements increases with increase in data set and several features. KNNs are likely to yield better results in conjunction with supervised learning methods.

Decision Tree

A Decision tree is a tree-like graph representation that is widely used for predicting PPIs, determining protein function, splice site etc. Decision tree works by applying a set of questions about the attributes (features) associated with items or data. Each of the nodes performs a test on the features, each branch represents feature values or the test outcome and the leaf node corresponds to class label (i.e., decision after all computation). The training dataset is divided into subsets on basis of feature values at the training step and this process continues until it does not affect classification. Obtaining an optimal decision tree is a NP-complete problem. Hence, a heuristic approach is employed by decision tree algorithms like ID3 (Gnocchi, Massimi, Alisi, Incerpi, & Bruscalupi, 2014), C4.5 (Quinlan, 2015) and CART (Breiman, Friedman, Olshen, & Stone, 1984).

Scope and usage: Decision trees can efficiently explain the patterns in the data but may not provide generalized results for some applications.

Random Forest *(RF)*

RF is an ensemble classification algorithm employing multitude of decision trees. Individual trees are built from random feature vectors extracted independently from that datasets. Further, variables are randomly selected in small fraction for tree nodes and a decision tree is grown. For classification of new entities, new vectors are placed down each tree. Each of the trees provides a classification to the new vector objects. Based on the majority vote, a class is decided for the new object. Thus, RF methods can be used to classify large datasets or large quantity features and can rank features according to their importance in classification. Moreover, RF can be employed for recovery of missing data. For further details refer (Chen & Liu, 2005; Qi, Klein-Seetharaman, & Bar-Joseph, 2005; Xia, Han, & Huang, 2010).

Scope and usage: The performance of RF methods is inherently dependent on the training sets, choice of parameters and choice of initial nodes. Choosing this with a wide base of experience and knowledge will help improve performance of RF algorithms.

Naïve Bayes

It is a probabilistic classifier based on Bayes theorem and is widely used for PPI prediction. It is based on the assumption that features are statistically independent and therefore the method is considered simple. The method works well for real world problems that involve normal distribution.

Scope and usage: Small data set can be used for training naïve Bayes classifiers through maximum likelihood method, but may not work well in case of more complex classification. Naïve Bayes methods can increase rapidly in complexity with the increase in amount of data.

TOOLS AND DATABASES FOR PPI PREDICTION

There has been a substantial increase in known PPIs. To make these data publically available, a host of databases have been established. There are six main databases for retrieval of PPI's. The databases, namely: BioGRID (Biological General Repository for Interaction Datasets), IntAct (IntAct molecular interaction database), BIND (Biomolecular Interaction Network Database), MINT (Molecular INTeraction database), DIP (Database of Interacting Proteins) and HPRD (Human Protein Reference Database) vary with respect to content and scope. Table 3 briefly describes the statistics of all six databases.

Scientific publications are the primary sources of PPI's. Publically available databases curate the interaction data and provide data to the researchers. Since there is a wide range of experiments to de-

Table 3. Statistics of protein-protein interaction databases

Database	Proteins	Interactions	URL	References
BioGrid	56322	787370	http://thebiogrid.org/_	(Breitkreutz et al., 2008; Stark et al., 2011; Stark et al., 2006)
MINT	35553	241458	http://mint.bio.uniroma2.it/mint/_	(Zanzoni et al., 2002)
DIP	27183	78322	http://dip.doe-mbi.ucla.edu/dip/Main.cgi_	(Xenarios et al., 2000)
BIND	23643	43050	http://bond.unleashedinformatics.com/_	(Bader, Betel, & Hogue, 2003)
IntAct	84391	300353	http://www.ebi.ac.uk/intact/_	(Hermjakob et al., 2004)
HPRD	30047	41327	http://www.hprd.org_	(Peri et al., 2004)

tect PPI's, different databases have different schema. Hence, all the data may not be covered by single database. Recently, the International Molecular Exchange (IMEx) was created that allows exchange of information from various sources, prevents duplication of data and reduces curation efforts (Lehne & Schlitt, 2009). BIND was the first interaction database created by University of Toronto and University of British Columbia. IntAct, MINT and DIP are members of IMEx. HPRD deals completely with human proteins providing information about protein-protein interactions along with some specific information like post translational modification, substrate-enzyme relationship and involvement in disease.

After construction of Protein-Protein Interaction network, visualization and analysis of PPI network is needed. A large number of tools have been developed for this purpose. Table 4 lists the available tools, servers and Plugins for visualizing and analysis of PPI networks. Some well known tools are (Pavlopoulos, et al., 2008):

- **Cytoscape:** Cytoscape is well known free software package for visualization and analysis of biological networks. It can further integrate annotation data, expression data or other type of data in these biological networks. Cytoscape supports a variety of network file formats such as text delimited files, excel files, SIF, GML, SBML, XGMML, OBO, BioPAX, GraphML, PSI-MI, Gene Association and KGML (KEGG XML). It provides node graphics, different layouts for the network like cyclic, tree, force-directed, edge-weight etc. Along with basic features, Cytoscape provides additional features through plugins that can be easily downloaded, managed and updated.
- **Medusa:** Medusa is highly interactive standalone software for visualization and clustering of biological network. It is extremely interactive and can handle multi-edged and weighted networks. It is currently supplemented with variety of layouts like Grid, Random, Parallel Coordinates, Hierarchical, Spring Embedding, Fruchterman-Reingold, Distance geometry and Circular. Clustering algorithm embedded in Medusa are Predefined clustering, Spectral, k-Means, Affinity Propagation.
- **Navigator:** Network Analysis, Visualization, & Graphing TORonto is a freely available visualizing and graphing tool for 2D and 3D biological network. Network file in tab-delimited, NAViGaTOR XML, BioPAX or PSI formats can be loaded. Multiple network panels can be handled in Navigator workspace and can be modified by cutting, copying and pasting nodes and edges. For analysis the highly connected sub-networks and hubs can be automatically detected.

Table 4. Tools, servers, and plugins for network visualization and analysis

Name	Standalone/Web-based/Plugin	URL	Reference
APID	Web-based	http://bioinfow.dep.usal.es/apid/index.html	(Prieto & De Las Rivas, 2006)
BioLayout	Standalone	http://www.biolayout.org.	(Enright & Ouzounis, 2001)
Cytoscape	Standalone	http://cytoscapeweb.cytoscape.org/	(Shannon, et al., 2003)
BioNoM	Cytoscape plugin	https://binom.curie.fr/	(Zinovyev, Viara, Calzone, & Barillot, 2008)
Cerebral	Cytoscape plugin	http://www.pathogenomics.ca/cerebral/	(Barsky, Munzner, Gardy, & Kincaid, 2008)
InterProSurf	Standalone	http://curie.utmb.edu/prosurf.html	(Negi, Schein, Oezguen, Power, & Braun, 2007)
iSPOT	Web-based	http://cbm.bio.uniroma2.it/iSPOT/	(Brannetti & Helmer-Citterich, 2003)
MCODE	Cytoscape plugin	http://baderlab.org/Software/MCODE	(Bader & Hogue, 2003)
InterViewer	Standalone	http://interviewer.inha.ac.kr/	(Ju, Park, Park, & Han, 2003)
Medusa	Standalone	https://sites.google.com/site/medusa3visualization/	(Pavlopoulos, Hooper, Sifrim, Schneider, & Aerts, 2011)
Navigator	Standalone	http://ophid.utoronto.ca/navigator/	(Brown et al., 2009)
Pajek	Standalone	http://vlado.fmf.unilj.si/pub/networks/pajek/	(Batagelj & Mrvar, 2009)
Meta-PPISP	Web-based	http://pipe.scs.fsu.edu/meta-ppisp.html	(Qin & Zhou, 2007)
NoxClass	Web-based	http://noxclass.bioinf.mpi-inf.mpg.de/	(H. Zhu, Domingues, Sommer, & Lengauer, 2006)
Osprey	Standalone	http://biodata.mshri.on.ca/osprey/servlet/Index	(Breitkreutz, Stark, & Tyers, 2003)
VisANT	Cytoscape plugin	http://visant.bu.edu/	(Hu et al., 2009)
UVCLUSTER	Standalone	http://www.uv.es/genomica/UVCLUSTER/	(Arnau, Mars, & Marin, 2005)
PathBlast	Web-based	http://www.pathblast.org/	(Kelley et al., 2004)
Ondex	Standalone	http://ondex.rothamsted.ac.uk/OndexWeb/	(Kohler et al., 2006)
ProViz	Standalone	http://www.cbib.ubordeaux2.fr/eng/proviz.html	(Iragne, Nikolski, Mathieu, Auber, & Sherman, 2005)
PIVOT	Standalone	http://acgt.cs.tau.ac.il/pivot/	(Orlev, Shamir, & Shiloh, 2004)
PATIKA	Web-based	http://www.patika.org/	(Demir et al., 2002)

SOLUTIONS AND RECOMMENDATIONS

There has been a substantial increase in the number of reported proteins, and the information about proteins function and characteristics. Owing to drawbacks related to experimental methods of PPI detection, computational methods for PPI predictions have been developed and they have overcome problems related to experimental methods. Yet, to minimize number of false positives, more accurate statistical and validation methods are needed. With advancement in technology, there has also been an increase in number of solved genomes that further increase the number of reference genomes for PPI prediction. More the genome information incorporated in the prediction study better will be the coverage and accuracy of the method. Several verification methods such as Expression Profile Reliability (EPR index), Interaction Generalities Measures IG1 and IG2, Paralogous Verification Method (PVM) and Protein Localization Method (PLM) can be used for eliminating false positives that are detected in high-throughput PPI measurement methods. Performance of machine learning PPI prediction methods improves with increase in data from various sources in training set. PPI prediction methods that incorporate data from all sources such as gene expression data, evolutionary profile, codon usage, structural data, and sequence data may produce more accurate results. It is recommended to use methods based on different approaches synchronously to predict PPIs with high confidence. Weightage of a PPI increases if it is predicted through different methods. Also use of a vigorous validation method assists in distinguishing between false positive and true positives.

FUTURE RESEARCH DIRECTIONS

PPIs hold an excellent future in developing new therapeutics that makes PPI identification an important task. Due to disadvantages that experimental methods of PPI detection hold, there is a need to develop computational approaches for PPI prediction. These *in silico* methods should be based on data from various sources like gene expression, codon usage, evolutionary profiles, sequence and structural information to increase performance and coverage of PPI prediction. Methods that utilize combination of different approaches for PPI prediction should be developed as they may give more precise results. One of the greatest problems with PPI prediction methods is prediction of false positive interactions. Therefore, strong validation methods should be developed to distinguish between false positives and true positives. Furthermore, there has been an increase in number of reported proteins and data regarding their function, structure and characteristics, therefore constant updates are needed in existing databases. Beside this, development of new databases and repositories are also required to maintain vast amount of data.

CONCLUSION

PPIs control a wide range of cellular processes including signal transduction, enzyme inhibition, cell growth, proliferation, antigen-antibody detection, DNA transcription, replication, translation, splicing, assemblage of multi-domain proteins etc. Any alteration in PPIs results in changes in downstream signaling processes that affect normal functioning of cellular machinery. PPI have also become an attractive target for developing new therapeutics. Thus, identification and characterization of PPI have become essential to understand molecular basis of a biological process. PPI detection through experimental methods is expensive, time consuming, prone to experimental errors. They do not cover transient interactions. Therefore, computational approaches to predict PPI have been developed. These approaches work on genomic, structural, evolution, sequence, gene expression and other biological data. In recent times, computational prediction of PPI is categorized into genomic context based methods, structure context based method, network topology, machine learning and literature and data mining based methods. However, computational methods require a strong validation method to filter out false positive hits. PPI prediction methods should also use a combination of approaches based on genomic context, structural context, network topology, machine learning and data mining methods to improve performance, coverage and accuracy of the program. Due to increase in number of reported proteins, data concerning function and characteristics of proteins, the need for maintenance of this information have also increased. A large number of databases and repositories such as BioGRID, IntAct, BIND, MINT, DIP and HPRD are available for this purpose. An array of softwares and servers are also available for network construction and visualization. Still the accuracy of PPI prediction methods is a matter of concern and development of new approaches with improved accuracy and coverage is in demand.

CASE STUDY

Study of Pathology and Treatment Strategy of Ocular Effect of Atherosclerosis using Systems Biology Approach

This case study is based on "Gupta A, Mohanty P, Bhatnagar S (2014) Integrative analysis of ocular complications in atherosclerosis unveils pathway convergence and crosstalk. J Recept Signal Transduct Res. 23:1-16".

Atherosclerosis is a deadly disease and is a foremost cause of mortality worldwide. Atherosclerosis has microvascular effect on eyes, brain, kidney etc. Microvascular complications resulting due to atherosclerosis can easily be visualized in eye as ophthalmic artery is first major branch of carotid artery. However, the mechanisms leading to microvascular complications in eye are still unknown, thus a systems biology approach particularly analysis of protein-protein interaction network was applied to get insights into the causable mechanisms.

Methodology

Genes involved in atherosclerosis and ophthalmic diseases were retrieved using Polysearch text mining system which on basis of users' query searches multiple sources like Pubmed, OMIM, SwissProt, Drugbank etc. Search was performed individually for atherosclerosis and ophthalmic diseases resulting into two datasets of proteins/genes involved in atherosclerosis and ophthalmic diseases respectively. From two data sets, seed genes involved in both atherosclerosis and ophthalmic diseases were identified. PPI network (Figure 6) was then developed using seed genes and their first interactors through PathwayLinker (Farkas, Szanto-Varnagy, & Korcsmaros, 2012). Disconnected components were discarded from the original network and the resulting network was subjected to further analysis which involves:

Figure 6. The PPI network where seed proteins are shown in yellow, high BC nodes in Green, high degree protein nodes (hubs) in Red. Seed Proteins having high degree is shown in Orange while Violet depicts seed proteins with high BC. Proteins having high BC and high degree are in Blue while the proteins having high BC and Degree (Bottleneck Hubs) are in Pink.

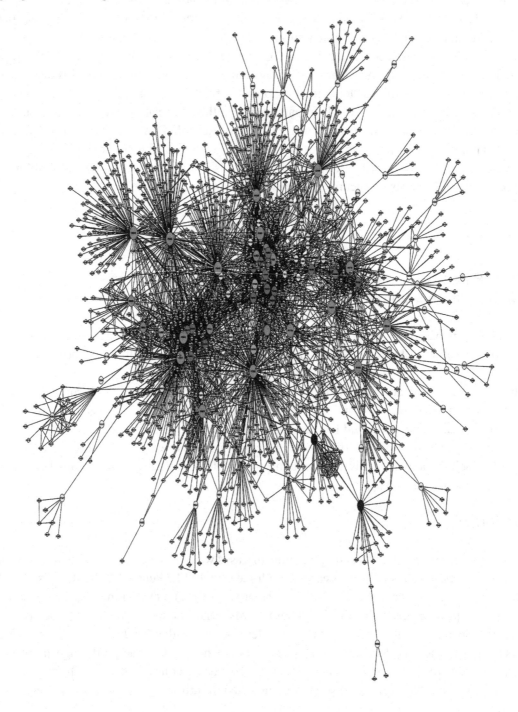

Figure 7. Graph of node degree distribution against number of nodes representing the PPI network follows power law

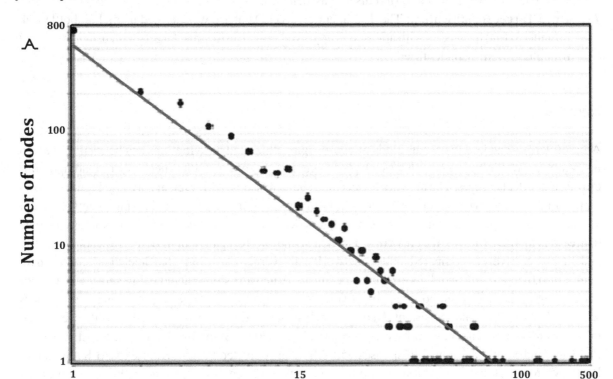

1. **Topological Analysis of The PPI Network:** Topological analysis consisted of determining degree, clustering coefficient, CC, BC, characteristic path length, power law fit and was done using Cytoscape 2.8.3.

2. **Network Validation by Comparison With Randomized Networks:** The confidence of the PPI network was evaluated by comparing clustering coefficient of the PPI network with that of random networks formed by shuffling the edges but keeping the node degree constant.

3. **Creation of High BC Backbone Network:** The nodes with high BC (value greater than the mean of BC of all nodes) were extracted from the original network and a backbone network was created (Figure 7).

4. **Candidate Gene Prioritization:** Candidate disease genes were identified using GPEC plugin of cytoscape 2.8.3. Seed genes identified from the literature search were used as training dataset. The neighboring genes within the topological distance less than or equal to 1 were considered as candidate disease gene.

5. **Biological Complex Detection:** MCODE plugin of cytoscape 2.8.3 was employed to detect the major clusters or subgraphs within the network. MCODE program was used with haircut option and clustering cutoff score of 0.2 for clustering.

6. **Data Annotation:** Database for annotation, visualization and integrated discovery was used to identify overrepresented pathways and processes. Complete list of network protein was given as input in DAVID and initial filter of p-value/ease score of 0.05 with Fisher's exact test was applied.

Pathways with p-value lower than 0.05 were strongly enriched. Genetic Association DB disease class database was mapped to find disease association.

7. **Drug Target Identification:** The Therapeutic Target Database was queried using hub bottleneck proteins to find the targets with atleast one approved drug. Beside this, targets with drugs in clinical trial phase were also identified.

Results

Atherosclerosis can lead to various kinds of microangiopathies and its symptoms can be easily observed in eyes. Systems biology approach was adapted to get insights of molecular mechanisms leading to microvascular effects in eyes. The network formed had characteristics of biological network. Figure 7 shows that PPI network follows Power law with straight line passing through few nodes (hubs) and exponent γ value -1.459. Topological analysis revealed that largest degree of network was 193, whereas average degree was 5.6089. The average clustering coefficient and shortest path length of the network was 0.185 and 3.62 respectively as compared random network with average clustering coefficient and shortest path length of 0.029 ± 0.003 and 4.74 ± 0.06 respectively. A network constructed using shortest path connecting high BC nodes resulted in a sub-network of 33 nodes and 82 edges representing core element was highly connected and consistent. Network analysis showed that atherosclerosis and its eye related microvascular effects are caused by crosstalks of Neurotrophin Signaling Pathways, Focal Adhesion Pathways and Multiple Immune Responses with Mitogen Activated Protein Kinase (MAPK) Signaling Pathways. MAPK1 and PKC, through topological and pathway analysis came out to be central proteins regulating both atherosclerosis and the related ocular diseases. MAPK pathway gets activated and in turn activates NFKB signaling pathways. This results in uncontrolled endothelial cell proliferation and pericyte loss and disruption of tight junctions of Blood –Retinal –Barrier (BRB). The dysfunctional BRB becomes more permeable for inflammatory cytokines and proteins and the ophthalmic complications increases due to entry of these proinflammatory molecules into eye tissues.

In this work, a total of 24 central proteins were identified that had an important role in atherosclerosis induced eye diseases. The network showed features of vasoregression (which further leads to diabetic retinopathy) when compared to other known models of ophthalmic diseases. The network was also enriched with proteins involved in diabetic retinopathy. These proteins had a close relationship with central proteins of the network demonstrating how atherosclerotic proteins lead to vasoregressive changes in eyes. The paper proposes that a large number of eye diseases are caused by vasoregression. Moreover, five drug targets among all the central proteins were identified and each of the drug targets has one therapeutic modulator. Thus, novel therapies can be developed for treatment of ophthalmic diseases induced by atherosclerosis.

REFERENCES

Aloy, P., & Russell, R. B. (2003). InterPreTS: Protein interaction prediction through tertiary structure. *Bioinformatics (Oxford, England)*, *19*(1), 161–162. doi:10.1093/bioinformatics/19.1.161 PMID:12499311

Arnau, V., Mars, S., & Marin, I. (2005). Iterative cluster analysis of protein interaction data. *Bioinformatics (Oxford, England), 21*(3), 364–378. doi:10.1093/bioinformatics/bti021 PMID:15374873

Bader, G. D., Betel, D., & Hogue, C. W. (2003). BIND: The Biomolecular Interaction Network Database. *Nucleic Acids Research, 31*(1), 248–250. doi:10.1093/nar/gkg056 PMID:12519993

Bader, G. D., & Hogue, C. W. (2003). An automated method for finding molecular complexes in large protein interaction networks. *BMC Bioinformatics, 4*(1), 2. doi:10.1186/1471-2105-4-2 PMID:12525261

Barsky, A., Munzner, T., Gardy, J., & Kincaid, R. (2008). Cerebral: Visualizing multiple experimental conditions on a graph with biological context. *IEEE Transactions on Visualization and Computer Graphics, 14*(6), 1253–1260. doi:10.1109/TVCG.2008.117 PMID:18988971

Baspinar, A., Cukuroglu, E., Nussinov, R., Keskin, O., & Gursoy, A. (2014). PRISM: a web server and repository for prediction of protein-protein interactions and modeling their 3D complexes. *Nucleic Acids Res, 42*(Web Server issue), W285-289. doi:10.1093/nar/gku397nar/gku397

Batagelj, V., & Mrvar, A. (2009). Pajek - Program for Large Network Analysis. *Connections, 21*, 47–57.

Berggard, T., Linse, S., & James, P. (2007). Methods for the detection and analysis of protein-protein interactions. *Proteomics, 7*(16), 2833–2842. doi:10.1002/pmic.200700131 PMID:17640003

Berman, H. M., Westbrook, J., Feng, Z., Gilliland, G., Bhat, T. N., Weissig, H., . . . Bourne, P. E. (2000). The Protein Data Bank. *Nucleic Acids Res, 28*(1), 235-242. doi:gkd090

Brannetti, B., & Helmer-Citterich, M. (2003). iSPOT: A web tool to infer the interaction specificity of families of protein modules. *Nucleic Acids Research, 31*(13), 3709–3711. doi:10.1093/nar/gkg592 PMID:12824399

Breiman, L., Friedman, J. H., Olshen, R. A., & Stone, C. J. (1984). *Classification and regression trees.* Chapman and Hall/CRC.

Breitkreutz, B. J., Stark, C., Reguly, T., Boucher, L., Breitkreutz, A., Livstone, M., . . . Tyers, M. (2008). The BioGRID Interaction Database: 2008 update. *Nucleic Acids Res, 36*(Database issue), D637-640. doi:10.1093/nar/gkm1001

Breitkreutz, B. J., Stark, C., & Tyers, M. (2003). Osprey: A network visualization system. *Genome Biology, 4*(3), R22. doi:10.1186/gb-2003-4-3-r22 PMID:12620107

Brown, K. R., Otasek, D., Ali, M., McGuffin, M. J., Xie, W., Devani, B., & Jurisica, I. et al. (2009). NAViGaTOR: Network Analysis, Visualization and Graphing Toronto. *Bioinformatics (Oxford, England), 25*(24), 3327–3329. doi:10.1093/bioinformatics/btp595 PMID:19837718

Chen, X. W., & Liu, M. (2005). Prediction of protein-protein interactions using random decision forest framework. *Bioinformatics, 21*(24), 4394-4400. doi:10.1093/bioinformatics/bti721

Chien, C. T., Bartel, P. L., Sternglanz, R., & Fields, S. (1991). The two-hybrid system: A method to identify and clone genes for proteins that interact with a protein of interest. *Proceedings of the National Academy of Sciences of the United States of America, 88*(21), 9578–9582. doi:10.1073/pnas.88.21.9578 PMID:1946372

Chung, F., Lu, L., Dewey, T. G., & Galas, D. J. (2003). Duplication models for biological networks. *Journal of Computational Biology, 10*(5), 677–687. doi:10.1089/106652703322539024 PMID:14633392

De Las Rivas, J., & Fontanillo, C. (2010). Protein-protein interactions essentials: Key concepts to building and analyzing interactome networks. *PLoS Computational Biology, 6*(6), e1000807. doi:10.1371/journal.pcbi.1000807 PMID:20589078

Demir, E., Babur, O., Dogrusoz, U., Gursoy, A., Nisanci, G., Cetin-Atalay, R., & Ozturk, M. (2002). PATIKA: An integrated visual environment for collaborative construction and analysis of cellular pathways. *Bioinformatics (Oxford, England), 18*(7), 996–1003. doi:10.1093/bioinformatics/18.7.996 PMID:12117798

Dobzhansky, T. (1946). Genetics of Natural Populations. Xiii. Recombination and Variability in Populations of Drosophila Pseudoobscura. *Genetics, 31*(3), 269–290. PMID:17247197

Dunker, A. K., Cortese, M. S., Romero, P., Iakoucheva, L. M., & Uversky, V. N. (2005). Flexible nets. The roles of intrinsic disorder in protein interaction networks. *FEBS J, 272*(20), 5129-5148. doi:10.1111/j.1742-4658.2005.04948.x

Enright, A. J., & Ouzounis, C. A. (2001). BioLayout--an automatic graph layout algorithm for similarity visualization. *Bioinformatics (Oxford, England), 17*(9), 853–854. doi:10.1093/bioinformatics/17.9.853 PMID:11590107

Farkas, I. J., Szanto-Varnagy, A., & Korcsmaros, T. (2012). Linking proteins to signaling pathways for experiment design and evaluation. *PLoS One, 7*(4), e36202. doi:10.1371/journal.pone.0036202

Fernandez-Recio, J., Totrov, M., & Abagyan, R. (2004). Identification of protein-protein interaction sites from docking energy landscapes. *J Mol Biol, 335*(3), 843-865.

Fields, S., & Sternglanz, R. (1994). The two-hybrid system: An assay for protein-protein interactions. *Trends in Genetics, 10*(8), 286–292. doi:10.1016/0168-9525(90)90012-U PMID:7940758

Gnocchi, D., Massimi, M., Alisi, A., Incerpi, S., & Bruscalupi, G. (2014). Effect of fructose and 3,5-diiodothyronine (3,5-T(2)) on lipid accumulation and insulin signalling in non-alcoholic fatty liver disease (NAFLD)-like rat primary hepatocytes. *Hormone and Metabolic Research. Hormon- und Stoffwechselforschung. Hormones et Metabolisme, 46*(5), 333–340. doi:10.1055/s-0034-1371858 PMID:24816759

Goldberg, D. S., & Roth, F. P. (2003). Assessing experimentally derived interactions in a small world. *Proc Natl Acad Sci U S A, 100*(8), 4372-4376. doi:10.1073/pnas.0735871100

Golemis, E. A. (2002). *Protein-protein interactions: A molecular cloning manual.* Cold Spring Harbor, NY: Cold Spring Harbor Laboratory Press.

Hermjakob, H., Montecchi-Palazzi, L., Lewington, C., Mudali, S., Kerrien, S., Orchard, S., . . . Apweiler, R. (2004). IntAct: an open source molecular interaction database. *Nucleic Acids Res, 32*(Database issue), D452-455. doi: 10.1093/nar/gkh052

Hu, Z., Hung, J. H., Wang, Y., Chang, Y. C., Huang, C. L., Huyck, M., & DeLisi, C. (2009). VisANT 3.5: multi-scale network visualization, analysis and inference based on the gene ontology. *Nucleic Acids Res, 37*(Web Server issue), W115-121. doi:10.1093/nar/gkp406

Huynen, M., Snel, B., Lathe, W. III, & Bork, P. (2000). Predicting protein function by genomic context: Quantitative evaluation and qualitative inferences. *Genome Research, 10*(8), 1204–1210. doi:10.1101/gr.10.8.1204 PMID:10958638

Iragne, F., Nikolski, M., Mathieu, B., Auber, D., & Sherman, D. (2005). ProViz: protein interaction visualization and exploration. *Bioinformatics, 21*(2), 272-274. doi: 10.1093/bioinformatics/bth494

Jones, S., & Thornton, J. M. (1996). Principles of protein-protein interactions. *Proceedings of the National Academy of Sciences of the United States of America, 93*(1), 13–20. doi:10.1073/pnas.93.1.13 PMID:8552589

Ju, B. H., Park, B., Park, J. H., & Han, K. (2003). Visualization and analysis of protein interactions. *Bioinformatics (Oxford, England), 19*(2), 317–318. doi:10.1093/bioinformatics/19.2.317 PMID:12538268

Kelley, B. P., Yuan, B., Lewitter, F., Sharan, R., Stockwell, B. R., & Ideker, T. (2004). PathBLAST: a tool for alignment of protein interaction networks. *Nucleic Acids Res, 32*(Web Server issue), W83-88. doi:10.1093/nar/gkh411

Keskin, O., Ma, B., Rogale, K., Gunasekaran, K., & Nussinov, R. (2005). Protein-protein interactions: organization, cooperativity and mapping in a bottom-up Systems Biology approach. *Phys Biol, 2*(2), S24-35. doi: S1478-3975(05)94487-2

Kim, W. K., Henschel, A., Winter, C., & Schroeder, M. (2006). The many faces of protein-protein interactions: A compendium of interface geometry. *PLoS Comput Biol, 2*(9), e124. doi:10.1371/journal.pcbi.0020124

Kim, W. K., & Ison, J. C. (2005). Survey of the geometric association of domain-domain interfaces. *Proteins, 61*(4), 1075–1088. doi:10.1002/prot.20693 PMID:16247798

Kohler, J., Baumbach, J., Taubert, J., Specht, M., Skusa, A., Ruegg, A., . . . Philippi, S. (2006). Graph-based analysis and visualization of experimental results with ONDEX. *Bioinformatics, 22*(11), 1383-1390. doi:10.1093/bioinformatics/btl081

Koike, A., & Takagi, T. (2004). Prediction of protein-protein interaction sites using support vector machines. *Protein Eng Des Sel, 17*(2), 165-173. doi:10.1093/protein/gzh020

Lawson, C. L., Baker, M. L., Best, C., Bi, C., Dougherty, M., Feng, P., . . . Chiu, W. (2011). EMData-Bank.org: unified data resource for CryoEM. *Nucleic Acids Res, 39*(Database issue), D456-464. doi: 10.1093/nar/gkq880

Lehne, B., & Schlitt, T. (2009). Protein-protein interaction databases: keeping up with growing interactomes. *Hum Genomics, 3*(3), 291-297.

Mellor, J. C., Yanai, I., Clodfelter, K. H., Mintseris, J., & DeLisi, C. (2002). Predictome: A database of putative functional links between proteins. *Nucleic Acids Research, 30*(1), 306–309. doi:10.1093/nar/30.1.306 PMID:11752322

Mosca, R., Ceol, A., Stein, A., Olivella, R., & Aloy, P. (2014). 3did: a catalog of domain-based interactions of known three-dimensional structure. *Nucleic Acids Res, 42*(Database issue), D374-379. doi: gkt887 [pii]10.1093/nar/gkt887

Negi, S. S., Schein, C. H., Oezguen, N., Power, T. D., & Braun, W. (2007). InterProSurf: a web server for predicting interacting sites on protein surfaces. *Bioinformatics, 23*(24), 3397-3399. doi:10.1093/bioinformatics/btm474

Orlev, N., Shamir, R., & Shiloh, Y. (2004). PIVOT: protein interactions visualizatiOn tool. *Bioinformatics, 20*(3), 424-425. doi: 10.1093/bioinformatics/btg426

Overbeek, R., Fonstein, M., D'Souza, M., Pusch, G. D., & Maltsev, N. (1999). Use of contiguity on the chromosome to predict functional coupling. Silico Biol, 1(2), 93-108.

Pavlopoulos, G. A., Hooper, S. D., Sifrim, A., Schneider, R., & Aerts, J. (2011). Medusa: A tool for exploring and clustering biological networks. *BMC Res Notes*, 4, 384. doi:10.1186/1756-0500-4-384

Pavlopoulos, G. A., Wegener, A. L., & Schneider, R. (2008). A survey of visualization tools for biological network analysis. *BioData Min*, 1, 12. doi:10.1186/1756-0381-1-12

Pedamallu, C. S., & Posfai, J. (2010). Open source tool for prediction of genome wide protein-protein interaction network based on ortholog information. *Source Code Biol Med.*, 5, 8. doi:10.1186/1751-0473-5-8

Peri, S., Navarro, J. D., Kristiansen, T. Z., Amanchy, R., Surendranath, V., Muthusamy, B., . . . Pandey, A. (2004). Human protein reference database as a discovery resource for proteomics. *Nucleic Acids Res, 32*(Database issue), D497-501. doi: 10.1093/nar/gkh070

Phizicky, E. M., & Fields, S. (1995). Protein-protein interactions: Methods for detection and analysis. *Microbiological Reviews*, *59*(1), 94–123. PMID:7708014

Pieper, U., Webb, B. M., Barkan, D. T., Schneidman-Duhovny, D., Schlessinger, A., Braberg, H., . . . Sali, A. (2011). ModBase, a database of annotated comparative protein structure models, and associated resources. *Nucleic Acids Res, 39*(Database issue), D465-474. doi:10.1093/nar/gkq1091

Prieto, C., & De Las Rivas, J. (2006). APID: Agile Protein Interaction DataAnalyzer. *Nucleic Acids Res, 34*(Web Server issue), W298-302. doi:10.1093/nar/gkl128

Qi, Y., Klein-Seetharaman, J., & Bar-Joseph, Z. (2005). Random forest similarity for protein-protein interaction prediction from multiple sources. *Pacific Symposium on Biocomputing. Pacific Symposium on Biocomputing*, 2005, 531–542. PMID:15759657

Qin, S., & Zhou, H. X. (2007). meta-PPISP: a meta web server for protein-protein interaction site prediction. *Bioinformatics, 23*(24), 3386-3387. doi:10.1093/bioinformatics/btm434

Quinlan, A. (2015). Response to "A Comparison of Paper Documentation to Electronic Documentation for Trauma Resuscitations at a Level I Pediatric Trauma Center". *J Emerg Nurs*. doi:10.1016/j.jen.2015.02.010

Rao, V. S., Srinivas, K., Sujini, G. N., & Kumar, G. N. (2014). Protein-protein interaction detection: Methods and analysis. *International Journal of Proteomics*, *147648*. doi:10.1155/2014/147648 PMID:24693427

Ratner, D. (1974). The interaction bacterial and phage proteins with immobilized Escherichia coli RNA polymerase. *Journal of Molecular Biology, 88*(2), 373–383. doi:10.1016/0022-2836(74)90488-4 PMID:4616088

Roche P, M. X. (n. d.). *Protein-Protein Interaction Inhibition (2P2I): Mixed Methodologies for the Acceleration of Lead Discovery*: Bentham Science Publishers

Sarmady, M., Dampier, W., & Tozeren, A. (2011). HIV protein sequence hotspots for crosstalk with host hub proteins. *PLoS One, 6*(8), e23293. doi: PONE-D-11-07403 [pii]10.1371/journal.pone.0023293

Shannon, P., Markiel, A., Ozier, O., Baliga, N. S., Wang, J. T., Ramage, D., . . . Ideker, T. (2003). Cytoscape: a software environment for integrated models of biomolecular interaction networks. *Genome Res, 13*(11), 2498-2504. doi: 10.1101/gr.1239303

Shoemaker, B. A., & Panchenko, A. R. (2007). Deciphering protein-protein interactions. Part I. Experimental techniques and databases. *PLoS Comput Biol, 3*(3), e42. doi:10.1371/journal.pcbi.0030042

Skrabanek, L., Saini, H. K., Bader, G. D., & Enright, A. J. (2008). Computational prediction of protein-protein interactions. *Molecular Biotechnology, 38*(1), 1–17. doi:10.1007/s12033-007-0069-2 PMID:18095187

Smith, G. P. (1985). Filamentous fusion phage: Novel expression vectors that display cloned antigens on the virion surface. *Science, 228*(4705), 1315–1317. doi:10.1126/science.4001944 PMID:4001944

Snel, B., Lehmann, G., Bork, P., & Huynen, M. A. (2000). STRING: A web-server to retrieve and display the repeatedly occurring neighbourhood of a gene. *Nucleic Acids Research, 28*(18), 3442–3444. doi:10.1093/nar/28.18.3442 PMID:10982861

Stark, C., Breitkreutz, B. J., Chatr-Aryamontri, A., Boucher, L., Oughtred, R., Livstone, M. S., . . . Tyers, M. (2011). The BioGRID Interaction Database: 2011 update. *Nucleic Acids Res, 39*(Database issue), D698-704. doi: 10.1093/nar/gkq1116

Stark, C., Breitkreutz, B. J., Reguly, T., Boucher, L., Breitkreutz, A., & Tyers, M. (2006). BioGRID: a general repository for interaction datasets. *Nucleic Acids Res, 34*(Database issue), D535-539. doi:10.1093/nar/gkj109

Surade, S., & Blundell, T. L. (2012). Structural biology and drug discovery of difficult targets: the limits of ligandability. *Chem Biol, 19*(1), 42-50. doi: 10.1016/j.chembiol.2011.12.013

Szilagyi, A., Grimm, V., Arakaki, A. K., & Skolnick, J. (2005). Prediction of physical protein-protein interactions. *Phys Biol, 2*(2), S1-16. doi:10.1088/1478-3975/2/2/S01

Tamames, J., Casari, G., Ouzounis, C., & Valencia, A. (1997). Conserved clusters of functionally related genes in two bacterial genomes. *Journal of Molecular Evolution, 44*(1), 66–73. doi:10.1007/PL00006122 PMID:9010137

Tatusov, R. L., Koonin, E. V., & Lipman, D. J. (1997). A genomic perspective on protein families. *Science, 278*(5338), 631–637. doi:10.1126/science.278.5338.631 PMID:9381173

Teyra, J., Doms, A., Schroeder, M., & Pisabarro, M. T. (2006). SCOWLP: a web-based database for detailed characterization and visualization of protein interfaces. *BMC Bioinformatics, 7*, 104. doi:10.1186/1471-2105-7-104

Teyra, J., Paszkowski-Rogacz, M., Anders, G., & Pisabarro, M. T. (2008). SCOWLP classification: structural comparison and analysis of protein binding regions. *BMC Bioinformatics, 9*, 9. doi: 10.1186/1471-2105-9-9

Teyra, J., Samsonov, S. A., Schreiber, S., & Pisabarro, M. T. (2011). SCOWLP update: 3D classification of protein-protein, -peptide, -saccharide and -nucleic acid interactions, and structure-based binding inferences across folds. *BMC Bioinformatics, 12*, 398. doi: 10.1186/1471-2105-12-398

Traut, R. R., Casiano, C., & Zecherle, N. (1989). Crosslinking of protein subunits and ligands by the introduction of disulphide bonds. In T. E. Creighton (Ed.), *Protein function: a practical approach* (pp. 101–133). Oxford: IRL Press.

Tuncbag, N., Gursoy, A., Nussinov, R., & Keskin, O. (2011). Predicting protein-protein interactions on a proteome scale by matching evolutionary and structural similarities at interfaces using PRISM. *Nat Protoc, 6*(9), 1341-1354. doi: 10.1038/nprot.2011.367

UniProt: a hub for protein information. (2015). *Nucleic Acids Res, 43*(Database issue), D204-212. doi: 10.1093/nar/gku989

Valencia, A., & Pazos, F. (2002). Computational methods for the prediction of protein interactions. *Curr Opin Struct Biol, 12*(3), 368-373.

Valencia, A., & Pazos, F. (2003). Prediction of protein-protein interactions from evolutionary information. *Methods of Biochemical Analysis, 44*, 411–426. PMID:12647397

Wilson, C. G., & Arkin, M. R. (2011). Small-molecule inhibitors of IL-2/IL-2R: Lessons learned and applied. *Current Topics in Microbiology and Immunology, 348*, 25–59. doi:10.1007/82_2010_93 PMID:20703966

Winter, C., Henschel, A., Kim, W. K., & Schroeder, M. (2006). SCOPPI: a structural classification of protein-protein interfaces. *Nucleic Acids Res, 34*(Database issue), D310-314. doi:10.1093/nar/gkj099

Xenarios, I., Rice, D. W., Salwinski, L., Baron, M. K., Marcotte, E. M., & Eisenberg, D. (2000). DIP: the database of interacting proteins. *Nucleic Acids Res, 28*(1), 289-291.

Xia, J. F., Han, K., & Huang, D. S. (2010). Sequence-based prediction of protein-protein interactions by means of rotation forest and autocorrelation descriptor. *Protein and Peptide Letters, 17*(1), 137–145. doi:10.2174/092986610789909403 PMID:20214637

Young, R. A., & Davis, R. W. (1983). Yeast RNA polymerase II genes: Isolation with antibody probes. *Science, 222*(4625), 778–782. doi:10.1126/science.6356359 PMID:6356359

Zahiri, J., Bozorgmehr, J. H., & Masoudi-Nejad, A. (2013). Computational Prediction of Protein-Protein Interaction Networks: Algo-rithms and Resources. *Curr Genomics, 14*(6), 397-414. doi:10.2174/1389202911314060004

Zanzoni, A., Montecchi-Palazzi, L., Quondam, M., Ausiello, G., Helmer-Citterich, M., & Cesareni, G. (2002). MINT: a Molecular INTeraction database. *FEBS Lett, 513*(1), 135-140.

Zhu, H., Domingues, F. S., Sommer, I., & Lengauer, T. (2006). NOXclass: prediction of protein-protein interaction types. *BMC Bioinformatics, 7*, 27. doi:10.1186/1471-2105-7-27

Zhu, X., Gerstein, M., & Snyder, M. (2007). Getting connected: analysis and principles of biological networks. *Genes Dev, 21*(9), 1010-1024. doi:10.1101/gad.1528707

Zinovyev, A., Viara, E., Calzone, L., & Barillot, E. (2008). BiNoM: a Cytoscape plugin for manipulating and analyzing biological networks. *Bioinformatics, 24*(6), 876-877. doi:10.1093/bioinformatics/btm553

KEY TERMS AND DEFINITIONS

Empirical Function: Function based on counting number of different types of interactions (hydrophobic, H-bonds and other Vander wall forces) between interfaces of binding partners.

Feature Vector: It is a vector with n-dimensions that stores numerical and measurable features representing some objects.

Feature Space: Space associated feature vector.

Hyperplane: Hyperplane of an object is a subspace with one dimension less than the space surrounding the object. For example, if a space is three dimensional then two dimensional planes constitute its hyperplane.

Knowledge based Interfacial Potential: These are statistics based energy function that is derived from previously available protein complexes in various 3D structure repositories like PDB.

Pattern Recognition: A branch of machine learning that deals with identification of regularities and patterns in a given data.

SIF: Simple interaction file.

SBML: Systems Biology Markup Language.

XGMML: Graph modeling language XML file.

Z-Score: Z-Score is a standard score which signifies how much a score deviates from mean. Z-Score of zero means score is equal to mean.

Chapter 11
Analysis of Microarray Data using Artificial Intelligence Based Techniques

Khalid Raza
Jamia Millia Islamia, India

ABSTRACT

Microarray is one of the essential technologies used by the biologists to measure genome-wide expression levels of genes in a particular organism under some particular conditions or stimuli. As microarrays technologies have become more prevalent, the challenges of analyzing these data for getting better insight about biological processes have essentially increased. Due to availability of artificial intelligence based sophisticated computational techniques, such as artificial neural networks, fuzzy logic, genetic algorithms, and many other nature-inspired algorithms, it is possible to analyse microarray gene expression data in a better way. In this chapter, we present artificial intelligence based techniques for the analysis of microarray gene expression data. Further, challenges in the field and future work direction have also been suggested.

INTRODUCTION

The bioinformatics is an interdisciplinary area of study where one of the objectives is to deal with the analysis and interpretation of large sets of data generated from various large-scale biological experiments. The example of one such large-scale biological experiment is measuring the expression levels of tens of thousands of genes simultaneously under some environmental condition. Microarray is one of the essential technologies used by the biologists to measure genome-wide expression levels of genes in a particular organism. As microarrays technologies have become more prevalent, the challenges associated with collecting, managing, and analyzing the data from each experiment have essentially increased. Robust laboratory protocols, improved understanding of the complex experimental design and falling prices of commercial platforms, all these have combined to drive the field to more complex experiments, generating huge amounts of data (Brazma & Vilo, 2000).

DOI: 10.4018/978-1-5225-0427-6.ch011

With the help of measured transcription levels of genes under different biological conditions (e.g. at various developmental stages and in different tissues), biologists are able to develop gene expression profiles that differentiate the functionality of each gene in the genome. The gene expression profiles are organized in the form of a matrix, where rows represent genes, columns represent samples/replicas, and each cell of the matrix contains a numeric value representing the expression level of a gene in a particular sample. Generally, such a table is called gene expression matrix. These gene expression matrices can be used to correlate the over expression of certain genes with a certain disease and can help researchers to discover other conditions affecting the expression level of these genes. The gene expression matrix can also be used to identify other set of genes having co-expression profile patterns. Hence, suitable compounds (potential drugs) can be investigated that can lower the expression level of these overexpressed genes (Babu, 2004).

Many sophisticated statistical and computational tools have been developed to help biologists analyse gene expression data and to identify novel targets from their experimental data (Deng et al., 2009; Debouck et al., 1999). Among these techniques, clustering and statistical methods are most commonly used data analysis methods. Clustering generally groups the gene expression data with similar expression pattern, i.e. co-expressed genes. However, clustering approach suffers from several drawbacks (Bassett et al., 1999). The statistical methods help to analyse gene expression data and infer relationships between genes. However, it fails to provide complex regulatory relationships among genes.

The chapter is organized as follows. Section 2 describes the background of Microarray experiments and data generation. Section 3 covers the applications of Microarrays and Section 4 describes artificial intelligence based techniques, and reviews its application in the analysis of Microarray data. Section 5 summarizes the chapter and presents research challenges and future work directions.

Microarray Technology

With the help of Microarray technology, one can measure the expression level of all genes in a genome simultaneously. By measuring and comparing the expression level of genes in an normal and diseased cell, it would be possible to identify genes which are responsible for various diseases. Due to unprecedented amount of large biological data generated out of microarray experiments, the focus of research has shifted from the generation of data to analysis, interpretation, and presentation of data in the most efficient manner (Hood, 2003; Kitano, 2002; Kitano, 2002a). With the help of these technologies, researchers can find answers to some of the challenging questions like;

1. What are the functions of different genes?
2. In what cellular processes do these genes participate?
3. How genes are regulated?
4. How genes and their products (proteins) do interact, and what are these interaction networks?
5. How expression level of genes differs in different cell types and states?
6. How expressions of genes are affected by various disease or drug treatments?

Microarrays are frequently used in biomedical research to tackle a number of problems, including classification of tumors, and gene expression response to different stress conditions. A central and frequently asked question in microarray is the identification of differentially expressed genes (DEGs). The DEGs are those genes whose expression levels are associated with a response or covariate of interest

Figure 1. Step involved in microarray experiments

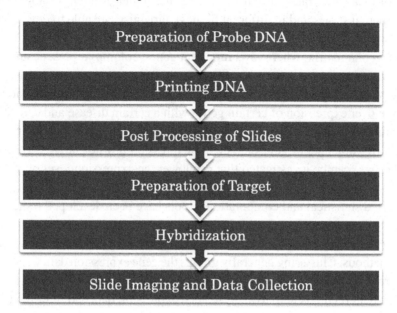

(Dudoit, 2002). The covariates can be either polytomous (for instance, treatment/control status, cell type, drug type) or continuous (for instance, drug doses), and the responses can be, for instance, censored survival times or any other clinical outcomes (Dudoit, 2002; Lee et al., 2012). Scientists from different disciplines such as biology, statistics, computer science, mathematics, bioinformatics, etc. are working in this area to identify some new insight from DNA microarray data such as identification of differentially expressed genes, classification between cancerous and non-cancerous genes, identification of potential genes for drug target, identification of gene function, and so on. In the following section, various steps involved in Microarray experiments are discussed.

Experimental Setup

Basically microarray is a solid base having grid of spots where genetic material of known sequence is arranged systematically. It is mostly made up of glass on which single stranded DNA molecules are attached at fixed positions. The size of the arrays can vary from microscope slide to square silicon chips. On an array, there can be thousands of spots and each spot contain number of identical DNA molecules. The microarray fabrication can be done in two ways:

1. cDNA and
2. Oligonucleotide.

The steps involved in microarray experiments are shown in Figure 1.

Step 1 – Preparation of Probe DNA: For the study of large-scale expression, a specific DNA sequence is needed for all genes whose expression values are to be measured. The selection of probe is done on the basis of resources available for obtaining the representation of the genes under study. The simplest way is to amplify every known ORF in the genome and use it as a probe. PCR is used for the amplification purpose and allows multiplication of DNA fragments by millions in just few hours. ESTs may be used to identify distinct mRNA transcripts.

Step 2 – Printing Array: In cDNA array, arrays are mostly printed on Poly-L-lysine coated glass microscope slide using arraying robot. During the arraying operation, a large number of slides are placed on and secured to a platter. The samples of DNA are placed in microliter plates on the stand. The reservoir slot of each tip is filled with ~1µ liter of DNA solutions. The tips are then lightly tapped at identical positions on each slide leaving a small drop of DNA solution on the poly-L-lysine coated slide. In Oligonucleotide array, oligos are printed at the spots instead of cDNA. Same robotics can be applied to manufacture both types of arrays. However, the preparation of oligonucleotide array is quite different from that of cDNA's. During fabrication of array, the probes are synthesized on the chip using photolithography.

Step 3 – Post Processing of Slides: This step consists of Rehydration and Blocking. The spots on the microarray are rehydrated to distribute DNA more evenly. In the blocking process, free reactive groups on the slide surface are modified to minimize their ability to bind to labeled target DNA. If these groups are not blocked, the labeled DNA target can bind to the surface of the slide.

Step 4 – Preparation of Target: In this step, isolate mRNA from the samples and purify it. Since, mRNA degrades very fast; hence it is reverse-transcribed into more stable cDNA.

Step 5 – Hybridization: In hybridization process, a single stranded DNA molecule is bound to another single strand DNA molecule with a precisely matching sequence. After hybridization process, the microarray is properly washed to eliminate any excess labeled sample and finally dried using a centrifuge. Sometimes two types of target mRNA samples are simultaneously hybridized on the array, called two channel microarray experiment. In that case, two types of molecules are added to targets and uses fluorescent dyes like *Cy3* and *Cy5*, which can be separated spectrally. The *Cy3* is green and *Cy5* is red when excited by laser light at specific wavelength.

Step 6 – Slide Imaging: Under this step, the microarray is scanned to measure the fluorescent signal emitted at every spot that determines the amount of labeled sample bound to each spot. The laser scanning confocal microscope is used for this purpose. For single channel array, the array is scanned once but for two-channel experiment, it is scanned in two phases. In the obtained image, the intensity of each spot is proportional to the amount of mRNA from the sample, matching cDNA sequence of given spot. A gene expressed in a sample labeled with red dye and not expressed in the other sample will produce a red spot and vice versa. A gene expressed in both the samples will produced equal amount of red and green intensities and a spot is given yellow (Figure 2).

Quantification of Images

The images generated by scanner of microarray are the raw data. There is one image per array for a single channel microarray, while there are two images per array for two channel microarrays. The image intensity is scanned by detector at a high spatial resolution, where every probe spots are represented by several pixels. The intensity values of each probe are identified and these intensities are quantified to numeric values. Image quantification process involves following steps:

1. Identification of position of spots on the array
2. For every spot on the array, pixel identification on the image

Figure 2. Preparation of cDNA probe and microarray

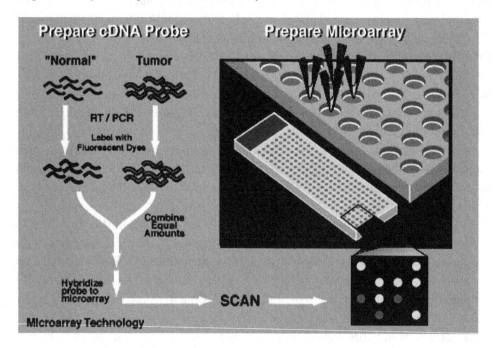

3. For every spot on the array, identifying pixels so that it may be used for background calculation
4. Computation of numeric value for the intensity of the spot, intensity of background image and quality control information.

There are several methods for segmentation and quantification which are available in software packages but they differ in their robustness. To a microarray project, quantification of image involves the transition of workflow from wet-lab procedure to computational (dry-lab). During the computation of numeric information at the microarray spot, image processing software provides a number of measures such as mean, median and standard deviation of signal and background, along with diameter and number of pixels. Among these measures, the most important measure is hybridization intensity for each spot that can be either mean or median of the pixel intensities. The second important information is signal standard deviation that helps in computation of coefficient of variation for spot as well as for the background. Once the spotted image and other statistics are computed then it is suggested that quality of the array and individual spots on the array be assessed because sometimes array may have a few defected spots.

The obtained microarray gene expression data is presented in a tabular form, called gene expression matrix, as shown in Figure 3. The first column specifies the identity of genes and first rows represents "samples" (replicas), "condition" or "time-series" observations. The element of the matrix gives expression values of genes under various conditions or samples.

Figure 3. A Sample format of microarray data

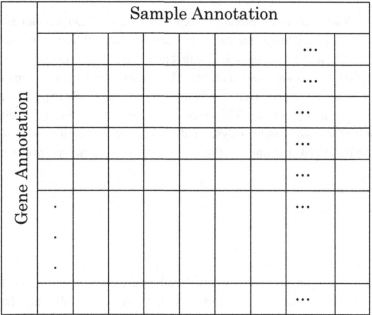

Data Preprocessing and Normalization

Once the spotted images have been quantified to generate datasets, these datasets should be preprocessed before their analysis and interpretation. In this step, meaningful characteristics are extracted or enhanced and prepare the dataset for its analysis and interpretation. In data preprocessing step, generally two issues are addressed:

1. To adjust background intensities, and
2. To transform data into a scale suitable for analysis and interpretation.

A simple example of preprocessing microarray data is taking the Log of the raw intensity values. The main purpose of normalization is to ensure that variation in the expression values are because of biological differences between the mRNA samples and not because of experimental artifacts.

The adjustment of background intensities is needed because despite of washing done after hybridization in microarrays, there are chances of genes annealing in the background of the spot and during scanning time it may give rise to background intensity. Another issue in the gene expression data which need to be addressed is the difference between the data generated by two microarray technologies (cDNA and oligonucleotide microarrays). The cDNA reports differences in gene expression, while oligonucleotide microarray report absolute expression values (Butte, 2002). Hence, same normalization techniques may not be applied to these different microarray technologies. In a given experiment, most genes do not change their expression levels and if equal numbers of genes are up-regulated and down-regulated, then differential expression measurements might be normally distributed.

Normalization for Single Channel Experiment

Suppose that one needs to find out differentially expressed genes (DEGs) under various experimental conditions, such as normal sample against cancerous sample, control tissue versus treatment, etc. in a single channel experiment. It is generally expected that gene expression values in both the conditions are more or less similar but it is seldom found in reality. This variation is because of many factors including different arrays used for each samples. Hence, it is natural that one would expect distribution of expression values would more or less be similar. Therefore, it is necessary to remove variation between arrays. The methods to remove variation among arrays, is called array normalization methods. There are several methods to make empirical distribution of expression values over all arrays. Some of the methods are:

1. Normalization by mean
2. Median or Q2 normalization
3. Q3 normalization
4. Quartile normalization

In normalization by mean method, the expression values are transformed so that that mean of all the arrays is same. Median method transforms the expression values so that all arrays have median same as that of some reference array. The Q3 method is defined as similar to Q2. In Q3, third quartiles of the arrays are calculated to the third quartile of the mock array. Quartile normalization method is an extension of Q2 and Q3 normalization. This method is based on transforming each array specific distribution of intensities so that they all have similar values of quartiles.

Normalization for Two Channel Experiment

In a two channel microarray experiment, two different samples are labeled by two fluorescent dyes R and G, hybridized on an array. The difference of intensities between two channels gives DEGs, provided that these variations are only because of biological functioning of the genes in different conditions. Here, to identify DEGs it is necessary to compare the intensity of R and G. These methods are applied on the Log of the ratio R/G.

APPLICATIONS OF MICROARRAYS

Microarrays have been utilized in several biomedical problems including gene discovery, disease diagnosis, pharmacogenomics, and toxicology. For instance, microarrays can be used to identify disease genes by comparing expression patterns of genes in disease versus normal cell samples. Similarly, it can also be used to identify possible abnormal gene expressions and abnormal interaction between genes for a disease.

For a majority of applications, microarrays address four broad categories of problems (Xu et al., 2008):

1. Gene selection/gene filtering or identification of differentially expressed genes (DEGs)
2. Finding natural groupings among genes, conditions or both (clustering)
3. Patient classification using gene expression
4. Finding regulatory relationships among given set of genes

Gene Selection or Identification of DEGs

An important purpose for monitoring expression level of genes is to identify those genes which are differentially expressed across two different kinds of tissue samples or samples observed under two different experimental conditions. Set of genes differentially expressed over two different samples, i.e., normal and cancerous tissue, are expected to give clues about cancer mechanism. A large variety of methods exist for finding differentially expressed genes and most of these methods are based on statistical techniques, such as fold-change (Schena et al., 1995), t-test statistics (Peck & Devore,2011; Draghici, 2003), ANOVA (Kerr et al., 2000), rank product (Breitling et al., 2004), Significant Analysis of Microarray (Tusher et al., 2001), Random Variance Model (Wright & Simon, 2003), Limma (Smyth, 2004), and so on. Review on the various methods can be found in: Pan, 2002; Jeffery et al., 2006.

Fold change is one of the simplest ad-hoc methods often used in microarray analysis. A fold change is a measure that describes how much expression level of a gene changes over two different samples (conditions) or groups. To calculate a fold change, the average of expression values for each probes are calculated across the samples in each group, and then ratios of these average are taken. The levels of fold change are observed and genes under or above a thresholds are selected. For example, fold change below 0.5 is considered as down-regulated and fold change above 2.0 is considered as up-regulated. The Rank Products method is based on the statement that an experiment examining for n genes in m replicas, will have probability to be ranked first of $1/nm$, if the list values were totally random. Hence, it is improbable that single gene to have top position in all the given replicas, if given gene was not expressed differentially. Then, genes can be sorted based on likelihood of observing their rank product values (Jeffery et al., 2006). The two-sample t-test is widely used parametric hypothesis testing method for the identification of DEGs. The t-statistics gives a probability value (p-value) for each gene. A small p-value indicates that genes are differentially expressed under the hypothesis that there is no differential expression, which is not true. The t-statistic is calculated as the difference in the means over the standard deviation. Raza & Mishra (2012) proposed an anti-clustering gene algorithm for the identification of genes as drug targets, where they applied a combination of statistical techniques.

Clustering Genes, Samples, or Both

Clustering is a means of analysing set of objects by grouping them into different clusters based on some similarity measure. Basically clustering is an unsupervised technique that groups the similar objects into clusters. Researchers can apply clustering techniques to cluster gene expression data. Hence, genes belonging to a particular cluster are supposed to share common properties. If gene expression profiles (genes) are clustered, one may discover set of genes co-regulated in a certain sample. Similarly, gene expression can be grouped by clustering its samples. Sample clustering is done when it is needed to identify subgroups of certain condition (for instance, disease). The third means of grouping the gene expression data is to cluster both rows (genes) as well as columns (samples), which are known as co-clustering or bi-clustering. This kind of clustering helps us to find groups of genes associated with group of samples (patient). Some of the most popularly used clustering techniques are k-means, hierarchical, SOM, fuzzy c-means, non-Euclidean relational fuzzy c-means.

Using Microarray gene expression data, distance between two expressed genes can be computed to find out interrelationship between genes, so that genes with similar expressions can be placed in a single cluster. Euclidean distance, Manhattan distance and Pearson correlation distance are some of the commonly applied distance measures to compute the similarity matrix of the gene expression data. In Raza (2014), four different clustering techniques viz., k-means, Hierarchical clustering, density based clustering and Euclidean method based clustering have been applied on five different types of cancer gene expression data (lung cancer, prostate cancer, colon cancer, breast cancer and ovarian cancer). In all these five datasets, there are large numbers of genes compared to numbers of samples. The Microaaray data is normalised in order to avoid the dimensioanlity curse and enable machine learning algorithms to learn these data in a better way. After data normalization, attribute reduction using t-test has been done at a significance level of 0.001. There is no single clustering algorithm that can work well in all the situations. Selection of a particular clustering approach depends on the problem at hand and the dataset under study.

Patient Classification

Gene expression data can be used to train a classifier so that it can recognize a given condition (e.g. class label such as normal or cancerous). The advantage of this kind of classification is that once a classifier is trained with gene expression profiles to recognize a patient class, then it can recognize a class of unknown patient for which the classifier has not been trained. There are several supervised techniques available for patient classification, such as Bayesian networks, M5 model tree, k-nearest neighborhood, Random forest, neural networks, and support vector machines.

In Raza & Hasan (2015), authors have done a comparative evaluation of various machine learning techniques for their accuracy in class prediction of prostate cancer based on Microarray dataset. As per their evaluation, Bayes Net gave the best accuracy for prostate cancer class prediction with an accuracy of 94.11%. Bayes Net is followed by Naïve Bayes with an accuracy of 91.17%. The objective of evaluating various machine learning techniques is to come up with the best technique in terms of prediction accuracy and to reveal a good procedure for meaningful attribute reduction. A similar kind of process may be used to classify other types of cancers. One of the biggest challenges is to develop a single universal classifier which would be capable of classifying all types of cancer gene expression data into meaningful number of classes.

Finding Regulatory Relationship among Genes

A gene regulatory network (GRN) is a network of interactions among genes, where nodes represent genes and interconnection between them represent their regulatory relationships. Today, one of the most exciting problems in systems biology research is to decipher how the genome controls the development of complex biological system. Microarrays have been widely used to find out new (unknown) regulatory relationship. The discovery of GRN using gene expression data is known as reverse-engineering of GRN. The GRNs help in identifying the interactions between genes and provide fruitful information about the functional role of individual genes in a cellular system. They also help in diagnosing various diseases including cancer (Raza, 2016).

In the last several decades, many computational methods have been proposed to discover complex regulatory interactions among genes based on microarray data. These techniques can be clubbed into different groups, such as Boolean networks (Liang et al., 1998; Akutsu et al., 1999; Shmulevich et al., 2002; Martin et al., 2007; Raza & Jaiswal, 2013; Raza & Parveen, 2013), Bayesian networks (Friedman et al., 2000; Husmeier, 2003), Petri nets (Koch et al., 2005; Remy et al., 2006), linear and non-linear ordinary differential equations (ODEs) (Chen et al., 1999; Tyson et al., 2002; Jong & Page, 2008), machine learning approaches (Weaver et al., 1999; Kim et al., 2000; Vohradsky, 2001; Keedwell et al., 2002; Huang et al., 2003; Tian & Burrage, 2003; Zhou et al., 2004; Hu et al., 2006; Jung & Cho, 2007, Xu et al., 2007a; Xu et al., 2007b; Chiang & Chao, 2007; Lee & Yang, 2008; Datta et al., 2009; Zhang et al., 2009; Maraziotis et al., 2010; Ghazikhani et al., 2011; Liu et al., 2011; Kentzoglanakis, 2012; Noman et al., 2013), etc. For review of the modeling techniques and the subject, refer to (Jong, 2002; Wei et al., 2004; Schlitt & Brazma, 2007; Cho et al., 2007; Karlebach & Shamir, 2008; Swain et al., 2010; Sirbu et al., 2010; Mitra et al., 2011, Raza & Parveen, 2012).

ARTIFICIAL INTELLIGENCE TECHNIQUES AND MICROARRAY ANALYSIS

Artificial Intelligence (AI) is an interdisciplinary field of study where the goal is to design intelligent machines or computer programs. Most of the researchers defines AI as "the study and design of intelligent agents", where an intelligent agent is a system that can perceive given environment to take actions and maximize its probability of being success. John McCarthy coined this term in 1955 and defined AI as "the science and engineering of making intelligent machine". AI encompasses a vast domain of research including reasoning, knowledge, learning, natural language processing, perception, etc. Most popularly used AI techniques for solving real-life problems, including bioinformatics problems such as analysis of microarray array data to extract valuable knowledge are statistical methods and computational intelligence. Among the computational intelligence, artificial neural networks, fuzzy systems, evolutionary computations and many statistical tools are mostly applied AI based approaches.

In this section, few computational intelligence approaches and their applications in Microarray data analysis have been briefly described.

Artificial Neural Networks

Artificial Neural Networks (ANNs) are massively parallel computing system inspired by biological system of neurons. It is collection of extremely large number of simple processing elements, called neurons, having many interconnections. These elements have inputs, which are multiplied by weights and then computed by a mathematical function, called activation function, regulating the activation of the neuron. A weight value w_{ij} is assigned to each connection and hence the net input to the neuron is the weighted sum of its n input signals, x_i, i=1, 2,…, n. Each neuron has an activation function f (generally a sigmoidal function), which is used to compute the neuron's current activation a_i, and output function g (generally identity function) which is used to compute value O_i. By adjusting the weights of neurons, the desired output can be obtained from the inputs. The process of adjusting the synaptic weights is known as *learning* or *training process*. The most widely applied training algorithm is Backpropagation algorithm.

The first neural network model was proposed by McCulloch and Pitts in 1993 and since then hundreds of different models have been developed (Gershenson, 2003). The differences in the neural networks might be in their architecture, activation function, and topology, training algorithm and accepted input and output values. On the basis of architecture (connection pattern), neural networks can be broadly clubbed into two groups (Jain et al., 1996): i) feedforward networks, where there is no loop and ii) recurrent networks, which contain loops because of feedback connections. A typical network from each category is shown in Fig. 4. Feedforward networks are memory-less, i.e., their output is independent

Figure 4. A taxonomy of feed-forward and recurrent network architectures

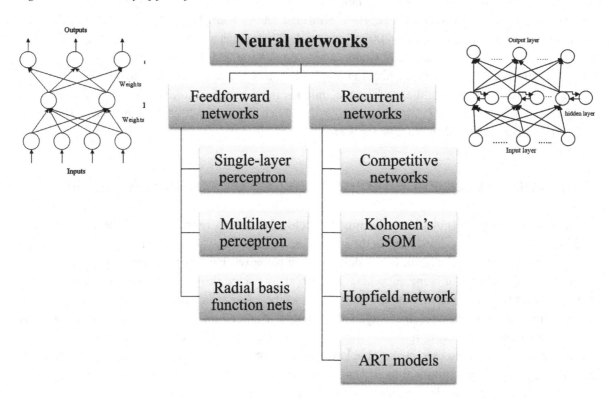

of the previous network state but recurrent networks consider network feedback paths, which are with memory, i.e., the current output is dependent on the previous state of the network. Different network architecture needs appropriate training algorithm. The learning paradigms can be categorized as: supervised, unsupervised and hybrid (reinforcement).

Vohradsky (2001) applied ANN to model gene regulation by assuming that the regulatory effect on gene expression of a particular gene can be expressed in the form of ANN. Each neuron in the neural network represents a gene and connectivity between them represents regulatory interactions. Here each layer of the ANN represents the level of gene expression at time t and output of a neuron at time $t+\Delta t$ can be determined from the expression at time t. The advantage the model is that it is continuous, uses a transfer function to transform the inputs to a shape close to those observed in natural processes and does not use artificial elements. Keedwell and his collaborators (Keedwell et al., 2002) also applied ANN in the purest form for the reconstruction of GRNs from microarray data. The architecture of the neural network was quite simple when dealing with Boolean networks. Hu et al. (Hu et al., 2006) has proposed a general recurrent neural network (RNN) model for the reverse-engineering of GRNs and to learn their parameters. RNN has been deployed due to its capability to deal with complex temporal behaviour of genetic networks. In this model, time delay between the output of a gene and its effect on another gene has been incorporated. A more recent work by Noman and his colleagues (Noman et al., 2013) proposed a decoupled-RNN model of GRN. Here, decoupled means dividing the estimation problem of parameters for the complete network into several sub-problems, each of which estimate parameters associated with single gene. This decoupled approach decreases the dimensionality problem and makes the reconstruction of large network feasible. In our recent work (Raza et al., 2014), we also proposed a RNN based hybrid model of GRN that uses extended Kalman filter to estimate and update synaptic weights using Backpropagation Through Time (BPTT) training algorithm.

The ANN approach of GRN inference works well for small size network, i.e., a network of up to 100 genes. This is because of less number of available samples in a Microarray experiment. As the size of the network grows, the number of unknown parameters (interactions) also grows, and that requires a very large number of Microarray samples, which is rarely available in Microarray data.

Fuzzy System

Fuzzy logic is based on the concept of partial truth, i.e., truth values between "completely true" and "completely false". For example, using fuzzy logic, propositions can be denoted with degrees of truthfulness and falsehood with the help of a membership function. L.A. Zadeh (Zadeh, 1996) was the first who introduced the concept of fuzzy logic to represent vagueness in linguistics and implement and express human knowledge and inference capability in a natural way. In broad sense, fuzzy logic is an extension of multivalue logic. In specific sense, fuzzy logic is a logic system which can be used to model approximate reasoning (Cao, 2006). Fuzzy logic has been proved to be useful in expert system and other artificial intelligence applications. A fuzzy system generally consists of three parts:

1. Fuzzy input and output variables, and their fuzzy values,
2. Fuzzy rules, such as Zadeh-Mamdani's fuzzy rules, Takagi-Sugeno's fuzzy rules, gradual fuzzy rules and recurrent fuzzy rules,
3. Fuzzy inference methods, which may include fuzzification and defuzzification.

The biological systems behave in a fuzzy manner. Fuzzy logic provides a mathematical framework for modeling and describing biological systems. Literature reports that fuzzy logic has been successfully used for the analysis of microarray data due to its capability to represent non-linear systems, its friendly language to incorporate and edit domain knowledge in the form of fuzzy rules (Raza & Parveen, 2012). Woolf and Wang (Woolf & Wang, 2000) proposed a fuzzy logic based algorithm for analysing gene expression data. The proposed fuzzy model was designed to extract gene triplets (activators, repressors, targets) in yeast gene expression data. The model took ~200 hours to analyse the relationships between 1,898 genes on an 8-processor SGI Origin 2000 system. Later, Ressom and his colleagues (Ressom et al., 2003) extended and improved the work of Woolf and Wang (Woolf & Wang, 2000) in terms of reducing computation time and generalizing the model to accommodate co-activator and co-repressors, in addition to activators, repressors and targets. Reduction in computation time is achieved by applying clustering as a pre-processing step. The improved algorithm achieves a reduction of 50% computation time. After 3 years, Ram and his colleagues (Ram et al., 2006) also improved the Woolf and Wang's fuzzy logic model to predict changes in gene expression values and extracted causal relationship between genes. They have improved searching for activator/repressor regulatory relationship between gene triplets in the microarray data. A pre-processing technique for the fuzzy model has also been proposed to remove redundant data present that makes the model faster. Sun and colleagues (Sun *et al, .*2010) applied dynamic fuzzy approach by incorporating structural knowledge to model gene regulatory networks using microarray gene expression data. This technique infers gene interactions in the form of fuzzy rules and able to reveal biological relationships among genes and their products. The distinguishing feature of this model is that:

1. Prior structural knowledge on GRN can be incorporated for the purpose of faster convergence of the identification process and
2. Non-linear dynamic property of the GRN can be well captured for the better prediction.

As discussed in previous section, clustering (grouping) Microarray data is also one aspect of analysing it, that gives clues about a set of co-regulated genes. Fuzzy based clustering algorithm, called fuzzy c-means (FCM) was first introduced by Dunn in 1973(Dunn, 1973) but implemented by Bezdek (Bezdek, 1981). The FCM has now become most popular fuzzy clustering algorithm and considered as robust to scale the dataset (Wang et al., 2008). A major problem with FCM algorithm for clustering microarray data is the selection of the fuzziness parameter m. The work of Dembélé & Kastner (2003) shows that the commonly used value m = 2 is not always appropriate. The optimal value for m varies from one dataset to another. Dembélé & Kastner (2003) also proposed an empirical method to estimate an adequate value for m, based on the distribution of distances between genes in the given dataset.

In addition to fuzzy-clustering hybrid, fuzzy logic has been hybridized with other computational intelligence techniques, including fuzzy and neural network hybrid (called neuro-fuzzy) and fuzzy and genetic algorithm (called fuzzy-genetic). Neuro-fuzzy and fuzzy-genetic hybrid have been successfully applied for GRN inference using Microarray data. The review of the application of neuro-fuzzy and neuro-genetic for GRN inference can be found in Mitra et al., 2011 and Raza & Parveen, 2012.

Evolutionary Computation

Evolutionary computing is a collection of problem-solving techniques based on principles of biological evolution. The functional analogy of evolutionary computing is the natural evolution that relates to a particular kind of problem solving grounded on trial-and-error process. Natural selection means that we have a population of individuals that strive for survival and reproduction. The fitness of these individuals determines how well they succeed in achieving their goals, i.e., presenting their chance for survival and reproduction. Charles Darwin formulated the theory of natural evolution. Over several generations, biological organism evolves according to the principle of natural selection like "survival of the fittest". The history of evolutionary computing goes back to 1940s. After many decades of research in this area, researchers came up with many evolutionary computing techniques such as *evolutionary programming*, *evolution strategies*, *genetic algorithm* (Holland, 1975) and *generic programming* (Koza, 1992).

Genetic algorithms (GAs) are basically optimization techniques inspired by Darwin's theory of evolution. In fact, it is a search algorithm based on the mechanism of natural selection and survival for the fittest. Here, searching in a population is done from a single point and competitive selection is done in each iterations. The solutions having high "fitness" are recombined with other solutions and then "mutated" by changing the single element of the solution. The purpose of genetic operators, such as crossover and mutation, are to generate new population of solutions for the next generation. Genetic algorithms belong to probabilistic algorithms and are different from random search algorithms because former combines elements of directed and stochastic search. Due to this reason, GAs are found to be more robust than directed search methods. Further, GAs maintain a population of potential solutions; on the other hand, other search techniques process a single point of search space (Raza & Parveen, 2012a).

Noman and Iba (Noman & Iba, 2005) applied decoupled S-system approach for the inference of effective kinetic parameters from time series gene expression data and applied Trigonometric Differential Evolution (TDE) for the optimization and captures the dynamics of gene expression. Later, Chowdhury and Chetty (Chowdhury & Chetty, 2011) extended the work of Noman and Iba (Noman & Iba, 2005) and applied GA for scoring the networks' several useful features, such as a Prediction Initialization (PI) algorithm to initialize the individuals, a Flip Operation (FO) for matching values. A refinement algorithm for optimizing sensitivity and specificity of inferred networks was also proposed. Xu et al., 2009 proposed genetic programming based method for the analysis of microarray datasets, where genetic programming performs classification and feature selection simultaneously. Maulik (2011) studied the performance of three most commonly used computational techniques such as genetic algorithm, simulated annealing and differential evolution for developing fuzzy clusters of gene expression data. Clustering is an unsupervised analysis approach for grouping co-expressed genes together. To improve results of clustering, support vector machine (SVM) has been utilized. A review of application of evolutionary computation for Microarray analysis can be found in Sirbu et al., (2010), Mitra et al., (2011) and Raza and Parveen (2012a).

Other AI Based Methods

Machine learning algorithms, like ANN, are also used to predict interactions between genes of a GRN using Microarray data. But, these algorithms are so complex and work like a black-box. Black-box model means what is happening inside the algorithm is hidden (Sîrbu et al., 2010). On the other hand, nature-inspired algorithms, in comparison to other algorithms, are simpler in nature and they have been found to be applied in various biological problems from simplest like alignment of sequences to the complex like protein structure prediction (Pal et al., 2006). One such type of nature-inspired algorithm is Genetic algorithm which has already been discussed in the previous section.

In the last two decades, several nature-inspired metaheuristic optimization algorithms have been proposed and successfully applied in many optimization problems, including microarray analysis. Fister and colleagues (Fister et al., 2013) have done a survey of nature-inspired optimization algorithm and list ~75 nature-inspired algorithms proposed by different researchers, and classified these algorithms into four groups: Swarm intelligence based, Bio-inspired based, Physics-based and Chemistry-based, and Others. algorithms. Ant colony optimization (ACO) is one of the nature-inspired swarm-based optimization algorithm proposed by Marco Dorigo in 1992 (Dorigo, 1992) in his PhD thesis. ACO is a metaheuristic optimization technique where a set of artificial ants search for optimal solutions in a given optimization problem. Ants use pheromones laid by the other ants as footmarks to follow. Hence, ant reaches the food source by the shortest path using knowledge gained by the other ants. This algorithm can be used for optimization problems, including gene interaction network optimization. ACO has been applied to several bioinformatics problems including sequence alignment, drug designing, 2D protein folding and biological network optimization. Raza and Kohli (2015) applied ACO algorithm for inferring highly correlated key gene interactions in a GRN that plays an important role in identifying biomarkers for disease which further helps in drug design. The limitation of proposed algorithm by Raza and Kholi (2015) is that it can find out a total number of interactions equal to total number of genes.

PSO has been applied for clustering and feature (genes) selection in microarray data. A k-means clustering based upon PSO has been proposed for microarray data clustering by Deng et al. (2005). The algorithm discovers clusters in microarray data without having any prior knowledge of feasible number of clusters. Chuang et al., (2009) applied Binary PSO for feature selection in microarray data. Sahu and Mishra (2012) also proposed a PSO based feature selection algorithm for cancer microarray data. For the selection of efficient genes from thousands of genes, Chen at al. (2014) proposed an approach utilizing

PSO combined with a decision tree classifier. For the biclustering of microarray data, a comparative study on three nature-inspired algorithms, such as PSO, Shuffled Frog Leaping (SFL) and Cuckoo Search (CS) algorithms, have been done on benchmark gene expression dataset by Balamurugan and colleagues (Balamurugan et al., 2014). The result reports that CS outperforms PSO and SFL for 3 out of 4 datasets. The classification accuracy of simple statistical learning techniques can be enhanced when nature-inspired algorithm is applied for the feature selection. One such study has been carried out by Gunavathi and Premalatha (2014). They performed a comparative analysis of swarm intelligence techniques, such as PSO, cuckoo search (CS), SFL, and SFL with Lévy flight (SFLLF), for feature selection in cancer classification. The k-nearest neighbour (kNN) classifier is applied to classify the samples. The result shows that k-NN classifier through SFLLF feature selection method outperform PSO, CS, and SFL. Sometimes, DEGs techniques are used for gene selection/filtering or dimension reduction in microarray data where we have a large number of genes (features). The dimension reduction is a preprocessing step whenever we use a machine learning technique for training with gene expression datasets where number of gene are larger than the available samples (generally known as "curse of dimensionality problem").

Due to advancement in data mining algorithms and tools, it is a keen interest of the researchers to apply these tools to identify patterns of interest in the gene expression data. Association rule mining is one of the most widely used data mining technique that have been applied for gene expression mining by a number of researchers (Creighton et al., 2003). Association rules mining may discover biologically useful associations between genes, or between different biological conditions using microarray gene expression data. An association rules are written in the form A1 → A2, where A1 and A2 are disjoint sets of data items. The set A2 is likely to occur whenever the set A1 occurs. Here, the data items may present either highly expressed or repressed genes, or any other facts that state the cellular environment of genes (e.g. diagnosis of a disease samples) (Raza, 2015). Formal Concept Analysis (FCA), introduced by R. Wille in early 1980s, is another data mining technique based on lattice theory. It has been widely used for the analysis of binary relational data. Like other computational techniques, FCA has also been applied in microarray analysis, gene expression mining, gene expression clustering, finding genes in gene regulatory networks, and so on. A review FAC for the analysis and knowledge discovery from gene expression and other biological data can be found in Raza, (2015).

CONCLUSION AND FUTURE CHALLENGES

The bioinformatics is an interdisciplinary area of study where one of the objectives is to deal with the analysis and interpretation of large sets of data generated from various large-scale biological experiments, including Microarrays. Microarray technology is one of the powerful tools used to measure genome wide expression levels of genes. As microarrays technologies have become more prevalent, the challenges associated with collecting, managing, and analyzing the data from each experiment have essentially increased. With the help of these technologies, researchers can find out answer of some challenging questions like:

1. What are the functions of different genes?
2. In what cellular processes do they participate?
3. How genes are regulated?
4. How genes and its products (proteins) do interact, and what are these interaction networks?

5. How expression level of genes differs in different cell types and states?
6. How expressions of genes are affected by various disease or drug treatments?

In this chapter, four broad categories of problems have been tackled for the analysis of Microarrays:

1. **Identification of Differentially Expressed Genes:** It helps us in the selection of few relevant genes and elimination of irrelevant genes for further study. It also solves the dimensionality problem of machine learning techniques by filtering differentially expressed genes over various samples and training a classifier with the selected number of genes only.
2. **Cancer Classification using Gene Expression:** Classification of patient based on gene expression profile is another important issue for the analysis of microarray data. The application of AI-based techniques for cancer classification based microarray data has been discussed.
3. **Clustering Genes, Conditions, or Both:** Another important aspect of analyzing microarray data is finding natural groupings among genes, which can be done using clustering techniques. Clustering is an unsupervised learning technique that plays a vital role in providing a "class label" to unlabeled data and it can be used to identify set of co-regulated genes.
4. **Inferring Gene Interaction Network:** The gene interaction network plays an important role in identifying root-cause of various diseases. Inferring gene interaction network from gene expression profiles is one of other aspect of analyzing microarray data. The application of AI-based techniques for GRN inference has been covered in length and various resources for further study has been listed.

FUTURE CHALLENGES

Microarray technology is a high-throughput experimental approach that measures the genome-wide expression of genes and data are produced in large-scale. Hence, analysing these data to infer useful information is big challenge. Some of the future directions for the analysis of microarray data are as follows:

1. One of the main drawbacks of microarray technology is that data generated by these experiments contain noises and are not much reliable. Hence, before the data is analysed, we must apply sophisticated noise removal and data normalization technique.
2. Application of machine learning techniques in genome-wide analysis of microarray data creates the problem of dimensionality. Hence, some techniques are required to identify differentially expressed genes (DEGs). Statistical techniques, such as fold change, t-test, ANOVA, etc. dominate in the identification of DEGs. Hence, it is needed to explore the application of computational intelligence to tackle the problem of DEGs.
3. Another biggest challenge is to develop a single classifier which is best suitable for classification of all types of cancer gene expression data into meaningful number of classes. Nature inspired optimization techniques such as Ant Colony Optimization (ACO) (Dorigo, 1992), Artificial Bee Colony optimization (ABC) (Karaboga, 2005), Cuckoo Search (Yang & Deb, 2009), Particle Swarm Optimization (PSO) (Kennedy & Eberhart, 1995), Spider Monkey Algorithm (Bansal et al., 2014) and so on are successfully being used in many challenging problems. In the future work, one can

hybridize these nature-inspired optimization techniques with different classifiers for better classification accuracy.

4. For the gene clustering problem, one can apply fuzzy based clustering techniques (such as Fuzzy C-Means) to group genes or patient or both. Even, ranked based classification techniques can be applied.

5. Inference of gene interaction networks using gene expression profile is another open area where computational intelligence can be applied to identify interactions among given set of genes. Hybrid algorithms (for example, fusion of neural networks, genetic algorithms and/or fuzzy logic and other nature-inspired algorithms) can be applied for the said purpose.

ACKNOWLEDGMENT

The author acknowledges the funding received from University Grants Commission, Govt. of India through research grant 42-1019/2013(SR).

REFERENCES

Akutsu, T., Miyano, S., & Kuhara, S. (1999). Identification of genetic networks from a small number of gene expression patterns under the Boolean network model. In Pacific symposium on biocomputing (Vol. 4, pp. 17-28).

Babu, M. M. (2004). Introduction to microarray data analysis. In *Computational Genomics: Theory and Application*, 225-249.

Balamurugan, R., Natarajan, A., & Premalatha, K. (2014). Comparative study on swarm intelligence techniques for biclustering of microarray gene expression data. *International journal of computer, control, quantum and information engineering*, 8(2).

Bansal, J. C., Sharma, H., Jadon, S. S., & Clerc, M. (2014). Spider monkey optimization algorithm for numerical optimization. *Memetic computing*, 6(1), 31-47.

Bassett, D. E., Eisen, M. B., & Boguski, M. S. (1999). Gene expression informatics: it's all in your mine. *Nature Genetics*, 21, 51–55. doi:10.1038/4478 PMID:9915502

Bezdek, J. C. (1981). *Pattern recognition with fuzzy objective function algorithms*. New York: Plenum Press. doi:10.1007/978-1-4757-0450-1

Brazma, A., & Vilo, J. (2000). Gene expression data analysis. *FEBS Letters*, 480(1), 17–24. doi:10.1016/S0014-5793(00)01772-5 PMID:10967323

Breitling, R., Armengaud, P., Amtmann, A., & Herzyk, P. (2004). Rank products: A simple, yet powerful, new method to detect differentially regulated genes in replicated microarray experiments. *FEBS Letters*, 573(1), 83–92. doi:10.1016/j.febslet.2004.07.055 PMID:15327980

Butte, A. (2002). The use and analysis of microarray data. *Nature Reviews. Drug Discovery, 1*(12), 951–960. doi:10.1038/nrd961 PMID:12461517

Cao, Y. (2006). *Fuzzy logic network theory with applications to gene regulatory networks* [Unpublished doctoral dissertation]. Duke University.

Chen, K.-H., Wang, K.-J., Tsai, M.-L., Wang, K.-M., Adrian, A. M., Cheng, W.-C., & Chang, K.-S. et al. (2014). Gene selection for cancer identification: A decision tree model empowered by particle swarm optimization algorithm. *BMC Bioinformatics, 15*(1), 49. doi:10.1186/1471-2105-15-49 PMID:24555567

Chen, T., He, H. L., & Church, G. M. (1999). Modeling gene expression with differential equations. In Pacific symposium on Biocomputing (Vol. 4, p. 4).

Chiang, J.-H., & Chao, S.-Y. (2007). Modeling human cancer-related regulatory modules by ga-rnn hybrid algorithms. *BMC Bioinformatics, 8*(1), 91. doi:10.1186/1471-2105-8-91 PMID:17359522

Cho, K.-H., Choo, S.-M., Jung, S., Kim, J.-R., Choi, H.-S., & Kim, J. (2007). Reverse engineering of gene regulatory networks. *Systems Biology, IET, 1*(3), 149–163. doi:10.1049/iet-syb:20060075 PMID:17591174

Chowdhury, A. R., & Chetty, M. (2011). An improved method to infer gene regulatory network using s-system. Proceedings of the 2011 IEEE congress on Evolutionary computation (CEC) (pp. 1012-1019). doi:10.1109/CEC.2011.5949728

Chuang, L.-Y., Yang, C.-H., & Yang, C.-H. (2009). Tabu search and binary particle swarm optimization for feature selection using microarray data. *Journal of Computational Biology, 16*(12), 1689–1703. doi:10.1089/cmb.2007.0211 PMID:20047491

Creighton, C., & Hanash, S. (2003). Mining gene expression databases for association rules. *Bioinformatics (Oxford, England), 19*(1), 79–86. doi:10.1093/bioinformatics/19.1.79 PMID:12499296

Datta, D., Choudhuri, S. S., Konar, A., Nagar, A., & Das, S. (2009). A recurrent fuzzy neural model of a gene regulatory network for knowledge extraction using differential evolution. Proceedings of the IEEE congress on Evolutionary computation CEC '09 (pp. 2900-2906). doi:10.1109/CEC.2009.4983307

Debouck, C., & Goodfellow, P. N. (1999). DNA microarrays in drug discovery and development. *Nature Genetics, 21*, 48–50. doi:10.1038/4475 PMID:9915501

Dembele, D., & Kastner, P. (2003). Fuzzy c-means method for clustering microarray data. *Bioinformatics (Oxford, England), 19*(8), 973–980. doi:10.1093/bioinformatics/btg119 PMID:12761060

Deng, X., Xu, J., Hui, J., & Wang, C. (2009). Probability fold change: A robust computational approach for identifying differentially expressed gene lists. *Computer Methods and Programs in Biomedicine, 93*(2), 124–139. doi:10.1016/j.cmpb.2008.07.013 PMID:18842321

Deng, Y., Kayarat, D., Elasri, M. O., & Brown, S. J. (2005). Microarray data clustering using particle swarm optimization k-means algorithm.*Proc. 8th JCIS* (pp. 1730-1734).

Dorigo, M. (1992). *Optimization, learning and natural algorithms* {Ph.D. Thesis]. Politecnico di Milano, Italy.

Draghici, S. (2003). *Data analysis tools for DNA microarrays*. CRC Press. doi:10.1201/9780203486078

Dudoit, S., Yang, Y. H., Callow, M. J., & Speed, T. P. (2002). Statistical methods for identifying differentially expressed genes in replicated cDNA microarray experiments. *Statistica Sinica, 12*(1), 111–140.

Dunn, J. C. (1973). A fuzzy relative of the isodata process and its use in detecting compact well-separated clusters.

Fister, I., Jr., Yang, X.-S., Fister, I., Brest, J., & Fister, D. (2013). A brief review of nature-inspired algorithms for optimization. arXiv preprint arXiv:1307.4186.

Friedman, N., Linial, M., Nachman, I., & Pe'er, D. (2000). Using Bayesian networks to analyze expression data. *Journal of Computational Biology, 7*(3-4), 601–620. doi:10.1089/106652700750050961 PMID:11108481

Gershenson, C. (2003). Artificial neural networks for beginners. arXiv preprint cs/0308031.

Ghazikhani, A., Akbarzadeh, T. M. R., & Monse, R. (2011). Genetic regulatory network inference using recurrent neural networks trained by a multi agent system. In Computer and knowledge engineering (ICCKE), 2011 1st international e-conference on (pp. 95-99). doi:10.1109/ICCKE.2011.6413332

Gunavathi, C., & Premalatha, K. (2014). A comparative analysis of swarm intelligence techniques for feature selection in cancer classification. *TheScientificWorldJournal*, 2014. PMID:25157377

Holland, J. H. (1975). Adaptation in natural and artificial systems: An introductory analysis with applications to biology, control, and artificial intelligence.

Hood, L. (2003). Systems biology: Integrating technology, biology, and computation. *Mechanisms of Ageing and Development, 124*(1), 9–16. doi:10.1016/S0047-6374(02)00164-1 PMID:12618001

Hu, X., Maglia, A., & Wunsch, D. C. (2006). A general recurrent neural network approach to model genetic regulatory networks. *Proceedings of the 27th annual international conference of the Engineering in medicine and biology society IEEE-EMBS '05* (pp. 4735-4738).

Huang, J., Shimizu, H., & Shioya, S. (2003). Clustering gene expression pattern and extracting relationship in gene network based on artificial neural networks. *Journal of Bioscience and Bioengineering, 96*(5), 421–428. doi:10.1016/S1389-1723(03)70126-1 PMID:16233550

Husmeier, D. (2003). Sensitivity and specificity of inferring genetic regulatory interactions from microarray experiments with dynamic Bayesian networks. *Bioinformatics (Oxford, England), 19*(17), 2271–2282. doi:10.1093/bioinformatics/btg313 PMID:14630656

Jain, A. K., Mao, J., & Mohiuddin, K. (1996). Artificial neural networks: A tutorial. *Computer, 29*(3), 31–44. doi:10.1109/2.485891

Jeffery, I. B., Higgins, D. G., & Culhane, A. C. (2006). Comparison and evaluation of methods for generating differentially expressed gene lists from microarray data. *BMC Bioinformatics, 7*(1), 359. doi:10.1186/1471-2105-7-359 PMID:16872483

Jong, H. (2002). Modeling and simulation of genetic regulatory systems: A literature review. *Journal of Computational Biology, 9*(1), 67–103. doi:10.1089/10665270252833208 PMID:11911796

Jong, H., & Page, M. (2008). Search for steady states of piecewise-linear differential equation models of genetic regulatory networks. *IEEE/ACM transactions on Computational biology and bioinformatics*, 5(2), 208-222.

Jung, S. H., & Cho, K.-H. (2007). Reconstruction of gene regulatory networks by neuro-fuzzy inference systems. In *Frontiers in the convergence of bioscience and information technologies, 2007* (pp. 32–37). FBIT. doi:10.1109/FBIT.2007.53

Karaboga, D. (2005). An idea based on honey bee swarm for numerical optimization (Tech. Rep. tr06). Erciyes university.

Karlebach, G., & Shamir, R. (2008). Modelling and analysis of gene regulatory networks. *Nature Reviews. Molecular Cell Biology*, 9(10), 770–780. doi:10.1038/nrm2503 PMID:18797474

Keedwell, E., Narayanan, A., & Savic, D. (2002). Modelling gene regulatory data using artificial neural networks. Proceedings of the 2002 international joint conference on Neural networks IJCNN '02. (Vol. 1, pp. 183-188). doi:10.1109/IJCNN.2002.1005466

Kennedy, J., & Eberhart, R. (1995). Particle swarm optimization. Proceedings of the IEEE international conference on Neural networks (Vol. 4, pp. 1942-1948). doi:10.1109/ICNN.1995.488968

Kentzoglanakis, K., & Poole, M. (2012). A swarm intelligence framework for reconstructing gene networks: searching for biologically plausible architectures. *IEEE/ACM Transactions on Computational Biology and Bioinformatics*, 9(2), 358-371.

Kerr, M. K., Martin, M., & Churchill, G. A. (2000). Analysis of variance for gene expression microarray data. *Journal of Computational Biology*, 7(6), 819–837. doi:10.1089/10665270050514954 PMID:11382364

Kim, S., Dougherty, E. R., Chen, Y., Sivakumar, K., Meltzer, P., Trent, J. M., & Bittner, M. (2000). Multivariate measurement of gene expression relationships. *Genomics*, 67(2), 201–209. doi:10.1006/geno.2000.6241 PMID:10903845

Kitano, H. (2002a). Computational systems biology. *Nature*, 420(6912), 206–210. doi:10.1038/nature01254 PMID:12432404

Kitano, H. (2002b). Systems biology: A brief overview. *Science*, 295(5560), 1662–1664. doi:10.1126/science.1069492 PMID:11872829

Koch, I., Schueler, M., & Heiner, M. (2005). STEPP-search tool for exploration of petri net paths: A new tool for petri net-based path analysis in biochemical networks. *In Silico Biology*, 5(2), 129–138. PMID:15972017

Koza, J. R. (1992). *Genetic programming: on the programming of computers by means of natural selection* (Vol. 1). MIT press.

Lee, C.-P., Leu, Y., & Yang, W.-N. (2012). Constructing gene regulatory networks from microarray data using GA/PSO with DTW. *Applied Soft Computing*, 12(3), 1115–1124. doi:10.1016/j.asoc.2011.11.013

Lee, W.-P., & Yang, K.-C. (2008). A clustering-based approach for inferring recurrent neural networks as gene regulatory networks. *Neurocomputing*, 71(4), 600–610. doi:10.1016/j.neucom.2007.07.023

Liang, S., Fuhrman, S., & Somogyi, R. (1998). REVEAL, a general reverse engineering algorithm for inference of genetic network architectures. In Pacific symposium on biocomputing (Vol. 3, pp. 18-29).

Liu, G., Liu, L., Liu, C., Zheng, M., Su, L., & Zhou, C. (2011). Combination of neuro-fuzzy network models with biological knowledge for reconstructing gene regulatory networks. *Journal of Bionics Engineering*, *8*(1), 98–106. doi:10.1016/S1672-6529(11)60008-5

Maraziotis, I. A., Dragomir, A., & Thanos, D. (2010). Gene regulatory networks modelling using a dynamic evolutionary hybrid. *BMC Bioinformatics*, *11*(1), 140. doi:10.1186/1471-2105-11-140 PMID:20298548

Martin, S., Zhang, Z., Martino, A., & Faulon, J.-L. (2007). Boolean dynamics of genetic regulatory networks inferred from microarray time series data. *Bioinformatics (Oxford, England)*, *23*(7), 866–874. doi:10.1093/bioinformatics/btm021 PMID:17267426

Maulik, U. (2011). Analysis of gene microarray data in a soft computing framework. *Applied Soft Computing*, *11*(6), 4152–4160. doi:10.1016/j.asoc.2011.03.004

Mitra, S., Das, R., & Hayashi, Y. (2011). Genetic networks and soft computing. *IEEE/ACM Transactions on Computational Biology and Bioinformatics*, 8(1), 94-107.

Noman, N., & Iba, H. (2005). Reverse engineering genetic networks using evolutionary computation. *Genome Informatics*, *16*(2), 205–214. PMID:16901103

Noman, N., Palafox, L., & Iba, H. (2013). Reconstruction of gene regulatory networks from gene expression data using decoupled recurrent neural network model. In *Natural computing and beyond* (pp. 93–103). Springer. doi:10.1007/978-4-431-54394-7_8

Pal, S.K., Bandyopadhyay, S., & Ray, S. S. (2006). Evolutionary computation in bioinformatics: A review. *IEEE transactions on Systems, man, and cybernetics, Part c: Applications and reviews*, 36(5), 601-615.

Pan, W. (2002). A comparative review of statistical methods for discovering differentially expressed genes in replicated microarray experiments. *Bioinformatics (Oxford, England)*, *18*(4), 546–554. doi:10.1093/bioinformatics/18.4.546 PMID:12016052

Peck, R., & Devore, J. (2011). *Statistics: The exploration & analysis of data*. Cengage Learning.

Ram, R., Chetty, M., Dix, T., ... (2006). Fuzzy model for gene regulatory network. Proceedings of the IEEE congress on Evolutionary computation CEC '06 (pp. 1450-1455). doi:10.1109/CEC.2006.1688479

Raza, K. (2014). Clustering analysis of cancerous microarray data. *Journal of Chemical and Pharmaceutical Research*, *6*(9), 488–493.

Raza, K. (2015). Formal concept analysis for knowledge discovery from biological data. *arXiv preprint arXiv*:1506.00366.

Raza, K. (2016). Reconstruction, topological and gene ontology enrichment analysis of cancerous gene regulatory network modules. *Current Bioinformatics*, *11*(2), 243–258. doi:10.2174/157489361166616 0115212806

Raza, K. & Alam, M. (2014). Recurrent neural network based hybrid model of gene regulatory network. *arXiv preprint arXiv*:1408.5405.

Raza, K., & Hasan, A. N. (2015). A comprehensive evaluation of machine learning techniques for cancer class prediction based on microarray data. *International Journal of Bioinformatics Research and Applications*, *11*(5), 397–416. doi:10.1504/IJBRA.2015.071940 PMID:26558300

Raza, K., & Jaiswal, R. (2013). Reconstruction and analysis of cancer specific gene regulatory networks from gene expression profiles. *International Journal on Bioinformatics & Biosciences*, *3*(2), 25–34. doi:10.5121/ijbb.2013.3203

Raza, K., & Kohli, M. (2015). Ant colony optimization for inferring key gene interactions. *Proceedings of the 9th indiacom-2015, 2nd international conference on computing for sustainable global development* (pp. 1242-1246).

Raza, K., & Mishra, A. (2012). A novel anticlustering filtering algorithm for the prediction of genes as a drug target. *American journal of biomedical engineering*, 2(5), 206-211.

Raza, K., & Parveen, R. (2012). Evolutionary algorithms in genetic regulatory networks model. *Journal of Advanced Bioinformatics Applications and Research*, *3*(1), 271–280.

Raza, K., & Parveen, R. (2013). Soft computing approach for modeling genetic regulatory networks. In *Advances in computing and information technology* (pp. 1–11). Springer. doi:10.1007/978-3-642-31600-5_1

Remy, E., Ruet, P., & Mendoza, L. Thieffry, D., & Chaouiya, C. (2006). From logical regulatory graphs to standard petri nets: Dynamical roles and functionality of feedback circuits. In Transactions on computational systems biology VII (pp. 56-72). Springer.

Ressom, H., Wang, D., Varghese, R. S., & Reynolds, R. (2003). Fuzzy logic-based gene regulatory network. *Proceedings of the 12th IEEE international conference on Fuzzy systems FUZZ '03*. (Vol. 2, pp. 1210-1215). doi:10.1109/FUZZ.2003.1206604

Sahu, B., & Mishra, D. (2012). A novel feature selection algorithm using particle swarm optimization for cancer microarray data. *Procedia Engineering*, *38*, 27–31. doi:10.1016/j.proeng.2012.06.005

Schena, M., Shalon, D., Davis, R. W., & Brown, P. O. (1995). Quantitative monitoring of gene expression patterns with a complementary DNA microarray. *Science*, *270*(5235), 467–470. doi:10.1126/science.270.5235.467 PMID:7569999

Schlitt, T., & Brazma, A. (2007). Current approaches to gene regulatory network modelling. *BMC Bioinformatics*, *8*(Suppl. 6), S9. doi:10.1186/1471-2105-8-S6-S9 PMID:17903290

Shmulevich, I., Dougherty, E. R., Kim, S., & Zhang, W. (2002). Probabilistic Boolean networks: A rule-based uncertainty model for gene regulatory networks. *Bioinformatics (Oxford, England)*, *18*(2), 261–274. doi:10.1093/bioinformatics/18.2.261 PMID:11847074

Sirbu, A., Ruskin, H. J., & Crane, M. (2010). Comparison of evolutionary algorithms in gene regulatory network model inference. *BMC Bioinformatics*, *11*(1), 59. doi:10.1186/1471-2105-11-59 PMID:20105328

Smyth, G. (2004). Statistical applications in genetics and molecular biology. Linear models and empirical Bayes methods for assessing differential expression in microarray experiments.

Sun, Y., Feng, G., & Cao, J. (2010). A new approach to dynamic fuzzy modelling of genetic regulatory networks. *IEEE Transactions on NanoBioscience*, *9*(4), 263–272.

Swain, M. T., Mandel, J. J., & Dubitzky, W. (2010). Comparative study of three commonly used continuous deterministic methods for modelling gene regulation networks. *BMC Bioinformatics*, *11*(1), 459. doi:10.1186/1471-2105-11-459 PMID:20840745

Tian, T., & Burrage, K. (2003). Stochastic neural network models for gene regulatory networks. Proceedings of the 2003 congress on Evolutionary computation CEC '03. (Vol. 1, pp. 162-169). doi:10.1109/CEC.2003.1299570

Tusher, V. G., Tibshirani, R., & Chu, G. (2001). Significance analysis of microarrays applied to the ionizing radiation response. *Proceedings of the National Academy of Sciences of the United States of America*, *98*(9), 5116–5121. doi:10.1073/pnas.091062498 PMID:11309499

Tyson, J. J., Csikasz-Nagy, A., & Novak, B. (2002). The dynamics of cell cycle regulation. *BioEssays*, *24*(12), 1095–1109. doi:10.1002/bies.10191 PMID:12447975

Vohradskffy, J. (2001). Neural network model of gene expression. *The FASEB Journal*, *15*(3), 846-854.

Wang, F., Pan, D., & Ding, J. (2008). A new approach combined fuzzy clustering and bayesian networks for modeling gene regulatory networks. Proceedings of the international conference on Biomedical engineering and informatics BMEI '08 (Vol. 1, pp. 29-33). doi:10.1109/BMEI.2008.117

Weaver, D. C., Workman, C. T., & Stormo, G. D. (1999). Modeling regulatory networks with weight matrices. In Pacific symposium on biocomputing (Vol. 4, pp. 112-123).

Wei, G., Liu, D., & Liang, C. (2004). Charting gene regulatory networks: Strategies, challenges and perspectives. *The Biochemical Journal*, *381*(1), 1–12. doi:10.1042/BJ20040311 PMID:15080794

Woolf, P. J., & Wang, Y. (2000). A fuzzy logic approach to analyzing gene expression data. *Physiological Genomics*, *3*(1), 9–15. PMID:11015595

Wright, G. W., & Simon, R. M. (2003). A random variance model for detection of differential gene expression in small microarray experiments. *Bioinformatics (Oxford, England)*, *19*(18), 2448–2455. doi:10.1093/bioinformatics/btg345 PMID:14668230

Xu, C.-G., Liu, K.-H., & Huang, D.-S. (2009). The analysis of microarray datasets using a genetic programming. In Computational intelligence in bioinformatics and computational biology, 2009. CIBCB'09. IEEE symposium on (pp. 176-181). doi:10.1109/CIBCB.2009.4925725

Xu, D. (2008). *Applications of fuzzy logic in bioinformatics* (Vol. 9). Imperial College Press.

Xu, R., Venayagamoorthy, G. K., & Wunsch, D. C. II. (2007a). Modeling of gene regulatory networks with hybrid differential evolution and particle swarm optimization. *Neural Networks*, *20*(8), 917–927. doi:10.1016/j.neunet.2007.07.002 PMID:17714912

Xu, R., Wunsch, I. I. D., & Frank, R. (2007b). Inference of genetic regulatory networks with recurrent neural network models using particle swarm optimization. *IEEE/ACM Transactions on Computational Biology and Bioinformatics*, *4*(4), 681–692. doi:10.1109/TCBB.2007.1057 PMID:17975278

Yang, X.-S., & Deb, S. (2009). Cuckoo search via levy flights. In Nature & biologically inspired computing, 2009. NABIC 2009. world congress on (pp. 210{214).

Zadeh, L. A. (1996). Fuzzy logic= computing with words. *IEEE Transactions on Fuzzy Systems*, *4*(2), 103–111.

Zhang, Y., Xuan, J., de los Reyes, B. G., Clarke, R., & Ressom, H. W. (2009). Reverse engineering module networks by pso-rnn hybrid modeling. *BMC Genomics*, *10*(Suppl. 1), S15. doi:10.1186/1471-2164-10-S1-S15 PMID:19594874

Zhou, X., Wang, X., Pal, R., Ivanov, I., Bittner, M., & Dougherty, E. R. (2004). A Bayesian connectivity-based approach to constructing probabilistic gene regulatory networks. *Bioinformatics (Oxford, England)*, *20*(17), 2918–2927. doi:10.1093/bioinformatics/bth318 PMID:15145802

Chapter 12
Extraction of Protein Sequence Motif Information using Bio-Inspired Computing

Gowri Rajasekaran
Periyar University, India

Rathipriya R
Periyar University, India

ABSTRACT

Nowadays there are many people affected by the genetic disorder, hereditary diseases, etc. The protein complexes and their functions are detected, in order to find the irregularity in the gene expression. In a group of related proteins, there exist some conserved sequence patterns (motifs) either functionally or structurally similar. The main objective of this work is to find the motif information from the given protein sequence dataset. The functionalities of the proteins are ideally found from their motif information. Clustering approach is a main data mining technique. Besides the clustering approach, the biclustering is also used in many Bioinformatics related research works. The PSO K-Means clustering and biclustering approach is proposed in this work to extract the motif information. The Motif is extracted based on the structure homogeneity of the protein sequence. In this work, the clusters and biclusters are compared based on homogeneity and motif information extracted. This study shows that biclustering approach yields better result than the clustering approach.

INTRODUCTION

Protein Sequence

Proteins (Vincent, Bernard, & SinanKockara, n.d.) are present in every cell of the organisms. They are involved virtually almost in all cellular activities. They are responsible for the various metabolic activities, nutrition transportation, regulations and etc. They exist as single chain molecule, as a three dimensional structures or even in the bundle or complex forms. The protein plays a vital role in cellular processes.

DOI: 10.4018/978-1-5225-0427-6.ch012

Table 1. Amino acid codes

1-LETTER	3-LETTER	DESCRIPTION
A	Ala	Alanine
R	Arg	Arginine
N	Asn	Asparagine
D	Asp	Aspartic acid
C	Cys	Cysteine
Q	Gln	Glutamine
E	Glu	Glutamic acid
G	Gly	Glycine
H	His	Histidine
I	Ile	Isoleucine
L	Leu	Leucine
K	Lys	Lysine
M	Met	Methionine
F	Phe	Phenylalanine
P	Pro	Proline
S	Ser	Serine
T	Thr	Threonine
W	Trp	Tryptophan
Y	Tyr	Tyrosine
V	Val	Valine
B	Asx	Aspartic acid or Asparagine
Z	Glx	Glutamine or Glutamic acid

The protein consists of twenty amino acids. They possess different characteristics such as hydrophobic, hydrophilic, polar, non-polar and etc. It is the great challenge to the bioinformatics that to find which combination of proteins are responsible for what kind of activities. The structure and function discovery of proteins in living organisms is vital role in understanding the background of various cellular processes. It is helpful in treating various diseases, in detecting the drugs to peculiar diseases.

The irregularity in the proteins can be found if their actual functionality and their protein complex are known. The biologist will interpret the functionality of the protein complex based on their chemical properties.

These significant protein complexes of various organisms are discovered using the computational techniques. Protein complexes are an assembly of proteins that build up some cellular machinery; commonly spans a dense Sub-network of proteins in a protein interaction network. The gene expression would not help much in detecting the functionalities of the gene. Protein sequence can be generated from the DNA/mRNA sequence that codes for the protein are shown in the Figure 1. The four basic amino acid combines to form the protein that is shown. The 20 different amino acids that are present in the protein sequence along with their chemical name are listed in the Table 1.

Figure 1. The IUPAC code for PROTEIN from DNA code

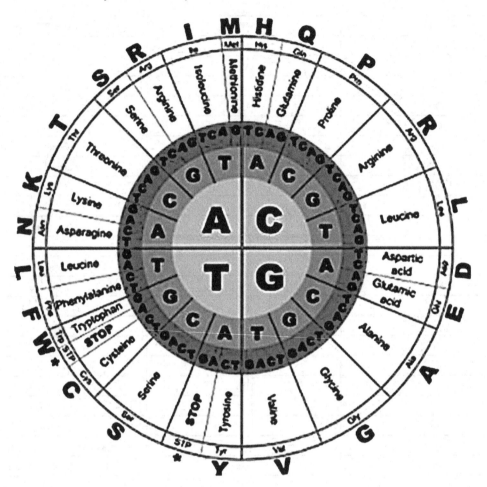

As the protein sequences are in the form of long amino acid sequence, the repeated protein groups are not found manually. These protein groups are denoted as motifs. The protein structure is of many types secondary, tertiary, quaternary, 3 fold and so on. The secondary structures are used in this work. The structural similarity of the detected protein complexes is used to extract the homologous complexes. The functionality of proteins is discovered by various methods like sequence-motif based method, homology based methods, and structure based methods. The motifs can be extracted from the clusters that are generated by various computational techniques.

Roles of Proteins

The proteins[1] are responsible for various activities of the biological system. They present in various parts of the human body. The Figure 2 shows the basic roles of protein in the human body. Besides this, the protein also has various other roles. The motifs are helpful in predicting these functionalities of the protein. The proteins are present in

- **Blood**: The hemoglobin protein carries oxygen in our blood to every part of our body.
- **Hair and Nail**: Protein called alpha-keratin forms our hair and fingernails, and also the major component of feathers, wool, claws, scales, horns and hooves
- **Muscles**: Muscle proteins called actin and myosin enable all muscular movement- from blinking to breathing to rollerblading.
- **Cellular Messengers**: Receptor proteins stud the outside of your cells and transmit signals to partner proteins on the inside of the cells.
- **Cellular Construction Workers**: Huge clusters of proteins form molecular machines that do your cells' heavy work, such as copying genes during cell division and making new proteins.
- **Brain and Nerves**: Ion channel proteins control brain signaling by allowing small molecules into and out of nerve cells.
- **Enzymes**: Enzymes in our saliva, stomach, and small intestine are proteins that help you digest food.
- **Antibodies**: Antibodies are proteins that help defend your body against foreign invaders, such as bacteria and viruses.

Figure 2. Various roles of protein in human body

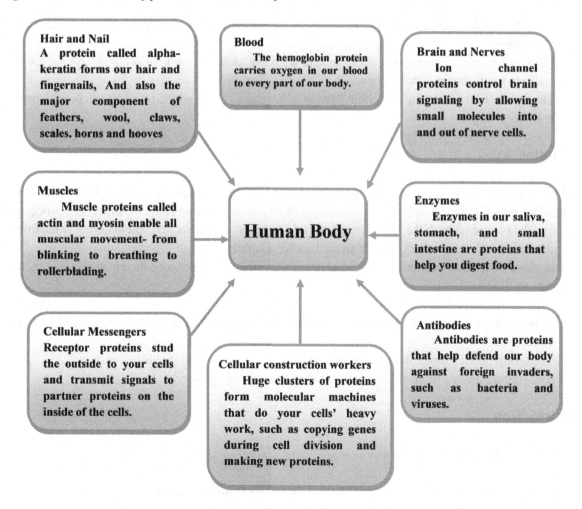

Clustering

Clustering (Berkhin, 2002) is one of the known data mining technique used to group similar kind of data elements. It is used to discover similar patterns from a sea of data. The similarity among objects in the same cluster is greater than in different clusters. It is one of the unsupervised learning algorithms. The clustering (DEIB, n.d) is helpful in intrinsic grouping the unknown data based on our objective. It is a main task of exploratory data mining (Wikipedia, n.d.), and a common technique for statistical data analysis, used in many fields, including machine learning, pattern recognition, image analysis, information retrieval, and Bioinformatics. The motif information is extracted using various techniques like clustering with K-Means, hybrid K-Means, Self-Organizing Maps, etc., in the literature. As all these areas are dealing with the unclassified data, the clustering is well suited to these kinds of research areas. The clusters can be found based on various similarities between the data, such as intra distance and inter distance of the clusters. The quality of clusters will be evaluated based on our objective.

There are a number of problems with clustering. Some of them are as follows.

- Current clustering techniques do not address all the requirements adequately (and concurrently).
- Dealing with large number of dimensions and large number of data items can be problematic because of time complexity.
- The effectiveness of the method depends on the definition of "distance" (for distance-based clustering).
- If an obvious distance measure doesn't exist, we must "define" it, which is not always easy, especially in multi-dimensional spaces.
- The result of the clustering algorithm (that in many cases can be arbitrary itself) can be interpreted indifferent ways.

Biclustering

Biclustering (Madeira & Oliveira, 2004) is another data mining technique. It is also named as Co-Clustering, Two Way Clustering. It generates biclusters of different sizes and characteristics. The process of grouping data based on both the rows (segments) and columns (amino acids). Biclustering is useful for Bioinformatics and many other research areas. It is NP-Complete.

The major difference (Berkhin, 2002; Madeira & Oliveira, 2004) between the clustering and biclustering are as follows.

1. Clustering applied to any one of the dimensions of the dataset, but biclustering applies to both dimensions.
2. Clustering derives the global model, biclustering derives the local model.
3. Biclustering groups more similar patterns than the clustering process.

Contribution

The contributions of the thesis are as follows.

1. Studying various methods of extracting protein motifs from the literature.

Figure 3. Overview of the proposed work

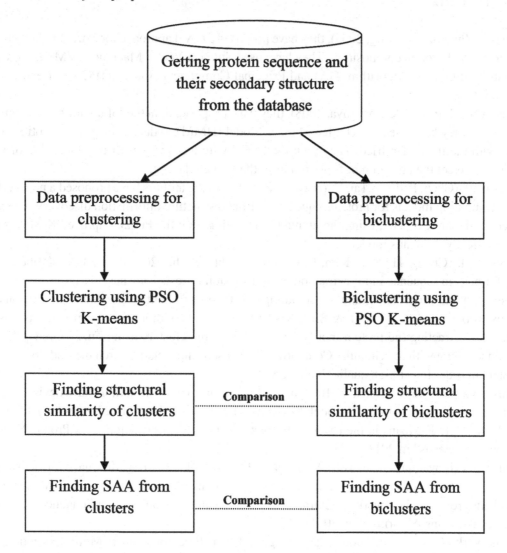

2. The proposed work is to extract the motif from the protein by clustering the given protein sequence with PSO K-Means.
3. The proposed work is to extract the motif from the protein by biclustering the given protein sequence with PSO K-Means.
4. Comparison between the quality of the clusters and biclusters based on structural similarity.
5. Comparison between significant amino acids extracted from clusters and biclusters.
6. The overview of the proposed work is shown in the Figure 3.

The protein sequence is extracted from the databases that are available for the protein sequence and motifs such as BLOCKS (Pietrokovski, Henikoff, & Henikoff, 1996), PROSITE (Bairoch, 8ucher & Hofmann, 1996), PISCES (Wang & Dunbrack, 2003) and so on. The protein sequence is preprocessed for both clustering and biclustering processes. The clusters and biclusters are compared based on their structural similarity, extracted significant amino acids and protein motifs extracted.

BACKGROUND

In this work (Zhaoa-Xing-Ming, 2005), they have proposed a novel approach for extracting features from motif content and protein composition. They have used Support Vector Machine (SVM) along with the combination of Genetic Algorithm (GA) and Principal Component Analysis (PCA) for extracting the protein motif.

In this work (Fujiwara & Konagaya, 2008), they have proposed a methodology for protein extraction in their work, they have used the Hidden Markov Model (HMM) to detect the protein motifs from the proteins with motifs unidentified. They train the HMM with test samples of protein motifs of various categories to detect the protein motifs as similar to the trained dataset.

In this work (Chen, Pellicer, Tai, Harrison, & Pan, 2009), the authors have proposed a novel efficient granular computing models for protein sequence motif and structure information discovery. The protein sequence motifs are extracted using the granular computing with the Fuzzy improved K-Means model and Fuzzy greedy K-Means model.

In this work (Cheng, Hudson, Kim, Crawford, Wright, & Che, 2011), they have defined another method for protein sequence motif extraction using Decision Forest. They have used the decision forest combined with fuzzy logic and granular computing to get more efficient results than their previous work.

In this work (Vincent, Bernard, & SinanKockara, n. d.), the authors have proposed a biclustering algorithm for extracting the protein motifs. They obtained the clusters using Fuzzy Greedy K-Means (FGK) model along with the Granular Computing. They used Cheng and Church methodology to shrink the clusters in order to get high quality biclusters.

In this work (Elayaraja, Thangavel, Ramya, & Chitralegha, 2011), the authors have devised a method for motif extraction process using the rough K-Means. They have used Rough K-Means to yield the better results than simple K-Means in their work, "Extraction of Motif Information from Protein Sequences using Rough K-Means" in 2011

In this work (Elayaraja, Thangavel, Chitralega, & Chandrasekhar, 2012), they have further suggested another method for motif extraction process using the SVD in addition to the rough K-Means in order to attain better results. Their work is "Extraction of Motif Patterns from Protein Sequences Using SVD with Rough K-Means Algorithm" in 2011

In this work (Chang, 2012), they have suggested a method for Protein Motif Extraction Using Neuro-Fuzzy optimization in 2002, they attempted to improve the speed and flexibility of protein motif identification. They proposed an algorithm to extract both rigid and flexible protein motifs and to detect consensus pattern, or motif, from a group of related protein sequences.

In this work (Chen, KripamoyAguan, Yang, Wang, Pal, & Chung, 2011), they have suggested a method for the discovery of Protein Phosphorylation Motifs through Exploratory Data Analysis, they proposed an F-Motif algorithm for motif extraction using clustering methods in 2011.

The various works in the literature show that the different hybrid methods were used for extracting the Motif Information. Those methods are any combination of Support Vector Machine (SVM), hidden Markov Model (HMM), Neural Networks, Fuzzy system, Rough set, Clustering technique and so on. Some authors were used optimization technique to improve the extraction process, such as Genetic Algorithm (GA). From the literature, it shows the combination of optimization technique can improve the results. The PSO is one of the best optimization techniques that does not stuck with local optimum. The clustering technique is better suits for unidentified data. The biclustering further improves results than the clustering process, the combination of PSO with clustering and biclustering on protein sequences is proposed and yield better results. This proposed work is further discussed in the following chapters.

METHODS AND MATERIAL

The protein motifs are extracted using various data mining techniques. In this study, clustering and biclustering technique are used. The K-Means algorithm is used for this clustering process. The PSO K-Means algorithm is proposed for the protein sequence to extract motif information.

K-Means

The K-Means (Ahmadyfard & Modares, 2008) algorithm is one of the simplest, ever using and known clustering algorithms. It is suitable for many research areas. K-Means is one of the simplest unsupervised learning algorithms that solve the well-known clustering problem. It is numerical, unsupervised, non-deterministic and iterative clustering method.

The given dataset is partitioned into k clusters. The data points are assigned randomly to the clusters resulting in clusters that have roughly the same number of data points. This algorithm works faster for the larger dataset. It produces the tighter clusters than hierarchical clustering. The simple K-Means algorithm is shown in the Figure 4.

Particle Swarm Optimization

Optimization is the process of determining the best possible or desirable solution. There are a number of nature inspired optimization algorithms that imitate the natural behaviors. Swarm intelligence (2006) is devised based on the collective behavior of the decentralized and self-organized system of the natural swarms. The particle swarm optimization (AshaGowdaKaregowda & SeemaKumari, 2013) is one of the swarm intelligence techniques. It is a stochastic optimization technique. It is a population based method that is designed based on the birds flocking behavior. Selecting the initial population is decided based on the problem criteria. The steps involved in PSO algorithm are given in the Figure 5. The number of individuals in the population is decided based on the objective of the problem. The particle at each time interval updates its position and velocity based on its own best position achieved so far and the global best position achieved by any one of the particles in its swarm. The random terms are used to weigh the acceleration of the particle. The best position is evaluated based on the objective function of the problem. The basic particle swarm optimization algorithm (Vora, 2013; Riccardo, James, & Tim, 2007) is in 0.

Figure 4. Simple K-Means algorithm

1. Select k objects from the search space represented by the objects that are to be clustered. These are initial cluster centroid.

2. Assign each object to the group that has the closest centroid.

3. When all objects have been assigned, recalculate the positions of the centroid.

4. Repeat Steps 2 and 3 until the centroid no longer move. This produces a separation of the objects into groups from which the metric to be minimized can be calculated.

Figure 5. Particle swarm optimization algorithm

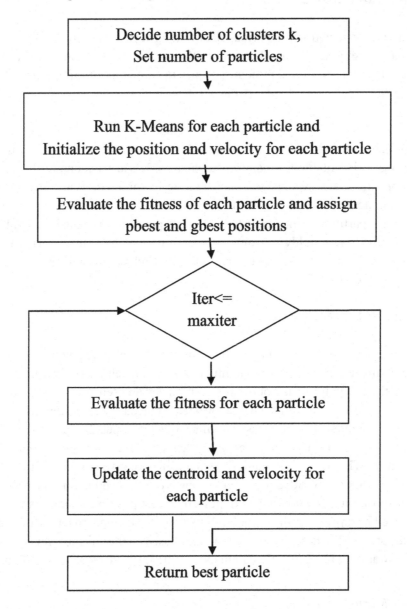

The velocity of the particle is updated based on equation 1, here the first term is based on the velocity of the previous iteration t, second term is cognition part, based on the local best position of the particle and the third term is social part, based on the global best position of the particle. The w represents the inertia weight of the previous velocity of the particle; it is calculated using the equation 2. The c1 and c2 are constant values chosen randomly, the R1 and R2 are random numbers where R1, R2 [0,1].

$$vel_{ij}(t+1) = wv_{ij}(t) + c_1 R_1 \left(pbest_{ij} - x_{ij}(t) \right) + c_2 R_2 \left(gbest_{ij} - x_{ij}(t) \right) \tag{1}$$

where,

$$w = W_{max} - \frac{W_{max} - W_{min}}{iter(max)} - iter(x) \tag{2}$$

The w_{max} is the initial weight of the particle and w_{min} is the final weight of the particle. The position of the particle at each iteration is updated using the equation 3 based on the updated velocity of the particle.

$$x_{ij}(t+1) = x_{ij}(t) + v_{ij}(t+1) \tag{3}$$

Homology Secondary Structure of Proteins

HSSP (Homology-derived Secondary Structures of Proteins) (Reinhard, Antoine & Chris, 1996) is a derived database merging information from three-dimensional structures and one-dimensional sequences of proteins.

HSSP file of any protein sequence will contain the following parts:

- Header information
- Protein sequence
- Alignment information
- Sequence profiles

Distance Measure

The city block distance (Vincent, Bernard, & SinanKockara, n. d.; Elayaraja, Thangavel, Chitralega & Chandrasekhar, 2012) is suitable for this type of data. Since this measure deals with n-dimensional data element, it is suitable for this type of sequence profiles. The distance measure is calculated using the equation 4.

$$distance = \sum_{i=1}^{R}\sum_{j=1}^{A} V_k(i,j) - V_c(i,j) \tag{4}$$

where R is the number of residues and A is the number of amino acids (20). The $V_k(i,j)$ is the value of the profile matrix in row i and column j of segment k. The $V_c(i,j)$ is the value at row i and column j of the centroid of the cluster c.

Cluster Validity Measure

The clusters detected by each particle are evaluated for their fitness. The intra cluster distance (Ahmady-fard & Modares, 2008) is used as the cluster validity measure. The intra distance of the cluster shows how close the elements of the cluster are placed. The average intra distance value of each particle is calculated. The particle with the minimum distance is taken as the best particle.

$$\text{intra distance} = \sum_{i=1}^{n} \text{distance}(A_k(i), \text{cent}_k) \tag{5}$$

where distance(A_k(i),cent$_k$) is calculated using the city block distance as defined earlier in the equation 5.

Bicluster Validity Measure

The biclusters detected by each particle are evaluated for their fitness. The Mean Square Residue (MSR) (Madeira & Oliveira, 2004) value is used to validate the biclusters of each particle. The particle with minimal MSR value is considered as best particle. It is calculated using the equation 6.

$$\text{MSR}(b) = \frac{1}{|I||J|} \sum_{i \in I, \ j \in J} \left(b_{ij} - b_{iJ} - b_{Ij} + b_{IJ} \right)^2 \tag{6}$$

Where MSR(b) is the mean square residue of a bicluster b with I rows and J columns, b_{iJ} represents the column average and b_{Ij} represents the row average.

Structural Similarity Measure

Similarity measure for the protein sequences is calculated based on the secondary structure of the protein sequence. A cluster's or bicluster's average structure (Vincent, Bernard, & SinanKockara, n.d.) is calculated using the equation 7.

$$\text{Structural similarity} = \frac{\sum_{i=1}^{ws} \max \left(P_{i,H}, \ P_{i,E}, \ P_{i,C} \right)}{ws} \tag{7}$$

Where ws is the window size and $P_{i,H}$ shows the frequency of occurrence of helix among the segments for the cluster in position i. $P_{i,E}$ and $P_{i,C}$ are defined in a similar way. If the structural homology for a cluster or bicluster exceeds 70%, then it can be considered as structurally identical. If the structural homology for the cluster or bicluster is between 60% and 70%, then it can be considered weakly structurally homologous.

PROPOSED METHOD: MOTIF EXTRACTION USING PSO K-MEANS

PSO K-Means

Initially the numbers of groups (k) have to be given data. This will differ for different dataset. The k value plays vital role in the K-Means, the k value that suits the given dataset can be estimated by the trial and error process. Then decide the number of particles to perform our clustering process to find the optimal result. The initial velocity and position of the particle can be set based on the objective.

Each particle will cluster the source data into k clusters. The centroid of their clusters is taken as the position of that particle. Initially, each particle will take the random position and random velocity. Then the fitness of each particle is calculated. Then for each particle the pbest position is evaluated, the velocity and position of each particle are updated until the termination criteria are met. The gbest position is updated at each iteration. The various steps involved in PSO K-Means is shown in the Figure 6.

Clustering Using PSO K-Means

The K-Means algorithm is one of the simplest, ever using and known clustering algorithms. K-means algorithm highly depends on the initial state and converges to the local optimum solution. So the optimization method is used to obtain the optimum result of the K-Means algorithm. PSO (Kunik, Solan, Edelman, Ruppin & Horn, 2005) is ideal for identifying the global optimal cluster i.e. global significant amino acid. This method suffers from local minima problem which can be eliminated by the optimization technique like PSO (Youcheng et al., 2012; AshaGowdaKaregowda & SeemaKumari, 2013)

The number of particles is set as per the user's need not greater than 100. It is set in order to overcome the complexity of the computation. The initial velocities of each particle are set to random values. The position of each particle is the cluster centroid. The number of cluster taken is fixed for each particle. The cluster intra distance is taken as the fitness in the PSO algorithm (Fitness$_{clus}$) using equation 8.

$$\text{Fitness}_{clus} = \frac{\sum_{k=1}^{K} \sum_{i=1}^{n} P_{ik} - P_{ibest}}{K} \qquad (8)$$

The particle with minimum fitness value is taken as the best particle. In the equation 4.1K represents the number of clusters, P_{ik} is the position of the i[th]particle in the cluster k, P_{ibest} is the personal best of the i[th]particle and n is the number of particles. The various steps involved in PSO K-Means are shown in theFigure 6.

The pseudo code for psokmeansprocedureis given in theFigure 7. the preprocessed sequence (A), number of clusters required (k) and number of particles (n) to generate are given as input to the this procedure. The procedure kmeans(A, k) is used to cluster the given dataset A into k clusters for each particle with different centroid. The max_iter is the maximum number of iterations to be performed. The evaluateFitness(pop$_i$) is used to evaluate the fitness value of the i[th] particle using the equation 4.1. The evaluatePBest(p$_{besti}$) is used to find the local best (pbest) position of the i[th] particle. The updateVelocity(vel$_i$) procedure is used to update the velocity of the i[th]particlein the current iteration. The updatePosition(pop$_i$) procedure is used to update the position of the i[th]particle in the current iteration. The global best (gbest) value is evaluated at the end of each iteration using evaluateGBest(pbest) procedure.

Figure 6. Steps in PSO K-Means

1. Generate the initial population by choosing number of individuals in the population.
2. For each particle initialize the parameters like velocity and position.
3. While the iteration <= iteration max or termination condition
   a. Evaluate the fitness of each particle position and Update the 'pbest' and 'gbest' positions.
   b. Update the particle velocity and position using eq. 1 & 3.
4. End

Figure 7. Pseudocode for PSO K-Means procedure

```
Procedure psokmeans
Input :
        A    //preprocessed dataset
        n    // number of particles
        k    // number of clusters
Output :
        gbest    //global best particle
start procedure
        for each particle i
                    // call kmeans for each particle
                pop_i=kmeans(A,k)
                pbest_i=evaluateFitness(pop_i)
                vel_i=rand val
        end for
        gbest=pbest_1
                    //initialize gbest with pbest of first particle
        while iter<=max_iter
                for each particle i
                        evaluateFitness(pop_i)
                        pbest_i = evaluatePBest(pop_i)
                        vel_i = updateVelocity(pop_i)
                        updatePosition(pop_i)
                end
                gbest=evaluateGBest(pbest)
        end while
        return gbest

end procedure
```

Biclustering Using PSO K-Means

Biclustering is viewed as an optimization problem with the objective of finding the biclusters with minimum MSR and high volume. PSO is ideal for identifying the global optimal bicluster i.e. global optimal sequence motif. This method suffers from local minima problem which can be eliminated by the optimization technique like PSO. A Biclustering (Das & Idicula, 2010; Rathipriya, Thangavel & Bagyamani, 2011; Cui & Potok, 2005) algorithm along with Particle Swarm Optimization (PSO) technique for protein sequence is proposed. The main objective of this algorithm is to identify the minimal subset of amino acids with coherent in their presence in the sequences. These biclusters have low MSR value, where MSR value is the quality measure of correlation between various residues and amino acids. PSO is initialized with initial biclusters which is obtained by using PSO K-Means on both the dimensions of the normalized protein frequency matrix A. This result in faster convergence compared to random particle initialization of the PSO and it also maintains high diversity in the population. Each particle of PSO (Rathipriya, Thangavel & Bagyamani, 2011; Thangavel, Bagyamani & Rathipriya, 2011) explores a possible solution. It adjusts its flight, according to its own and its companions flying experience.

The personal best (pbest) position is the best solution found by the particle during the course of the flight. This is denoted by the pbest and the optimal solution is attained by the global best (gbest). BPSO updates iteratively the velocity of each particle towards the pbest and gbest. For finding an optimal or near optimal solution to the problem, PSO keeps updating the current generation of particles. This process is repeated until the stopping criterion is met or maximum number of iterations is reached. The MSR is taken as the fitness of the bicluster (Fitness$_{bic}$) using the equation (9).

$$\text{Fitness}_{bic} = \frac{1}{|I||J|} \sum_{i \in I, j \in J} \left(b_{ij} - b_{iJ} - b_{Ij} + b_{IJ} \right)^2 \tag{9}$$

Where fitness is the mean square residue of a biclusterb with I rows and J columns, b_{iJ} represents the column average and b_{Ij} represents the row average.

The pseudo code for psokmeansbic procedure is given in the Figure 8 9. the preprocessed sequence (B), number of row clusters (rk) and column clusters (ck) required and number of particles (n) to generate are given as input to this procedure. The procedure kmeansbic(B, rk, ck) is used to cluster the rows of given dataset B into rk clusters and cluster the columns of given dataset B into ck clusters, then combines the row clusters and column clusters into sub-clusters known as biclusters for each particle with different centroid.

The max_iter is the maximum number of iterations to be performed. The evaluateFitness(popbic$_i$) is used to evaluate the fitness value of the ith particle. The evaluatePBest(pbestbic$_i$) is used to find the local best (pbestbic) position of the ith particle. The updateVelocity(vel$_i$) procedure is used to update the velocity of the ith particle in the current iteration. The updatePosition(popbic$_i$) procedure is used to update the position of the ith particle in the current iteration. The global best (gbestbic) value is evaluated at the end of each iteration using evaluateGBest(pbestbic) procedure.

Figure 8. Pseudocode for psokmeansbic

```
Procedure psokmeansbic
Input :
        B    //preprocessed dataset for biclustering
        n    // number of particles
        rk   // number of row clusters
        ck   //number of column clusters
Output :
        gbestbic    //global best particle

start procedure
        for each particle i
                popbic_i=kmeansbic(B, rk, ck)
                        // call kmeansbic for each particle
                pbestbic_i=evaluateFitness(popbic_i)
                vel_i=rand val
        end for
        gbestbic=pbestbic_1
                //initialize gbest with pbest of first particle
        while iter<=max_iter
                for each particle i
                        evaluateFitness(popbic_i)
                        pbestbic_i = evaluatePBest(popbic_i)
                        vel_i = updateVelocity(popbic_i)
                        updatePosition(popbic_i)
                end
                gbestbic=evaluateGBest(pbestbic)
        end while
        return gbestbic
end procedure
```

Experimental Analysis

The proposed work is implemented in MATLAB 2012, the system has 3 GHz Intel core processor, 2GB RAM and Windows7 Operating System. This section discusses the experimental analysis of each step involved in this proposed work.

Protein Sequence Dataset

In this empirical study, more than 2710 protein sequences are taken from the Protein Sequence Culling Server (PISCES) (Wang & Dunbrack, 2003) as the dataset. In this database, none of the sequences shares more than 25% sequence identity.

The frequency profiles from the HSSP is constructed based on the alignment of each protein sequence from the protein data bank (PDB) where 300 sequences are considered as homologous in the sequence

Table 2. List of parameters

Number of sequences	30
Number of segments	10,635
Number of residues	9
Number of clusters	50-100
Number of biclusters	Row clusters: 50-100 Column clusters: 3-5
Number of particles	30-100

database. The Sliding windows with nine consecutive residues are taken. Each window contains one sequence segment of nine continuous positions. In addition, all the sequences are considered homologous in the sequence database. Secondary structures are also taken from DSSP. DSSP is a database of secondary structure assignments for all protein entries in the PDB. The various parameters used in our work are listed in the Table 2. The 30 sample protein sequences are taken and it is converted into 10,635 segments.

Sequence Representation

Each sequence is represented using sliding window (Vincent, Bernard & SinanKockara, n.d.; Elayaraja, Thangavel, Chitralega & Chandrasekhar, 2012). A sliding window contains residues as rows and amino acids as columns. In this study nine consecutive residues are taken. Normally, twenty Amino Acids are used to represent the protein sequence. The size of each sequence differs from the other. In order to make all the sequence of same size and to convert the categorical data into numerical the following steps are performed. First arrange the one-dimensional sequence data into two-dimensional by taking the HSSP profile frequency values of every nine consecutive residues as one segment. Now each segment will be in the size nine by twenty. This preprocessing step is shown in the Figure 9. The secondary structures of the protein sequence are collected from the DSSP database. There are eight classes in secondary structure which is mapped to three classes the following conversion model: assigning H, G, and I to H (Helices), assigning B and E to E (Sheets), and assigning all others to C (Coils).

These sliding windows are used for clustering process, whereas for biclustering each window is normalized to a single row. For this purpose, the normalization techniques like average value, difference between max and min value and most frequent value can be taken. Now the data become two-dimensional with each row representing a segment and the column represents the average composition of the 20 Amino acids in that segment. This preprocessing step is shown in the Figure 10.

RESULTS AND DISCUSSIONS

The result of both the clustering and biclustering process using PSO K-Means model as proposed in this work are tabulated and interpreted below. The comparison between the clustering and biclustering process is performed based on their secondary structure similarity is discussed. The significant amino acids of the protein sequence are extracted and visualized using logo representation. The motifs detected for the given sequences are taken as superset for the significant amino acids and their interpretation is also tabulated.

Figure 9. Motif comparator preprocessing protein sequence for clustering

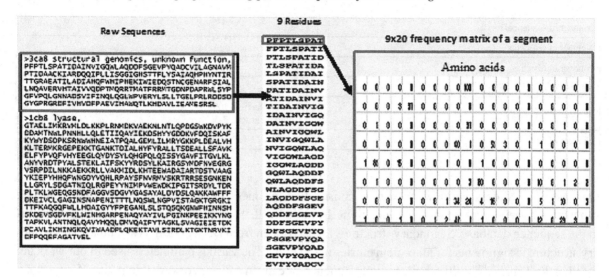

Figure 10. Motif comparator preprocessing protein sequence for biclustering

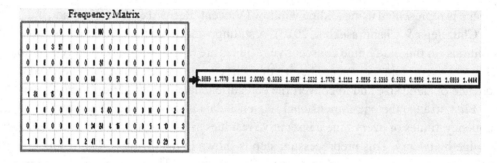

Structural Similarity Comparison

The clustering technique is quite inefficient when compared to the biclustering process. This is proven from the secondary structure similarity value. The number of clusters (Vincent, Bernard, & SinanKockara, n. d.) with higher similarity value generated by our model is less when compared to the number of biclusters generated.

The Table 3 shows that biclustering can detect the biclusters with more similarity value. So the biclustering technique is better when compared to the clustering technique for protein motif extraction process. The structural similarity value is calculated using the equation 7. The clusters or biclusters with similarity value greater than 70% is taken as highly homologous and with a similarity greater than 60% and less than 70% is taken as a weakly homologous sequence. The Figure 11 is the plot with the number of clusters and biclusters with structural similarity as given in the Table 3. From this figure, it is clear that the biclustering model can detect more homologous sequence than the clustering model.

Sequence Motif Representation

The PSO K-Means Biclustering Model is chosen to improve the cluster quality which extracts the motif information efficiently without converging to the local minima. The Figure 12 and Figure 13 are the sequence logo representation of the cluster 1 and 2. Similarly the Figure 14 and Figure 15 are the logo representation of the bicluster 1 and 2.

The logo representations of the clusters and biclusters show that the biclusters are more conserved to specific amino acids than the clusters. The horizontal axis shows the positions and the vertical axis shows the bits of amino acids. The PSO K-Means-Biclustering Model is chosen to improve the cluster quality because it clusters the columns of the data matrix in addition to clustering the rows. The corresponding amino acid sequence columns that are purged by the PSO K-MeansBiclustering Model (Motif) (Vincent, Bernard, & SinanKockara, n. d.) are shown to be either the full or the partial superset of the significant amino acids (SAA): amino acids with appearing frequency greater than 8%. Table 4 and Table 5 illustrate the SAA and Motif relationship for the entire nine positions of the bicluster 1 and 2. Thus, biclustering are proven to have the potential to select meaningful amino acids that biologists are interested in.

Figure 11. Comparison between clusters and biclusters based on structural similarity

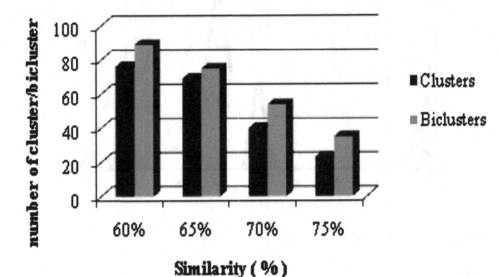

Table 3. Comparison between clustering and biclustering based on secondary structural similarity

Number of clusters= 147 *Number of biclusters=147 (49× 3)*		
Structural Similarity Value Above	**Clusters**	**Biclusters**
75%	23	35
70%	40	54
65%	69	75
60%	76	89

Figure 12. Cluster 1 SAA logo representation

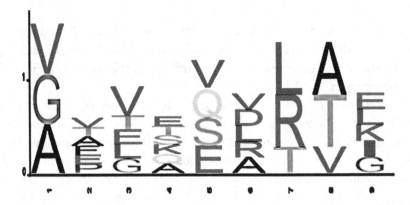

Figure 13. Cluster 2 SAA logo representation

Figure 14. Bicluster 1 SAA logo representation

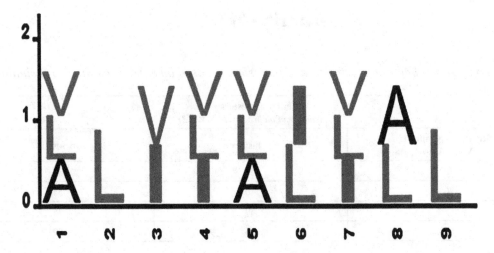

Figure 15. Bicluster 2 SAA logo representation

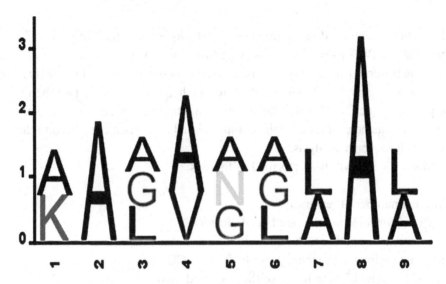

Table 4. Full and partial superset of protein sequence motif on Bicluster 1

Position	SAA	Motif	SAA ⊑ Motif
1	ALV	ADEGILKTV	Full
2	L	ADEGILKTV	Full
3	VI	ADEGILKTV	Full
4	VLI	ADEGILKTV	Full
5	ALV	ADEGILKTV	Full
6	LI	ADEGILKTV	Full
7	VLI	ADEGILKTV	Full
8	AL	ADEGILKTV	Full
9	L	ADEGILKTV	Full

Table 5. Full and partial superset of protein sequence motif on Bicluster 2

Position	SAA	Motif	SAA ⊑ Motif
1	AK	ADEGILKTV	Full
2	A	ADEGILKTV	Full
3	AGL	ADEGILKTV	Full
4	AV	ADEGILKTV	Full
5	ANG	ADEGILKTV	Partial
6	AGL	ADEGILKTV	Full
7	LA	ADEGILKTV	Full
8	A	ADEGILKTV	Full
9	LA	ADEGILKTV	Full

CONCLUSION

The motif information is extracted using this PSO-K-Means model efficiently than simple K-Means. The results show that the PSO-K-Means Biclustering Model is capable of preserving more original data points and obtaining better cluster quality. The biclustering model can detect the highly homologous sequences than the clustering model. The motifs extracted are helpful for biologist for their further research works on new protein sequence. This will be an apt computational process for the biologists handling the two dimensional sequences. It reduces the computational cost when compared to the computations on multi-dimensional sequence analysis.

The future enhancements will be performed as follows:

- Select different number of residues
- Use any criteria for selecting the number of clusters
- Combine granular computing technique with this technique further
- Use some other optimization techniques like BCO, ACO etc.,
- Prediction of biological functionality of the extracted motifs

REFERENCES

Ahmadyfard, A., & Modares, H. (2008). Combining PSO and K-Means to enhance data clustering. *Proceedings of theInternational Symposium on Telecommunication* (pp. 688 – 691). doi:10.1109/IS-TEL.2008.4651388

AshaGowdaKaregowda, & SeemaKumari. (2013). Particle Swarm Optimization Algorithm Based K-Means and Fuzzy c-means clustering. *International Journal of Advanced Research in Computer Science and Software Engineering, 3*(7).

B.Chen, S.Pellicer, P.C.Tai, R.Harrison, & Y.Pan. (2009). Novel efficient granular computing models for protein sequence motifs and structure information discovery. *International Journal of Computational Biology and Drug Design.*

Cheng, B., Hudson, C., Kim, M., Crawford, A., Wright, J., & Che, D. (2011). Protein Sequence Motif Extraction using Decision Forest. Proceedings of the World Congress in Computer Science, Computer Engineering.

Bairoch, A., Bucher, P., & Hofmann, K. (1996). The PROSITE database, its status in 1995. *Nucleic Acids Research, 24*(1), 189-196.

Bill, C. H., & Chang, S. (2012). Protein Motif Extraction Using Neuro-Fuzzy optimization. *Bioinformatics (Oxford, England), 18*(8), 1084–1090. PMID:12176831

Chen, Y.-C., KripamoyAguan, Yang, C.-W., Wang, Y.-T., Pal, N. R., & Chung, I.-F. (2011). Discovery of Protein Phosphorylation Motifs through Exploratory Data Analysis. Discovery of Protein Phosphorylation Motifs(PLoS ONE).

Cui, X., & Potok, T. E. (2005). Document Clustering Analysis Based on Hybrid PSO K-means Algorithm. *Journal of Computer Sciences*, 2005, 27-33.

Das, S., & Idicula, S. M. (2010). Greedy Search-Binary PSO Hybrid for Biclustering Gene Expression Data. *International Journal of Computers and Applications*, 2(3), 1–5. doi:10.5120/651-908

DEIB. (n. d.). K Means. Retrieved from: www.home.deib.polimi.it/matteucc/clustering/tutorial_html/k_means.html

Elayaraja, E., Thangavel, K., Chitralega, M., & Chandrasekhar, T. (2012). Extraction of Motif Patterns from Protein Sequences Using SVD with Rough K-Means Algorithm. *International Journal of Computer Science Issues*, 9(6), 350–356.

Elayaraja, E., Thangavel, K., Ramya, B., & Chitralegha, M. (2011). Extraction of Motif Patterns from Protein Sequence using Rough K-Means Algorithm. *Procedia Engineering*, 30, 814–820. doi:10.1016/j.proeng.2012.01.932

Thangavel, K., Bagyamani, J., & Rathipriya, R. (2011). Novel Hybrid PSO-SA Model for Biclustering of Expression Data. *Proceedings of theInternational Conference on Communication Technology and System Design* (pp. 1048 – 1055).

Youcheng, L., Nan, T., Majie, S., Kedi, F., Yuan, D., Lincong, Q., et al. (2012). K-means optimization clustering algorithm based on Particle swarm optimization and multiclass merging. In *Advances in CSIE* (Vol. 1, pp. 569-578).

Madeira, S. C., & Oliveira, A. L. (2004). Biclustering Algorithms for Biological Data Analysis. *Survey (London, England)*, 2004, 1–31. PMID:17048406

Riccardo, P., James, K., & Tim, B. (2007). Particle swarm optimization An Overview. In *Swarm Intell.* (pp. 33-57).

Berkhin. (2002). Survey of Clustering Data Mining Techniques. *Accrue Software*.

Vora. (2013). A Survey on K-mean Clustering and Particle Swarm Optimization. *International Journal of Science and Modern Engineering*, 1(3), 24-26.

Rathipriya, R., Thangavel, K., & Bagyamani, J. (2011). Binary Particle Swarm Optimization based Biclustering of Web usage Data. *International Journal of Computers and Applications*, 25(2), 43–49. doi:10.5120/3001-4036

Pietrokovski, S., Henikoff, J. G., & Henikoff, S. (1996). The BLOCKS database - a system for protein classification. *Nucleic Acids Research*, 24(1), 197–200. doi:10.1093/nar/24.1.197 PMID:8594578

Reinhard, S., Antoine, D., & Chris, S. (1996). The HSSP database of protein structure–sequence alignments. *Nucleic Acids Research*, 1996, 226–230. PMID:9016541

Swarm Intelligence. (2006). Particle Swarm Optimization. Retrieved from www.swarmintelligence.org

Kunik, V., Solan, Z., Edelman, S., Ruppin, E., & Horn, D. (2005). Motif Extraction and Protein Classification. proceedings of IEEE. *Computational Systems Bioinformatics / Life Sciences Society. Computational Systems Bioinformatics Conference.*

Wang, G., & Dunbrack, R. (2003). PISCES: a protein sequence culling server in Bioinformatics, 19(12), 1589-1591.

Cluster Analysis. (n. d.) *Wikipedia*. Retrieved from: en.wikipedia.org/wiki/Cluster_analysis

Fujiwara, Y., & Konagaya, A. (2008). Protein Motif Extraction using Hidden Markov Model. Proceedings of the Genome Informatics Workshop IV (pp. 57-64).

Vincent, Y., Bernard, C., & Kockara, S. (n. d.). Extraction of Protein Sequence Motifs Information by Bi-Clustering Algorithm.

Zhaoa-Xing-Ming. (2005). A novel approach to extracting features from motif content and protein composition for protein sequence classification. Neural Networks, 2005, 1019–1028. PubMed PMID:16153801

KEY TERMS AND DEFINITIONS

Biclustering: The process of grouping data based on both the rows (segments) and columns (amino acids)

Bio-Inspired Computing: Bio-inspired computing is a field devoted to tackling complex problems using computational methods modeled after design principles encountered in nature

Clustering: Grouping similar kind of data elements. It is used to discover similar patterns from a sea of data. The similarity between the objects in the same cluster is greater than that of the different clusters.

Protein Motif: Motifs are the patterns that present repeatedly in the sequence which are responsible for various cellular processes

Protein Sequence: Sequence of Amino Acids responsible for various cellular activities of the biological systems

PSO: Particle Swarm Optimization is one of the swarm based optimization technique. It is devised based on the bird flocking behavior

Significant Amino Acids (SAA): SAA represents the protein pattern that present in the set of protein sequences that shows the dominant characteristic present in that Protein group.

ENDNOTE

[1]   Structures of life (Book)

Chapter 13
Study of Basic Concepts on the Development of Protein Microarray – Gene Expression Profiling:
Protein Microarray

P. Sivashanmugam
National Institute of Technology, India

Arun C.
National Institute of Technology, India

Selvakumar P.
National Institute of Technology, India

ABSTRACT

The physical and biological activity of any organisms is mainly depended on the genetic information which stored in DNA. A process at which a gene gives rise to a phenotype is called as gene expression. Analysis of gene expression can be used to interpret the changes that occur at biological level of a stressed cell or tissue. Hybridization technology helps to study the gene expression of multiple cell at a same time. Among them microarray technology is a high- throughput technology to study the gene expression at transcription level (DNA) or translation level (Protein). Analysis the protein only can predict the accurate changes that happens in a tissue, when they are infected by a disease causing organisms. Protein microarray mainly used to identify the interactions and activities of proteins with other molecules, and to determine their function for a system at normal state and stressed state. The scope of this chapter is to outline a detail description on the fabrication, types, data analysis, and application of protein microarray technology towards gene expression profiling.

DOI: 10.4018/978-1-5225-0427-6.ch013

INTRODUCTION

Molecular biology is study of biological activity of living organisms at molecular level, it also comprises the braches of biology, genetics, chemistry, and biochemistry. Molecular biology basically deals with the interactions between the various types of macromolecules. The two main types of macromolecules are nucleic acids (Deoxyribonucleic acid -DNA and ribonucleic acid- RNA) and proteins. Since the study of structure, function and relationship between these two types of macromolecules are called as molecular biology.

In 1957, Crick formulated the term the central dogma of molecular biology, which describes the information-flow in the replication of DNA and in the making of protein from DNA. In 1958 the mechanisms of replication were understood by the Meselson–Stahl experiment which predicts the double helical structure of DNA. The double helical structures are made up of sugar, phosphates and nucleotide or base pairs (adenine-A, thymine-T, guanine-G and cytosine-C).

In transcription process the genetic information from double strand DNA molecule was copied as a single stranded messenger ribonucleic acid (m-RNA) by the process of transcription (Figure 1.). The term m-RNA is called as codons. Codon is a sequence of three nucleotides which contains a message for specific amino acids. The information for the building of proteins is written in DNA using the genetic codes which consist of codon. In translation process at the initial stage m-RNA attaches to ribosomes, then the t-RNA (Transfer-RNA) attaches to m-RNA and releases the amino acids to produce proteins i.e. Poly peptides.

The study on synthesis of functional gene product by the process of m-RNA transcription is called as gene expression. Any changes in physiology characterization (structural mutation) of a cell or organisms are complemented by the changes in the configuration of gene expression (Nicole et al., 2000). Since analysis of gene expression is important to find the flow of genetic information from a gene which is used in the synthesis of protein (Functional gene product).

Methods like northern blot, quantitative reverse transcription PCR, serial analysis of gene expression, dot plot analysis are used to analysis the expression of particular gene (m-RNA) in a cell or organisms. All the above conventional analysis of gene expression was studied using one gene at a time, thus these methods are become inappropriate when analysis large numbers of functional gene products simultaneously. The limitation of above methods are overcome by hybridization array technology which is simultaneously generating the labelled copies of multiple sample RNAs and then hybridizing them to numerous different gene specific fixed DNA molecules (Willard et al 2000).

Figure 1. Central dogma of life

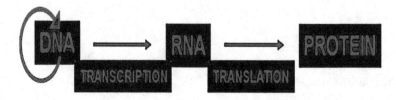

Microarray Technology

Microarray technology has more advantages among the hybridization methodology of measuring gene expression. Microarray technology becomes one of the mile stone in the strengthening of experimental molecular biology. Microarrays are used to detect and measure gene expression at the mRNA (DNA Microarray, oligonucleotides microarray) or protein level (protein microarray). This technology rapidly and efficiently helps to detect the mutations and genotype of cell or organisms, to locate chromosomal changes etc. by measuring the multi gene in a cell or organisms. The major 5 steps involved of microarray technology is as follows:

1.   Coupling of biomolecules to a matrix (glass or plastic slides),
2.   Preparing samples for detection,
3.   Hybridization,
4.   Scanning,
5.   Analyzing the data.

Microarray is defined as an assembly of microscopic spots organized in an array or grid-like format and attached to a standard blotting membrane or solid surface (nylon, glass etc.). A spot indicates the hybridization of particular gene to the probe fixed target (DNA or protein) gene. Generally, dye or detectable molecules are used to label the target gene. The fluorescence or signal emitted by the labelling dye in all spot is used to determine the association between the probe and target. The microarray assembly is scanned using laser beam to develop an image of all spots, each spots is evaluated using refined software to generate the general profile of gene expression level to determine the specific gene sequence in target gene for the experimental and control conditions.

According to sample preparation and identification the microarray was classified as:

1.   DNA microarray,
2.   Protein microarray,
3.   Tissue microarray,
4.   Antibody microarrays,
5.   Carbohydrate arrays (glycoarrays)
6.   Phenotype microarrays.

Among the above classification most widely used microarray technology was DNA and protein microarray. This chapter discuss in detail about

1.   The reason why the protein microarrays technology become predominant in drug development research?
2.   The Fabrication and different type of protein array
3.   The data analysis of protein microarray
4.   The different application of protein microarray.

NEED FOR PROTEIN MICROARRAY

DNA microarray helps to study the gene (whole genome) which encodes specific functional product by evaluating the mRNA produced by transcription process in tissue or cells. DNA microarrays can be constructed using PCR-amplified cDNA (100–3000 base-pairs) or oligonucleotides (short chain - 15–25 nucleotides or long chain - 50–120 nucleotides). In drug development and design, the DNA microarrays is used to study the difference in expression of gene in normal and infected states of tissue or cell. DNA microarray can be subdivided into two type according to the probe hybridization techniques i.e., One- and two-fluorescent probe hybridization. In one fluorescent probe hybridization, one colour fluorescent probe is used to produce expression profile of single sample on single microarray. Thus each sample generates separate expression profile images which can be compared. In two fluorescent probe hybridization, two colours fluorescent probe hybridization is used to label two samples separately with different fluorescent codes or dyes on a single microarray and same was scanned to produce two different images. These images are overlaid in order to analyse and compare the induced, suppressed or expressed gene between the two samples (Stears et al, 2003). Thus this type of DNA microarray can be used to compare the gene expression of different tissue types simultaneously.

In drug discovery phenomenon, the main scope is to suppress the active of receptors of protein structure. But DNA microarrays analyse the expression of gene by measuring the transcribed mRNA in a sample and not measuring the functional gene product (protein). DNA microarray cannot be used to analyse the translational products of genes for determination of gene expression, because such analysis required polypeptide-based arrays.

Discovery of genomics and proteomics help us to understand the deeper mechanisms of disease development by generating individual protein expression profiles for every patient (Yu et al., 2011). Dasgupta, (2007) stated that proteomics can be used to develop a strategy for analysis the personalized medicine for an individual by following five "Rs" principles: right patient/target, right diagnosis, right treatment, right drug/target and right dose/time. On other hand the limitation of DNA microarray can be overcome by studying the gene expression according to the target (protein) produced from stressed organisms or cell. The proteome is the complete gene product (protein) produced or modified by an organisms or a cell or a system at different time, when they undergo stresses. The study of protein structure and its function is called as proteomics (Parag et al, 2011). However, the function based assay technology is required to analyses and validates the protein receptors. The conventional methods like ELISA and Western blotting are the common method used to find and validate the protein receptors and they require only fewer sample and perform the validation at lesser time. In current circumstances the most of the disease causing organisms develop a resistance for given drug and changes the structure or function of protein receptors often, as a result a newer technology is required to validate these mutated protein receptor 10 -100 times faster than conventional methods. One such technology is protein microarray, which helps in massive screening of drug for a specific target at accurate and rapid rate using chip based methodology (Greenbaum et al., 2002; Wilson & Nock, 2003). Protein microarray mainly used to identify the interactions and activities of proteins with other proteins, and to determine their function for a system at normal state and stressed state. Thus the protein microarrays technology become more important during the last decade, primarily due to its ability to analysing thousands of proteins in a single experiment at rapid rate and accurate format (Merbl & Kirschner, 2011).

FABRICATION OF PROTEIN MICROARRAY

The biomarkers play an important role in drug discovery. Biomarker is a cell, gene, molecule, gene product, hormones or an enzyme which shows the difference in biological characteristics of normal or disease individual. The determination of biomarkers is done by many studies like proteomics, genomics, metabolomics and image technologies. As previously discussed DNA microarray can be used to determine the potentiality of a gene using the m-RNA present in them. Griffin et al. (2002) showed that mRNA level is not necessarily proportional to changes at the protein level because biochemical activity of protein majorly depends on the state of protein (post translations modification, reverse covalent modification and interaction with other protein). Protein microarray helps to study the following interaction like Protein–Protein, Peptide–Protein, Antibody–Antigen, Protein–Peptide, Protein–Carbohydrate, Protein–DNA and Aptamer–Protein.

In general protein array are developed by coupling the analytes (proteins, antigen, peptide, carbohydrate etc.) on to the support surface in an array (planar or bead) format for multiplex analysis (Zhu & Snyder, 2003). In this type of array, one captures molecules bind to one analytes in the mixture. In protein array technology number of capture molecules is involved to bind on different analytes of the complex mixture. Glass slide, micro titre plate, bead, nitrocellulose membrane, are used as a support medium on which capture molecules are bound in an array format. The desired analytes are labelled properly and the same is hybridised directly or indirectly on these capture molecules. The signal formed by the interaction between the capture molecules and analytes are detected by image processing tools with that protein expression profile are estimated (Fig.2.).

Figure 2. General steps in the preparation and analysis of protein microarray

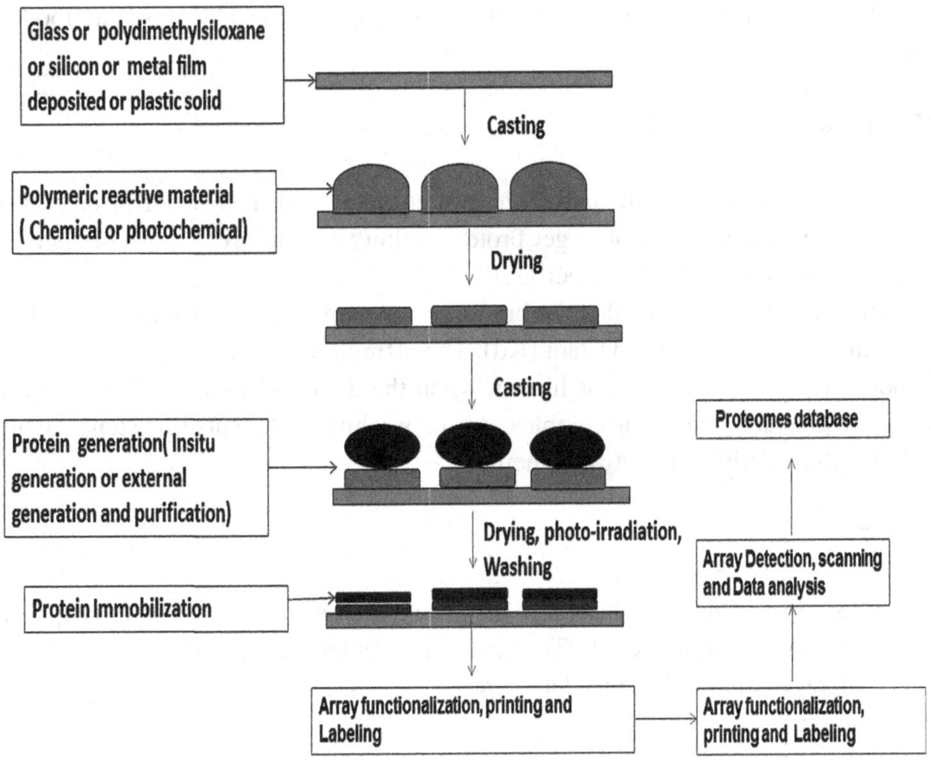

267

The protein analysis by protein microarray are mainly depends on three major challenges:

1. Manufacturing of functional capture molecules or agents.
2. Surface chemistry of solid support.
3. High throughput detection methods.

Capture Molecule

A capture molecule is a specific molecule for a given target, which is immobilized onto a microarray solid support (Phelan & Nock, 2003). The higher affinity of capture molecule towards its specific target is very much essential for quantification and identification of target proteins. Various molecules used as capture agent are:

1. Monoclonal antibody (Goldman, 2000).
2. Polyclonal sera (Zhang, 2003).
3. Antibody fragments (Knappik et al., 2000).
4. Aptamers- Peptide/DNA/RNA (Brody & Gold, 2000).

In many proteins profiling using microarray process the antibody is used as common capture molecule (Huang, 2003). Development of technology like animal immunization and culturing of hybridoma cells produce large quantity of highly specific monoclonal antibody. Thus, these types of antibody are preferred as capture molecules for microarray fabrication. However, the production of monoclonal antibody is a time consuming and expensive process. Li, 2002 used phage display techniques with synthetic libraries for the isolation of antibody fragments against target proteins at a shorter time. Thus phage-display libraries of antibody fragments become an important process for the production of antibody fragments in large scale.

Dissociation Rate Constant

The affinity between capture molecule and target protein play important factor in protein microarray technology. Since the quantification of target protein affinity on capturing molecule is needed to the select a specific capture molecule for a specific

target protein. Wild 2001 reported that the binding of protein to capture molecule can be quantified by determining the dissociation rate constant (Kd). The affinity between

Capture molecule and target protein is higher, when the dissociation rate is lower and Vice versa. The loss of capture and target molecule complex, during washing and incubation step, can be prevented by maintain lower dissociation rate between them.

Solid Support

Selection of solid support is also a key factor to produce higher and accurate protein expression profiling from protein microarray. Kumble (2003) stated that to obtain an optimal solid support for protein microarrays the characteristics to be considered are:

1. Binding capacity,
2. Preservation of capture agent functionality after immobilization,
3. Ease of manufacture,
4. High reproducibility,
5. High signal-to-noise ratio, and
6. Ease to manipulate.

Among the above most important factor is maintaining the activity of capture agent after immobilizing on to the solid support. This can be achieved by preparing the capturing agents using a buffer solution with similar properties to the physiological fluid before immobilization. In many case the addition of stabilizer like 30-40% glycerol (Zhu & Snyder 2003) is used to maintain the intrinsic properties of antibodies (capture molecule) and also ensure the uniformity in physical properties of different capture molecule spots in protein microarray.

Surface Substrate

The significant factors to be considered for developing of protein expression profiling are surface substrates and bonding force between the surface substrates and capture molecule. Espina et al. 2004 reported that polystyrene a hydrophobic plastic is commonly used as surface substrates, because most of the proteins are easily bound to it by physical adsorption (hydrophobic, van der Waals, and electrostatic Interactions). Advantage for this type of immobilization is that it does not require any modifications of the protein for its attachment to the surface. But the disadvantage of using this substrate is multiple uncontrolled physical interactions developed between protein and surface material, resulting in denaturing of protein molecules. Haab et al 2001 used the non- covalent, hydrophilic and positively charged poly-lysine as substrate on glass for the fabrication of protein microarray. The adsorption of proteins onto hydrophobic and hydrophilic surfaces substrates can also lead to problems with protein desorption during the assay, which can lead to signal loss. Another alternated method used to bind protein to the surface is by covalent attachment, achieved by chemically (aldehyde, epoxy or ester functional groups) activated surface. The advantage of this type of attachment is its stability, and the capture molecules are immobilized at very high densities (Lahiri et al. 1999). Thus this type of attachment helps directly to interpret and produce highly sensitive detection. The above discussed types of attachment determine the random orientation of protein bound to the glass slide by passive adsorption principle. The uniform orientation of the different proteins onto the chip surface can be achieved by utilization of site-oriented immobilization methodologies (Templin et al. 2002). The site –oriented immobilization can be attained by using streptavidin-biotin or His-tag-nickel-chelates which produce specific bimolecular interactions. This type of attachment shows six-fold higher active of antibody (capture molecule) when compared to random orientation (Peluso et al. 2003).

PRINTING TECHNOLOGY

Accurate, reliable and repeatability of assay for the production of protein array in large scale can be achieved by printing technology in a multiplicity of configurations (Schena, 2000). Printing technologies are highly desired with less deterioration on biosamples during the manufacturing of protein microarray (Cheng-En Ho et al, 2008). Basically Printing technologies are of two types 1) contact printing 2) non-contact printing.

Contact Printing Technologies

Contact printing is accomplished by direct contact between a metal pin head and the solid surface. Contact printing methodology is further classified into three major as:

1. **Solid Pin Contact Printing:** A solid pin printing assembly is composed of a solid pin with a flat end. Immersing the pin in a fluid sample and a sub-nanolitre volume of sample is taken by the tip of the pin. The pin will come in direct contact with the solid surface and delivers the fluid to the surface. In this methodology the spot size can be determined by estimating the volume of fluid deposited. The volume of fluid deposited greatly is dependent on the diameter of the pin and sample fluid properties. Schena (2000) reported for each spot printing, it is necessary to re-immerse the solid pin into the sample fluid, thus the solid pin format does not offer duplicate or triplicate printing.
2. **Quill Type Contact Printing:** This type of printing assembly generally contains a flat pin head with a demarcated hollow bore (bag like structure). In this printing, first the flat pin head in quill type device is immersed into sample fluid and collected them in a hollow bore structure attached to the head. Secondly when this flat pin head come in contact, they start depositing the sample fluid on the solid surface. Quill type contact printing offer multiple spot printing from each sample fluid (Schena, 2000).
3. **Pin and Ring Type Contact Printing:** This type of printing device contains a ring like structure to which sample fluid and quill type contact printing, which has a flat head pin. The flat head pin is immersed into the sample and start collecting a microliter of the sample, stored in ring like structure. When the flat pin head comes in contact with a solid surface it starts depositing the sample on the solid surface. The pin and ring contact printing assembly is capable of replicate spot printing (Schena, 2000). Espina et al. (2003) showed that the dispensed volume (0.3 -2 nL per drop) into the spot or well.

The disadvantages of contact printing process are as follows:

1. Pin head touching the solid surfaces will denature the protein.
2. Cross contamination of sample due to washing of pin head.
3. Less homogenous protein spotting causing assay variability.

Non-Contact Printing Technologies

Espina et al. 2003 explained that this type of printing technologies operates with help of a sensor for depositing printing sample solution on to the solid surface. Non-contact printing technologies are classified according to material used and they are of two types

1. **Piezoelectric Crystal:** Piezoelectric non-contact printing technologies contains of a glass capillary tube which is surrounded by piezoelectric material (Espina et al., 2003; Schena, 2000). In general, piezoelectric material usually a ceramic material which will undergo deformation when induced by

electric Thus the induced deformation provides a pressure on the sample containing glass capillary, which result in dispensing of sample fluid on to the solid surface of protein microarray platform. Piezoelectric non-contact printing has an ability to dispense picoliter quantities of sample fluid on to the solid surface and deliver a maximum volume of 0.1-0.3 nL of sample

2. **Syringe Solenoid**: Syringe solenoid printing system develops a pressure by a syringe to dispense the sample fluid into a sample tip and by opening the solenoid valve, droplets of sample fluid is ejected from the tip to the solid surface of protein array. Schena 2000 stated syringe solenoid system provided ejects the sample fluid volume of 4–8 nL.

Non-contact printing is becoming predominant nowadays than contact printing for the following reasons:

1. Yield the lowest spot to spot variability in the amount of sample deposited.
2. Provide less harm to the protein structure as the capillary tube does not touch the solid surface of protein array.

DIFFERENT TYPES OF PROTEIN MICROARRAY

The multiplex measurement of protein expression profile using protein microarray platform are broadly classified as spot based array and bead based array format.

Spot Based Array

Spot-based arrays generated by printing of capture molecules onto the planar solid support surfaces (Wiese et al., 2001). In this array format, protein is immobilized on planar surfaces made from glass, polydimethylsiloxane, silicon, metal film deposited or plastic. The array is made using the following steps:

1. Preparation and selection of capture molecule,
2. Sample (analytes) preparation,
3. Labelling of analytes,
4. Immobilization of capture molecule onto solid planar surface,
5. Sample fixing with capture molecule,
6. Detection and imaging of signal produce by the interaction between capture and sample.

Assay sensitivity and sample amount needed are the two important advantages on spot microarray platform. Microarray system has higher sensitivity (signal intensity) only when the binding reaction occurs at the highest possible concentration and it also depends on immobilization of the capture-detection complex in the microarray spot. Espina et al. (2003) reported when the size of spot increases the signal intensity produced from capture-detection complex sequentially reduced.

The planar array surface is chosen for protein array platform due to its simplicity and its surface-to-volume ratio is higher surface larger than macroscopic surfaces. As result the planar array surface has higher capacity to bind capture molecule with surface than by macroscopic surfaces. This Random surface immobilization of multiple fixing points can also cause a protein to be denatured and cause them to lose their activity (Nakanishi et al, 2008).

Bead Based Array

Bead-based fluidic arrays prepared with help of beads of different colour or size will conjugate with capture molecules. Protein immobilization is done with the materials namely glass beads, silica beads, polymeric beads and agarose beads. The surface materials used bead based array are having 3D structure as result it produces 3D surface for immobilization of capture molecules which has more advantages over planar surface. The increased effective surface area found in this type of 3D material offers a larger number of immobilization sites for capture molecules, when compared with planar surface. In such bead based microarray format, the identification of each specific binding is done according to the size, color and mean fluorescence intensity of conjugated fluorochromes by coupling the flow cytometer along with the microarray platform.

According to the application the protein microarray (Figure 3) are broadly classified as follows:

Figure 3. General classification of protein microarray technology

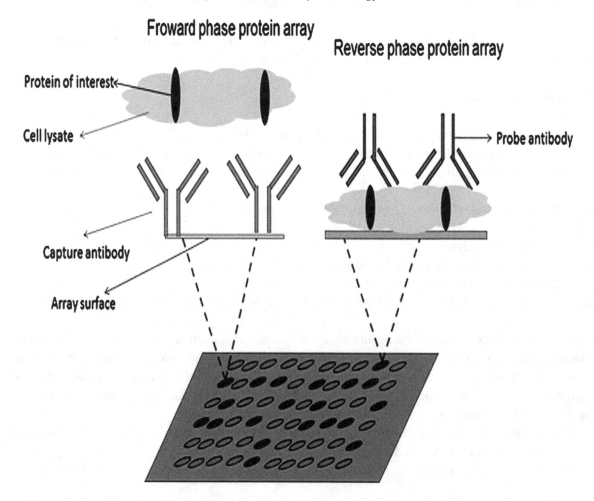

Analytical Protein Microarray

Analytical arrays also called as capture array, in this type of array, capture or affinity molecules like antibody or antigen are immobilized onto the solid support of microarray platform along with the test samples. Each target molecules (protein) from the extract of cell or tissue (test sample) are detected by means of specific labelled secondary antibodies. In general, this type of array is used mainly to determine the protein expression level in a complex mixture, and also helps to find factor like bio affinity and specificity of test sample. Among the capture molecule antibody is used commonly for fabrications of this type of protein array, but the major disadvantage is cross reactivity with test sample and sometimes loss its activity by immobilization on the solid surface (Labaer & Ramachandran, 2005). Currently in many application aptamers (short single stranded oligonucleotides) are become favourable molecule for microarray format, because of its stability and also it has an ability to bind with various range of test sample with accurate specificity and affinity (Walter et al, 2008). Renberg et al 2007 investigated the use of affibody molecules (protein engineered small protein bundles) in microarray format and showed that it has the specificity for wide range of test samples taken from human, bacterial and viral proteins. Major application of capture array is to determine the interaction effects of antigen – antibody, biomarker for specific disease conditions and also helps to check the immunological properties of test samples. This type of array also is used to find the profile of carbohydrate post translation modification to determine the specify glycan of diseased condition (Chen et al, 2007). The capture array can be used to monitor differential protein expression profiles in response to environmental stress and also determine differences among a healthy cell or tissue and with respect to a pathological sample cell or tissue. The disadvantage is direct labelling protocols of thousands of protein onto the surface and the usage to find the protein expression for some specific targets only (Gonzalez et al, 2012; Dasilva et al, 2012).

Reverse-Phase Protein Microarrays

In this protein array the test sample from cellular or tissue lysate or serum sample are bound to the array solid surface. To the immobilized sample the antibody detection probes for specific target protein was attached. The signal produced from the interaction effect is detected with help of the secondary tagging present on the test sample. The interaction effects are mainly depends on the analytes, analytes specific reagent, concentration of test sample binding affinities. In this reverse phase protein array a single analytes endpoint is measured and directly compared across multiple samples. The reverse phase protein array is successfully used to produce a functional map of cell signalling pathway from the cell or tissues of a patient to develop personalized therapies for that individual (Espina et al, 2009).

Functional Protein Microarrays

Functional microarrays are used to investigate the biochemical characteristics and functional activity of proteins, peptides or domains immobilized onto the solid surface, these functional molecules are highly purified by the process of cell-based methods or by cell-free expression on the microarray (Chen & Zhu, 2006; Hall & Ptacek, 2007). Functional microarray is used to study the whole proteome in a single assay methodology. It is also operated to find the different type of protein interaction like protein-protein, protein-small molecules, protein-RNA, Protein-phospholipids and protein-DNA.

CELL BASED MICROARRAY TECHNOLOGIES

Cell-based assays are significantly used in drug discovery process. Cell-based technologies use heterologous host system like *Escherichia coli* and *Saccharomyces cerevisiae*, to produce a functionally expressed protein which is extracted from the cell and then purified using suitable methods like electrophoretic and chromatographic techniques. The purified functionally expressed proteins are printed onto the solid surface to generate a functional protein microarray. The interaction effects of captured antibody or antigen on the solid surface with protein test sample produce a signal, whose intensity is calculated to find the expression of given test sample. The proper folding and modification of protein in the host system, expression of eukaryotic proteins, protein shelf life, stability and purity are the parameters highly important for whole proteomic investigation. The major drawback of the cell based array are not having the capacity to achieve above condition and at the same time this process is highly time consuming, expensive and need many steps like protein generation and purification before protein microarray generation.

The above drawbacks related with cell based protein microarrays can be overcome by developing protein microarray using cell-free expression format, in which DNA templates are used to produce in situ protein synthesis directly on the microarray surface. In this type of techniques different type of DNA templates are used and which has a capacity to express proteins with higher reproducibility. Another advantage of this process is that the protein can be generated on demand, thus loss of protein activity during storage after purification can be avoided.

CELL-FREE EXPRESSION BASED PROTEIN MICROARRAYS

The Cell-free expression based protein microarrays are further developed or classified (Fig.4.) are as follows

Protein in Situ Array (PISA)

He and Taussig (2003) state that PISA can also be called as Discern array technology. This type of array generated protein array from DNA fragments by cell–free transcription and translation, which was then immobilized onto a solid support. In this process the DNA is produced by PCR which was encoded with protein of interest, along with transcription and translation initiation sequences and an appropriate N- or C-terminal tag sequence for immobilization. PISA offer several advantages over the conventional cell based method of printing protein arrays and it also helps to overcome the problems like aggregation, degradation and insolubility of protein, when eukaryotic function gene product expression in bacterial cell.

In PISA, the DNA fragments are synthesised in PCR based on the genome data to generate whole protein or domains. The limitation of this technology:

1. Immediate utilization of DNA generated from PCR.
2. Required higher volume of cell free lysate (extract from cell or tissue).
3. Interference of tag sequence with protein folding structure may affect the activity of functional protein.

Figure 4. Classification of cell-free expression based protein microarrays

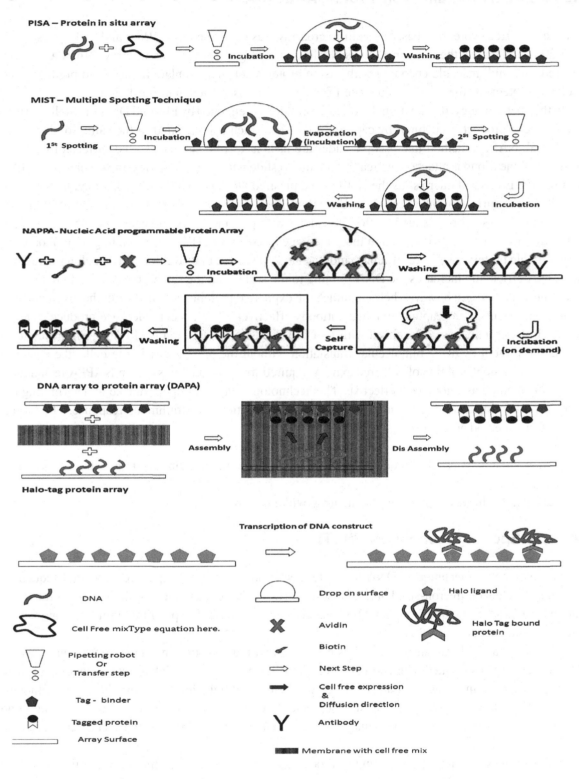

Nucleic Acid Programmable Protein Array (NAPPA)

A novel cell free expression based protein microarray was developed by LaBaer and colleagues in the year 2004 and named the array method as Nucleic acid programmable protein array (NAPPA). In this method, plasmid molecule encoding with fusion proteins act as a template molecule to produce gene product (protein) on the protein chip by cell free in vitro transcription and translation.

In this methodology, the functional protein expression is generated by Plasmid DNA on a solid surface and the gene product is captured by capture molecules which is co spotted in the same solid surface. In general, NAPPA method microscopic slides are used as a solid surface. To the surface of the slide primary amine group is attached by treating the micro slide with aminopropyltriethoxysilane (APTES). To this APTES coated micro slide the biotinylated plasmid DNA is bound with help of avidin molecule present on the surface of the micro slide. BS[3] (Bissulfosuccinimidyl suberate) a homobifunctional primary amine cross-linker is coded on the slide along with plasmid DNA and capture antibody (anti tag antibody) because it helps to maintain the effective expression of cDNAs and binding of antibodies to form reliable protein microarray. Ramachandran et al 2004 stated that addition of BSA along with plasmid DNA efficiently increases the DNA binding to the surface, at the same time it helps to reduce the undefined interactions; however, helps to attach the expressed protein generated from the given plasmid DNA components to the capture anti –tag antibody effectively. These techniques also produce an array in which the protein was co-localized with its DNA. Cell-free expression NAPPA system generates a functional protein by using bimolecular translation without the presence of living cells like bacterial or others. The small volume of cell-free extract required for protein expression in NAPPA techniques, made this method as a good cost effective. This technology plays an important role in determining the protein-protein interaction, vaccine development and estimation of autoimmune response. The limitations of this method are as follows

1. Huge time is required to produce the cDNA along with the protein of interest and its respective tag.
2. Dose not achieves to produce protein array with pure protein.

Multiple Spotting Techniques (MIST)

In multiple spotting techniques, DNA template, detection agent and sample are deposited sequential as small droplets on micron-sized area of a solid surface. These techniques is similar to micron-sized sandwich ELISA technique, however MIST generate immense parallel profiling with lesser amount of samples (Angenendt *et al.* 2004).

MIST uses a solid chip surface which is pre-coated with the capture molecule, mostly an antibody. The chip surface also coated with 100-nanometer-thin Ta_2O_5 film with a high refractive index. This film coating helps to illuminates every area of the chip, when a laser light falls on them. The above methodology also helps to visible only the detected molecules bounded assay. At the same time the background signal is suppressed to improve the signal to noise ratio factor by 50-100 (Duveneck et al, 2002; Pawlak et al, 2002).

MIST follows two steps drop spotting methodology to produce protein expression profile. In the first steps a drop containing DNA template coding for a desired protein of interest, is spotted on the solid chip surface. The second spotting step, the cell free lysate along with detection molecule and BSA blocking molecules is spotted exactly on the first drop. The spots are incubated with detection antibodies conjugated with fluorophores. By tag- capturing agent or by non-specific interaction, the protein sis generated by cell free expression from the corresponding DNA template and detected using the capturing molecule (antibodies) used for protein array formation.

The advantages of MIST is that it can produce high density protein expression array with un-purified PCR products (DNA template) and sample required for this process is very minimal. The major disadvantages of this techniques is time consuming process, non-specific protein binding with capture molecule and loss of signal intensity at prolonged incubation time.

DNA Array to Protein Array (DAPA)

DNA array to protein array is a well-established cell-free protein expression technique, to generate the protein expression profiling array by direct printing of DNA array as template (He, et al., 2008). DAPA technique use two glass slides (i.e.) solid support whose surface are coated with Nickel-nitrilotriacetic acid (Ni-NTA). To one glass slide, PCR based amplified DNA array template, which codes for a specific protein of interest, is immobilized onto the Ni-NTA surface. To another glass slide protein Tag – capturing agent is immobilized, to capture the protein produced from cell free expression system. These two slides are kept face to face as sandwich model and between them a membrane layer is placed, where the protein generation will take place. The newly synthesised protein easily penetrates through the membrane and bound to the protein tag capturing molecule on the opposite slide surface. The interaction between the synthesised protein and protein tag capturing agent produce as signal with high intensity, this is detected and used for a protein microarray for parallel investigation of protein expression profile.

DAPA generates purely expressed protein and it is easily scaled up to sub proteome array (hundreds of protein) with help of DNA construct and thus followed to produce a whole set of proteomes. The advantage of this process is that it produces a pure protein array without any DNA contamination, as they are kept separated and another advantage is reusability of DNA template to produce the protein array many times. Thus this process requires less time and cost as DAPA generates purely expressed protein and it is easily scaled up to sub proteome array (hundreds of protein) and thus followed to produce a whole set of proteomes effective. The major disadvantage is the diffusion of protein through membrane, enlarges the size of spot.

Halo-Tag Protein Array

Halo tag protein array is used to produce a tightly bounded protein array. This was developed by promega. Halo tag protein array uses a glass slide coated with Polyethylene glycol, which in turn activated by immobilizing the Halo tag ligand for capturing of protein expressed. This type of array contains a DNA construct (codes for desired protein expression), which is bonded with halo tag. Halo tag is a 33kDa engineered derivative of bacterial hydrolase Georgyi et al (2008). The protein of interest is produced using WGE (Wheat Germ Extract) and RRL (Rabbit reticulocyte lysate) cell free expression based process. Halo tag is bounded on the protein of interest, which in turn binds to the halo ligand of slide by covalent bonding interaction. This type of interaction enables the capture of desired protein without affecting the protein activity and also prevents material loss during washing process.

DETECTION SYSTEM FOR PROTEIN MICROARRAYS

Now day's microarray technology is used widely for early detection or diagnosis of disease by measuring the gene product. Protein microarray is mainly developed to identify and quantify protein of interest, to screen biomarkers and also to investigate the protein function and its intermolecular interaction in a high throughput manner. Amir Syahir et al., (2015) stated that the detection method should possess following properties to offer effective and good quality result from microarray analysis:

1. Higher signal to noise ratio.
2. High spatial resolution.
3. Good reproducibility.
4. Require a simple and low cost instrumentation.

To investigate the protein expression from the developed protein array, many novel detection systems are developed. In general, they are classified as:

1. Label based system, and
2. Label free system.

Label Based Detection System

In most of the microarray technology, label based detection system is used because it needs only simple instruments and uses easily available reagents. This kind of detection methods has simple working methodology for detection of molecule or compound by attaching the labelling agents or molecule. A foreign molecule which is chemically or temporarily attached to the molecule (protein) of interest, to determine the presence of that protein molecule is called as a label molecule. The label based systems are broadly classified as 1) conventional labelling system 2) Novel labelling system

The labelling system uses the molecules like radioisotopes (Adamczyk et al, 2003), fluorescent dyes (Espina et al., 2004) and chemiluminescent agent (Angenen, et al., 2005) are called as conventional labelling systems. When using novel labels like inorganic quantum dots, gold nano particles, dye-doped silica nano particles, single-walled carbon nanotubes and ultrasensitive bio-barcodes for microarray detection, then that method of detection is called as Novel labelling system.

Fluorescent Label Based Detection System (FLBD)

The FLBD are most appropriate techniques to determine the information from molecular events of biological systems. Silva et al (1997) reported that this technique uses a molecular labels or probes or dyes which are stable and easily manipulated to provide a good and high resolution images for data analysis. In general, FLBD system uses dyes like nitrobenzoxadiazole, fluorescein, acridines, cyanine compounds and rhodamine, are used for protein microarray detection. Among them the most commonly used dye for protein microarray detection is Cyanine dyes (Cy3 and Cy5), as it is easily attached to the charged lysine residues of protein chain. The major factors that governs the selection of fluorophore molecules are 1) type of sample used,2) nature of substrate used,3) the spectral characteristics of light emitted due the binding of sample to the capture antibody, 4) Number of protein to be analysed. The labelling of

Figure 5. Classification of fluorescent label based detection system

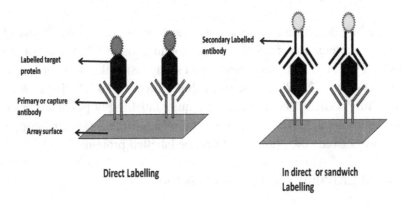

FLBD system are classified into two types one is called as direct labelling system and another one is called as indirect system (Figure 5).

Direct Labelling FLBD System

In direct labelling FLBD system, the Cyanine dyes are labelled directly to the of protein interest which are immobilized onto the antibody bound to the solid array surface (Haab, 2003).

This system required only a single capture molecule for multiplexed detection of proteins for producing hundreds of accurate protein array for data analysis. The advantage of this technique is that it can reproduce the result for the adequate proteins of interest. The demerits of direct labelling are:

1. Produce low sensitivity array images.
2. Lack of specificity between the label and the protein of interest.
3. Label molecule reduces the interaction binding between the protein and capture molecule.
4. Label molecule may alter the chemical nature of the sample.
5. Increase the cross- reactivity between the protein samples and capture antibody.

Indirect Labelling FLBD System

In this type of labelling system, first the unlabelled protein molecule is immobilized to the capture antibody bound on the solid array surface. Then to the protein of interest a second antibody with fluorophore molecule is attached, which is used for detection molecule. These techniques use two type of antibody, each antibody binds to different epitopes of the analytes of interest. Thus this labelling system offers higher specificity and higher sensitivity due to low background labelling (Haab, 2003). The Indirect labelling system also called as sandwich array based assay system. In general, the FLBD system is not suitable for all kinds of substrate due to the intrinsic auto fluorescence property of some fluorescent dye molecule, which may reduce the signal to noise ratio.

Radioisotopes Labelling Detection System

The radioisotopes labelling detection system are one the earliest method which uses the radioisotope molecule to determine the interaction effect of protein-protein, protein-DNA, protein –RNA and protein-ligand. This methodology is producing some health and safety issue like waste disposal etc., made them to decline over years. Ong et al (2002) reported a method called SILAC (Stable isotope labelling using amino acids in cell culture). SILAC method doesn't require labelling or purification step as that in normal label based detection method. This method is combined with mass spectroscopy to determine the relative protein quantity between the normal and isotope labelled proteins.

Chemiluminescent Labelling Detection System

Chemiluminescent labelling detection system is one of best detection method in which the molecular interaction is determined according to the colour formation. The colour is developed according to the energy exerted by interaction of chemiluminescent molecule with protein of interest. The different wavelength is emitted from the chemiluminescent molecule attached to the protein, when these molecules come to ground state. The amount of energy exerted is equal to the amount of energy uptake by the chemiluminescent molecule. This kind of detection methodology can be used for either smaller or larger size sample. Addition of poly horse radish peroxidase to the chemiluminescent microarray immunoassay complex will amplify the signal produced by chemiluminescence molecule, thus result in low detection limits to microgram or sub microgram level of sample molecule (Szkola et al 2014). This type of detection produces higher sensitivity dynamic microarray assay but quantum yield is lower than 1% due to poor energy transfer rate during the chemical interaction of chemiluminescence molecule with sample.

Novel Labelling Detection System

Quantum Dots

Quantum dots are inorganic nano sized crystal consisting of a semiconductor fluorescent core (cadmium selenide) covered by another semiconductor shell (Zinc sulphide or cadmium sulphide). These quantum dots have larger spectral band gap and emit a stable light, when higher energy light incident on them. Thus the quantum dots are helpful in detection of protein interaction with other molecules. The quantum dots are mainly used to find the biomarkers for cancer, to produce diagnostic images and also help in tumor biopsy test (Ghazani et al, 2006; Zajac et al, 2007; Hu et al, 2010). These quantum dots have excellent photo stability and produce higher quality multicolour fluorescence image for detection of protein expression profiling, when compare to organic dyes.

Gold Nano Particles

In this detection system gold nano particles are labelled with the appropriate capture biomolecule. The specific bio molecular interaction between the GNPs with the analyte of interest (protein mixture) may change the emission spectrum of scattered light, (i.e.) it changes the surface plasmon resonance. The changes in the surface plasmon resonance may shift the wavelength from visible to mid-infrared region. The determination of shift occurred due to molecular interaction can be used to generate the protein expression profile for the specific protein of interest. The addition of silver to gold nano particle attached to capture molecule will enhance detection of protein of interest (Liang et al, 2004).The carbohydrate –protein interactions can be determined by the gold nano particles microarray based resonance light – scattering method (Gao et al, 2008). Gao et al (2010) reported that the GNPs can be used for vivo studies to determine the carbohydrate–lectin and glycoprotein–lectin interactions due to their biocompatibility and low cellular toxicity.

Dye-Doped Silica Nano Particles

The large quantity of fluorescent dyes is packed inside the silica based nanoparticles(SNPs) which can be used to tag number of biomolecules, cancer cell and bacteria. This kind of nano particles possess the property like:

1. Eco-friendly in nature,
2. Easy to manipulate and recover after interaction reaction,
3. Nontoxic to biomolecules,
4. Biocompatible,
5. Activity of SNPs is not affected by the pH of the environment,
6. Have microbe growth resistant property.

Deng et al (2006) reported and successfully employed near infrared fluorescent silica based NPs for the production of immunoagglutinaion assay for detection of fetoprotein in blood samples. This kind of SNPs system can be used to determine the biomarker for particular disease, helps in drug delivery systems and also helps to produce multiple signalling in biomolecule interaction analysis.

Nano Particle Based Barcoded Detection Techniques

In 2003, Mirkin's group developed an ultrasensitive protein detection technology using functionalized nano particles called as bio- barcode detection technology (Nam et al., 2003). Goluch et al (2006) reported that bio- barcode system consist of a magnetic micro particles coated with antibody for specific targets of interest and a nano particles encodes the DNA for the protein of interest along with secondary antibody, which binds to the protein of interest captured by magnetic micro particles. The nano particle - protein - magnetic micro particles complex can be separated using magnetic field and the oligonucleotide strands are removed from hybridized complex and whose sequences are determined to identify the target protein.

Detection System for Suspension Microarray Methodology

The suspension microarray systems are detected using two type of detection system:

1. **Flow Cytometer**: Flow cytometer is a special type of fluorescent detection technique for fast, multiplexes and quantitative detection of biomolecules. In this methodology a microsphere with a different colour and size bounded with capture molecule are used and they are incubated along with protein of interest. These target proteins bind to another or secondary capture molecule which is tagged with fluorescent molecule or dye for detection process. In general flow cytometer has

two laser sources one is to detect the capture molecule bounded to the microsphere and second laser for estimating the quality and quantity of protein that bound to the microsphere with help of tagged secondary capture molecule (Edwards et al, 2004). The advantages of flow cytometer with conventional method of fluorescent detection are as follows:

a. Required lesser sample to perform a fast, accurate, reproducible detection of multiple bio-molecules simultaneously.

b. The detection process is cost effective and highly sensitive in nature.

2. **Magnetic Bead-Based Detection:** In this technology the fluorescent tagged secondary capture molecule is immobilized on to the magnetic beads were used to detect the target protein which binds to primary capture molecule. This methodology is highly sensitivity, reproducible and rapid when compare to conventional methods. Leblanc et al reported a novel magnetic bead microarray platform for the simultaneous detection of four kinds of pestiviruses

LABEL-FREE DETECTION TECHNOLOGY

Amir Syahir et al 2015 stated that the system that determine the actual bio molecular events or interaction directly by using the phenomenon like mechanical, electrical or optical signals without any labelling agent is called as label free detection system. The different types of label free detection systems (Amir Syahir et al, 2015) are mass spectrometry (MS), micro cantilevers, quartz-crystal microbalance (QCM), localized surface plasmon resonance (LSPR).

Mass Spectrometry

Mass spectroscopy permits the direct identification of target protein by determining the molecular mass of specific protein of interest but this analysis cannot provide high throughput screening of protein in protein mixture. Bischoff et al (2004) developed a Surface-enhanced laser desorption/ionization - Time of flight – mass spectroscopy system (SELDI TOF MS) to overcome the disadvantages possessed by ordinary mass spectroscopy. In SELDI TOF MS system provides on-chip purification of target protein by solid phase chromatographic surface and consequent ionization and detection of retained protein in the chromatographic surface by TOF MS systems. Unbound or non-retained or interfering molecules are washed from chromatographic surface using proper washing process. Thus this technique provides a high throughput screening of protein expression profiling of given tissue or cell. The major disadvantages of this system is that it can only perform a profiling for lower molecular weight proteins and it is unable to identify the protein after recovery process.

Micro Cantilevers

Atomic force microscopy is one of the scanning probe microscopy, which helps to determine the surface topology using micro cantilevers. This instrument helps to measure the repulsive force produced between the protein sample and the tip of micro cantilever. In general the space between the tip of cantilever to protein on the surface is kept constant. When the tip moves closer to the protein, a repulsive force is produced by the interaction and which in turn induce the bending or deforms of cantilever. This deforms or changes in the cantilever produce a nano mechanical signals (venam (2007), Giljohann and Mirkin

(2008)). These signals are detected by the laser beam and which is reflected back to the cantilever. Thus this method helps to determine the surface characterization of protein microarrays, monitor the protein – protein interaction, DNA –protein binding and also helps to analysis biomarkers in serum (Lee et al, 2006; Breitenstein et al, 2010).

Quartz-Crystal Microbalance (QCM)

Acoustic waves are used in quartz crystal microbalance and by observing the changes in resonant frequency of acoustic waves, this method provides the information about the mass, film thickness, molecular adsorption and surface reaction for a give sample surface. When the sample (protein) adsorbed by quartz crystal microbalance results in effective changes in quartz frequency, as it follows piezoelectric principle, the frequency changes produce a detectable electric filed. Thus this method is used to find the protein adsorption and many biological reactions directly on a one chip multichannel detection method (Cooper et al., 2007; Mori et al., 2009; Ogi et al., 2010).

Surface Plasmon Resonance

In this detection technology the binding interaction between the protein of interest and the probe cause the changes in the refractive index at the surface, which changes the reflection angle in the sensor gram. Thus this method helps to measure the interaction between the biomolecules and also helps to detect the potential biomarkers for cancer, antibody screening and cancer diagnosis etc. (Wassaf et al, 2006; Ladd et al., 2009). Campbell and Kim 2007 reported that surface plasmon resonance imaging can monitor less than 1000 interaction in a real time i.e. about (1020 spots/108 mm^2). Nand et al 2014 studied the interaction between the antibody and protein in high throughput array format (7 x 6 spots) using Surface plasmon resonance system.

PROTEIN MICROARRAY DATA ANALYSIS

The protein microarray generates valuable information on protein functions, interaction effects of protein with different bio molecules and also it gives information about the participation of protein molecule in cell signalling pathways. These data are very much important in the field of clinical diagnostics of particular disease for an individual and thus it helps for the development of a drug for a specific disease according to the individual profile. Protein microarrays are used to develop large quantities of proteomics data by high throughput screening method. Several steps are involved to convert of large quantities of protein microarray raw data into significant biological information are as follows

Protein Array Design Sequence

Design of protein microarray represents the number of samples and type of array performed. In general there are two types of design are used in protein microarray one is called as single channel protein microarray and another one is called as dual channel protein microarray.

Single channel arrays are considered as a standard experiment, in which two arrays are studied with two standard applied conditions. For example, the array one the sample molecule is hybridized with dye 1 (emits red colour) and in another array sample molecules is hybridized with dye 2 (emits green colour).

Dual channel array is single array hybridized with two labels compounds which are not symmetric in character (produce signal at different intensity). For example, in an array the analyte molecule hybridized with two label compounds, one of the label produce red colour and another will produce green colour.

The most commonly used array design within the biological molecules is Reference Design.

Reference Design

In this design a single sample was taken and to it a single fluorescent label is hybridized and the intensity is estimated. For the same sample another fluorescent label are hybridized and its intensity is estimated. In this design both the intensity produced by two fluorescent labels for a single sample is compared by taking log ratio of fluorescent label intensities.

Loop Design

In this design the sample is hybridized in different array using different fluorescent labels i.e. this system simply compares the two conditions of array using a chain of other condition. Thus this type of design doesn't require a reference sample for a give array condition.

Pre-Processing of Protein Microarray Data

Quality Control

The main aim of quality control is to ensure the reliability of the data obtained from whole protein microarray process. The quality control step is important for different level or stages of protein microarray system. Among them the two most important levels to be considered are as follows:

- Array level (check each spot and surrounding).
- Experiment level (compare all protein array generated to identify the outliers and batch effects).

The quality control is mainly tested based on the following factors:

1. Inspection of image (To find the irregularities like bubbles, scratches, missing spots or high background effect).
2. Studying the signal and signal to noise histograms plots (To determine the possible defects or to find the high background effect).
3. Spot analysis by scanners to find the quality of spot generated.
4. Compare the quality of all types of array generated by protein microarray systems.

Table 1. Qualitative Image analysis according to colour generated by spots.

Colour of Spot	Signal Intensity	Gene Expression
Blue colour	Control values equal to predicted values	Unchanged
Red colour	Control values less than predicted values	Induced
Green colour	Control values greater than predicted values	Suppressed

Image Analysis

Image analysis is one of the important steps in data analysis of microarray technology. It helps to find the difference in key features (gene expression – unchanged, induced, repressed) from the background intensity values obtained from the image.

The good quality images have a low background with a high signal to noise ratio and the bad quality images have higher background effects with a low signal to noise ratio.

In general, nowadays software is commonly used to analyse the images generated from the protein microarray experiments. For example, the two fluorescence 16 bit images are generated from the microarray experiment. These images are compressed into 8 bit images (pseudo- colour overlay). The software codes images with three intensity values they are Blue values (B) are set to 0, red values (R) are used for one fluorescence dye (for example cy5), green values (G) are used for another fluorescence dye (for example cy3). Table 1 will show the qualitative result of image analysis.

Eugene and Emmanuel (2007) presented software package MAIA (Automatic microarray image analysis) processing of two-colour images from protein microarray data base. This software can be used to find spot localization, image quality characterization, signal to noise ratio, pixel regression outliers, and quality plot testing etc. the above software can be downloaded from the web site http://bioinfo.curie.fr/projects/ma.

Normalization

Normalization is method by which unwanted systematic variability from protein microarray data can be removed.

In normalization method two types of plots are used to visualise the microarray normalization data are:

- **Scatter Plot:** This plot is drawn between the red intensities (induced) Vs. green (Suppressed) intensities. After normalization most of points are to stay around the diagonal line. (Dov stekel, 2003).

$A= \frac{1}{2}(\log_2(R*G))$: the average log – intensity of the two channels

- **MA Plot:** The normalisation of data to produce a scatterplot of the log ratio against the average intensity of each features, this type of plots are called as MA plot. This plot is drawn between the intensity Vs. log –ratio. (Dov Stekel, 2003).

M= $\log_2(R*G)$: The (logarithm) of the relative expression between both channel (usually known a "log-ratio")

Two common approach are used for protein microarray normalisation namely within-array normalisation to remove the effects of dye bias and spatial bias and between array-normalisation to enable comparison of multiple arrays.

The uniformity between array distributions can be achieved by using the following methods:

- **Scale Normalization:** This method is to scale the log ratio of all the data on the array to have the same median absolute –deviation (MAD) across the arrays.
- **Quantile Normalization:** This type of normalization can be used for both one and two-colour arrays. The intensities values have the same empirical distribution across arrays and across channels can be achieved by using this kid of normalization.

The accurate signal intensity can be calculated by normalization process in microsphere based protein microarray methodology as follows:

- Correction of noise generated by empty microspheres and the calculation of signal intensity from them.
- Correction of noise generated by antibody bounded microspheres and then calculation of signal intensity from them.
- The accurate signal intensity produced by the microsphere population of interest is equal to the difference between signal intensity produced by antibody bounded microspheres and signal intensity produced by empty microspheres.

Now days many number of software is used in normalization process are as given below:

- Gene ARMADA (Chatziioannou et al, 2009).
- Gene Trail Express (Keller et al, 2008).
- μ- CS (Guzzi et al, 2010).

Statistical Inference

Statistical inference lies at the core of both science and classical statistics. The t-test is a commonly used in statistical inference in both biological and medical application. t-test require a normal distribution of the data for analysing and it is of two types one is paired and another one is unpaired t-test.

Paired t-test is called one sample t- test and this method is used to compare the average log ratio with a threshold to determine the protein expressed as the quantity x.

$$t = \frac{x}{s / \sqrt{n}}$$

where x=average of the log ratios of each of the sample, n=number of samples, s=standard deviation of the sample.

Unpaired t-test is called two sample t- test and it is used similar to paired t-test

$$t = \frac{x_1 - x_2}{\left(\dfrac{s_1^2}{n_1} + \dfrac{s_2^2}{n_2}\right)}$$

where x_1, x_2=mean of the two sample, n_1, n_2=size of the two samples, s_1, s_2=standard deviation of the two sample.

Now days number of software is used in statistical inference are as given below:

- Iron chip evaluation package (Vainshtein et al, 2010).
- Nexus Expression (http://www.biodiscovery.com/Index/nexus-expression).

Clustering, Classification, and Validation

Clustering techniques are used to formulate the proper classification of protein microarray for the particular experimental conditions. The clustering process helps to find the following factors:

- Groups of co-regulated genes.
- Spatial or temporal expression patterns.
- Reduce redundancy in prediction models.

Another important advantage of clustering is that it can be used to identify new class of biological expression classes or gene product.

Now days many types of software are used in clustering and classification and these are as follows:

- SEURAT (Gribov, et al., 2010).
- VISHIC (Krushevskaya, et al., 2009).
- Filter-based gene selection (Hwang, et al., 2010).
- Clustering analysis of large microarray data with individual dimension based clustering (Seiler et al., 2010).

VALIDATION

Validation of the results obtained by classification algorithms are done by two methods:

- Training and test sets: More effective method for validation of large number of microarray data set but it doesn't produce valuable results for smaller data set.
- Cross validation: This is often used as a part of training stages to optimise the classification algorithm. It can be used to validate the smaller data set.

APPLICATION OF PROTEIN MICROARRAY

Protein microarrays are quickly becoming essential tools for large-scale and high throughput molecular biology and biochemistry. Recent progress has been made in all the key steps of protein microarray application, such as diagnostics, proteomics, protein functional analysis, antibody characterization, and treatment development. Diagnostics involves the detection of antigens and antibodies in blood samples; the profiling of sera to discover new disease biomarkers and indicators; the monitoring of disease states and responses to therapy in personalized medicine; forensics (scientific investigation of criminal activities),the monitoring of environment and food. Proteomics pertains to protein expression profiling i.e. which proteins are expressed in the lysate of a particular cell. Protein functional analysis is the identification of protein-protein interactions (e.g. identification of members of a protein complex), protein-phospholipid interactions, small molecule targets, enzymatic substrates and receptor ligands. Treatment development involves the development of antigen-specific therapies for cancer and allergies; the identification of small molecule targets and autoimmunity disease that could potentially be used as new drugs. They are also used for things such as kinase/phosphatase substrate determination and antibody cross-reactivity.

ISSUE AND RESOLUTION PROTEIN MICROARRAY FABRICATION AND DETECTION

The protein microarray technology is become more complicated by the inherent structural diversity and complexity nature of proteins. The protein molecules do not have a straight forward binding with other molecules as it possesses diverse biochemical features. Moreover, the comprehensive collection of protein concentration in real samples presents great challenges for printing, arraying and detection strategies in microarray formulation. Some of the major issues and it resolution are as follows:

1. The problems arise while going for the process of printing an array format are inconsistent spotting pattern, merging of spots, missing of spots, compression of membrane surface and variability of slide surface. Many research suggested the ways to overcome the above problems are by ensuring the clean and dry nature of head assembly of printing device, clean the debris under the slide, allow the sample to dry in between multiple spot printing, ensure the calibration of print head assembly of printing device, proper resetting of pin on printing device to ensure proper membrane contact without any damage to the membrane surface and also properly ensuring the consistency in the slide membrane surface.
2. The major issue when going for processing and storage of protein microarray plates is formation of water droplets; which can be prevented by storing the printed slides in container at 20°C with desiccant and before staining process one should ensure that the slides reach room temperature.
3. The problems found in detection of protein microarray are improper staining, usage of defective condition of reagents, dissociation of primary capture molecule, not showing any difference between the target and background. The above problems can be overcome by proper selection of sample i.e. Properly diluted sample with adequate quantity of proteins and protease inhibitors, confirming the proper storage of reagents at particular temperature, by avoiding drying of slide during detection and by confirming the primary antibody for specific protein of interest. Some microarrays may also interfere with certain image analysis techniques due to high levels of background noise. This

noise is often due to nonspecific binding of sample proteins to the chemical coating on the surface of the array. Such noise may be reduced to a certain extent by tailoring the coating of the array, and also by increasing the signal intensity of specific binding proteins. Some fluorescent labels used for detection may alter the probe's ability to interact with target proteins, thereby impairing protein interactions on the microarray and interfering with results. This may be improved by using fluorescent tags that do not interfere with targeted protein interactions.

CONCLUSION

The continuous growth of genomic and proteomic information helps the protein microarray data to grow faster in various application like drug discovery and clinical diagnostics. The protein microarray generates valuable information on protein functions, interaction effects of protein with different bio molecules and also it gives information about the participation of protein molecule in cell signaling pathways. These data are very much important in the field of clinical diagnostics as it helps in the development of a drug for a specific disease according to the individual cellular and molecular profile. This chapter gives the detailed information about the importance of the protein microarray in drug discovery, fabrication of protein array, types of protein array, various methodologies for detection and analysis of protein array data. These give a significant idea for the research for the development of protein microarray for gene expression study and which in turn generated number of protein database. Thus the larger the protein data base helps to understand each and every bio molecular mechanisms of life.

REFERENCES

Adamczyk, J., Hesselsoe, M., Iversen, N., Horn, M., Lehner, A., Nielsen, P. H., & Wagner, M. et al. (2003). The isotope array, a new tool that employs substrate-mediated labeling of rRNA for determination of microbial community structure and function. *Applied and Environmental Microbiology*, *69*(11), 6875–6887. doi:10.1128/AEM.69.11.6875-6887.2003 PMID:14602652

Angenendt, P. (2005). Progress in protein and antibody microarray technology. *Drug Discovery Today*, *10*(7), 503–511. doi:10.1016/S1359-6446(05)03392-1 PMID:15809196

Angenendt, P., Kreutzberger, J., Glokler, J., & Hoheisel, J. D. (2007). Generation of highdensity protein microarrays by cell-free in situ expression of unpurified PCR products. *Molecular & Cellular Proteomics*, *5*(9), 1658–1666. doi:10.1074/mcp.T600024-MCP200 PMID:16825183

Bischoff, R., & Luider, T. M. (2004). Methodological advances in the discovery of protein and peptide disease markers. *Journal of Chromatography. B, Analytical Technologies in the Biomedical and Life Sciences*, *803*(1), 27–40. doi:10.1016/j.jchromb.2003.09.004 PMID:15025996

Breitenstein, M., Holzel, R., & Bier, F. F. (2010). Immobilization of different biomolecules by atomic force microscopy. *Journal of Nanobiotechnology*, *8*(1), 10. doi:10.1186/1477-3155-8-10 PMID:20478017

Brody, E. N., & Gold, L. (2000). Aptamers as therapeutic and diagnostic agent. *Journal of Biotechnology*, *74*(1), 81–91. PMID:10943568

Campbell, C. T., & Kim, G. (2010). SPR microscopy and its applications to high-throughput analyses of biomolecular binding events and their kinetics. *Biomaterials*, *28*(15), 2380–2392. doi:10.1016/j. biomaterials.2007.01.047 PMID:17337300

Chatziioannou, A., Moulos, P., & Kolisis, F. N. (2009). Gene ARMADA: An integrated multi-analysis platform for microarray data implemented in MATLAB. *BMC Bioinformatics*, *10*(1), 354. doi:10.1186/1471-2105-10-354 PMID:19860866

Chen, C. S., & Zhu, H. (2006). Protein microarrays. *BioTechniques*, *40*(4), 423–429, 425, 427. doi:10.2144/06404TE01 PMID:16629388

Chen, S., Zheng, T., Shortreed, M. R., Alexander, C., & Smith, L. M. (2007). Analysis of cell surface carbohydrate expression patterns in normal and tumorigenic human breast cell lines using lectin arrays. *Analytical Chemistry*, *79*(15), 5698–5702. doi:10.1021/ac070423k PMID:17580952

Cooper, M. A., & Singleton, V. T. (2007). A survey of the 2001 to 2005 quartz crystal microbalance biosensor literature: Applications of acoustic physics to the analysis of biomolecular interactions. *Journal of Molecular Recognition*, *20*(3), 154–184. doi:10.1002/jmr.826 PMID:17582799

Dasgupta, A. (2007). *Handbook of Drug Monitoring Methods: Therapeutics and Drugs of Abuse* (pp. 5400–5411). New York, NY, USA: Humana Press.

Dasilva, N., Diez, P., Matarraz, S., Gonzalez-Gonzalez, M., Paradinas, S., Orfao, A., & Fuentes, M. (2012). Biomarker discovery by novel sensors based on nanoproteomics approaches. *Sensors (Basel, Switzerland)*, *12*(12), 2284–2308. doi:10.3390/s120202284 PMID:22438764

De Silva, A. P., Gunaratne, H. Q., Gunnlaugsson, T., Huxley, A. J., McCoy, C. P., Rademacher, J. T., & Rice, T. E. (1997). Signaling recognition events with fluorescent sensors and switches. *Chemical Reviews*, *97*(5), 1515–1566. doi:10.1021/cr960386p PMID:11851458

Deng, T., Li, J. S., Jiang, J. H., Shen, G. L., & Yu, R. Q. (2006). Preparation of near-IR fluorescent nanoparticles for fluorescence-anisotropy-based immunoagglutination assay in whole blood. *Advanced Functional Materials*, *16*(16), 2147–2155. doi:10.1002/adfm.200600149

Díez, P., González-González, M., Lourido, L., Dégano, R. M., Ibarrola, N., Casado-Vela, J., & Fuentes, M. et al. (2015). NAPPA as a Real New Method for Protein Microarray Generation. *Microarrays*, *4*(2), 214–227. doi:10.3390/microarrays4020214

Duveneck, G. L., Abel, A. P., Bopp, M. A., Kresbach, M. G., & Ehrat, M. (2002). Planar waveguides for ultra-high sensitivity of the analysis of nucleic acids. *Analytica Chimica Acta*, *469*(1), 49–61. doi:10.1016/S0003-2670(01)01593-8

Edwards, B. S., Oprea, T., Prossnitz, E. R., & Sklar, L. A. (2004). Flow cytometry for high-throughput, high-content screening. *Current Opinion in Chemical Biology*, *8*(4), 392–398. doi:10.1016/j. cbpa.2004.06.007 PMID:15288249

Espina, V., Liotta, L. A., & Petricoin, E. F. (2009). Reverse-phase protein microarrays for theranostics and patient tailored therapy. *Methods in Molecular Biology (Clifton, N.J.)*, *520*, 89–105. doi:10.1007/978-1-60327-811-9_7 PMID:19381949

Espina, V., Woodhouse, E. C., Wulfkuhle, J., Asmussen, H. D., Petricoin, E. F. III, & Liotta, L. A. (2004). Protein microarray detection strategies: Focus on direct detection technologies. *Journal of Immunological Methods*, *290*(1–2), 121–133. doi:10.1016/j.jim.2004.04.013 PMID:15261576

Fischer, M., Wellnhofer, G., Hoess, A., Wolle, J., Pluckthun, A., & Virnekas, B. (2000). Fully synthetic human combinatorial Knappik, A., Ge, L., Honegger, A., Pack, antibody libraries (HuCAL) based on modular consensus frameworks and CDRs randomized with trinucleotides. *Journal of Molecular Biology*, *296*(1), 57–86. doi:10.1006/jmbi.1999.3444 PMID:10656818

Freeman, W. M., Robertson, D. J., & Vrana, K. E. (2000). Fundamentals of DNA Hybridization Arrays for Gene Expression Analysis. *BioTechniques*, *29*, 1042–1055. PMID:11084867

Gao, J., Liu, C., Liu, D., Wang, Z., & Dong, S. (2008). Antibody microarray-based strategies for detection of bacteria by lectin-conjugated gold nanoparticle probes. *Talanta*, *81*(4–5), 1816–1820. PMID:20441979

Gao, J., Liu, D., & Wang, Z. (2008). Microarray-based study of carbohydrate-protein binding by gold nanoparticle probes. *Analytical Chemistry*, *80*(22), 8822–8827. doi:10.1021/ac8015328 PMID:18855407

Georgyi, V. Los, Al Darzins, Chad Zimprich, B.S., Natasha Karassina, M.S., Randall Learish, Mark G. McDougall, Lance P. Encell,Rachel Friedman-Ohana, Monika Wood, M.S., Gediminas Vidugiris, Kris Zimmerman, B.S., Paul Otto, M.S., Dieter H. Klaubert & Wood, K. (2005). *HaloTag™ Interchangeable Labeling Technology for Cell Imaging, Protein Capture and Immobilization.* www.promega.com, accessed on 17. 05. 2015

Ghazani, A. A., & Jeongjin, A. (2006). High throughput quantification of protein expression of cancer antigens in tissue microarray using quantum dot nanocrystals. *Nano Letters*, *6*(12), 2881–2886. doi:10.1021/nl062111n PMID:17163724

Giljohann, D. A., & Mirkin, C. A. (2008). Tiny tiles, tiny targets. *Nature Biotechnology*, *26*(3), 299–300. doi:10.1038/nbt0308-299 PMID:18327241

Goldman, R. D. (2000). Antibodies: Indispensable tools for biomedical research. *Trends in Biochemical Sciences*, *25*(12), 593–595. doi:10.1016/S0968-0004(00)01725-4 PMID:11116184

Goluch, E. D., Nam, J. M., Georganopoulou, D. G., Chiesl, T. N., Shaikh, K. A., Ryu, K. S., & Liu, C. et al. (2006). A bio-barcode assay for on-chip attomolar-sensitivity protein detection. *Lab on a Chip*, *6*(10), 1293–1299. doi:10.1039/b606294f PMID:17102842

Gonzalez-Gonzalez, M., Jara-Acevedo, R., Matarraz, S., Jara-Acevedo, M., Paradinas, S., Sayagues, J. M., & Fuentes, M. et al. (2010). Nanotechniques in proteomics: Protein microarrays and novel detection platforms. *European Journal of Pharmaceutical Sciences*, *45*(4), 499–506. doi:10.1016/j.ejps.2011.07.009 PMID:21803154

Greenbaum, D., Baruch, A., Hayrapetian, L., & Darula, Z. (2002). Chemical approaches for functionally probing the proteome. *Molecular & Cellular Proteomics*, *1*(1), 60–68. doi:10.1074/mcp.T100003-MCP200 PMID:12096141

Gribov, A., Sill, M., Luck, S., Rucker, F., Dohner, K., Bullinger, L., & Unwin, A. et al. (2010). SEUR-AT: Visual analytics for the integrated analysis of microarray data. *BMC Medical Genomics*, *3*(1), 21. doi:10.1186/1755-8794-3-21 PMID:20525257

Griffin, T. J., Gygi, S. P., Ideker, T., Rist, B., Eng, J., Hood, L., & Aebersold, R. (2002). Complementary profiling of gene expression at the transcriptome and proteome levels in Saccharomyces cerevisiae. *Molecular & Cellular Proteomics*, *1*(4), 323–333. doi:10.1074/mcp.M200001-MCP200 PMID:12096114

Guzzi, P. H., & Cannataro, M. (2010). mu-CS: An extension of the TM4 platform to manage Affymetrix binary data. *BMC Bioinformatics*, *11*(1), 315. doi:10.1186/1471-2105-11-315 PMID:20537149

Haab, B. B. (2003). Methods and applications of antibody microarrays in cancer research. *Proteomics*, *3*(11), 2116–2122. doi:10.1002/pmic.200300595 PMID:14595810

Hall, D. A., Ptacek, J., & Snyder, M. (2007). Protein microarray technology. *Mechanisms of Ageing and Development*, *128*(1), 161–167. doi:10.1016/j.mad.2006.11.021 PMID:17126887

He, M., Stoevesandt, O., Palmer, E. A., Khan, F., Ericsson, O., & Taussig, M. J. (2008). Printing protein arrays from DNA arrays. *Nature Methods*, *5*(2), 175–177. doi:10.1038/nmeth.1178 PMID:18204456

He, M., & Taussig, M. J. (2003). Discern Array technology: A cell-free method for the generation of protein arrays from PCR DNA. *Journal of Immunological Methods*, *274*(1-2), 265–270. doi:10.1016/S0022-1759(02)00521-5 PMID:12609552

Hu, M., Yan, J., He, Y., Lu, H., Weng, L., Song, S., & Wang, L. et al. (2010). Ultrasensitive, multiplexed detection of cancer biomarkers directly in serum by using a quantum dot-based microfluidic protein chip. *ACS Nano*, *4*(1), 488–494. doi:10.1021/nn901404h PMID:20041634

Huang, R. P. (2003). Protein arrays, an excellent tool in biomedical research. *Frontiers in Bioscience*, *8*(1-3), d559–d576. doi:10.2741/1017 PMID:12700043

Hwang, T., Sun, C. H., Yun, T., & Yi, G. S. (2008). FiGS: A filter based gene selection workbench for microarray data. *BMC Bioinformatics*, *11*(1), 50. doi:10.1186/1471-2105-11-50 PMID:20100357

Keller, A., Backes, C., Al-Awadhi, M., Gerasch, A., Kuntzer, J., Kohlbacher, O., & Lenhof, H. P. et al. (2008). GeneTrailExpress: A web-based pipeline for the statistical evaluation of microarray experiments. *BMC Bioinformatics*, *9*(1), 552. doi:10.1186/1471-2105-9-552 PMID:19099609

Krushevskaya, D., Peterson, H., Reimand, J., Kull, M., & Vilo, J. (2009). VisHiC--hierarchical functional enrichment analysis of microarray data. *Nucleic Acids Research*, *37*(Web Server), W587–W592. doi:10.1093/nar/gkp435 PMID:19483095

Labaer, J., & Ramachandran, N. (2005). Protein microarrays as tools for functional proteomics. *Current Opinion in Chemical Biology*, *9*(1), 14–19. doi:10.1016/j.cbpa.2004.12.006 PMID:15701447

Ladd, J., Taylor, A. D., Piliarik, M., Homola, J., & Jiang, S. (2009). Label-free detection of cancer biomarker candidates using surface plasmon resonance imaging. *Analytical and Bioanalytical Chemistry*, *393*(4), 1157–1163. doi:10.1007/s00216-008-2448-3 PMID:18958451

Leblanc, N., Gantelius, J., Schwenk, J. M., Ståhl, K., Blomberg, J., Andersson-Svahn, H., & Belák, S. (2009). Development of a magnetic bead microarray for simultaneous and simple detection of four pestiviruses. *Journal of Virological Methods, 155*(1), 1–9. doi:10.1016/j.jviromet.2008.04.010 PMID:18514335

Lee, M., Kang, D.-K., Yang, H.-K., Park, K.-H., Choe, S. Y., Kang, C. S., & Kang, I.-C. et al. (2006). Protein nanoarray on Prolinker surface constructed by atomic force microscopy dip-pen nanolithography for analysis of protein interaction. *Proteomics, 6*(4), 1094–1103. doi:10.1002/pmic.200500392 PMID:16429461

Liang, R. Q., Tan, C. Y., & Ruan, K. C. (2004). Colorimetric detection of protein microarrays based on nanogold probe coupled with silver enhancement. *Journal of Immunological Methods, 285*(2), 157–163. doi:10.1016/j.jim.2003.11.008 PMID:14980430

Merbl, Y., & Kirschner, M. W. (2011). Protein microarrays for genome-wide posttranslational modification analysis. *Wiley Interdiscip. Rev. Syst. Biol. Med., 3*(3), 347–356. doi:10.1002/wsbm.120 PMID:20865779

Mori, T., Toyoda, M., Ohtsuka, T., & Okahata, Y. (2009). Kinetic analyses for bindings of concanavalin A, To dispersed and condensed mannose surfaces on a quartz crystal microbalance. *Analytical Biochemistry, 395*(2), 211–216. doi:10.1016/j.ab.2009.08.029 PMID:19703406

Nakanishi, K., Sakiyama, T., Kumada, Y., Imamura, K. & Imanaka, H.. (2008). Recent Advances in Controlled Immobilization of Proteins onto the Surface of the Solid Substrate and Its Possible Application to Proteomics. *Current Proteomics*, 5, 3,161-175(15)

Nam, J. M., Thaxton, C. S., & Mirkin, C. A. (2003). Nanoparticle-based bio-bar codes for the ultrasensitive detection of proteins. *Science, 301*(5641), 1884–1886. doi:10.1126/science.1088755 PMID:14512622

Nand, A., Singh, V., Perez, J. B., Tyagi, D., Cheng, Z., & Zhu, J. (2014). In situ protein microarrays capable of real-time kinetics analysis based on surface plasmon resonance imaging. *Analytical Biochemistry, 464*, 30–35. doi:10.1016/j.ab.2014.06.002 PMID:24953011

Newman, A. M., & Cooper, J. B. (2010). AutoSOME: A clustering method for identifying gene expression modules without prior knowledge of cluster number. *BMC Bioinformatics, 11*(1), 117. doi:10.1186/1471-2105-11-117 PMID:20202218

Nicole, L. W. (2000). The application of DNA microarrays in gene expression Analysis. *Journal of Biotechnology, 78*(3), 271–280. doi:10.1016/S0168-1656(00)00204-2 PMID:10751688

Novikov, E. & Barillot, E. (2007). Software package for automatic microarray image analysis (MAIA). bioinformatics application notes, 23(5), 639–640.

Ogi, H., Nagai, H., Fukunishi, Y., Yanagida, T., Hirao, M., & Nishiyama, M. (2010). Multichannel wireless-electrodeless quartz-crystal microbalance immunosensor. *Analytical Chemistry, 82*(9), 3957–3962. doi:10.1021/ac100527r PMID:20387824

Ong, S. E., Blagoev, B., Kratchmarova, I., Kristensen, D. B., Steen, H., Pandey, A., & Mann, M. (2002). Stable isotope labelling by amino acids in cell culture, SILAC, as a simple and accurate approach to expression proteomics. *Molecular & Cellular Proteomics, 1*(5), 376–386. doi:10.1074/mcp.M200025-MCP200 PMID:12118079

Parag A. Pathad., Vinod A.Bairagi., Yogesh S. Ahir. & Neela M. Bhatia, (2011). Proteomics: Opportunities and challenges. *International Journal Of Pharmaceuticals Science And Nanotechnology*, 3(4), 1165-1173.

Pawlak, M., Schick, E., Bopp, M. A., Schneider, M. J., Oroszlan, P., & Ehrat, M. (2002). Zeptosens' protein microarrays: A novel high performance microarray platform for low abundance protein analysis. *Proteomics*, 2(4), 383–393. doi:10.1002/1615-9861(200204)2:4<383::AID-PROT383>3.0.CO;2-E PMID:12164697

Phelan, M. L., & Nock, S. (2003). Generation of bioreagents for protein chips. *Proteomics*, 3(11), 2123–2134. doi:10.1002/pmic.200300596 PMID:14595811

Ramachandran, N., Hainsworth, E., Bhullar, B., Eisenstein, S., Rosen, B., Lau, A. Y., & LaBaer, J. et al. (2004). Self-assembling protein microarrays. *Science*, 2(305), 86–90. doi:10.1126/science.1097639 PMID:15232106

Ramachandran, N., Raphael, J. V., Hainsworth, E., Demirkan, G., Fuentes, M. G., Rolfs, A., & LaBaer, J. et al. (2008). Next-generation high-density self-assembling functional protein arrays. *Nature Methods*, 5(6), 535–538. doi:10.1038/nmeth.1210 PMID:18469824

Renberg, B., Nordin, J., Merca, A., Uhlén, M., Feldwisch, J., Nygren, P.-Å., & Eriksson Karlström, A. (2007). Affibody molecules in protein capture microarrays: Evaluation of multidomain ligands and different detection formats. *Journal of Proteome Research*, 6(1), 171–179. doi:10.1021/pr060316r PMID:17203961

Seiler, M., Huang, C. C., Szalma, S., & Bhanot, G. (2010). Consensus Cluster: A software tool for unsupervised cluster discovery in numerical data. *OMICS: A Journal of Integrative Biology*, 14(1), 109–113. doi:10.1089/omi.2009.0083 PMID:20141333

Stears, R. L., Martinsky, T., & Schena, M. (2003). Trends in microarray analysis. *Nature Medicine*, 9(1), 140–145. doi:10.1038/nm0103-140 PMID:12514728

Syahir, A., Usui, K., Tomizaki, K., Kajikawa, K. & Mihara, H. (2015). Label and Label-Free Detection Techniques for Protein Microarrays. *Microarrays journal*, 4, 228-244.

Szkola, A., Linares, E. M., Worbs, S., Dorner, B. G., Dietrich, R., Martlbauer, E., & Seidel, M. et al. (2014). Rapid and simultaneous detection of ricin, staphylococcal enterotoxin B and saxitoxin by chemiluminescence-based microarray immunoassay. *Analyst (London)*, 139(22), 5885–5892. doi:10.1039/C4AN00345D PMID:25237676

Vainshtein, Y., Sanchez, M., Brazma, A., Hentze, M. W., Dandekar, T., & Muckenthaler, M. U. (2010). The Iron Chip evaluation package: A package of pemodules for robust analysis of custom microarrays. *BMC Bioinformatics*, 11(1), 112. doi:10.1186/1471-2105-11-112 PMID:20193060

Venema, L. (2007). Applied physics: Weight inside. *Nature*, 7, 446, 994.

Walter, J. G., Kokpinar, O., Friehs, K., Stahl, F., & Scheper, T. (2008). Systematic investigation of optimal aptamer immobilization for protein-microarray applications. *Analytical Chemistry*, 80(19), 7372–7378. doi:10.1021/ac801081v PMID:18729475

Wassaf, D., Kuang, G., Kopacz, K., Wu, Q.-L., Nguyen, Q., Toews, M., & Sexton, D. J. et al. (2006). High-throughput affinity ranking of antibodies using surface plasmon resonance microarrays. *Analytical Biochemistry*, *351*(2), 241–253. doi:10.1016/j.ab.2006.01.043 PMID:16510109

Wilson, D. S., & Nock, S. (2003). Recent developments in protein microarray, technology. *Angewandte Chemie International Edition in English*, *42*(5), 494–500. doi:10.1002/anie.200390150 PMID:12569479

Yu, X., Schneiderhan-Marra, N., & Joos, T. O. (2011). Protein microarrays and personalized medicine. *Annales de Biologie Clinique*, *69*, 17–29. PMID:21463992

Yun, T., Hwang, T., Cha, K., & Yi, G. S. (2010). CLIC: Clustering analysis of large microarray datasets with Individual dimension-based clustering. *Nucleic Acids Research*, *2010*, 38. PMID:20529873

Zajac, A., Song, D., Qian, W., & Zhukov, T. (2007). Protein microarrays and quantum dot probes for early cancer detection. *Colloids and Surfaces. B, Biointerfaces*, *58*(2), 309–314. doi:10.1016/j.colsurfb.2007.02.019 PMID:17408931

Zhang, W. W. (2003). The use of gene-specific IgY antibodies for drug target discovery. *Drug Discovery Today*, *8*(8), 364–371. doi:10.1016/S1359-6446(03)02655-2 PMID:12681940

KEY TERMS AND DEFINITIONS

Affibody Molecules: It is a term meant as the protein engineered small protein bundles.

Array: An array is a systematic arrangement of similar objects, usually in rows and columns.

Biomarker: A characteristic that is objectively measured and evaluated as an indicator of normal biological processes, pathogenic processes or pharmacological responses to a therapeutic intervention.

Capture Molecules: The capture molecules arrayed on the solid surface may be full length proteins, antigens antibodies, nucleic acid-based ligands, small molecules engineered to mimic monoclonal antibodies.

Chemiluminescence: Chemiluminescence is the emission of light (luminescence), as the result of a chemical reaction.

Gene Expression: Gene expression is the process by which information from a gene is used in the synthesis of a functional gene product such as proteins.

Hybridization: It is the process of combining two complementary single-stranded DNA or RNA molecules and allowing them to form a single double-stranded molecule through base pairing.

Hybridoma Cells: A hybrid cell produced by the fusion of an antibody-producing lymphocyte with a tumor cell and used to culture continuously a specific monoclonal antibody.

Immobilization: It is a term meant as the restriction of material's mobility in a fixed space.

Chapter 14
Personalized Medicine in the Era of Genomics

Navneet Kaur Soni
Delhi Technological University, India

Nitin Thukral
Delhi Technological University, India

Yasha Hasija
Delhi Technological University, India

ABSTRACT

Personalized medicine is a model that aims at customizing healthcare and tailoring medicine according to an individual`s genetic makeup. It classifies individuals that differ in their susceptibility to a particular disease or response to a particular treatment into subpopulations based on individual's unique genetic and clinical information along with environmental factors. The completion of Human Genome Project and the advent of high-throughput genome analysis tools has helped in building and strengthening this model. There lies a huge potential in the implementation of personalized medicine to significantly improve the clinical outcomes; however, its implementation into clinical practice remains slow and is a matter of concern. This chapter aims at acquainting readers with the underlying concepts and components of personalized medicine supplemented with some disease-based case studies, discussing challenges and recent advancements in the implementation of the model of personalized medicine.

INTRODUCTION

Personalized medicine is one of the most exciting topics revolutionizing healthcare industry today. It is a concept that has the potential to transform medical interventions by providing effective, tailored therapies based on the genetic profile of an individual by utilizing vast information contained in our genetic code. It simply means studying the person in the framework of disease rather than just studying the disease itself. The kind of genetic makeup a person has, the kind of protein produced in them and bio-signatures or biomarkers present in their genome are considered while tailoring treatment for an

DOI: 10.4018/978-1-5225-0427-6.ch014

individual. Offering right drug to the right disease at the appropriate time with the optimal dosage is what is required to improve clinical outcomes and this is what personalized medicine stands for (The Case for Personalized Medicine, 2014)

Traditionally healthcare industry followed a reactive approach to treatment, in which the treatment only begins after signs and symptoms appear. The same prescription is given to different people suffering from the same disease. The physicians only considered family history, social-economic and environmental factors. As a result, every year large number of people die due to severe effects of the medicine and even larger gets hospitalized from adverse effects of medication (ADR-Adverse Drug Reaction). According to a report, patient's response rate to medicines can be as low as 20% depending upon the drug (range= 20-75% response rate). The pharmaceutical industry is still developing medicine based on the observation and the mechanism of the disease. Thus, just treating the disease and not the person.

The modern medical treatment focusses on patient's disease to investigate exactly the state and the pathophysiology of disease, in order to "select" the most appropriate medication. "One drug size fits all" paradigm has lost its validity and it is also clear now that the drug response varies from patient to patient. Genetics play an important role in individual's response to a drug and in deciding optimal drug dose. So we have a model that takes into consideration all the aspects affecting a person's state of health from genetics to lifestyle, termed precision or personalized medicine. The following quote can easily summarize the concept behind personalized medicine *It's far more important to know what person, the disease has than what disease the person has* (Hippocrates of Cos (c. 460 BC – c. 370 BC)).

The development of personalized medicine as an approach to medicine, and as a new dimension in medicine, took off when the human genome was sequenced in 2001. A tectonic shift has started since then which is though subtle and perhaps imperceptible for ordinary individuals, but it is bound to influence the entire backdrop of how we look at our physical and emotional well-being. Modern techniques and the completion of Human Genome project have made it possible to understand the genetic part of the diseases and helped in making significant advancements in the drug development process. Personalized medicine is the new paradigm shift in the field of drugs or medicine which formulates treatment or medicine following genetic testing, proteome profiling, and metabolomic analysis to identify the impact of genetic variations on drug response. However, personalized medicine also requires doctors to collect the patient's personal information including the genotype, so as to understand the nature of the particular patient. Based on which the doctor will decide the most suitable medical treatment for that particular patient.

In particular, each person has different ability of drug metabolism owing to the activity of their metabolic enzymes. For instance, if a person has very weak enzymatic activity, the drug will not get completely metabolized and its concentration in the blood increases. Contrary to this, if a person has very strong enzymatic activity towards a particular drug, the drug gets metabolized very quickly and its concentration in the blood would remain low. In simpler words, when several patients are prescribed the same dosage of a drug, the actual effect of the drug would vary depending on its enzymatic activity and thus its genotype. Based on this observation, a new process of drug development requires studying the effectiveness of the drug against the genotype, including the adverse effects.

The whole genome is sequenced using next generation sequencing methods and the obtained genomic reads are then filtered, aligned and variants identified. Variants and Mutations are then annotated using publically available bioinformatics resources. Personalized treatment could then be suggested based on the biomarkers present and other molecular aspects.

It could be possible to assess patient`s susceptibility for diseases such as high blood pressure, stroke, diabetes, cancer etc. On the basis of the collected information, a new type of medical treatment, called "preventive therapy" to prevent these risks is developed. This implies that even though a person is identified as susceptible to a particular disease based on the genomic examination, changes to prevent the disease by performing the preventive therapy which is designed on the basis of personal information, still prevails. The preventive therapy is expected to gain more importance in the near future.

One of the earliest and most important examples of precision medicine is related to breast cancer. In about one-third of the breast cancer patients, HER2 protein is overexpressed which is non-responsive to standard therapy. FDA has approved Trastuzumab for patients with such condition and research in further years showed that it reduced recurrence by about 52% in combination with chemotherapy (The Case for Personalized Medicine,2009). Another example of personalized medicine is known in melanoma. It is shown that a mutation exists in gene BRAF encoding for protein B-Raf, which is responsible for sending signals inside cells for directing its growth in the majority of melanoma patients. Vemurafenib, an inhibitor of B-Raf and the companion BRAF V600E mutation test were approved in 2011 for the treatment of these melanomas. Vemurafenib is only beneficial for patients with a positive test for BRAF V600E mutation (Ascierto et al., 2011).

A non-invasive genetic diagnostic test is available as an alternative to endomyocardial biopsy for heart transplant recipients to help manage the care of patients post-transplant. This test may be helpful for longer-term patient management as it will aid in predicting the risk of rejection and prescribing more precise immunosuppressive drug regimes.

The prevailing medical treatment is exercised majorly in large centralized hospitals where the focus is on "patients of the average population". However, when it comes to personalized medicine, the current medical system may fall short in expectations. If a patient particularly requires the personalized or the preventive therapy, a modern system would be required to fulfill the requirements. In future, a new system is believed to be a reality with the combination of a "family doctor" and a large centralized hospital. In this system, the role of the family doctor would be to convince the patient and establishing mutual trust as well as understanding the patient`s characteristics. On the other hand, the centralized hospital equipped with an advanced and the latest technologies and instruments would be dealing with the patients whom family doctor is unable to handle.

Personalized Medicine or Precision Medicine is a model that customizes and tailors medication according to an individual's genetic information and determines its predisposition to a particular disease or condition. With the help of personalized treatment model, the healthcare industry will be seen shifting its focus from illness to wellness, and from curing disease to maintaining health. The realization of this model is not without challenges such as lack of infrastructure to support the requirements of this model, the lacking recommendations for the implementation and follow-up of personalized therapy, ethical, legal and social issues, economic issues. But on the whole, it seems evident from the outcomes of the traditional trial and error medicinal approach, that personalized medicine was not a promise made hastily, but a realizable dream. Although the investment in precision medicine is not trivial, it is providing the foundation and systematic methods for prospective progress.

This chapter explains the very concept and the key components of the personalized therapy, dwelling deep into behind the scene factors affecting the implementations of the model of personalized medicine. The chapter also focuses on the advancements in other branches of science such as nanotechnology, metabolomics, molecular biology, immunoinformatics and bioinformatics which has significantly added more value to this model.

PHARMACOGENOMICS AND PHARMACOPROTEOMICS: KEY COMPONENTS OF PERSONALIZED THERAPY

Pharmacogenomics (PGx)uses 'omics' approaches that have led to a revolution in unraveling the underlying cause and mechanism of disease susceptibility, thus providing enormous potential for novel therapeutic strategies.

In general, pharmacogenomics can be defined by splitting the word into two words:

1. **Pharmacology**: The science of drug development and discovery, and
2. **Genomics**: The study of genes and their functional aspects.

Pharmacogenomics – the study of how genetic differences among individuals or alterations in gene expression that are linked to pharmacological function and therapeutic response. It is also sometimes referred to as science differentiating how individual's genetic makeup influences a person's reaction to drugs. The therapeutic response in many disease processes is gene-specific and multifactorial. Therefore, tailoring medication based on patient genomes maximizes efficacy and compliance while avoiding side-effects and drug-drug interactions. Basically, genomics knowledge would help optimize drug therapy for patients that would deliver the best results based on the patient's genotype. Thus, separating responders from non-responders and predicting the efficacy and toxicity of the drug.

PGx involves better pharmaceutical outcomes for patients and possibly finding the right mix of therapy thereby reducing the need for polypharmacy. "Pharmacogenomics" should be implemented in drug development Pipeline. It is introduced in Phase IIA/IIB of clinical trials with the aim of accelerating and facilitating the development of new molecules while reducing the associated risks and costs (Adams, 2008). Thus, aids in understanding how genetic variation among individuals contributes to differences in reactions to the drugs.

PGx play the following role in clinical trials:

*   Identification of variations in a large number of genes that affect drug action.
*   Stratification of Patients in Clinical Trials according to genotype.
*   Prediction of optimal doses of the drug in different patient populations.
*   Reduction in Drug Development time by predicting the populations having good efficacy.
*   Prediction of adverse reactions or therapeutic failures based on the Genotype of the patient.
*   Prediction of Drug-Drug interactions

In PGx, genomic information is used to study individual responses to drugs (Adams, 2008). The two major determinants for studying drug action in individuals are:

1. How much of a drug is needed to reach its target in the body – *Pharmacokinetics.*
2. How well the target cells such as heart tissue, liver respond to the Drug- *Pharmacodynamics.*

Figure 1. Advancement in PGxhas allowed for more tailored treatment for a wide range of health problems, including cardiovascular diseases, cancer, HIV/AIDS etc.

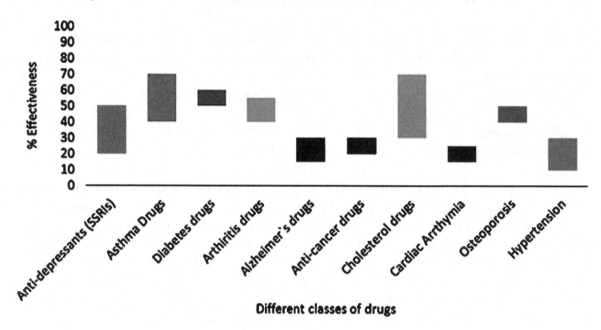

Factors Affecting Response to Medication

Genetic variations are not the only determinant of variations in response to the medications but age, sex, diet, intake of supplement drugs can each influence individual`s response to a medication (Personalized Medicine, Coriell Personalised Medicine Collaborative).

Non-Genetic Risks

- Interactions between drugs and lifestyle factors.
- A person's Gender, Age, and Weight.
- Drug-Drug Interactions like taking clopidogrelas a combination therapy with proton pump inhibitors like Prilosec (commonly used to treat heartburn) reduces the clopidogrel effectiveness in preventing blood clots.
- Interact of existing Medical conditions with Medications. For example, a person that has hypertension or high blood pressure cannot take many anti-inflammatory drugs, such as aspirin and steroids, as they could cause an unsafe rise in blood pressure.
- Environmental risk factors such as sun exposure, air quality, and job-related hazards involving exposure to chemicals, radiation, and carcinogens.

Genetic Risks

Family History for a particular disease may increase the risk of developing a disease.

Figure 2. Different set of population respond differently to same treatment owing to their genetic differences

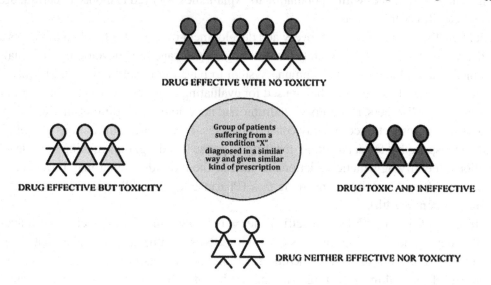

As pharmacogenetic testing become widely recognized and easily available, precision medicine will make use of the obtained genetic information to evaluate the multifaceted representation of variability in drug response and manifestation of side effects. In conclusion, while adopting pharmacogenomic testing for the design of personalized prescriptions still has hurdles to cross for integration into clinical practice, but the knowledge of drug response at the molecular level, risk factors, and disease susceptibility can increase the susceptibility towards achieving the aim of Precision Medicine.

Potent Applications

The application of PGx has focused on the studying genetic variations in the population to explore linkages between genes, diseases, and environmental factors, and developed new therapies and diagnostic tests. One such application is mentioned below.

Anti-cancer therapy was the foremost area of medicine to use PGx. Nowadays it is common to treat certain cancers by testing the tumor tissue for its genetic "signature" (Squassina et al., 2010; Xie & Frueh, 2005). The information obtained thus can be helpful for doctors to prescribe the effective therapy based on the tumor's specific genetic makeup. A successful example of this approach was observed in leukemia treatment, breast cancer treatment, and colon cancer treatment. The most promising applications of PGx has also been implemented in defining the risk for adverse effects, dosages and response to medications in Cardiovascular Diseases, Psychiatric Diseases, Infectious Diseases.

Pharmacogenetics (PG)

Most of the articles use the term Pharmacogenetics (PG) and Pharmacogenomics interchangeably though they only differ in the initial approach of science. Pharmacogenetics begins with the unexpected drug response to a given therapy and investigates the genetic cause behind it whereas PGx begins with identifying genetic differences with a population to explain the observed response to certain drugs or to define the susceptibility to a disease.

Potential benefits of PG include discovery and development of drugs for targeted therapies and with minimized adverse effects, more accurately determining drug dosages and development of amalgamated DNA vaccines that could activate the immune system to have the benefits of multiple vaccines with reduced infection risks. It is currently being used for evaluating drug responses in a number of diseases such as cardiological disorders, respiratory syndrome and neurological conditions, investigating fast and slow metabolizers in respect to commonly consumed drugs. It has certain limitations as well. Multiple genes could be responsible for determining the drug response to a drug, thus making drug development process tedious. Identifying genetic variations in each of the individuals that may influence drug metabolism is very difficult and time-consuming task (Pharmacogenetics/Pharmacogenomics, Fact sheet 25 NSW Government Health).

PG is the study of specific SNPs in specific genes with known functions that could be linked to drug response. Pharmacogenetic testing involves examining SNPs identified in advance, that are linked to Neurotransmitters, receptors or growth factors. Pharmacogenetic testing is an alternative to "Hit-&-Miss" approach of prescribing any drug. The knowledge of patient drug metabolizing gene variants (poor metabolizers, rapid metabolizers, and ultra-rapid metabolizers) can help in finding the appropriate therapy and optimal dosage of many of the commonly prescribed drugs, including Antidepressants, Beta blockers, Warfarin (Scott, 2012).

Determining Drug-Drug Interactions

The wider use of Pharmacogenetic testing is an opportunity for prescribing safety and efficacy. It is a very important and useful tool in predicting which drug will be effective in various patients. For instance, the drug "Plavix" is the best-selling prescription drug that blocks Platelet reception. It is being given to patients who had received a stent in the coronary artery to prevent clotting but Genome Wide Association Studies (GWAS) have identified the gene CYP2C19 in those who are unable to metabolize Plavix (Pharmacogenetics, Wikipedia)

Applying Pharmacogenetics into Clinical Practice

When physicians are equipped well evaluating a patient's genetic make-up will help them diagnose more accurately and prescribe the right drug. The variation extends among people beyond our phenotype (Pharmacogenomics, The University of Utah).

Case Study: An 18-year old person "X" who has been diagnosed with Leukemia type of Cancer involving the bone marrow and blood cells. His doctor wants to start his Chemotherapy as soon as possible.

"Purinethol" is a common chemotherapy drug. It incorporates itself into cancer cells and killing them. While most patients were benefitted from the drug, doctors knew that it canal so cause severe and fatal side effects in certain patients. Previously doctors were unable to understand that why these patients responded so negatively to the drug. After a long time, they discovered that TPMT (Thiopurine Methyltransferase) enzyme is responsible for metabolizing and inactivating the drug, Purinethol. The people also vary in their TPMT enzyme activity level. Because Purinethol is a toxic substance, it is important that it should only remain in the body for a limited amount of time, affecting mainly cancer cells and not the healthy cells. Therefore, before prescribing the drug, it is critical for doctors to know if a patient has enough TPMT enzymes to effectively inactivate Purinethol. If patients are unable to break down Purinethol they will suffer toxic side effects. About 89% of the population has the ability to fully breakdown the toxic anti-cancer drug. This population carries the variation in TPMT responsible for maximum enzymatic activity and will be resistant to severe ill-effects from Purinethol. 10.66% of the population has a TPMT variation with partial activity, leading to the less efficient breakdown of Purinethol. Thus, they will suffer severe side-effects if given a full dose of the drug. However, they will benefit from a much lower dose. 0.33% of the population has TPMT with insufficient enzymatic activity. As a result, Purinethol breakdown will not occur to the greater extent and the toxic substance will persist in the body. So they will suffer fatal side-effects if given any Purinethol.

Therefore, knowing which genetic variant of TPMT the person "X" has will influence his treatment tremendously. To determine the dosage of Purinethol that "X" will need, his doctor takes a DNA sample from his blood and sends it to a lab. After running a diagnostic test based on SNP Profiling, it was determined that person "X" has 'partial TPMT activity' variation. With this knowledge, he can confidently start "X" on a reduced dosage of Purinethol.

This case study illustrates just one-way doctors can apply PG into clinical practice to deliver with the correct dosage of a chemotherapeutic drug.

Pharmacoproteomics (PP)

Pharmacoproteomics is another key component of personalized medicine along with PG and PGx that uses proteomic technologies to discover and develop novel drugs. Genotyping just provides variations at the DNA level whereas pharmacoproteomics is the functional representation of those variations. Designing therapeutic strategies on the basis of differential protein expression would be more beneficial than just based on genetic polymorphism. Protein chips like microarray chips will be used more frequently in the near future in clinical diagnostics, particularly in Point of Care diagnostics. Proteomics will help in the development of molecular diagnostics, Characterization of complex disorders thereby defining a targeted therapy for a particular biomarker, Drug discovery and development, designing precision medicine based on proteomic profile rather than genetic polymorphism.

PP will be a useful adjunct to PGx and PG in developing the model of personalized medicine by connecting genotype with the phenotype and classifying the patients into responders and non-responders. Several important applications of Pharmacogenomics are already in clinical practice and some of them have the FDA approval (for example, cetuximab/panitumumab and KRAS; vemurafenib and BRAF; warfarin and CYP2C9/VKORC1; abacavir andHLA-B*5701; carbamazepin and HLA-B*1502; thiopurines and TPMT) (Meyer, Zanger, & Schwab, 2013)

METABOLOMIC ANALYSIS FOR PERSONALIZED MEDICINE

Despite technological advancements and enormous financial inputs, PGx has the success that has limitations too like in predicting drug response with absolute certainty using biomarkers. This can be attributed to the fact that PGx takes into account only genotypes and not the phenotypes, which is the result of interactions between genotype and environmental factors such as diet, gut microbiome, nutrition, age, sex, dietary supplements, and lifestyle. Therefore, it becomes critical to determine individual`s phenotype in deciding the correct drug and optimal dosage and thus predicting the response to a given therapy.

The metabolomic/metabolic profiling takes into account the influence of individual`s physiological state, microbiome diversity and functional composition, genetic polymorphism and other environmental factors. Thus, could be useful in predicting the possible outcomes following a therapeutic intervention. A new approach called Pharmacometabolomics is emerging that combines the effect of metabolic profiling and metabolite assessment tools for linking the inherent variations in the metabolite and drug efficacy. Some reviews have typically described the potential of metabolomics, especially pharmacometabolomics in clinical trials and thus personalized medicine (Nicholson, Wilson & Lindon, 2011; Nicholson, Everett & Lindon, 2012).

One advantage that pharmaco-metabolomics enjoys over the other 'omics' technologies is that the metabolic profile represents the phenotype of the organism and reflects the overall biological impact which no other technology represents. It involves metabolite profiling of the biofluids or fecal extracts in the pre-dose and post-dose individuals to envisage his/her responses for a therapeutic intervention and in the process identifies surrogate markers for subsequent therapies. Furthermore, it is also capable of providing useful drug pharmacokinetic and drug metabolite information for an individual, which can provide a mechanistic understanding of variations in responses.

Pharmacometabolomics along with other 'omics' technologies can be helpful in determining response phenotype, evaluating toxicity and predicting individual response to targeted drug therapy (Kaddurah-Daouk et al., 2010). For example, metabolic profiling was employed to investigate the metabolic pathways of ritonavir which is a protease inhibitor used with HIV chemotherapy (Li, Lu & Ma, 2011). Four bioactivation pathways associated with CYP3A were found to be related to ritonavir-induced toxicity. Additional data obtained from pharmacokinetics for a drug could provide relevant information to determine individual responses for the drug. Recently, to profile pre and post-dose urinary metabolites scientists applied metabolomics approach in individuals given a single toxic dose of APAP-s (acetaminophen sulfate). It was discovered that human subjects with high pre-dose levels of p-cresol (metabolites related to human gut microbiome) had lower concentrations of APAP-S, which is due to the competition of the binding site to the sulfotransferase enzyme. The individuals with lower pre-dose urinary concentrations of p-cresol might be more susceptible to APAP-induced toxicity since less APAP will be conjugated with sulfate to produce APAP-S. The findings indicated that each individual, colonized by a unique assortment of trillions of microbes, could respond to a drug differently, either beneficially or adversely. This study demonstrates that evaluation of metabolic phenotype by metabolic profiling could play an important role in drug toxicity and metabolism, as well as in personalized healthcare system (Clayton et al., 2006).

BIOMARKERS

The sole aim of precision medicine is to utilize the growing understanding of biology so that patients receive the right drug for their disease, at an accurate dose and in adequate time. But personalizing medication includes the use of different biomarkers driven by a decision-making process in which a diagnostic test is essential.

Biomarkers are organic substances that are known to indicate certain biological processes. A biomarker is a term used to indicate a measurable character that can indicate a biological state. Biomarkers vary from one branch of science to others. In the field of medicine, biomarkers such as DNA (copy number variations, methylation states, and mutations), RNA (mRNA, microRNA), Protein (phosphorylation sites, post-translational modifications), polysaccharides, metabolic products, single nucleotide polymorphism

Figure 3. Biomarker classification
(Drucker & Krapfenbauer, 2013; Buyse, Sargent, Grothey, Matheson, & de Gramont, 2007)

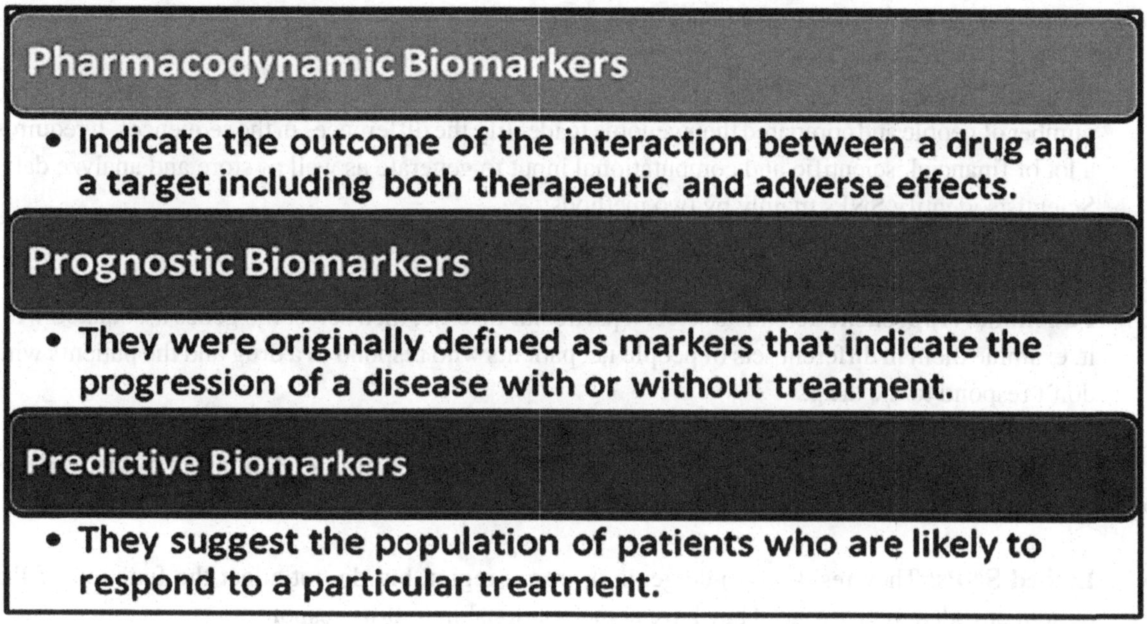

Pharmacodynamic Biomarkers

- Indicate the outcome of the interaction between a drug and a target including both therapeutic and adverse effects.

Prognostic Biomarkers

- They were originally defined as markers that indicate the progression of a disease with or without treatment.

Predictive Biomarkers

- They suggest the population of patients who are likely to respond to a particular treatment.

and gene variants and cells serve to diagnose diseases (Escamilla, 2013). Tests that screen for biomarkers can help medical practitioners to learn more about the patient's condition, for example, if he or she is afflicted with a certain type of cancer or is he/she at greater risk of suffering a heart attack. In medical diagnostics, biomarkers also serve to detect gene mutations that can cause diseases.

Ideal biomarkers for use in diagnostics and prognostics, and for drug development and targeting, should be measurable, safe, modifiable upon treatment, consistent across different populations, highly specific and sensitive (Issaq, Waybright & Veenstra, 2011).

Clinical Biomarkers can also be categorized as shown in Figure 3.

DNA Sequence-Based (SNPs) Biomarkers

Identifying, cataloging and studying small genetic variations among humans will lead to more efficient drug therapies. Reliable SNPs could serve as biomarkers to predict the response of various drugs.

SNP is defined as the single base change occurring in the DNA sequence such that it is present in at least 1% of the population. SNPs can be of two types:

- **Synonymous SNPs**: The single base change occurring at the DNA level will not reflect in the protein sequence as one amino acid can be coded by different codon triplets.
- **Non-Synonymous SNPs**: The single base change occurring at the DNA level will reflect in the protein sequence, thus leading to altered protein. These SNPs are of much importance in personalized medicine approach.

Finding and Identifying SNPs

It is generally done by following two major approaches:

1. **Genomic Approach:** Large scale projects are started to sequence the whole genome of a large number of people and compared their genome to identify the differences in the sequences. It requires a lot of financial, scientific and computational input to generate as well as store and analyze data. Scientists identify SNPs mainly by two methods:
   - Sequencing complete DNA of a large number of people and then a comparison of results.
   - Primer extension Method.
2. **Functional Approach:** Scientists select a particular disease, then select the genes associated with it, examine them in different sets of people i.e. patients who respond to a drug and the patients who don`t respond to the drug.

SNPs are categorized into two main categories when studying them in relationship to their effects on drug:

- **Linked SNPs**: They resides on intergenic or intron region but do not affect the function of the protein encoded by the gene. They have some relationship to drug response.
- **Causative SNPs**: These are those SNPs that affects the function of the protein and corresponds to a disease or abnormality or influence the person`s drug response. These are further of two types:
   - **Non-Coding SNPs:** They are present in the regulatory regions of the gene and they affect the gene expression.
   - **Coding SNPs:** They are present in the coding regions or within a gene, change the amino acid sequence in the protein and alters the protein function. [36]

Haplotypes (or Haplotyping)

Characterizing the combination of SNPs in a fragment of DNA. Most of the time a single SNP does not reveal everything about a person. Haplotypes influence the drug response and can be a more accurate predictor of phenotypes than SNPs.

Pharmacogenetics studies on candidate gene have been performed based on haplotype approach. Positive results have been obtained. This approach has also been applied to clinical trials making it the first genetically personalized medicine approach.

Companion Diagnostic (CDx)

Measurement of different markers (RNA, DNA, and/or proteins) needs different diagnostic assays; therefore, different qualification and validation strategies are needed. Pharmaceutical companies are increasingly looking to develop a drug and diagnostic test simultaneously, in a process referred to as drug-diagnostic-co-development, also called companion diagnostic (CDx), to significantly define the appropriate patient population for treatment. A companion diagnostic test is essentially a biomarker test that enables better decision making on the use of a therapy. In other words, they are often developed concurrently with a therapeutic, but can also be developed to optimize treatment with a therapeutic that has already been approved (Simoncelli, 2013). Pharmaceutical and device sponsors have become increasingly interested in pursuing "co-development" strategies for the development of a therapeutic product and an accompanying IV-D companion diagnostic device. As described earlier, the concept of co-development was first applied in 1998, when the approval of the therapeutic Trastuzumab (Herceptin), was paired with approval of an immune histochemical IVD companion diagnostic device (HercepTest™) that measures expression levels of human epidermal growth factor receptor 2 (HER-2) in breast cancer tissue (Elkin et al., 2004).

The goal here is to increase the safety and the efficacy of the drug (Buyse et al., 2007). CDxis increasingly important tools in drug development because they have following advantages:

1. Reduced costs through pre-selected (smaller) patient population;
2. Improved chances of approval through more focused therapies;
3. Offer better outcomes, less toxicity, and fewer treatment delays;
4. Significantly increased market uptake;
5. Added value for core business (late phase);
6. Regulatory trend to have CDx mandatory.

Tafinlar/Mekinist/THxID BRAF test: In May 2013, FDA approved Tafinlar (dabrafenib) and Mekinist (trametinib) for patients with advanced or unresectable melanoma, the leading cause of death from skin disease. The FDA approved Tafinlar and Mekinist with a genetic test called the THxID BRAF test, a companion diagnostic that will help determine if a patient's melanoma cells have the V600E or V600K mutation in the BRAF gene. Approximately half of melanomas arising in the skin have a BRAF gene mutation. Tafinlar is intended for patients whose tumors express a single BRAF gene mutation, V600E. Mekinist is intended for patients who express that mutation or the V600K mutation (Simoncelli, 2013).

A list of companion diagnostics that have been approved to date can be viewed athttp://www.fda.gov/MedicalDevices/ProductsandMedicalProcedures/InVitroDiagnostics/ucm301431.htm.

But actual co-development seems to be a rare phenomenon until now because of following reasons:

1. Clinically useful biomarkers are usually established late in the drug validation process because it is quite difficult to find clinically useful predictive biomarkers early on in a drug development program, simply because they can only be determined on the basis of the patients' responses to the drug. A number of biomarkers, such as KRAS and EGFR mutations, could only be established after a sufficient number of patients for a Phase III trial had elicited a better understanding of differential drug response. And still 30% of the drugs fail during Phase III, diagnostic manufacturers will not be able to afford the huge investment in the development of companion diagnostics (Collins, 2013).
2. The worlds of drug development and diagnostics, although both part of health care, are parallel universes in many ways. In general, they have different development timelines, product lifecycles, return on investment, customers, and regulations. Drugs are valued and reimbursed as products, typically of high value. Diagnostics are valued and paid for as services, typically at a much lower value. Drugs are protected by patents, but in the companion diagnostic arena, biomarkers are considered to be within the public domain and there is less emphasis on intellectual property. It is even debated whether biomarkers should be patented at all because biomarkers are not invented but already exist in cells.

3. The challenge of timing and alignment of the development strategies of the two products: if the diagnostic is going to be used to select patients for the trial, an analytically validated test should be available at the time of initiation of the trial. This can be challenging since sometimes the need for the companion diagnostic may not be evident until late in the development of the drug, or the need to change the test might arise during the course of the trial. The purpose of the trial is not only to assess the safety and effectiveness of the drug but also to investigate the performance of the diagnostic in that specific therapeutic context. A test that does not perform adequately may negatively impact the outcome of the trial and harm patients. Changes made to the test after initiation of the trial can make it difficult if not impossible to interpret the study results (Simoncelli, 2013).

4. Lastly, is the design of the trial itself. Identifying patients at the beginning who are most likely to benefit from a drug or biological product (or excluding those likely to suffer toxicities) can allow for smaller, faster, and less expensive clinical trials with a higher likelihood of success. However, there are some challenges associated with designing very small trials, such as being able to build insufficient statistical power to yield convincing results. Designing a trial to test whether a drug is effective for a subpopulation of patients also sometimes raises complex technical and ethical questions about whether to include marker-negative patients (i.e., those that are note expected to benefit from the drug) in the trial (Simoncelli, 2013).

Improvised treatment strategies and healthcare expenditure may reduce up to a greater extent with successful biomarker discovery and validation. For example, the American Society of Clinical Oncology estimates that routinely testing people with colon cancer for mutations in the K-RAS oncogene would save at least US $600 million a year (Drucker & Krapfenbauer, 2013). On the other side, thousands of projects in the course of potential biomarker discovery projects have been proposed, but only a few clinically useful biomarkers have been successfully validated for routine clinical practice (Poste, 2011). The following are the major pitfalls in the translation from biomarker discovery to clinical utility:

1. Lack of making different selections before initiating the discovery phase.
2. Lack in biomarker characterization/validation strategies.
3. Robustness of analysis techniques used in clinical trials.
4. The lack of characterization and validation of technologies such as protein chip, multiplex, etc. Besides technical characterization, it also needs quality requirements for correct characterization of the predictive value of biomarkers.
5. **Regulatory Hurdles:** Each of these details is hardly documented and can dramatically affect the predictive response of biomarker results. However, the selection of useful biomarkers must be carefully assessed and depends on different important parameters, such as on sensitivity (it should correctly identify a high proportion of true positive rate), specificity (it should correctly identify a high proportion of true negative rate), predictive value etc. Unfortunately, biomarkers with ideal specificity and sensitivity are difficult to find. One potential solution is to use the combinatorial power of different biomarkers, each of which alone may not offer satisfaction in specificity or sensitivity. Besides traditional immunoassays such as ELISA, recent technological advances in protein chip and multiplex technology offer a great opportunity for the simultaneous analysis of a large number of different biomarkers in a single experiment, which has expanded at a rapid rate in the last decade.

NANOBIOTECHNOLOGY IN PERSONALIZED MEDICINE

Nanobiotechnology is also an important contributor in the refinement of various molecular diagnostic technologies, biomarkers identification and other diagnostic and therapeutic technologies and useful field of science for personalized medicine.

Nanobiotechnology and Biomarkers

As already discussed in the previous chapter what biomarkers are, how important they are in personalized medicine approach and how important it is to identify novel biomarkers, Nanomaterials can be used for bio-labeling for identifying and characterizing biomarkers. Various new composites have shown high potential for cell labeling. One of such composite is made of biocompatible, water-soluble having fluorescence and being stable is nature silver dendrimernanocomposite for labeling cells in various *in-vitro* studies. Trials using quantum dots for molecular labels for detecting early signs of tumors and tracking drug efficacy and efficiency have shown significant results.

Nanoproteomics which is the application of Nanobiotechnology in proteomics helps in improving available protocols/procedures and analyzing less abundant proteins. Using Nanobiotech, we may design and build devices that can be implanted in the body to detect and identify biomarkers, thus enhancing the diagnosis of various diseases. It is now possible to mold certain known nanoparticles to selectively attach to a small set of biomarkers and help in sequestering them (Geho, Jones, Petricoin, & Liotta, 2006).

NanoDiagnostics

It refers to the appliance of nanotechnology in molecular diagnostics. It is believed that the use of nanotechnology in molecular diagnostics will enhance the sensitivity (Emerich, & Thanos, 2006). Nanopore technology has already been available to sequence single molecule of DNA providing higher sensitivity and offers correlation between gene and its expressed proteins with specific disease using not reusable and portable nanodevices. Molecular diagnostic tests used to detect and measure the activity of biomarkers will become speedier and reliable. Tagging of biomolecules with nanoparticles will provide an additional edge. It is viewed that nanotech has potential application in Point of Care (POC) diagnostics and thus will be helpful in personalized treatments.

Nanobiotechnology in Discovering and Delivering Personalized Medicine

Nanobiotechnology is making a noteworthy contribution to the pharmaceutical industry in developing personalized medicine. Nanobiosensors and Nanobiochips are being used for improving drug development process. Drug delivery to the targeted tissue/organ with precision is important for personalized medicine. Using nanocarriers in conjugation with ligands and aptamer allows precise targeting and improved clinical efficacy (Debbage, 2009). Nanobiotech will improve detection of cancer biomarkers. Scientists have applied Alpha-mu-beta 3 targeted paramagnetic nanoparticles for safely finding very minute regions of angiogenesis associated with cancer (Schmieder, Winter, Caruthers, Harris, Williams et al., 2005).

The contrast of MRI scans was enhanced by using particle filled with thousands of molecules of metal. The surface of each particle is coated with a substance that could connect to newly emerging blood vessels at the site of cancer, thus enabling detection of sparse biomarkers. Additionally, nanoparticles used for detection could also be used for precisely delivering doses of anti-cancer medication directly at the target site avoiding side-effects, thus posing another advantage of using nanoparticles. Furthermore, it would be easy for the physicians to evaluate MRI scans, thus fulfilling certain important criteria of a personalized therapy such as timely detection and amalgamation of diagnostics with therapeutics.

Similarly polyvalent dendrimers can be conjugated with several biofunctional moieties for targeting cancer cells. One such example is conjugating dendrimers with folic acid using complimentary DNA oligonucleotides to produce clustered molecules for targeting folate receptor overexpressing cancer cells (Choi, Thomas, Kotlyar, Islam, & Baker, 2005).

Investigations on multifactorial and multiplex nanoparticles linked with antibodies or other small molecules are speeding up for being using them to target malignant tumors with higher sensitivity and affinity (Cho, Wang, Nie, Chen, & Shin, 2008; Wang, Shin, Simons & Nie,2007).

Nanobiotech, when applied to the nervous system, will help us in improving our understanding of neurological disorders and help us design drug delivery systems for them (Jain, 2005). The first and foremost thing in applying nanobiotechnology to neurological disorders is to understand the pathomechanisms of it. The development of targeted drug delivery systems to brain that crosses blood-brain barrier is another important component of personalized treatment (nanobiotechnology-based drug delivery to the central nervous system).

NanoBiotechnology has already started establishing its foothold in the area of cardiovascular disorders diagnosis and treatment using targeted drug delivery (Wickline, Neubauer, Winter, Cauthers, & Lanza, 2006; Iverson, Plourde, Chnari, Nackman, & Moghe, 2008). For example, using perfluorocarbonnano particles for visualization and targeted drug delivery in cardiovascular disease. Such nanoparticles will ensure that the drug reaches the target and a subsequent molecular influence is taking place, a vital component of personalized treatment. For instance, with the technological improvement, it would be possible to screen and target biomarkers associated with atherosclerotic lesions expansion.

The main aim to personalized medicine is to improve healthcare and nanobiotechnology is surely all set to play an important role in it. Advancement in technology and availability of cheaper nanomaterials will surely help in cheaper and reliable molecular diagnostic technologies and personalized treatments. Both nanomedicine and personalized medicine will continue to advance and will play an important role in the development of healthcare industry towards personalized medicine. Safety and regulatory issues along with ethical and economic issues are being resolved. It is believed that nanotechnology will pace up the development of personalized medicine by integrating diagnostics with therapeutics.

BIOINFORMATICS TOOLS AND DATABASES AIDING PERSONALIZED MEDICINE

Systems biology along with the key components of personalized medicine i.e., pharmacogenomics, pharmacogenetics, and pharmacokinetics are developing as one of the most promising fields that give a complete understanding of diseases and enable targeted therapy. Although, there are a lot of hurdles that has to be overcome while preparing for personalized medicine (Yan, 2010). Few of the challenges are:

- The scientific challenges, such as determining which genetic markers have the most clinical significance, limiting the off-targeting effects of gene-based therapies, and conducting clinical studies to identify genetic variants that are correlated with a drug response.

- The policy challenges, such as finding a level of regulation for genetic tests that both protects patients and encourages innovation.

In order to make progress, the NIH and the FDA will invest in advancing translational and regulatory science, better define regulatory pathways for coordinated approval of co-developed diagnostics and therapeutics, develop risk-based approaches for appropriate review of diagnostics to more accurately assess their validity and clinical utility, and make information about tests readily available.

Translation of scientific discoveries into better therapeutic outcomes requires better information and workflow management, efficient literature and resource retrieval, and communication improvement. Translational bioinformatics is a powerful method to bridge the gap between systems biology research and clinical practice which provides biological and medical information to allow for individualized therapy. Such computational approaches encompass the development and application of informatics techniques in the biological sciences (Chang, 2005). It serves following purposes:

- It would enable the identification of biomarkers based on systemic analyzes.
- It enables researchers to search online biological databases and use the biological information in their medical practices. For instance, the data obtained from a microarray is extremely complicated and bioinformatics aids in selecting appropriate software to analyze the microarray data for medical decision making.
- It can improve the understanding of the correlations between genotypes and phenotypes.
- It would enable novel insights of interactions and interrelationships among different parts in a whole system.
- In translational bioinformatics biological databases have been managed in EHR to improve health care and clinical practice moves toward personalized medicine. Bioinformaticians hope to pull all available genomic data into electronic health records (EHRs) that also consider the effects of genetic mutations. The EHRs will allow researchers to assess the contribution of genomic variations to disease (Schmidt, 2003). A virtual patient system has been developed and used to model obesity, diabetes, and asthma.
- Methods based on data integration, data mining, and knowledge representation can provide decision support for both researchers and clinicians.

Moreover, advances in molecular-based information have led to a deeper understanding of the complexity of life. Translational bioinformatics using the high volume of biological information will contribute to changes in practice standards in healthcare systems. It is believed that bioinformatics tools will provide potential benefits to patients by means of improved healthcare, disease prevention and health maintenance as we move towards the era of personalized medicine.

IMMNUNOINFORMATICS AND PERSONALIZED MEDICINE

Immunoinformatics refer to the use of bioinformatics to study immunology. The immune system plays a critical role in the precision medication advance for some chronic, infectious and inflammatory immune-mediated diseases. The genetic capability to generate a diversity of adaptive immune responses is critical to fighting pathogens and differentiates between self and non-self-components. This diversity will also aid in defining patient subgroups for individualized vaccine or drug development. The accumulation of huge amount of immunological relevant information requires efficient informatics methods for analyzing data and its management.

Research areas of Immunoinformatics are:

- Immune system response modeling and simulation of laboratory experiments.
- T-cell and B-Cell epitope prediction.
- Host-pathogen interaction.
- Identify novel functions of existing genes.
- Performing NGS and RNA-Seqin healthy and diseased states.
- Epigenetic Studies (Allergy prediction)
- Design and engineering of immune therapeutics and diagnostics.
- *In silico* vaccination

Out of above-mentioned research areas, the most studied is the T-cell and B-cell epitopes prediction because they play a crucial role in disease understanding, host-pathogen interaction, antimicrobial target discovery and vaccine design (Bette, Montiago & Karina, 2006). Epigenetic studies provide the understanding of how environmental changes can affect complex immune diseases such as allergy.

With the help of Immunoinformatics, we can develop personalized medicine for chronic, infectious and inflammatory immune-mediated diseases.

DISEASE-BASED CASE STUDIES ON PERSONALIZED MEDICINE

Several genes have been found responsible for variations in drug response and metabolism among different individuals. The most important and common among them are the *Cytochrome P450* (*CYP*) genes. These genes encode enzymes involved in regulating in one way or the other the metabolism of about three-fourth of the prescribed drugs. Individuals carrying variations in certain *CYP* genes often differ in their ability to metabolize the drug. There are a number of other genes that affect drug response such as the ones encoding the regulatory molecule`s receptors, growth hormones, structural proteins, transcription factors and some cellular proteins. Diminished drug response and occurrence of adverse drug reactions (ADR) can often be due to polymorphism in these genes. Polymorphism in these genes can either hyperactive or inactive their protein proteins; or disable or interfere with the functioning of their protein, thus forcing physicians to discontinue the medication. A list mentioning drugs, and genetic variations affecting their response or safety, is available at U.S. Food and Drug Administration website for physicians, researchers and individual`s reference (Pharmacogenetics, FDA)

Also, it has been observed that certain drugs can lead to changes in the phenotype of individuals and influences the metabolizing capacity of enzymes by mimicking the effect of genetic variations. Quinidine is a known inhibitor of CYP2D6 activity. In case if an individual is prescribed quinidine, then he/she will be a poor metabolizer of CYP2D6, compared to someone who carries a loss-of-function polymorphism in *CYP2D6*. In those patients, drugs requiring the activity of CYP2D6, such as atomoxetine, will not be metabolized at the same rate as in most people. Mimicking the effect of genetic variations is also a known phenomenon in certain foods. For example, grapefruit juice, an inhibitor of CYP3A4 can lead to poor metabolism of drugs like diazepam, requiring the activity of CYP3A4.The following three case

Table 1. List of bioinformatics tools, databases used in different fields of personalized medicine

S.No.	Program/Databases	Description
Software for Analysis of Microarray Data		
1	Cluster	For clustering, SOM
2	TreeView	Graphically browse and analyzes results of clustering
3	ScanAlyze	Processes fluorescent images of microarrays
4	ArrayMiner	Set of analysis tools
5	Expression Profiler	Analysis & clustering of gene expression data
6	GeneX-Lite	Integrated toolset, provides an interface to RDBMS
7	BASE	Microarray database and analysis platform
8	dChip	Analysis of oligonucleotide arrays
9	ArrayDB	Mining and analysis of microarray data
Proteomics Strategy Tools		
1	ExPASy (Expert Protein Analysis System)	Analyzes protein sequences and structures
2	PROSITE	Protein database describing protein domains, families, and functional sites
3	Swiss-Prot	A manually curated protein sequence database
4	SWISS-3DIMAGE	An image database provides high-quality pictures of biological macromolecules with known 3D-structure
5	ENZYME	Repository of information relative to the nomenclature of enzymes
6	Protein Explorer	Software to display the protein structure
7	Cn3D	A structure viewer and a helper application
Pharmacogenomics Strategy Tools		
1	dbSNP (The database of Single Nucleotide Polymorphisms)	Free public archive for studying genetic variations.
2	OMIM (Online Mendelian Inheritance in Man)	Catalogues all the known diseases with a genetic component
3	dbGaP (The database of Genotypes and Phenotypes)	Archives the results of the studies of interaction of genotype and phenotype
4	PharmGKB (Pharmacogenomics Knowledgebase)	Encompasses clinical information including dosing guidelines and drug labels, potentially clinically actionable gene-drug associations
Systems Biology Strategy Tools		
1	KEGG (The Kyoto Encyclopedia of Genes and Genomes)	A knowledge base for systematic analysis of gene functions, linking genomic information
2	AfCS (Alliance for Cellular Signaling)	A large-scale collaboration designed to answer global questions about signaling networks
3	STKE (Signal Transduction Knowledge Environment)	Combines the traditional, albeit electronic, publishing of articles, such as reviews, perspectives, and protocols, with tools for organizing and collating information in the cross-disciplinary field of signal transduction

Table 2. Immunoinformatics databases and tools for epitope analyses

Name	URL
Immune Epitope Database and Analysis Resource (IEDB)	http://www.immuneepitope.org
AntiJen Database	http://www.jenner.ac.uk/antijen/
Epitome	http://cubic.bioc.columbia.edu/services/epitome/submit.php
MHCPred	http://www.jenner.ac.uk/MHCPred/
Macrophages.com	http://www.macrophages.com/content/macrophages/home/
Inflenza Research Database	http://www.fludb.org/brc/home.do?Decorator=influenza

studies illustrate three categories for which pharmacogenomic knowledge can help take better decisions for medication respectively.

Case Study 1: In Predicting and Preventing Adverse Drug Reactions

Aman, a 30-year-old man has recently been diagnosed of HIV infection. Before initiating Abacavirantiretroviral therapy, his physician decided to go for genetic testing to determine whether he carries any relevant variation. The test confirmed the presence of the *HLA-B*5701* allele.

How did genetic testing help Aman and his physician?

Abacavir (Ziagen) marketed by GlaxoSmithKline is a nucleoside reverse transcriptase inhibitor often used in amalgamation with other antiretroviral medication to treat HIV infection. An immunologically-mediated hypersensitivity reaction is known to occur in about 5–8 percent of patients taking Abacavir, usually during the first six weeks after initiation of therapy. (GlaxoSmithKline. Ziagen, product labelling. 2010)

Knowing that Aman carried the *HLA-B*5701* variation and he would likely experience a hypersensitivity reaction and would develop fever, rash, nausea, and fatigue if he is given Abacavir, thus, the physician would avoid prescribing him Abacavir.

Case Study 2: To Predict Effectiveness

JS, a 55-year-old man recently had an acute myocardial infarction. The physician recommended him anti-platelet therapy and prescribed clopidogrel. 6-months following the anti-platelet therapy, JS surprisingly

Table 3. Databases and tools for analysis of genetic variations of the immune system

Name	URL
IPD	http://www.ebi.ac.uk/ipd/_
MHC Haplotype Project	http://www.sanger.ac.uk/HGP/Chr6/MHC
dbSNP	http://www.ncbi.nlm.nih.gov/SNP/_
Allele Frequencies Database	http://www.allelefrequencies.net/_
International HapMap Project	http://snp.cshl.org/

suffered another acute myocardial infarction. The physician suspected that clopidogrel therapy may have been ineffective or less effective. Following genotyping it was found to carry a variation on *CYP2C19*.

How would genetic testing help JS and his physician?

Clopidogrel is a prodrug and it is converted to an active metabolite by cytochrome P450 enzyme, CYP2C19 to exert its anti-platelet properties. Individuals carrying certain variations in CYP2C19 are considered poor metabolizers and show decreased ability to convert clopidogrel into its active metabolite (Shuldiner, O'Connell, Bliden, Gandhi, & Ryan, 2009). Further, these patients are more likely to have an ischemic event following clopidogrel therapy (Mega, Close, Wiviott, Shen & Hockett, et al., 2009). It was found that JS carried a variation in its *CYP2C19*. This variant has been known to be associated with the diminished antiplatelet effect of clopidogrel. The physician would have to re-examine him and consider giving him some other anti-platelet therapies, thus decreasing his chance of getting another cardiac attack.

Case Study 3: In Predicting Optimal Dose

Mitchell, age 66, has been recently diagnosed with atrial fibrillation. The physician recommended her warfarin therapy in order to reduce the risk of further getting any stroke and leading to other thrombotic events. In order to estimate the optimal dose, the patient has to undergo INR monitoring every day until a stable dose is determined, and then every few weeks thereafter for maintenance monitoring.

How would genetic testing help Mitchell`s physician to determine the optimal dose for her?

The most commonly prescribed anti-coagulant is Warfarin (Coumadin), to treat and prevent thrombosis. CYP2C9 enzyme metabolizes it and further action by the enzyme VKORC1 mediates its anticoagulant effect. It is observed that polymorphism in the *CYP2C9* gene causes some individuals to slowly metabolize warfarin and increasing the half-life of the drug, resulting in higher than usual blood concentrations of warfarin and greater anticoagulant effect. On the other hand, certain variation in the VKORC1 gene reduce the activity of the enzyme encoded by it and subsequently decreases the production of coagulation factors. The blend of reduced warfarin metabolism causedby*CYP2C9* gene polymorphism and subsequent decreased coagulation due to*VKORC1* gene variations has been found to increases the chances of bleeding during warfarin therapy. Warfarin has a narrow therapeutic index; variations in *CYP2C9* and *VKORC1*, in addition to several other patient characteristics, make it difficult to predict the effective dose. (Reider, Reiner, Gage, Nickerson, & Eby, et al., 2005) (Bristol-Meyers Squibb Company. Coumadin (warfarin sodium) product labeling 2010). If Mitchell carries any mutation on *CYP2C9* and *VKORC1* genes then it would be difficult to optimize the dosage for warfarin but surely it would surely reduce the risk of bleeding. This would help thephysician to decide more appropriately decide the initial dosage.

The following case study which will demonstrate the application of personalized medicine/genetic testing in efficiently treating dreadful diseases.

Case Study 4

A clinician sends two samples for molecular analysis of the patients suffering from Chronic Myeloid Leukemia (CML) and been administered a drug called Imatinib, showing clinical signs of drug resistance. The samples are sent to the laboratory to confirm drug resistance and investigate the reason for drug resistance. A standard laboratory test called "IRMA" was performed to detect a point mutation in chromosome 9, as it is a known prognostic factor for drug resistance. One of the samples showed a positive result for IRMA and other showed a negative result.

How would one go through the rest of the process for personalized medicines for these 2 patients?

First of all, we have to identify all the other biomarkers present in the patient`s genome and understand their effect on the drugs available. For CML, not all the biomarkers are known yet, so it calls for studies regarding biomarkers. One such biomarker has been identified as single nucleotide polymorphisms of ABCB1. Also, one marker is surrogate for the other. Depending upon the biomarkers or the variants present in the patient we can go by tailoring a treatment specific to that patient only.

For more information on pharmacogenomics, visit the following websites:

- UC San Diego Skaggs School of Pharmacy and Pharmaceutical Sciences.
- Pharmacogenomics Education Program (http://pharmacogenomics.ucsd.edu/home.aspx).
- American College of Clinical Pharmacology.
- The Future of Medicine: Pharmacogenomics (http://user.accp1.org/Sample_Home.htm).
- Indiana University School of Medicine, Division of Clinical Pharmacology.
- Defining Genetic Influences on Pharmacologic Responses (www.drug-interactions.com).
- U.S. Food and Drug Administration Genomics (www.fda.gov/Drugs/ScienceResearch/ ResearchAreas/Pharmacogenetics/default.htm).
- Pharmacogenomics Research Network (www.nigms.nih.gov/initatives/pgrn).

ELSI (ETHICAL, LEGAL, AND SOCIAL IMPLICATIONS) OF PERSONALIZED MEDICINE

Introduction to Ethical Issues

Ethical issues of personalized medicine are based on PG, genetic information and impact on healthcare. We need to take care how the personal information of the patient, genetic information and information important for pharma companies flows during the implementation of personalized medicine approach. It is recognized that there are a number of barriers that need to be addressed before PGx will be part of routine clinical care.

Ethical Aspects of PG

Some of the ethical issues that are bound to rise by PG in implementation of personalized medicine are:

- When the geneticists can predict which patients are likely to benefit from the available pharmaco-therapy and which are less likely, the issue of inequality may arise. We have to ensure that equality remains in medical healthcare.
- Confidentiality of patient`s Genetic information. Protecting patient privacy is one of the most important concerns that must be addressed before implementation of individualized medicine in clinical practice and just about everyone agrees that patients have a right to keep details about their health private from most people (even if not from, say, their insurance company or in some cases state or local governments).

- Another issue is to protect the right of a medical practitioner or scientist to reject a patient the available therapy on the basis of its genetic makeup.
- Cost is also a significant ethical issue as well. Still millions of people are without health insurance today, and many more have insurance plans that cover only the most basic things. How can 'payers' provide access to personalized medicine to everyone?

Ethical Aspects of Genetic Information

It covers the following aspects:

- **Ethical Issues of Whole Genome Analysis**: A large amount of data generated by genetic studies and their analysis predicting the patient's response to different disease and the diseases they are likely to develop can have ethical issues as to what information is to be revealed to the patient and what is to be concealed.
- **Privacy Issues in Personalized Medicine:** As personalized medicine approach involves dealing with the complete information about a person, privacy issues are bound to rise. The patient might not be comfortable in sharing his/her personal information either due to social issues or some personal/moral issues. The information generated from genetic analysis of patient's data may not be emotional good for the patient and physician might try to conceal it for better treatment of the patient. Sometimes the patient is reluctant to reveal his information even before the diagnosis is done.

Molecular tests challenge two aspects: How comprehensive these tests are and how the access to this information is regulated:

- Accessibility of diagnostic tests and targeted treatments within and across countries with companies seeking orphan status for new targeted treatments.
- Patients' understanding and patients' role in future decision making.
- **Human Dignity:** Potential for stigmatization and discrimination.
- **Human Integrity:** How this affects moral convictions, preferences, and commitments
- **The Input-Output Problem:** Though personalized medicine aims at segregating populations into small subgroups based on their genotype and response to drug or susceptibility to a disease but in all these studies racial and ethnic minorities have been left unexplored. Even the GWAS studies take in account only European or in some cases Asian populations. The proportion of GWAS conducted with minorities suffered from health disparities. The input–output problem arises because allele frequencies and environmental exposures tend to vary among population groups (Fullerton, 2011). Because of this, the assumptions that inform personalized medicine practice in well-studied populations are not necessarily generalized to poorly studied populations.

Regulatory Aspects

All the above ethical issues need to be resolved for efficient implementation of personalized medicine approach in the healthcare industry. Regulatory authorities have to set some standards for this approach and ensure that the rights of the patient, physician, and Pharma companies are protected as well as ensuring that personalized medicine approach does not create any social differences (King, Casavant, & Lang, 2013).

Role of Regulatory Authorities

- Sometimes the patient is reluctant to reveal his information even before the diagnosis is done, in that case, it is needed to be ensured that patient is properly supported and informed about the personalized medicine approach.
- Medical products should be carefully evaluated to find out their benefits and risks.
- Regulatory authorities should remain updated about the new technology and must keep the pharma companies on the toes to inform the author about each and every aspect of drug development.
- Provide clarity to the pharma industry and the consumer/patient about the recent therapies available in the market.
- They should address "pipeline" problems about the drugs by identifying the opportunities for streamlining the processes.
- Scientific barriers, regulatory issues and ethical issues have to be tackled beforehand so that there is the smooth implementation of personalized medicine in clinical practice.

The need of an hour is to expand the amount of work and effort to address ELSI. This requires expanding our current list of experts in the field of bioethics and clinical policies along with collaborations with quality control experts, health economists, and strategists. It is also clear that new approaches towards informed consent, intellectual property, protection of individual`s privacy and data required to be established for facilitating the suitable and active application of new technologies to personalized medicine (Brothers, & Rothstein, 2015).

CHALLENGES IN THE JOURNEY TOWARDS PERSONALIZED MEDICINE

As every coin has two sides, personalized medicine too has another side to it. There is a need to take care how the personal information of the patient, genetic information and information important for pharma companies flows during the implementation of personalized medicine approach.

Whenever a new technology or a model is found, there are always some concerns in its implementation in the initial phase. Personalized medicine model`s implementation also have some concerns and limitations:

Economic Limitations

- Personalized medicine could raise issues for those who pay for treatment, people in developing countries like India. The cost of new assessment tests and personalized medication is more and predictive potential of personalized medicine could add more to the expense after the disease has been detected. Though health insurance is not a trending business in India, as the insurance premium are based on actuarial statistics that apply to large and predictable population, insured people might have to end up paying more for getting an insurance.

- It is difficult to convince pharma companies to manufacture drugs according to a group of people carrying a certain genotype. Pharma companies see more benefits in producing traditional drugs that work on 50-60% of the population and still being prescribed to patients who do not respond to it or have side effects after consuming these medicines.

- Genome-wide association studies (GWASs) have been used to assess the SNPs with many important common diseases. But only a limited number of variants have been characterized, and understanding the functional relationship between associated variants and phenotypic traits has been difficult. SNP Prediction methods are not to be solely relied on as they don`t provide much information about the pathophysiology of the diseases. So we have to switch to the wet lab and conduct experimental tests to validate genetic predictions. As we know Laboratory validations are always expensive and time-consuming and so there is a need for fast and accurate methods for gene prioritization.

Limitations in Identifying Disease Biomarkers

- To unravel DNA variants so as to predict common, complex diseases that result from a combination of genes and environmental factors will require cost-effective, high-throughput genotyping; large, well-characterized patient populations; sophisticated computational methodologies; and a detailed understanding of the biological pathways of disease.

- Uncovering mRNA and protein markers for application in screening, diagnosis & prognosis and monitoring of disease will have its own set of challenges. Access to optimal relevant tissues might not be possible for many diseases. Proteomic technologies still need further development, because computational approaches for analyzing massive amounts of gene and protein profile data. To realize the vision of personalized medicine, the agenda for medical and pharmaceutical research must include the assembly and integration data from many sources on large numbers of patients. Clinical investigations should incorporate genotyping and molecular profiling technologies along with traditional clinical data collection and should establish a repository of patient samples where possible.

- New molecular markers might face many hurdles before they can be implemented in patient care. The issues range from FDA regulation and acceptance of these new markers to developing tractable assay platforms, to resolving issues around the ethical, legal and social implications of obtaining highly sensitive genetic information. Foremost among these, in our opinion, is the education and engagement of physicians and patients in the paradigm shift to objective, quantitative marker-based clinical care. If appropriate patient management systems, integrated databases, educational tools and genetic counseling are not in place, then it will be difficult to realize the significant benefits forecast from this approach.

Bioinformatics Challenges

- **Processing Large-Scale Robust Genomic Data:** Sequencing technologies are becoming affordable and are replacing the microarray-based genotyping methods, which were limited to interrogating regions of known variation. Now a whole genome can be sequenced in less than 15 days with an error rate of ~ 1 error per 100 kb. Even such low error rates can lead to a significant number of errors, which is around ~30 000 errors in a 3 GB human. The error rate from these technologies is a source of significant challenges in applications, including discovering novel variants (Fernald, Capriotti, Daneshiou, Karczewski, & Altman, 2011). Whenever a novel variant is identified, it will still have to be verified due to this false positive rate. Even high-quality sequence reads must be placed into their genomic context to identify variants, which is an active area of research since, for example, different mapping and alignment algorithms often yield different results. Because de novo assembly (Shendure & Ji, 2008) is slow and complicated by repetitive elements, sequences are usually mapped to a genomic reference sequence instead. Algorithms such as BLAST (Altschul, Gish, Miller, Myers, & Lipman, 1990) or Smith–Waterman (Smith & Waterman, 1981) have been traditionally used, but their execution speed depends on the genome size. While individual queries may only take seconds per CPU, aligning 100 million of them would require more than 3 CPU years.

- **Interpretation of the Functional Effect and Impact of Genomic Variation:** After genomic data has been processed, the functional effect and the impact of the genetic variations must be analyzed. Genome-wide association studies (GWASs) have been used to assess the statistical association of SNPs with many important common diseases. These methods are providing new insights, but only a limited number of variants have been characterized, and understanding the functional relationship between associated variants and phenotypic traits has been difficult (Frazer, Murray, Schork & Topol, 2009).The important resources for obtaining SNP data are adbSNP database, Online Mendelian Inheritance in Man, Human Gene Mutation Database. But such prediction methods do not provide any information about the pathophysiology of the diseases and so experimental tests are required to validate genetic predictions. Laboratory validation is expensive and time-consuming and so there is a need for fast and accurate methods for gene prioritization.

- **Integrating Systems and Data to Capture Complexity:** Given the complex phenotypes involved in personalized medicine, the simple 'one-SNP, one-phenotype' approach taken by most studies is insufficient. Most medically relevant phenotypes are thought to be the result of gene–gene and gene–environment interactions (Manolio et al., 2009). For example, drug response often depends on multiple pharmacokinetic and pharmacodynamic interactions, which form a robust and tolerant system with highly polymorphic enzymes and many interaction partners (Wilke, Reif & Moore, 2005). As a result, of this complexity, a drug–response phenotype of interest is likely to depend on many genes and environmental factors. Basic GWAS approaches for pharmacogenomics have given some success. There is concern that pharmacogenomics GWAS themselves are susceptible to many limitations: insufficient sample size, selection biases for genetic variants, environmental interactions that may affect the outcome measures and multiple gene–gene interactions that may underlie unexplained effects (Motsinger-Reif et al., 2010).

- **Making it All Clinically Relevant:** The ultimate challenge for this research is to apply the results for improved patient care. Much of this research has yet to be translated to the clinic. In fact, many physicians are unprepared to incorporate personal genetic testing into their practice and it is unclear how to best apply research results to improve patient care (McGuire & Burke, 2008). Bioinformatics also translates discoveries to the clinic by disseminating discoveries through curated, searchable databases like PharmGKB, dbGaP, HGMD, OMIM (Mailmanet al., 2007; Thorn, Klein, & Altman, 2010). A major bottleneck for these databases is manual curation of the data. Biologically and medically focused text mining algorithms can speed the collection of this structured data, such as methods that use sentence syntax and natural language processing to derive drug–gene and gene–gene interactions from scientific literature (Garten, Coulet, & Altman, 2010).

These databases and methods need to be developed and used carefully. All these data sources are susceptible to errors and so validation of data is essential, especially before the information is applied in the clinic. Finally, there are challenges and opportunities for bioinformatics to integrate with the electronic medical record (EMR) (Busis, 2010). For example, the BioBank system at Vanderbilt links patient DNA with a de-identified EMRs to provide a rich research database for additional translational research in disease–gene and drug–gene associations (Denny et al., 2010; Roden et al., 2008).

Other Limitations

- **Limited Understanding of the Intrinsic Biology of Disease:** The tools of the last two decades have left us overflowing in data, yet we still have a relatively limited understanding of what it all means. Its implementation in clinical practices remains in its infancy. Scientific understanding will likely remain the most important limiting factor for the momentum of this field. Physicians will have to be well equipped with the knowledge of genomics and proteomics to understand the new data.

- **Common Conditions Involving Multiple Genes/Biomarkers:** Common conditions are often influenced by multiple genetic, as well as environmental and social factors, in ways that are not yet well understood. Realization of the benefits of personalized patient management for common conditions affected by multiple genes will be a complex process that will depend on substantial investment in clinical research well beyond the initial demonstration of gene-disease correlations (Simoncelli, 2013).

- **An Outdated Disease Classification System:** Currently used disease classification systems define diseases primarily on the basis of their signs and symptoms. These systems do not easily accommodate emerging information about disease mechanisms, particularly when it is at odds with traditional physical descriptions. As a result, many disease subtypes with distinct molecular causes are still classified as one disease, while multiple, different diseases that share a common molecular cause are not properly linked. The failure of our outdated disease classification systems to incorporate optimally new biological insights serves as a fundamental barrier to progress in personalized medicine. The National Academy of Sciences has called for the creation of a "New Taxonomy" of disease that is designed to advance our understanding of disease pathogenesis and improve health and that defines and describes diseases on the basis of their intrinsic biology in addition to traditional signs and symptoms. (National Research Council: Committee on a Framework for Developing a New Taxonomy of Disease. (2011). Toward Precision Medicine: Building a Knowledge Network for Biomedical Research and a New Taxonomy of Disease. Washington, DC: The National Academies Press).

- **Lack of Infrastructure:** Costs of genetic sequencing have plummeted over the past decade, resulting in an explosion of information. Yet, while information is becoming easier and easier to obtain, the infrastructure to collect, analyze, integrate, share, and mine that information remains lacking.

- **Clinical Implementation of New Diagnostics:** Many clinicians have been reluctant to use new diagnostics. Part of this reluctance may be due to the ongoing controversy over clinical utility and the fact that biomarker clinical utility can often be a moving target. Clinicians also commonly face the general problem of "information overload," making adoption of new tests difficult without decision-support tools in place that could be accessed to help the clinician to identify, order, and interpret the appropriate tests.

- We don`t know whether it will be a good idea to inform an individual that he/she is likely to develop a disease or is suffering from a disease for which there is no cure.

- Realization of personalized management in diseases with multiple genes affecting the diseased state is a complex process and will ask for higher financial input as well as in-depth clinical research.

- *Poor sequence quality* from sequencing technologies is a challenge in discovering novel variants. Moreover, it is difficult to detect INDELS, Copy number variants, and structural variants. The cost of sequencing is another major concern. Efforts are being made to reduce the cost of sequencing the whole genome under $1000.

CURRENT STATUS AND FUTURE IMPLICATIONS OF PERSONALIZED MEDICINE

Personalized medicine has just moved out of its infant shell and it is expected that it will enter its teen years by the end of this year. It is of outmost important that we design and device strategies for efficient implementation of the personalized medicine model in clinical practice. Currently, personalized treatment is employed in only few of the diseases such as Cancer, cardiovascular disorders, respiratory syndrome and psychiatric maladies. Most research and success has been achieved in case of anti-cancer therapies. But to reciprocate the success in other disorders, we need to work on areas such as lowering down the cost of sequencing, applying exome sequencing for better diagnosis and treatment, improving the available infrastructure for the implementation of personalized medicine in clinics and all these is to be supported by new regulatory policies. New technology, new models require new regulatory policies to ensure safer and smoother implementation. Government and regulatory authorities like FDA have to draw in more stern regulations for personalized medicine thus ensuring the availability of safe and effective diagnostics. The regulatory science has to catch up with all that is happening in relation to personalized medicine and help in its faster, safer and regulated implementation. Drug labeling provides important information about the drug which is useful for both clinician and the patient. As personalized medication will be designed for a group of population, product labeling becomes important. Integration of nanobioscience and high throughput proteomics techniques with personalized medicine and development of point of Care Medication.

A good amount of work on electronic health records is being carried out in the USA along with an additional emphasis on the storage of genetic data and developing point-of-service prompts to assist busy clinicians in identifying and utilizing relevant genomic data at the proper time in diagnostics or treatment planning. A 10 years down the line we could reach a point where the analytical validity of sequencing technologies are high, with the easy ability to access and clinically interpret genomic information, and knowledge about patient responses to genomic information.

Owing to recent developments with respect to personalized medicine, it is expected that this model will eventually be turned into clinical practice by the end of this decade. Besides the application of PG and PGx, pharmacoproteomics will gain more application in identification of novel biomarkers, design-

Figure 4. Flow chart for the case study 4

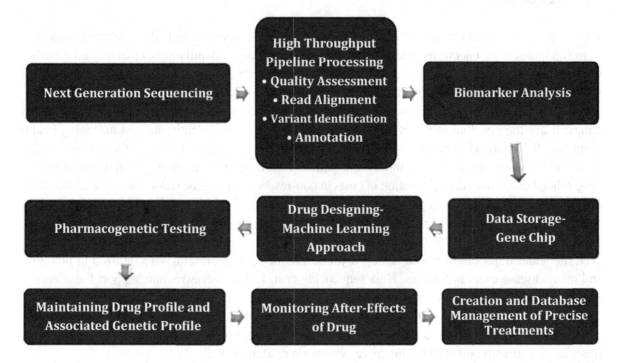

ing new drugs in accordance with the protein profile and understanding disease pathophysiology. By combining the three key components of personalized medicine, it would be possible to strictly define responsive populations and effectively monitor drug responses. Protein chips are expected to make it to the clinics within next five years thus aiding point-of-care diagnostics.

Efficient Next Generation Sequencing (NSG)

1. High-Throughput Pipeline Processing. Better and efficient bioinformatics tools for quality assessment, alignment, and variation calling.
2. Database for identifying biomarkers.
3. Storing the patient`s data in a Gene Chip. It will give easy an access to the Clinician.
4. Designing a probable drug molecule through machine learning.
5. Virtual Biological systems that will analyze the drug path, molecular interactions, signal transduction pathways and some other parameters.
6. A complete profile of the drug will be generated.
7. Store the Drug profile in association with a genetic profile in a database or some records.
8. Administer the drug, if found suitable for a group of patients.
9. Analyze the After effects. A Chip will keep the record of the patient`s physiological parameters.
10. Create and manage a database of such personalized treatments.

CONCLUSION

This chapter has tried to present the very model of personalized medicine from different angles, emphasizing on its key components, its potential applications and trying to identify issues that may arise during implementation of such a model in clinical practice. It also summarizes the current developments and future potential of personalized medicine.

We believe it would be fair enough to say that personalized medicine has started spreading out its wings. It has the potential to re-define the approach we have about identifying and managing health problems. It has already shown it significant impact on the healthcare industry. Since personalized medicine has the potential of revolutionizing patient care targeting patient population; avoidance of drug-related toxicities and optimization of costs in non-responder patients; reduction in the cost of drug development, and reduction in patients to be tested in clinical trials. There lies a huge potential in the application of precision medicine to significantly improve the clinical outcomes in terms of treatments, prevention strategies, medication types and dosages- that may have inter-individual variability. However, the wider impact hasn`t been achieved yet despite of being increasingly recognized in literature and many disease cases in humans. High sequencing cost, lack of infrastructure support for scientists and physicians, ELSI, lack of regulatory measures and economic factors additionally are hindering the translation of this model into reality. In short, we could say that though catering medicine specifically to an individual`s requirement is a farfetched but certainly possible reality following more research, high financial investments and establishing more systematic guidelines.

REFERENCES

Adams, J. (2008). Pharmacogenomics and Personalised Medicine. *Nature Education*, *1*(1), 194.

Agus, D. B. (2012). A Doctor in Your Pocket. *The Wall Street Journal*. Retrieved from http://online.wsj.com/news/articles/SB10001424052970204124204577155162382326848

Ascierto, P., Larkin, J., Dummer, R., Testori, A., Maio, M., Hogg, D., & Kirkwood, J. M. et al. (2011). Improved Survival with Vemurafenib in Melanoma with BRAF V600E Mutation. *The New England Journal of Medicine*, *364*(26), 2507–2516. doi:10.1056/NEJMoa1103782 PMID:21639808

Biomarker. (n. d.). Retrieved from http://en.wikipedia.org/wiki/Biomarker

Cho, K., Wang, X., Nie, S., Chen, Z. G., & Shin, D. M. (2008). Therapeutic nanoparticles for drug delivery in cancer. *Clinical Cancer Research*, *14*(5), 1310–1316. doi:10.1158/1078-0432.CCR-07-1441 PMID:18316549

CNS Spectrums. (n. d.). Retrieved from www.cnsspectrums.com

Coriell Personalised Medicine Collaborative. (n. d.). Retrieved from http:// cpmc.coriell.org/

Debbage, P. (2009). Targeted drugs, and nanomedicine: Present and future. *Current Pharmaceutical Design*, *15*(2), 153–172. doi:10.2174/138161209787002870 PMID:19149610

Emerich, D. F., & Thanos, C. G. (2006). The pinpoint promise of nanoparticle-based drug delivery and molecular diagnosis. *Biomolecular Engineering*, 23(4), 171–184. doi:10.1016/j.bioeng.2006.05.026 PMID:16843058

Eurofins Medigenomix Gmb, H. (n. d.). Retrieved from: www.medigenomix.de

Fruch, F. W., & Xie, H. G. (2005). *Pharmacogenomics steps towards Personalised Medicine*. Future Medicine.

Hamburg, A. M. (2013). Personalized medicine the future is now. *U.S. Food and Drug Administration*. Retrieved from: http://blogs.fda.gov/fdavoice/index.php/2013/11/personalized-medicine-the-future-is-now/

Huang, R., & Gamazon, E. R.Huang & Gamazon. (2013). Translating pharmacogenomics discoveries into the clinic: An implementation framework. *Genome Medicine*, 5(10), 94. doi:10.1186/gm497 PMID:24134796

Jain, K. (2015). Textbook of Personalised Medicine. Springer.

Jain, K.K. (2005). Personalized neurology. *Per. Med.*, 2(1), 15–21. doi:10.1517/17410541.2.1.15

Jain, K.K. (2006). The role of nanobiotechnology in developing new therapies for disease of the nervous system. *Nanomed.*, 1(1), 9–12. doi:10.2217/17435889.1.1.9 PMID:17716203

Karczewski, & Altman. (2012). Translational Bioinformatics. *PLOS Computational Biology*.

King, J. D., Casavant, B. P., & Lang, J. M. (2013). *Rapid translation of circulating tumor cell biomarkers into clinical practice: technology development, clinical needs, and regulatory requirements*. Royal Society of Chemistry.

Korber, B., Labute, M. & Yusim, K. (2006). Immunoinformatics Comes of Age. *PLoS Computational Biology*.

Learn Genetics. (n. d.) Retrieved from http://learn.genetics.utah.edu/content/health/pharma/snips/

Leung, E. Y., Malick, S. M., & Khan, K. S. (2013). On-the-Job Evidence-Based Medicine Training for Clinician-Scientists of the Next Generation. *Clinical Biochemistry*, 34. PMID:24151345

Mansour, J. C., & Schwarz, R. E. (2008). Molecular mechanisms for individualized cancer care. *Journal of the American College of Surgeons*, 207(2), 250–258. doi:10.1016/j.jamcollsurg.2008.03.003 PMID:18656055

Menden, M. P., Iorio, F., Garnett, M., McDermott, U., Benes, C. H., Ballester, P. J., & Saez-Rodriguez, J. (2013). Machine Learning Prediction of Cancer Cell Sensitivity to Drugs Based on Genomic and Chemical Properties. *PLoS ONE*, 8(4), e61318. doi:10.1371/journal.pone.0061318 PMID:23646105

Nair, R. (2010). Personalised Medicine: Striding from genes to medicine. *Perspectives in Clinical Research*, 1(4).

Nutritional Immunology and Molecular Medicine Lab. (n. d.). Retrieved from www.nimml.org

Nutritional Immunology and Molecular Medicine Laboratory. (n. d.). Personalized Medicine. Retrieved from http://www.nimml.org/programs/personalized-medicine/

Pabinger, S., Dander, A., Fisher, M., Snaider, R., Sperk, M., Efremova, M., ... Trajanoski, Z. (2012). A survey of tools for variant analysis of next-generation genome sequencing data. *Briefings in Bioinformatics,* 15(2), 256-278.

Personalised Medicine. (n. d.). Retrieved from http://en.wikipedia.org/wiki/Personalized_medicine

Personalised Prescribing Systems. (n. d.). Retrieved from http://youscript.com

Personalised Systems & Integrative Medicine. (n. d.). Retrieved from http://immune.pharmtao.com

Personalized Medicine Coalition. (n. d.). Personal Med Backgrounder. Retrieved from http://www.personalizedmedicinecoaliton.org/sites/default/files/personalmed_backgrounder.pdf

Perundurai, S.D., Sakthivel, S., Xue, Y., Powell, G.T., Rani, D.R., Nallari, P., ... Thangaraj, K. (2009). A common MYBPC3 (cardiac myosin binding protein C) variant associated with cardiomyopathies in South Asia.

Rabbani, B., Tekin, M. & Mahdieh, N. (2013). The promise of whole-exome sequencing in medical genetics. *J. Hum. Genet.*, 59(1), 5-15.

Scheider, A. H., & Winter, P. M. (2005). Molecular MR imaging of melanoma with alpha-mu-beta 3 targeted paramagnetic nanoparticles. *Magnetic Resonance in Medicine*, 53(3), 621–627. doi:10.1002/mrm.20391 PMID:15723405

Scott, A. (2012) Personalizing Medicine with Clinical Pharmacogenetics. National Institute of Health, 13(12).

Squassina, A., Manchia, M., Manolopoulos, V. G., Artac, M., Lappa-Manakou, C., Karkabouna, S., & Patrinos, G.P. et al. (2010). Realities, and Expectations of Pharmacogenomics and Personalized Medicine: Impact of translating Genetic knowledge into Clinical Practice. *Future Medicine*, 11(8), 1149–1167. PMID:20712531

The Daily Neuron. (n. d.). Intelligence. Retrieved from http://thedailyneuron.com/intelligence/

The University of Utah. (n. d.). Retrieved from www.learn.genetics.utah.edu

U.S. Food and Drug Administration. (2013). Paving the way for Personalized Medicine.

Van't Veer, L. J., & Bernards, R. (2008). Enabling personalized cancer medicine through analysis of gene-expression patterns. *Nature*, 452(7187), 564–570. doi:10.1038/nature06915 PMID:18385730

Whirl-Carrillo, M., McDonagh, E.M., Hebert, J.M., Gong, L., Sangkuhl, K., Thorn, C.F., Altman, R.B. & Klein, T.E. (2012) Pharmacogenomics knowledge for Personalised Medicine. *Clin. Pharmcol. Ther.*, 92(4).

Wikipedia. (n. d.). Pharmacogenetics. Retrieved from http://en.wikipedia.org/wiki/pharmacogenetics

Yan, Q. (2010). Immunoinformatics and systems biology methods for personalized medicine. *Methods in Molecular Biology (Clifton, N.J.)*, 662, 203–220. doi:10.1007/978-1-60761-800-3_10 PMID:20824473

Yang, Y., Yao, Q., Chen, Z., Xiang, J., William, F. E., Gibbs, R. A., & Chen, C. (2013). Genetic and molecular alterations in pancreatic cancer: Implications for personalized medicine. *Medical Science Monitor*. doi:10.12659/MSM.889636

KEY TERMS AND DEFINITIONS

Biomarker: It is measurable indicator for a biological state or physiological condition

Personalized Medicine: An approach followed for disease prevention and treatment that takes into account differences in people's genes, environments and lifestyles

Pharmacodynamics: The study of the biochemical and physiological effects of drugs on the body and the mechanisms of drug action and the relationship between drug and response

Pharmacokinetics: It refers to the study of drug pathway inside the body. It involves studying absorption, metabolism, distribution and excretion of a drug.

Pharmacoproteomics: It refers to the use of proteomic technologies in drug development and molecular diagnosis. It helps more clearly demarcate patient-to-patient variations as compared to genotyping

Risk Assessment: It refers to identifying sensible measures to control the risks associated with different trials especially where live organisms are involved.

Section 4
Bio-Inspired Algorithms and Engineering Applications

This section gives in-depth information about bio-inspired algorithms and its application in finding optimized solutions for engineering problems. Different evolutionary computing techniques are discussed to identify complex systems effectively in engineering applications. A popular technique like Bacteria Foraging Algorithm is quite faster in optimization such that there is reduction in the computational burden and also minimal use of computer resource utilization is discussed. Solution of some Differential Equation in Fuzzy Environment by Extension Principle method and its application in Biomathematics problems are explained here. Last chapter discusses application of computational intelligence techniques in wireless sensor networks on the coverage problem in general and area coverage in particular.

Chapter 15
Evolutionary Computing Approaches to System Identification

Bidyadhar Subudhi
NIT Rourkela, India

Debashisha Jena
National Institute of Technology, India

ABSTRACT

In this chapter, we describe an important class of engineering problem called system identification which is an essential requirement for obtaining models of system of concern that would be necessary for controlling, analyzing the systems. The system identification problem is essentially to pick up the best model out of the several candidate models. Thus, the problem of system identification or modeling building turns out to be an optimization problem. The chapter explain what are different evolutionary computing techniques used in the past and the state- of the art technologies on evolutionary computation. Then, some case studies have been included how the system identification of a number of complex systems effectively achieved by employing these evolutionary computing techniques.

1. INTRODUCTION

System identification or obtaining mathematical models of complex real-world is an important task in many fields of engineering. Identification of a dynamic system i.e. model building is essential for developing control, analysis, prediction, supervision and optimization. System parametric identification is usually achieved in two steps: the first step is selecting a model family from which a candidate model is produced by minimizing some error criterion. The second step is validating the identified candidate model in terms of verifying some performance indicators, such as noise independence, error auto-correlation, input/error correlation and real response following among others. If results do not satisfy some of the performance indicators, an alternative model must be produced over a different model family. Figure 1 describes the concept of system identification, where u is the input to the system,

DOI: 10.4018/978-1-5225-0427-6.ch015

Figure 1. System identification

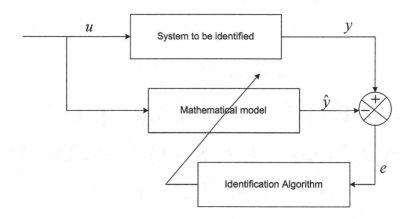

y is the system output, $\hat{y}$ is the output of the identified model and e is the error between the actual and the identified model outputs.

An identification problem can be transformed into an optimization problem for which an evolutionary approach can be employed. Evolutionary computation uses computational models of evolutionary processes occur in nature as key elements in the design and implementation of computer-based problem solving systems. There are a variety of evolutionary computational methods that have been reported during the last three decades. These evolutionary algorithms share a common conceptual base of simulating the evolution of individual structures via processes of selection and reproduction. These processes depend on the performance (fitness) of the individual structures as defined by an environment. More precisely, evolutionary algorithms maintain a population of structures that evolve according to rules of selection and other operators, such as recombination and mutation. Each individual in the population receives a measure of its fitness in the environment. Selection focuses attention on high fitness individuals, thus exploiting the available fitness information. Recombination and mutation perturb those individuals, providing general heuristics for exploration. Figure 2 outlines a generic evolutionary algorithm (EA).

A population of individual structures is initialized and then evolved from generation to generation by repeated applications of evolutionary operators evaluation, selection, recombination, and mutation. The population size N is generally constant in an evolutionary algorithm. An evolutionary algorithm typically initializes its population randomly, although domain specific knowledge can also be used to bias the search. Evaluation measures the fitness of each individual according to its worth in some environment. Selection decides who become parents in the next generation and how many children the parents have. Children are created via recombination, which exchanges information between parents, and mutation, which further perturbs the children. The children are then evaluated. Finally, the survival step decides who survives in the population.

2. EVOLUTIONARY ALGORITHMS PARADIGMS

The origin of evolutionary algorithms has dated back to early fifties (Fraser, 1957; Box, 1957). The earliest EAs that predominated in many engineering and related applications are, GA, GP, ES and EP.

Figure 2. A Generic evolutionary algorithm

```
procedure EA; {
    t = 0;
    initialize population P(t);
    evaluate P(t);
    until (done) {
        t = t + 1;
        parent_selection P(t);
        recombine P(t);
        mutate P(t);
        evaluate P(t);
        survive P(t);
    } }
```

Each of these varieties implements an evolutionary algorithm in a different manner which includes the choices of representation for the individual structures, types of selection mechanism used, forms of genetic operators, and measures of performance. These approaches in turn have inspired the development of additional evolutionary algorithms such as "classifier systems (Holland,1986), the LS systems (Smith,1983), "adaptive operator" systems (Davis,1989), Scheduling problems (Whitley,1989), "genetic programming" (Garis,1990). Recent advances of EAs are the following. Particle swarm optimization (PSO), Bacteria Foraging, Clonal Algorithm, Ant Colony Optimization, Differential evolution (DE) (Engelbrecht, 2005; Dasgupta, 2009) etc. Table 1 describes the similarities and dissimilarities of the different evolutionary algorithms.

3. RECENT EVOLUTIONARY COMPUTING APPROACHES

3.1 Bacteria Foraging Optimization (BFO)

The details of BFO are given in (Dong, 2006; Guney, 2008; Lin,2006 and Abraham et al., 2007). A group of bacteria move in search of food and away from noxious elements known as foraging. All bacteria try to move upward the food concentration gradient individually. At the initial location they measure the food concentration and then tumble to take a random direction and swim for a fixed distance and measure the concentration there. This tumble and swim make one chemotactic step. If the concentration is greater at next location then they take another step in that direction. When concentration at next location is lesser that of previous location they tumble to find another direction and swim in this new direction. This process is carried out up to a certain number of steps, which is limited by the lifetime of the bacteria. At the end of its lifetime the bacteria that have gathered good health that are in better

Table 1. Similarities and dissimilarities: Different evolutionary computing algorithms

GAs (Engelbrecht, 2005; Dasgupta, 2009)	EP (Davis,1989)	ES (Das & Konar, 2007; Das, Abraham & Konar, 2008)
First formulated by Holland for adaptive search and by his students for optimisation from mid 1960s to mid 1970s.	First proposed by Fogel *et al.* in mid 1960s for simulating intelligence.	First proposed by Rechenberg and Schwefel in mid 1960s for numerical optimisation.
Binary strings have been used extensively as individuals (chromosomes).	Finite state machines (FSMs) were used to represent individuals, although real-valued vectors have always been used in numerical optimisation.	Real-valued vectors are used to represent individuals.
Simulate Darwinian evolution.	It is closer to Lamarckian evolution.	They are closer to Larmackian evolution.
Search operators are only applied to the *genotypic* representation (chromosome) of individuals.	Search operators (mutations only) are applied to the *phenotypic* representation of individuals.	They do have recombination.
Emphasise the role of recombination (crossover). Mutation is only used as a background operator.	It does *not* use any recombination.	They use self-adaptive mutations.
Often use roulette-wheel selection.	Usually use tournament selection.	

pseudo code is given as:
procedure GA; {
t = 0;
initialize population P(t);
evaluate P(t);
until (done) {
t = t + 1;
parent_selection P(t);
recombine P(t)
mutate P(t);
evaluate P(t);
survive P(t);}}
	pseudo code is given as:
	Procedure EP; {
	t = 0;
	initialize population P(t);
	evaluate P(t);
	until (done) {
	t = t + 1;
	parent_selection P(t);
	mutate P(t);
	evaluate P(t);
	survive P(t);}}
		pseudo code is given as:
		procedure ES; {
		t = 0;
		initialize population P(t);
		evaluate P(t);
		until (done) {
		t = t + 1;
		parent_selection P(t);
		recombine P(t)
		mutate P(t);
		evaluate P(t);
		survive P(t);}}

concentration region divide into two cells. Thus in the next reproductive step the next generation of bacteria start from a healthy position. The better half reproduces to generate next generation where as the worse half dies. This reproduction step is also carried out a fixed number of times. In the optimization technique we can take the variable we want to optimize as the location of bacteria in the search plane (the plane where the bacteria can move). The specifications such as number of reproductive steps, number chemotactic steps which are consisted of run (or swim) and tumble, swim length, maximum allowable swims in a particular direction are given for a particular problem then the variable can be optimized using this Bacteria Foraging Optimization technique. The *E. coli* bacteria that are present in our intestines have a foraging strategy governed by four processes, namely, chemotaxis, swarming, reproduction, and elimination and dispersal.

3.1.1 Chemotaxis

This process is achieved through swimming and tumbling. Depending upon the rotation of the flagella in each bacterium, it decides whether it should move in a predefined direction (swimming) or an altogether different direction (tumbling), in the entire lifetime of the bacterium. To represent a tumble, a unit length random direction, $\varphi(j)$ say, is generated; this will be used to define the direction of movement after a tumble. In particular,

$$\theta^i\left(j+1,k,l\right) = \theta^i\left(j,k,l\right) + C(i)\phi(j) \tag{3.1}$$

where $\theta i(j, k, l)$ represents the ith bacterium at jth chemotactic kth reproductive, and lth elimination and dispersal step. $C(i)$ is the size of the step taken in the random direction specified by the tumble. "C" is termed as the "run length unit".

3.1.2 Swarming

It is always desired that the bacterium that has searched the optimum path of food should try to attract other bacteria so that they reach the desired place more rapidly. Swarming makes the bacteria congregate into groups and hence move as concentric patterns of groups with high bacterial density. Mathematically, swarming can be represented by

$$
\begin{aligned}
J_{cc} &= \sum_{i=1}^{s} J_{cc}^i\left(\theta,\theta^i(j,k,l)\right) \\
&= \sum_{i=1}^{s}\left[-d_{attract}\ \exp\left(-w_{attract}\sum_{m=1}^{p}\left(\theta_m-\theta_m^i\right)^2\right)\right] + \\
&\quad \sum_{i=1}^{s}\left[h_{repellent}\ \exp\left(-w_{repellent}\sum_{m=1}^{p}\left(\theta_m-\theta_m^i\right)^2\right)\right]
\end{aligned}
\tag{3.2}
$$

where $J_{cc}\ (\theta, P(j, k, l))$ is the cost function value to be added to the actual cost function to be minimized to present a time varying cost function. "S" is the total number of bacteria. "p" is the number of parameters to be optimized that are present in each bacterium. $d_{attract}$, $w_{attract}$, $h_{repellent}$, and $w_{repellent}$ are different coefficients that are to be chosen judiciously.

3.1.3 Reproduction

The least healthy bacteria die, and the other healthiest bacteria each split into two bacteria, which are placed in the same location. This makes the population of bacteria constant.

3.1.4 Elimination and Dispersal

It is possible that in the local environment, the life of a population of bacteria changes either gradually by consumption of nutrients or suddenly due to some other influence. Events can kill or disperse all the bacteria in a region. They have the effect of possibly destroying the chemotactic progress, but in contrast, they also assist it, since dispersal may place bacteria near good food sources. Elimination and dispersal helps in reducing the behavior of *stagnation* (i.e., being trapped in a premature solution point or local optima).

3.2 Particle Swarm Optimization (PSO)

PSO is a stochastic global optimization method which is based on simulation of social behavior. As in GA and ES, PSO exploits a population of potential solutions to probe the search space. In contrast to the aforementioned methods in PSO no operators inspired by natural evolution are applied to extract a new generation of candidate solutions. Instead of mutation PSO relies on the exchange of information between individuals, called particles, of the population, called swarm. In effect, each particle adjusts its trajectory towards its own previous best position, and towards the best previous position attained by any member of its neighborhood (Kennedy & Eberhart,1995). In the global variant of PSO, the whole swarm is considered as the neighborhood. Thus, global sharing of information takes place and particles profit from the discoveries and previous experience of all other companions during the search for promising regions of the landscape. Several variants of PSO have been proposed up to date, following Eberhart and Kennedy who were the first to introduce this method (Kennedy & Eberhart, 2001; Kenedy, 1998; Parsopoulos et al.,2001;Parsopoulos & Vrahatis, 2002).

Initially, assuming that the search space is D dimensional, so the i-th particle of the swarm is represented by a D dimensional vector Xi = (xi1; xi2;::: ; xiD) and the best particle of the swarm, i.e. the particle with the lowest function value, is denoted by index g. The best previous position (i.e. the position corresponding to the best function value) of the i-th particle is recorded and represented as Pi = (pi1; pi2;::: ; piD), and the position change (velocity) of the i-th particle is Vi = (vi1; vi2;::: ; viD). The particles are manipulated according to the following equations (the superscripts denote the iteration):

$$V_i^{k+1} = \chi \left(\omega V_i^k + c_1 r_{i_1}^k \left(P_i^k - X_i^k \right) + c_2 r_{i_2}^k \left(P_g^k - X_i^k \right) \right) \tag{3.3}$$

$$X_i^{k+1} = X_i^k + V_i^{k+1} \tag{3.4}$$

where i = 1; 2;::::;N, and N is the size of the population which is used to control and constrict velocities; w is the inertia weight; c1 and c2 are two positive constants, called the cognitive and social parameter respectively; ri1 and ri2 are random numbers uniformly distributed within the range [0; 1]. Eq. (3.3) is used to determine the i-th particle's new velocity, at each iteration, while Eq. (3.4) provides the new position of the i-th particle, adding its new velocity, to its current position. The performance of each particle is measured according to a fitness function. In optimization problems, the fitness function is usually identical with the objective function under consideration. The role of the inertia weight w is considered important for the PSO's convergence behavior. The inertia weight is employed to control the impact of the previous history of velocities on the current velocity. A large inertia weight facilitates exploration while a small one tends to facilitate exploitation, current search area. A proper value for the inertia weight w provides balance between the global and local exploration ability of the swarm, and, thus results in better solutions.

3.3 Differential Evolution Technique

(Storn,1999) and (Storn & Price,1995) developed DE to be a reliable and versatile function optimizer that is also easy to use. Like nearly all EAs, DE is a population-based optimizer that attacks the starting point problem by sampling the objective function at multiple, randomly chosen initial points. Each vector is indexed with a number from 0 to number of population (i.e. N_p).DE generates new points that are perturbations of existing points, but these deviations are not the samples from a predefined probability density function, like those in the ES. Instead, DE perturbs vectors with the scaled difference of two randomly selected population vectors. To produce the trial vector, DE adds the scaled, random vector difference to a third randomly selected population vector. In the selection stage, the trial vector competes against the population vector of the same index in which the vector with the lower objective function value is marked as a member of the next generation. Once the last trial vector has been tested, the survivors of the competitions become parents for the next generation in the evolutionary cycle.

DE (Lin et al., 2002; Ilonen & Lampinen, 2003) is capable of handling non-differentiable, non-linear and multimodal objective functions. It has been used to train neural networks having real and constrained integer weights. In a population of potential solutions within a d-dimensional search space, a fixed number of vectors are randomly initialized, then evolved over time to explore the search space and to locate the minima of the objective function. At each generation, new vectors are generated by the combination of vectors randomly chosen from the current population (mutation). The out coming vectors are then mixed with a predetermined target vector. This operation is called recombination and produces the trial vector. Finally, the trial vector is accepted for the next generation if and only if it yields a reduction in the value of the objective function. This last operator is referred to as a selection. There are many different variants of DE the variants are as follows.

- **DE/best/1/exp**
- **DE/rand/1/exp**
- **DE/rand-to-best/1/exp**
- **DE/best/2/exp**
- **DE/rand/2/exp**

Now we explain the working steps involved in employing a DE cycle.

Step 1: Parameter setup.

Choose the parameters of population size, the boundary constraints of optimization variables, the mutation factor (F), the crossover rate (C), and the stopping criterion of the maximum number of generations (g).

Step 2: Initialization of the Population.

Set generation g=0. Initialize a population of i=1, P individuals (real-valued d-dimensional solution vectors) with random values generated according to a uniform probability distribution in the d dimensional problem space. These initial values are chosen randomly within user's defined bounds.

Step 3: Evaluation of the Population.

Evaluate the fitness value of each individual of the population. If the fitness satisfies predefined criteria save the result and stop, otherwise go to step 4.

Step 4: Mutation Operation (or Differential Operation).

Mutation is an operation that adds a vector differential to a population vector of individuals. For each target vector $x_{i,g}$ a mutant vector is produced using the following relation,

$$v_{i,g} = x_{r_1,g} + F\left(x_{r_2,g} - x_{r_3,g}\right)$$

(3.5)

In Eqn. (3.5), F is the mutation factor, which provides the amplification to the difference between two individuals $(x_{r_2,g} - x_{r_3,g})$ so as to avoid search stagnation and it is usually taken in the range of [0, 1], where $i, r_1, r_2, r_3 \in \{1, 2, ...P\}$ are randomly chosen numbers but they must be different from each other. P is the number of population.

Step 5: Recombination Operation.

Following the mutation operation, recombination is applied to the population. Recombination is employed to generate a trial vector by replacing certain parameters of the target vector with the corresponding parameters of a randomly generated donor (mutant) vector. There are two methods of recombination in DE, namely, binomial recombination and exponential recombination. In binomial recombination, a series of binomial experiments are conducted to determine which parent contributes which parameter to the offspring. Each experiment is mediated by a crossover constant, C, $(0 \leq C \leq 1)$. Starting at a randomly selected parameter, the source of each parameter is determined by comparing C to a uniformly distributed random number from the interval [0, 1) which indicates the value of C can exceed the value 1. If the random number is greater than C, the offspring gets its parameter from the target individual; otherwise, the parameter comes from the mutant individual. In exponential recombination, a single contiguous block of parameters of random size and location is copied from the mutant individual to a copy of the target individual to produce an offspring. A vector of solutions are selected randomly from the mutant individuals when $rand_j$ ($rand_j \in [0,1]$, is a random number) is less than C.

$$t_{j,i,g} = \begin{cases} v_{j,i,g} & \text{if } (rand_j \leq C) \text{ or } j = j_{rand} \\ x_{j,i,g} & \text{otherwise} \end{cases}$$

(3.6)

$j = 1, 2......d$, where d is the number of parameters to be optimized.

Step 6: Selection Operation.

Selection is the procedure of producing better offspring. If the trial vector $t_{i,g}$ has an equal or lower value than that of its target vector, $x_{i,g}$ it replaces the target vector in the next generation; otherwise the target retains its place in the population for at least one more generation.

$$x_{i,g+1} = \begin{cases} t_{i,g}, & \text{if } f\left(t_{i,g}\right) \leq f\left(x_{i,g}\right) \\ x_{i,g}, & \text{otherwise} \end{cases} \tag{3.7}$$

Once new population is installed, the process of mutation, recombination and selection is replaced until the optimum is located, or a specified termination criterion is satisfied, e.g., the number of generations reaches a predefined maximum g_{max} .

At each generation, new vectors are generated by the combination of vectors randomly chosen from the current population (mutation). The upcoming vectors are then mixed with a predetermined target vector. This operation is called recombination and produces the trial vector. Finally, the trial vector is accepted for the next generation if it yields a reduction in the value of the objective function. This last operator is referred to as a selection. The block diagram for DE are given in Figure 3.

3.4 Opposition Based Mutation Differential Evolution (OMDE)

In evolutionary algorithm optimization approaches generally a uniform random guess is taken for the initial population. In each generation the solution obtained moves towards the optimal solution and the search process terminates when some predefined criteria is satisfied. The time of computation generally depends on the initial guess i.e. more is the distance between the initial guess to optimal solution more time it will take to terminate and vice versa. Opposition based learning improves the chance of starting with better initial population by checking the opposite solutions. Of course, in the absence of any a-priori knowledge, it is not possible that we can make the best initial guess. "Logically, we should be looking in all directions simultaneously, or more concretely, in the opposite direction. Therefore, starting with the closer of the two guesses (as judged by fitness values) has the potential to accelerate convergence" (Tizhoosh, 2005; Shokri et al., 2006; Tizhoosh & Ventesca, 2008; Rahnamayan et al., 2008; Rahnamayan *et al.,* 2008)).

At the same time, it also known that if the cross over is applied between two good parents there is fair chance of reproducing better offsprings. So the same approach can be applied to each solution after the mutation and before the crossover in the current population. However, before concentrating on OBL, we need to define the concept of opposite numbers (Tizhoosh et al., 2008). Like DE, there exits ten variants of OMDE which depend on the type of cross over and mutation. The variants of the MDE are as follows.

- **OMDE/best/1/exp,**
- **OMDE/rand/1/exp,**
- **OMDE/rand-to-best/1/exp,**
- **OMDE/best/2/exp,**
- **OMDE/rand/2/exp,**
- **OMDE/best/1/bin,**
- **OMDE/rand/1/bin,**
- **OMDE/rand-to-best/1/bin,**
- **OMDE/best/2/bin,**
- **OMDE/rand/2/bin.**

Figure 3. Block diagram for DE algorithm

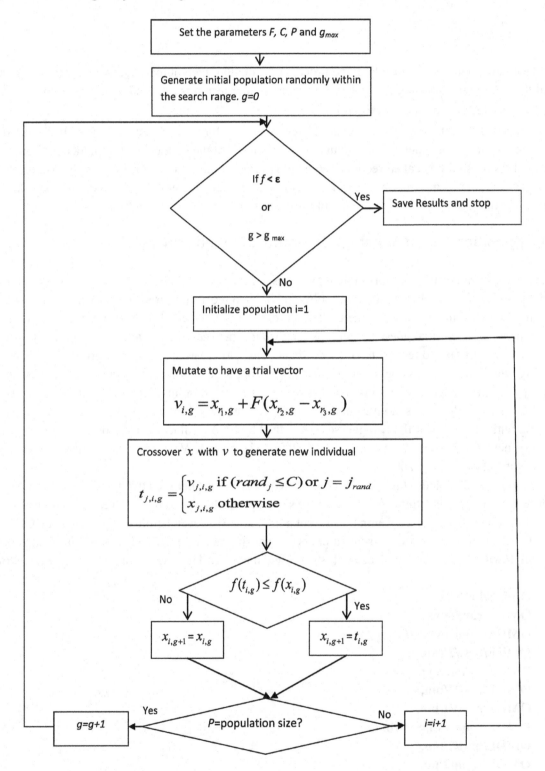

3.4.1 Definition of Opposite Number

Let $x \in [a, b]$ be a real number. The opposite number is $\tilde{x}$ which is defined by $\tilde{x} = a + b - x$

Definition of opposite point:

"Let $p = (x_1, x_2 \ldots \ldots x_d)$ be a point in the D dimensional space where $x_1, x_2 \ldots \ldots x_d \in R$ and $x_i \in [a_i, b_i]$. The opposite point $\tilde{p} = (\tilde{x}_1, \tilde{x}_2 \cdots, \tilde{x}_d)$ where $\tilde{x}_i = a_i + b_i - x_i$." [33-37].

3.4.2 Opposition Based Optimization

"Let $p = (x_1, x_2 \ldots \ldots x_d)$ be a point in the D dimensional i.e. a candidate solution. Assume $f(.)$ is the fitness function which is used to measure the candidate's fitness. According to the definition of the opposite point $\tilde{p} = (\tilde{x}_1, \tilde{x}_2 \cdots, \tilde{x}_d)$ is the opposite of $p = (x_1, x_2 \ldots \ldots x_d)$. Now if $f(\tilde{p}) \geq f(p)$ then point p can be replaced by $\tilde{p}$ otherwise we will continue with p. Hence the point and its opposite point are evaluated simultaneously in order to continue with the fitter one" [33-37].

OMDE Algorithm

Similar to all population-based optimization algorithms, two main steps are distinguishable for OMDE, namely, population initialization and opposition based mutation. We will enhance these two steps using the OBL scheme. The original DE is chosen as a parent algorithm and the proposed opposition-based ideas are embedded in DE to accelerate its convergence speed. Corresponding block diagram for the proposed approach (OMDE) are respectively given in Figure 4.

Opposition-Based Population Initialization

According to our review of optimization literature, random number generation, in absence of *a priori* knowledge, is the common choice to create an initial population. Therefore, by utilizing OBL, we can obtain fitter starting candidate solutions even when there is not *a priori* knowledge about the solution(s). The following steps present opposition-based initialization for OMDE that procedure. Initialize the population pop (P) randomly Calculate opposite population

$$\text{opop}_{i,j} = a_j + b_j - \text{pop}_{i,j}$$

$$i = 1, 2, \ldots \ldots P \qquad j = 1, 2, \ldots \ldots \ldots D$$

where $\text{pop}_{i,j}$ and $\text{opop}_{i,j}$ denote the jth variable of the ith vector of the population and opposite population respectively. Select P fittest individual from (pop U opop) as initial population.

Opposition-Based Mutation

By applying the same approach described above, to the current population, after the mutation, the evolutionary process can be forced to create new solution candidate, which ideally is fitter than the current one. After generating populations using mutation, the opposite population is calculated and the fittest individuals are selected from the union of the current population and the opposite population. Unlike

Figure 4. Block diagram for OMDE algorithm

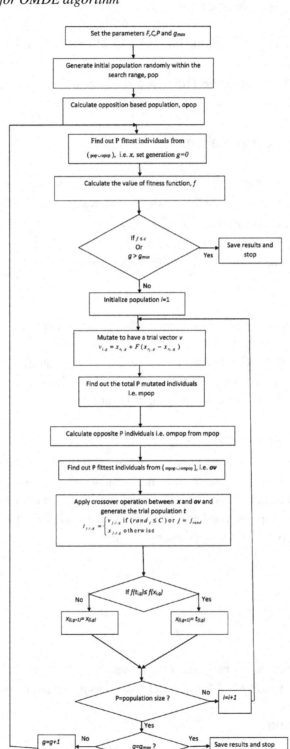

opposition-based initialization, opposition based mutation calculates the opposite population dynami-cally i.e. instead of using variables within predefined boundaries, opposition based mutation calculates the opposite of each variable based on minimum and maximum values of that variable in the current population as given by the equation below.

$$\mathrm{onpop}_{i,j} = \min\ (\mathrm{npop}_j) + \max\ (\mathrm{npop}_j) - \mathrm{npop}_{i,j}$$

By staying within variables' interval static boundaries, we would jump outside of the already shrunken search space and the knowledge of the current reduced space (converged population) would be lost. Hence, we calculate opposite points by using variables' current interval in the population which is, as the search does progress, increasingly smaller than the corresponding initial range.

4. PARAMETER IDENTIFICATION OF INDUCTION MOTOR USING DE AND OMDE

The objective of the parameter estimation of induction motor is to determine a mathematical model of the motor with sufficient accuracy. To develop robust methods for parameter estimation, it is important to quantify the information content about machine parameters on measured signals. This is of particular importance when we restrict only to electrical terminal quantities, such as stator voltages and currents. Most of the existing parameter estimation methods such as Least Mean Square (LMS) and Recursive Least Square (RLS) methods use the regressor equation i.e.

$$Y = X^T\theta + \varepsilon \tag{4.1}$$

where Y is the output vector, X is the regressor matrix, θ is the parameters to be estimated and ε is the system noise. However, difficulties are encountered in the regression equation (4.1) and in turn this method may be a viable choice for all situations in induction motor parameter estimation problems. Therefore, we explore an alternative way of solving the parameter estimation problem by using evolu-tionary method i.e. the DE and OMDE which do not require the description of equation (4.1) for param-eter estimation.

Recently differential evolution (DE) algorithm has been considered as a novel evolutionary computa-tion technique used for optimization problems. The DE has been preferred to many other evolutionary techniques such as GA and PSO due to its attractive characteristics such as its simple concept, easy imple-mentation and quick convergence. Generally speaking, all population-based optimization algorithms, no exception for DE, suffer from long computational times because of their evolutionary/stochastic nature. This crucial drawback sometimes limits their application to offline problems with little or no real-time constraints. The concept of *opposition-based learning* (OBL) was introduced by (Tizhoosh, 2008) and has thus far been applied to accelerate reinforcement learning . The main idea behind OBL is the simul-taneous consideration of an estimate and its corresponding opposite estimate i.e., guess and opposite guess in order to achieve a better approximation for the current candidate solution. The main aim using OBL inside DE is to accelerate the convergence rate of DE. There are number of ways in introducing opposition based learning at different points inside the evolutionary computation. The concept of using

OBL for initialization and for generation jumping which is known as opposition based differential evolution (ODE). Our proposed approach has been called opposition-based mutation differential evolution (OMDE). OMDE uses opposite numbers during population initialization and also for generating new populations after mutation during the evolutionary process. Here opposite numbers have been utilized to speed up the convergence rate of an optimization algorithm. Purely random resampling or selection of solutions from a given population has the chance of visiting or even revisiting unproductive regions of the search space. As the chance of this occurring is lower for opposite numbers than it is for purely random ones. In fact, a mathematical proof has been proposed to show that, in general, opposite numbers are more likely to be closer to the optimal solution than purely random ones. In (Rahnamayan et al., 2008), the usefulness of opposite numbers is investigated by replacing them with random numbers and it is applied for population initialization for different versions of DE. As in differential evolution the cross over is done after the mutation, we have put the OBL just after mutation so that better individuals can take part in crossover as a result we could able to get fitter individuals in the next generation. The focus of parameter estimation using evolutionary computation here are as follows.

1. Instead of being confronted with difficulties in finding expressions to represent the system by $Y = X^T \theta + \varepsilon$, the DE and OMDE method estimate the parameters directly.
2. An extensive study on finding of an efficient OMDE strategy with a view of obtaining faster convergence for parameter estimation of induction motor has been pursued.

4.1 A Brief Review of Induction Motor Dynamics

Although there are many models to describe induction motors, most of them are highly complex and not suitable to be used in control. Also, since modern induction motor control is field oriented, d-q models will be analyzed. An excellent presentation on available model types can be found in (Ursem & Vadstrup, 2004). The classical induction motor model (used in most control schemes) has identical d and q axis circuits. Since the classical model is a fourth order system with six elements of storage (inductances) the model can be reduced to a simpler model without any loss of information . The following notations are used.

$v_{ds,} v_{qs}$: stator voltages in stationary reference frame
$i_{ds,} i_{qs}$: stator currents in stationary reference frame
$\lambda_{dr,} \lambda_{qr}$: rotor fluxes in stationary reference frame
$L_{ls,,} L_{ms}$: leakage and magnetizing inductance for stator
$L_{lr,,} L_{mr}$: leakage and magnetizing inductance for rotor
$R_{s,} R_{r}$: stator and rotor resistances

Figure 5 and Figure 6 show the classical induction motor model (used in most control schemes) has identical d and q axis circuits. Figure 7 and Figure 8 shows the reduced induction motor model used in this work in stationary reference frame. Since the core loss resistance is much larger than the rotor resistance, it is neglected in this part of modeling. The following basic equations of induction machine can be derived as follows (Ursem & Vadstrup, 2004).

$$\frac{d\omega_r}{dt} = \mu\left(\lambda_{dr}i_{qs} - \lambda_{qr}i_{ds}\right) - \frac{B}{J}\omega_r - \frac{T_L}{J} \tag{4.2}$$

$$\frac{d\lambda_{qr}}{dt} = n_p\omega_r\lambda_{dr} - \eta\lambda_{qr} + \eta L_m i_{qr} \tag{4.3}$$

$$\frac{d\lambda_{dr}}{dt} = -n_p\omega_r\lambda_{qr} - \eta\lambda_{dr} + \eta L_m i_{dr} \tag{4.4}$$

$$\frac{di_{qs}}{dt} = -\beta n_p\omega_r\lambda_{dr} + \eta\beta\lambda_{qr} - \gamma i_{qs} + \frac{1}{\sigma L_s}v_{qs} \tag{4.5}$$

$$\frac{di_{ds}}{dt} = \beta n_p\omega_r\lambda_{qr} + \eta\beta\lambda_{dr} - \gamma i_{ds} + \frac{1}{\sigma L_s}v_{ds} \tag{4.6}$$

where, $\eta = \dfrac{1}{T_R} = \dfrac{R_r}{L_m}$: Inverse of the rotor time constant and $\sigma = 1 - \dfrac{L_m}{L_s}$: Leakage coefficient

$\beta = \dfrac{1}{L_l}$: Inverse of leakage inductance

Figure 5. Equivalent circuit in d-q stationary frame (d-axis)

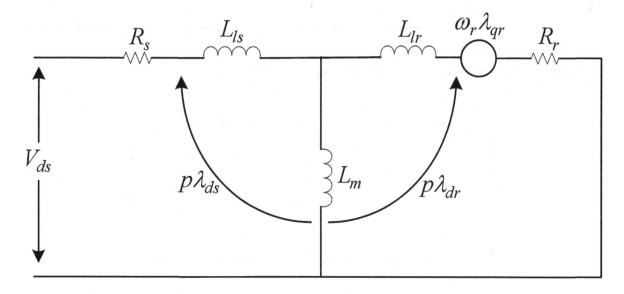

Figure 6. Equivalent circuit in d-q stationary frame (q-axis)

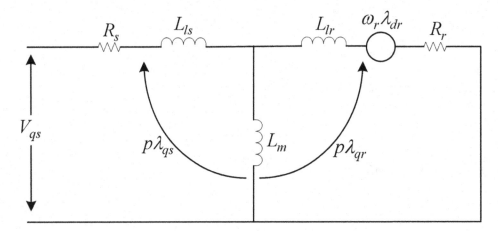

Figure 7. Reduced equivalent circuit in d-q stationary frame (d-axis)

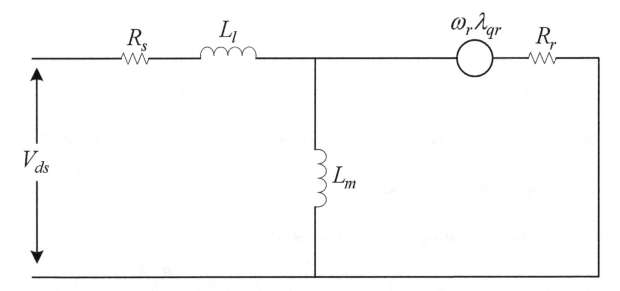

Figure 8. Reduced equivalent circuit in d-q stationary frame (q-axis)

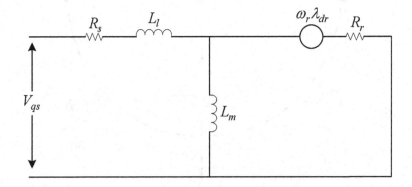

$$\gamma = \frac{R_s + R_r}{L_l} : \text{Inverse of stator time constant}$$

n_p : number of pole pairs

$$\mu = \frac{n_p}{J} \text{ where } J \text{ is the moment of inertia}$$

The above five equations (4.2)-(4.6) can be rewritten in state variable form as:

$$\dot{X} = AX + BU \tag{4.7}$$

and the output equation is:

$$Y = CX \tag{4.8}$$

where, $X = \begin{bmatrix} i_{qs} & i_{ds} & \lambda_{qr} & \lambda_{dr} \end{bmatrix}$

$$A = \begin{bmatrix} -\dfrac{R_s + R_r}{L_l} & 0 & \dfrac{R_r}{L_l L_m} & -\dfrac{\omega_r}{L_l} \\[2ex] 0 & -\dfrac{R_s + R_r}{L_l} & \dfrac{\omega_r}{L_l} & \dfrac{R_r}{L_l L_m} \\[2ex] -R_r & 0 & -\dfrac{R_r}{L_m} & \omega_r \\[2ex] 0 & R_r & -\omega_r & -\dfrac{R_r}{L_m} \end{bmatrix}$$

$$B = \frac{1}{L_l}\begin{bmatrix} 1 & 0 \\ 0 & 1 \\ 0 & 0 \\ 0 & 0 \end{bmatrix}, \quad C = \begin{bmatrix} 1 & 0 & 0 & 0 \\ 0 & 1 & 0 & 0 \end{bmatrix}, \text{ and } U = \begin{bmatrix} v_{ds} \\ v_{qs} \end{bmatrix}.$$

The dynamics of the induction motor can be described by a set of differential equations (4.2-4.6). Let the motor be supplied by three voltages from mains or from an electronic unit that can convert the main voltages to user specified voltages v_1, v_2 and v_3. In order to simplify the notation, we introduce complex voltages and currents. The transformation of the voltages from a three phase system to a complex system can be achieved by using the following formula.

$$v_s = v_{ds} + j v_{qs} = \frac{2}{3}\left(v_1 + a v_2 + a^* v_3\right) \text{ , where } a = e^{j\frac{2\pi}{3}}$$

The real and imaginary parts of the voltages then can be obtained as:

$$v_{ds} = \frac{1}{3}\left(2v_1 - v_2 - v_3\right) \qquad v_{qs} = \frac{1}{\sqrt{3}}\left(v_2 - v_3\right)$$

The inverse transformation from the complex notation to the three phase system is for the currents given by the following set of equations:

$$i_1 = i_{ds} \quad , \quad i_2 = -\frac{1}{2}i_{ds} + \frac{\sqrt{3}}{2}i_{qs} \quad , \quad i_3 = -\frac{1}{2}i_{ds} - \frac{\sqrt{3}}{2}i_{qs}$$

4.2 Induction Motor Parameter Estimation Problem Definition

The induction motor given in equations (4.7 and 4.8 can be written in compact form as:,
$\dot{X} = f(\theta, X, u)$, $y = g(X, \theta)$ where f and g are known nonlinear functions,

$\theta = \begin{bmatrix} R_s & R_r & L_1 & L_m \end{bmatrix}^T$, $u = [v_1 \ v_2 \ v_3]^T$, $X = \begin{bmatrix} i_{qs} & i_{ds} & \lambda_{qr} & \lambda_{dr} \end{bmatrix}^T$, and $y = [i_1 \ i_2 \ i_3]^T$.

In Figure 9, we present the parameter scheme of the induction motor drive system, where the optimization is to be performed using different variants of DE and OMDE algorithm.

The error, e between model and measurements can be calculated as:

$$e = \sqrt{\sum_{k=1}^{N} \left(\hat{i}_{ds(k)} - i_{ds(k)}\right)^2 + \left(\hat{i}_{qs(k)} - i_{qs(k)}\right)^2} \tag{4.9}$$

where $\wedge$ denotes the estimated values. The objective of the estimation problem is to determine θ such that the error given by (4.9) is minimized.

Assumptions: In our model, we assume that the load torque T_L is zero, which eliminates the load torque as an additional input.

4.3 Obtaining IM Parameter Estimates Using EC

The parameter estimation schemes as described in above have been applied to the induction motor by using the input-output data i.e. the stator voltage (transformed d-q axis, equation) and the stator current (d-q transformed, equation) to estimate motor resistance and inductance. Table 2 gives the rating of the induction motor and the actual value of the parameters to be identified.

All the ten variants of the DE and OMDE schemes for identifying the motor parameters R_s, R_r, L_s and L_m have been implemented using the following common parameters given in Table 3.

Convergence Characteristic of Different DE and OMDE Strategies

Figures 10-14 show the RMSE plot for the exponential crossover scheme. From these figures it is clear that the OMDE strategies outperform over the corresponding DE strategies in terms of faster conver-

Figure 9. Parameter estimation scheme for induction motor drive system

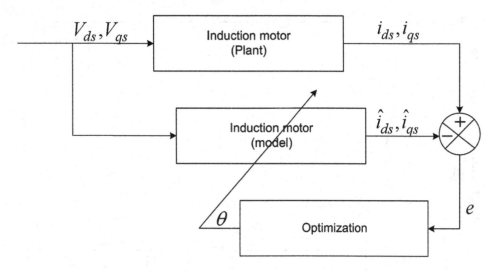

Table 2. Parameters of the induction motor drive

Voltage	220V
Power	5hp
Frequency	50Hz
Stator Resistance	0.39 ohm
Rotor Resistance	0.22ohm
Leakage Inductance	0.006 Henry
Magnetizing Inductance	0.0680 Henry
RPM	1750rpm

Table 3. Parameters for DE and OMDE simulation

Number of generations	50
Population size, S	20
Upper and lower bound of stator resistance	[0 1]
Upper and lower bound of rotor resistance	[0 1]
Upper and lower bound of leakage inductance	[0 1]
Upper and lower bound of magnetizing inductance	[0 1]
Mutation constant factor, F	0.6
Cross over constant, CR	0.5

Figure 10. RMSE for DE/best/1/exp and OMDE/best/1/exp

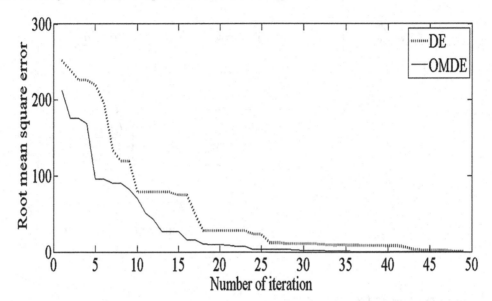

Figure 11. RMSE for DE/rand/1/exp and OMDE/rand/1/exp

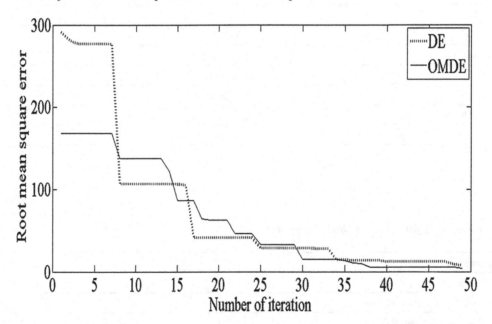

gence and less estimated error, and the RMSE is maximum for DE/rand/2/exp i.e. 25.08 and minimum for OMDE/best/1/exp i.e. 0.0307.

Figures 15-19 give the root mean square error (RMSE) characteristic for different DE and OMDE strategies for the binomial cross scheme. From all the Figures 10-19 it is clear that the OMDE has the better convergence characteristic in comparison to classical DE irrespective of any crossover scheme.

Figure 12. RMSE for DE/rand-to-best/1/exp and OMDE /rand-to-best/1/exp

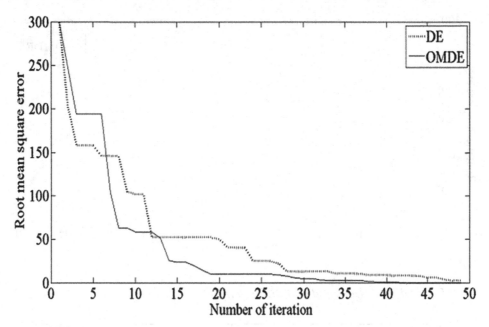

Figure 13. RMSE for DE/best/2/exp and OMDE/best/2/exp

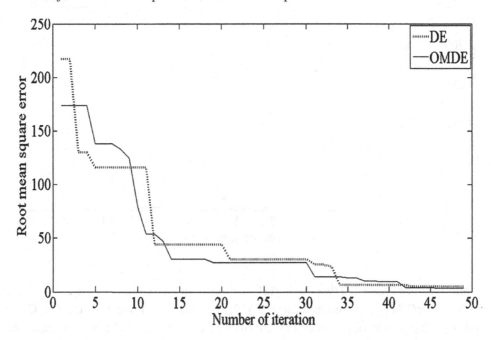

Figures 20-23 give the value of the estimated stator resistance, rotor resistance, magnetizing inductance and leakage inductance respectively, for the strategy *OMDE/best/1/bin* those values becomes approximately equal to its actual value after 30 iterations. Table 3 shows the comparison of the performance of all the ten variants of DE and OMDE terms of the means squared error after fifty iterations. From the

Figure 14. RMSE for DE/rand/2/exp and OMDE/rand/2/exp

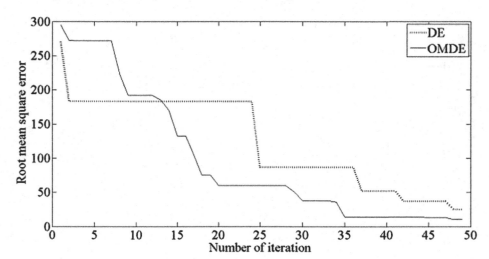

Figure 15. RMSE for DE/best/1/bin and OMDE/best/1/ bin

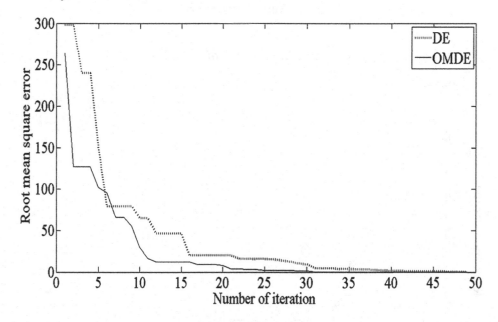

results it is found that for *DE/best/1/bin* the RMSE is minimum i.e. 0.4060 among all the DE strategies similarly *OMDE/best/1/bin* gives the minimum RMSE i.e. 0.0168 amongst all the OMDE strategies. This shows that the superiority of proposed OMDE over the conventional DE. In some cases the value of the parameters exceed their boundary values because we have defined the boundaries only for initialization, but when the evolutionary process continues the parameter values depend on the type of mutation scheme. The process converges to its optimal value after few numbers of iterations i.e. only 30 number of iterations as shown in Figures 17-21 for the strategy *OMDE/best/1/bin*.

Figure 16. RMSE for DE/rand/1/bin and OMDE/rand/1/ bin

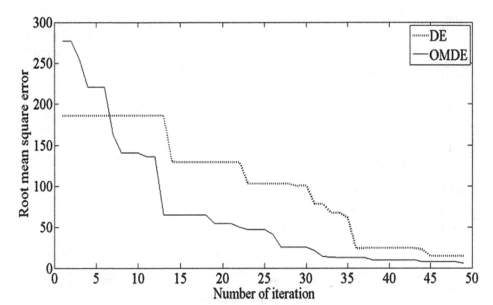

Figure 17. RMSE for DE/rand-to-best/1/ bin and OMDE /rand-to-best/1/ bin

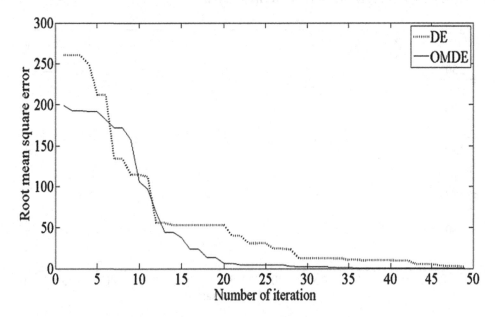

4.5 Concluding Remarks on IM Parameter Estimation

This work presents a new differential evolution (DE) algorithm called opposition based mutation differential evolution (OMDE). In this work; we described the application of the DE and OMDE strategies for efficiently solving the identification problem of an induction motor. We have considered ten different DE and OMDE formulations towards estimating the parameters i.e. stator and rotor resistances, leakage

Figure 18. RMSE for DE/best/2/bin and OMDE/best/2/ bin

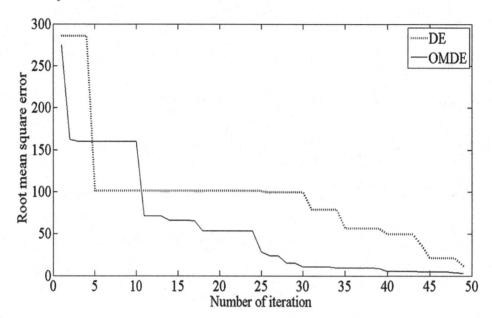

Figure 19. RMSE for DE/rand/2/bin and OMDE/rand/2/bin

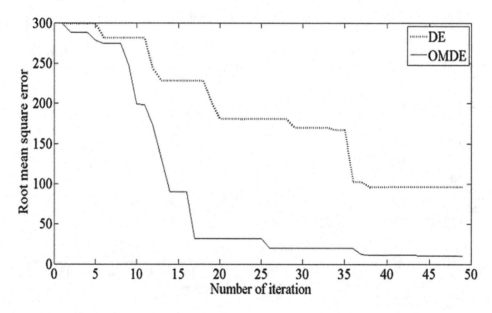

inductance and magnetizing inductance of the Induction Motor Drive System. For a given induction motor, the unknown parameters are successively evolved by using DE and OMDE algorithm to approximate the actual parameters accurately. From results obtained above, it is concluded that OMDE/best/1/exp gives the better result in terms of faster convergence and accuracy in estimating parameters. The main advantage of DE over other algorithms is that it requires less number of tuning parameters even if opposition based differential evolution (ODE) converges faster than DE but it requires some extra parameters such

Figure 20. Estimation of stator resistance

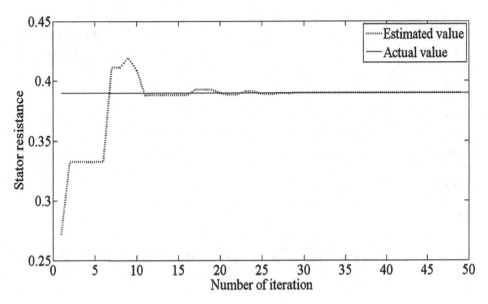

Figure 21. Estimation of rotor resistance

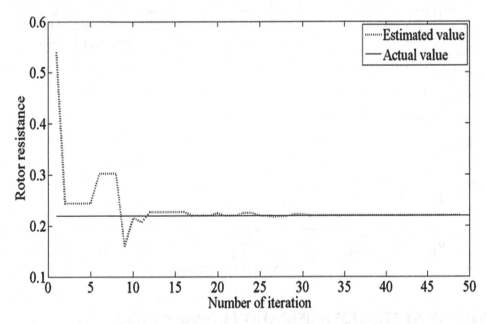

as jumping rate J_r to be tuned properly. The advantage of OMDE over ODE is that the proposed method does not require any extra parameters to be tuned which provides more flexibility than its counterpart i.e. ODE. The authors also tried the same problem using ODE it was found that ODE performance was at par with OMDE for the jumping rate of 0.3 and for other jumping rates OMDE outperforms over ODE.

Figure 22. Estimation of magnetizing inductance

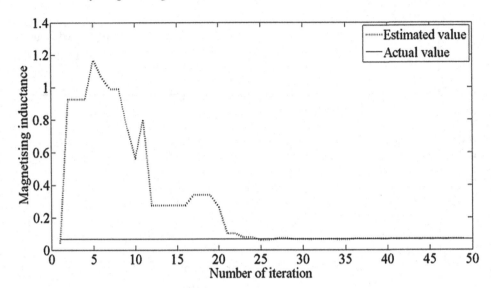

Figure 23. Estimation of leakage inductance

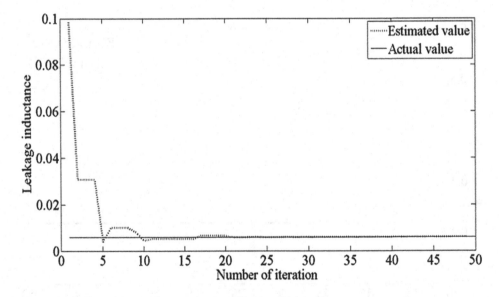

5. NONLINEAR SYSTEM IDENTIFICATION USING HYBRID DIFFERENTIAL EVOLUTION TRAINING ALGORITHM

Here, we describe how a hybrid differential evolution (DE) is applied for training neural network in the frame work of system identification (see Algorithm-1). DE can be applied to global searches within the weight space of a typical feed-forward neural network. Output of a feed-forward neural network is a function of synaptic weights $\mathbf{w}$ and input values $\mathbf{x}$, i.e. $\mathbf{y} = f(\mathbf{x}, \mathbf{w})$. The role of BP in the proposed algorithm has been described in section I. In the training process, both the input vector $\mathbf{x}$ and the output vector $\mathbf{y}$ are known and the synaptic weights in $\mathbf{w}$ are adapted to obtain appropriate functional mappings from the input $\mathbf{x}$ to the output $\mathbf{y}$. Generally, the adaptation can be carried out by minimizing the network error function $\mathbf{E}$ which is of the form $\mathbf{E}(\mathbf{y}, f(\mathbf{x}, \mathbf{w}))$. In this work we have taken $\mathbf{E}$ as mean squared error i.e. $\mathbf{E} = \dfrac{1}{N} \sum_{k=1}^{N} \left[\mathbf{y} - f(\mathbf{x}, \mathbf{w}) \right]^2$, where N is the number of data considered. The optimization goal is to minimize the objective function $\mathbf{E}$ by optimizing the values of the network weights, $\mathbf{w} = (w_1, \ldots, w_d)$.

ALGORITHM-1: Differential Evolution Back-Propagation (DEBP) Identification Algorithm

Step 1: Initialize population pop: Create a population from randomly chosen object vectors with dimension P, where P is the number of population

$$\mathbf{P}_g = (\mathbf{w}_{1,g}, \ldots, \mathbf{w}_{P,g})^T, \quad g = 1, \ldots, g_{max}$$

$$\mathbf{w}_{i,g} = (w_{1,i,g}, \ldots, w_{d,i,g}), \quad i = 1, \ldots, P$$

where d is the number of weights in the weight vector. In $\mathbf{w}_{i,g}$, i is index to the population and g is the generation to which the population belongs.

Step 2: Evaluate all the candidate solutions inside the pop for a specified number of iterations.

Step 3: For each ith candidate in pop, select the random population members, $r_1, r_2, r_3 \in \{1, 2, \ldots P\}$

Step 4: Apply a mutation operator to each candidate in a population to yield a mutant vector i.e.

$$v_{j,i,g+1} = w_{j,r_1,g} + F(w_{j,r_2,g} - w_{j,r_3,g}), \text{ for } j = 1, \ldots, d$$
$$(i \neq r_1 \neq r_2 \neq r_3) \in \{1, \ldots, P\} \text{ and } F \in (0, 1+]$$

where "F" denotes the mutation factor.

Step 5: Apply crossover i.e. each vector in the current population is recombined with a mutant vector to produce trial vector.

$$t_{j,i,g+1} = \begin{cases} v_{j,i,g+1} & \text{if } rand_j[0,1] \leq C \\ w_{j,i,g} & \text{otherwise} \end{cases}$$

where $C \in [0, 1]$

Step 6: Apply Local Search (back propagation algorithm) i.e. each trial vector will produce a lst-trial vector $lst_{j,i,g+1} = bp\left(t_{j,i,g+1}\right)$

Step 7: Apply selection i.e. between the local search trial (lst-trial) vector and the target vector. If the lst-trial vector has an equal or lower objective function value than that of its target vector, it replaces the target vector in the next generation; otherwise, the target retains its place in the population for at least one more generation

$$\mathbf{w}_{i,g+1} = \begin{cases} lst_{i,g+1}, & \text{if } \mathbf{E}(\mathbf{y}, f(\mathbf{x}, \mathbf{w}_{i,g+1})) \leq \mathbf{E}(\mathbf{y}, f(\mathbf{x}, \mathbf{w}_{i,g})) \\ \mathbf{w}_{i,g}, & \text{otherwise} \end{cases}$$

Step 8: Repeat steps 1 to 7 until stopping criteria (i.e. maximum number of generation) is reached

5.1 Application of EC to a Bench Mark Problem

In this section we present the performance of the proposed Differential Evolution Back-Propagation (DEBP) Identification Algorithm using the simulation studies on a bench mark problem and a laboratory based twin rotor multi-input-multi-output system. The output equation of the bench mark problem

$$y_p(k+1) = \frac{y_p(k)[y_p(k-1)+2][y_p(k)+2.5]}{8.5 + [y_p(k)]^2 + [y_p(k-1)]^2} + u(k) \tag{5.1}$$

where $y_p(k)$ is the output of the system at the kth time step and $u(k)$ is the plant input which is uniformly bounded function of time. The plant is stable for $u(k) \in [-2\ 2]$.

For the identification of the plant described in Eqn. (6.1), let the neural model be in the form of

Figure 24. Neural network based identification scheme

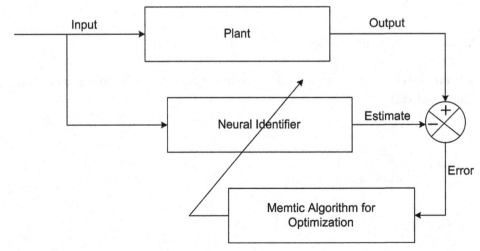

$$\hat{y}(k+1) = f(y_p(k), y_p(k-1)) + u(k) \qquad (5.2)$$

where $f(y_p(k), y_p(k-1))$ is the nonlinear function of $y_p(k)$ and $y_p(k-1)$. The inputs to the neural network are $y_p(k)$ and $y_p(k-1)$. The output from neural network is $\hat{y}(k+1)$. The goal is to train the neural network such that when an input $u(k)$ is simultaneously presented to the nonlinear system (5.1) as well as to neural network (5.2), the neural network outputs $\hat{y}(k+1)$ will finally approach the nonlinear system output $y_p(k+1)$ as close as possible.

In the following discussions, we will present our observation on nonlinear system identification schemes using seven different identification algorithms with comparison of their identification performances.

Figure 24 shows the neural network based system identification scheme for the given plant employing the proposed hybrid algorithm. The role of MA here is to train the weights of the neural network optimally.

In applying different system identification techniques to nonlinear systems considered in equation 5.1 we conducted several sets of simulation experiments with different number of hidden units. During these experiments we observed the pattern of estimation errors corresponding to the number of hidden nodes taken. By the process we end up with choice of twenty one number of hidden units leading lowest estimation error. After 100 epochs the training of the neural identifier has been stopped. During training period, input $u(k)$ was a random white noise signal, but after the training is over, its prediction capability were tested for input given by

$$u(k) = \begin{cases} 2\cos(2\pi k / 100) & \text{if} \quad k \leq 200 \\ 1.2\sin(2\pi k / 20) & \text{if} \quad 200 < k \leq 500 \end{cases} \qquad (5.3)$$

Figure 25. BP identification performances

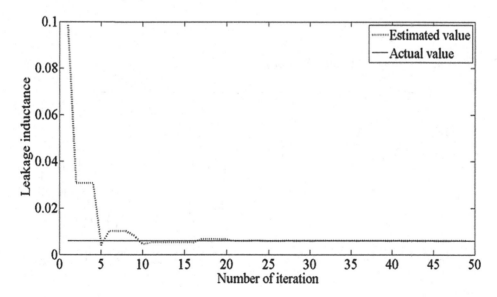

Figure 26. Error in modeling (BP identification)

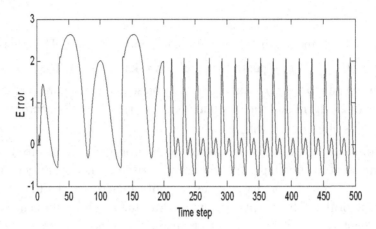

Figure 27. GA identification performances

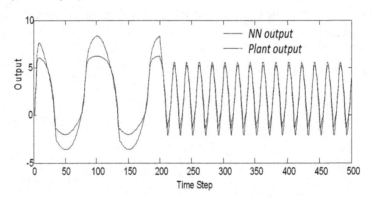

Figure 28. Error in modeling (GA identification)

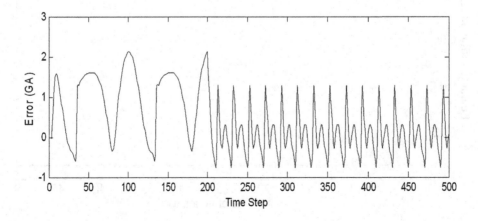

Identification Using Back-Propagation Algorithm (BP) (Figures 25 and 26)

Figure 25 shows the system identification results obtained using the back propagation algorithm for training the feed-forward neural network. Figure 26 shows the identification error plot obtained with BP identification.

Identification Using Genetic Algorithm (GA) (Figures 27 and 28)

Figure 27 shows the identification performance of the system using genetic algorithm as learning algorithm for the given neural network. The same neural network configuration i.e. twenty one number of neurons are taken into account. After 100 epochs it was found that the squared error is more than conventional back propagation also taking more time to converge. Figure 28 shows the error between actual and GA identification. We have considered one point crossover in this case.

Genetic Algorithm Back-Propagation (GABP) Identification (Figures 29 and 30)

Figure 29 shows the comparison of identification performance between the GABP identification scheme and the actual plant output. The identification error is shown in Figure 30.

Identification Using Particle Swarm Optimization (PSO) (Figures 31 and 32)

Figure 31 shows the identification performance between the particle swarm optimization and the actual output. The identification error between the actual output and the PSO output is shown in Figure 32.

Figure 29. GABP identification. Performances

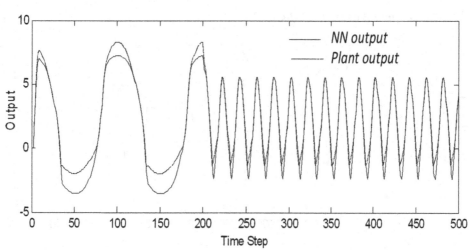

Figure 30. Error in modeling (GABP identification)

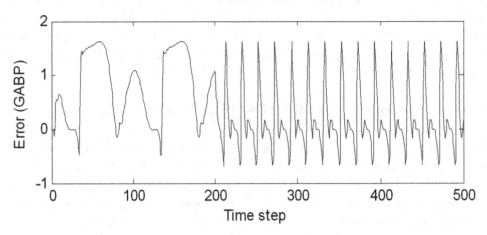

Figure 31. PSO identification performances

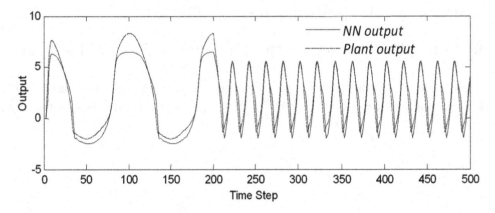

Figure 32. Error in modeling (PSO identification)

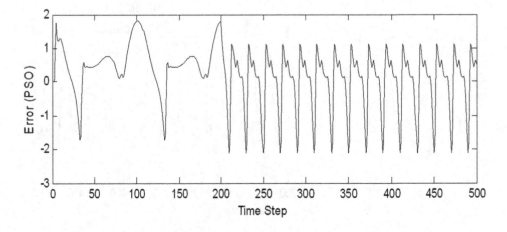

Figure 33. PSOBP identification performances

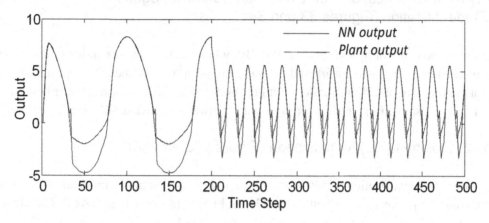

Figure 34. Error in modeling (PSOBP identification)

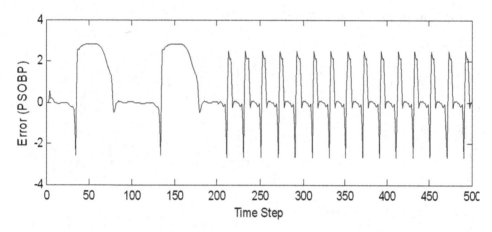

Figure 35. DE identification performances

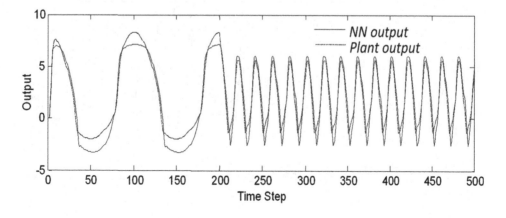

Particle Swarm Optimization Combined with Back-Propagation (PSOBP) Identification (Figures 33 and 34)

Figure 33 shows the result of hybrid scheme (PSOBP) where particle swarm optimization is hybridized with back propagation. The result clearly indicates even if the above scheme gives less sum squared error than PSO at the moment of testing, but does not give better identification of nonlinear system at validation stage. Figure 34 shows its identification error curve between actual and GABP system identification.

Differential Evolution (DE) Identification (Figures 35 and 36)

Figure 35 shows the identification performance between the differential evolution and the actual output. It was found that the performance is better than GA and PSO but worse than GABP. The identification error between the actual output and the DE output is shown in Figure 36.

Figure 36. Error in modeling (DE identification)

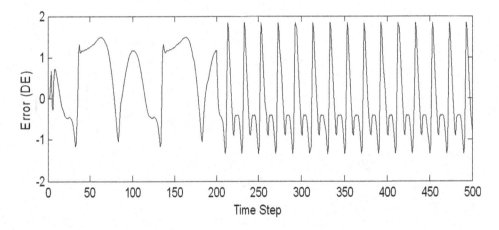

Figure 37. DEBP identification performances

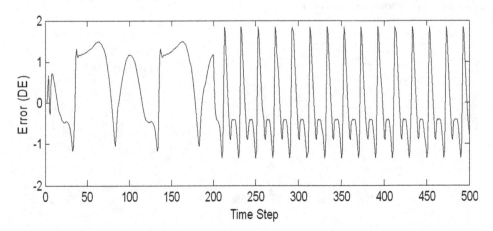

Figure 38. Error in modeling (DEBP identification)

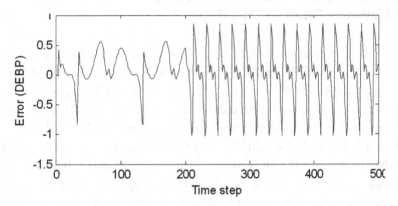

Differential Evolution Plus the Back-Propagation (DEBP) Identification (Figures 37 and 38)

From Figure 37 it is clear that the proposed method, i.e. DEBP identification is more effective than other mentioned approaches as per as identification performance and speed of convergence is concerned. Figure 38 shows the error between the plant output and NN identified model output.

Figure 39. A comparison on the convergence on the mean squared error (MSE) for all the seven methods (1-BP, 2-GA, 3-GABP, 4-PSO, 5-PSOBP, 6-DE, 7-DEBP)

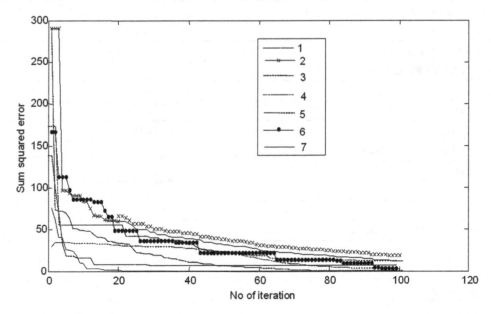

5.2 Performance Comparison of All the Seven Identification Methods Cited in This Paper

Figure 39 depicts the mean square error (MSE) profiles for all the seven different identification methods (BP, GA, GABP, PSO, PSOBP, DE and DEBP). In these seven methods, we have proposed a new identification scheme, namely the Differential Evolution plus the Back-propagation (DEBP) identification approach. From this figure it is clear that the SSE with the proposed method DEBP converges to zero very fast taking only about 20th iteration while the error curves with the other system identification methods (BP, GA,GABP, PSO, PSOBP and DE) converges to zero taking over 70th iterations. Hence it is important to note that the proposed DEBP system identification exhibits better convergence characteristics. All the simulations have been performed in MATLAB using same set of parameters i.e. population size, number of generations, upper and lower bounds of weights and number of hidden layer neurons.

Table 4 gives the value of parameters used in all the seven identification schemes. Table 5 gives the comparison of performance of all the seven methods in terms of MSE. From the results it is clear that for a particular number of generations i.e. 100, the proposed DEBP algorithm has a MSE of 0.0625. It is found that out of all the seven methods the hybrid approaches i.e. GABP, DEBP, and PSOBP are having faster convergence in comparison to other local search and evolutionary computing approaches. Finally it is concluded that the proposed hybrid DEBP is having better identification performance and faster convergence in comparison to hybrid GABP and PSOBP algorithm which indicates DE is outperforming than its counterpart GA and PSO.

Table 4. Parameters used in simulation studies

Total sampling number (T)	500
Population size (S)	20
Number of iteration (generation)	100
Upper and lower bounds of weights	[-1 1]
BP learning parameter (η)	0.55
Number of hidden layer neurons	21
Parameters for DE & DEBP algorithm	
Mutation constant factor (*F*)	0.6
Crossover constant (*C*)	0.5
BP learning parameter (η)	0.55
Parameters for GA & GABP algorithm	
Mutation probability	0.002
Crossover constant probability	1
BP learning parameter (η)	0.55
Parameters for PSO & PSOBP algorithm	
Learning factor (C_1)	1.9
Learning factor (C_2)	1.9
BP learning parameter (η)	0.55

Table 5. Comparison of performances of seven methods

SI. No	Identification Method	Computation Time (Sec) for 100 Iterations	Mean Squared Error (MSE)	Number of Iterations for Which the MSE Converges to Zero
1	BP	4.76	2.6086	>100
2	GA	40.42	11.4156	>100
3	GABP	131.42	0.2852	70
4	PSO	42.15	5.49	>100
5	PSOBP	142.79	0.2074	50
6	DE	42.19	3.9645	>100
7	DEBP	136.73	0.0625	20

5.3 Concluding Remarks on Nonlinear System Identification

In this section we have provided an extensive study of hybrid algorithms applied to nonlinear system identification. From the results presented it has been found that the proposed DEBP hybrid algorithm applied to neural network learning exhibits better result in terms of faster convergence and lowest mean squared error (MSE) amongst all the seven methods (i.e. BP, GA, GABP, PSO, PSOBP, DE. and DEBP). The proposed method DEBP exploits the advantages of both the local search and global search. It is interesting to note that the local search pursued after the mutation and crossover operation that helps in intensifying the region of search space which leads to faster convergence. We investigated the performance of the proposed version of the DEBP algorithm using a benchmark nonlinear system identification problem and a real time multi input multi output highly nonlinear TRMS system. The simulation studies showed that the proposed algorithm of DEBP outperforms in terms of convergence velocity among all the seven discussed algorithms. The overall performance of the DEBP scheme was better than the other approaches and the overall performance of the newly proposed DEBP algorithm was superior to other methods i.e. GABP and PSOBP. This shows it is advantageous to use DEBP over other evolutionary computation such as GA and PSO in nonlinear system identification.

6. CHAPTER SUMMARY

In this chapter we have discussed about the parameter estimation techniques using evolutionary computation applied to induction motor. The results show a high degree of accuracy of estimating the induction motor parameters and eliminate the problem of expressing the system parameters in terms of regressor equation. These methods used to estimate parameters directly. In this chapter we have considered one of the evolutionary computing techniques i.e. DE and its variation OMDE to estimate different parameters of an induction motor which analyses the understanding of the use of evolutionary algorithms for parameter estimation problems.

In the second part of the chapter we have discussed the identification of nonlinear systems using different hybrid approaches. Hybridization of a global search algorithm with a local search is a challenging approach for optimization problems where the individual methods without hybridization may suffer from slow convergence and trapped by local minima. In this chapter we have considered one bench mark problem of nonlinear system and another highly nonlinear TRMS system and applied the proposed approached for identifying the above two systems. From the statistical analysis it was found that the proposed approach is able to identify the accurate model with faster convergence without being trapped into a local optimum.

REFERENCES

Banks, A., Vincent, J., & Anyako, C. (2008). A review of particle swarm optimization". Part II: Hybridisation, combinatorial, multicriteria and constrained optimization, and indicative applications. *Natural Computing, 7*(1).

Box, G. E. P. (1957). Evolutionary operation: A method of increasing industrial productivity. *Applied Statistics, 6*, 81–101.

Das, S., & Konar, A. (2007). Swarm Intelligence in Production Management and Engineering. In Dipak Laha and Purnendu Mandal (Eds.), Handbook of Computational Intelligence in Manufacturing and Production Management. Hershey, PA, USA: IGI Global.

Das, S. A., Abraham, A., & Konar, A. (2008). Particle Swarm Optimization and Differential Evolution Algorithms: Technical Analysis, Applications and Hybridization Perspectives. In Ying Liu et al. (Eds.), Advances of Computational Intelligence in Industrial Systems. Springer Verlag, Germany.

Dasgupta, S., Das, S., Abraham, A., & Biswas, A. (2009). Adaptive computational chemotaxis in bacterial foraging optimization: an analysis. *IEEE Transactions on Evolutionary Computing, 13*(4), 919-941

Davis, L. (1989). Adapting operator probabilities in genetic algorithms. *Proceedings of the Third International Conference on Genetic Algorithms*, La Jolla, CA (pp. 60-69). Morgan Kaufmann.

De Garis, H. (1990).Genetic programming: modular evolution for darwin machines.*Proceedings of the 1990 International Joint Conference on Neural Networks*, Washington, DC (pp. 194-197). Lawrence Erlbaum.

De Jong, K. A., K.A.(1992). Are genetic algorithms function optimizers. *Proceedings of the Second International Conference on Parallel Problem Solving from Nature* (pp. 20-27). Kaufmann.

Dong, Z., & Ze, H., P, Wang,D. & Jiao,S.(2006).Thermal Process System Identification Using Particle Swarm Optimization. *Proceedings of theIEEE International Symposium on* Industrial Electronics(*Vol. 1*, pp. 194-198).

Engelbrecht, A. P. (2005, July 9 – 13). Fundamentals of Computational Swarm Intelligence, John Wiley & Sons. *Proceedings of theGenetic and Evolutionary Computation Conference*.

Fogel, L. J., Owens, A. J., & Walsh, M. J. (1966). *Artificial Intelligence through Simulated Evolution*. New York: Wiley Publishing.

Fraser, A. S. (1957). Simulation of genetic systems by automatic digital computers". *Australian Journal of Biological Sciences, 10*, 484–491.

Grefenstette, J. G., & Baker, J. E. (1989).How genetic algorithms work: a critical look at implicit parallelism. *Proceedings of the Third Int.l Conference on Genetic Algorithms*, Fairfax, VA, USA. Morgan.

Guney, K., & Basbug, S. (2008). Interference suppression of linear antenna arrays by amplitude-only control using a bacterial foraging algorithm. *Progress In Electromagnetics Research*, *79*, 475–497.

Holland, J. H. (1975). *Adaptation in Natural and Artificial Systems*. Ann Arbor, Michigan: The University of Michigan Press.

Holland, J. H. (1986). Escaping brittleness: The possibilities of general-purpose learning algorithms applied to parallel rule-based systems. In R. Michalski, J. Carbnell, & T. Mitchell (Eds.), *Machine Learning: An Artificial Intelligence Approach* (pp. 593–623). Los Altos: Morgan Kaufmann.

Ilonen, J., Kamarainen, J. K., & Lampinen, J. (2003). Differential Evolution Training Algorithm for Feed Forward Neural Networks. *Neural Processing Letters*, *17*(3), 93–105.

Kennedy, J. (1998). The Behavior of Particles. *Proc. of the 7th Intl. Conference on Evolutionary Programming VII* (pp. 581-587).

Kennedy, J., & Eberhart, R. C. (1995). Particle Swarm Optimization.*Proceedings of IEEE International Conference on Neural Networks*, Piscataway, NJ (pp. 1942-1948).

Kennedy, J., & Eberhart, R. C. (2001). *Swarm Intelligence*. Morgan Kaufmann.

Kim, D. H., Abraham, A., & Cho, J. H. (2007). A hybrid genetic algorithm and bacterial foraging approach for global optimization. *Information Sciences*, *177*, 3918–3937.

Lin,W. & Liu, P.X. (2006). Hammerstein model identification based on bacterial foraging. *Electronics Letters*, *42*(23), 1332-1333.

Lin, Y.C., Hwang, K.S., & Wang, F.-S. (2002, May 12-17). Hybrid Differential Evolution with Multiplier Updating Method for Nonlinear Constrained Optimization. *Proceedings of the 2002 Congress on Evolutionary Computation, CEC'02*, Honolulu, Hawaii(*Vol.1*, pp. 872–877).

Parsopoulos, K.E., Plagianakos, V.P., & Magoulas, , G.D., & Vrahatis, M.N. (2001). Objective Function Stretching to Alleviate Convergence to Local Minima. *Nonlinear Analysis*, *47*(5), 3419–3424.

Parsopoulos, K. E., & Vrahatis, M. N. (2002). Initializing the Particle Swarm Optimizer Using the Nonlinear Simplex Method. In *Advances in Intelligent Systems* (pp. 216–221). Fuzzy Systems, Evolutionary Computation.

Rahnamayan, S. Tizhoosh, H.R. & Salama,M.A.(2008).Opposition-Based Differential Evolution," *IEEE Trans. Evolutionary Computation, 12*(1), 64–79. Retrieved from http://ieeexplore.ieee.org/xpl/tocresult.jsp?isnumber=4444540

Rahnamayan, S., Tizhoosh, H. R., & Salama, A. (2008). Opposition versus randomness in soft computing techniques. *J. Applied Soft Computing*, *8*(2), 906–918.

Rechenberg, I. (1973). *Evolutionsstrategie: Optimierung Technischer Systeme nach Prinzipien der Biologischen Evolution* [PhD Thesis]. Frommann-Holzboog, Stuttgart.

Schwefel, H. P. (1981). *Numerical Optimization of Computer Models*. New York: John Wiley & Sons.

Shokri, M., Tizhoosh, H. R., & Kamel, M. (2006).Opposition-based Q (λ) algorithm.*Proceedings of the IEEE World Congr. Comput. Intell.*, Vancouver,BC, Canada (pp. 646–653).

Smith, S. (1983).Flexible learning of problem solving heuristics through adaptive search. *Proceedings of the Eighth Intl. Joint Conference on Artificial Intelligence*, Karlsruche, Germany (pp. 422-425). William Kaufmann

Storn, R., & K. Price, K. (1995). Differential Evolution - a Simple and Efficient Adaptive Scheme for Global Optimization over Continuous Spaces (Technical Report TR-95-012). ICSI.

Storn, R. (1999). System Design by Constraint Adaptation and Differential Evolution. *IEEE Transactions on Evolutionary Computation*, *3*(1), 22–34.

Tizhoosh, H. R. (2005). Opposition-based learning: A new scheme for machine intelligence.*Proceedings. Int. Conf. Comput. Intell. Modeling Control and Autom.*, Vienna(Vol. 1, pp. 695–701).

Tizhoosh, H.R., & Ventesca, M.M. (2008). Oppositional Concepts. In Computational Intelligence. Springer.

Ursem, R. K., & Vadstrup, P. (2003, December 8-12). Parameter identification of induction motors using differential evolution. *Proceedings of the 2003 Congress onEvolutionaryComputation CEC2003*, Canberra (pp. 790-796).

Ursem, R. K., & Vadstrup, P. (2004). Parameter identification of induction motors using stochastic optimization algorithm. *Applied Soft Computing*, *4*(1), 49–64.

Voss, M. S., & Feng, X. (2002).A New Methodology For Emergent System Identification Using Particle Swarm Optimization (PSO) And The Group Method Data Handling (GMDH).*Proceedings of the Genetic and Evolutionary Computation Conference* (pp. 1227-1232).

Whitley, D., Starkweather, T., & Fuquay, D. (1989).Scheduling problems and traveling salesmen: the genetic edge recombination operator.*Proceedings of the Third Intl. Conference on Genetic Algorithms*, Fairfax, VA (pp. 133-140). Morgan Kaufmann.

KEY TERMS AND DEFINITIONS

DE: DE is an abbreviation used for Differential evolution is an evolutionary computation technique.

Estimation Error: Estimation error is the difference between actual parameter and estimated parameter.

Evolutionary Computation: Evolutionary Computation is a stochastic optimization approach which provides a global optimal solution.

Neural Network: Neural network is a soft computing paradigm inspired by the working of human brain to inculcate intelligence in machines.

Optimization: Optimization is the method of determining the optimal value of a system.

Parameter Estimation: Parameter Estimation is the optimal parameter determination.

PSO: PSO is the abbreviation used for particle swarm optimization evolutionary computation technique.

System Identification: System Identification is model building procedure using the data set of a physical system.

Chapter 16
BFO Optimized Automatic Load Frequency Control of a Multi-Area Power System

Pravat Kumar Ray
National Institute of Technology Rourkela, India

Sushmita Ekka
National Institute of Technology Rourkela, India

ABSTRACT

This chapter presents an analysis on operation of Automatic Load Frequency Control (ALFC) by developing models in SIMULINK which helps us to understand the principle behind ALFC including the challenges. The three area system is being taken into account considering several important parameters of ALFC like integral controller gains (KIi), governor speed regulation parameters (Ri), and frequency bias parameters (Bi), which are being optimized by using Bacteria Foraging Optimization Algorithm (BFOA). Simultaneous optimization of certain parameters like KIi, Ri and Bi has been done which provides not only the best dynamic response for the system but also allows us to use much higher values of Ri than used in practice. This will help the power industries for easier and cheaper realization of the governor. The performance of BFOA is also investigated through the convergence characteristics which reveal that that the Bacteria Foraging Algorithm is quite faster in optimization such that there is reduction in the computational burden and also minimal use of computer resource utilization.

INTRODUCTION

Power systems are very large and complex electrical networks consisting of generation networks, transmission networks and distribution networks along with loads which are being distributed throughout the network over a large geographical area as per Yao (2007). In the power system, the system load keeps changing from time to time according to the needs of the consumers. So properly designed controllers are required for the regulation of the variations in the system so as to maintain the stability of the power system and ensure its reliable operation.

DOI: 10.4018/978-1-5225-0427-6.ch016

The rapid growth of the industries has further lead to the increased complexity of the power system. Frequency greatly depends on active power and the voltage greatly depends on the reactive power. So the control difficulty in the power system can be divided into two parts. One is related to the control of the active power and the frequency whereas the other is related to the reactive power and the control of voltage. The active power control and the frequency control is generally known as the Automatic Load Frequency Control (ALFC).

Basically the Automatic Load Frequency Control (ALFC) deals with the regulation of the real power output of the generator and its frequency (speed). The primary loop is relatively fast where changes occur in one to several seconds. The primary control loop responds to frequency changes through the speed governor and the steam (or hydro) flow is managed accordingly to counterpart the real power generation to relatively fast load variations. Thus maintain a megawatt balance and this primary loop performs a course speed or frequency control.

The secondary loop is slower compared to the primary loop. The secondary loop maintains the excellent regulation of the frequency, furthermore maintains appropriate real power exchange among the rest of the pool members. This loop being insensitive to quick changes in load as well as frequency, it focuses on swift changes which occur over periods of minutes.

Load disturbance due to the occurrence of continuous and frequent variation of loads having smaller values always creates problem for ALFC. Due to the change in the active power demand/load in an area, tie-line power flows from the interconnected areas and the frequency of the system changes and thus the system becomes unstable. So we need Automatic Load Frequency Control to maintain the stability during the load variations. This is done by minimizing transient deviations of frequency as well as tie-line power exchange and also making the steady state error to zero [3,4]. Inequality involving generation with demand causes frequency deviations. If the frequency is not maintained within the scheduled values then it may lead on the way to tripping of the lines, system collapse as well as blackouts.

BACKGROUND

Literature Review

A lot of work has been done related to automatic load frequency control in power systems. Load variations give rise to drifts in frequency along with voltage consequential in reduction of generation because of line tripping as well as blackouts. These variations are reduced by AGC that constitutes of two sections namely LFC and AVR. Adil et. al. (2012) discussed simulation analysis is dispensed to comprehend operation of LFC by rising models in SIMULINK that helps to know the principles and various challenges relating to LFC.

The PI controller parameters derived from conventional or trial-and-error methods can't have sensible dynamical act for a large variety of operating circumstances and changes in load in multi-area power system. To solve this difficulty, decentralized LFC combination is developed as an H-∞ control problem and furthermore solved by means of iterative linear matrix inequalities algorithmic rule to style sturdy PI controllers in multi-area power systems as discussed by Bevrani et. al. (2004).

Rout et. al. (2013) discussed, a unified PID tuning technique dependent on two-degree-of-freedom for LFC of power system. Also time domain act and robustness of consequential PID controller is associated to two regulation parameters and its robustness is discussed. Simulation results shows improvement in damping of power systems. The additional degree-of-freedom cancels the impact of unwanted poles of the disturbance, improving the disturbance reduction performance of closed-loop system.

FA is used in control of the frequency in CCGT plant for controller gain optimization in Saikia (2013). Also Performance of traditional controllers I, PI, PID and ID are also compared.

Investigation of differential evolution algorithmic program based on PI controller designed for AGC of interrelated power system is shown in the work of Mohammad (2013) and Rout et. al. (2013). The outcomes are made a comparison by means of BFOA and GA based on PI controller.

Pradhan and Majhi (2013) used a tuning method to model PID load frequency controller meant for power systems and relay based recognition technique is considered for estimation of power system dynamics. Robustness investigations on stability as well as performance are given in relation to uncertainties in plant parameters and it is seen that on the whole the system remains asymptotically steady for all enclosed uncertainties in addition to system oscillations.

Characteristics of a Properly Designed Power System

- It should supply power everywhere the customer demands practically.
- It should always supply power.
- It should always supply the ever changing load demand.
- The supplied power should be of good quality.
- The supplied power should be economical.
- The necessary safety requirements should be satisfied.

The power delivered must satisfy certain minimal necessities with regards to the supply quality. The quality of the power supply can be determined as follows:

1. The system frequency must be kept around the specified value i.e. 50 Hz.
2. The magnitude of the bus voltage is maintained within prescribed limits around the normal value.

Voltage and frequency controls are the necessary requirements for the effective operation of the power systems.

Major Objectives of ALFC in a Power System

- To take care of the required megawatt power output of a generator matching with the changing load.
- To take care of the appropriate value of exchange of power linking control areas.
- To facilitate control of the frequency for larger interconnection.

Advantages of ALFC in Multi Area System

- The ALFC helps to minimize the transient deviations and make the steady state error to zero.
- It also holds system frequency at a specified value.
- The ALFC also collaborate in keeping the net power interchange between the pool members at the predetermined values.

Types of Control

1. **Primary Control**: This type of control is endeavored locally to keep the balance involving generation along with demand within the network. It is apprehended by speed of turbine governors that adjusts the generators output as a response to the frequency divergence in the area. If there is a major disturbance, then the primary control permits the balance of generated as well as utilized power at a frequency distinguishable from the set-point quantity in order to make the network stable.
2. **Secondary Control**: This type of control is exerted by means of an automatic centralized procedure in the control building block. It has two purposes:
    a. It keeps the interchange power connecting the control block and its adjoining blocks according to the planned value.
    b. In case of major frequency drop, it brings back the set point value of the frequency.

Need for the Inter-Connection of Areas

Earlier electric power systems were usually operated as individual units. But a need for the inter-connection was realized due to the following reasons:

- There was a demand for larger bulk of power with increased reliability so there was interconnection of neighboring plants.
- It is also beneficial economically since fever machines are necessary as reserve for action at peak loads (reserve capacity) and also less machines are needed to be run without load to take care of sudden jumps in load(spinning reserve).

Therefore, several generating units are connected with each other forming state, regional and national grids respectively. Also for the control of power flow in these grids the Load dispatch centers are needed.

Advantages of Interconnected System

- Reserve capacity is reduced and thus there is reduction in the installed capacity.
- For larger units the capital cost/kW is reduced. (In India a particular unit can hold up >500MW due to interconnection).
- Generators are used effectively.
- Generation is optimized so there is reduction in the installed capacity.
- The reliability of the system is increased.

Disadvantages of Having Interconnected System

- Faults gets propagated which is responsible for faster switchgear operation.
- Circuit breaker rating increases.
- Proper management is required.

Motivation

- There are numerous works pertaining to ALFC of interconnected areas of the power system by using various control methods like classical, optimal, suboptimal and adaptive control etc. to obtain better dynamic response characteristics but there are a very small number of works concerned to primary control/governor control characteristic i.e. suitable choice of speed regulation constraint 'R'.
- Also the works are concerned with the selection of the speed regulation constraint 'R' more willingly than the optimized value.
- Also few works have been presented about the study of the significance of the tie line power alterations and its effect on the dynamic response of the system. The changes in the system response due to imbalanced ties which are present in actual operation in a multi area system have not been investigated properly.
- Through simulations, the objective is to maintain constant frequency and fulfill the load demand and also minimize the overall generated steady state error but it poses some demerits.
- The general hit and trial method seems very tiresome for finding the suitable parameters so we are using an optimization tool i.e. BFOA for tuning of the parameters such as KIi, Ri and Bi.
- Along with the optimized parameters the steady state error is to be minimized.
- Convergence characteristics can ensure reduction in computational burden as it is faster.

Problem Statement

Load Frequency Problem

In a system as the load changes, the frequency of the system also changes. No regulation control would be required if it was not important to keep the frequency of the system constant. Normally the frequency would vary by 5% approx. from light load to full load conditions.

Tie Line Power Problem

In case of a two machine system having two loads, the change in load is to be taken care of by both the machines such that there is equal participation by both the machines in sharing the tie-line power and also maintaining the stability of the system by reducing the error to zero value.

How Estimation Problem Becomes Optimization Problem

Estimation problem is based on the empirical or measured data so as to approximate the values of the unknown parameters used from among the group of measured data.

Optimization problem is based on the process of finding the best solution from among the feasible solutions with respect to a particular goal, obtained through the process of several steps. The best solution is known as the optimal value.

Here the optimization technique is used to find the values of the controllable factors that determine the system behavior and minimize the objective function constituting the errors which occur due to variation in load.

Figure 1. Block diagram of automatic load frequency control

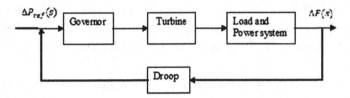

Why to Go for BFOA

An effort has been done to initiate a new-fangled optimization technique known as Bacteria Foraging Optimization Technique (BFOA) by Nanda et. al (2009), intended for optimization of the parameters of the Automatic Load Frequency Control (ALFC) which would otherwise have been very difficult. BFOA technique gives us a chance to optimize several parameters simultaneously. Simultaneous optimization of the parameters controls the relative effects of the variation of the parameters. The most vital achievement of using this method is the optimization of 'R' together with the controller gain parameters as discussed by Ali and Abd-Elazim (2011) and Ali and Abd-Elazim (2013).

DYNAMICS OF THE POWER SYSTEM

The automatic load frequency control loop is mainly associated with the large size generators. The main aim of the automatic load frequency control (ALFC) is to keep the desired unvarying frequency, so as to divide loads among generators and also to manage the tie line power interchange according to the scheduled values as per Fosha and Elgerd (1970). Various components of the automatic load frequency control loop is shown in the Figure 1.

Turbines

Turbines are used in power systems for the conversion of the natural energy, like the energy from the steam or water, into mechanical power (P_m) which can be conveniently supplied to the generator. There are three kinds of turbines commonly used in power systems: non-reheat, reheat and hydraulic turbines, all of which can be modeled by transfer functions. We have non-reheat turbines which are represented as first-order units where the delay in time known as time delay (T_{ch}) takes place between the interval during switching of the valve and producing the torque in the turbine. Design of reheat turbines is done by using second-order units as there are different stage because of high and low steam pressure. Because of the inertia of the water hydraulic turbines are non-minimum phase units.

The turbine model represents changes in power output of the steam turbine to changes in its steam valve opening. Here we have considered a non-reheat turbine with a single gain factor K_T and single time constant T_T. In the model the representation of the turbine is,

$$\frac{\Delta P_T(s)}{\Delta P_v(s)} = \frac{K_T}{1 + sT_T} \tag{1}$$

where

$\Delta P_v(s)$ = the input to the turbine

$\Delta P_T(s)$ = the output from the turbine

Generators

Generators receive mechanical power from the turbines and then convert it to electrical power. However, our interest concerns the speed of the rotor rather than the power transformation. The speed of the rotor is proportional to the frequency of the power system. We need to keep the balance between the power generated and the power demands of the load because the electrical power cannot be stored in bulk amounts. When there is a change in load, the mechanical power sent by the turbine does not match the electrical power generated by the generator which results in an error which is being integrated into the rotor speed deviation $(\Delta\omega)$. Frequency bias $\Delta f = 2\pi\Delta\omega$. The power loads can be decomposed into resistive loads (P_L), which remain constant when the rotor speed is changing, and motor loads that change with load speed. If the mechanical power remains unchanged, the motor loads will compensate the load change at a rotor speed that is completely different from a scheduled value.

Mathematically,

$$\frac{\Delta P_v(s)}{\Delta P_g(s)} = \frac{1}{1 + sT_g} \tag{2}$$

where

$\Delta P_v(s)$ = the output from the generator

$\Delta P_g(s)$ = the input to the generator

T_g = time constant of the generator

Governors

Governors are employed in power systems for sensing the frequency bias which is caused by the load change and cancel it by varying the turbine inputs such as the speed regulation characteristic(R) and the time constant of the governor(T_g). If the change in load occurs without the load reference, then some part of the change can be compensated by adjusting the valve/gate and the remaining part of the change can be depicted in the form of frequency deviation. LFC aims to regulate the deviation in frequency in the presence of varying active power load. Thus, the load reference set point can be used for adjusting the valve/gate positions so as to cancel all the load change by controlling the power generation rather than resulting in a frequency deviation.

Mathematically,

$$\Delta P_g\left(s\right) = \Delta P_{ref}\left(s\right) - \frac{1}{R}\Delta F\left(s\right)$$

(3)

where

$\Delta P_g\left(s\right)$ = governor output

$\Delta P_{ref}\left(s\right)$ = the reference signal

R = regulation constant or droop

$\Delta F\left(s\right)$ = frequency deviation due to speed

Load

The load on a power system consists of a variety of electrical devices. The resistive loads such as lighting and heating loads are independent of frequency, but the motor loads are sensitive to frequency depending on the speed-load characteristics as shown below:

$$\Delta P_e = \Delta P_L + D\Delta\omega$$

(4)

where

ΔP_L = non frequency sensitive load change

$D\Delta\omega$ = frequency sensitive load change

$$D = {\%\text{change in load}}\Big/{\%\text{change in frequency}}$$

Tie-Lines

Various areas can be connected with one another by one or more transmission lines in an interconnected power grid through the tie-lines. When two areas are having totally different frequencies, then there's an exchange of power between the two areas which are linked by the tie lines. The tie-line power trade in area i and area j (ΔPij) and the tie-line synchronizing torque coefficient (Tij). Thus we can also say that the integral of the divergence in frequency among the two areas is an error in the tie-line power.

The objective of tie-lines is to trade power with the systems or areas in the neighborhood whose costs for operation create such transactions cost-effective. Moreover, even though no power is being transmitted through the tie-lines to the neighborhood systems/areas and it so happens that suddenly there is a loss of a generating unit in one of the systems. During such type of situations all the units in the interconnection experience a alteration in frequency and because of which the desired frequency is regained. Let there be two control areas and power is to be exchanged from area 1 to area 2.

Mathematically,

$$P_{12} = \frac{|V_1||V_2|}{X_{12}} \sin\left(\delta 1 - \delta 2\right)$$

(5)

where suffix 1 refers to control area 1 and suffix 2 refers to control area 2

X_{12} = series reactance involving area 1 and 2

$|V_1|$ and $|V_2|$ = magnitude of voltages of area 1 plus area 2

Area Control Error

The aim of LFC is not just to terminate frequency error in all areas, but as well to enable the exchange of the tie-line power as scheduled. In view of the fact that the tie-line power error is the integral of the difference in frequency between every pair of areas, but when we control frequency error back to zero, all steady state errors in the system frequency will give rise to in tie-line power errors. For this reason, it is necessary to consider the control input in the deviation in the tie-line power. Consequently, an area control error (ACE) is stated. Each of the power generating area considers ACE signal to be used as the output of the plant. By making the ACEs zero in all areas makes all the frequency along with tie-line power errors in the system as zero.

In order to take care of the total interchange of power among its areas within the neighborhood, ALFC uses real power flow determinations of all tie lines a emanating through the area and there after subtracts the scheduled interchange to compute an error value. The total power interchange, jointly with a gain, B (MW/0.1Hz), known as the frequency bias, as a multiplier with the frequency deviation is known as the Area Control Error (ACE) specified by,

$$ACE = \sum_{k=1}^{k} P_k - P_s + B\left(f_{act} - f_0\right) MW$$

(6)

where,

P_k = power in the tie line (if out of the area then +ve)

P_s = planned power exchange

f_0 = base frequency

f_{act} = actual frequency

Positive (+ve) ACE shows that the flow is out of the area.

Figure 2. Block diagram for parallel operation of generators

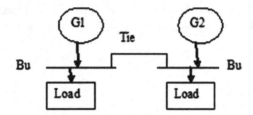

Parallel Operation of Generators

If there is a number of power generating units operational in parallel in the same particular area, a counterpart generator will be created for simplicity. The corresponding generator inertia constant (M_{eq}), damping constant of load (D_{eq}) and frequency response characteristic (B_{eq}) may be shown. Tie line flows as well as frequency droop represented for interconnecting power areas may be composite characteristics derived from parallel operation of generators. Each one of the areas could retain its speed $\omega = 2\pi f$, then a load general to both areas; by superposition include the terminal voltage. Two generators paralleled include completely different governor-speed-droop characteristics. Since they may be in parallel, power exchange linking them forces them to synchronize at a general frequency. Block diagram of parallel operation of generators is shown in Figure 2.

Modeling of ALFC

Modeling for the Change in Frequency

Let us consider an automatic load frequency control loop of an isolated system intended for the analysis of the steady state and dynamic responses as shown in Figure 3:

Steady State Analysis

Let $\Delta P_{ref}(s)$ be the speed changer setting and ΔP_D be the alteration in load demand. Considering a simple situation where the speed changer might have fixed setting i.e.

$$\Delta P_{ref}(s) = 0 \tag{7}$$

as well as there is change in the load demand. This may be known to be free governor operation. For such a process the steady modification in the system frequency for a step change in load i.e. is obtained as follows:

$$\left\{ \Delta P_{ref}(s) - \frac{1}{R} \Delta F(s) \right\} \frac{K_T}{(1 + sT_H)(1 + sT_T)} - \Delta P_D(s)] \frac{K_p}{(1 + sT_p)} = \Delta F(s) \tag{8}$$

Figure 3. Automatic load frequency control loop

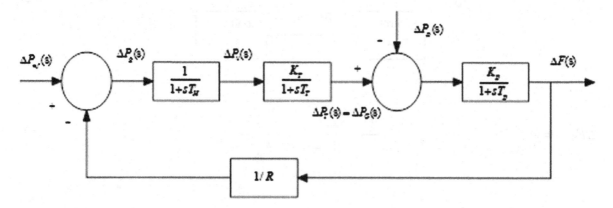

This implies that,

$$\Delta F\left(s\right) = \frac{-K_p \Delta P_D\left(s\right)/s\left(1+sT_p\right)}{\left(K_T K_p / R\right)/\left(1+sT_H\right)\left(1+sT_T\right)\left(1+sT_p\right)} \tag{9}$$

After simplification we get,

$$\Delta F\left(s\right) = -\frac{\Delta P_D}{\beta} \tag{10}$$

where β is the area frequency response characteristics.

Dynamic Analysis

For a step change in load,

$$\Delta F\left(s\right) = \frac{-K_p \Delta P_D\left(s\right)/s\left(1+sT_p\right)}{\left(K_T K_p / R\right)/\left(1+sT_H\right)\left(1+sT_T\right)\left(1+sT_p\right)} \tag{11}$$

Assuming amplifier and turbine response to be instantaneous i.e. $T_T = T_H = 0$ and $K_T = 1$, we have

$$\Delta F\left(s\right) = \frac{-K_p}{\left(1+sT_p\right)+K_p / R}\frac{\Delta P_D}{s} \tag{12}$$

After simplification we get,

Figure 4. Power transfer through tie line

$$\Delta F\left(s\right) = \frac{-RsK_p\left(1+sT_H\right)\left(1+sT_T\right)}{Rs\left(1+sT_H\right)\left(1+sT_T\right)\left(1+sT_p\right)+\left(s+RK_i\right)K_p}\frac{\Delta P_D}{s} \tag{13}$$

Modeling of the Tie-Line

Let us consider that area 1 is having surplus power and it transfers power to the area 2 by the tie-line as shown in Figure 4.

P_{12} = power exchanged from area 1 to area 2 via tie lines.

Then the power transfer equation the tie-line is specified as follows:

$$P_{12} = \frac{\left|V_1\right|\left|V_2\right|}{X_{12}}\sin\left(\delta1-\delta2\right) \tag{14}$$

where $\delta1$ and $\delta2$ = power angles of end voltages V_1 and V_2 of corresponding machine of the two areas.

X_{12} = reactance of the tie line.
$\left|V_1\right|$ and $\left|V_2\right|$ = magnitude of voltages of area 1 and area 2

The sequence of the subscripts depicts that the tie line power flow is positive in the direction from 1 to 2.
For little deviation in the angles $\delta1$ and $\delta2$ changes by $\Delta\delta1$ and 2, the tie line power changes as follows:

$$\Delta P_{12} = \frac{\left|V_1\right|\left|V_2\right|}{X_{12}}\cos\left(\delta1-\delta2\right)\left(\Delta\delta_1-\Delta\delta_2\right) \tag{15}$$

i.e.

$$\Delta P_{12} = T^0\left(\Delta\delta_1-\Delta\delta_2\right) \tag{16}$$

i.e.

$$\Delta P_{12}\left(s\right) = \frac{2\Pi T^0}{s}\left(\Delta F_1\left(s\right) - \Delta F_2\left(s\right)\right) \tag{17}$$

where, $T^0 = \dfrac{|V_1||V_2|}{X_{12}}\cos\left(\delta 1 - \delta 2\right) = $ Torque produced

In a control area which is isolated, the incremental power ($\Delta P_G - \Delta P_D$) is the rate of rise of preserved kinetic energy due to increase in the load followed by an increase in the frequency. The tie-line power for each area is as below:

$$\Delta P_1\left(s\right) = \Delta P_{12}\left(s\right) + a_{31}\Delta P_{31}\left(s\right) \tag{18}$$

$$\Delta P_2\left(s\right) = \Delta P_{23}\left(s\right) + a_{12}\Delta P_{12}\left(s\right) \tag{19}$$

$$\Delta P_3\left(s\right) = \Delta P_{31}\left(s\right) + a_{23}\Delta P_{23}\left(s\right) \tag{20}$$

Control of tie line bias is utilized to get rid of the steady state error in frequency in the tie-line power exchange. This shows that each one of the control areas should put in their share in frequency control, besides dealing with their own particular net interchange of power.

Let,

ACE$_1$ = area control error of area 1
ACE$_2$ = area control error of area 2
ACE$_3$ = area control error of area 3

ACE$_1$, ACE$_2$ and ACE$_3$ are shown as linear arrangement of frequency along with tie-line power error as follows:

$$ACE_1 = \Delta P_{12} + b_1\Delta f_1 \tag{21}$$

$$ACE_2 = \Delta P_{23} + b_2\Delta f_2 \tag{22}$$

$$ACE_3 = \Delta P_{31} + b_3\Delta f_3 \tag{23}$$

Figure 5. Model of single area ALFC without secondary control

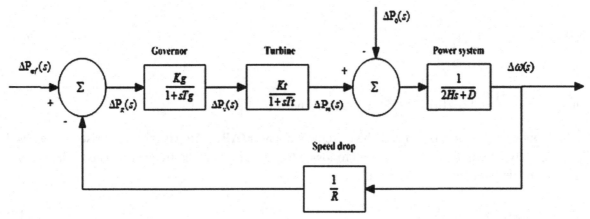

where $b_1, b_2 and b_3$ are known as area frequency bias of area 1, area 2 and area 3 respectively.

Area control error (ACE) is negative when the net power flow output from an area is very low or else when the frequency has dropped or both. During such situations we need to increase the generation.

DESIGN MODEL FOR VARIOUS SYSTEMS

Single Area System

Figure 5 shows the Automatic Load Frequency Control (ALFC) loop. The frequency which changes with load is contrasted with reference speed setting. The frequency can be set to the desired value by making generation and demand equal with the help of steam valve controller which regulate steam valve and increases power output from generators. It serves the primary/basic purpose of balancing the real power by regulating turbine output (ΔP_m) according to the variation in load demand (ΔP_0).

The transfer function of the model of the single area system as shown in Figure 1 is as below:

$$KG\left(s\right)H\left(s\right) = \frac{1}{R} \frac{1}{\left(2Hs + D\right)\left(1 + \tau_g s\right)\left(1 + \tau_T s\right)} \tag{24}$$

$$\frac{\Delta \acute{E}\left(s\right)}{-\Delta P_L\left(s\right)} = \frac{\left(1 + \tau_g s\right)\left(1 + \tau_T s\right)}{\left(2Hs + D\right)\left(1 + \tau_g s\right)\left(1 + \tau_T s\right) + 1/R} \tag{25}$$

$$\Delta\omega\left(s\right) = -\Delta P_0\left(s\right)T\left(s\right) \tag{26}$$

For the case with load which is not sensitive to frequency load (D=0):

$$\Delta \omega_{ss} = \left(-\Delta P_0\right) R \tag{27}$$

From the above equations we can get the steady state value of new system frequency which is less than the initial value. But we have to make the frequency drift ($\Delta \omega$) to zero or to an acceptable value with the help of secondary loop for stable operation. This is shown in Figure 2.

Due to change in load there is change in the steady state frequency ($\Delta \omega$) so we need another loop apart from primary loop to convey the frequency to the initial value, before the load disturbance occurs. The integral controller which is responsible in making the frequency deviation zero is put in the secondary loop as shown in Figure 2.

Therefore, the signal from $\Delta \omega \left(s\right)$ is being fed back all the way through an integrator block (1/s) to regulate ΔP_{ref} to get the frequency value to steady state. Thus $\Delta \omega \left(s\right) = 0$. Thus integral action is responsible for automatic adjustment of ΔP_{ref} making $\Delta \omega = 0$. So this act is known as Automatic Load Frequency Control transfer function with integral group is shown in Figure 6.

$$\omega = \cfrac{1}{D + \cfrac{1}{R}} \left[\Delta P_{ref} - \Delta P_0\right] \tag{28}$$

Two Area System

Two area interconnected system which is connected by tie-line for the flow of tie-line power is shown in Figure 7. Let the additional input be ΔP_{12}, ΔP_{01} be the change in load in area1 and frequencies of the two areas be

$$\Delta \omega = \Delta \omega_1 = \Delta \omega_2 \tag{29}$$

Let X_{12} be the reactance of the tie line, then power delivered from area 1 to area 2 is

$$P_{12} = \frac{\left|E_1\right|\left|E_2\right|}{X_{12}} \sin \delta_{12} \tag{30}$$

when $X_{12} = X_1 + X_{tie} + X_2$ and $\delta_{12} = \delta_1 - \delta_2$

Equation can be linearized as:

$$\Delta P_{12} = \frac{dP_{12}}{d\delta_{12}} \big|_{\delta_{12}} \Delta \delta_{12} = P_s \Delta \delta_{12} \tag{31}$$

Figure 6. Model of single area ALFC with secondary control

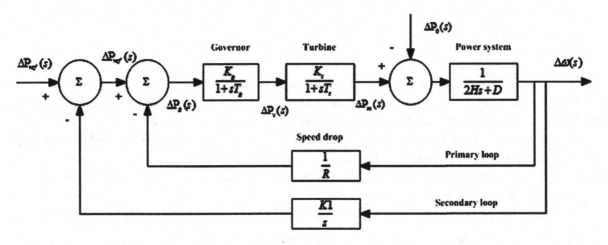

The tie-line power deviation:

$$\Delta P_{12} = P_s \left(\Delta \delta_1 - \Delta \delta_2 \right) \tag{32}$$

Figure 7. Model of two area system without secondary loop or only primary loop control

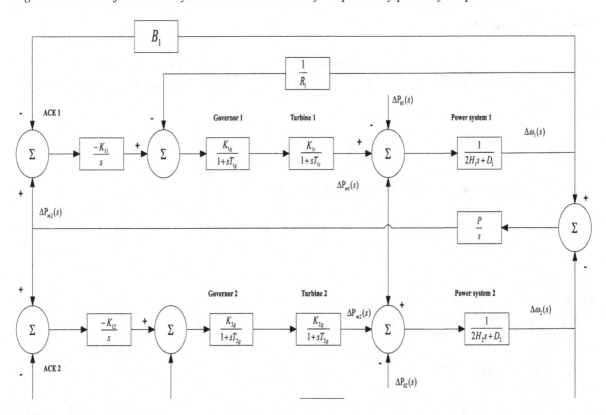

Let $\Delta\omega = \Delta\omega_1 = \Delta\omega_2$

For area 1,

$$\Delta P_{m1} - \Delta P_{12} - \Delta P_{01} = \Delta\omega D_1 \tag{33}$$

$$\Delta P_{m1} = -\Delta P_{m2} = \Delta P_{12} = \Delta\omega D_2 \tag{34}$$

For area 2,

$$\Delta P_{m1} = \frac{-\Delta\omega}{R_1} \tag{35}$$

$$\Delta P_{m2} = \frac{-\Delta\omega}{R_2} \tag{36}$$

$$\Delta P_{12} = \frac{-\Delta P_{01}\beta_1}{\beta_1 + \beta_2} \tag{37}$$

Thus increase in load in area 1 reduces the frequency of both the areas and causes the flow of tie-line power. If ΔP_{12} is negative then power flows from area 2 to area 1. Similarly, for change in load in area 2 (ΔP_{02}),

$$\Delta\omega = \frac{-\Delta P_{02}}{\beta_1 + \beta_2} \tag{38}$$

$$\Delta P_{12} = -\Delta P_{21} = \frac{-\Delta P_{02}\beta_1}{\beta_1 + \beta_2} \tag{39}$$

The secondary control basically restores balance between each area load generation which is possible by maintaining the frequency at scheduled value. This is shown in Figure 8 If there is load change in area 1 then the secondary control is in area 1 and not in area 2 so area control error (ACE) is used [1]. The ACE of two areas is given as follows

For area 1: $\text{ACE1} = \Delta P_{12} + \beta_1 \Delta\omega \tag{40}$

Figure 8. Model of two area system with secondary loop

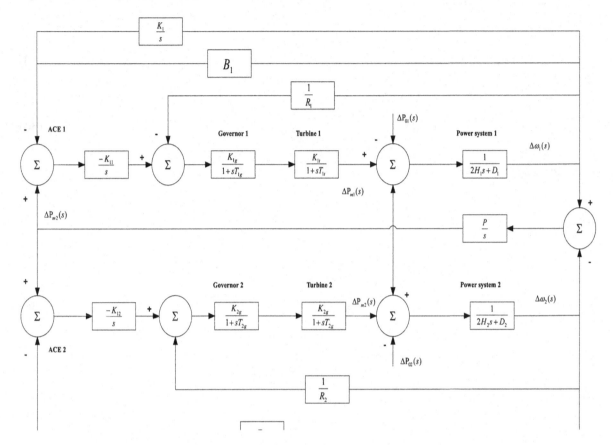

For area 2: $ACE2 = \Delta P_{21} + \beta_2 \Delta \omega$ (41)

For a total change in load of ΔP_D the steady state deviation in frequency in two areas is

$$\Delta \omega = \frac{-\Delta P_{L1}}{(\frac{1}{R_1} + D_1) + (\frac{1}{R_2} + D_2)} = \frac{-\Delta P_{L1}}{\beta_1 + \beta_2}$$ (42)

There will be one ALFC for each control area in an interconnected multi area system. ACEs are the actuating signals that activate changes in reference power set points such that ΔP_{12} and $\Delta \omega$ becomes zero when steady-state is reached.

Each area ACE is a combination of frequency and tie-line error.

$$ACEi = \sum nj = \Delta Pij + Ki\Delta \omega$$ (43)

Three Area System

The control in three area system is similar to the two area system. The integral control loop which is applied to the single area system and two area system can also be applied to the three area systems. Due to change in load there is change in the steady state frequency $\left(\Delta\omega\right)$ so we need another loop apart from primary loop to bring the frequency to the initial value, before the load disturbance occurs. This is shown in Figure 9.

The integral controller which is responsible in making the frequency deviation zero is put in the secondary loop. Three area interconnected system consists of three interconnected control areas. There is flow of tie line power as per the changes in the load demand due to the interconnection made between the control areas.

Thus the overall stability of the system is maintained at a balanced condition in spite of the constant variations in the load and load changes.

Change in frequency for the three areas is as follows:

$$\Delta f_1(s) = \frac{R_1 K_p m_1 (sT_g + 1)(sT_t + 1)}{K_p(s + Ki_1 R_1) + R_1 s(sT_g + 1)(sT_p + 1)(sT_t + 1)} \tag{44}$$

$$\Delta f_2(s) = \frac{R_2 K_p m_2 (sT_g + 1)(sT_t + 1)}{K_p(s + Ki_2 R_2) + R_2 s(sT_g + 1)(sT_p + 1)(sT_t + 1)} \tag{45}$$

$$\Delta f_3(s) = \frac{R_3 K_p m_3 (sT_g + 1)(sT_t + 1)}{K_p(s + Ki_3 R_3) + R_3 s(sT_g + 1)(sT_p + 1)(sT_t + 1)} \tag{46}$$

The tie-line power flow between three areas is as below:

$$\Delta P_{12}(s) = \frac{2\pi T^0}{s}\left[\Delta f_1(s) - \Delta f_2(s)\right] \tag{47}$$

$$\Delta P_{13}(s) = \frac{2\pi T^0}{s}\left[\Delta f_1(s) - \Delta f_3(s)\right] \tag{48}$$

$$\Delta P_{23}(s) = \frac{2\pi T^0}{s}\left[\Delta f_2(s) - \Delta f_3(s)\right] \tag{49}$$

Figure 9. Model of three area system with secondary loop

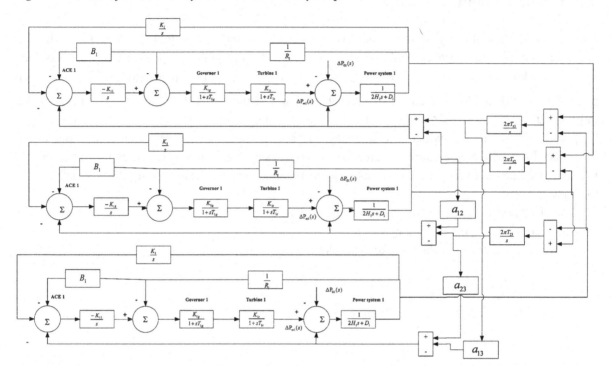

SIMULATION RESULTS OF AUTOMATIC LOAD FREQUENCY CONTROL

By using simulation models we can obtain the performance characteristics of the system very easily and quickly for analysis purposes. Below are the various systems simulink models with their respective responses plotted against time. Here we considered two area and three area systems.

Single Area System without Secondary Loop

The plot in Figure 11 which is obtained by simulating the model as shown in Figure 10 shows that the change in load causes change in speed which causes variation in frequency $\Delta\omega$. From the plot we can understand that the frequency drift will settle down to a finite value and the new operating frequency will be lower than the nominal value.

Single Area System with Secondary Loop

In Figure 12 an integral controller with a gain Ki is used to adjust the speed reference signal ΔP_{ref} (as shown in Figure 15) so that $\Delta\omega_s$ returns to zero (as shown in Figure 14). Figure 13 shows the variation in turbine output with time. The frequency drift has been made zero due to the integral loop.

Figure 10. Simulink model of single area system without secondary loop

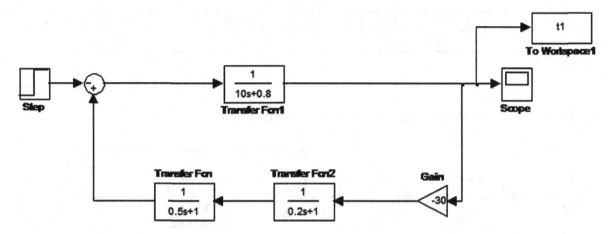

Figure 11. Frequency deviation vs. time for single area system without secondary loop

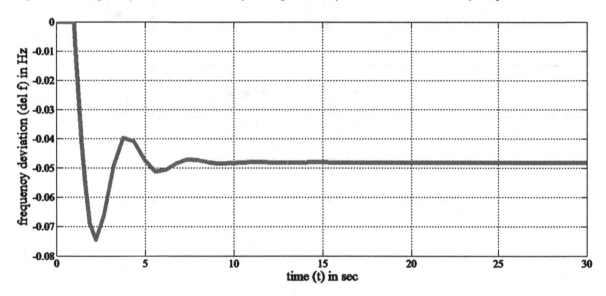

Table 1. System parameters for single area system without secondary control

Name	Kg	Tg(s)	Kt	Tt(s)	H(s)	D(puMW /Hz)	1/R
Value	1	0.20	1	0.50	5	0.80	30

Two Area System without Secondary Loop

Figure 16 shows that the two systems are interconnected so the frequency drifts of the two will settle down to equal value after some oscillations. The mechanical inputs of the two vary to reduce the mis-

Table 2. System parameters for single area system with secondary control

Name	Kg	Tg(s)	Kt	Tt(s)	H(s)	D(p.u.MW/Hz)	1/R	K1
Value	1	0.20	1	0.50	5	0.8	20	7

Figure 12. Simulink model for single area system with secondary loop

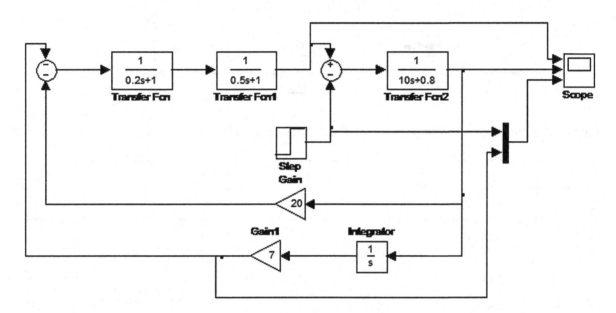

Figure 13. Change in turbine output vs. time for single area system with secondary loop

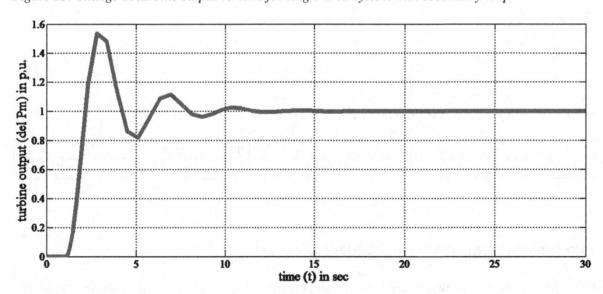

Figure 14. Change in frequency vs. time for single area system with secondary loop

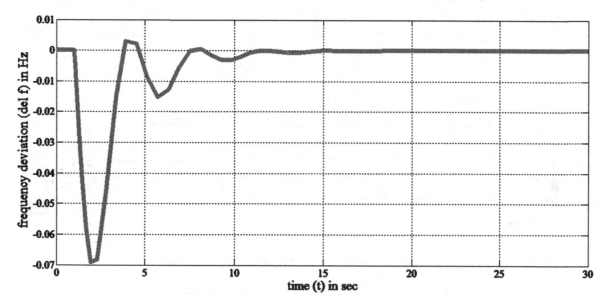

Figure 15. Incremental speed reference signal vs. time for single area with secondary loop

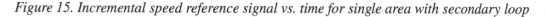
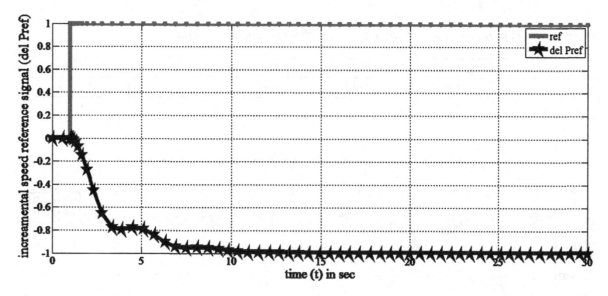

match power between electrical load in area 1 and the mechanical inputs. Area 2 will generate excess power to share the load change in area 1.

Changes in tie-line power flow can be observed with changes in load disturbance in area 1 as shown in Figure 18. Figure 17 shows that the frequency will settle to a finite value which is less than the actual frequency. Although we get same results as area 1 but stability is improved with interconnection.

Figure 16. Simulink model of two area system without secondary loop

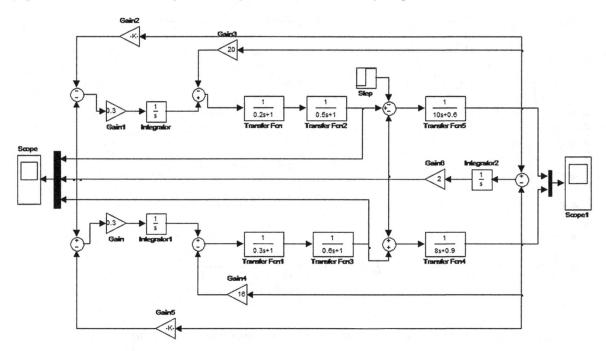

Table 3. System parameters for two area system without secondary control

Name	Kg	Tg(s)	Kt	Tt(s)	H(s)	D(p.u.MW/Hz)	1/R	ΔPL(p.u)
Area 1	1	0.20	1	0.50	5	0.60	20	0
Area 2	1	0.30	1	0.60	4	0.90	16	1

Figure 17. Frequency deviation vs. time for two area system without secondary loop

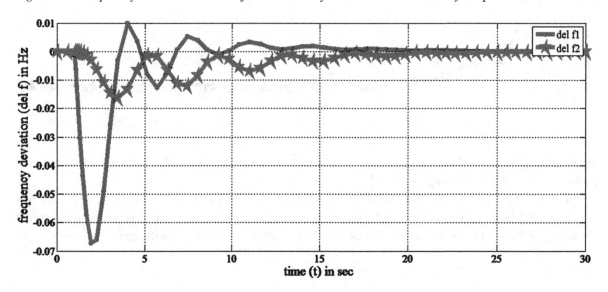

Figure 18. Change in power output vs. time for two area without secondary loop

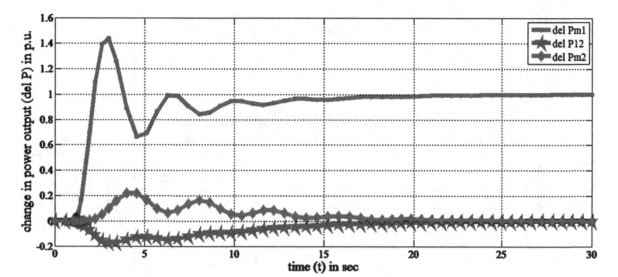

Two Area System with Secondary Loop

Two area systems with secondary loop are shown in Figure 19. The secondary loop causes the return of frequency drifts to zero as shown in Figure 20. By changing the gain of the secondary loop we can observe the change in the dynamic response of the system through tie line power as shown in Figure 21.

Three Area System without Secondary Loop

Three area interconnected systems without secondary loop is shown in Figure 22. Figure 23 shows that the frequency will settle to a finite value which is less than the actual frequency. Figure 24 shows the change in tie-line power due to the variation in the load. Here stability is improved with interconnection.

Three Area System with Secondary Loop

The model for the three area system with secondary control is shown in Figure 25. The results of the change in frequency and tie line power output with respect to time are being shown in Figure 26 and Figure 27. The system operates in a similar way to that of the two area system, taking into consideration the changes in the load.

OBSERVATION

From the above simulation plots it can be observed that the system experiences frequency drift following a load disturbance and it is mainly due to the mismatch between the electrical load and the mechanical input to the turbine. System oscillation is serious in the single area system compared to two area system because all the load change in the load is to be met by one area. Also change in frequency is brought to

Figure 19. Simulink model for two area system with secondary loop

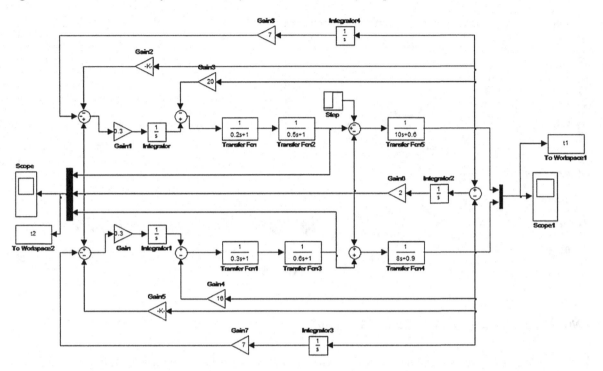

Figure 20. Frequency deviation vs. time for two area with secondary loop

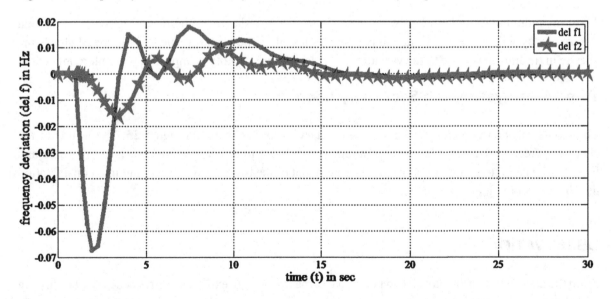

Figure 21. Change in power output vs. time for two area with secondary loop

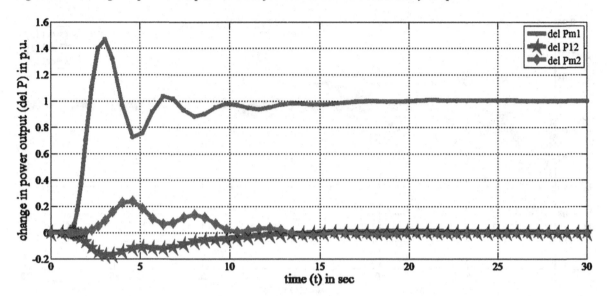

Table 4. System parameters for two area system with secondary control

Name	Kg	Tg(s)	Kt	Tt(s)	H(s)	D(p.u.MW/Hz)	1/R	ΔPL(p.u)	K1
Area 1	1	0.20	1	0.50	5	0.60	20	0	7
Area 2	1	0.30	1	0.60	4	0.90	16	1	7

Figure 22. Simulink model of three area system without secondary loop

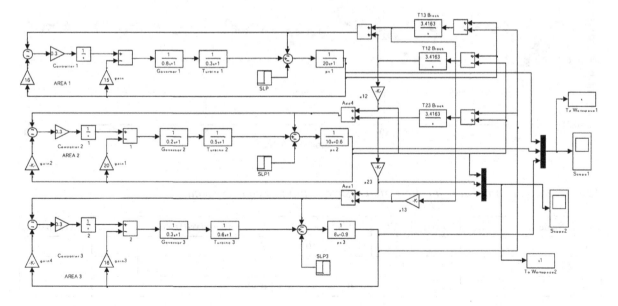

Figure 23. Frequency deviation vs. time for three area system without secondary loop

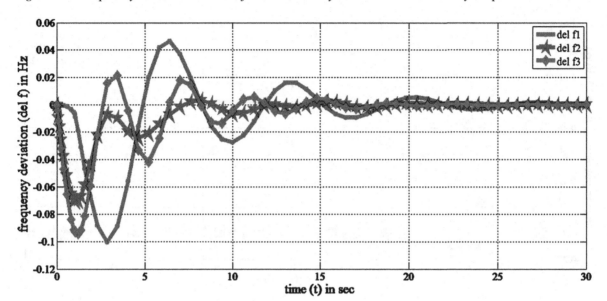

Figure 24. Tie line power deviation vs. time for three area system without secondary loop

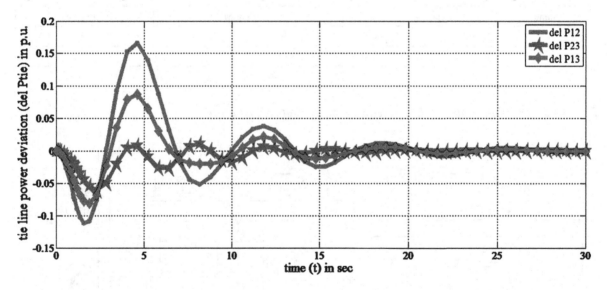

Table 5. System parameters for three area system without secondary control

Name	Kg	Tg (s)	Kt	Tt (s)	H(s)	D(p.u.MW/Hz)	1/R	ΔPL(p.u)
Area 1	1	0.80	1	0.30	10	1.00	15	1
Area 2	1	0.20	1	0.50	5	0.60	20	0
Area 3	1	0.30	1	0.60	4	0.90	16	0

Figure 25. Simulink model of three area system with secondary loop

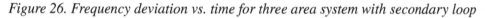

Figure 26. Frequency deviation vs. time for three area system with secondary loop

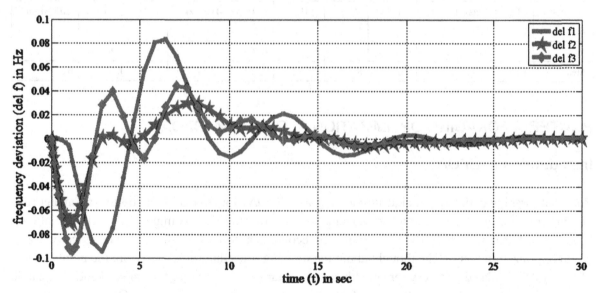

zero by using a secondary loop in both single area and two area systems. we also see that the three area system also operates in a similar manner like that of two area system.

Figure 27. Change in tie line power vs. time for three area system with secondary loop

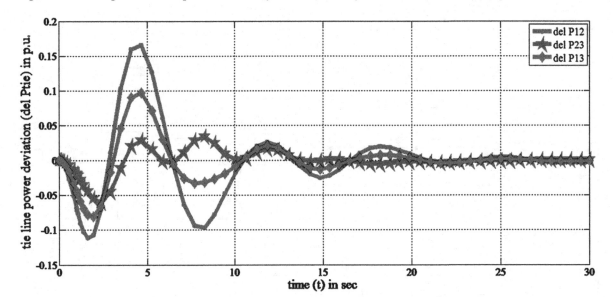

Table 6. System parameters for three area system with secondary control

Name	Kg	Tg(s)	Kt	Tt(s)	Tp (s)	H(s)	D (p.u.MW/Hz)	Ki	1/R	Δ/R.Mp.u.)
Area 1	1	0.80	1	0.30	20	10	1.00	7	17	1
Area 2	1	0.20	1	0.50	10	5	0.60	7	20	0
Area 3	1	0.30	1	0.60	8	4	0.90	7	16	0

BACTERIA FORAGING OPTIMIZATION ALGORITHM (BFOA)

Introduction of BFOA

Bacterial foraging optimization algorithmic program (BFOA) could be a global optimization algorithmic program for distributed control, management and optimization. It is impressed by the social hunt behavior of Escherichia coli. BFOA is extremely economical to find a solution for dealing with real-world optimization issues. The thought about the foraging procedure of E. coli from the point of view of biology is emulated in a very remarkable and peculiar manner and used as an easy and reasonable optimization program. Bacteria Foraging Optimization Algorithmic program (BFOA), is one amongst the many optimization algorithms those are being inspired from the nature. Following a similar trend of swarm-based algorithms, Passino presented the BFOA. Application of group hunt strategy of a swarm of E. coli bacterium in multi-optimal function optimization is the key thought of the new algorithmic program. Each bacterium looks around for nutrients in order to maximize energy obtained per unit time. Individual bacterium simultaneously communicates with others by delivering signals. A bacterium takes foraging judgment after considering two previous factors. The process when a bacterium is all set for finding the nutrients with small steps, is named as chemo taxis and key concept of BFOA is mimicking chemo tactic movement within the region of problem search for the virtual bacterium as per Saikia (2013).

Bacteria discover the direction to food in the surroundings on the basis of the gradients of chemicals. Similarly, bacterium secretes attracting and repellant chemicals into the surroundings and can discover one another in the similar way. Locomotion mechanisms (such as flagella) bacterium is used to make it able to move around in their surroundings, sometimes moving chaotically (tumbling and spinning), and other times moving in a determined path (swimming). Bacterial cells are usually treated like agents in particular surroundings, using their perception of food and various other cells as a motivating factor to move, and random tumbling and swimming like movement to re-locate. Based on the cell-cell interactions, cells may swarm a food source, and/or might directly repel or ignore one another.

Bacterial Foraging Optimization Algorithmic program is being used for minimizing a cost function. A bacterium cost is derated by its interaction with various other cells. This interaction function is calculated by using the parameters such as: a given cell, attraction coefficients, repulsion coefficients, the number of cells within the population, the number of dimensions on a given cells position vector, the number of cells maintained within the population, the number of elimination-dispersal steps, the number of reproduction steps, the number of chemo taxis steps, the number of swim steps for a given cell, a random direction vector with identical range of dimensions because the problem region, and also the probability of a cell being subjected to elimination and dispersal. Some of the Features of BFOA are

- The algorithmic program was designed for application to continuous function optimization problem domains.
- Given the loops within the algorithmic program, it can be configured in various ways to elicit completely different search behavior. It is common to possess a large number of chemo taxis iterations, and small numbers of the other iterations.
- The swarming behavior coefficients with their default values.
- The step size is usually a small fraction of the search region, such as 0.1.
- During reproduction, generally half the population having a low profile according to the health meter are discarded, and two copies of each member from the first (high-health) half of the population are being retained.
- The probability of elimination and dispersal (P_{ed}) is usually set quite high, such as 0.25.

Description

During foraging of the real bacterium, locomotion is achieved by a group of tensile flagella. Flagella facilitate an *E. coli* bacterium to undergo tumble or swim. These two are the basic operations performed by a bacterium at the time of foraging. When they rotate the flagella in the clockwise direction, every flagellum pulls on the cell such that the flagella move independently and eventually the bacterium tumbles with lesser number of tumbling whereas during a harmful place it tumbles often to seek out a nutrient gradient.

Moving the flagella in the counterclockwise direction helps the bacterium to swim at quite a very faster rate and the bacterium undergoes chemo taxis in which they prefer to move towards a nutrient gradient and avoid toxic surroundings. Typically, the bacterium moves for an extended distance during a favorable surrounding.

When they get sufficient food they elongate in length and in presence of appropriate temperature they breakdown in the middle portion to form two exact duplicates. This phenomenon shows reproduction in BFOA. Occurrence of unexpected environmental changes or attack destroys the chemo tactic progress and a set of bacteria move to another places or some other are introduced to the concerned swarm. Thus the process of elimination-dispersal takes place in the population. All the bacteria in that particular region are either killed or a group of bacteria is moved to a new location.

Thus it can be said that BFOA consists of four principal mechanisms as seen in a real bacterial system: chemo taxis, swarming, reproduction, and elimination-dispersal to resolve an optimization problem. A virtual bacterium is actually one trial answer or a search agent that moves on the functional surface to find the global optimum.

Let us consider

j = The index for the chemo tactic step
k = The index for the reproduction step
l = The index of the elimination-dispersal event
p = Dimension of the search space,
S = Total number of bacteria within the population,
Nc = The number of chemo tactic steps,
N_s = The swimming length.
N_{re}= The number of reproduction steps,
N_{ed} = The number of elimination dispersal events,
P_{ed} = Elimination-dispersal probability,
C(i) = Step size considered randomly in any direction specified by the tumble.
$P\left(j,k,l\right) = \{\theta^i\left(j,k,l\right) \mid i = 1,2,..S\}$ = Position of individual bacterium within the population of S number of bacterium at the j-th chemo tactic step, k-th reproduction step and l-th elimination-dispersal step.

The four processes in BFOA are described below:

- **Chemo Taxis**: In this process the bacteria moves in search of food in two different ways: swimming and tumbling with the help of flagella. The bacterium will swim in the predetermined direction and it will tumble by moving in different directions. By deciding upon the flagella rotation of each bacterium, the decision is made about going for swimming or tumbling in their whole lifetime. During chemo taxis the movement of the bacterium can be represented by

$$\theta^i\left(j+1,k,l\right) = \theta^i\left(j,k,l\right) + C\left(i\right)\varphi\left(i\right) \tag{50}$$

i.e.

$$\theta^i\left(j+1,k,l\right) = \theta^i\left(j,k,l\right) + C\left(i\right)\frac{\Delta\left(i\right)}{\sqrt{\Delta^T\left(i\right)\Delta\left(i\right)}} \tag{51}$$

i.e. where Δ indicates a vector in the random direction whose elements lie in [-1, 1].

- **Swarming**: During this process a group of bacteria move concentrically and arrange themselves as it moves towards the richest food location. As a result of which it attracts other bacteria and rapidly converges to a point which gives us the desired solution point. Mathematically it can be represented by the following function.

$$J_{cc}\left(\theta, P\left(j, k, l\right)\right) = \sum_{i=1}^{S} J_{cc}^{i}\left(\theta, \theta^{i}\left(j, k, l\right)\right)$$

$$= \sum_{i=1}^{S}\left[-d_{attract}\, exp\left(-\omega_{attract}\sum_{m=1}^{P}\left(\theta_m - \theta_m^i\right)^2\right)\right]$$

$$+ \sum_{i=1}^{S}\left[-h_{repelent}\, exp\left(-\omega_{repelent}\sum_{m=1}^{P}\left(\theta_m - \theta_m^i\right)^2\right)\right]$$

where

$J_{cc}\left(\theta, P\left(j, k, l\right)\right)$ = the objective function value to be added to the actual objective function (to be minimized) to show a time varying objective function

S = total number of bacteria

p = number of variables to be optimized those are present in each bacterium

$d_{attarct}, w_{attract}, h_{repelent}\ and\ w_{repelent}$ = various coefficients that must be chosen properly.

- **Reproduction**: After going through the chemo tactic process the bacteria moves on to the reproduction stage. During this process the bacteria having low health profile eventually die where as each of the healthier bacteria (those yielding lower value of the objective function) asexually split into two bacterium, which are then placed in the same location. This keeps the constant value of the population of the bacteria.

$$j_{health}^{i} = \sum_{j=1}^{N_c+1} J\left(i, j, k, l\right) \tag{52}$$

- **Elimination and Dispersal**: This process deals with the removal of bacteria as a result of gradual or unexpected changes in the local surroundings where the population of the bacteria might degrade due to various reasons like significant rise of temperature or some other sudden influence might kill a set of bacteria that are present in a particular region. Sometimes there may be some cases which might kill all the bacteria in a region or disperse a set of bacteria to a new favorable location. Rather than disturbing the whole process the bacteria can find the desired food location during this particular process only so that we can obtain the desired solution point. To simulate this event in BFOA some bacteria are being liquidated randomly with a very small probability whereas the new replacements are being initialized randomly over the region of search.

Steps for Solving a Problem Using BFO Algorithm

BFO Parameters Initialization

Algorithm for optimization:

1. Elimination-dispersal loop: $l=l+1$
2. Reproduction loop: $k=k+1$
3. Chemo taxis loop: $j=j+1$
   a. For $i=1, 2, \ldots S$ take a chemo tactic step for bacterium i and calculate fitness function, J (i, j, k, l).
   Let,

$$J_{sw}\left(i,j,k,l\right) = J\left(i,j,k,l\right) + J_{cc}\left(\theta^i\left(j,k,l\right), P\left(j,k,l\right)\right) \tag{53}$$

(i.e. add on the cell-to cell attractant–repellant profile/effect to simulate the swarming behavior)

Where, $J_{cc}(\theta, P(j,k,l)) = \sum_{i=1}^{S} J^i{}_{cc}(\theta, \theta^i(j,k,l))$

$$
\begin{aligned}
J_{cc}\left(\theta, P\left(j,k,l\right)\right) &= \sum_{i=1}^{S} J^i{}_{cc}\left(\theta, \theta^i\left(j,k,l\right)\right) \\
&= \sum_{i=1}^{S}\left[-d_{attract}\,exp\left(-\omega_{attract}\sum_{m=1}^{P}\left(\theta_m - \theta_m^i\right)^2\right)\right] \\
&+ \sum_{i=1}^{S}\left[-h_{repelent}\,exp\left(-\omega_{repelent}\sum_{m=1}^{P}\left(\theta_m - \theta_m^i\right)^2\right)\right]
\end{aligned}
$$

Let $J_{last}=J_{sw}$ (i, j, k, l) to preserve this value because we may get a better cost via a run.
End for this loop
   b. For i=1, 2,..S tumble/swim decision is taken.
   Tumble: random vector $\Delta(i)$ is generated on [-1, 1].
   Move: Let

$$\theta^i\left(j+1,k,l\right) = \theta^i\left(j,k,l\right) + C\left(i\right)\frac{\Delta\left(i\right)}{\sqrt{\Delta^T\left(i\right)\Delta\left(i\right)}} \tag{54}$$

This results in a step of size C (i) in the direction of the tumble for i-th bacterium.
Calculate J $(i, j + 1, k, l)$ and let

$$J_{sw}\left(i,j+1,k,l\right) = J\left(i,j+1,k,l\right) + J_{cc}\left(\theta^i\left(j+1,k,l\right), P\left(j+1,k,l\right)\right) \tag{55}$$

Swim

i.   Let *mswim*=0 (counter for swim length).

ii. While *mswim*< N_s (if haven't climbed down too long).
Let *mswim*=*mswim*+*1*.
If J$_{sw}$ $(i, j + 1, k, l)$ =J$_{last}$ (if doing better), let J$_{last}$ = J$_{sw}$ $(i, j + 1, k, l)$ and let

$$\theta^i \left(j+1,k,l\right) = \theta^i \left(j,k,l\right) + C\left(i\right)\frac{\Delta\left(i\right)}{\sqrt{\Delta^T\left(i\right)\Delta\left(i\right)}} \tag{56}$$

and use this θ^i $(j + 1, j, k)$ to find the new J $(i, j + 1, k, l)$.
Else, let *mswim*= N_s.
This ends the while statement.

c.   Go to next bacterium (i+1) if $i \neq S$ (i.e., go to [b] to process the successive bacterium).

4.   If $j < N_c$, go to step 3 and continue the chemo taxis process since the lifetime of the bacteria isn't over.

5.   Reproduction:

a.   For the given k and l, and for every $i = 1,2,..., S$, let

$$J^i_{health} = \sum_{j=1}^{N_c+1} J_{sw}\left(i, j, k, l\right) \tag{57}$$

be the health of the bacterium i (a quantity of the number of nutrients it got over its lifespan and how efficient it was at avoiding toxic substances). Arrange bacteria and chemotactic parameters C (i) in order of ascending cost J_{health} (higher cost means that lower health).

b.   The $S_r = S / 2$ bacterium with the maximum J_{health} values die and the remaining S_r bacteria with the best values split (this method is performed by the copies that are placed at the same location as their parent).

6.   If $k < N_{re}$, go to step 3 because we haven't reached the specified number of reproduction steps and therefore we begin the next generation of the chemotactic loop.

7.   Elimination-dispersal: For $i = 1,2..., S$ with probability *Ped* every bacterium is eliminated and dispersed so as to keeps the quantity of bacteria in the population to a constant value. During this process if a bacterium is eliminated then simply disperse another one to a random location on the optimization domain. If l = Ned then move on to step 2 else end it.

8.   Obtain the optimized values of the parameters.

9.   Employ BFO for final updating of the various parameters as desired in the system.

The flow chart for the Bacteria Foraging Optimization algorithm is as below in the Figure 28

Application of BFOA to Three Area Power System

The effective application of bacteria foraging (BF) to optimize many vital parameters in automatic load frequency control (ALFC) of interconnected three unequal area thermal systems, like integral controller

Figure 28. Flowchart of the Bacteria Foraging Algorithmic program

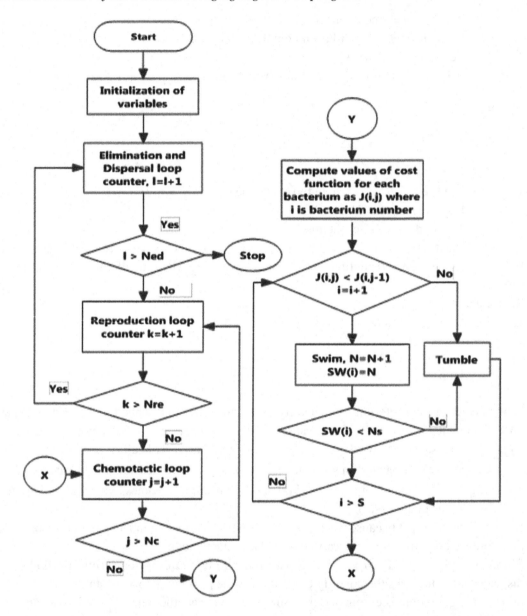

gains for the secondary control, governor speed regulation parameters for primary control and frequency bias parameters. BF algorithmic program is very fast to optimize the various parameters which results in reduction in computational burden and giving rise to minimal computer resource utilization. Simultaneous optimization of Ki, Ri and Bi parameters provides not only the best dynamic response for the system but also make it possible for us to use much higher values of R which will prove to be helpful to the power industries for easier and cheaper realization of governor.

An electric energy system should be maintained at a desired operational level characterized by desired frequency, voltage and load flow. This is often achieved by close control and management of real and reactive powers generated through the manageable supply of the system. Automatic generation control

(AGC) or Automatic load frequency control (ALFC) plays a major role in the power grid by maintaining scheduled system frequency and tie line flow throughout the course of normal operating condition and also through small perturbations. Numerous investigations of isolated and interconnected power systems is being performed and presented in the past.

For any optimization technique the convergence and also the optimal value achieved are necessary. Classical integral or proportional integral controllers considering integral sq. error (ISE) criterion for optimization of their gains are quite in trend. The optimization of gains for such classical controller is sort of involved and time taking process.

When the number of parameters to be optimized is large enough, classical technique for optimization is never chosen. Some authors have used genetic algorithmic program (GA) to optimize controller gains of a multi-area AGC system at the same time a lot more effectively than is feasible with traditional approach. Here the optimization of parameters of secondary control, primary control and frequency bias is being carried out simultaneously for an AGC system so as to explore and examine their optimum values for every area under consideration and their specific impact on the complete dynamics of the system as compared to the case when only secondary control gains is being optimized, considering values of governor speed regulation parameters (Ri) and frequency bias parameters (Bi) same as generally employed in reality. Optimization of parameters simultaneously at the same time additionally throws new findings for governor operation and layout.

To overcome the chances of being captured into local minima, only two operations crossover and mutation is being performed. Recent research and analysis has brought to notice some deficiencies in GA performance i.e. the premature convergence of GA degrades its efficiency and reduces search capability. To get out of this problem a more advanced and powerful computational intelligence technique bacterial foraging (BF) is employed where we have the number of parameters used for searching the whole solution space is far more higher compared to those in GA and therefore the chance of overriding local minimum in BF is far more higher than in GA. BF technique in the meantime has been applied successfully in a number of the areas of electrical engineering where the superiority of BF over GA is shown clearly.

Thus we've got the application of BF technique for simultaneous optimization of many parameters like integral controller gains (KIi), for secondary control, governor speed regulation parameters (Ri) for primary control loops and frequency bias parameters (Bi) for AGC of a three unequal area thermal power grid. It provides through analysis of the dynamic responses and compares them with those obtained with simultaneous optimization of KIi only (keeping Ri and Bi at values used in practice) or simultaneous optimization of KIi and Ri only (keeping Bi at values used in practice) such that one can explore what valuable findings are lost when we aren't optimizing all the parameters (KIi, Ri, and Bi) at the same time. The performance of BF technique is seen.

System Investigated

Investigations have been dispensed on three unequal area systems. The systems are designed with single reheat turbines, integral controllers. MATLAB version 7.01 has been used to acquire dynamic responses. During the modeling of interconnected areas of unequal capacities, the quantities $a_{12} = -P_{r1} / P_{r2}$, $a_{23} = -P_{r2} / P_{r3}$ and $a_{13} = -P_{r1} / P_{r3}$ are taken into account. The thought given by Elgerd and Fosha [4] has been used for modeling the system. The transfer function model of a three-area system is shown in Figure 29.

Figure 29. Model of a three-area thermal system

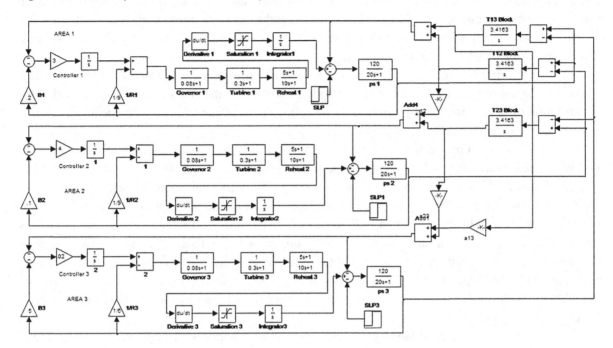

SIMULATION RESULTS AND DISCUSSIONS

Three cases are being considered for the study and examination of the three area system based on the number of parameters that are being optimized at a time using the bacteria foraging technique. These are as follows:

CASE A: Here only one parameter is optimized i.e. the integral gains (KIi) of the three areas are only optimized and the values of speed regulation parameter Ri=2.4 and frequency bias setting Bi=βi=0.425 for three areas respectively.

CASE B: Here two parameters are optimized i.e. the integral gains (KIi) and also the values of speed regulation parameter (Ri) for the three areas are optimized. The frequency bias setting for the three areas is Bi=βi=0.425 respectively.

CASE C: Here there is simultaneous optimization of all the three parameters, the integral gains (KIi), the values of speed regulation parameter (Ri) and also the frequency bias setting (Bi) which is usually considered equal to βi.

$$J = cost = \int_{0}^{T} \left\{ \left(\Delta f_i\right)^2 + \left(\Delta P_{tiei-j}\right)^2 \right\} dt$$

In case A just one of the parameters i.e. integral control gain of the system is being optimized for the three areas and the remaining two parameters are kept constant. In case of case B two parameters

Figure 30. Frequency deviation in area 1 vs. time

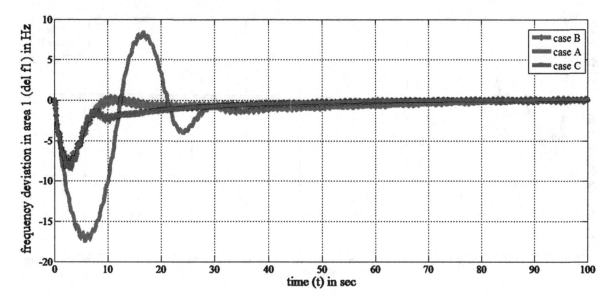

Figure 31. Frequency deviation in area 2 vs. time

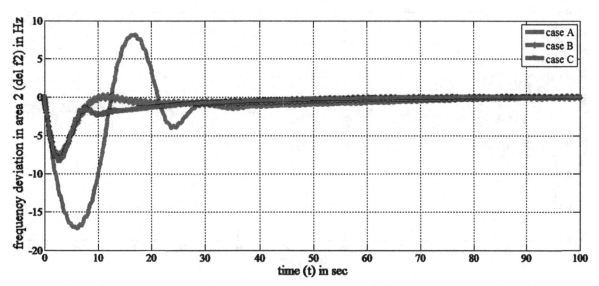

are optimized viz. integral control gain and speed regulation constant for the three areas and also the frequency bias parameter is kept constant. In case of case C all the three parameters for the three area system is being optimized. Frequency deviations of area 1, area2 and area3 for all the three cases are shown in Figure 30, Figure 31 and Figure 32 respectively.

Tie line power flow between area 1-2, area 2-3 and area 1-3 are shown in Figure 33, Figure 34 and Figure 35 respectively. By examination and comparison of the responses for the three cases viz. case A, case B and case C we are able to say that we obtained the best results in case C where the values of all the three parameters are optimized. This can be said in view of settling time, peak deviation and

Figure 32. Frequency deviation in area 3 vs. time

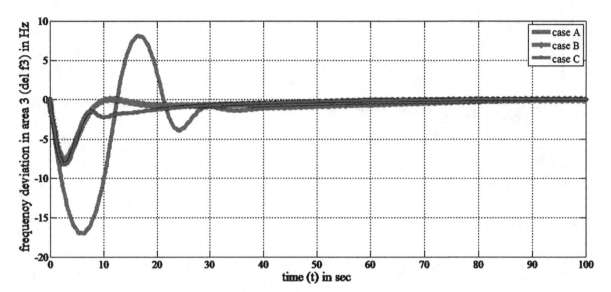

Figure 33. Tie line power deviation connecting area 1 and 2 vs. time

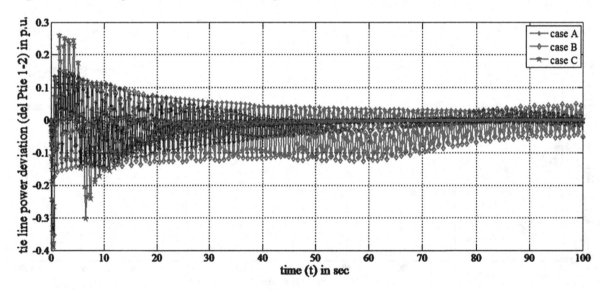

oscillation value. Also in case C we see that the settling time is reduced as compared to case A and case B. at the same time the deviation and oscillation value is reduced to a greater extent. Additionally, we observe that quiet higher values of R can be thought of in case of simultaneous optimization of the three parameters. Therefore, we've the best dynamic response of the system. The importance of optimizing the value of Bi rather than making it equal to βa_i is also seen.

The convergence characteristics of bacteria foraging technique is shown in Figure 36 by considering the x-axis to be the number of J evaluations and the y-axis to be the minimum value of J. The calculation of J takes most of the computation time; thus the number of J evaluation is almost equal to the scaled value of computational time. The convergence characteristic is also fast.

Figure 34. Tie line power deviation connecting area 2 and 3 vs. time

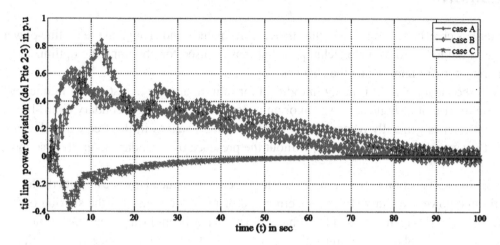

Figure 35. Deviation of tie line power connecting area 1 and 3 vs. time

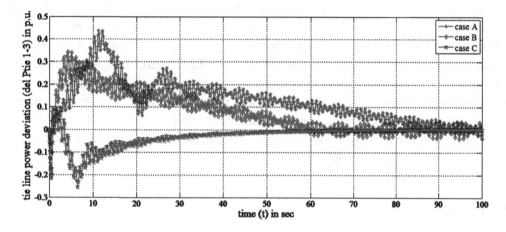

Figure 36. Convergence characteristics of BF algorithm

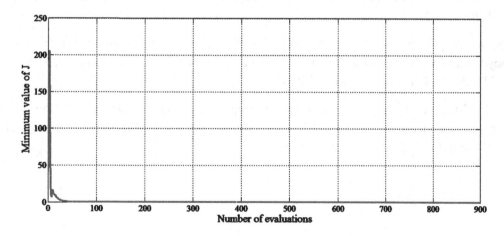

CONCLUSION

The chapter has chiefly investigated on the change in frequency and change in the tie line power due to the change in the load and also the techniques that may be used for obtaining the optimized values of various parameters for minimizing the changes.

Firstly, a secondary control is being introduced for minimizing the deviations in frequency. This is usually vital in case of a single area system or an isolated system as the secondary control loop i.e. an integral controller is generally responsible for reducing the changes in the frequency deviations and maintains the system stability. Therefore, without the presence of secondary loop the system losses its stability.

Secondly interconnection of two or more systems is being introduced to cope up with the load changes through tie line power exchange. Interconnecting two or more areas ensures the sharing of the power among the systems during the times of load changes which may occur in any area at any time. Therefore, the burden on the controllers to minimize the changes in the frequency is reduced as a result of the rise in the power demand can be fulfilled by drawing power from the neighboring areas and thus maintains the stability of the system.

Thirdly there's introduction of an optimization technique i.e. Bacteria Foraging Optimization Algorithmic program to change the values of the various parameters present in the power system under investigation so it can cope up with the changes in the load demand. As a result of which the changes in the frequency and also the tie line power is reduced and also the stability of the system is maintained. It is also seen that BF technique has quicker convergence characteristics. BF technique serves to be quite useful for obtaining the optimized values of the various parameters as compared to the general hit and trial technique which is extremely tedious and time taking method.

The investigations have been done for single area system, two area systems and three area systems and the result is being given accordingly.

REFERENCES

Ali, E. S., & Abd-Elazim, S. M. (2011). Bacteria foraging optimization algorithm based load frequency controller for interconnected power system. *Electrical Power Energy System*, *33*(3), 633–638. doi:10.1016/j.ijepes.2010.12.022

Ali, E. S., & Abd-Elazim, S. M. (2013). BFOA based Design of PID Controller for Two Area Load Frequency Control with Nonlinearities. *International Journal of Electrical Power & Energy Systems*, *51*, 224–231. doi:10.1016/j.ijepes.2013.02.030

Bevrani, H., Mitani, Y., & Tsuji, K. (2004). Robust decentralized load frequency control using an iterative linear matrix inequalities algorithm. *IEE Proceedings. Generation, Transmission and Distribution*, *151*(3), 347–354. doi:10.1049/ip-gtd:20040493

Elgerd, O., & Fosha, C. (1970). Optimal megawatt frequency control of multi area electric energy systems. *IEEE Trans Electric Power Apparatus System*, *89*, 63–556.

Elgerd, O. (2000). Electric energy systems theory- an introduction (2nd ed.). Tata McGraw Hill

Fosha, C. E., & Elgerd, O. (1970). The megawatt-frequency control problem: A new approach via optimal control theory. *IEEE Transactions on Power Systems*, *89*(4), 563–577. doi:10.1109/TPAS.1970.292603

Mohammad, T. H. (2013). Robust multivariable predictive based load frequency control considering generation rate constant. *International Journal of Electrical Power & Energy Systems*, *46*, 405–413. doi:10.1016/j.ijepes.2012.10.039

Nagrath, I. J., & Kothari, D. P. (1993). *Modern power system analysis*. TMH.

Nanda, J., Mishra, S., & Saikia, L. C. (2009). Maiden Application of Bacterial Foraging Based Optimization Technique in Multiarea Automatic Generation Control. *IEEE Transactions on Power Systems*, *22*(2), 602–609. doi:10.1109/TPWRS.2009.2016588

Padhan, D. G., & Majhi, S. (2013). A new control scheme for PID load frequency controller of single area and multi area power systems. *ISA Transactions*, *52*(2), 242–251. doi:10.1016/j.isatra.2012.10.003 PMID:23141877

Rout, U. K., Sahu, R. K., & Panda, S. (2013). Design and analysis of differential evolution algorithm based automatic generation control for interconnected power system. *Ain Shams Engineering Journal*, *4*(3), 409–419. doi:10.1016/j.asej.2012.10.010

Saikia, L. C., & Sahu, S. K. (2013). Automatic Generation Control of a combined cycle gas turbine plant with classical controllers using firefly algorithm. *International Journal of Electrical Power & Energy Systems*, *53*, 27–33. doi:10.1016/j.ijepes.2013.04.007

Tan, W. (2010). Unified tuning of PID load frequency controller for power systems via IMC. *IEEE Transactions on Power Systems*, *25*(1), 341–350. doi:10.1109/TPWRS.2009.2036463

Usman, A., & Divakar, B. P. (2012). Simulation study of load frequency control of single and two area systems. *Proceedings of theIEEE Global Humanitarian Technology Conference* (pp. 214-219). doi:10.1109/GHTC.2012.38

Zang, Y. (2007). Load Frequency Control of Multiple-Area Power Systems [Master of Science in Electrical Engineering]. Tsinghua University.

KEY TERMS AND DEFINITIONS

AGC: Automatic Generation Control
ALFC: Automatic Load Frequency Controller
Area Control Error (ACE): It is the difference between scheduled and actual electrical generation within a control area on the power grid, taking frequency bias into account.

Chemo Taxis: In this process of BFO, the bacteria move in search of food in two different ways: swimming and tumbling with the help of flagella.

Control Area: a control area is defined as a power system, a part of a power system or a combination of systems to which a common generation control scheme is applied.

Elimination and Dispersal: This process of BFO deals with the removal of bacteria as a result of gradual or unexpected changes in the local surroundings.

Reproduction: During this process of BFO, the bacteria having low health profile eventually die whereas each of the healthier bacteria asexually split into two bacterium

Tie-Line: A Tie line is a connecting line between two control areas in a power system.

Chapter 17
Solution of Some Differential Equation in Fuzzy Environment by Extension Principle Method and Its Application in Biomathematics

Sankar Prasad Mondal
National Institute of Technology, India

ABSTRACT

The concept of fuzzy differential equations is very important for new developments of model in various fields of science and engineering problems in uncertain environments because this theory represent a natural way to modeling dynamical system under uncertain environment. In this way we can modeled mathematical biology problem associated with differential equation in fuzzy environment and solved them. In this chapter we solve two mathematical biology models which are taken in fuzzy environment. A one species prey predator model is considered with fuzzy initial data. Whereas an insect population model are described with fuzzy initial value. The solution procedures of the fuzzy differential equation are taken as extension principle method.

1. INTRODUCTION

1.1 Fuzzy Differential Equation

The topic "fuzzy differential equation" (FDE) has been speedily developing in recent years. The appliance of fuzzy differential equations is an inherent way to model dynamic systems under possibilistic uncertainty (Zadeh (2005)). The concept of the fuzzy derivative was first initiated by Chang and Zadeh (1972). It was followed up by Dubois and Prade (1982). Other methods have been smeared by Puri and Ralescu (1983) and Goetschel and Voxman (1986). The concept of differential equations in a fuzzy envi-

DOI: 10.4018/978-1-5225-0427-6.ch017

ronment was first formulated by Kaleva (1987). In fuzzy differential equation all derivative is deliberated as either Hukuhara or generalized derivatives. The Hukuhara differentiability has a deficiency (Bede et al., 2005; Diamond et al., 1994). The solution turns fuzzier as time goes by. Bede (2006) exhibited that a large class of BVPs has no solution if the Hukuhara derivative is applied. To exceeds this difficulty, the concept of a generalized derivative was developed (Bede & Gal, 2005; Cano & Flores, 2008) and fuzzy differential equations were smeared using this concept (Bede & Rudas, 2007; Cano et al., 2007; Cano et al., 2008; Stefanini & Bede, 2009). Khastan and Nieto (2010) set up the solutions for a large enough class of boundary value problems using the generalized derivative. Obviously the disadvantage of strongly generalized differentiability of a function in comparison H-differentiability is that, a fuzzy differential equation has no unique solution (Bede & Gal, 2005). Recently, Stefanini and Bede (2008) by the concept of generalization of the Hukuhara difference for compact convex set, introduced generalized Hukuhara differentiability (Stefanini & Bede, 2009) for fuzzy valued function and they displayed that, this concept of differentiability has relationships with weakly generalized differentiability and strongly generalized differentiability.

There are many approaches for solving FDE. Some researchers transform the FDE into equivalent fuzzy integral equation and then solve this (Allahviranloo et al., 2011; Chen et al., 2008; Regan et al., 2003). Another one is Zadeh extension principle method. In this method first solve the associated ODE and lastly fuzzify the solution and check whether it is satisfied or not. For details see Buckley and Feuring (2000, 2001). In the third approach, the fuzzy problem is converted to a crisp problem. Hüllermeier (1997), uses the concept of differential inclusion. In this way, by taking an α-cut of the initial value and the solution, the given differential equation is converted to a differential inclusion and the solution is accepted as the α-cut of the fuzzy solution. Laplace transform method is use many where in linear FDE (Allahviranloo & Ahmadi, 2010; Tolouti & Ahmadi, 2010). Recently, Mondal and Roy (2013) solve the first order Linear FDE by Lagrange multiplier method. Using generalized Hukuhara differentiability concept we transform the given FDE into two ODEs. And this ODEs also a differential equation involving the parametric form of a fuzzy number.

1.2 Work Done on Biomathematics Problem in Fuzzy Environment

In Barros et al. (2000) take fuzzy population dynamics model with fuzzy initial value and solve the problem. Akin and Oruc (2012) consider a prey predator model with fuzzy initial value. Here they solve the equation by generalized derivative of fuzzy function concept. Zarei et al. (2012) give a formulation on fuzzy HIV modeling. Diniz et al. (2001) consider a fuzzy Cauchy problem and apply in the behavior of decay of the biochemical oxygen demand in water. Nounou et al. (2012) discuss fuzzy intervention in biological phenomena. Fuzzy delay predator-prey system and their existence theorem and oscillation property of solution is nicely delivered by Barzinji (2014). Symptomatic HIV virus infected population with fuzzy concept is done by Jafelice et al (2004). The interaction of predator prey with uncertain initial population sizes was considered in Omar et al. (2011). Predator–prey fuzzy model is solved by Peixoto (2008) by fuzzy rule base method. Ahmad et al. (2012) solve a biological population model by numerical method, Euler's method. Here system of fuzzy differential equation is solved. Zaini and Baets (2009), solve the predator-prey model with fuzzy initial populations by Runge-Kutta method. Optimal control of HIV infection by using fuzzy dynamical systems is discussed by Najariyan et al. (2011). Mann et al. (2013) use delay differential equation in predator-prey interaction and analysis on the stability of steady state. Pal and Mahapatra (2014) solve a bio-economic modeling of two-prey and one-predator fishery model with optimal harvesting policy through hybridization approach. They solve the differential equation in interval and fuzzy environment whereas Pal et al. (2013a) take optimal harvesting of prey–predator system with interval biological parameters. Pandit et al. (2014) solve Prey predator model with fuzzy initial conditions. Quota harvesting model for a single species population under fuzziness is discuss by Pal et al. (2013b). Tapaswani and Chakraverty (2013) solve the fuzzy arbitrary order predator-prey equations by Homotopy perturbation method. A Proportional harvesting dynamical model with fuzzy intrinsic growth rate and harvesting quantity is taken by Pal et al. (2012).

1.3 Motivation

Impreciseness can become in every model for biological systems. The necessity for taking some parameter as imprecise in a model is important topic today. There are so many works done on biological model with imprecise data. Some-times parameters are taken as fuzzy sometime it is interval. Our main aim is modeled a biological problem associated with differential equation with some imprecise parameters and solve them.

1.4 Novelties

Although some developments are done but some new interest and new work have done here which is mentioned bellow:

1.   How a differential equation is solved in fuzzy environment is addressed here.
2.   Biological system can be modeled in imprecise environment i.e.; fuzzy environment is discussed briefly.
3.   Finding the solution of differential equation in fuzzy environment by extension principle method.
4.   Fuzzy predator-prey model for a one species system is solved in fuzzy environment.
5.   Fuzzy Insect population model is solved in fuzzy environment.

Moreover, we can say the all developments can help for the researchers who engage with uncertainty modeling, differential equation and its application.

1.5 Structure of the Chapter

In first section we give introduction on related work. Second section belongs to preliminaries. In third section we define fuzzy differential equation. Fourth section belongs to the solution procedure. The differentiability and extension principle approach is addressed here. In section fifth we consider two bio mathematical models in fuzzy environment and solve by extension principle method. After these the future research scope on the topic is also described. And lastly the conclusion part is there.

2. PRELIMINARIES

2.1 Fuzzy Sets and Number

Definition 2.1: Fuzzy Set: A fuzzy set $\bar{A}$ is defined by $A = \left\{ \left(x, \mu_{A}(x) \right) : x \in A, \mu_{A}(x) \in [0,1] \right\}$. In the

pair $\left(x, \mu_{A}(x) \right)$ the first element x belong to the classical set A, the second element $\mu_{A}(x)$,

belong to the interval $[0,1]$, called Membership function.

Definition 2.2: α**-Cut of a Fuzzy Set**: The α-evel set (or interval of confidence at level α or α-cut) of the fuzzy set $\tilde{A}$ of X is a crisp set A_{α} that contains all the elements of X that have membership

values in $\bar{A}$ greater than or equal to α i.e.,.

Definition 2.3: Fuzzy Number: (Zadeh (2005)) A fuzzy number is fuzzy set like $u : R \to I = [0,1]$

which satisfies

1. u is upper semi-continuous.
2. $u(x) = 0$ outside the interval $[c,d]$
3.   There are real numbers a, b such $c \leq a \leq b \leq d$ and
   3.1. $u(x)$ is monotonic increasing on $[c,a]$,
   3.2. $u(x)$ is monotonic decreasing on $[b,d]$,
   3.3. $u(x) = 1$, $a \leq x \leq b$

Let E^{1} be the set of all real fuzzy numbers which are normal, upper semi-continuous, convex and compactly supported fuzzy sets.

Definition 2.4: Fuzzy Number (Parametric Form): (Chang and Zadeh (1972)) A fuzzy number u in a parametric form is a pair (u_{1}, u_{2}) of function $u_{1}(r), u_{2}(r), 0 \leq r \leq 1$, which satisfies the following requirements:

1. $u_{1}(r)$ is a bounded monotonic increasing left continuous function,
2. $u_{2}(r)$ is a bounded monotonic decreasing left continuous function,
3. $u_{1}(r) \leq u_{2}(r), 0 \leq r \leq 1$.

A crisp number x is simply represented by $\left(u_{1}(r), u_{2}(r) \right) = (x, x), 0 \leq r \leq 1$. By appropriate definitions, the fuzzy number space $\{ \left(u_{1}(r), u_{2}(r) \right) \}$ becomes a convex cone E^{1} which could be embedded isomorphically and isometrically into a Banach space.

Definition 2.5: (Goetschel and Voxman (1986)) Let $x = \left(x_{1}(r), x_{2}(r) \right), y = \left(y_{1}(r), y_{2}(r) \right) \in E^{1}$, $0 \leq r \leq 1$ and arbitrary $k \in R$.

Then

$x = y$ iff $x_{1}(r) = y_{1}(r)$ and $x_{2}(r) = y_{2}(r)$,

1. $x + y = \left(x_1\left(r \right) + y_1\left(r \right), x_2\left(r \right) + y_2\left(r \right) \right),$

2. $x - y = \left(x_1\left(r \right) - y_2\left(r \right), x_2\left(r \right) - y_1\left(r \right) \right),$

3. $kx = \begin{cases} \left(kx_1\left(r \right), kx_2\left(r \right) \right), k \geq 0 \\ \left(kx_2\left(r \right), kx_1\left(r \right) \right), k < 0 \end{cases}$

Definition 2.6: (Kaleva (1987)) For arbitrary $u = \left(u_1, u_2 \right)$, $v = \left(v_1, v_2 \right) \in E^1$, the quantity

$$D\left(u, v \right) = \left[\int\limits_0^1 \left(u_1 - v_1 \right)^2 + \int\limits_0^1 \left(u_2 - v_2 \right)^2 \right]^{\frac{1}{2}}$$

is the distance between fuzzy numbers u and v.

Definition 2.7: Triangular Fuzzy Number: A Triangular fuzzy number (TFN) denoted by A is defined as (a, b, c) where the membership function

$$\mu_{\tilde{A}}\left(x \right) = \begin{cases} 0, x \leq a \\ \dfrac{x - a}{b - a}, a \leq x \leq b \\ 1, x = b \\ \dfrac{c - x}{c - b}, b \leq x \leq c \\ 0, x \geq c \end{cases}$$

Definition 2.8: α-**Cut of a Fuzzy Set** A: The α-cut of $A = (a, b, c)$ is given by

$$A_\alpha = \left[a + \alpha\left(b - a \right), c - \alpha\left(c - b \right) \right], \forall \alpha \in \left[0, 1 \right]$$

Definition 2.9: Generalized Fuzzy Number (GFN): Generalized Fuzzy number $\tilde{A}$ as

$A = (a_1, a_2, a_3, a_4; \omega)$, where $0 < \omega \leq 1$, and a_1, a_2, a_3, a_4 $(a_1 < a_2 < a_3 < a_4)$ are real numbers. The generalized fuzzy number $\tilde{A}$ is a fuzzy subset of real line R, whose membership function $\mu_{\tilde{A}}\left(x \right)$ satisfies the following conditions:

1. $\mu_{\tilde{A}}\left(x \right) = R \rightarrow \left[0,\ 1 \right]$

2. $\mu_{\tilde{A}}\left(x \right) = 0$ for $x \leq a_1$

3. $\mu_{\underset{A}{.}}\left(x\right)$ is strictly increasing function for $a_1 \leq x \leq a_2$

4. $\mu_{\underset{A}{.}}\left(x\right) = w$ for $a_2 \leq x \leq a_3$

5. $\mu_{\underset{A}{.}}\left(x\right)$ is strictly decreasing function for $a_3 \leq x \leq a_4$

6. $\mu_{\underset{A}{.}}\left(x\right) = 0$ for $a_4 \leq x$

Definition 2.10: Generalized TFN: If $a_2 = a_3$ then A is called a GTFN as $A = (a_1, a_2, a_4; \omega)$ or

$(a_1, a_3, a_4; \omega)$ with membership function $\mu_{\underset{A}{.}}\left(x\right) = \begin{cases} \omega \dfrac{x - a_1}{a_2 - a_1} & if a_1 \leq x \leq a_2 \\ \omega \dfrac{a_4 - x}{a_4 - a_2} & if a_2 \leq x \leq a_4 \\ 0 otherwise \end{cases}$

Definition 2.11: (Bede, 2006) Let $x, y \in E^1$. If there exists $z \in E^1$ such that $x = y + z$, then z is called the Hukuhara-difference of fuzzy numbers x and y, and it denoted by $z = x \ominus y$.

Remark that $x \ominus y \neq x + \left(-1\right) y$.

2.2 Fuzzy Derivative

Definition 2.12: (Bede and Gal (2005)) Let $f : \left[a, b\right] \to E^1$ and $t_0 \in \left[a, b\right]$. We say that f is Hukuhara differential at t_0, if there exist an element $f'\left(t_0\right) \in E^1$ such that for all $h > 0$ sufficiently small, there exists $f\left(t_0 + h\right) \ominus f\left(t_0\right)$, $f\left(t_0\right) \ominus f\left(t_0 - h\right)$ and the limits exists in metric D.

$$\lim_{h \to 0} \frac{f\left(t_0 + h\right) \ominus f\left(t_0\right)}{h} = \lim_{h \to 0} \frac{f\left(t_0\right) \ominus f\left(t_0 - h\right)}{h} = f'\left(t_0\right)$$

Definition 2.13: (Cano & Flores, 2008) Let $f : (a, b) \times E \to E$ and $x_0 \in \left(a, b\right)$. We say that f is strongly generalized differential at x_0 (Bede-Gal differential) if there exists an element $f'\left(x_0\right) \in E$, such that

For all $h > 0$ sufficiently small, there exist $f\left(x_0 + h\right) -^h f\left(x_0\right)$ and $f\left(x_0\right) -^h f\left(x_0 - h\right)$ and the limits exist in the metric D

$$\lim_{h \searrow 0} \frac{f\left(x_0 + h\right) -^h f\left(x_0\right)}{h} = \lim_{h \searrow 0} \frac{f\left(x_0\right) -^h f\left(x_0 - h\right)}{h} = f'\left(x_0\right)$$

or

For all $h > 0$ sufficiently small, there exist $f(x_0) -^h f(x_0 + h)$ and $f(x_0 - h) -^h f(x_0)$ and the limits exist in the metric D

$$\lim_{h \searrow 0} \frac{f(x_0) -^h f(x_0 + h)}{-h} = \lim_{h \searrow 0} \frac{f(x_0 - h) -^h f(x_0)}{-h} = f'(x_0)$$

or

For all $h > 0$ sufficiently small, there exist $f(x_0 + h) -^h f(x_0)$, and $f(x_0 - h) -^h f(x_0)$ and the limits exist in the metric D

$$\lim_{h \searrow 0} \frac{f(x_0 + h) -^h f(x_0)}{h} = \lim_{h \searrow 0} \frac{f(x_0 - h) -^h f(x_0)}{-h} = f'(x_0)$$

or

For all $h > 0$ sufficiently small, there exist $f(x_0) -^h f(x_0 + h)$ and $f(x_0) -^h f(x_0 - h)$ and the limits exists in the metric D

$$\lim_{h \searrow 0} \frac{f(x_0) -^h f(x_0 + h)}{-h} = \lim_{h \searrow 0} \frac{f(x_0) -^h f(x_0 - h)}{h} = f'(x_0)$$

(h and $-h$ at denominators mean $\dfrac{1}{h}$ and $-\dfrac{1}{h}$, respectively).

Definition 2.14: (Bede et al. (2007)) Let $f : R \to E$ be a function and denote $f(t) = \left(f_1(t, r), f_2(t, r) \right)$, for each $r \in [0, 1]$. Then

1. If f is (i)-differentiable, then $f_1(t, r)$ and $f_2(t, r)$ are also differentiable function and
   $$f'(t) = \left(f_1'(t, r), f_2'(t, r) \right)$$
2. If f is (ii)-differentiable, then $f_1(t, r)$ and $f_2(t, r)$ are also differentiable function and
   $$f'(t) = (f_2'(t, r), f_1'(t, r))$$

Definition 2.15: (Cano et al., 2007, 2008) Let $f : (a, b) \times E \to E$ and $x_0 \in (a, b)$. We define the nth-order derivative of f as follows: we say f is strongly generalized differentiable of the nth-order at x_0 . If there exists an element $f^{(s)}(x_0) \in E$, $\forall s = 1, \ldots, n$, such that

For all $h > 0$ sufficiently small, there exist

$$f^{(s-1)}\left(x_0 + h\right) \ominus f^{(s-1)}\left(x_0\right) \text{ and } f^{(s-1)}\left(x_0\right) \ominus f^{(s-1)}\left(x_0 - h\right)$$

and the limits exist in the metric D

$$\lim_{h \searrow 0} \frac{f^{(s-1)}\left(x_0 + h\right) \ominus f^{(s-1)}\left(x_0\right)}{h} = \lim_{h \searrow 0} \frac{f^{(s-1)}\left(x_0\right) \ominus f^{(s-1)}\left(x_0 - h\right)}{h} = f^{(s)}\left(x_0\right)$$

or,

For all $h > 0$ sufficiently small, there exist

$$f^{(s-1)}\left(x_0\right) \ominus f^{(s-1)}\left(x_0 + h\right) \text{ and } f^{(s-1)}\left(x_0 - h\right) \ominus f^{(s-1)}\left(x_0\right)$$

and the limits exist in the metric D

$$\lim_{h \searrow 0} \frac{f^{(s-1)}\left(x_0\right) \ominus f^{(s-1)}\left(x_0 + h\right)}{-h} = \lim_{h \searrow 0} \frac{f^{(s-1)}\left(x_0 - h\right) \ominus f^{(s-1)}\left(x_0\right)}{-h} = f^{(s)}\left(x_0\right)$$

or,

For all $h > 0$ sufficiently small, there exist

$$f^{(s-1)}\left(x_0 + h\right) \ominus f^{(s-1)}\left(x_0\right) \text{ and } f^{(s-1)}\left(x_0 - h\right) \ominus f^{(s-1)}\left(x_0\right)$$

and the limits exist in the metric D.

$$\lim_{h \searrow 0} \frac{f^{(s-1)}\left(x_0 + h\right) \ominus f^{(s-1)}\left(x_0\right)}{h} = \lim_{h \searrow 0} \frac{f^{(s-1)}\left(x_0 - h\right) \ominus f^{(s-1)}\left(x_0\right)}{-h} = f^{(s)}\left(x_0\right)$$

or,

For all $h > 0$ sufficiently small, there exist

$$f^{(s-1)}\left(x_0\right) \ominus f^{(s-1)}\left(x_0 + h\right) \text{ and } f^{(s-1)}\left(x_0\right) \ominus f^{(s-1)}\left(x_0 - h\right)$$

and the limits exist in the metric D

$$\lim_{h \searrow 0} \frac{f^{(s-1)}(x_0) \ominus f^{(s-1)}(x_0 + h)}{-h} = \lim_{h \searrow 0} \frac{f^{(s-1)}(x_0) \ominus f^{(s-1)}(x_0 - h)}{h} = f^{(s)}(x_0)$$

(h and $-h$ at denominators mean $\dfrac{1}{h}$ and $-\dfrac{1}{h}$, respectively $\forall s = 1, \dots, n$)

Definition 2.16: Generalized Hukuhara Difference: The generalized Hukuhara difference of two fuzzy numbers $u, v \in \mathcal{R}_{\mathcal{F}}$ is defined as follows

$$u -_g v = w \Leftrightarrow \begin{cases} (i)\, u = v \oplus w \\ or\, (ii)\, v = u \oplus (-1)\, w \end{cases}$$

Consider $\left[w \right]_\alpha = \left[w_1(\alpha), w_1(\alpha) \right]$, then

$$w_1(\alpha) = \min \left\{ u_1(\alpha) - v_1(\alpha), u_2(\alpha) - v_2(\alpha) \right\}$$

and

$$w_2(\alpha) = \max \left\{ u_1(\alpha) - v_1(\alpha), u_2(\alpha) - v_2(\alpha) \right\}$$

Here the parametric representation of a fuzzy valued function $f : (a,b) \to \mathcal{R}_{\mathcal{F}}$ is expressed by

$$\left[f(t) \right]_\alpha = \left[f_1(t,\alpha), f_2(t,\alpha) \right], t \in [a,b], \alpha \in [0,1].$$

Definition 2.17: Generalized Hukuhara Derivative: The generalized Hukuhara derivative of a fuzzy valued function $f : (a,b) \to \mathcal{R}_{\mathcal{F}}$ at t_0 is defined as

$$f'(t_0) = \lim_{h \to 0} \frac{f(t_0 + h) -_g f(t_0)}{h}$$

In parametric form we say that

$f(t)$ is (i)-gH differentiable at t_0 if $\left[f'(t_0) \right]_\alpha = \left[f_1'(t_0,\alpha), f_2'(t_0,\alpha) \right]$

and

$f(t)$ is (ii)-gH differentiable at t_0 if $\left[f'\left(t_0\right) \right]_\alpha = \left[f_2'\left(t_0,\alpha\right), f_1'\left(t_0,\alpha\right) \right]$.

Definition 2.18: Generalized Hukuhara Derivative for Second Order: The second order generalized Hukuhara derivative of a fuzzy valued function $f : \left(a,b\right) \to \mathcal{R}_{\mathcal{F}}$ at t_0 is defined as

$$f''\left(t_0\right) = \lim_{h\to0} \frac{f'\left(t_0+h\right) -_g f'\left(t_0\right)}{h}$$

If $f''\left(t_0\right) \in \mathcal{R}_{\mathcal{F}}$, we say that $f'\left(t_0\right)$ is generalized Hukuhara at t_0.

Also we say that $f'\left(t_0\right)$ is (i)-gH differentiable at t_0 if

$$f''\left(t_0;\alpha\right) = \begin{cases} \left[f_1''\left(t_0,\alpha\right), f_2''\left(t_0,\alpha\right) \right] if\ f\ be\left(i\right)-gH\ differentiable\ on\left(a,b\right) \\ \left[f_2''\left(t_0,\alpha\right), f_1''\left(t_0,\alpha\right) \right] if\ f\ be\left(ii\right)-gH\ differentiable\ on\left(a,b\right) \end{cases}$$

for all $\alpha \in \left[0,1\right]$, and that $f'\left(t_0\right)$ is (ii)-gH differentiable at t_0 if

$$f''\left(t_0;\alpha\right) = \begin{cases} \left[f_2''\left(t_0,\alpha\right), f_1''\left(t_0,\alpha\right) \right] if\ f\ be\left(i\right)-gH\ differentiable\ on\left(a,b\right) \\ \left[f_1''\left(t_0,\alpha\right), f_2''\left(t_0,\alpha\right) \right] if\ f\ be\left(ii\right)-gH\ differentiable\ on\left(a,b\right) \end{cases}$$

for all $\alpha \in \left[0,1\right]$.

2.3 Extension Principle

Definition 2.19: Extension Principle: The extension principle is an important tool in fuzzy set theory.

If a function $f : R^m \to R^n$ induces to another function $f : F(R^m) \to F(R^n)$ defined for each fuzzy set u in R^m by

$$f\left(u\right)\left(y\right) = \begin{cases} \sup_{x\in f^{-1}(y)} \sup_{x\in f^{-1}(y)} u\left(x\right) if\ y \in range\left(f\right) \\ 0 y \notin range\left(f\right) \end{cases}$$

If f is one to one mapping, then

$$f(u)(y) = \begin{cases} uf^{-1}(y) \, if \ y \in range(f) \\ 0y \notin range(f) \end{cases}$$

2.4 Behavior of Solution

Definition 2.20: Strong and Weak Solution of FODE: Consider the 1st order linear homogeneous fuzzy ordinary differential equation

$$\frac{dx(t)}{dt} = f(x(t)) \text{ with } x(t_0) = x_0.$$

Here k or (and) x_0 be fuzzy number(s).

Let the solution of the above FODE be $x(t)$ and its α-cut be $x(t,\alpha) = \left[x_1(t,\alpha), x_2(t,\alpha)\right]$. If $x_1(t,\alpha) \le x_2(t,\alpha) \forall \alpha \in [0,1]$ then $x(t)$ is called strong solution otherwise $x(t)$ is called weak solution and in that case the α-cut of the solution is given by

$$x(t,\alpha) = \left[\min\left\{x_1(t,\alpha), x_2(t,\alpha)\right\}, \max\left\{x_1(t,\alpha), x_2(t,\alpha)\right\}\right]$$

3. FUZZY DIFFERENTIAL EQUATION: LINEAR AND NON LINEAR

Let us consider the differential equation

$$x'(t) = f(t,k,x(t)), \ x(t_0) = x_0, \ a \le t \le b \tag{3.1}$$

where k is constant, x_0 is initial condition, $f(t,k,x(t))$ is the function may be linear or non-linear.

The differential equation (3.1) can be fuzzy differential equation if

1. x_0 i.e., initial condition is fuzzy number.
2. k i.e., coefficient is a fuzzy number.
3. x_0 and k i.e., initial condition and coefficient are both fuzzy number.

4. TECHNIQUES FOR SOLVING FUZZY DIFFERENTIAL EQUATION

Let us consider the fuzzy initial value problem(FIVP)

$$x'\left(t\right) = f\left(t, x\left(t\right)\right), \tilde{x}\left(t_0\right) = \tilde{x}_0 , \ a \leq t \leq b \tag{4.1}$$

If we denote

$$\left[\tilde{x}\left(t\right)\right]^{\alpha} == \left[x_1^{\alpha}\left(t\right), x_2^{\alpha}\left(t\right)\right], \ \left[\tilde{x}_0\right]^{\alpha} = \left[x_{0,1}^{\alpha}, x_{0,2}^{\alpha}\right]$$

and

$$\left[f\left(t, \tilde{x}\left(t\right)\right)\right]^{\alpha} = \left[f_1^{\alpha}\left(t, x_1^{\alpha}\left(t\right), x_2^{\alpha}\left(t\right)\right), f_2^{\alpha}\left(t, x_1^{\alpha}\left(t\right), x_2^{\alpha}\left(t\right)\right)\right]$$

4.1 Solution Using Fuzzy Differentiability Concept

We have the following results

Case 1: If we consider $x'(t)$ in the first from (1), then we have to solve the following system of ODEs

$$\frac{d}{dt}\left(x_1^{\alpha}\left(t\right)\right) = f_1^{\alpha}\left(t, x_1^{\alpha}\left(t\right), x_2^{\alpha}\left(t\right)\right), \ x_1^{\alpha}\left(a\right) = x_{0,1}^{\alpha}$$

$$\frac{d}{dt}\left(x_2^{\alpha}\left(t\right)\right) = f_2^{\alpha}\left(t, x_1^{\alpha}\left(t\right), x_2^{\alpha}\left(t\right)\right), \ x_2^{\alpha}\left(t\right) = x_{0,2}^{\alpha}$$

Case 2: If we consider $x'(t)$ in the first from (ii), then we have to solve the following system of ODEs

$$\frac{d}{dt}\left(x_1^{\alpha}\left(t\right)\right) = f_2^{\alpha}\left(t, x_1^{\alpha}\left(t\right), x_2^{\alpha}\left(t\right)\right), \ x_1^{\alpha}\left(a\right) = x_{0,1}^{\alpha}$$

$$\frac{d}{dt}\left(x_2^{\alpha}\left(t\right)\right) = f_1^{\alpha}\left(t, x_1^{\alpha}\left(t\right), x_2^{\alpha}\left(t\right)\right), \ x_2^{\alpha}\left(t\right) = x_{0,2}^{\alpha}$$

In both case, we should ensure that the solution $[x_1^{\alpha}\left(t\right), x_2^{\alpha}\left(t\right)]$ are valid level sets of a fuzzy number valued function and $\left[\frac{d}{dt}\left(x_1^{\alpha}\left(t\right)\right), \frac{d}{dt}\left(x_2^{\alpha}\left(t\right)\right)\right]$ are valid level sets of a fuzzy valued function.

Example: We consider the differential equation

$$y' = 6y - 6 \tag{4.2}$$

with initial condition

$$y(0) = 3 \tag{4.3}$$

We fuzzify the initial conditions producing

$$\tilde{\gamma}_0 = \left(2 / 3 / 4\right) \tag{4.4}$$

Let $\tilde{Y}_c(x)$ be the classical solution.
Let $Y_c[\alpha] = \left[y_1(x, \alpha), y_2(x, \alpha)\right]$.

We substitute the α-cuts of $\tilde{Y}_c(x)$ into equation (4.2) giving

$$\left[y'_1(x, \alpha), y'_2(x, \alpha)\right] = 6\left[y_1(x, \alpha), y_2(x, \alpha)\right] - \left[6, 6\right] \tag{4.5}$$

The initial condition (4.4) becomes,

$$\left[y_1(0, \alpha), y_2(0, \alpha)\right] = \left[2 + \alpha, 4 - \alpha\right] \tag{4.6}$$

From (4.5), we get two differential equations

$$y'_1(x, \alpha) = 6y_1(x, \alpha) - 6 \tag{4.7}$$

With initial condition

$$y_1(0, \alpha) = 2 + \alpha \tag{4.8}$$

and

$$y'_2(x, \alpha) = 6y_1(x, \alpha) - 6 \tag{4.9}$$

with initial condition

$$y_2(0, \alpha) = 4 - \alpha \tag{4.10}$$

The solution is,

$$y_1\left(x,\alpha\right) = c_1 e^{6x} + 1 \qquad\qquad (4.11)$$

$$y_2\left(x,\alpha\right) = c_2 e^{6x} + 1 \qquad\qquad (4.12)$$

Using initial conditions, we get

$$y_1\left(x,\alpha\right) = \left(1+\alpha\right)e^{6x} + 1 \qquad\qquad (4.13)$$

$$y_2\left(x,\alpha\right) = \left(3-\alpha\right)e^{6x} + 1 \qquad\qquad (4.14)$$

Now,

$$\frac{\partial}{\partial\alpha}\left[y_1\left(x,\alpha\right)\right] = e^{6x} > 0$$

$$\frac{\partial}{\partial\alpha}\left[y_2\left(x,\alpha\right)\right] = -e^{6x} < 0$$

$$y_1\left(x,1\right) = 2e^{6x} + 1$$

$$y_2\left(x,1\right) = 2e^{6x} + 1$$

$$\therefore y_1\left(x,1\right) = y_2\left(x,1\right)$$

Therefore we see that equations (4.13) and (4.14) do define a fuzzy number for all $x \geq 0$.

So the classical solution $Y_c(x)$ exist and it is $Y_c(x) \approx \left(1,2,3\right)e^{6x} + 1$.

4.2 Solution by Extension Principle Method

By using the extension principle we have the membership function

$$f\left(t,x\left(t\right)\right)\left(s\right) = \sup\left\{x\left(t\right)\left(\tau\right)\,|\, s = f\left(t,\tau\right)\right\},\; s \in R$$

The result $f\left(t, x\left(t\right)\right)$ is a fuzzy function.

Where,

$$f_1^\alpha\left(t, x_1^\alpha\left(t\right), x_2^\alpha\left(t\right)\right) = \min\left\{f\left(t, u\right) \mid u \in \left[x_1^\alpha\left(t\right), x_2^\alpha\left(t\right)\right]\right\}$$

and

$$f_2^\alpha\left(t, x_1^\alpha\left(t\right), x_2^\alpha\left(t\right)\right) = \max\left\{f\left(t, u\right) \mid u \in \left[x_1^\alpha\left(t\right), x_2^\alpha\left(t\right)\right]\right\}$$

Example: We again consider the differential equation (4.2) with initial condition (4.3) $y_0 = 3 = \gamma_0$, say.

We fuzzify the initial condition producing $\tilde{\gamma}_0 = (2 \, / \, 3 \, / \, 4)$

$$\gamma_{01}\left(\alpha\right) = 2 + \alpha, \; \gamma_{02}\left(\alpha\right) = 4 - \alpha$$

The crisp solution is,

$$y\left(x\right) = ce^{6x} + 1 \tag{4.15}$$

Substituting the initial condition in (4.15), we get

$$\gamma_0 = c + 1$$

or, $c = \gamma_0 - 1$

$$\therefore y\left(x\right) = \left(\gamma_0 - 1\right)e^{6x} + 1$$

$$= \gamma_0 e^{6x} - e^{6x} + 1$$

$$= \gamma_0 e^{6x} + \vdots \left(x\right)$$

where $\vdots \left(x\right) = -e^{6x} + 1$

To obtain $Y_e\left(x\right)$, we substitute $\tilde{\gamma}_0$ for γ_0 in equation (4.15) where

$$\gamma_0\left[\alpha\right] = \left[\gamma_{01}\left(\alpha\right), \gamma_{02}\left(\alpha\right)\right] = \left[2 + \alpha, 4 - \alpha\right]$$

Let, $Y_e[\alpha] = \left[y_{e1}(x,\alpha), y_{e2}(x,\alpha)\right]$ where

$$y_{e1}(x,\alpha) = \min\left\{\gamma_0 e^{6x} + \mid (x) \mid \gamma_0 \in \gamma_0[\alpha]\right\}$$

$$y_{e2}(x,\alpha) = \max\left\{\gamma_0 e^{6x} + \mid (x) \mid \gamma_0 \in \gamma_0[\alpha]\right\}$$

now, $e^6 x > 0$ for all $x \geq 0$.

Therefore,

$$y_{e1}(x,\alpha) = (2+\alpha)e^{6x} + \mid (x)$$

$$y_{e2}(x,\alpha) = (4-\alpha)e^{6x} + \mid (x)$$

$$\frac{\partial}{\partial \alpha}\left[y_1(x,\alpha)\right] = e^{6x} > 0$$

$$\frac{\partial}{\partial \alpha}\left[y_2(x,\alpha)\right] = -e^{6x} < 0$$

Therefore, $y_{e1}(x,\alpha)$ is a monotonically increasing function of α and $y_{e2}(x,\alpha)$ is a monotonically decreasing function of α and $y_{e1}(x,1) = y_{e2}(x,1)$.

Therefore, the solution $\tilde{Y}_e(x)$ exists and it is a triangular shaped fuzzy number.

$$\tilde{Y}_e(x) \approx (2,3,4)e^{6x} + (1 - e^{6x}) = (1,2,3)e^{6x} + 1$$

5. BIO-MATHEMATICAL PROBLEM IN FUZZY ENVIRONMENT AND ITS SOLUTION

5.1 Fuzzy Predator-Prey Model for a One Species System

Consider the general predator-prey model for an one species system

$$\frac{dR}{dt} = R(b + aR) \tag{5.1}$$

where $a < 0, b >, = 0$ are constant and initial condition $R(0) = \tilde{R}_0$ is triangular fuzzy number.

5.1.1 Solution in Crisp Case

The differential equation is

$$\frac{dR}{dt} = R\left(b + aR\right) \tag{5.2}$$

with initial condition $R\left(0\right) = R_0$

The solution of (5.1) is

$$R\left(t\right) = \frac{be^{bt}}{\dfrac{b + aR_0}{R_0} - ae^{bt}} \quad \text{for } b \neq 0 \tag{5.3}$$

$$= \frac{R_0}{1 - aR_0 t} \quad \text{for } b = 0 \tag{5.4}$$

5.1.2 Solution in Fuzzy Case by Extension Principle

Let $\left[R_{e1}\left(t,\alpha\right), R_{e2}\left(t,\alpha\right)\right]$ be the α-cut solution of (5.1) by extension principle when initial condition is fuzzy

$$R_{e1}\left(t,\alpha\right) = \min\left\{ \frac{be^{bt}}{\dfrac{b + aR_0}{R_0} - ae^{bt}} : R_0 \in \left[R_{01}\left(\alpha\right), R_{02}\left(\alpha\right)\right] \right\} \text{ when for } b \neq 0$$

$$= \min\left\{ \frac{R_0}{1 - aR_0 t} : R_0 \in \left[R_{01}\left(\alpha\right), R_{02}\left(\alpha\right)\right] \right\} \text{ when for } b = 0$$

and

$$R_{e2}\left(t,\alpha\right) = \max\left\{ \frac{be^{bt}}{\dfrac{b + aR_0}{R_0} - ae^{bt}} : R_0 \in \left[R_{01}\left(\alpha\right), R_{02}\left(\alpha\right)\right] \right\} \text{ when for } b \neq 0$$

$$= \max \left\{ \frac{R_0}{1 - aR_0 t} : R_0 \in \left[R_{01}(\alpha), R_{02}(\alpha) \right] \right\} \text{ when for } b = 0$$

Now two cases arise

Case 1: $b \neq 0$

Here

$$R_{e1}(t, \alpha) = \min \left\{ \frac{be^{bt}}{\dfrac{b + aR_0}{R_0} - ae^{bt}} : R_0 \in \left[R_{01}(\alpha), R_{02}(\alpha) \right] \right\}$$

and

$$R_{e2}(t, \alpha) = \max \left\{ \frac{be^{bt}}{\dfrac{b + aR_0}{R_0} - ae^{bt}} : R_0 \in \left[R_{01}(\alpha), R_{02}(\alpha) \right] \right\}$$

Let

$$f(R_0) = \frac{be^{bt}}{\dfrac{b + aR_0}{R_0} - ae^{bt}}$$

Now

$$\frac{\partial f}{\partial R_0} = \frac{\partial}{\partial R_0} \left(\frac{be^{bt}}{\dfrac{b + aR_0}{R_0} - ae^{bt}} \right) = \frac{b^2 e^{bt}}{\left(b + aR_0 - aR_0 e^{bt} \right)^2} > 0$$

Hence

$$R_{e1}(t,\alpha) = \frac{bR_{01}(\alpha)e^{bt}}{b + aR_{01}(\alpha) - aR_{01}(\alpha)e^{bt}}$$

and

$$R_{e2}(t,\alpha) = \frac{bR_{02}(\alpha)e^{bt}}{b + aR_{02}(\alpha) - aR_{02}(\alpha)e^{bt}}$$

Numerical Example: when $b = 1$, $a = -3$ and $R(0) = (0.08, 0.1, 0.12)$

The solution is

$$R_{e1}(t,\alpha) = \frac{e^t}{\dfrac{0.76 - 0.06\alpha}{0.08 + 0.02\alpha} + 3e^t}$$

$$R_{e2}(t,\alpha) = \frac{e^t}{\dfrac{0.64 + 0.06\alpha}{0.12 - 0.02\alpha} + 3e^t}$$

Case 2: $b = 0$

Here

$$R_{e1}(t,\alpha) = \min\left\{\frac{R_0}{1 - aR_0 t} : R_0 \in \left[R_{01}(\alpha), R_{02}(\alpha)\right]\right\}$$

and

$$R_{e2}(t,\alpha) = \max\left\{\frac{R_0}{1 - aR_0 t} : R_0 \in \left[R_{01}(\alpha), R_{02}(\alpha)\right]\right\}$$

Let

$$f(R_0) = \frac{R_0}{1 - aR_0 t}$$

Now

Table 1. Value of $R_{e1}(t,\alpha)$ and $R_{e2}(t,\alpha)$ at $t = 0.6$

α	$R_{e1}(t,\alpha)$	$R_{e2}(t,\alpha)$
0	0.1217	0.1687
0.1	0.1243	0.1665
0.2	0.1268	0.1643
0.3	0.1293	0.1621
0.4	0.1318	0.1599
0.5	0.1342	0.1577
0.6	0.1366	0.1554
0.7	0.1390	0.1531
0.8	0.1414	0.1508
0.9	0.1438	0.1485
1	0.1462	0.1462

Note: Clearly from Table 1 and Figure 1 we see that $R_{e1}(t,\alpha)$ is increasing and $R_{e2}(t,\alpha)$ is a decreasing function. Hence the solution is a strong solution.

Figure 1. Graph of $R_{e1}(t,\alpha)$ and $R_{e2}(t,\alpha)$ at $t = 0.6$

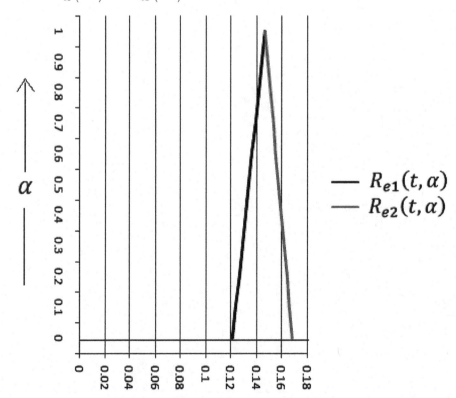

$$\frac{\partial f}{\partial R_0} = \frac{\partial}{\partial R_0}\left(\frac{R_0}{1 - aR_0 t}\right) = \frac{1}{\left(1 - aR_0 t\right)^2} > 0$$

Hence here

$$R_{e1}\left(t,\alpha\right) = \frac{R_{01}\left(\alpha\right)}{1 - aR_{01}\left(\alpha\right)t}$$

and

$$R_{e2}\left(t,\alpha\right) = \frac{R_{02}\left(\alpha\right)}{1 - aR_{02}\left(\alpha\right)t}$$

Numerical Example: $b = 0, a = -4$ and $R\left(0\right) = \left(0.07, 0.1, 0.12\right)$

The solution is

$$R_{e1}\left(t,\alpha\right) = \frac{0.07 + 0.03\alpha}{1 + 4\left(0.07 + 0.03\alpha\right)t}$$

and

$$R_{e2}\left(t,\alpha\right) = \frac{0.12 - 0.02\alpha}{1 + 4\left(0.12 - 0.02\alpha\right)t}$$

5.2 Fuzzy Insect Population Model

Suppose that an insect population P shows seasonal growth model by differential equation $\frac{dP}{dt} = kP \cos \xi t$, where k and ξ are positive constants. Here the cosine factor suggests periodic fluctuation. is the population at $t = 0$. If $k = 2$ and $\xi = \pi$ then determine the solution if $P(0)$ is a generalized triangular fuzzy number $\left(\gamma_1, \gamma_2, \gamma_3; \omega\right)$. (take realistic values of $\gamma_1, \gamma_2, \gamma_3$).

Solution: $\frac{dP}{dt} = kP \cos \xi t$ with fuzzy initial condition $P(0) = \left(\gamma_1, \gamma_2, \gamma_3; \omega\right)$

We first consider the problem $\frac{dP}{dt} = kP \cos \xi t$ with $P\left(0\right) = P_0$

The general solution of this equation is $P = P_0 e^{\frac{k}{\xi}\sin \xi t}$

Table 2. Value of $R_{e1}(t,\alpha)$ and $R_{e2}(t,\alpha)$ at $t = 0.7$

α	$R_{e1}(t,\alpha)$	$R_{e2}(t,\alpha)$
0	0.0585	0.0898
0.1	0.0606	0.0887
0.2	0.0627	0.0876
0.3	0.0647	0.0864
0.4	0.0667	0.0853
0.5	0.0687	0.0841
0.6	0.0706	0.0829
0.7	0.0725	0.0817
0.8	0.0744	0.0805
0.9	0.0763	0.0793
1	0.0781	0.0781

Note: Clearly from Table 2 and Figure 2 we see that $R_{e1}(t,\alpha)$ is increasing and $R_{e2}(t,\alpha)$ is a decreasing function. Hence the solution is a strong solution.

Figure 2. Graph of $R_{e1}(t,\alpha)$ and $R_{e2}(t,\alpha)$ at $t = 0.7$

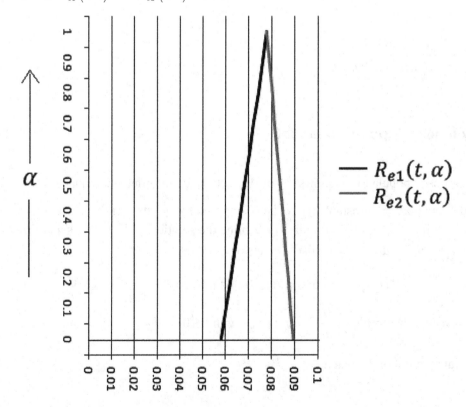

Let $P_e\left(t\right)$ be the solution by extension principle and its α-cut be $\left[P_{e_1}\left(t,\alpha\right), P_{e_2}\left(t,\alpha\right)\right]$

Now by extension principle

$$P_{e_1}\left(t,\alpha\right) = \min\left\{P_0 e^{\frac{k}{\xi}\sin\xi t} \mid P_0 \in \left[\gamma_1 + \frac{\alpha l_{P_0}}{\omega}, \gamma_3 - \frac{\alpha r_{P_0}}{\omega}\right]\right\}$$

and

$$P_{e_2}\left(t,\alpha\right) = \max\left\{P_0 e^{\frac{k}{\xi}\sin\xi t} \mid P_0 \in \left[\gamma_1 + \frac{\alpha l_{P_0}}{\omega}, \gamma_3 - \frac{\alpha r_{P_0}}{\omega}\right]\right\}$$

where $l_{P_0} = \gamma_2 - \gamma_1$ and $r_{P_0} = \gamma_3 - \gamma_2$

Here $f\left(P_0\right) = P_0 e^{\frac{k}{\xi}\sin\xi t}$

Now $\dfrac{df}{dP_0} = e^{\frac{k}{\xi}\sin\sin\xi t} > 0$

Therefore,

$$P_{e_1}\left(t,\alpha\right) = \left(\gamma_1 + \frac{\alpha l_{P_0}}{\omega}\right) e^{\frac{k}{\xi}\sin\xi t}$$

and

$$P_{e_2}\left(t,\alpha\right) = \left(\gamma_3 - \frac{\alpha r_{P_0}}{\omega}\right) e^{\frac{k}{\xi}\sin\xi t}$$

Hence,

$$\left(P_e\left(t\right)\right)_\alpha = \left[\gamma_1 + \frac{\alpha l_{P_0}}{\omega}, \gamma_3 - \frac{\alpha r_{P_0}}{\omega}\right] e^{\frac{k}{\xi}\sin\xi t}$$

Numerical example:

$P_0 = \left(950, 1000, 1100; 0.8\right), k = 2$ and $\xi = \pi$

$P_{e_1}\left(t,\alpha\right) = \left(950 + 62.5\alpha\right) e^{\frac{2}{\pi}\sin\pi t}$ and $P_{e_2}\left(t,\alpha\right) = \left(1100 - 125\alpha\right) e^{\frac{2}{\pi}\sin\pi t}$

Table 3. Value of $P_{e_1}(t,\alpha)$ and $P_{e_2}(t,\alpha)$ at $t = 1$

α	$P_{e_1}(t,\alpha)$	$P_{e_2}(t,\alpha)$
0	983.7296	1139.0554
0.1	990.2015	1126.1116
0.2	996.6734	1113.1677
0.3	1003.1454	1100.2239
0.4	1009.6173	1087.2801
0.5	1016.0892	1074.3363
0.6	1022.5611	1061.3925
0.7	1029.0330	1048.4487
0.8	1035.5049	1035.5049

Note: Clearly from Table 3 and Figure 3 we see that $P_{e_1}(t,\alpha)$ is increasing and $P_{e_2}(t,\alpha)$ is a decreasing function. Hence the solution is a strong solution.

Figure 3. Graph of $P_{e_1}(t,\alpha)$ and $P_{e_2}(t,\alpha)$ at $t = 1$

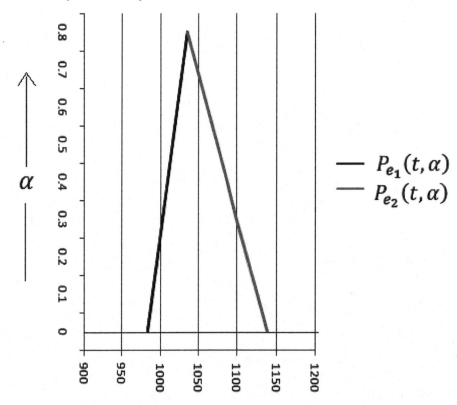

6. FUTURE SCOPE

Though the assumption in the models presented in the chapter are new, not considered by earlier investigators, still here for some limitations we not give various examples and hence there is a lot of scope of extension of these models and methods for future research work which we do.

The following works can be made for future extension:

1. There are several types of imprecise environments: such as stochastic environment, non-stochastic imprecise environment (rough environment, fuzzy rough environment, intuitionistic fuzzy environment.). We have solved the differential equations in such environments. Here we only solved in fuzzy environment.
2. In future we solve the different type's fuzzy differential equation such as fuzzy partial differential equation, fuzzy delay differential equation and fuzzy stochastic differential equation analytically and numerically in different imprecise environments by different method.
3. Most of the models in bio mathematics are described by stability analysis. We may further consider different fuzzy bio-mathematical models and work with fuzzy stability analysis.
4. There are several models with differential equation associated with biological science engineering science and economics. We may develop and discussed these models in imprecise environment and solve them.

7. CONCLUSION

1. Calculation of the solutions of nonlinear fuzzy differential equation using fuzzy differentiability concept is in general very difficult but we can easily solve by extension principle method.
2. For natural way of modeling of a mathematical biology problem, the uncertain parameter can play important role. It is need to be takes some parameter as uncertain variable (such as fuzzy).
3. A one species prey predator model and an insect population model can be formulated in fuzzy environment and it can be easily solved by extension principle method.
4. The extension principle method is also a promising method for solving nonlinear fuzzy differential equation which can be very helpful who deal with nonlinear fuzzy differential equation and its application.

REFERENCES

Ahmad, M. Z., & Baets, B. D. (2009). *A Predator-Prey Model with Fuzzy Initial Populations*. IFSA-EUSFLAT.

Ahmad, M. Z., & Hasan, M. K. (2012). Modeling of biological populations using fuzzy differential equations, International Conference Mathematical and Computational Biology 2011. *International Journal of Modern Physics: Conference Series, 9*, 354–363.

Akin, O., & Oruc, O. (2012). A Prey predator model with fuzzy initial values. *Hacettepe Journal of Mathematics and Statistics, 41*(3), 387–395.

Allahviranloo, T., Abbasbandy, S., Salahshour, S., & Hakimzadeh, A. (2011). A., A new method for solving fuzzy linear differential equations. *Computing, 92*(2), 181–197. doi:10.1007/s00607-010-0136-6

Allahviranloo, T., & Ahmadi, M. B. (2010). Fuzzy Laplace transforms. *Soft Computing, 14*(3), 235–243. doi:10.1007/s00500-008-0397-6

Barros, L. C., Bassanezi, R. C., & Tonelli, P. A. (2000). Fuzzy modelling in population dynamics. *Ecological Modelling, 128*(1), 27–33. doi:10.1016/S0304-3800(99)00223-9

Barzinji, K. (2014). Fuzzy Delay Predator-Prey System: Existence Theorem and Oscillation Property of Solution, *Int. Journal of Math. Analysis, 8*(17), 829–847.

Bede, B. (2006). A note on "two-point boundary value problems associated with non-linear fuzzy differential equations". *Fuzzy Sets and Systems, 157*(7), 986–989. doi:10.1016/j.fss.2005.09.006

Bede, B., & Gal, S. G. (2005). Generalizations of the differentiability of fuzzy-number-valued functions with applications to fuzzy differential equations. *Fuzzy Sets and Systems, 2005*, 151581–151599.

Bede, B., Rudas, I. J., & Bencsik, A. L. (2007). First order linear fuzzy differential equations under generalized differentiability. *Inf. Sci., 177*(7), 1648–1662.

Buckley, J. J., & Feuring, T. (2000). Fuzzy differential equations. *Fuzzy Sets and Systems, 110*(1), 43–54. doi:10.1016/S0165-0114(98)00141-9

Buckley, J. J., & Feuring, T. (2001). Fuzzy initial value problem for Nth-order linear differential equations. *Fuzzy Sets and Systems, 121*(2), 247–255. doi:10.1016/S0165-0114(00)00028-2

Cano, Y. C., & Flores, H. R. (2008). On the new solution of fuzzy differential equations. *Chaos, Solitons, and Fractals, 38*(1), 112–119. doi:10.1016/j.chaos.2006.10.043

Cano, Y. C., Flores, H. R., & Medar, M. A. R. (2008). Fuzzy differential equations with generalized derivative. *Proceedings of the 27th North American Fuzzy Information Processing Society International Conference, IEEE.*

Cano, Y. C., Medar, M. A. R., & Flores, H. R. (2007). Sobre ecuaciones diferencial esdifusas. *Bol. Soc. Esp. Mat. Apl., 41*, 91–99.

Chang, S. L., & Zadeh, L. A. (1972). On fuzzy mapping and control. *IEEE Transactions on Systems, Man, and Cybernetics, 2*(1), 30–34. doi:10.1109/TSMC.1972.5408553

Chen, M., Wu, C., Xue, X., & Liu, G. (2008). On fuzzy boundary value problems. *Inf. Sci, 178*(7), 1877–1892. doi:10.1016/j.ins.2007.11.017

Diamond, P., & Kloeden, P. (1994). *Metric Spaces of Fuzzy Sets*. Singapore: World Scientific. doi:10.1142/2326

Diniz, G. L., Fernandes, J. F. R., Meyer, J. F. C. A., & Barros, L. C. (2001). *A fuzzy Cauchy problem modelling the decay of the biochemical oxygen demand in water*. IEEE.

Dubois, D., & Prade, H. (1982). Towards fuzzy differential calculus: Part 3, Differentiation. *Fuzzy Sets and Systems, 8*(3), 225–233. doi:10.1016/S0165-0114(82)80001-8

Goetschel, R. Jr, & Voxman, W. (1986). Elementary fuzzy calculus. *Fuzzy Sets and Systems, 18*(1), 31–43. doi:10.1016/0165-0114(86)90026-6

Hullermeier, E. (1997). An approach to modeling and simulation of uncertain dynamical systems. *International Journal of Uncertainty, Fuzziness and Knowledge-based Systems, 5*(02), 117–137. doi:10.1142/S0218488597000117

Jafelice, R. M., Barros, L. C., Bassanezi, R. C., & Gomide, F. (2004). Fuzzy Modeling in Symptomatic HIV Virus Infected Population. *Bulletin of Mathematical Biology, 66*(6), 1597–1620. doi:10.1016/j.bulm.2004.03.002 PMID:15522347

Kaleva, O. (1987). Fuzzy differential equations. *Fuzzy Sets and Systems, 24*(3), 301–317. doi:10.1016/0165-0114(87)90029-7

Khastan, A., & Nieto, J. J. (2010). A boundary value problem for second-order fuzzy differential equations. *Nonlinear Analysis, 72*(9-10), 3583–3593. doi:10.1016/j.na.2009.12.038

Maan, N., Barzinji, K., & Aris, N. (2013, July 3 - 5). Fuzzy Delay Differential Equation in Predator-Prey Interaction: Analysis on Stability of Steady State. *Proceedings of the World Congress on Engineering WCE '13, London, UK.*

Mondal, S.P., & Roy, T.K. (2013). First Order Linear Homogeneous Fuzzy Ordinary Differential Equation Based on Lagrange Multiplier Method. *Journal of Soft Computing and Applications.*

Najariyan, M., Farahi, M. H., & Alavian, M. (2011). Optimal Control of HIV Infection by using Fuzzy Dynamical Systems. *The Journal of Mathematics and Computer Science 2*(4), 639–649.

Nounou, H. N., Nounou, M. N., Meskin, N., Datta, A., & Dougherty, E. R. (2012). Fuzzy Intervention in Biological Phenomena. *IEEE/ACM Transactions on Computational Biology and Bioinformatics, 9*(6), 1819–1825. doi:10.1109/TCBB.2012.113 PMID:23221089

Omar, A. H. A., & Hasan, Y. A. (2011). The interaction of predator prey with uncertain initial population sizes. *Journal of Quality Measurement and Analysis, 7*(2), 75–83.

Pal, D., & Mahapatra, G. S. (2014). A bioeconomic modeling of two-prey and one-predator fishery model with optimal harvesting policy through hybridization approach. *Applied Mathematics and Computation, 242*, 748–763. doi:10.1016/j.amc.2014.06.018

Pal, D., Mahaptra, G. S., & Samanta, G. P. (2012). A Proportional harvesting dynamical model with fuzzy intrinsic growth rate and harvesting quantity. *Pacific-Asian Journal of Mathematics, 6*(2), 199–213.

Pal, D., Mahaptra, G. S., & Samanta, G. P. (2013). Optimal harvesting of prey–predator system with interval biological parameters: A bioeconomic model. *Mathematical Biosciences, 241*(2), 181–187. doi:10.1016/j.mbs.2012.11.007 PMID:23219573

Pal, D., Mahaptra, G. S., & Samanta, G. P. (2013). Quota harvesting model for a single species population under fuzziness. *IJMS, 12*(1-2), 33–46.

Pandit, P., & Singh, P. (2014). Prey Predator Model with Fuzzy Initial Conditions, *International Journal of Engineering and Innovative Technology, 3*(12).

Peixoto, M.S., Barros, L.C., & Bassanezi, R.C. (2008). Predator–prey fuzzy model. *Ecological Modeling*, 214, 39–44.

Puri, M. L., & Ralescu, D. A. (1983). Differentials of fuzzy functions. *Journal of Mathematical Analysis and Applications*, *91*(2), 552–558. doi:10.1016/0022-247X(83)90169-5

Regan, D. O., Lakshmikantham, V., & Nieto, J. (2003). Initial and boundary value problems for fuzzy differential equations. *Nonlinear Analysis*, *54*, 405–415. doi:10.1016/S0362-546X(03)00097-X

Stefanini, L. (2008). A generalization of Hukuhara difference for interval and fuzzy arithmetic. In D. Dubois, M. A. Lubiano, H. Prade, M. A. Gil, P. Grzegorzewski, & O. Hryniewicz (Eds.), *Soft Methods for Handling Variability and Imprecision, in: Series on Advances in Soft Computing, 48*. doi:10.1007/978-3-540-85027-4_25

Stefanini, L., & Bede, B. (2009). Generalized Hukuhara differentiability of interval-valued functions and interval differential equations. *Nonlinear Analysis*, *71*(3-4), 1311–1328. doi:10.1016/j.na.2008.12.005

Tapaswini, S., & Chakraverty, S. (2013). Numerical Solution of Fuzzy Arbitrary Order Predator-Prey Equations, Appl. *Applications of Mathematics*, *8*(2), 647–672.

Tolouti, S. J., & Ahmadi, M. B. (2010). Fuzzy Laplace Transform on Two Order Derivative and Solving Fuzzy Two Order Differential Equation. *Int. J. Industrial Mathematics*, *2*(4), 279–293.

Zadeh, L. (2005). Toward a generalized theory of uncertainty (GTU) – an outline. *Information Sciences*, *172*(1-2), 1–40. doi:10.1016/j.ins.2005.01.017

Zarei, H., Kamyad, A. V., & Heydari, A. A. (2012). Fuzzy Modeling and Control of HIV Infection, Computational and Mathematical Methods in Medicine, Volume 2012, Article ID 893474, 17 pages.

KEY TERMS AND DEFINITIONS

Bio-Mathematical Modeling: Modeling natural phenomena by mathematics.

Bio-Mathematical Modeling with Uncertainty: Uncertainty came in bio mathematical model.

Extension Principle: A rule for operating fuzzy operation.

Fuzzy Derivative: Since fuzzy difference are different than crisp difference so fuzzy derivative are different

Fuzzy Difference: The fuzzy number is not like crisp number. So the fuzzy difference is not same as crisp difference.

Fuzzy Differential Equation: The differential equation associated with fuzzy sets theory.

Fuzzy Number: The element of fuzzy sets is called fuzzy number.

Fuzzy Sets: A set which is a collection of object with graded membership function.

Chapter 18
Application of Computational Intelligence Techniques in Wireless Sensor Networks the State of the Art

Subhendu Kumar Pani
Biju Patnaik University of Technology, India

ABSTRACT

A wireless sensor network may contain hundreds or even tens of thousands of inexpensive sensor devices that can communicate with their neighbors within a limited radio range. By relaying information on each other, they transmit signals to a command post anywhere within the network. Worldwide market for wireless sensor networks is rapidly growing due to a huge variety of applications it offers. In this chapter, we discuss application of computational intelligence techniques in wireless sensor networks on the coverage problem in general and area coverage in particular. After providing different types of coverage encountered in WSN, we present a possible classification of coverage algorithms. Then we dwell on area coverage which is widely studied due to its importance. We provide a survey of literature on area coverage and give an account of its state-of-the art and research directions.

INTRODUCTION

Revolutionary advances in Micro-Electro-Mechanical Systems (MEMS), wireless networking, and information processing have taken place during the past decade, resulting in the emergence of small-size and low-cost wireless sensors. These miniature sensors are self-content and capable of sensing the environment, data processing, and reporting via wireless network. The availability of such wireless sensor networks has opened up an exciting new opportunity to monitor the physical world like never before. WSN is mainly differentiated from the traditional wireless ad hoc network by their unique and dynamic network topology which owing to the time-varying link condition and node variation, diverse applications emphasizes on different sensory date requirement in terms of quality of service (QoS) and

DOI: 10.4018/978-1-5225-0427-6.ch018

Figure 1. Typical WSN components

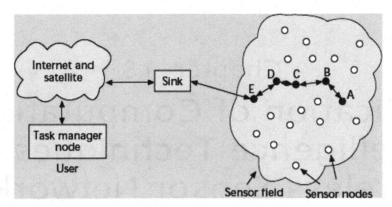

reliability. Furthermore, sensor nodes' limitation in power, computational capacities and memory are often deployed in large numbers and high density, for example to sense, process, and disseminate information of physical environments, thus resulting in upstream direction traffic from the sensor nodes to the sink whereas traditional networks are mostly point-to point or point-to-multipoint data forwarding (Lyas et al.,2005). Hence, one needs to carefully cope with such problems as energy conservation, reliability, and quality of services (QoS) to meet application requirements. Our major in this chapter focuses on the coverage problem of WSN. Coverage is a basic research issue in WSN because it can be considered as the measure of QoS of sensing function for a sensor network. For example, in an application of forest monitoring, one may ask how well the network can monitor a given area and what the chances are that a fire starting in a specific location of forest will be detected in a given time frame. Additionally, coverage formulations can try to find weak points in a sensor field and suggest future deployment or reconfiguration schemes for improving the coverage performance. The major components of a typical sensor network are: sensor nodes, the sensor field, the sink and the task manager, as shown in Figure 1.

- **Sensor Nodes:** Sensor nodes (also called Field devices) are capable sensing the environment, process data; transmit data to other devices and route data packets on behalf of other devices.
- **Sink (Access Points):** A Sink enables communication between Host application and field devices.
- **Task Manager:** A Task Manager is responsible for configuration of the network, scheduling communication between devices (i.e., configuring super frames), management of the routing tables and monitoring and reporting the health of the network.

A sensor node plays a major role in the sensor network. A typical sensor node is made up of a sensor board and a mote. A mote is made up of a processor, memory, radio transceiver (communication device), and power supply.

Wireless sensor networks are mugged with lots of challenges, mainly due to the communication failure, storage and computing constraints and limited power supply. Computational Intelligence CI paradigm has been effectively used in recent years to address issues such as the optimal allocation, data aggregation and integration, energy aware routing, task scheduling, security, and localization challenges. CI presents exhibit complex dynamic environment, intelligent behavior as adaptation mechanism for wireless sensor networks. CI fetches flexibility, autonomous behavior, as well as changes in the topology, communication failures and scene changes robustness. All sensor data is forwarded to the cluster head node, in turn, it is routed to a unique multi hop wireless communication node called sink nodes or base station. Though, very often, the sensor network is quite small, a single cluster with a single base station. Extra programs, such as a plurality of base station or mobile node are also possible. Resource constraints and dynamic network topology discovery constituted, network control and routing technology challenges, collaborative information processing, queries and tasks. However, while a various research organizations are implementing these applications, and an overview of its absence. Their goal is to bridge the CI methods and applications, WSN provides researchers with fresh ideas and motivation gap between (Haenggi, 2005). Challenges in wireless sensor networks have not yet untapped, as well as wireless sensor networks to confer the potential application of the projection of CI are encouraged to study with an aim to use CI techniques in wireless sensor network applications.

Several researchers are currently involved in developing solutions that fulfill diverse requirements, at the same time, various algorithms that relating to coverage have been proposed. Some algorithms work on pure coverage problems to characterize the coverage of WSN (Szewczy et al., 2004). Others combine some considerations for optimizing the utilization of network resources or for supporting specific application requirements (for example, network connectivity, energy consumption) into coverage problem. To offer guaranteed coverage, the necessary point is to solve the coverage problem with sufficient available resources and possibly to incorporate optimizations. Among many challenges, when designing an efficient coverage scheme, maintaining connectivity and maximizing the network lifetime stand out as the critical challenges.

APPLICATIONS OF WSN

The low-cost sensing technology combined with processing power and wireless communication makes WSN lucrative for a wide range of applications. These networks are widely being implemented to perform a number of tasks, ranging from environmental and natural habitat monitoring to home networking, medical applications and smart battlefields. Sensor network can signal a machine malfunction to the control centre in a factory or it can warn about smoke on a remote forest hill indicating that a forest fire is about to start. On the other hand, wireless sensor nodes can be designed to detect the ground vibrations generated by silent footsteps of a burglar and trigger an alarm. The following are some examples of applications:

- **Environmental Monitoring**: Sensors can be deployed to monitor an environment where it is labor intensive or hazardous to mankind. Some examples include using sensors to do precision measurements of fertilizer concentration and seismic activity, monitoring of water quality, tracking of wild animals, detection of fire or floods, and checking contamination levels of air or soil. One such example is using a wireless sensor network to observe the breeding behavior of a small bird called Leach's Storm Petrel on Great Duck Island, Maine, USA (Mainwaring et al., 2002). Previously it was almost impossible to collect data like their usage patterns of the nesting burrows, yet now variations among breeding sites to changes in environmental conditions inside and outside of the burrow can be done with wireless sensor networks. Nodes with humidity, pressure, temperature and light sensors are installed inside the burrows and surface to collect these statistics. Data are then relayed back to the back-end station through the multi-hop network.

- **Seismic/Glacier Detection**: Sensors can be placed to detect seismic activity along a fault line or coastline. This will give early detection to a natural disaster like a tsunami, a volcanic eruption or an earthquake. They can also be deployed to glaciers to monitor the displacements and dynamics inside the glacier (Martinez et al., 2004). Such monitoring normally requires a few months to years of monitoring in order to have any meaningful results.
- **Disaster Operations**: A wireless sensor network can be a helpful tool in times of disaster operations. These disaster scenarios can range from chemical or biological contamination, a forest fire, and flooding to an earthquake. A network of communication can be deployed without existing infrastructure to help the authorities have better command and control over the operations. It can also be setup to monitor the situation without risking any life. Sensors have been deployed to assist rescue teams in saving people buried in avalanches (Michahelles et al., 2003). By using this solution, the rescue team is able to locate the victim and have access to the health state of the victim for prioritization.
- **Medical Monitoring**: A wireless sensor network can be setup to monitor vital signs of patients either in the hospital or out of the hospital. It can also be used as a tool for doctors to retrieve past data collected since the last visit. Another use of a wireless sensor network is to track suspected infectious patients so that further spread of a contagious virus is minimized or prevented. Such implementation has been used and proved to improve data accuracy and provide more convenience for the patient (Baldus et al.,2004). Cancer Detection represents one of the key concerns in healthcare. Nowadays, one of largest treat for human life is cancer. Cancer is the second leading cause of death in US with rising numbers each year: currently 9 million people had a cancer diagnosis; with 1,221,800 new cases in 1999Glucose Level Monitoring is necessary for controlling another rising disease: diabetes. The US national institute of health (NIH), US national institute of diabetes, and digestive and kidney disease reported 15.7 million persons had diabetes in 1999 in the US. Complications that can arise from diabetes include heart disease, stroke, high blood pressure, blindness, kidney disease, and amputations. Characteristic treatment for diabetes includes a strict diet, exercise, insulin injections, and blood monitoring.
- **Military Surveillance**: Wireless sensor networks are increasingly being used by the military in recent years and form a critical part of military command, control and communication. There are even routing protocols specifically designed for military applications (Ye et al.,2002). The small form factor of a node makes it attractive to use it as an area monitoring tool. In addition to that, WSNs can be easily deployed, and they are coupled with self-organization capability and high fault tolerance, which is an essential requirement in a military environment. By fixing sensors on to equipment and personnel, weapons and troop status information can be gathered and sent back to a command center to provide information and better battlefield intelligence. An ad hoc network can be setup easily where wiring is not feasible or possible. Sensors can be deployed as a smart minefield with intelligence that can differentiate between a friendly or enemy force. In biological or chemical warfare, sensors can be deployed to determine the presence of a toxic substance in the monitored area without unnecessarily risking human life. It can also be used to track movement of troops or vehicles over an area (Zhao et al.,2004).
- **Civil Engineering and Home Intelligence**: Monitoring of structures like bridges in order to detect and to warn of structural weakness, or the reaction of tall buildings to wind and earthquakes

are some of the civil engineering applications of WSNs (Akyildiz et al.,2002). In the area of home intelligence, WSN applications can provide smoke detection in order to prevent fires and their spread; automate the reading of gas, water and electricity reading/levels; and facilitate safety monitoring through remote surveillance to detect intruders.

CONSTRAINTS AND CHALLENGES

A sensor network is a wireless network that comprises many sensing devices scattered in an area as guards to record and eventually to control surrounding environment conditions such as temperature, humidity, sound, vibration, and pressure. In a sensor network, sensors cooperatively work to sense, process and route data. The recent development in many supporting technologies has enabled the productions of low-cost, low-power, multifunction, and tiny sensors (Pottie et al.,2000), so that a redundant number of sensors can be densely deployed to a monitored area to prolong network lifetime and to enhance the surveillance quality. Although a huge number of protocols have been devised and applied to wired and traditional wireless networks (such as wireless LAN), those protocols cannot directly be employed to sensor network since sensor network possesses some special characteristics and restrictions that distinguish it from the other types of networks.

WSN are restricted in their energy, computation, and communication capabilities. Contrary to traditional networks, sensor nodes are frequently deployed in accessible areas, presenting a threat of physical attacks. Sensor networks interact strongly with their physical environment and with people, posing additional security issues. Because of these reasons current security mechanisms are insufficient for WSN. These fresh constraints pose new research challenges on key establishment, secrecy and authentication, privacy, robustness to denial-of-service attacks, secure routing, and node capture. To get a secure system, security must be integrated into every component, since components designed without security can become a point of attack. Therefore, security and privacy pervade every aspect of system design. If the transmission is strong enough, the entire system could be jammed. More complicated attacks are also possible: the adversary can inhibit communication by violating the MAC protocol, for instance by transmitting while a neighbor is also transmitting or by continuously requesting channel access with a RTS (requestto-send). New techniques for managing with this simple yet potentially devastating attack are needed. Many other security-related problems need further research. One challenge is how to make safe wireless communication links against eavesdropping and tampering. Overall, security is a not easy challenge for any system. The severe constraints and demanding environments of WSN make computer security for these systems even more challenging.

Constraints of WSN

There are several constraints of sensor network which include the following:

- **Limited Support for Networking**: The sensor nodes can only communicate with very low quality, high latency and variance, limited bandwidth, and high failure-rate. A sensor's transmission range is short and greatly affected by energy. In a WSN, the communication mainly relies on broadcasting. Moreover, the network is peer-to-peer, with a mesh topology and dynamic, mobile, and unreliable connectivity.

- **Energy Constraint**: The most precious resource of a sensor is energy. In most cases, the battery is irreplaceable, while all the sensor's operations consume a certain amount of energy. Therefore, energy conservation is always the most critical requirement on designing a sensor network protocol. It has been shown that the power to transmit 1 bit is enough for executing at least 3000 instructions (Ilyas et al., 2005). That means a sensor consumes much more energy on communication than on computation, thus the designed protocols for WSN usually try to make good uses of computation to get the jobs done to compensate for expensive and unreliable communication.
- **Dynamic Topology:** The topology of a WSN changes very frequently due to the movement of sensors, the sensors' temporary or permanent failure, the death of sensors, the addition of sensors to the network, or even the temporary sensors' malfunction.
- **Scalability and Heterogeneity**: WSN may consist of a large number of different sensors in terms of sensing units, communicational ability, computational power, memory size, and manufacturer. Huge number of sensors is deployed into hostile environment under tough condition, thus it is very difficult to maintain and manage the network. Due to the same reason, sensor nodes may not have global ID in the network.
- **Limited Support for Software Development:** The tasks are typically real-time and massively distributed. They require involved dynamic collaboration among nodes and they must handle multiple competing events. Also, sensors are limited in computational capability and memory sizes. This limits the types of algorithms and results processed on a sensor.
- **Prone to Failure**: A tiny sensor node tends to fail to operate due to numerous reasons such as depletion of energy and environmental interference making it very vulnerable to the environment, e.g., easy to be physically damaged. Sensing data is prone to bias under the environment effects such as noise and obstacle. Moreover, sensors have to operate unattended, since it is impossible to service a large number of nodes in remote, possibly inaccessible locations.

Challenges

There are several challenges which arise from the constraints and limitations of the network. These challenges draw the most attention from the research community.

- **Algorithm Type:** Energy is the most critical resource of a sensor since every operation requires a certain amount of energy while sensor is battery-driven but battery is not always replaceable. Thus, energy-efficiency should be and have been the foremost concern of any protocol designed for a WSN. Other limitations of a sensor that require thorough awareness when designing a WSN protocol include sensor's limited memory size, communication and computation capability, thus, algorithms for WSNs need to be simple but robust and fault-tolerant. That is also the reason why decentralized algorithm is always preferable (if it is not the only suitable ones) in WSNs. Some requirements that a "good" protocol aims to are simplicity, energy-efficiency, localized, distributed, and parallel type, scalability and flexibility to the enlargement of the network, robustness, fault-tolerance, and low communication overhead.
- **Topology Control**: For a prone-to-failure network as WSN, the sensors may malfunction at any time or any place for various reasons. It follows that the topology of a WSN is highly dynamic and unpredictable. For each kind of applications, an appropriate topology may be required.

- **Routing**: After sensors collect the information, enormous streams of information need to be made available to some data consuming centers. The question of how to efficiently, reliably, and securely route the data through a high-density network is also a challenging issue for sensor networks.
- **Data Management**: A WSN is supposed to frequently collect information about the physical world, e.g., surrounding environment or objects. Information is exchanged on a multiple-source-multiple-destination basis and the number of sensors in a WSN is in the order of hundreds, thousands or even more. Thus, the amount of data collected by a WSN is extremely large. How to manage, process and route the data is truly a challenge. Researchers have considered the following sub-problems for this kind of issue: in-network data processing, data dissemination (multicast, unicast, broadcast) and aggregation (or converge cast).
- **Coverage**: The primary function of a WSN is to watch over the physical world. To accomplish this function, it is compulsory to schedule, organize the network in such a way that it can effectively observe the interested environment or set of objects, and then collect information that it is desired and supposed to gather. This problem is thoroughly investigated in this chapter.
- **Programming Abstractions**: A key to the growth of WSN is the increasing level of abstraction for programmers. Presently, programmers' pact with too many low levels details regarding sensing and node to node communication. For example, they usually deal with sensing data, fusing data and moving data. They deal with particular node to node communication and details. If we increase the level of abstraction to judge aggregate behavior, application functionality and direct maintain for scaling issues then productivity increases. Current research in programming abstractions for WSN can be categorized into 7 areas:
  - Environmental,
  - Middleware APIs,
  - Database centric,
  - Event based,
  - Virtual machines,
  - Scripts
  - Component-based.

As an example, consider an environmental based abstraction called EnviroTrack. Here the programmer deals with entities found in an application. If the application ways people and vehicles, then the programmer can identify people and vehicle entities and utilize library routines that support low level sensing functions that can detect and classify objects of these types. They can also easily specify the application level processing associated with each type of entity. This permits programmers to deal with application level functionality rather than low level details. Since WSN deal primarily with collecting, analyzing and acting on data, a database view of such systems is popular. In this vision, a programmer deals with queries written in an SQL-like format. Though, real-world data problems such as probabilistic data, various levels of confidence in data and missing or late data occasionally make the SQL paradigm insufficient. It is likely that no one programming abstraction for WSN will exist. Rather, a number of solutions will emerge, each better for certain domains.

- **Security**: It is no use if the sensed data of a WSN is illegally modified, blocked, or redirected to some illegal data centers. It is the responsibility of security protocols to protect the WSNs from such undesired actions. Because a WSN is usually an ad hoc wireless network and is usually deployed to an unattended and hostile region, attacks in sensor networks are relatively easy to carry out, but are exceptionally difficult to defend. Also, types of attacks in WSN are very multiform.

Some aspects of security issues in WSNs are to guarantee the integrity, confidentiality of the data or to verify the authenticity of entities exchanging the data.

- **Power Management**: Low-cost deployment is one acclaimed gain of sensor networks. Limited processor bandwidth and micro memory are two arguable constraints in sensor networks, which will have vanished with the development of fabrication techniques. On the other hand, the energy restriction is unlikely to be solved soon due to slow progress in developing battery capacity. Additionally, the untended nature of sensor nodes and hazardous sensing environments preclude battery replacement as a feasible solution. However, the surveillance nature of many sensor network applications requires a long lifetime; therefore, it is a very significant research issue to provide a form of energy-efficient surveillance service for a geographic area. Much of the current research focuses on how to present full or partial sensing coverage in the context of energy conservation. In such an approach, nodes are set into a dormant state as long as their neighbors can give sensing coverage for them. These solutions consider the sensing coverage to a certain geographic area as binary, either it provides coverage or not. However, we argue that, in the majority scenarios such as battlefields, there are assured geographic sections such as the general command center that are much more security-sensitive than others. Based on the fact that individual sensor nodes are not consistent and subject to failure and single sensing readings can be easily distorted by background noise and cause false alarms, it is simply inadequate to rely on a single sensor to safeguard a critical area. In this case, it is needed to provide higher degree of coverage in which multiple sensors monitor the same location at the same time in order to obtain high confidence in detection. On the other hand, it is overkill and energy overwhelming to support the same high degree of coverage for some non-critical area.

Besides the above issues, there are numerous other important issues that are being worked on such as time synchronization, localization, positioning and location tracking, sensor management protocol (Ilyas et al., 2005) link-layer protocols (e.g., MAC), and transport-layer protocols (e.g., real-time traffic, reliable transfer).

COVERAGE PROBLEM

Coverage is a fundamental problem in wireless sensor networks. Such problem is centered around a basic question: "How well can the sensors observe the physical world?" Given a collection of nodes X in a bounded domain D of the plane, it is assumed that each node can sense and broadcast, or monitor a region of fixed radius about the node for any occurrence of the event of interest. In that case, how much region of the domain D monitored by the collection of nodes X is defined as the coverage. Coverage holes are areas not covered by any node due to random aerial deployment creating voids, presence of obstructions, and more likely, node failures etc.

Coverage problem in WSN basically is caused by three main reasons; not enough sensors to cover the whole region of interest, limited sensing range and random deployment. Since the sensors are operated using limited power supply, some of them might die out thereby resulting in inadequate sensors to fully cover the whole region of interest. A sensor's sensing range is restricted to certain radius which consequently brings coverage problem.

Thus, coverage problem can be seen as a maximization problem, where the objective is to maximize the coverage percentage, i.e. the ratio of area covered by at least one sensor to the total area of the region of interest. Coverage problem can also be seen as a minimization problem, where the objective is to make the coverage holes in the network as small as possible (Cardei et al., 2005).

The coverage concept is used as a measure of quality of service provided by the sensing function in various ways depending on sensor devices and applications.

Types of Coverage

Sensor coverage problems can be classified into three categories: area coverage, point coverage (or target coverage), and barrier coverage (Chakrabarty et al., 2002).

1. **Area Coverage**: The most studied coverage problem is the area coverage problem, where the main objective of the sensor network is to cover (monitor) an area (also referred sometimes as region). The connected black nodes form the set of active sensors, as the result of a node scheduling mechanism. This is the minimal set of nodes cover the region of interest. A random deployment of sensors to cover a given square-shaped area as shown in Figure 2.
2. **Point Coverage**: In the point (also called target) coverage problem, the objective is to cover a set of points in a region (Gage, 1992). The connected black nodes form the set of active sensors, the result of a scheduling mechanism. An example of a set of sensors randomly deployed to cover a set of points (small square nodes) as shown in Figure 3.
3. **Barrier Coverage**: The notion of barrier coverage was firstly introduced in the context of robotics sensors (Xing et al., 2005) . In this category of coverage, the goal is to minimize the probability of undetected intrusion behavior that attempts to cross from one side of a strip-like area to the opposite side (called path) existing in the sensing region. The selection of the path depends on the objective of the application. A general barrier coverage problem where start and end points of the path are selected from bottom and top boundary lines of the sensing region is shown in Figure 4.

Classification of Coverage Algorithms

Coverage algorithms found in literature can be classified into following categories:

1. **Sensors Placement**: This category concerns with the following issue and the algorithms are usually carried out prior or at the time of deploying the sensors.
2. **Coverage Conditions**: Find out the conditions (e.g., the number of sensors, sensor's sensing range) to provide certain level of coverage for a sensor network.
3. **Deployment Schemes (Deterministic Deployments)**: Concerned with schemes on how to place the sensors to achieve a number of optimal objectives such as the best coverage quality or maximum network lifetime with least number of sensors possible.

Figure 2. Area coverage

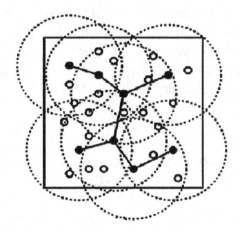

Figure 3. Point coverage

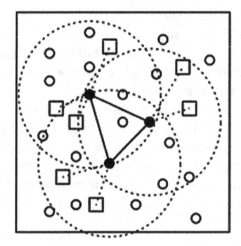

Figure 4. Barrier coverage

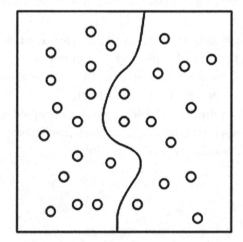

Sensors Scheduling

To discover the schedule for a set of sensors to provide coverage or a WSN with the assumption that the network has already been (randomly) deployed.

1. **Centralized Algorithms:** Algorithms that require global information (such as sensors' sensing ranges, sensors' location, sensors' residual energy, etc.) of the whole sensor network. Besides, the algorithms are always executed at a powerful central node, after that the result is scattered to each sensor in the network. We further divide this type of algorithms into two smaller groups:
   a. Algorithms result in disjoint sets.
   b. Algorithms result in non-disjoint sets.
2. **Decentralized (Localized and Distributed) Algorithms**: Algorithms that require only the local information (the fix-number-of-hop neighbors' information, usually 1- or 2-hop information) to function and are run at large number of sensor nodes (usually at all nodes). Each sensor then makes its own decision of turning on or off (although its neighbors may have contribution on that decision). We further divide this type of algorithms into two smaller groups:
   a. Decentralized algorithms based on back-off (or off-duty) mechanism.
   b. Decentralized algorithms work in rounds.

AREA COVERAGE IN LITERATURE

The area coverage problem is mostly studied in literature. It also emphasizes coverage with minimum sensor nodes and energy consumption when the region is covered by connected WSN. We provide a survey of some selected work here.

The work in (Wang et al., 2008) proposed a protocol called Coverage Configuration Protocol (CCP). The goal of this protocol is to achieve to the guaranteed different degrees of coverage and connectivity while maximize the number of sleeping, and to allow WSN to self-configure for a wide range of applications when the communication range is more than twice as the sensing range.

The work in (Cerpa et al., 2004) shows that coverage will imply connectivity if the communication range is greater or equal to twice the sensing range. To ensure K-coverage, a node only needs to check whether the intersection points inside its sensing area are K-covered. Note that it cannot guarantee network connectivity when the radio transmission range is less than twice the sensing range. Therefore, by combing CCP with SPAN (a distributed connectivity preserving mechanism for multi-hop ad hoc wireless networks that reduces energy consumption without significantly diminishing the connectivity of the network), the coverage and connectivity can be guaranteed in any case. In CCP, sensor nodes need accurate location information and a neighborhood table.

Adaptive Self-Configuring sensor Networks Topologies (ASCENT) is proposed in (Zhang et al., 2005).

In this work sensors self-configure to automatically establish network topology, while allowing redundant sensors to stay asleep in order to conserve energy. The main idea of ASCENT is to let sensors measure their connectivity as well as their data loss rate and activate their neighbors based on these local measurements. However, ASCENT does not guarantee network connectivity in any sense (the network could be partitioned), although the delivery of data indicates that there is a certain level of connectivity. Each node assesses its connectivity as well as their data loss ratio and each of them adapts its participation in the multi-hop network topology based on the measured monitoring region. In ASCENT, nodes require per neighbor state to keep track of the number of active neighbors, and do not need accurate location information. It is a disadvantage of ASCENT that working nodes never go back to sleep.

Optimal Geographical Density Control (OGDC) (Podur let al., 2004) is a decentralized and localized density control scheme based on the proof that if communication range is at least twice of the sensing range, then a complete coverage of a convex area implies connectivity. It can configure a sensor network with the characteristics of full-coverage, network connectivity, and maximum energy conservation by assuming that the sensor density is high enough so that a sensor could be found at any desirable position and the sensing range could be different for sensors. The goal of OGDC is to maximize the number of sleeping sensors while ensuring that the working sensors provide 1-coverage and 1-connectivity. By using its own location and the working sensors' locations, a sensor can verify whether or not it turns on. When a sensor minimizes the overlapping area with the existing working sensors and when it covers an intersection point of two working sensors, itself will be activated. When the radio transmission range is at least twice the sensing range, OGDC can maintain both 1-coverage and 1-connectivity. In OGDC, sensor nodes need accurate location information and time synchronization, and working nodes never go back to sleep, but different nodes may be working in different rounds so energy consumption may still be balanced among all the nodes.

K-neighbors Constrained Coverage Strategy (KCCS) proposed in (Kumar et al., 2004) is a self-deployment strategy for mobile sensor network. In KCCS, by using virtual forces governing the pair-wise interaction between sensor nodes, every node tries to maximize its coverage while maintaining the required number of neighbors. In KCCS, the pair-wise interaction between nodes is governed by two kinds of virtual forces - one cause the nodes to repel each other to improve their coverage and the other is an attractive force that prevents the nodes from losing connectivity. The goal of KCCS is to maximize the area coverage of the network with the constraint that each of the nodes has at least K neighbors by using a combination of the above two forces. The disadvantage of KCCS is that there is a strong assumption it makes on the capabilities of the nodes - in particular the ability of each node to measure the exact range and bearing of the neighboring nodes and obstacles.

The goal of Random independent scheduling (RIS) (Wu et al., 2002) is to determine the appropriate number of sensors that are enough to achieve k-coverage of a region when sensors are allowed to sleep most of their lifetime for extending network lifetime. It assumes that time is divided into cycles based on a time synchronization method. In RIS, independently sleeping approach that is energy-efficient and light-weight because each sensor doesn't require any interaction with their neighbor that can make a sensor is active with probability p or go to sleep with probability 1-p. RIS does not require location information and the table of neighborhoods, but it is not robust against unexpected failures that destroy the sensors before they run out of energy because the sensors do not dynamically evaluate their situation.

Connected Dominating Coverage Set (CDCS) (Cardei et al., 2005) is based on the observation that all sensors can be divided into disjoint sets such as that every set completely covers all points (targets) (Wu et al.,1999). When each set can cover all points (point coverage) and monitoring region (area coverage), by activating disjoint set successively, the sensor network lifetime can be extended (Lazos et al., 2006).

Lightweight deployment-aware scheduling (LDAS) (Heinzelman et al., 2000) is proposed to maintain long network lifetime as well as sufficient sensing areas. Similarly, the previous technique turning off redundant sensors, the method of LDAS analyzes the redundant sensing areas among neighboring wireless sensors. Because it is assumed that sensor nodes are not equipped with GPS or other devices to obtain location information, LDAS provides tight upper and lower bounds on the probability of complete redundancy and on the average partial redundancy. In LDAS, when the number of working neighbors exceeds a threshold determined by the application's requirement on sensing coverage, the node randomly selects some of its neighbors to turn off and sends tickets to them. When a node collects enough tickets from its neighbors, it may enter the off duty mode after a random back-off period.

Low-energy adaptive clustering hierarchy (LEACH) (Andries et al., 2007), a cluster-based protocol architecture for micro sensor networks that combines the ideas of energy-efficient cluster-based routing and media access together with application-specific data aggregation to achieve good performance in terms of system lifetime, latency, and application-perceived quality. The goal of LEACH is turning off non-head nodes as much as possible. In LEACH, the operation is divided into cycles and each cycle includes a set-up phase and a steady phase. During the set-up phase, cluster heads are selected and each sensor joins a cluster by choosing the cluster head that requires the minimum communication energy. During the steady phase, each cluster head aggregates the data from the sensors in its cluster and then transmits the compressed data to the base station. LEACH enables self-organization of large numbers of nodes, algorithms for adapting clusters and rotating cluster head positions to evenly distribute the energy load among all the nodes, and techniques to enable distributed signal processing to save communication resources.

Since sensors are frequently powered by batteries, sensors' on-duty time should be right scheduled to conserve energy. If some nodes distribute the common sensing region and task, then we can turn off various of them to conserve energy and thus extend the lifetime of the network. This is feasible if turning off such a node still provides the alike "coverage" (i.e., the provided coverage is not affected).

A heuristic to select mutually exclusive sets of sensor nodes such that each set of sensors can give a complete coverage of the monitored area. They claim that this trouble is a NP-complete problem by reducing it to the least cover problem. The key idea of the heuristic is to find out which sensors cover up fields that are less covered by other sensors and then avoid including those sensors into the same set. After a sleeping node wakes up, it broadcasts a probing message within a assured range and then waits for a reply. If no reply is received within a pre-defined time period, it will keep active until it depletes its energy. The coverage degree (density) is controlled by sensor's probing range and wake-up rate. However, this probing-based approach has no guarantee of sensing coverage and thus blind points could appear.

A coverage preserving node scheduling scheme is in attendance in to determine when a node can be turned off and when it should be reorganized to become active again. It is based on an eligibility rule which permits a node to turn itself off as long as other neighboring nodes can cover its sensing area. After evaluating its eligibility for off-duty, each sensor accepts a back-off scheme to avoid the appearance of blind points. If a node is eligible for off-duty, it will delay a random back-off time before actually turning itself off. During this period of time, if it accepts any message from its neighbors requesting to go to sleep, it marks the sender as an off-duty node and evaluates its eligibility. If the eligibility still holds after the back-off time, this node broadcasts a message to notify its neighbors, waits for a short period of time, and then actually turns itself off. A sleeping node will sporadically wake up to check if it is still eligible for off-duty and then decide to keep sleeping or go back to on-duty.

However, the solution might lead to excess energy consumption. Based on the eligibility rule, a sensor only regards a node whose sensing range can cover up the sensor as a neighboring node grid point is covered by at least one sensor at any moment of a round. Then a sensor's on-duty time in each round is the union of schedules of grid points covered by the sensor. However, this scheme may suffer from the time synchronization problem in a large-scale sensor network.

We observe that area coverage schemes usually assume that sensors have a simplistic model of propagation, where sensors have a homogeneous or heterogeneous disk model. By formulating coverage problem as a set of intersection problem that studied in integral geometry, the coverage problem for sensing areas of sensors having any arbitrary shape is researched in (Heinzelman et al., 2000). However, other constraints (e.g., connectivity, energy consumptions) have not been analyzed.

COMPUTATIONAL INTELLIGENCE (CI) AND CLUSTERING IN WIRELESS SENSOR NETWORK

Clustering has been successfully applied to control the WSN energy consumption. Traditional techniques have some constraints. Recently, CI paradigms are used to cluster WSN. This section summarizes the work done by CI paradigms to cluster WSN. CI is an intelligent computational methodology that uses heuristic algorithms to find approximate solutions to NP hard problems efficiently. CI paradigms are appropriate to adapt to the dynamic nature of WSN. The next subsections briefly explain some CI paradigms used in clustering WSN. Optimization problems due to its adaptive nature and distributive system properties. WSN nodes based on AIS using Antigen expressions, antibody expressions and the initialization of antibody optimizes the problems. The idea of genetic evolution of nature has immensely make an impact on the humans to use the ideology behind them in different disciplines of life and this gave birth to the energy consciousness. SI is a computational technique, which is originality from ant colonies, bird flocking, animal herding, and fish schoolings. A collective behavior in each BI system shows that single agent is not efficient and so their collective collaboration makes system intelligent. Decentralized and self-organized behavior of SI helps to solve the various optimization problems SI are Ant Colony Optimization (ACO).

Genetic Algorithm

Genetic Algorithm inspired by Charles Darwin's theory of evolution: 'the survival of the fittest", Genetic Algorithm (GA) was introduced formally by John Holland in 1970s. GA is an adaptive heuristic search algorithm that models biological genetic evolution. It proved to be a strong optimizer that searches among a population of solutions, and showed flexibility in solving dynamic problems. It has been successfully applied to many NP-hard problems. The main challenge in solving a problem with GA is the encoding of the problem into a set of chromosomes; each representing a solution to the problem. The quality of each chromosome is evaluated using a fitness function. Based on their fitness value, crossover and mutation procedures are applied on selected chromosomes. The crossover method produces new solutions, called offspring, by concatenating parts of two selected chromosomes. Mutation modifies one or more genetic element in the produced offspring to prevent being trapped in local minima.

Initialization

The genetic algorithm begins with an elementary population comprised of random chromosomes which includes genes with a sequence of 0s or 1s. Afterward, the algorithm leads individuals to achieve an optimum solution by the way of repetitive processes including crossover and selection operators. There are two ways to expand a new population. Steady-state GA and generational GA. In the case of the former, one or two members in the population are changed and at the same time, the generational GA replaces all the generated individuals of a generation.

Fitness

In the genetic algorithm, the fitness function, by meaning, is a process for scoring each chromosome based on their qualification. The allocated score is a trait for continuation of further reproduction. Dependence to difficulty by the fitness function is considerable, so that in case of some problems, it is not possible to define the problem. Naturally, individuals are allowed to go to the new generation based on their fitness score. Therefore, the score read outs the fate of individuals.

Selection

All through every successive generation, a fresh generation is developed through adopting members of the current generation to mate on the bases of their fitness. The individuals with higher fitness score have higher chance for being chosen, the process which outcomes in preferential adoption of the best solution. Common functions include a stochastically designed element for adopting small number of less fit individuals for sake of keeping diversity in the population. Among the several selection methods, Roulette-Wheel is adopted to differentiate proper individuals.

Crossover

The crossover or reproduction method constitutes the major step toward production. Indeed, sexual reproductive process by which inherited characteristics are moved from one generation to the next generation is simulated. In the reproduction process, crossover method adopts a couple of individuals as the parents through breeding selection process. The process continues to reach the desired size in the new population. Generally, several crossover operations take place, each of which with different aims. The easiest way is single point, where a random point is adopted to divide the role of the patents.

Particle Swarm Optimization

Particle Swarm Optimization (PSO) was developed in 1995 by James Kennedy, and Russell Eberhart (Bratton et al., 2007). PSO is a strong stochastic nonlinear- optimization technique based on movement and intelligence of swarms. It is motivated from social behavior of bird or fish, where a group of birds randomly look for food in an area by following the nearest bird to the food. It merges local search methods with global search methods depending on social interaction between particles to locate the best achieved position so far. PSO and GA are very similar (Cristian et al., 2003). Both are population based stochastic optimization that begins with a group of a randomly generated population. They have fitness values to estimate their population, and update the population and search for the optimum with random techniques. However, PSO varies from GA in that there is no crossover and mutation. PSO particles do not expire. They update themselves with the internal velocity. Finally, the information sharing mechanism in PSO is significantly different. Each particle is treated as a point in a multi-dimensional space, and changes its position influenced by two components: the cognitive component and the social component outcomes from neighbor communication. Several enhancements on the standard PSO equation are listed in (Braik et al., 2008).

Cuckoo Search

It is Developed by Yang and Deb in 2009, Cuckoo Search is a new met heuristic optimization algorithm that is motivated from the behavior of some cuckoo species. The cuckoo lays an egg in a host's nest with risk of surviving. If the egg is to find out by the host, it can either throw the egg away, or abandon the nest and build a completely new nest. This behavior is converted to Algorithm. It can also be taken form Levy Flight distribution which is a random walk ` with step length depending on the current state plus a transition probability. This algorithm is characterized by its simplicity and fast convergence. However, the improper tuning of the CS parameters could result in decrease of the algorithm efficiency. Several improvements are made to the CS algorithm.

Neural Networks

A Neural Network (NN) is a big system containing parallel or distributed processing components called neurons connected in a graph topology. These neurons are connected through weighted connections known as synapses. Weight vectors (synapses) connect the network input layer to output layer. Indeed, the knowledge of NN is stored on weights of its connections and it doesn't need to any data storage. In other words, Artificial Neural Networks are arithmetic algorithms which are able to find out complicated mappings between input and output according to supervised training or they can categorize input data in an unsupervised manner.

One of the problems with NNs is selecting of appropriate topology for the problem. This selection depends on attributes of the problem, the most possible techniques for solving the problem and also the properties of NN. Moreover, there are different types of training rules which are motivated from biology science which decides the way NNs learn. In most of these networks, training is based on learning by example. Thus, a set of correct input-output data are often given to the network and using these examples, the network should change the weights values so that by inputting new data the network can return correct answers as output what we call "learning". One of the most important properties of NNs is ability to recognize the data affected by noise or intentional change and to remove those variations after learning. There are different types of NN's topologies, each have different capabilities according to the application needed.

The network's efficiencies depend on its structure, dynamics and training rules. The most important applications of NN include prediction, classification and identification. The most significant question is: how can Neural Networks help out to energy conservation of Wireless Sensor Networks? In fact, Neural Networks are not energy conservation techniques and cannot independently assist to conserve energy but they can help energy conservation methods as intelligent tools to work in more efficient, useful and easier way. So the energy conservation methods are the same previous methods which can use neural network as a tool to better approach to their goals. However, there is enough enthusiasm to implement full ANNs on each single sensor node due to analogy between WSNs and ANN as in. Neural Network based energy efficient method can also be classified according to the role Neural Networks play on them or according to the appropriated neural topologies applied.

Fuzzy Logic

Dynamic Channel allocation problem in a hierarchical cellular system, which consists of a macro layer and a micro layer. The macro cells find fast mobile users. Though, if one directs too much mobile users to the macro cells, the system capacity becomes low. Alternatively, the microcells are manufactured to increase capacity, but they cause a lots of handoffs. The aim is to maximize the system capacity while keeping the number of handoffs small. The DCA algorithm reduce the handoff rate by a fuzzy layer selection algorithm, which makes use of the past cell residence times of a user and the channel occupancy of the target cell. To maximize the capacity, they use a distributed channel assignment algorithm to dynamically allocate the channels among the two layers. Exchange of data is allowed between neighboring macrocells. The state of channel allocation in a macro cell and its interfering cells are tabulated in a channel allocation table, which provides all information needed in the integrated resource allocation scheme, a novel call admission control (CAC) scheme using fuzzy logic is used for the reverse link transmission in wideband Code Division Multiple Access (CDMA) cellular communications. The fuzzy CAC scheme first uses the effective bandwidths of the call request from a mobile station and its mobility information, then decides a decision to accept or reject the connection request based on the estimation and system resource availability

OPEN CHALLENGES

The existing research works in literature focus on evaluating and improving coverage performance of area and target coverage, while maintaining connectivity and maximizing the network lifetime. Although many schemes have been proposed and progress has been made in coverage problems of WSN, there are still many open research issues.

More authentic model of sensor nodes must be incorporated with the coverage schemes in order to perform various real-time applications excellently. Effective coverage scheme should be proposed to implement real-time applications. Therefore, most existing centralized solutions need to be developed including the distributed and localized algorithms or protocols. The mobile sensor problem in WSN must be solved perfectly.

As we discuss in literature sections, current researches in coverage of WSN consider either area (point) coverage or path coverage, except for mobile sensor. Some ideas focus on evaluating the coverage performance and others improving the coverage performance. Some proposals consider about stationary network and others mobile network. However, the current schemes for the coverage of WSN have two primary limitations. Firstly, in the literature most existing works assume that the boundary of sensing and communication of sensor node is a perfect circle which is a known and static radius in considering the coverage problem. That is, the sensor coverage model is the sensing disk model where a sensor can face a disk centered at itself with a radius equal to a fixed sensing range. In this model all events within the circular disc are assumed to be detected with probability 1. However, the sensing pattern of sensor node is controlled by themselves (for example, insufficient hardware calibration) and other factors (such as obstacles, environmental conditions, and noise). The effect of obstacles on the sensing region of sensor node. Hence, the sensing ranges are very irregular and dynamic in real situation for wireless sensor network, which generally employ small quality radio modules to decrease the cost. In addition, there are some sensors having a sector sensing range, such as the directional antenna. Despite the outcomes based on the simplified theoretical sensing coverage model could expose high-level insights or guidelines, it could cause an all-too-common problem found today where solutions developed by simulation and analysis do not work in the real world. The irregularity is a ordinary issue in wireless sensor networks, so it is unwise for developers to continue to ignore this reality. Additionally, most of the coverage protocols assume location-aware nodes. However, location estimates using existing sensor localization protocols is not very accurate. Therefore, there is a need to assess the effect of location in-accuracies on the performance of various coverage protocols.

Secondly, by leveraging mobile nodes, more network wide performance metrics inclusive coverage can be greatly improved than the conventional approach by deploying a great amount of stationary sensor nodes and then apply coverage control algorithms to schedule sensors' activity in an efficient way. on the other hand the movement of sensors may be caused by the environment they are in (such as winds, currents, and etc.) or by the actuator they have. Mobile nodes are usually expensive than their stationary compeers, and they are often considered as rich of resources such as more battery supply, advanced computing and more storage. In addition, the earlier works assume random movement of nodes without considering any mobility models. In applications where nodes go around in a certain pattern, mobility could further be exploited to develop coverage and connectivity. On the other hand, mobility poses challenges in guaranteeing coverage at all times, while alternatively, it enables nodes to cover areas that would have been left uncovered using only static nodes.

Thirdly, with the developing research interest in underwater sensor networks for marine life and coral reef monitoring, a range of applications, such as oceanographic data collection, pollution monitoring, and offshore explorations pose a lot of challenges to the coverage–connectivity problem. Several extensive researches have been done in the context of 2D terrestrial networks. Though, since a 3D network is still a novelty, many basic problems have largely been unexplored in the context of a 3D network. There are several important problems in sensor network design where the physical dimensionality of the network participates a very significant role and the optimal solution of such a problem in a 3D network is quite different from the optimal solution in a 2D network. Since the density of nodes to completely cover a three-dimensional region is prohibitively higher than the corresponding two-dimensional case, sensors set up in a three-dimensional setting, like in underwater or in the atmosphere, should collaborate with each other to regulate their depths according to their sensing ranges in order to achieve complete three-dimensional coverage.

Fourthly, in keeping with the application necessity the existing coverage schemes for WSN adjust the state of sensor nodes. Although the connectivity of WSN is considered, the other properties (e.g., routing, location) are not incorporated the coverage schemes. In practice, the coverage scheme can make the changes of nodes' states to bring the change of other properties. For example, when a node is from active to asleep, some routings will break.

CONCLUSION

In this chapter, the state-of-the art research for coverage problem in wireless sensor networks is reviewed. It is observed that several approaches have been explored to address the different coverage problems. Among them area coverage is widely studied. Since coverage problem is fundamental to many applications of wireless sensor network, research and investigation activities remain active in this area. The Main constraints of WSNs are energy consumption and lifetime of the network, which are common concerns almost for any WSN application. In general, the operational stages of WSNs include node placement, network coverage, clustering, data aggregation, and routing. A technical survey was performed on these operational stages. By finding the disadvantages and optimizing them, ideal parameters of the network were achieved.

It is expected that future approaches will be simple, effective and energy efficient in addressing coverage problem in WSN. The Problem of Energy consumption problem was arising. Clustering was used to solve the problem of energy consumption. Clustering has major problem such as latency, data accuracy. To manage the clustering problems, CI techniques proved promising results in solving energy consumption problem in WSN.

REFERENCES

Akyildiz, F., Su, W. Sankarasubramaniam, Y., & Cayirci, E. (2002). Wireless sensor networks: a survey. *Computer Networks*, 38, 393-422,

Andries, P., & Engelbrecht, H. (2007). *Computational Intelligence: An Introduction*. Wiley Publishing.

Baldus, H., Klabunde, K., & Muesch, G. (2004). Reliable Set-Up of Medical Body-Sensor Networks. Proc. of EWSN '04, Berlin, Germany.

Braik, M., Sheta, A., & Arieqat, A. (2008). A comparison between GA and PSO in training ANN to model the chemical process reactor. *Proceedings of the AISB symposium on swarm intelligence algorithms and applications*.

Bratton, D., & Kennedy, J. (2007). Defining a standard for particle swarm optimization. *Proceedings of theIEEE Swarm Intelligence Symposium*. doi:10.1109/SIS.2007.368035

Cardei, M., & Du, D.Z. (2005). Improving wireless sensor network lifetime through power aware organization. *ACM Wireless Networks*, 11(3), 333–340.

Cardei, M., & Wu, J. (2005). Coverage in Wireless Sensor Networks. In M. Ilyas & I. Mahgoub (Eds.), *Handbook of Sensor Networks: Compact Wireless and Wired Sensing Systems*. CRC Press.

Cerpa, A., & Estrin, D. (2004). ASCENT: Adaptive Self-Configuring sEnsor Networks Topologies. *IEEE Transactions on Mobile Computing* (Vol. 3, pp. 272–284).

Chakrabarty, K., Iyengar, S. S., Qi, H., & Cho, E. (2002). Grid Coverage for Surveillance and Target Location in Distributed Sensor Networks. *IEEE Transactions on Computers*, 51(12), 1448–1453. doi:10.1109/TC.2002.1146711

Cristian, I., & Trelea, T. (2003). The particle swarm optimization algorithm: convergence analysis and parameter selection. *Information Processing Letters*, 85(6), 317–325.

Gage, D. (1992). Command control for many-robot systems. *Proceedings of the 19th Annual AUVS Technical Symposium*.

Haenggi, M. (2005). Opportunities and Challenges in Wireless Sensor Networks. In I. Mahgoub (Ed.), *Handbook of Sensor Networks: Compact Wireless and Wired Sensing Systems*. Boca Raton: CRC Press.

Heinzelman, W., Chandrakasan, R., & Balakrishnan, H. (2000). Energy-efficient communication protocols for wireless microsensor networks. *Proceedings of Hawaiian International Conference on Systems Science*. doi:10.1109/HICSS.2000.926982

Ilyas, I., Mohammad, H., & Imad, M. (2005). *Handbook of Sensor Networks: Compact Wireless and Wired Sensing Systems*. CRC Press.

Ilyas, M., & Mahgoub, I. (2005). *Handbook of Sensor Networks: Compact Wireless and Wired Sensing Systems*. CRC Press LLC.

Kumar, S., Lai, T. H., & Balogh, J. (2004). On K-Coverage in A Mostly Sleeping Sensor Network. *Proceedings of the tenth Annual International Conference on Mobile Computing and Networking (MobiCom)*. doi:10.1145/1023720.1023735

Lazos, L., & Poovendran, R. (2006). Stochastic Coverage in Heterogeneous Sensor Networks. *ACM Transactions on Sensor Network*, 2(3), 325-358.

Mainwaring, A., Polastre, J., Szewczyk, R., Culler, D., & Anderson, J. (2002). Wireless Sensor Networks for Habitat Monitoring, *Proceedings of WSNA*, Atlanta, USA. doi:10.1145/570738.570751

Martinez, K., Ong, R., Hart, J. K., & Stefanov, J. (2004). Sensor Web for Glaciers. In the Proceedings of (EWSN 2004). Berlin, Germany.

Michahelles, F., Matter, P., Schmidt, A., & Schiele, B. (2003). Applying Wearable Sensors to Avalanche Rescue. *Computers & Graphics*, 27(6), 839–847. doi:10.1016/j.cag.2003.08.008

Podurl, S., & Sukhatme, G. S. (2004). Constrained coverage for mobile sensor networks.*Proceedings of the IEEE International Conference on Robotics and Automation*.

Pottie, G. J., & Kaiser, W. J. (2000). Wireless integrated network sensors. *Communications of the ACM*, 43, 51-58.

Shen, X., & Chen, J., Wang, Zhi., & Sun, Y. (2006). Grid Scan: A Simple and Effective Approach for Coverage Issue in Wireless Sensor Networks. *Proceedings of theIEEE International Communications Conference* (Vol. 8, pp. 3480-3484). doi:10.1109/ICC.2006.255611

Szewczy, K. R., Osterweil, E., Polastre, J., & Hamilton, A. (2004). Habitat monitoring with sensor networks. *Communications of the ACM*, 47(6), 34–44. doi:10.1145/990680.990704

Wang, W., Chua, K. C., & Srinivasan, V. (2008). Coverage in Hybrid Mobile Sensor Networks. *IEEE Transactions on Mobile Computing*, 7(11), 1374–1387. doi:10.1109/TMC.2008.68

Wu, J., Dai, F., Gao, M., & Stojmenovic, I. (2002). On calculating power aware connected dominating sets for efficient routing in ad hoc wireless networks. *Journal of Communications and Networks.*, 4(1), 59–70. doi:10.1109/JCN.2002.6596934

Wu, J., & Li, H. (1999). On calculating connected dominating set for efficient routing in ad hoc wireless networks. *Proceedings of the Third International Workshop on Discrete Algorithms and Methods for Mobile Computing and Communications*. doi:10.1145/313239.313261

Xing, G., Wang, X., & Zhang, Y. LU, C., Pless, R., & Gill, C. (2005). Integrated coverage and connectivity configuration for energy conservation in sensor networks. ACM Transactions on Sensor Network (Vol. 1, pp. 36–72).

Ye, F., Luo, H., Cheng, J., Lu, S., & Zhang, L. (2002). A two-tier data dissemination model for large-scale wireless sensor networks. *Proceedings of the 8th Annual International Conference on Mobile Computing and Networking*, Atlanta, Georgia, USA. doi:10.1145/570645.570664

Zhang, H., & Hou, J. C. (2005). Maintaining Sensing Coverage and Connectivity in Large Sensor Networks. *Ad Hoc & Sensor Wireless Networks.*, *1*, 89–124.

Zhao, F., & Guibas, L. (2004). *Wireless Sensor Networks. An Information Processing Approach*. Morgan Kaufmann.

KEY TERMS AND DEFINITIONS

Area Coverage: Area Coverage in sensor networks measures how closely target area is observed by the sensor nodes.

Computational Intelligence: It is a set of nature-inspired computational techniques and approaches to address complex real-world problems to which mathematical or traditional modeling can be of no use for a few reasons: the processes might be too difficult for mathematical reasoning, it might contain some uncertainties during the process, or the process might simply be stochastic in nature.

Genetic Algorithm: GA is an adaptive heuristic search algorithm that models biological genetic evolution. It proved to be a strong optimizer that searches among a population of solutions, and showed flexibility in solving dynamic problems.

Particle Swarm Optimization: It is motivated from social behavior of bird or fish, where a group of birds randomly look for food in an area by following the nearest bird to the food.

Sensor Node: A sensor node is a node in a sensor network that is capable of performing some processing, gathering sensory information and communicating with other connected nodes in the network.

Signal: A signal is a function that conveys information about the behavior or attributes of some phenomenon.

Wireless Sensor Network (WSN): WSNs are spatially distributed autonomous sensors to monitor physical or environmental conditions.

Compilation of References

Abraham, A. (2004). Meta-Learning Evolutionary Artificial Neural Networks. *Neurocomputing, 56*, 1–38. doi:10.1016/S0925-2312(03)00369-2

Adamczyk, J., Hesselsoe, M., Iversen, N., Horn, M., Lehner, A., Nielsen, P. H., & Wagner, M. et al. (2003). The isotope array, a new tool that employs substrate-mediated labeling of rRNA for determination of microbial community structure and function. *Applied and Environmental Microbiology, 69*(11), 6875–6887. doi:10.1128/AEM.69.11.6875-6887.2003 PMID:14602652

Adams, J. (2008). Pharmacogenomics and Personalised Medicine. *Nature Education, 1*(1), 194.

Adlassnig, K. P. (1986). Fuzzy set theory in medical diagnosis. *IEEE Transactions on Systems, Man, and Cybernetics, 16*(2), 260–265. doi:10.1109/TSMC.1986.4308946

Agus, D. B. (2012). A Doctor in Your Pocket. *The Wall Street Journal.* Retrieved from http://online.wsj.com/news/articles/SB10001424052970204124204577155162382326848

Ahlqvist, O., Keukelaar, J., & Oukbir, K. (2003). Rough and fuzzy geographical data integration. *International Journal of Geographical Information Science, 17*(3), 223–234. doi:10.1080/13658810210157750

Ahmad, M. S. (2009). Iris recognition using the discrete cosine transform and artificial neural networks. *J. Computer Science, 5*(4), 369373.

Ahmad, M. Z., & Baets, B. D. (2009). *A Predator-Prey Model with Fuzzy Initial Populations.* IFSA-EUSFLAT.

Ahmad, M. Z., & Hasan, M. K. (2012). Modeling of biological populations using fuzzy differential equations, International Conference Mathematical and Computational Biology 2011. *International Journal of Modern Physics: Conference Series, 9*, 354–363.

Ahmadyfard, A., & Modares, H. (2008). Combining PSO and K-Means to enhance data clustering. *Proceedings of theInternational Symposium on Telecommunication* (pp. 688 – 691). doi:10.1109/ISTEL.2008.4651388

Ahmed, N., Natarajan, T., & Rao, K. R. (1974). Discrete cosine transforms. *IEEE Transactions on Computers, C-32*, 9093.

Ahmed, Z., Salama, M. A., Hefny, H., & Hassanien, A. E. (2012). A Hepatitis C Virus Data Sets, Rough Sets-Based Rules Generation Approach. *Proceedings of AMLTA 2012, CCIS,* (Vol. *322,* pp. 52–59).

Ahn, J. Y., Han, K. S., Oh, S. Y., & Lee, C. D. (2011). An Application of Interval-Valued Intuitionistic Fuzzy Sets for Medical Diagnosis of Headache. *International Journal of Innovative Computing, Information, & Control, 7*(5B), 2755–2762.

Ahn, J. Y., Kim, Y. H., & Kim, S. K. (2003). A fuzzy differential diagnosis of headache applying linear regression method and fuzzy classification. *IEICE Transactions on Information and Systems, E86-D*(12), 2790–2793.

Ahn, J. Y., Mum, K. S., Kim, Y. H., Oh, S. Y., & Han, B. S. (2008). A fuzzy method for medical diagnosis of headache. *IEICE Transactions on Information and Systems, E91-D*(4), 1215–1217. doi:10.1093/ietisy/e91-d.4.1215

Akin, O., & Oruc, O. (2012). A Prey predator model with fuzzy initial values. *Hacettepe Journal of Mathematics and Statistics, 41*(3), 387–395.

Akutsu, T., Miyano, S., & Kuhara, S. (1999). Identification of genetic networks from a small number of gene expression patterns under the Boolean network model. In Pacific symposium on biocomputing (Vol. 4, pp. 17-28).

Akyildiz, F., Su, W. Sankarasubramaniam, Y., & Cayirci, E. (2002). Wireless sensor networks: a survey. *Computer Networks, 38*, 393-422,

Ali, E. S., & Abd-Elazim, S. M. (2011). Bacteria foraging optimization algorithm based load frequency controller for interconnected power system. *Electrical Power Energy System, 33*(3), 633–638. doi:10.1016/j.ijepes.2010.12.022

Ali, E. S., & Abd-Elazim, S. M. (2013). BFOA based Design of PID Controller for Two Area Load Frequency Control with Nonlinearities. *International Journal of Electrical Power & Energy Systems, 51*, 224–231. doi:10.1016/j.ijepes.2013.02.030

Ali, R., Hussain, J., Siddiqi, M. H., & Lee, S. (2015). H2RM: A Hybrid Rough Set Reasoning Model for Prediction and Management of Diabetes Mellitus. *Sensors (Basel, Switzerland), 15*(7), 15921–15951. doi:10.3390/s150715921 PMID:26151207

Allahviranloo, T., Abbasbandy, S., Salahshour, S., & Hakimzadeh, A. (2011). A., A new method for solving fuzzy linear differential equations. *Computing, 92*(2), 181–197. doi:10.1007/s00607-010-0136-6

Allahviranloo, T., & Ahmadi, M. B. (2010). Fuzzy Laplace transforms. *Soft Computing, 14*(3), 235–243. doi:10.1007/s00500-008-0397-6

Allan, M., Collins, A., & Quillian, M. R. (1969). Retrieval time from semantic memory. *Journal of Verbal Learning and Verbal Behavior, 8*(2), 240–248. doi:10.1016/S0022-5371(69)80069-1

Allan, M., Collins, A., & Quillian, M. R. (1970). Does category size affect categorization time? *Journal of Verbal Learning and Verbal Behavior, 9*(4), 432–438. doi:10.1016/S0022-5371(70)80084-6

Allen, J., & Frisch, A. (1982). What's in a Semantic Network. *Proceedings of the 20th. annual meeting of ACL*, Toronto (pp. 19-27). doi:10.3115/981251.981256

Aloy, P., & Russell, R. B. (2003). InterPreTS: Protein interaction prediction through tertiary structure. *Bioinformatics (Oxford, England), 19*(1), 161–162. doi:10.1093/bioinformatics/19.1.161 PMID:12499311

Ambroise, C., & McLachlan, G. J. (2002). Selection bias in gene extraction on the basis of microarray gene-expression data. *Proceedings of the National Academy of Sciences of the United States of America, 99*(10), 6562–6566. doi:10.1073/pnas.102102699 PMID:11983868

Andreeva, A., Howorth, D., Chandonia, J.M., Brenner, S.R., Hubbard, T.J., Clothia, C. & Murzin, A.G. (2008). Data growth and its impact on the SCOP database: New developments. *Nucleic Acids Research,* 36(Database issue), D419-D425.

Angenendt, P. (2005). Progress in protein and antibody microarray technology. *Drug Discovery Today, 10*(7), 503–511. doi:10.1016/S1359-6446(05)03392-1 PMID:15809196

Angenendt, P., Kreutzberger, J., Glokler, J., & Hoheisel, J. D. (2007). Generation of highdensity protein microarrays by cell-free in situ expression of unpurified PCR products. *Molecular & Cellular Proteomics, 5*(9), 1658–1666. doi:10.1074/mcp.T600024-MCP200 PMID:16825183

Anouncia, S. M., Clara Madonna, L. J., & Jeevitha, P. & Nandhini. (2013). Design of a Diabetic Diagnosis System Using Rough Sets. *Cybernetics and Information Technologies*, *13*(3), 124–139.

Arafat, H., Barakat, S., & Goweda, A. F. (2012). Using Intelligent Techniques for Breast Cancer Classification. *International Journal of Emerging Trends & Technology in Computer Science*, *1*(3), 26–36.

Armstrong, S. A., Staunton, J. E., Silverman, L. B., Pieters, R., den Boer, M. L., Minden, M. D., & Korsmeyer, S. J. et al. (2002). MLL translocations specify a distinct gene expression profile that distinguishes a unique leukemia. *Nature Genetics*, *30*(1), 41–47. doi:10.1038/ng765 PMID:11731795

Arnau, V., Mars, S., & Marin, I. (2005). Iterative cluster analysis of protein interaction data. *Bioinformatics (Oxford, England)*, *21*(3), 364–378. doi:10.1093/bioinformatics/bti021 PMID:15374873

Ascierto, P., Larkin, J., Dummer, R., Testori, A., Maio, M., Hogg, D., & Kirkwood, J. M. et al. (2011). Improved Survival with Vemurafenib in Melanoma with BRAF V600E Mutation. *The New England Journal of Medicine*, *364*(26), 2507–2516. doi:10.1056/NEJMoa1103782 PMID:21639808

AshaGowdaKaregowda, & SeemaKumari. (2013). Particle Swarm Optimization Algorithm Based K-Means and Fuzzy c-means clustering. *International Journal of Advanced Research in Computer Science and Software Engineering*, *3*(7).

Atanassov, K. T. (1986). Intuitionistic Fuzzy Sets. *Fuzzy Sets and Systems*, *20*(1), 87–96. doi:10.1016/S0165-0114(86)80034-3

Atanassov, K., & Gargov, K. (1989). Interval-valued intuitionistic fuzzy sets. *Fuzzy Sets and Systems*, *31*(3), 343–349. doi:10.1016/0165-0114(89)90205-4

Aversa, F., Gronda, E., Pizzuti, S., & Aragno, C. (2002). A fuzzy logic approach to decision support in medicine. *Proc. of the Conf. on Systemics, Cybernetics and Informatics*.

Aziz, N. A. A., Mubin, M., Mohamad, M. S., & Aziz, K. A. (2014). Scientific World Journal, 2014.

B.Chen, S.Pellicer, P.C.Tai, R.Harrison, & Y.Pan. (2009). Novel efficient granular computing models for protein sequence motifs and structure information discovery. *International Journal of Computational Biology and Drug Design*.

Babu, M. M. (2004). *An Introduction to Microarray Data Analysis*. Retrieved from www.mrc-lmb.cam.ac.uk/genomes/madanm/microarray

Babu, M. M. (2004). Introduction to microarray data analysis. In *Computational Genomics: Theory and Application*, 225-249.

Bader, G. D., Betel, D., & Hogue, C. W. (2003). BIND: The Biomolecular Interaction Network Database. *Nucleic Acids Research*, *31*(1), 248–250. doi:10.1093/nar/gkg056 PMID:12519993

Bader, G. D., & Hogue, C. W. (2003). An automated method for finding molecular complexes in large protein interaction networks. *BMC Bioinformatics*, *4*(1), 2. doi:10.1186/1471-2105-4-2 PMID:12525261

Bai, Q. (2010). Analysis of Particle Swarm Optimization Algorithm. *Computer and information science, 3*.

Bai, H., Ge, Y., Wang, J., & Liao, Y. L. (2010). Using Rough Set Theory to identify villages affected by birth defects: The example of Heshun, Shanxi, China. *International Journal of Geographical Information Science*, *24*(4), 559–576. doi:10.1080/13658810902960079

Bai, H., Ge, Y., Wangm, J., Li, D., Liao, Y., & Zheng, X. (2014). A method for extracting spatial rules from spatial data based on rough fuzzy sets. *Knowledge-Based Systems*, *57*, 28–50. doi:10.1016/j.knosys.2013.12.008

Bairoch, A., Bucher, P., & Hofmann, K. (1996). The PROSITE database, its status in 1995. *Nucleic Acids Research*, 24(1), 189-196.

Balamurugan, R., Natarajan, A., & Premalatha, K. (2014). Comparative study on swarm intelligence techniques for biclustering of microarray gene expression data. *International journal of computer, control, quantum and information engineering*, 8(2).

Baldus, H., Klabunde, K., & Muesch, G. (2004). Reliable Set-Up of Medical Body-Sensor Networks. Proc. of EWSN '04, Berlin, Germany.

Banks, A., Vincent, J., & Anyako, C. (2008). A review of particle swarm optimization". Part II: Hybridisation, combinatorial, multicriteria and constrained optimization, and indicative applications. *Natural Computing*, 7(1).

Bansal, J. C., Sharma, H., Jadon, S. S., & Clerc, M. (2014). Spider monkey optimization algorithm for numerical optimization. *Memetic computing*, 6(1), 31-47.

Barros, L. C., Bassanezi, R. C., & Tonelli, P. A. (2000). Fuzzy modelling in population dynamics. *Ecological Modelling*, 128(1), 27–33. doi:10.1016/S0304-3800(99)00223-9

Barsky, A., Munzner, T., Gardy, J., & Kincaid, R. (2008). Cerebral: Visualizing multiple experimental conditions on a graph with biological context. *IEEE Transactions on Visualization and Computer Graphics*, 14(6), 1253–1260. doi:10.1109/TVCG.2008.117 PMID:18988971

Barzinji, K. (2014). Fuzzy Delay Predator-Prey System: Existence Theorem and Oscillation Property of Solution, *Int. Journal of Math. Analysis*, 8(17), 829–847.

Baspinar, A., Cukuroglu, E., Nussinov, R., Keskin, O., & Gursoy, A. (2014). PRISM: a web server and repository for prediction of protein-protein interactions and modeling their 3D complexes. *Nucleic Acids Res, 42*(Web Server issue), W285-289. doi:10.1093/nar/gku397nar/gku397

Bassett, D. E., Eisen, M. B., & Boguski, M. S. (1999). Gene expression informatics: it's all in your mine. *Nature Genetics, 21*, 51–55. doi:10.1038/4478 PMID:9915502

Batagelj, V., & Mrvar, A. (2009). Pajek - Program for Large Network Analysis. *Connections, 21*, 47–57.

Bates, M. (1995, October24). Models of natural language understanding. *Proceedings of the National Academy of Sciences of the United States of America*, 92(22), 9977–9982. doi:10.1073/pnas.92.22.9977 PMID:7479812

Beaubouef, T., & Petry, F. (2002), A Rough Set Foundation for Spatial Data Mining Involving Vague Regions.*Proc. of IEEE Intl. Conference on Fuzzy Systems* (pp. 761–772). doi:10.1109/FUZZ.2002.1005090

Bede, B. (2006). A note on "two-point boundary value problems associated with non-linear fuzzy differential equations". *Fuzzy Sets and Systems, 157*(7), 986–989. doi:10.1016/j.fss.2005.09.006

Bede, B., & Gal, S. G. (2005). Generalizations of the differentiability of fuzzy-number-valued functions with applications to fuzzy differential equations. *Fuzzy Sets and Systems*, 2005, 151581–151599.

Bede, B., Rudas, I. J., & Bencsik, A. L. (2007). First order linear fuzzy differential equations under generalized differentiability. *Inf. Sci.*, 177(7), 1648–1662.

Belal, M., Gaber, J., El-Sayed, H., & Almojel, A. (2006). Swarm Intelligence. In Chapman & Hall (Eds.), Handbook of Bioinspired Algorithms and Applications (Vol. 7).

Bergeron, B. (2003). *Bioinformatics Computing*. New Delhi: Pearson Education.

Berggard, T., Linse, S., & James, P. (2007). Methods for the detection and analysis of protein-protein interactions. *Proteomics*, *7*(16), 2833–2842. doi:10.1002/pmic.200700131 PMID:17640003

Berkhin. (2002). Survey of Clustering Data Mining Techniques. *Accrue Software*.

Berman, H. M., Westbrook, J., Feng, Z., Gilliland, G., Bhat, T. N., Weissig, H., . . . Bourne, P. E. (2000). The Protein Data Bank. *Nucleic Acids Res, 28*(1), 235-242. doi:gkd090

Berners-Lee, T., Hendler, J., & Lassila, O. (2001). The Semantic Web. *Scientific American*, (May), 2001. PMID:11323639

Bevrani, H., Mitani, Y., & Tsuji, K. (2004). Robust decentralized load frequency control using an iterative linear matrix inequalities algorithm. *IEE Proceedings. Generation, Transmission and Distribution*, *151*(3), 347–354. doi:10.1049/ip-gtd:20040493

Bezdek, J. C. (1981). *Pattern recognition with fuzzy objective function algorithms*. New York: Plenum Press. doi:10.1007/978-1-4757-0450-1

Bharathi & Natarajan. (2010). Cancer Classification of Bioinformatics data using ANOVA. *International Journal of Computer Theory and Engineering*, *2*(3), 369–373.

Bhattacharjee, A., Richards, W. G., Staunton, J., Li, C., Monti, S., Vasa, P., & Meyerson, M. et al. (2001). Classification of human lung carcinomas by mRNA expression profiling reveals distinct adenocarcinoma subclasses. *PNAS. The National Academy of Sciences, USA*, *98*(24), 13790–13795. doi:10.1073/pnas.191502998 PMID:11707567

Big Data Now: 2014 Edition. (2015). O'Reilly Media, Inc. United States of America.

Big Data. (n. d.). Gartner IT Glossary. Retrieved from http://www.gartner.com/it-glossary/big-data/

Bill, C. H., & Chang, S. (2012). Protein Motif Extraction Using Neuro-Fuzzy optimization. *Bioinformatics (Oxford, England)*, *18*(8), 1084–1090. PMID:12176831

Biomarker. (n. d.). Retrieved from http://en.wikipedia.org/wiki/Biomarker

Bischoff, R., & Luider, T. M. (2004). Methodological advances in the discovery of protein and peptide disease markers. *Journal of Chromatography. B, Analytical Technologies in the Biomedical and Life Sciences*, *803*(1), 27–40. doi:10.1016/j.jchromb.2003.09.004 PMID:15025996

Blum, C., & Merkle, D. (2008). *Swarm Intelligence – Introduction and Applications. Natural Computing*. Berlin: Springer.

Boulos, M. N. K. (2004). Towards evidence-based, GIS driven national spatial health information infrastructure and surveillance services in the United Kingdom. *International Journal of Health Geographics*, *3*(1), 1. doi:10.1186/1476-072X-3-1 PMID:14748927

Box, G. E. P. (1957). Evolutionary operation: A method of increasing industrial productivity. *Applied Statistics*, *6*, 81–101.

Braik, M., Sheta, A., & Arieqat, A. (2008). A comparison between GA and PSO in training ANN to model the chemical process reactor. *Proceedings of the AISB symposium on swarm intelligence algorithms and applications*.

Brannetti, B., & Helmer-Citterich, M. (2003). iSPOT: A web tool to infer the interaction specificity of families of protein modules. *Nucleic Acids Research*, *31*(13), 3709–3711. doi:10.1093/nar/gkg592 PMID:12824399

Bratton, D., & Kennedy, J. (2007). Defining a standard for particle swarm optimization. *Proceedings of the IEEE Swarm Intelligence Symposium*. doi:10.1109/SIS.2007.368035

Brazma, A., & Vilo, J. (2000). Gene expression data analysis. *FEBS Letters*, *480*(1), 17–24. doi:10.1016/S0014-5793(00)01772-5 PMID:10967323

Breiman, L. (1996). Bagging predictors. *Machine Learning*, *24*(2), 123–140. doi:10.1007/BF00058655

Breiman, L. (2001). Random forests. *Machine Learning*, *45*(1), 5–32. doi:10.1023/A:1010933404324

Breiman, L., Friedman, J. H., Olshen, R. A., & Stone, C. J. (1984). *Classification and regression trees*. Chapman and Hall/CRC.

Breitenstein, M., Holzel, R., & Bier, F. F. (2010). Immobilization of different biomolecules by atomic force microscopy. *Journal of Nanobiotechnology*, *8*(1), 10. doi:10.1186/1477-3155-8-10 PMID:20478017

Breitkreutz, B. J., Stark, C., Reguly, T., Boucher, L., Breitkreutz, A., Livstone, M., . . . Tyers, M. (2008). The BioGRID Interaction Database: 2008 update. *Nucleic Acids Res, 36*(Database issue), D637-640. doi:10.1093/nar/gkm1001

Breitkreutz, B. J., Stark, C., & Tyers, M. (2003). Osprey: A network visualization system. *Genome Biology*, *4*(3), R22. doi:10.1186/gb-2003-4-3-r22 PMID:12620107

Breitling, R., Armengaud, P., Amtmann, A., & Herzyk, P. (2004). Rank products: A simple, yet powerful, new method to detect differentially regulated genes in replicated microarray experiments. *FEBS Letters*, *573*(1), 83–92. doi:10.1016/j.febslet.2004.07.055 PMID:15327980

Briggs, D. (2000). *Environmental Health Hazard Mapping for Africa*. World Health Organization – Regional Office for Africa.

Brody, E. N., & Gold, L. (2000). Aptamers as therapeutic and diagnostic agent. *Journal of Biotechnology*, *74*(1), 81–91. PMID:10943568

Brown, K. R., Otasek, D., Ali, M., McGuffin, M. J., Xie, W., Devani, B., & Jurisica, I. et al. (2009). NAViGaTOR: Network Analysis, Visualization and Graphing Toronto. *Bioinformatics (Oxford, England)*, *25*(24), 3327–3329. doi:10.1093/bioinformatics/btp595 PMID:19837718

Buckley, J. J. (2006). *Fuzzy Probability and Statistics*. Springer.

Buckley, J. J., & Feuring, T. (2000). Fuzzy differential equations. *Fuzzy Sets and Systems*, *110*(1), 43–54. doi:10.1016/S0165-0114(98)00141-9

Buckley, J. J., & Feuring, T. (2001). Fuzzy initial value problem for Nth-order linear differential equations. *Fuzzy Sets and Systems*, *121*(2), 247–255. doi:10.1016/S0165-0114(00)00028-2

Burrough, P. A., & Frank, A. U. (1996). *Geographic objects with indeterminate boundaries*. Taylor & Francis.

Buscema, M., Grossi, E., Bronstein, A., Lodwick, W., Asadi-Zeydabadi, M., Benzi, R., & Newman, F. (2013). A new algorithm for possible epidemic sources with application to the German *E. coli* outbreak. *International Journal of Geographical Information Science*, *2*(1), 155–200.

Butte, A. (2002). The use and analysis of microarray data. *Nature Reviews. Drug Discovery*, *1*(12), 951–960. doi:10.1038/nrd961 PMID:12461517

Cai, Y. D., Liu, X. J., Xu, X., & Zhou, P. (2001). Support vector machines for predicting protein structural class. *BMC Bioinformatics*, *2*(1), 3. doi:10.1186/1471-2105-2-3 PMID:11483157

Cai, Y., & Zhou, G. (2000). Prediction of protein structural classes by neural network. *Biochimie*, *82*(8), 783785. doi:10.1016/S0300-9084(00)01161-5 PMID:11018296

Calvo, T., Mayor, G., & Mesiar, R. (2002). *Aggregation Operators: New Trends and Applications*. Physica-Verlag. doi:10.1007/978-3-7908-1787-4

Campbell, C. T., & Kim, G. (2010). SPR microscopy and its applications to high-throughput analyses of biomolecular binding events and their kinetics. *Biomaterials, 28*(15), 2380–2392. doi:10.1016/j.biomaterials.2007.01.047 PMID:17337300

Cano, Y. C., Flores, H. R., & Medar, M. A. R. (2008). Fuzzy differential equations with generalized derivative. *Proceedings of the27th North American Fuzzy Information Processing Society International Conference, IEEE.*

Cano, Y. C., & Flores, H. R. (2008). On the new solution of fuzzy differential equations. *Chaos, Solitons, and Fractals, 38*(1), 112–119. doi:10.1016/j.chaos.2006.10.043

Cano, Y. C., Medar, M. A. R., & Flores, H. R. (2007). Sobre ecuaciones diferencial esdifusas. *Bol. Soc. Esp. Mat. Apl., 41*, 91–99.

Cao, Y. (2006). *Fuzzy logic network theory with applications to gene regulatory networks* [Unpublished doctoral dissertation]. Duke University.

Cardei, M., & Du, D.Z. (2005). Improving wireless sensor network lifetime through power aware organization. *ACM Wireless Networks, 11*(3), 333–340.

Cardei, M., & Wu, J. (2005). Coverage in Wireless Sensor Networks. In M. Ilyas & I. Mahgoub (Eds.), *Handbook of Sensor Networks: Compact Wireless and Wired Sensing Systems*. CRC Press.

Carlin, U. S., Komoroski, J., & Ohrn, A. (1998): Rough set analysis of medical datasets and a case of patients with suspected acute Appendicitis. *Proceedings of theWorkshop on Intelligent Data Analysis in medicine and pharmacologyECAI 98* (pp. 1 -11).

Casadio, R., Compiani, M., Fariselli, P. & Vivarelli, F. (1995). Predicting free energy contributions to the conformational stability of folded proteins. *Journal of Intelligent System Molecular Biology, 3*, 81–88.

Cerpa, A., & Estrin, D. (2004). ASCENT: Adaptive Self-Configuring sEnsor Networks Topologies. *IEEE Transactions on Mobile Computing* (Vol. 3, pp. 272–284).

Chaira, T., & Chaira, T. (2008). Intuitionistic fuzzy sets: Application to medical image segmentation. *Studies in Computational Intelligence, 85*, 51–68. doi:10.1007/978-3-540-75767-2_3

Chakrabarty, K., Iyengar, S. S., Qi, H., & Cho, E. (2002). Grid Coverage for Surveillance and Target Location in Distributed Sensor Networks. *IEEE Transactions on Computers, 51*(12), 1448–1453. doi:10.1109/TC.2002.1146711

Chang, S. L., & Zadeh, L. A. (1972). On fuzzy mapping and control. *IEEE Transactions on Systems, Man, and Cybernetics, 2*(1), 30–34. doi:10.1109/TSMC.1972.5408553

Chan, Z. S. H., Havukkala, I., Jain, V., Hu, Y., & Kasabov, N. (2008). Soft computing methods to predict gene regulatory networks: An integrative approach on time-series gene expression data. *Journalof Applied Soft Computing, 8*(3), 1189–1199. doi:10.1016/j.asoc.2007.02.023

Chatziioannou, A., Moulos, P., & Kolisis, F. N. (2009). Gene ARMADA: An integrated multi-analysisplatform for microarray data implemented in MATLAB. *BMC Bioinformatics, 10*(1), 354. doi:10.1186/1471-2105-10-354 PMID:19860866

Chen, T., He, H. L., & Church, G. M. (1999). Modeling gene expression with differential equations. In Pacific symposium on Biocomputing (Vol. 4, p. 4).

Chen, X. W., & Liu, M. (2005). Prediction of protein-protein interactions using random decision forest framework. *Bioinformatics, 21*(24), 4394-4400. doi:10.1093/bioinformatics/bti721

Chen, Y.-C., KripamoyAguan, Yang, C.-W., Wang, Y.-T., Pal, N. R., & Chung, I.-F. (2011). Discovery of Protein Phosphorylation Motifs through Exploratory Data Analysis. Discovery of Protein Phosphorylation Motifs(PLoS ONE).

Chena, C. B., & Wang, L. Y. (2006). Rough set-based clustering with refinement using Shannon's entropy theory. *Computers & Mathematics with Applications (Oxford, England)*, *52*(10–11), 1563–1576. doi:10.1016/j.camwa.2006.03.033

Chen, C. S., & Zhu, H. (2006). Protein microarrays. *BioTechniques*, *40*(4), 423–429, 425, 427. doi:10.2144/06404TE01 PMID:16629388

Cheng, B., Hudson, C., Kim, M., Crawford, A., Wright, J., & Che, D. (2011). Protein Sequence Motif Extraction using Decision Forest. Proceedings of the World Congress in Computer Science, Computer Engineering.

Cheng, J. & Baldi, P. (2007) Improved residue contact prediction using support vector machines and a large feature set. *BMC Bioinform*, 8, 113.

Chen, K.-H., Wang, K.-J., Tsai, M.-L., Wang, K.-M., Adrian, A. M., Cheng, W.-C., & Chang, K.-S. et al. (2014). Gene selection for cancer identification: A decision tree model empowered by particle swarm optimization algorithm. *BMC Bioinformatics*, *15*(1), 49. doi:10.1186/1471-2105-15-49 PMID:24555567

Chen, M., Wu, C., Xue, X., & Liu, G. (2008). On fuzzy boundary value problems. *Inf. Sci*, *178*(7), 1877–1892. doi:10.1016/j.ins.2007.11.017

Chen, S., Zheng, T., Shortreed, M. R., Alexander, C., & Smith, L. M. (2007). Analysis of cell surface carbohydrate expression patterns in normal and tumorigenic human breast cell lines using lectin arrays. *Analytical Chemistry*, *79*(15), 5698–5702. doi:10.1021/ac070423k PMID:17580952

Chiang, J.-H., & Chao, S.-Y. (2007). Modeling human cancer-related regulatory modules by ga-rnn hybrid algorithms. *BMC Bioinformatics*, *8*(1), 91. doi:10.1186/1471-2105-8-91 PMID:17359522

Chien, C. T., Bartel, P. L., Sternglanz, R., & Fields, S. (1991). The two-hybrid system: A method to identify and clone genes for proteins that interact with a protein of interest. *Proceedings of the National Academy of Sciences of the United States of America*, *88*(21), 9578–9582. doi:10.1073/pnas.88.21.9578 PMID:1946372

Chi, G., & Zhu, J. (2008). Spatial regression models for demographic models. *Population Research and Policy Review*, *27*(1), 17–42. doi:10.1007/s11113-007-9051-8

Cho, K.-H., Choo, S.-M., Jung, S., Kim, J.-R., Choi, H.-S., & Kim, J. (2007). Reverse engineering of gene regulatory networks. *Systems Biology, IET*, *1*(3), 149–163. doi:10.1049/iet-syb:20060075 PMID:17591174

Cho, K., Wang, X., Nie, S., Chen, Z. G., & Shin, D. M. (2008). Therapeutic nanoparticles for drug delivery in cancer. *Clinical Cancer Research*, *14*(5), 1310–1316. doi:10.1158/1078-0432.CCR-07-1441 PMID:18316549

Cho, S. B., & Ryu, J. (2002). Classifying gene expression data of cancer using classifier ensemble with mutually exclusive features *Proceedings of the IEEE*, *90*(11), 1744–1753. doi:10.1109/JPROC.2002.804682

Choubey, D. K., Paul, S., & Bhattachrjee, J. (2014). Soft Computing Approaches for Diabetes Disease Diagnosis: A Survey. *International Journal of Applied Engineering Research*, *9*(21), 11715–11726.

Chou, K. C. (1995). A novel approach to predicting protein structural classes in a (20-1)-D amino acid composition space. *Proteins*, *21*(4), 319344. doi:10.1002/prot.340210406 PMID:7567954

Chou, K. C. (1999). A key driving force in determination of protein structural classes. *Biochemical and Biophysical Research Communications*, *264*(1), 216224. doi:10.1006/bbrc.1999.1325 PMID:10527868

Chou, K. C. (2005). Using amphiphilic pseudo amino acid composition to predict enzyme. *Bioinformatics (Oxford, England)*, *21*(1), 1019. doi:10.1093/bioinformatics/bth466 PMID:15308540

Chou, K. C., & Shen, H. B. (2007). Review: Recent progresses in protein sub cellular location prediction. *Analytical Biochemistry*, *370*(1), 116. doi:10.1016/j.ab.2007.07.006

Chowdhury, A. R., & Chetty, M. (2011). An improved method to infer gene regulatory network using s-system. Proceedings of the 2011 IEEE congress on Evolutionary computation (CEC) (pp. 1012-1019). doi:10.1109/CEC.2011.5949728

Chuang, L. Y., Chang, H. W., Tu, C. J., & Yang, C. H. (2008). Improved binary PSO for feature selection using gene expression data. *Computational Biology and Chemistry*, *32*(1), 29–38. doi:10.1016/j.compbiolchem.2007.09.005 PMID:18023261

Chuang, L.-Y., Yang, C.-H., & Yang, C.-H. (2009). Tabu search and binary particle swarm optimization for feature selection using microarray data. *Journal of Computational Biology*, *16*(12), 1689–1703. doi:10.1089/cmb.2007.0211 PMID:20047491

Chung, F., Lu, L., Dewey, T. G., & Galas, D. J. (2003). Duplication models for biological networks. *Journal of Computational Biology*, *10*(5), 677–687. doi:10.1089/106652703322539024 PMID:14633392

Clote, P., & Backofen, R. (2000). *Computational Molecular Biology*. John Wiley & Sons Ltd.

Cluster Analysis. (n. d.) *Wikipedia*. Retrieved from: en.wikipedia.org/wiki/Cluster_analysis

CNS Spectrums. (n. d.). Retrieved from www.cnsspectrums.com

Cohen, J. (1960). A coefficient of agreement for nominal scales. *Educational and Psychological Measurement*, *20*(1), 37–46. doi:10.1177/001316446002000104

Cooper, M. A., & Singleton, V. T. (2007). A survey of the 2001 to 2005 quartz crystal microbalance biosensor literature: Applications of acoustic physics to the analysis of biomolecular interactions. *Journal of Molecular Recognition*, *20*(3), 154–184. doi:10.1002/jmr.826 PMID:17582799

Coriell Personalised Medicine Collaborative. (n. d.). Retrieved from http:// cpmc.coriell.org/

Corp, U. (2015). AI meets Big Data (White paper). Retrieved from http://etailwest.wbresearch.com/ai-meets-big-data-ml

Couzin, I. D., Krause, J., James, R., Ruxton, G. D., & Franks, N. R. (2002). Collective Memory and Spatial Sorting in Animal Groups. *Journal of Theoretical Biology*, *218*(1), 1–11. doi:10.1006/jtbi.2002.3065 PMID:12297066

Cox, M., & Ellsworth, D. (1997). Managing Big Data for Scientific Visualization. *Proc. of ACM Siggraph* (pp. 5-1–5-17).

Creighton, C., & Hanash, S. (2003). Mining gene expression databases for association rules. *Bioinformatics (Oxford, England)*, *19*(1), 79–86. doi:10.1093/bioinformatics/19.1.79 PMID:12499296

Cristian, I., & Trelea, T. (2003). The particle swarm optimization algorithm: convergence analysis and parameter selection. *Information Processing Letters*, *85*(6), 317–325.

Cui, X., & Potok, T. E. (2005). Document Clustering Analysis Based on Hybrid PSO K-means Algorithm. *Journal of Computer Sciences*, 2005, 27-33.

Cui, W., & Blockley, D. I. (1990). Interval provability theory for evidential support. *International Journal of Intelligent Systems*, *5*(2), 183–192. doi:10.1002/int.4550050204

Cui, Y., Chen, R. S., & Hung, W. (1998). Protein folding simulation with genetic algorithm and supersecondary structure constraints. *Proteins*, *31*(3), 247–257. doi:10.1002/(SICI)1097-0134(19980515)31:3<247::AID-PROT2>3.0.CO;2-G PMID:9593196

Cukier, K. (2010). Data, data everywhere: A special report on managing information. *The Economist*. Retrieved from http://www.economist.com/node/15557443

Cyran, K. A., & Mrzek, A. (2001). Rough sets in hybrid methods for pattern recognition. *International Journal of Intelligent Systems*, *16*(2), 149–168. doi:10.1002/1098-111X(200102)16:2<149::AID-INT10>3.0.CO;2-S

Das, S. A., Abraham, A., & Konar, A. (2008). Particle Swarm Optimization and Differential Evolution Algorithms: Technical Analysis, Applications and Hybridization Perspectives. In Ying Liu et al. (Eds.), Advances of Computational Intelligence in Industrial Systems. Springer Verlag, Germany.

Das, S., & Konar, A. (2007). Swarm Intelligence in Production Management and Engineering. In Dipak Laha and Purnendu Mandal (Eds.), Handbook of Computational Intelligence in Manufacturing and Production Management. Hershey, PA, USA: IGI Global.

Das, S., Panigrahi, B. K., & Pattnaik, S. S. (2009). Nature-Inspired Algorithms for Multi-objective Optimization. In Handbook of Research on Machine Learning Applications and Trends: Algorithms Methods and Techniques (Vol. 1, pp. 95–108). Hershey, PA, USA: IGI Global.

Dasgupta, S., Das, S., Abraham, A., & Biswas, A. (2009). Adaptive computational chemotaxis in bacterial foraging optimization: an analysis. *IEEE Transactions on Evolutionary Computing*, 13(4), 919-941

Dasgupta, A. (2007). *Handbook of Drug Monitoring Methods: Therapeutics and Drugs of Abuse* (pp. 5400–5411). New York, NY, USA: Humana Press.

Dash, S., & Dash, A. (2014). A correlation based multilayer perception algorithm for cancer classification with gene-expression dataset. *Proceedings of theInternational conference on Hybrid Intelligent Systems (HIS)*. doi:10.1109/HIS.2014.7086190

Dash, S., Patra, B., & Tripathy, B. K. (2012). A hybrid Data Mining Technique for Improving the Classification accuracy of Microarray Dataset. *I.J. Information engineering and electronics Business*, 2, 43-50.

Dash, M., Choi, K., Scheuermann, P., & Liu, H. (2002). Feature selection for clustering – a filter solution. *Proc.of theSecond International Conference on Data Mining* (pp. 115–122).

Dash, M., & Liu, H. (1997). Feature selection for classification, *Intelligent Data Analysis*. *International Journal (Toronto, Ont.)*, *1*(3), 131–156.

Dash, M., & Liu, H. (2003). Consistency-based search in feature selection. *Artificial Intelligence*, *151*(1-2), 155–176. doi:10.1016/S0004-3702(03)00079-1

Dash, N., Priyadarshini, R., & Misra, R. (2015). An Artificial Neural Network Model to Classify Multinomial Datasets with Optimized Target Using Particle Swarm Optimization Technique, *Springer-Smart Innovation. Systems and Technologies*, *31*, 355–364.

Dash, S. (2015). A Diverse Meta learning ensemble technique to handle imbalanced microarray dataset. *Proceedings of Seventh World Congress on Nature and Biologically Inspired Computing (NaBIC2015), Advances in Nature and Biologically Inspired Computing, Advances in Intelligent Systems and Computing*. Doi:10.1007/978-3-319-27400-3_1

Dasilva, N., Diez, P., Matarraz, S., Gonzalez-Gonzalez, M., Paradinas, S., Orfao, A., & Fuentes, M. (2012). Biomarker discovery by novel sensors based on nanoproteomics approaches. *Sensors (Basel, Switzerland)*, *12*(12), 2284–2308. doi:10.3390/s120202284 PMID:22438764

Das, S., Abraham, A., & Konar, A. (2008). Swarm Intelligence Algorithms in Bioinformatics, *Springer*[SCI]. *Studies in Computational Intelligence*, *94*, 113–147. doi:10.1007/978-3-540-76803-6_4

Das, S., & Idicula, S. M. (2010). Greedy Search-Binary PSO Hybrid for Biclustering Gene Expression Data. *International Journal of Computers and Applications*, 2(3), 1–5. doi:10.5120/651-908

Datta, D., Choudhuri, S. S., Konar, A., Nagar, A., & Das, S. (2009). A recurrent fuzzy neural model of a gene regulatory network for knowledge extraction using differential evolution. Proceedings of the IEEE congress on Evolutionary computation CEC '09 (pp. 2900-2906). doi:10.1109/CEC.2009.4983307

Davis, L. (1989). Adapting operator probabilities in genetic algorithms. *Proceedings of the Third International Conference on Genetic Algorithms*, La Jolla, CA (pp. 60-69). Morgan Kaufmann.

De Garis, H. (1990).Genetic programming: modular evolution for darwin machines.*Proceedings of the 1990 International Joint Conference on Neural Networks*, Washington, DC (pp. 194-197). Lawrence Erlbaum.

De Jong, K. A., K.A.(1992). Are genetic algorithms function optimizers. *Proceedings of the Second International Conference on Parallel Problem Solving from Nature* (pp. 20-27). Kaufmann.

De Las Rivas, J., & Fontanillo, C. (2010). Protein-protein interactions essentials: Key concepts to building and analyzing interactome networks. *PLoS Computational Biology*, 6(6), e1000807. doi:10.1371/journal.pcbi.1000807 PMID:20589078

De Silva, A. P., Gunaratne, H. Q., Gunnlaugsson, T., Huxley, A. J., McCoy, C. P., Rademacher, J. T., & Rice, T. E. (1997). Signaling recognition events with fluorescent sensors and switches. *Chemical Reviews*, 97(5), 1515–1566. doi:10.1021/cr960386p PMID:11851458

Debbage, P. (2009). Targeted drugs, and nanomedicine: Present and future. *Current Pharmaceutical Design*, 15(2), 153–172. doi:10.2174/138161209787002870 PMID:19149610

Deb, K., & Agrawal, R. B. (1995). Simulated binary crossover for continuous search space. *Complex Systems*, 9, 115148.

Deb, K., Pratap, A., Agarwal, S., & Meyarivan, T. (2002). A fast and elitist multi objective genetic algorithm: NSGA-II. *IEEE Transactions on Evolutionary Computation*, 6(2), 181–197. doi:10.1109/4235.996017

DeBock, K. W., Coussement, K., & VandenPoel, D. (2010). Ensemble classification based on generalized additive models. *Computational Statistics & Data Analysis*, 54(6), 1535–1546. doi:10.1016/j.csda.2009.12.013

Debouck, C., & Goodfellow, P. N. (1999). DNA microarrays in drug discovery and development. *Nature Genetics*, 21, 48–50. doi:10.1038/4475 PMID:9915501

DEIB. (n. d.). K Means. Retrieved from: www.home.deib.polimi.it/matteucc/clustering/tutorial_html/k_means.html

Deja, W. A., & Paszek, P. (2003). Applying rough set theory to multi stage medical diagnosing. *Fundamenta Informaticae*, 54(4), 387–408.

Dembele, D., & Kastner, P. (2003). Fuzzy c-means method for clustering microarray data. *Bioinformatics (Oxford, England)*, 19(8), 973–980. doi:10.1093/bioinformatics/btg119 PMID:12761060

Demir, E., Babur, O., Dogrusoz, U., Gursoy, A., Nisanci, G., Cetin-Atalay, R., & Ozturk, M. (2002). PATIKA: An integrated visual environment for collaborative construction and analysis of cellular pathways. *Bioinformatics (Oxford, England)*, 18(7), 996–1003. doi:10.1093/bioinformatics/18.7.996 PMID:12117798

Demystifying big data: A practical guide to transforming the business of Government. (2012). TechAmerica. Retrieved from http://www.techamerica.org/Docs/fileManager.cfm?f=techamerica-bigdatareport-final.pdf

Deng, T., Li, J. S., Jiang, J. H., Shen, G. L., & Yu, R. Q. (2006). Preparation of near-IR fluorescent nanoparticles for fluorescence-anisotropy-based immunoagglutination assay in whole blood. *Advanced Functional Materials*, 16(16), 2147–2155. doi:10.1002/adfm.200600149

Deng, X., Xu, J., Hui, J., & Wang, C. (2009). Probability fold change: A robust computational approach for identifying differentially expressed gene lists. *Computer Methods and Programs in Biomedicine*, *93*(2), 124–139. doi:10.1016/j.cmpb.2008.07.013 PMID:18842321

Deng, Y., Kayarat, D., Elasri, M. O., & Brown, S. J. (2005). Microarray data clustering using particle swarm optimization k-means algorithm.*Proc. 8th JCIS* (pp. 1730-1734).

Dervojeda, K., Verzijl, D., Nagtegaal, F., Lengton, M., & Rouwmaat, E. (2013, September). Big Data Artificial Intelligence, Business Innovation Observatory Contract No 190/PP/ENT/CIP/12/C/N03C01. *European Union*. Retrieved from http://ec.europa.eu/enterprise/policies/innovation/policy/business-innovation-observatory/files/case-studies/09-bid-artificial-intelligence_en.pdf

De, S. K., Biswas, R., & Roy, A. R. (2001). An application of intuitionistic fuzzy sets in medical diagnosis. *Fuzzy Sets and Systems*, *117*(2), 209–213. doi:10.1016/S0165-0114(98)00235-8

Diamond, P., & Kloeden, P. (1994). *Metric Spaces of Fuzzy Sets*. Singapore: World Scientific. doi:10.1142/2326

Diebold, F.X. (2000, August). Big data dynamic factor models for macroeconomic measurement and forecasting. *Presented at the 8th World Congress of the Econometric Society*, Seattle. Retrieved from http://www.upenn.edu/~fdiebold/papers107/ABCD_HOED.pdf

Dietterich, T. (2000). Ensemble methods in machine learning. *Proceedings of the Multiple Classifier System Conference* (pp. 1– 15). doi:10.1007/3-540-45014-9_1

Dietterich, T. G. (2000). An experimental comparison of three methods for constructing ensembles of decision trees: Bagging, boosting, and randomization. *Machine Learning*, *40*(2), 139–157. doi:10.1023/A:1007607513941

Díez, P., González-González, M., Lourido, L., Dégano, R. M., Ibarrola, N., Casado-Vela, J., & Fuentes, M. et al. (2015). NAPPA as a Real New Method for Protein Microarray Generation. *Microarrays*, *4*(2), 214–227. doi:10.3390/microarrays4020214

Ding, Y. S., Zhang, T. L., & Chou, K. C. (2007). Prediction of protein structure classes with pseudo amino acid composition and fuzzy support vector machines network. *Protein and Peptide Letters*, *14*, 811815. PMID:17979824

Diniz, G. L., Fernandes, J. F. R., Meyer, J. F. C. A., & Barros, L. C. (2001). *A fuzzy Cauchy problem modelling the decay of the biochemical oxygen demand in water*. IEEE.

Dobzhansky, T. (1946). Genetics of Natural Populations. Xiii. Recombination and Variability in Populations of Drosophila Pseudoobscura. *Genetics*, *31*(3), 269–290. PMID:17247197

Dong, Z., & Ze, H., P, Wang,D. & Jiao,S.(2006).Thermal Process System Identification Using Particle Swarm Optimization. *Proceedings of theIEEE International Symposium on* Industrial Electronics(*Vol. 1*, pp. 194-198).

Dorigo, M. (1992). Optimization, learning and natural algorithms (in Italian) [Ph.D. Thesis]. Dipartimento diElettronica, Politecnico di Milano, Italy.

Dorigo, M. (1992). *Optimization, learning and natural algorithms* {Ph.D. Thesis]. Politecnico di Milano, Italy.

Dorigo, M., Maniezzo, V., & Colorni, A. (1991). Positive feedback as a search strategy (Tech. Report 91-016). Dipartimento di Elettronica, Politecnico di Milano, Italy.

Dorigo, M., Bonabeau, E., & Theraulaz, G. (2000). Ant algorithms and stigmergy. *Future Generation Computer Systems*, *16*(8), 851–871. doi:10.1016/S0167-739X(00)00042-X

Draghici, S. (2003). *Data analysis tools for DNA microarrays*. CRC Press. doi:10.1201/9780203486078

Dubois, D., & Prade, H. (1982). Towards fuzzy differential calculus: Part 3, Differentiation. *Fuzzy Sets and Systems*, *8*(3), 225–233. doi:10.1016/S0165-0114(82)80001-8

Dubois, D., & Prade, H. (1990). Rough fuzzy sets and fuzzy rough sets. *International Journal of General Systems*, *17*(2–3), 191–208. doi:10.1080/03081079008935107

Duch, W., Krzysztof Gr, ., Adamczak, R., Grudzinski, K., & Hippe, Z. S. (2001). Rules for Melanoma Skin Cancer Diagnosis. *KOSYR*, *2001*, 59–68.

Dudoit, S., Yang, Y. H., Callow, M. J., & Speed, T. P. (2002). Statistical methods for identifying differentially expressed genes in replicated cDNA microarray experiments. *Statistica Sinica*, *12*(1), 111–140.

Duggan, D. J., Bittner, M., Chen, Y., Meltzer, P., & Trent, J. M. (1999). Expression profiling using cDNA microarrays. *Nature Genetics*, *21*, 10–14. doi:10.1038/4434 PMID:9915494

Dumbill, E. (2012, January 11). What is big data? An introduction to the big data landscape. O'Reilly Radar.

Dunker, A. K., Cortese, M. S., Romero, P., Iakoucheva, L. M., & Uversky, V. N. (2005). Flexible nets. The roles of intrinsic disorder in protein interaction networks. *FEBS J*, *272*(20), 5129-5148. doi:10.1111/j.1742-4658.2005.04948.x

Dunn, J. C. (1973). A fuzzy relative of the isodata process and its use in detecting compact well-separated clusters.

Dunn, C. E., Woodhouse, J., Bhopal, R. S., & Acquilla, S. D. (1995). Asthma and factory emissions in northern England: Addressing public concern by combining geographical and epidemiological methods. *Journal of Epidemiology and Community Health*, *49*(4), 395–400. doi:10.1136/jech.49.4.395 PMID:7650463

Du, Q. S., Jiang, Z. Q., He, W. Z., Li, D. P., & Chou, K. C. (2006). Amino acid principal component analysis (AAPCA) and its applications in protein structural class prediction. *Journal of Biomolecular Structure & Dynamics*, *23*(6), 635640. doi:10.1080/07391102.2006.10507088 PMID:16615809

Duveneck, G. L., Abel, A. P., Bopp, M. A., Kresbach, M. G., & Ehrat, M. (2002). Planar waveguides for ultra-high sensitivity of the analysis of nucleic acids. *Analytica Chimica Acta*, *469*(1), 49–61. doi:10.1016/S0003-2670(01)01593-8

Dy, J. G., & Brodley, C. E. (2004). Feature Selection for Unsupervised Learning. *Journal of Machine Learning Research*, *5*, 845–889.

Edwards, B. S., Oprea, T., Prossnitz, E. R., & Sklar, L. A. (2004). Flow cytometry for high-throughput, high-content screening. *Current Opinion in Chemical Biology*, *8*(4), 392–398. doi:10.1016/j.cbpa.2004.06.007 PMID:15288249

Elayaraja, E., Thangavel, K., Chitralega, M., & Chandrasekhar, T. (2012). Extraction of Motif Patterns from Protein Sequences Using SVD with Rough K-Means Algorithm. *International Journal of Computer Science Issues*, *9*(6), 350–356.

Elayaraja, E., Thangavel, K., Ramya, B., & Chitralegha, M. (2011). Extraction of Motif Patterns from Protein Sequence using Rough K-Means Algorithm. *Procedia Engineering*, *30*, 814–820. doi:10.1016/j.proeng.2012.01.932

Elgerd, O. (2000). Electric energy systems theory- an introduction (2nd ed.). Tata McGraw Hill

Elgerd, O., & Fosha, C. (1970). Optimal megawatt frequency control of multi area electric energy systems. *IEEE Trans Electric Power Apparatus System*, *89*, 63–556.

Emerich, D. F., & Thanos, C. G. (2006). The pinpoint promise of nanoparticle-based drug delivery and molecular diagnosis. *Biomolecular Engineering*, *23*(4), 171–184. doi:10.1016/j.bioeng.2006.05.026 PMID:16843058

Engelbrecht, A. P. (2005, July 9 – 13). Fundamentals of Computational Swarm Intelligence, John Wiley & Sons. *Proceedings of theGenetic and Evolutionary Computation Conference.*

Engelbrecht, A. P. (2002). *Computational Intelligence: An Introduction*. England: John Wiley & Sons.

Enright, A. J., & Ouzounis, C. A. (2001). BioLayout--an automatic graph layout algorithm for similarity visualization. *Bioinformatics (Oxford, England)*, *17*(9), 853–854. doi:10.1093/bioinformatics/17.9.853 PMID:11590107

Espina, V., Liotta, L. A., & Petricoin, E. F. (2009). Reverse-phase protein microarrays for theranostics and patient tailored therapy. *Methods in Molecular Biology (Clifton, N.J.)*, *520*, 89–105. doi:10.1007/978-1-60327-811-9_7 PMID:19381949

Espina, V., Woodhouse, E. C., Wulfkuhle, J., Asmussen, H. D., Petricoin, E. F. III, & Liotta, L. A. (2004). Protein microarray detection strategies: Focus on direct detection technologies. *Journal of Immunological Methods*, *290*(1–2), 121–133. doi:10.1016/j.jim.2004.04.013 PMID:15261576

Ester, M., Kriegel, H. P., & Sander, J. (1997). Spatial data mining: A database approach. In *Advances in spatial databases* (pp. 47–66). Springer Berlin Heidelberg. doi:10.1007/3-540-63238-7_24

Ester, M., Kriegel, H. P., Sander, J., & Xu, X. (1996) A density-based algorithm for Discovering cluster in large database with noise.*Proc of 2nd KDD, Portland* (pp 226-231).

Estivill-Castro, V., & Houle, M. E. (2001). Robust distance-based clustering with applications to spatial data mining. *Algorithmica*, *30*(2), 216–242. doi:10.1007/s00453-001-0010-1

Eurofins Medigenomix Gmb, H. (n. d.). Retrieved from: www.medigenomix.de

Farkas, I. J., Szanto-Varnagy, A., & Korcsmaros, T. (2012). Linking proteins to signaling pathways for experiment design and evaluation. *PLoS One, 7*(4), e36202. doi:10.1371/journal.pone.0036202

Fernandez-Recio, J., Totrov, M., & Abagyan, R. (2004). Identification of protein-protein interaction sites from docking energy landscapes. *J Mol Biol, 335*(3), 843-865.

FICO. (2014). Does AI + Big Data = Business Gain? *Insights White Paper*. Retrieved from http://www.fico.com/en/latest-thinking/white-papers/insightsdoes-ai--big-data--business-gain

Fields, S., & Sternglanz, R. (1994). The two-hybrid system: An assay for protein-protein interactions. *Trends in Genetics*, *10*(8), 286–292. doi:10.1016/0168-9525(90)90012-U PMID:7940758

Fischer, M., Wellnhofer, G., Hoess, A., Wolle, J., Pluckthun, A., & Virnekas, B. (2000). Fully synthetic human combinatorial Knappik, A., Ge, L., Honegger, A., Pack, antibody libraries (HuCAL) based on modular consensus frameworks and CDRs randomized with trinucleotides. *Journal of Molecular Biology*, *296*(1), 57–86. doi:10.1006/jmbi.1999.3444 PMID:10656818

Fister, I., Jr., Yang, X.-S., Fister, I., Brest, J., & Fister, D. (2013). A brief review of nature-inspired algorithms for optimization. arXiv preprint arXiv:1307.4186.

Fogel, L. J., Owens, A. J., & Walsh, M. J. (1966). *Artificial Intelligence through Simulated Evolution*. New York: Wiley Publishing.

Fortuna's Corner. (2014). Ten Big Data Start-Ups To Watch. Retrieved from http://fortunascorner.com/2014/04/17/ten-big-data-start-ups-to-watch/

Fosha, C. E., & Elgerd, O. (1970). The megawatt-frequency control problem: A new approach via optimal control theory. *IEEE Transactions on Power Systems*, *89*(4), 563–577. doi:10.1109/TPAS.1970.292603

Fraser, A. S. (1957). Simulation of genetic systems by automatic digital computers". *Australian Journal of Biological Sciences*, *10*, 484–491.

Freeman, W. M., Robertson, D. J., & Vrana, K. E. (2000). Fundamentals of DNA Hybridization Arrays for Gene Expression Analysis. *BioTechniques*, *29*, 1042–1055. PMID:11084867

Freund, Y., & Schapire, R. E. (1997). A decision-theoretic generalization of on-line learning and an application to boosting. *Journal of Computer and System Sciences*, *55*(1), 119–139. doi:10.1006/jcss.1997.1504

Friedman, N., Linial, M., Nachman, I., & Pe'er, D. (2000). Using Bayesian networks to analyze expression data. *Journal of Computational Biology*, *7*(3-4), 601–620. doi:10.1089/106652700750050961 PMID:11108481

Fruch, F. W., & Xie, H. G. (2005). *Pharmacogenomics steps towards Personalised Medicine*. Future Medicine.

Fujiwara, Y., & Konagaya, A. (2008). Protein Motif Extraction using Hidden Markov Model. Proceedings of the Genome Informatics Workshop IV (pp. 57-64).

Gage, D. (1992). Command control for many-robot systems. *Proceedings of the 19th Annual AUVS Technical Symposium*.

Gandomi, A., & Murtaza, H. (2015). Beyond the hype: Big data concepts, methods, and analytics *International Journal of Information Management*, *35*(2), 137–144. doi:10.1016/j.ijinfomgt.2014.10.007

Gangwal, C., & Bhaumik, R. N. (2012). Intuitionistic Fuzzy Rough Relation in Some Medical Applications. *International Journal of Advanced Research in Computer Engineering & Technology*, *1*(6), 28–32.

Gao, J., Liu, C., Liu, D., Wang, Z., & Dong, S. (2008). Antibody microarray-based strategies for detection of bacteria by lectin-conjugated gold nanoparticle probes. *Talanta*, *81*(4–5), 1816–1820. PMID:20441979

Gao, J., Liu, D., & Wang, Z. (2008). Microarray-based study of carbohydrate-protein binding by gold nanoparticle probes. *Analytical Chemistry*, *80*(22), 8822–8827. doi:10.1021/ac8015328 PMID:18855407

Gens, F. (2011). IDC 2012 Predictions: Competing for 2020. Retrieved from http://cdn.idc.com/research/Predictions12/Main/downloads/IDCTOP10Predictions2012.pdf

Georgyi, V. Los, Al Darzins, Chad Zimprich, B.S., Natasha Karassina, M.S., Randall Learish, Mark G. McDougall, Lance P. Encell,Rachel Friedman-Ohana, Monika Wood, M.S., Gediminas Vidugiris, Kris Zimmerman, B.S., Paul Otto, M.S., Dieter H. Klaubert & Wood, K. (2005). *HaloTag™ Interchangeable Labeling Technology for Cell Imaging, Protein Capture and Immobilization*. www.promega.com, accessed on 17. 05. 2015

Gershenson, C. (2003). Artificial neural networks for beginners. arXiv preprint cs/0308031.

Ghazani, A. A., & Jeongjin, A. (2006). High throughput quantification of protein expression of cancer antigens in tissue microarray using quantum dot nanocrystals. *Nano Letters*, *6*(12), 2881–2886. doi:10.1021/nl062111n PMID:17163724

Ghazikhani, A., Akbarzadeh, T. M. R., & Monse, R. (2011). Genetic regulatory network inference using recurrent neural networks trained by a multi agent system. In Computer and knowledge engineering (ICCKE), 2011 1st international e-conference on (pp. 95-99). doi:10.1109/ICCKE.2011.6413332

Ghosh, J. (2012): Modeling Intelligent System for Medical Diagnosis, Ph. D Thesis, The University of Burdwan, West Bengal, India.

Giljohann, D. A., & Mirkin, C. A. (2008). Tiny tiles, tiny targets. *Nature Biotechnology*, *26*(3), 299–300. doi:10.1038/nbt0308-299 PMID:18327241

Gnocchi, D., Massimi, M., Alisi, A., Incerpi, S., & Bruscalupi, G. (2014). Effect of fructose and 3,5-diiodothyronine (3,5-T(2)) on lipid accumulation and insulin signalling in non-alcoholic fatty liver disease (NAFLD)-like rat primary hepatocytes. *Hormone and Metabolic Research. Hormon- und Stoffwechselforschung. Hormones et Metabolisme*, *46*(5), 333–340. doi:10.1055/s-0034-1371858 PMID:24816759

Goel, N., Singh, S., & Aseri, T. C. (2013).A Review of Soft Computing Techniques for Gene Prediction. Hindawi Publishing Corporation.

Goetschel, R. Jr, & Voxman, W. (1986). Elementary fuzzy calculus. *Fuzzy Sets and Systems*, *18*(1), 31–43. doi:10.1016/0165-0114(86)90026-6

Goldberg, D. S., & Roth, F. P. (2003). Assessing experimentally derived interactions in a small world. *Proc Natl Acad Sci U S A, 100*(8), 4372-4376. doi:10.1073/pnas.0735871100

Goldman, R. D. (2000). Antibodies: Indispensable tools for biomedical research. *Trends in Biochemical Sciences*, *25*(12), 593–595. doi:10.1016/S0968-0004(00)01725-4 PMID:11116184

Golemis, E. A. (2002). *Protein-protein interactions: A molecular cloning manual*. Cold Spring Harbor, NY: Cold Spring Harbor Laboratory Press.

Goluch, E. D., Nam, J. M., Georganopoulou, D. G., Chiesl, T. N., Shaikh, K. A., Ryu, K. S., & Liu, C. et al. (2006). A bio-barcode assay for on-chip attomolar-sensitivity protein detection. *Lab on a Chip*, *6*(10), 1293–1299. doi:10.1039/b606294f PMID:17102842

Gomez-Chova, L., Calpe, J., Camps-Valls, G., Martin, J. D., Soria, E., Vila, J., & Moreno, J. (2003, September). Semi-supervised classification method for hyperspectral remote sensing images. Proceedings of the International Geoscience and Remote Sensing Symposium (Vol. 3, pp. III-1776). doi:10.1109/IGARSS.2003.1294247

Gonzalez-Gonzalez, M., Jara-Acevedo, R., Matarraz, S., Jara-Acevedo, M., Paradinas, S., Sayagues, J. M., & Fuentes, M. et al. (2010). Nanotechniques in proteomics: Protein microarrays and novel detection platforms. *European Journal of Pharmaceutical Sciences*, *45*(4), 499–506. doi:10.1016/j.ejps.2011.07.009 PMID:21803154

Goodchild, M. F., & Gopal, S. (Eds.). (1989). *The accuracy of spatial databases*. CRC Press.

Greenbaum, D., Baruch, A., Hayrapetian, L., & Darula, Z. (2002). Chemical approaches for functionally probing the proteome. *Molecular & Cellular Proteomics*, *1*(1), 60–68. doi:10.1074/mcp.T100003-MCP200 PMID:12096141

Greengard, S. (2014). Artificial Intelligence: Ready To Live Up To Its Hype? *Insight/ Market Research, CMO by Adobe*. Retrieved from http://www.cmo.com/articles/2014/11/5/artifical_intelligence.html

Grefenstette, J. G., & Baker, J. E. (1989).How genetic algorithms work: a critical look at implicit parallelism. *Proceedings of the Third Int.l Conference on Genetic Algorithms*, Fairfax, VA, USA. Morgan.

Gribov, A., Sill, M., Luck, S., Rucker, F., Dohner, K., Bullinger, L., & Unwin, A. et al. (2010). SEURAT: Visual analytics for the integrated analysis of microarray data. *BMC Medical Genomics*, *3*(1), 21. doi:10.1186/1755-8794-3-21 PMID:20525257

Griffin, T. J., Gygi, S. P., Ideker, T., Rist, B., Eng, J., Hood, L., & Aebersold, R. (2002). Complementary profiling of gene expression at the transcriptome and proteome levels in Saccharomyces cerevisiae. *Molecular & Cellular Proteomics*, *1*(4), 323–333. doi:10.1074/mcp.M200001-MCP200 PMID:12096114

Grigoris, A., & van Harmelen, F. (2008). *A Semantic Web* (2nd ed.). The MIT Press.

Gunavathi, C., & Premalatha, K. (2014). A comparative analysis of swarm intelligence techniques for feature selection in cancer classification. *TheScientificWorldJournal*, 2014. PMID:25157377

Guney, K., & Basbug, S. (2008). Interference suppression of linear antenna arrays by amplitude-only control using a bacterial foraging algorithm. *Progress In Electromagnetics Research*, *79*, 475–497.

Guo, X., Zhang, H., & Chang, Z. (2010). Image thresholding algorithm based on image gradient and fuzzy set distance. *ICIC Express Letters*, 4(3B), 1059-1064.

Guyon, I., & Elisseeff, A. (2003). An introduction to variable and feature selection. *Journal of Machine Learning Research*, 3, 1157–1182.

Guzzi, P. H., & Cannataro, M. (2010). mu-CS: An extension of the TM4 platform to manage Affymetrix binary data. *BMC Bioinformatics*, 11(1), 315. doi:10.1186/1471-2105-11-315 PMID:20537149

Haab, B. B. (2003). Methods and applications of antibody microarrays in cancer research. *Proteomics*, 3(11), 2116–2122. doi:10.1002/pmic.200300595 PMID:14595810

Haenggi, M. (2005). Opportunities and Challenges in Wireless Sensor Networks. In I. Mahgoub (Ed.), *Handbook of Sensor Networks: Compact Wireless and Wired Sensing Systems*. Boca Raton: CRC Press.

Hall, D. A., Ptacek, J., & Snyder, M. (2007). Protein microarray technology. *Mechanisms of Ageing and Development*, 128(1), 161–167. doi:10.1016/j.mad.2006.11.021 PMID:17126887

Hall, M. A. (2000). Correlation-based feature selection for discrete and numeric class machine learning. *Proc.Seventeenth International Conference on Machine Learning* (pp. 359–366).

Hamburg, A. M. (2013). Personalized medicine the future is now. *U.S. Food and Drug Administration*. Retrieved from: http://blogs.fda.gov/fdavoice/index.php/2013/11/personalized-medicine-the-future-is-now/

Hansen, L. K., & Salamon, P. (1990). Neural network ensembles. *IEEE Transactions on Pattern Analysis and Machine Intelligence*, 12(10), 993–1001. doi:10.1109/34.58871

Hassanien, A. E., Abraham, A., Peters, J. F. & Kacprzyk, J. (2001). Rough Sets in Medical Imaging: Foundations and Trends.

Hassanien, A. E., Abraham, A., Peters, J. F. & Kacprzyk, J. (2009). Rough Sets in Medical Informatics Applications, Application of Soft Computing. Advances in intelligent and soft computing, 58, 23-30.

Hassanien, A. E., Ali, J. M., & Hajime, N. (2004): Detection of spiculated masses in mammograms based on fuzzy image processing. *Proceedings of the7th Int. Conference on Artificial Intelligence and Soft Computing*, LNAI (Vol. *3070*, pp. 1002–1007). doi:10.1007/978-3-540-24844-6_156

Haykin, S. (1999). *Neural networks—a comprehensive foundation*. Englewood Cliffs: Prentice Hall.

Haykin, S. (2009). *Neural Network*. Prentice Hall.

Heinzelman, W., Chandrakasan, R., & Balakrishnan, H. (2000). Energy-efficient communication protocols for wireless microsensor networks. *Proceedings of Hawaiian International Conference on Systems Science*. doi:10.1109/HICSS.2000.926982

He, M., Stoevesandt, O., Palmer, E. A., Khan, F., Ericsson, O., & Taussig, M. J. (2008). Printing protein arrays from DNA arrays. *Nature Methods*, 5(2), 175–177. doi:10.1038/nmeth.1178 PMID:18204456

He, M., & Taussig, M. J. (2003). Discern Array technology: A cell-free method for the generation of protein arrays from PCR DNA. *Journal of Immunological Methods*, 274(1-2), 265–270. doi:10.1016/S0022-1759(02)00521-5 PMID:12609552

Hendler, J. A., & van Harmelen, F. (2008). The Semantic Web: webizing knowledge representation, In Hendler, J., & van Harmelen, F. (Eds.), Foundations of Artificial Intelligence (pp. 821-839). Springer.

Hermjakob, H., Montecchi-Palazzi, L., Lewington, C., Mudali, S., Kerrien, S., Orchard, S., . . . Apweiler, R. (2004). IntAct: an open source molecular interaction database. *Nucleic Acids Res, 32*(Database issue), D452-455. doi: 10.1093/nar/gkh052

Herrera, E. G., Ali, Y., Athanasius, T., Barnes, L. E., & Benjamin, D. (2011, August 30 - September 3). Rough Set Theory based Prognostication of Life Expectancy for Terminally Ill Patients. *Proceedings of the 33rd Annual International Conference of the IEEE EMBS*, Boston, Massachusetts USA (pp. 6438-6441).

Hof, R. (2014). Baidu Announces Breakthrough In Speech Recognition, Claiming To Top Google And Apple. *Forbes*. Retrieved from http://www.forbes.com/sites/roberthof/2014/12/18/baidu-announces-breakthrough-in-speech-recognition-claiming-to-top-google-and-apple/2/

Holland, J. H. (1975). Adaptation in natural and artificial systems: An introductory analysis with applications to biology, control, and artificial intelligence.

Holland, P. (2015). Characteristics of Big Data – Part One. Retrieved from http://makingdatameaningful.com/2015/05/26/characteristics-of-big-data-part-one/

Holland, J. H. (1975). *Adaptation in Natural and Artificial Systems*. Ann Arbor, Michigan: The University of Michigan Press.

Holland, J. H. (1986). Escaping brittleness: The possibilities of general-purpose learning algorithms applied to parallel rule-based systems. In R. Michalski, J. Carbnell, & T. Mitchell (Eds.), *Machine Learning: An Artificial Intelligence Approach* (pp. 593–623). Los Altos: Morgan Kaufmann.

Hood, L. (2003). Systems biology: Integrating technology, biology, and computation. *Mechanisms of Ageing and Development, 124*(1), 9–16. doi:10.1016/S0047-6374(02)00164-1 PMID:12618001

Horn, J., Nafploitis, N., & Goldberg, D. E. (1994). *A niched Pareto genetic algorithm for multi objective optimization* (p. 8287). IEEE Press.

Hsieh, Y.-Z., Su, M.-C., & Wang, P.-C. (2014). A PSO-based rule extractor for medical diagnosis. *Journal of Biomedical Informatics, 49*, 53–60. doi:10.1016/j.jbi.2014.05.001 PMID:24835617

Hsu, H. L., & Wu, B. (2010). An innovative approach on fuzzy correlation coefficient with interval data. *International Journal of Innovative Computing, Information, & Control, 6*(3), 1049–1058.

Hsu, H.-H., Hsieh, C.-W., & Lu, M.-D. (2011). Hybrid feature selection by combining filters and wrappers. *Expert Systems with Applications, 38*(7), 8144–8150. doi:10.1016/j.eswa.2010.12.156

Hu, X., Maglia, A., & Wunsch, D. C. (2006). A general recurrent neural network approach to model genetic regulatory networks. *Proceedings of the 27th annual international conference of the Engineering in medicine and biology society IEEE-EMBS '05* (pp. 4735-4738).

Hu, Z., Hung, J. H., Wang, Y., Chang, Y. C., Huang, C. L., Huyck, M., & DeLisi, C. (2009). VisANT 3.5: multi-scale network visualization, analysis and inference based on the gene ontology. *Nucleic Acids Res, 37*(Web Server issue), W115-121. doi:10.1093/nar/gkp406

Huang, J., Shimizu, H., & Shioya, S. (2003). Clustering gene expression pattern and extracting relationship in gene network based on artificial neural networks. *Journal of Bioscience and Bioengineering, 96*(5), 421–428. doi:10.1016/S1389-1723(03)70126-1 PMID:16233550

Huang, R. P. (2003). Protein arrays, an excellent tool in biomedical research. *Frontiers in Bioscience, 8*(1-3), d559–d576. doi:10.2741/1017 PMID:12700043

Huang, R., & Gamazon, E. R.Huang & Gamazon. (2013). Translating pharmacogenomics discoveries into the clinic: An implementation framework. *Genome Medicine*, 5(10), 94. doi:10.1186/gm497 PMID:24134796

Hullermeier, E. (1997). An approach to modeling and simulation of uncertain dynamical systems. *International Journal of Uncertainty, Fuzziness and Knowledge-based Systems*, 5(02), 117–137. doi:10.1142/S0218488597000117

Hu, M., Yan, J., He, Y., Lu, H., Weng, L., Song, S., & Wang, L. et al. (2010). Ultrasensitive, multiplexed detection of cancer biomarkers directly in serum by using a quantum dot-based microfluidic protein chip. *ACS Nano*, 4(1), 488–494. doi:10.1021/nn901404h PMID:20041634

Hung, X. M., & Zhang, Y. H. (2003). A new application of rough set to ECG recognition. *Proceeding of theInternational Conference on Machine Learning and Cybernetics* (Vol. 3, pp. 1729–1734).

Husmeier, D. (2003). Sensitivity and specificity of inferring genetic regulatory interactions from microarray experiments with dynamic Bayesian networks. *Bioinformatics (Oxford, England)*, 19(17), 2271–2282. doi:10.1093/bioinformatics/btg313 PMID:14630656

Huynen, M., Snel, B., Lathe, W. III, & Bork, P. (2000). Predicting protein function by genomic context: Quantitative evaluation and qualitative inferences. *Genome Research*, 10(8), 1204–1210. doi:10.1101/gr.10.8.1204 PMID:10958638

Hvidsten, T. R., & Komorowski, J. (2007). Rough sets in Bioinformatics. In Transactions on Rough Sets VII, *LNCS* (Vol. *4400*, pp. 225–243).

Hwang, T., Sun, C. H., Yun, T., & Yi, G. S. (2008). FiGS: A filter based gene selection workbench for microarray data. *BMC Bioinformatics*, 11(1), 50. doi:10.1186/1471-2105-11-50 PMID:20100357

Hyvarinen, A., & Oja, E. (1999). *Independent component analysis: A tutorial (Technical report)*. Laboratory of Computer and Information Science, Helsinki University of Technology.

Ilonen, J., Kamarainen, J. K., & Lampinen, J. (2003). Differential Evolution Training Algorithm for Feed Forward Neural Networks. *Neural Processing Letters*, 17(3), 93–105.

Ilyas, I., Mohammad, H., & Imad, M. (2005). *Handbook of Sensor Networks: Compact Wireless and Wired Sensing Systems*. CRC Press.

Innocent, P. R., & John, R. I. (2004). Computer aided fuzzy medical diagnosis. *Information Sciences*, 162(2), 81–104. doi:10.1016/j.ins.2004.03.003

Iragne, F., Nikolski, M., Mathieu, B., Auber, D., & Sherman, D. (2005). ProViz: protein interaction visualization and exploration. *Bioinformatics, 21*(2), 272-274. doi: 10.1093/bioinformatics/bth494

Jafelice, R. M., Barros, L. C., Bassanezi, R. C., & Gomide, F. (2004). Fuzzy Modeling in Symptomatic HIV Virus Infected Population. *Bulletin of Mathematical Biology*, 66(6), 1597–1620. doi:10.1016/j.bulm.2004.03.002 PMID:15522347

Jain, K. (2015). Textbook of Personalised Medicine. Springer.

Jain, A. K., Mao, J., & Mohiuddin, K. (1996). Artificial neural networks: A tutorial. *Computer*, 29(3), 31–44. doi:10.1109/2.485891

Jain, K.K. (2005). Personalized neurology. *Per. Med.*, 2(1), 15–21. doi:10.1517/17410541.2.1.15

Jain, K.K. (2006). The role of nanobiotechnology in developing new therapies for disease of the nervous system. *Nanomed.*, 1(1), 9–12. doi:10.2217/17435889.1.1.9 PMID:17716203

Jeffery, I. B., Higgins, D. G., & Culhane, A. C. (2006). Comparison and evaluation of methods for generating differentially expressed gene lists from microarray data. *BMC Bioinformatics*, *7*(1), 359. doi:10.1186/1471-2105-7-359 PMID:16872483

Jensen, R., & Shen, Q. (2004). Semantics-preserving dimensionality reduction: Rough and fuzzy-rough based approaches. *IEEE Transactions on Knowledge and Data Engineering*, *16*(12), 1457–1471. doi:10.1109/TKDE.2004.96

Jones, S., & Thornton, J. M. (1996). Principles of protein-protein interactions. *Proceedings of the National Academy of Sciences of the United States of America*, *93*(1), 13–20. doi:10.1073/pnas.93.1.13 PMID:8552589

Jong, H., & Page, M. (2008). Search for steady states of piecewise-linear differential equation models of genetic regulatory networks. *IEEE/ACM transactions on Computational biology and bioinformatics*, *5*(2), 208-222.

Jong, H. (2002). Modeling and simulation of genetic regulatory systems: A literature review. *Journal of Computational Biology*, *9*(1), 67–103. doi:10.1089/10665270252833208 PMID:11911796

Ju, B. H., Park, B., Park, J. H., & Han, K. (2003). Visualization and analysis of protein interactions. *Bioinformatics (Oxford, England)*, *19*(2), 317–318. doi:10.1093/bioinformatics/19.2.317 PMID:12538268

Jung, S. H., & Cho, K.-H. (2007). Reconstruction of gene regulatory networks by neuro-fuzzy inference systems. In *Frontiers in the convergence of bioscience and information technologies, 2007* (pp. 32–37). FBIT. doi:10.1109/FBIT.2007.53

Karaboga & Basturk, B. (2007). A Powerful and Efficient Algorithm For Numerical Function Optimization: Artificial Bee Colony (ABC) Algorithm. *Journal of Global Optimization, Springer Netherlands*, *39*(3), 459471.

Karaboga, (2005) An Idea Based On Honey Bee Swarm for Numerical Optimization (Technical Report-TR06). Erciyes University.

Karaboga, D. (2005). An idea based on honey bee swarm for numerical optimization (Tech. Rep. tr06). Erciyes university.

Karczewski, & Altman. (2012). Translational Bioinformatics. *PLOS Computational Biology*.

Karlebach, G., & Shamir, R. (2008). Modelling and analysis of gene regulatory networks. *Nature Reviews. Molecular Cell Biology*, *9*(10), 770–780. doi:10.1038/nrm2503 PMID:18797474

Kaufman, L & Rousseeuw, P.J. (2009). *Finding groups in data: an introduction to cluster analysis*. John Wiley & Sons.

Keedwell, E., Narayanan, A., & Savic, D. (2002). Modelling gene regulatory data using artificial neural networks. Proceedings of the 2002 international joint conference on Neural networks IJCNN '02. (Vol. 1, pp. 183-188). doi:10.1109/IJCNN.2002.1005466

Keller, A., Backes, C., Al-Awadhi, M., Gerasch, A., Kuntzer, J., Kohlbacher, O., & Lenhof, H. P. et al. (2008). GeneTrailExpress: A web-based pipeline for the statistical evaluation of microarray experiments. *BMC Bioinformatics*, *9*(1), 552. doi:10.1186/1471-2105-9-552 PMID:19099609

Kelley, B. P., Yuan, B., Lewitter, F., Sharan, R., Stockwell, B. R., & Ideker, T. (2004). PathBLAST: a tool for alignment of protein interaction networks. *Nucleic Acids Res, 32*(Web Server issue), W83-88. doi:10.1093/nar/gkh411

Kennedy, J. & Eberhart, R. (1995). An Introduction Particle Swarm Optimization. *IEEE Transaction*.

Kennedy, J., & Eberhart, R. (1995). Particle swarm optimization. Proceedings of the IEEE international conference on Neural networks (Vol. 4, pp. 1942-1948). doi:10.1109/ICNN.1995.488968

Kennedy, J. (1998). The Behavior of Particles. *Proc. of the 7th Intl. Conference on Evolutionary Programming VII* (pp. 581-587).

Kennedy, J., & Eberhart, R. C. (1995). Particle Swarm Optimization. *Proceedings of IEEE International Conference on Neural Networks*, Piscataway, NJ (pp. 1942-1948).

Kennedy, J., & Eberhart, R. C. (2001). *Swarm Intelligence*. Morgan Kaufmann.

Kentzoglanakis, K., & Poole, M. (2012). A swarm intelligence framework for reconstructing gene networks: searching for biologically plausible architectures. *IEEE/ACM Transactions on Computational Biology and Bioinformatics, 9*(2), 358-371.

Kerr, M. K., Martin, M., & Churchill, G. A. (2000). Analysis of variance for gene expression microarray data. *Journal of Computational Biology, 7*(6), 819–837. doi:10.1089/10665270050514954 PMID:11382364

Keskin, O., Ma, B., Rogale, K., Gunasekaran, K., & Nussinov, R. (2005). Protein-protein interactions: organization, cooperativity and mapping in a bottom-up Systems Biology approach. *Phys Biol, 2*(2), S24-35. doi: S1478-3975(05)94487-2

Khan, J., Wei, J. S., Ringner, M., Saal, L. H., Ladanyi, M., Westermann, F., & Meltzer, P. S. et al. (2001). Classification and diagnostic of cancers using gene expression profiling and Artificial neural networks. *NCBI, 7*(6), 673–679. PMID:11385503

Khastan, A., & Nieto, J. J. (2010). A boundary value problem for second-order fuzzy differential equations. *Nonlinear Analysis, 72*(9-10), 3583–3593. doi:10.1016/j.na.2009.12.038

Kim, W. K., Henschel, A., Winter, C., & Schroeder, M. (2006). The many faces of protein-protein interactions: A compendium of interface geometry. *PLoS Comput Biol, 2*(9), e124. doi:10.1371/journal.pcbi.0020124

Kim, D. H., Abraham, A., & Cho, J. H. (2007). A hybrid genetic algorithm and bacterial foraging approach for global optimization. *Information Sciences, 177*, 3918–3937.

Kim, S., Dougherty, E. R., Chen, Y., Sivakumar, K., Meltzer, P., Trent, J. M., & Bittner, M. (2000). Multivariate measurement of gene expression relationships. *Genomics, 67*(2), 201–209. doi:10.1006/geno.2000.6241 PMID:10903845

Kim, W. K., & Ison, J. C. (2005). Survey of the geometric association of domain-domain interfaces. *Proteins, 61*(4), 1075–1088. doi:10.1002/prot.20693 PMID:16247798

King, J. D., Casavant, B. P., & Lang, J. M. (2013). *Rapid translation of circulating tumor cell biomarkers into clinical practice: technology development, clinical needs, and regulatory requirements*. Royal Society of Chemistry.

Kitano, H. (2002a). Computational systems biology. *Nature, 420*(6912), 206–210. doi:10.1038/nature01254 PMID:12432404

Kitano, H. (2002b). Systems biology: A brief overview. *Science, 295*(5560), 1662–1664. doi:10.1126/science.1069492 PMID:11872829

Klein, S., & Simmons, R.F. (1963). Syntactic dependence and the computer generation of coherent discourse. *Mechanical Translation, 7*.

Kobashi, S., Kondo, K., & Hata, Y. (2004): Rough sets based medical image segmentation with connectedness. *Proceedings of the 5th Int. Forum on Multimedia and Image processing* (pp. 197-202).

Koch, I., Schueler, M., & Heiner, M. (2005). STEPP-search tool for exploration of petri net paths: A new tool for petri net-based path analysis in biochemical networks. *In Silico Biology, 5*(2), 129–138. PMID:15972017

Kohavi, R., & John, G. H. (1997). Wrappers for feature subset selection. *Artificial Intelligence, 97*(1-2), 273–324. doi:10.1016/S0004-3702(97)00043-X

Kohler, J., Baumbach, J., Taubert, J., Specht, M., Skusa, A., Ruegg, A., . . . Philippi, S. (2006). Graph-based analysis and visualization of experimental results with ONDEX. *Bioinformatics, 22*(11), 1383-1390. doi:10.1093/bioinformatics/btl081

Koike, A., & Takagi, T. (2004). Prediction of protein-protein interaction sites using support vector machines. *Protein Eng Des Sel, 17*(2), 165-173. doi:10.1093/protein/gzh020

Koperski, K., Han, J., & Nebojsa, S. (1998). An efficient two-step method for classification of spatial data. *Proceedings of International Symposium on Spatial Data Handling* (SDH'98) (pp. 45-54).

Koperski, K., Adhikary, J., & Han, J. (1996). Spatial data mining: progress and challenges survey paper.*Proc. ACM SIGMOD Workshop on Research Issues on Data Mining and Knowledge Discovery*, Montreal, Canada (pp. 1-10).

Korber, B., Labute, M. & Yusim, K. (2006). Immunoinformatics Comes of Age. *PLoS Computational Biology.*

Koza, J. R. (1992). *Genetic programming: on the programming of computers by means of natural selection* (Vol. 1). MIT press.

Krushevskaya, D., Peterson, H., Reimand, J., Kull, M., & Vilo, J. (2009). VisHiC--hierarchical functional enrichment analysis of microarray data. *Nucleic Acids Research, 37*(Web Server), W587–W592. doi:10.1093/nar/gkp435 PMID:19483095

Kumar, S., Lai, T. H., & Balogh, J. (2004). On K-Coverage in A Mostly Sleeping Sensor Network.*Proceedings of the tenth Annual International Conference on Mobile Computing and Networking (MobiCom)*. doi:10.1145/1023720.1023735

Kuncheva, L. I., & Rodriguez, J. J. (2007). An experimental study on Rotation Forest ensembles. Proceedings of MCS 2007, LNCS (Vol. 4472, pp. 459–468). Berlin: Springer. doi:10.1007/978-3-540-72523-7_46

Kuncheva, L. I., & Whitaker, C. J. (2003). Measures of diversity in classifier ensembles. *Machine Learning, 51*(2), 181–207. doi:10.1023/A:1022859003006

Kunik, V., Solan, Z., Edelman, S., Ruppin, E., & Horn, D. (2005). Motif Extraction and Protein Classification. proceedings of IEEE. *Computational Systems Bioinformatics / Life Sciences Society. Computational Systems Bioinformatics Conference.*

Labaer, J., & Ramachandran, N. (2005). Protein microarrays as tools for functional proteomics. *Current Opinion in Chemical Biology, 9*(1), 14–19. doi:10.1016/j.cbpa.2004.12.006 PMID:15701447

Ladd, J., Taylor, A. D., Piliarik, M., Homola, J., & Jiang, S. (2009). Label-free detection of cancer biomarker candidates using surface plasmon resonance imaging. *Analytical and Bioanalytical Chemistry, 393*(4), 1157–1163. doi:10.1007/s00216-008-2448-3 PMID:18958451

Lapkin, A. (2012). *Hype Cycle for Big Data.* Gartner.

Lapowsky, I. (2014). 4 Big Opportunities in Artificial Intelligence. *Inc.com.* Retrieved from http://www.inc.com/issie-lapowsky/4-big-opportunities-artificial-intelligence.html

Lawson, C. L., Baker, M. L., Best, C., Bi, C., Dougherty, M., Feng, P., . . . Chiu, W. (2011). EMDataBank.org: unified data resource for CryoEM. *Nucleic Acids Res, 39*(Database issue), D456-464. doi: 10.1093/nar/gkq880

Lazos, L., & Poovendran, R. (2006). Stochastic Coverage in Heterogeneous Sensor Networks. *ACM Transactions on Sensor Network, 2*(3), 325-358.

Learn Genetics. (n. d.) Retrieved from http://learn.genetics.utah.edu/content/health/pharma/snips/

Leblanc, N., Gantelius, J., Schwenk, J. M., Ståhl, K., Blomberg, J., Andersson-Svahn, H., & Belák, S. (2009). Development of a magnetic bead microarray for simultaneous and simple detection of four pestiviruses. *Journal of Virological Methods, 155*(1), 1–9. doi:10.1016/j.jviromet.2008.04.010 PMID:18514335

Lee, A. J., Hong, R. W., Ko, W. M., Tsao, W. K., & Lin, H. H. (2007). Mining spatial association rules in image databases. *Information Sciences*, *177*(7), 1593–1608. doi:10.1016/j.ins.2006.09.018

Lee, C. D., Oh, S. Y., Choi, H. M., & Ahn, J. Y. (2009). (Manuscript submitted for publication). A medical diagnosis based on interval-valued fuzzy sets. *Biomedical Engineering: Applications. Basis and Communications*.

Lee, C.-P., Leu, Y., & Yang, W.-N. (2012). Constructing gene regulatory networks from microarray data using GA/PSO with DTW. *Applied Soft Computing*, *12*(3), 1115–1124. doi:10.1016/j.asoc.2011.11.013

Lee, M., Kang, D.-K., Yang, H.-K., Park, K.-H., Choe, S. Y., Kang, C. S., & Kang, I.-C. et al. (2006). Protein nanoarray on Prolinker surface constructed by atomic force microscopy dip-pen nanolithography for analysis of protein interaction. *Proteomics*, *6*(4), 1094–1103. doi:10.1002/pmic.200500392 PMID:16429461

Lee, W.-P., & Yang, K.-C. (2008). A clustering-based approach for inferring recurrent neural networks as gene regulatory networks. *Neurocomputing*, *71*(4), 600–610. doi:10.1016/j.neucom.2007.07.023

Lehne, B., & Schlitt, T. (2009). Protein-protein interaction databases: keeping up with growing interactomes. *Hum Genomics, 3*(3), 291-297.

Leung, E. Y., Malick, S. M., & Khan, K. S. (2013). On-the-Job Evidence-Based Medicine Training for Clinician-Scientists of the Next Generation. *Clinical Biochemistry*, *34*. PMID:24151345

Leung, Y., Fung, T., Mi, J., & Wu, W. (2007). A rough set approach to the discovery of classification rules in spatial data. *International Journal of Geographical Information Science*, *21*(9), 1033–1058. doi:10.1080/13658810601169915

Levine, B. (2015). Persado scores $21M to become the Moneyball of marketing. VB News. Retrieved from http://venturebeat.com/2015/01/22/persado-scores-21m-to-become-the-moneyball-of-marketing/

Levitt. & Chothia. (1976). Structural patterns in globular proteins. *Nature,* 261(5561), 52558.

Liang, S., Fuhrman, S., & Somogyi, R. (1998). REVEAL, a general reverse engineering algorithm for inference of genetic network architectures. In Pacific symposium on biocomputing (Vol. 3, pp. 18-29).

Liang, R. Q., Tan, C. Y., & Ruan, K. C. (2004). Colorimetric detection of protein microarrays based on nanogold probe coupled with silver enhancement. *Journal of Immunological Methods*, *285*(2), 157–163. doi:10.1016/j.jim.2003.11.008 PMID:14980430

Liang, Z., & Shi, P. (2003). Similarity measures on intuitionistic fuzzy sets. *Pattern Recognition Letters*, *24*(15), 2687–2693. doi:10.1016/S0167-8655(03)00111-9

Liao, W. (2012). The rough method for spatial data subzone similarity measurement. *Journal of Geographic Information System*, *4*(01), 37–45. doi:10.4236/jgis.2012.41006

Li, B., Zheng, C. H., Huang, D. S., Zhang, L., & Han, K. (2010). Gene expression data classification using locally linear discriminant embedding. *Computers in Biology and Medicine*, *40*(10), 802–810. doi:10.1016/j.compbiomed.2010.08.003 PMID:20864095

Li, D. R., & Cheng, T. (1994), KDG-Knowledge Discovery from GIS.*Proceedings of the Canadian Conference on GIS, Ottawa* (pp. 123-145).

Li, D., & Cheng, C. (2002). New similarity measures of intuitionistic fuzzy sets and application to pattern recognitions. *Pattern Recognition Letters*, *23*(1-3), 221–225. doi:10.1016/S0167-8655(01)00110-6

Li, D.R., Wang, S.L., & Li, D.Y. (2006). *Spatial data mining theories and applications*. Beijing: Science Press.

Lim, C. P., Jain, L. C., & Dehuri, S. (2009). *Innovations in Swarm Intelligence: Studies in Computational Intelligence* (Vol. 248). Springer. doi:10.1007/978-3-642-04225-6_1

Lin, Y.C., Hwang, K.S., & Wang, F.-S. (2002, May 12-17). Hybrid Differential Evolution with Multiplier Updating Method for Nonlinear Constrained Optimization. *Proceedings of the 2002 Congress on Evolutionary Computation, CEC'02*, Honolulu, Hawaii(*Vol.1*, pp. 872–877).

Lin,W. & Liu, P.X. (2006). Hammerstein model identification based on bacterial foraging. *Electronics Letters,* 42(23), 1332-1333.

Liu, G., Liu, L., Liu, C., Zheng, M., Su, L., & Zhou, C. (2011). Combination of neuro-fuzzy network models with biological knowledge for reconstructing gene regulatory networks. *Journal of Bionics Engineering*, 8(1), 98–106. doi:10.1016/S1672-6529(11)60008-5

Liu, H., Liu, L., & Zhang, H. (2010). Ensemble gene selection for cancer classification. *Pattern Recognition*, 43(8), 2763–2772. doi:10.1016/j.patcog.2010.02.008

Liu, H., Meng, W., & Chou, K. C. (2005a). Low-frequency Fourier spectrum for predicting membrane protein types. *Biochemical and Biophysical Research Communications*, 336(3), 737739. doi:10.1016/j.bbrc.2005.08.160 PMID:16140260

Liu, H., Motoda, H., & Yu, L. (2002). Feature selection with selective sampling. *Proc. Nineteenth International Conference on Machine Learning* (pp. 395–402).

Liu, H., Yang, J., Wang, M., Xue, L., & Chou, K. C. (2005b). Using Fourier spectrum analysis and pseudo amino acid composition for prediction of membrane protein types. *The Protein Journal*, 24(6), 385–389. doi:10.1007/s10930-005-7592-4 PMID:16323044

Liu, K.-H., & Huang, D.-S. (2008). Cancer classification using Rotation Forest. *Computers in Biology and Medicine*, 38(5), 601–610. doi:10.1016/j.compbiomed.2008.02.007 PMID:18394595

Lu, W., Han, J., & Ooi, B. C. (1993) Discovery of general knowledge in large spatial databases. *In proceedings FarRast Workshop on Geographic Information System*, pp 275-289.

Luscombe, N. M., Greenbaum, D., & Gerstein, M. (2001). What is Bioinformatics? A Proposed Definition and Overview of the Field. *Methods of Information in Medicine*, 40(4), 346–358. PMID:11552348

Ma, R. J., Yu, N. Y., & Hu, J. Y. (2013). Application of Particle Swarm Optimization Algorithm in the Heating System Planning Problem. The Scientific World Journal.

Ma, R.J., Yu, N.Y., & Hu, J.Y. (2013). Application of Particle swarm Optimization Algorithm in the Heating System Planning Problem. *The Scientific World Journal.*

Maan, N., Barzinji, K., & Aris, N. (2013, July 3 - 5). Fuzzy Delay Differential Equation in Predator-Prey Interaction: Analysis on Stability of Steady State. *Proceedings of the World Congress on Engineering* WCE '13, London, UK.

Madeira, S. C., & Oliveira, A. L. (2004). Biclustering Algorithms for Biological Data Analysis. *Survey (London, England)*, 2004, 1–31. PMID:17048406

Mainwaring, A., Polastre, J., Szewczyk, R., Culler, D., & Anderson, J. (2002). Wireless Sensor Networks for Habitat Monitoring, *Proceedings of WSNA*, Atlanta, USA. doi:10.1145/570738.570751

Majhi, R., Panda, G., & Sahoo, G. (2009). Development and performance evaluation of FLANN based model for forecasting of stock markets. *Expert Systems with Applications*, 36(3), 6800–6808. doi:10.1016/j.eswa.2008.08.008

Mandal, S. & Saha, G. (2013): Rough Set Theory based Automated Disease Diagnosis using Lung Aden carcinoma as a Test Case. *The SIJ Transactions on Computer Science Engineering & its Applications (CSEA)*, 1(3), 75-82.

Mandal, S., Saha, G., & Pal, R. K. (2013). An Approach towards Automated Disease Diagnosis & Drug Design Using Hybrid Rough-Decision Tree from Microarray Dataset. *J. Comput Sci Syst Biol*, 6(6), 337–343. doi:10.4172/0974-7230.1000130

Mansour, J. C., & Schwarz, R. E. (2008). Molecular mechanisms for individualized cancer care. *Journal of the American College of Surgeons*, 207(2), 250–258. doi:10.1016/j.jamcollsurg.2008.03.003 PMID:18656055

Mansour, N., Kanj, F., & Khachfe, H. (2012). *Particle Swarm Optimization Approach for Protein Structure Prediction in the 3D HP Model*. Interdisciplinary Science Compute Life Science.

Maraziotis, I. A., Dragomir, A., & Thanos, D. (2010). Gene regulatory networks modelling using a dynamic evolutionary hybrid. *BMC Bioinformatics*, 11(1), 140. doi:10.1186/1471-2105-11-140 PMID:20298548

Marquez-Chamorroa, A. E. (2015). Soft computing methods for the prediction of protein tertiary structures: A survey. *Journal of Applied Soft Computing*, 35, 398–410. doi:10.1016/j.asoc.2015.06.024

Martinez, K., Ong, R., Hart, J. K., & Stefanov, J. (2004). Sensor Web for Glaciers. In the Proceedings of (EWSN 2004). Berlin, Germany.

Martin, S., Zhang, Z., Martino, A., & Faulon, J.-L. (2007). Boolean dynamics of genetic regulatory networks inferred from microarray time series data. *Bioinformatics (Oxford, England)*, 23(7), 866–874. doi:10.1093/bioinformatics/btm021 PMID:17267426

Maulik, U. (2011). Analysis of gene microarray data in a soft computing framework. *Applied Soft Computing*, 11(6), 4152–4160. doi:10.1016/j.asoc.2011.03.004

McKinsey Global Institute. (2011, May). Big data: The next frontier for innovation, competition, and productivity.

Mellor, J. C., Yanai, I., Clodfelter, K. H., Mintseris, J., & DeLisi, C. (2002). Predictome: A database of putative functional links between proteins. *Nucleic Acids Research*, 30(1), 306–309. doi:10.1093/nar/30.1.306 PMID:11752322

Menden, M. P., Iorio, F., Garnett, M., McDermott, U., Benes, C. H., Ballester, P. J., & Saez-Rodriguez, J. (2013). Machine Learning Prediction of Cancer Cell Sensitivity to Drugs Based on Genomic and Chemical Properties. *PLoS ONE*, 8(4), e61318. doi:10.1371/journal.pone.0061318 PMID:23646105

Meng, B., Wang, J., Liu, L., Wu, J., & Zhong, E. (2002). Understanding spatial diffusion process of severe acute respiratory syndrome in Beijing. *Public Health*, 119(12), 1080–1087. doi:10.1016/j.puhe.2005.02.003 PMID:16214187

Merbl, Y., & Kirschner, M. W. (2011). Protein microarrays for genome-wide posttranslational modification analysis. *Wiley Interdiscip. Rev. Syst. Biol. Med.*, 3(3), 347–356. doi:10.1002/wsbm.120 PMID:20865779

Merrett, R. (2015). Intelligent machines part 1: Big data, machine learning and the future. CIO. Retrieved from http://www.cio.com.au/article/576664/intelligent-machines-part-1-big-data-machine-learning-future/

Michahelles, F., Matter, P., Schmidt, A., & Schiele, B. (2003). Applying Wearable Sensors to Avalanche Rescue. *Computers & Graphics*, 27(6), 839–847. doi:10.1016/j.cag.2003.08.008

Miller, H. J. (2004). Tobler's first law and spatial analysis. *Annual Association – America,* 94(2), pp. 284-289.

Miller, H.J., & Han, J. (2001). *Geographic datamining and knowledge discovery*. London.

Mitchell, I., & Wilson, M. (2012). Linked data Connecting and exploiting big data (White paper). Retrieved from from www.fujitsu.com/.../Linked-data-connecting-and-exploiting-big-data-(v1.0). pdf

Mitra, S., Das, R., & Hayashi, Y. (2011). Genetic networks and soft computing. *IEEE/ACM Transactions on Computational Biology and Bioinformatics*, 8(1), 94-107.

Mitra, S., & Hayashi, Y. (2006). Bioinformatics with Soft Computing. *IEEE Transactions on Systems, Man and Cybernetics. Part C, Applications and Reviews*, 36(5), 616–635. doi:10.1109/TSMCC.2006.879384

Mitra, S., Mitra, M., & Chaudhuri, B. B. (2006). A rough set based inference engine for ECG classification. *IEEE Transactions on Instrumentation and Measurement*, 55(6), 2198–2206. doi:10.1109/TIM.2006.884279

Moein, S., Monadjemi, S. A., & Moallem, P. (2008). A novel fuzzy-neural based medical diagnosis system, *World Academy of Science. Engineering and Technology*, 37, 157–161.

Mohabey, A., & Ray, A. K. (2000): Fusion of rough set theoretic approximations and FCM for color image segmentation. *Proceedings of theIEEE Int. Conference on Systems, Man, and Cybernetics* (Vol. 2, pp. 1529–1534). doi:10.1109/ICSMC.2000.886073

Mohammad, T. H. (2013). Robust multivariable predictive based load frequency control considering generation rate constant. *International Journal of Electrical Power & Energy Systems*, 46, 405–413. doi:10.1016/j.ijepes.2012.10.039

Molodtsov, D.A. (1999) Soft Sets. *First Results, Computers and mathematics with applications*, 37, 19-31.

Mondal, S.P., & Roy, T.K. (2013). First Order Linear Homogeneous Fuzzy Ordinary Differential Equation Based on Lagrange Multiplier Method. *Journal of Soft Computing and Applications*.

Mongardi, S. (2015). 'What is the Grid and why it's a revolution. *The Web Mate*. Retrieved from http://www.thewebmate.com/2015/05/18/what-is-the-grid-and-why-its-a-revolution/

Mori, T., Toyoda, M., Ohtsuka, T., & Okahata, Y. (2009). Kinetic analyses for bindings of concanavalin A, To dispersed and condensed mannose surfaces on a quartz crystal microbalance. *Analytical Biochemistry*, 395(2), 211–216. doi:10.1016/j.ab.2009.08.029 PMID:19703406

Mosca, R., Ceol, A., Stein, A., Olivella, R., & Aloy, P. (2014). 3did: a catalog of domain-based interactions of known three-dimensional structure. *Nucleic Acids Res, 42*(Database issue), D374-379. doi: gkt887 [pii]10.1093/nar/gkt887

Murgante, B., Las Casas, G., & Sansone, A. (2007). *A spatial rough set for locating the periurban fringe*. SAGEO.

Nagrath, I. J., & Kothari, D. P. (1993). *Modern power system analysis*. TMH.

Nair, R. (2010). Personalised Medicine: Striding from genes to medicine. *Perspectives in Clinical Research, 1*(4).

Najafabadi, M., Villanustre, F., Khoshgoftaar, T. M., Seliya, N., Wald, R., & Muharemagic, E. (2015). Deep learning applications and challenges in big data analytics. *Journal of Big Data*. Retrieved from http://www.journalofbigdata.com/content/2/1/1

Najariyan, M., Farahi, M. H., & Alavian, M. (2011). Optimal Control of HIV Infection by using Fuzzy Dynamical Systems. *The Journal of Mathematics and Computer Science 2*(4), 639–649.

Nakanishi, K., Sakiyama, T., Kumada, Y., Imamura, K. & Imanaka, H.. (2008). Recent Advances in Controlled Immobilization of Proteins onto the Surface of the Solid Substrate and Its Possible Application to Proteomics. *Current Proteomics*, 5, 3,161-175(15)

Nam, J. M., Thaxton, C. S., & Mirkin, C. A. (2003). Nanoparticle-based bio-bar codes for the ultrasensitive detection of proteins. *Science*, *301*(5641), 1884–1886. doi:10.1126/science.1088755 PMID:14512622

Nand, A., Singh, V., Perez, J. B., Tyagi, D., Cheng, Z., & Zhu, J. (2014). In situ protein microarrays capable of real-time kinetics analysis based on surface plasmon resonance imaging. *Analytical Biochemistry*, *464*, 30–35. doi:10.1016/j.ab.2014.06.002 PMID:24953011

Nanda, J., Mishra, S., & Saikia, L. C. (2009). Maiden Application of Bacterial Foraging Based Optimization Technique in Multiarea Automatic Generation Control. *IEEE Transactions on Power Systems*, *22*(2), 602–609. doi:10.1109/TP-WRS.2009.2016588

Negi, S. S., Schein, C. H., Oezguen, N., Power, T. D., & Braun, W. (2007). InterProSurf: a web server for predicting interacting sites on protein surfaces. *Bioinformatics*, *23*(24), 3397-3399. doi:10.1093/bioinformatics/btm474

Newman, A. M., & Cooper, J. B. (2010). AutoSOME: A clustering method for identifying gene expression modules without prior knowledge of cluster number. *BMC Bioinformatics*, *11*(1), 117. doi:10.1186/1471-2105-11-117 PMID:20202218

Nicole, L. W. (2000). The application of DNA microarrays in gene expression Analysis. *Journal of Biotechnology*, *78*(3), 271–280. doi:10.1016/S0168-1656(00)00204-2 PMID:10751688

Noman, N., & Iba, H. (2005). Reverse engineering genetic networks using evolutionary computation. *Genome Informatics*, *16*(2), 205–214. PMID:16901103

Noman, N., Palafox, L., & Iba, H. (2013). Reconstruction of gene regulatory networks from gene expression data using decoupled recurrent neural network model. In *Natural computing and beyond* (pp. 93–103). Springer. doi:10.1007/978-4-431-54394-7_8

Nounou, H. N., Nounou, M. N., Meskin, N., Datta, A., & Dougherty, E. R. (2012). Fuzzy Intervention in Biological Phenomena. *IEEE/ACM Transactions on Computational Biology and Bioinformatics*, *9*(6), 1819–1825. doi:10.1109/TCBB.2012.113 PMID:23221089

Novikov, E. & Barillot, E. (2007). Software package for automatic microarray image analysis (MAIA). bioinformatics application notes, 23(5), 639–640.

Nutritional Immunology and Molecular Medicine Lab. (n. d.). Retrieved from www.nimml.org

Nutritional Immunology and Molecular Medicine Laboratory. (n. d.). Personalized Medicine. Retrieved from http://www.nimml.org/programs/personalized-medicine/

O'Dwyer, M. (2014). How companies can make the most of big data. *Dell.com*. Retrieved from http://techpageone.dell.com/technology/companies-can-make-big-data/

Ogi, H., Nagai, H., Fukunishi, Y., Yanagida, T., Hirao, M., & Nishiyama, M. (2010). Multichannel wireless-electrodeless quartz-crystal microbalance immunosensor. *Analytical Chemistry*, *82*(9), 3957–3962. doi:10.1021/ac100527r PMID:20387824

Ohlhorst, F. J. (2012). *Big Data Analytics: Turning Big Data into Big Money*. Cary, North Carolina, USA: SAS Institute Inc. doi:10.1002/9781119205005

Ohrn, A. (1999). Discernibility and Rough Sets in Medicine: Tools and Applications. Norwegian University of Science and Technology, Trondheim, Norway.

Oliviu, M. (2008). Applying Rough Sets Algorithm for Radiography Diagnosis. *Proceedings of the 9th International Conference on Development and Application Systems*, Suceava, Romania (pp. 272-277).

Omar, A. H. A., & Hasan, Y. A. (2011). The interaction of predator prey with uncertain initial population sizes. *Journal of Quality Measurement and Analysis, 7*(2), 75–83.

Ong, S. E., Blagoev, B., Kratchmarova, I., Kristensen, D. B., Steen, H., Pandey, A., & Mann, M. (2002). Stable isotope labelling by amino acids in cell culture, SILAC, as a simple and accurate approach to expression proteomics. *Molecular & Cellular Proteomics, 1*(5), 376–386. doi:10.1074/mcp.M200025-MCP200 PMID:12118079

Orlev, N., Shamir, R., & Shiloh, Y. (2004). PIVOT: protein interactions visualizatiOn tool. *Bioinformatics, 20*(3), 424-425. doi: 10.1093/bioinformatics/btg426

Osareh, A., & Shadgar, B. (2013). An efficient ensemble learning method for gene microarray classification. Biomed Research International, 2013.

Overbeek, R., Fonstein, M., D'Souza, M., Pusch, G. D., & Maltsev, N. (1999). Use of contiguity on the chromosome to predict functional coupling. Silico Biol, 1(2), 93-108.

Pabinger, S., Dander, A., Fisher, M., Snaider, R., Sperk, M., Efremova, M., … Trajanoski, Z. (2012). A survey of tools for variant analysis of next-generation genome sequencing data. *Briefings in Bioinformatics, 15*(2), 256-278.

Padhan, D. G., & Majhi, S. (2013). A new control scheme for PID load frequency controller of single area and multi area power systems. *ISA Transactions, 52*(2), 242–251. doi:10.1016/j.isatra.2012.10.003 PMID:23141877

Pal, S.K., Bandyopadhyay, S., & Ray, S. S. (2006). Evolutionary computation in bioinformatics: A review. *IEEE transactions on Systems, man, and cybernetics, Part c: Applications and reviews*, 36(5), 601-615.

Pal, D., & Mahapatra, G. S. (2014). A bioeconomic modeling of two-prey and one-predator fishery model with optimal harvesting policy through hybridization approach. *Applied Mathematics and Computation, 242*, 748–763. doi:10.1016/j.amc.2014.06.018

Pal, D., Mahaptra, G. S., & Samanta, G. P. (2012). A Proportional harvesting dynamical model with fuzzy intrinsic growth rate and harvesting quantity. *Pacific-Asian Journal of Mathematics, 6*(2), 199–213.

Pal, D., Mahaptra, G. S., & Samanta, G. P. (2013). Optimal harvesting of prey–predator system with interval biological parameters: A bioeconomic model. *Mathematical Biosciences, 241*(2), 181–187. doi:10.1016/j.mbs.2012.11.007 PMID:23219573

Pal, D., Mahaptra, G. S., & Samanta, G. P. (2013). Quota harvesting model for a single species population under fuzziness. *IJMS, 12*(1-2), 33–46.

Panda, B., Mishra, A. P, Majhi, B. & Rout, M. (2013). Performance evaluation of FLANN based model for Protein Structural Class Prediction. *International journal of Artificial Intelligence and Neural Networks*, 3(4).

Pandit, P., & Singh, P. (2014). Prey Predator Model with Fuzzy Initial Conditions, *International Journal of Engineering and Innovative Technology*, 3(12).

Panigrahi, K., Shi, Y., & Lim, M.-H. (2011). *Handbook of Swarm Intelligence. Series: Adaptation, Learning, and Optimization* (Vol. 7). Springer-Verlag Berlin Heidelberg. doi:10.1007/978-3-642-17390-5

Pan, W. (2002). A comparative review of statistical methods for discovering differentially expressed genes in replicated microarray experiments. *Bioinformatics (Oxford, England), 18*(4), 546–554. doi:10.1093/bioinformatics/18.4.546 PMID:12016052

Pao, Y. H. (1989). *Adaptive pattern recognition and neural networks*. Reading, MA: Addison Wesley.

Parag A. Pathad., Vinod A.Bairagi., Yogesh S. Ahir. & Neela M. Bhatia, (2011). Proteomics: Opportunities and challenges. *International Journal Of Pharmaceuticals Science And Nanotechnology*, 3(4), 1165-1173.

Park, J. H., Lim, K. M., Park, J. S., & Kwun, Y. C. (2008). Distances between interval-valued intuitionistic fuzzy sets. *Journal of Physics: Conference Series*, 96, 012089. doi:10.1088/1742-6596/96/1/012089

Parsopoulos, K. E., & Vrahatis, M. N. (2002). Initializing the Particle Swarm Optimizer Using the Nonlinear Simplex Method. In *Advances in Intelligent Systems* (pp. 216–221). Fuzzy Systems, Evolutionary Computation.

Parsopoulos, K.E., Plagianakos, V.P., & Magoulas, , G.D., & Vrahatis, M.N. (2001). Objective Function Stretching to Alleviate Convergence to Local Minima. *Nonlinear Analysis*, 47(5), 3419–3424.

Patra, J. C., Pal, R. N., Chatterji, B. N., & Panda, G. (1999). Identification of Nonlinear Dynamic Systems Using Functional-Link Artificial Neural Networks. *IEEE Trans. on Systems, Man, and Cybernetics-part B. Cybernetics*, 29(2), 254–262. PMID:18252296

Patterson, S. D., & Aebersold, R. H. (2003). Proteomics: The first decade and beyond. *Nature Genetics*, 33(Suppl. 3), 311–323. doi:10.1038/ng1106 PMID:12610541

Pavlopoulos, G. A., Hooper, S. D., Sifrim, A., Schneider, R., & Aerts, J. (2011). Medusa: A tool for exploring and clustering biological networks. *BMC Res Notes*, 4, 384. doi:10.1186/1756-0500-4-384

Pavlopoulos, G. A., Wegener, A. L., & Schneider, R. (2008). A survey of visualization tools for biological network analysis. *BioData Min*, 1, 12. doi:10.1186/1756-0381-1-12

Pawlak, M., Schick, E., Bopp, M. A., Schneider, M. J., Oroszlan, P., & Ehrat, M. (2002). Zeptosens' protein microarrays: A novel high performance microarray platform for low abundance protein analysis. *Proteomics*, 2(4), 383–393. doi:10.1002/1615-9861(200204)2:4<383::AID-PROT383>3.0.CO;2-E PMID:12164697

Pawlak, Z. (1982). Rough Sets. *International Journal of Computer and Information Sciences*, 11(5), 341–356. doi:10.1007/BF01001956

Pawlak, Z. (1982). Rough Sets. *International Journal of Man-Machine Studies*, 21(2), 127–134. doi:10.1016/S0020-7373(84)80062-0

Pawlak, Z. (1991). *Rough Sets: Theoretical Aspects of Reasoning About Data*. Kluwer Academic Publishing. doi:10.1007/978-94-011-3534-4

Peck, R., & Devore, J. (2011). *Statistics: The exploration & analysis of data*. Cengage Learning.

Pedamallu, C. S., & Posfai, J. (2010). Open source tool for prediction of genome wide protein-protein interaction network based on ortholog information. *Source Code Biol Med.*, 5, 8. doi:10.1186/1751-0473-5-8

Peixoto, M.S., Barros, L.C., & Bassanezi, R.C. (2008). Predator–prey fuzzy model. *Ecological Modeling*, 214, 39–44.

Pei, Z., Liu, X., & Zou, L. (2010). Extracting association rules based on intuitionistic fuzzy sets. *International Journal of Innovative Computing, Information, & Control*, 6(6), 2567–2580.

Peng, Y. (2006). A novel ensemble machine learning for robust microarray data classification. *Computers in Biology and Medicine*, 6(36), 553–573. doi:10.1016/j.compbiomed.2005.04.001 PMID:15978569

Perez-Rodriguez, J., & Garcia-Pedrajas, N. (2011). An evolutionary algorithm for gene structure prediction. *Journal of Industrial Engineering and Other Applications*.

Peri, S., Navarro, J. D., Kristiansen, T. Z., Amanchy, R., Surendranath, V., Muthusamy, B., . . . Pandey, A. (2004). Human protein reference database as a discovery resource for proteomics. *Nucleic Acids Res, 32*(Database issue), D497-501. doi: 10.1093/nar/gkh070

Personalised Medicine. (n. d.). Retrieved from http://en.wikipedia.org/wiki/Personalized_medicine

Personalised Prescribing Systems. (n. d.). Retrieved from http://youscript.com

Personalised Systems & Integrative Medicine. (n. d.). Retrieved from http://immune.pharmtao.com

Personalized Medicine Coalition. (n. d.). Personal Med Backgrounder. Retrieved from http://www.personalizedmedicinecoalition.org/sites/default/files/personalmed_backgrounder.pdf

Perundurai, S.D., Sakthivel, S., Xue, Y., Powell, G.T., Rani, D.R., Nallari, P., ... Thangaraj, K. (2009). A common MYBPC3 (cardiac myosin binding protein C) variant associated with cardiomyopathies in South Asia.

Petricoin, E. F. III, Ardekani, A. M., Hitt, B. A., Levine, P. J., Fusaro, V. A., Steinberg, S. M., & Liotta, L. A. et al. (2002). Use of Proteomic Patterns in Serum to Identify Ovarian Cancer. *Lancet, 359*(9306), 572–577. doi:10.1016/S0140-6736(02)07746-2 PMID:11867112

Phelan, M. L., & Nock, S. (2003). Generation of bioreagents for protein chips. *Proteomics, 3*(11), 2123–2134. doi:10.1002/pmic.200300596 PMID:14595811

Phizicky, E. M., & Fields, S. (1995). Protein-protein interactions: Methods for detection and analysis. *Microbiological Reviews, 59*(1), 94–123. PMID:7708014

Pieper, U., Webb, B. M., Barkan, D. T., Schneidman-Duhovny, D., Schlessinger, A., Braberg, H., . . . Sali, A. (2011). ModBase, a database of annotated comparative protein structure models, and associated resources. *Nucleic Acids Res, 39*(Database issue), D465-474. doi:10.1093/nar/gkq1091

Pietrokovski, S., Henikoff, J. G., & Henikoff, S. (1996). The BLOCKS database - a system for protein classification. *Nucleic Acids Research, 24*(1), 197–200. doi:10.1093/nar/24.1.197 PMID:8594578

Pingdom. (2012). Internet 2011 in Numbers. *Pingdom.com*. Retrieved from http://royal. pingdom.com/2012/01/17/internet-2011-in-numbers

Podraza, R., Dominik, A. and Walkiewicz, M. (2003). Decision support system for medical applications. In *Applied Simulation and Modeling*.

Podurl, S., & Sukhatme, G. S. (2004). Constrained coverage for mobile sensor networks.*Proceedings of the IEEE International Conference on Robotics and Automation.*

Pomeroy, S. L., Tamayo, P., Gaasenbeek, M., Sturla, L. M., Angelo, M., McLaughlin, M. E., & Golub, T. R. et al. (2002). Prediction of central nervous system embryonal tumor outcome based on gene expression. *Nature, 415*(6870), 436–442. doi:10.1038/415436a PMID:11807556

Pottie, G. J., & Kaiser, W. J. (2000). Wireless integrated network sensors. *Communications of the ACM*, 43, 51-58.

Press, G. (2014). 12 Big Data Definitions: What's Yours?" Forbes.com. Retrieved from http://www.forbes.com/sites/gilpress/2014/09/03/12-big-data-definitions-whats-yours/

Prieto, C., & De Las Rivas, J. (2006). APID: Agile Protein Interaction DataAnalyzer. *Nucleic Acids Res, 34*(Web Server issue), W298-302. doi:10.1093/nar/gkl128

Priya. G., Jaisankar, N., & Venkatesan, M. (2011). Mining Colocation patterns from Spatial Data using Rulebased Approach. *Journal of Global Research in Computer Science, 2*(7), 58-61.

Priyadarshini, R., Dash, N. & Rout, S. (2012). A Novel Approach for Protein Structure Prediction using Back Propagation Neural Network. *International Journal of Computer Science & Technology, 3*(2).

Puri, M. L., & Ralescu, D. A. (1983). Differentials of fuzzy functions. *Journal of Mathematical Analysis and Applications, 91*(2), 552–558. doi:10.1016/0022-247X(83)90169-5

Qin, S., & Zhou, H. X. (2007). meta-PPISP: a meta web server for protein-protein interaction site prediction. *Bioinformatics, 23*(24), 3386-3387. doi:10.1093/bioinformatics/btm434

Qi, Y., Klein-Seetharaman, J., & Bar-Joseph, Z. (2005). Random forest similarity for protein-protein interaction prediction from multiple sources. *Pacific Symposium on Biocomputing. Pacific Symposium on Biocomputing, 2005*, 531–542. PMID:15759657

Quinlan, A. (2015). Response to "A Comparison of Paper Documentation to Electronic Documentation for Trauma Resuscitations at a Level I Pediatric Trauma Center". *J Emerg Nurs*. doi:10.1016/j.jen.2015.02.010

Rabbani, B., Tekin, M. & Mahdieh, N. (2013). The promise of whole-exome sequencing in medical genetics. *J. Hum. Genet., 59*(1), 5-15.

Radwan, E., & Assiri, A. M. A. (2013). Thyroid Diagnosis based Technique on Rough Sets with Modified Similarity Relation. *International Journal of Advanced Computer Science and Applications, 4*(10), 120–126. doi:10.14569/IJACSA.2013.041019

Rahnamayan, S. Tizhoosh, H.R. & Salama,M.A.(2008).Opposition-Based Differential Evolution," *IEEE Trans. Evolutionary Computation, 12*(1), 64–79. Retrieved from http://ieeexplore.ieee.org/xpl/tocresult.jsp?isnumber=4444540

Rahnamayan, S., Tizhoosh, H. R., & Salama, A. (2008). Opposition versus randomness in soft computing techniques. *J. Applied Soft Computing, 8*(2), 906–918.

Ram, R., Chetty, M., Dix, T., ... (2006). Fuzzy model for gene regulatory network. Proceedings of the IEEE congress on Evolutionary computation CEC '06 (pp. 1450-1455). doi:10.1109/CEC.2006.1688479

Ramachandran, N., Hainsworth, E., Bhullar, B., Eisenstein, S., Rosen, B., Lau, A. Y., & LaBaer, J. et al. (2004). Self-assembling protein microarrays. *Science, 2*(305), 86–90. doi:10.1126/science.1097639 PMID:15232106

Ramachandran, N., Raphael, J. V., Hainsworth, E., Demirkan, G., Fuentes, M. G., Rolfs, A., & LaBaer, J. et al. (2008). Next-generation high-density self-assembling functional protein arrays. *Nature Methods, 5*(6), 535–538. doi:10.1038/nmeth.1210 PMID:18469824

Randell, D., Cui, Z., & Cohn, A. (1992), A spatial logic based on regions and connection. *Proc. of 3rd Intl. Conference on Knowledge Representation and Reasoning* (pp. 165-176).

Rao, V. S., Srinivas, K., Sujini, G. N., & Kumar, G. N. (2014). Protein-protein interaction detection: Methods and analysis. *International Journal of Proteomics, 147648*. doi:10.1155/2014/147648 PMID:24693427

Rashedi, Nezamabadi-pour & Saryazdi. (2009). GSA: a Grviational Search Algorithm. *Information Sciences, 6*, 2232-2248.

Rathipriya, R., Thangavel, K., & Bagyamani, J. (2011). Binary Particle Swarm Optimization based Biclustering of Web usage Data. *International Journal of Computers and Applications, 25*(2), 43–49. doi:10.5120/3001-4036

Ratner, D. (1974). The interaction bacterial and phage proteins with immobilized Escherichia coli RNA polymerase. *Journal of Molecular Biology, 88*(2), 373–383. doi:10.1016/0022-2836(74)90488-4 PMID:4616088

Raza, K. & Alam, M. (2014). Recurrent neural network based hybrid model of gene regulatory network. *arXiv preprint arXiv*:1408.5405.

Raza, K. (2015). Formal concept analysis for knowledge discovery from biological data. *arXiv preprint arXiv*:1506.00366.

Raza, K., & Kohli, M. (2015). Ant colony optimization for inferring key gene interactions. *Proceedings of the 9th india-com-2015, 2nd international conference on computing for sustainable global development* (pp. 1242-1246).

Raza, K., & Mishra, A. (2012). A novel anticlustering filtering algorithm for the prediction of genes as a drug target. *American journal of biomedical engineering*, 2(5), 206-211.

Raza, K. (2014). Clustering analysis of cancerous microarray data. *Journal of Chemical and Pharmaceutical Research*, 6(9), 488–493.

Raza, K. (2016). Reconstruction, topological and gene ontology enrichment analysis of cancerous gene regulatory network modules. *Current Bioinformatics*, 11(2), 243–258. doi:10.2174/1574893611666160115212806

Raza, K., & Hasan, A. N. (2015). A comprehensive evaluation of machine learning techniques for cancer class prediction based on microarray data. *International Journal of Bioinformatics Research and Applications*, 11(5), 397–416. doi:10.1504/IJBRA.2015.071940 PMID:26558300

Raza, K., & Jaiswal, R. (2013). Reconstruction and analysis of cancer specific gene regulatory networks from gene expression profiles. *International Journal on Bioinformatics & Biosciences*, 3(2), 25–34. doi:10.5121/ijbb.2013.3203

Raza, K., & Parveen, R. (2012). Evolutionary algorithms in genetic regulatory networks model. *Journal of Advanced Bioinformatics Applications and Research*, 3(1), 271–280.

Raza, K., & Parveen, R. (2013). Soft computing approach for modeling genetic regulatory networks. In *Advances in computing and information technology* (pp. 1–11). Springer. doi:10.1007/978-3-642-31600-5_1

Rechenberg, I. (1973). *Evolutionsstrategie: Optimierung Technischer Systeme nach Prinzipien der Biologischen Evolution* [PhD Thesis]. Frommann-Holzboog, Stuttgart.

Regan, D. O., Lakshmikantham, V., & Nieto, J. (2003). Initial and boundary value problems for fuzzy differential equations. *Nonlinear Analysis*, 54, 405–415. doi:10.1016/S0362-546X(03)00097-X

Reinhard, S., Antoine, D., & Chris, S. (1996). The HSSP database of protein structure–sequence alignments. *Nucleic Acids Research*, 1996, 226–230. PMID:9016541

Remy, E., Ruet, P., & Mendoza, L. Thieffry, D., & Chaouiya, C. (2006). From logical regulatory graphs to standard petri nets: Dynamical roles and functionality of feedback circuits. In Transactions on computational systems biology VII (pp. 56-72). Springer.

Renberg, B., Nordin, J., Merca, A., Uhlén, M., Feldwisch, J., Nygren, P.-Å., & Eriksson Karlström, A. (2007). Affibody molecules in protein capture microarrays: Evaluation of multidomain ligands and different detection formats. *Journal of Proteome Research*, 6(1), 171–179. doi:10.1021/pr060316r PMID:17203961

Ressom, H., Wang, D., Varghese, R. S., & Reynolds, R. (2003). Fuzzy logic-based gene regulatory network. *Proceedings of the 12th IEEE international conference on Fuzzy systems FUZZ '03.* (Vol. 2, pp. 1210-1215). doi:10.1109/FUZZ.2003.1206604

Revett, K., Gorunescu, F., Gorunescu, M., & E-Darzi, E. (2005, November 21-24). A breast cancer diagnosis system: a combined approach using rough sets and probabilistic neural networks. Proceedings of Marius Ene2, EUROCON 2005, Serbia & Montenegro, Belgrade (pp. 1124-1127).

Riccardo, P., James, K., & Tim, B. (2007). Particle swarm optimization An Overview. In *Swarm Intell.* (pp. 33-57).

Richens, R. H. (1956). Preprogramming for mechanical translation. *Machine Translation, 3*(1), 20–25.

Rissino, S., Martins, H. G., & Torres, G. L. (2009). Applying Rough Set Classification in Dengue Diagnosis. *Proceedings of the First International workshop on rough sets theory (RST09)*, Milano, Italy (pp. 25-27).

Roche P, M. X. (n. d.). *Protein-Protein Interaction Inhibition (2P2I): Mixed Methodologies for the Acceleration of Lead Discovery*: Bentham Science Publishers

Rout, U. K., Sahu, R. K., & Panda, S. (2013). Design and analysis of differential evolution algorithm based automatic generation control for interconnected power system. *Ain Shams Engineering Journal, 4*(3), 409–419. doi:10.1016/j.asej.2012.10.010

Rowland, T., Ohrn, A., & Ohno-Machado, L. (1998). Building manageable rough set classifiers. *Proceedings AMIA 1998 Annual Symposium*, Orlando, FL.

Sahu, B., & Mishra, D. (2012). A novel feature selection algorithm using particle swarm optimization for cancer microarray data. *Procedia Engineering, 38*, 27–31. doi:10.1016/j.proeng.2012.06.005

Sahu, S. S., & Panda, G. (2010). A novel feature representation method based on Chou's pseudo amino acid composition for protein structural class prediction. *Computational Biology and Chemistry, 34*(5-6), 320327. doi:10.1016/j.compbiolchem.2010.09.002 PMID:21106461

Saikia, L. C., & Sahu, S. K. (2013). Automatic Generation Control of a combined cycle gas turbine plant with classical controllers using firefly algorithm. *International Journal of Electrical Power & Energy Systems, 53*, 27–33. doi:10.1016/j.ijepes.2013.04.007

Saleha, R., Haider, J. N., & Danish, N. (2002, March 9–12). Rough Intuitionistic Fuzzy Set. *Proc. of 8th Int. conf. on Fuzzy Theory and Technology*, Durham, North Carolina, USA.

Samatsu, T., Tachikawa, K., & Shi, Y. (2008). GUI form for car retrieval systems using fuzzy theory. *ICIC Express Letters, 2*(3), 245–249.

Sanchez, E. (1979). *Medical diagnosis and composite fuzzy relations. In Advances in Fuzzy Set Theory and Applications* (M. M. Gupta, R. K. Ragade, & R. R. Yager, Eds.). Elsevier Science Ltd.

Sarhan, A. M. (2009). Cancer Classification Based on Micro array Gene Expression Data Using DCT and ANN. *Journal of Theoretical and Applied Information Technology, 6*(2), 208–216.

Sarmady, M., Dampier, W., & Tozeren, A. (2011). HIV protein sequence hotspots for crosstalk with host hub proteins. *PLoS One, 6*(8), e23293. doi: PONE-D-11-07403 [pii]10.1371/journal.pone.0023293

SAS. (2012). Big Data Meets Big Data Analytics (White Paper). SAS.com. Retrieved from http://www.sas.com/content/dam/SAS/en_us/doc/whitepaper1/big-data-meets-big-data-analytics-105777.pdf

Scheider, A. H., & Winter, P. M. (2005). Molecular MR imaging of melanoma with alpha-mu-beta 3 targeted paramagnetic nanoparticles. *Magnetic Resonance in Medicine, 53*(3), 621–627. doi:10.1002/mrm.20391 PMID:15723405

Schena, M., Shalon, D., Davis, R., & Brown, P. O. (1995). Quantitative monitoring of gene expression patterns with a complementary DNA microarray. *Science, 270*(5235), 467–470. doi:10.1126/science.270.5235.467 PMID:7569999

Schlitt, T., & Brazma, A. (2007). Current approaches to gene regulatory network modelling. *BMC Bioinformatics, 8*(Suppl. 6), S9. doi:10.1186/1471-2105-8-S6-S9 PMID:17903290

Schuh, C. (2005). *Fuzzy sets and their application in medicine. Proc. of the North American Fuzzy Information Society*(pp. 86–91). doi:10.1109/NAFIPS.2005.1548513

Schulze-Kremer, S. (2000). *Genetic algorithms and protein folding, Protein Struct* (pp. 75–222). Predict.

Schwefel, H. P. (1981). *Numerical Optimization of Computer Models.* New York: John Wiley & Sons.

Sciences, G. (n. d.). Deep Learning from Big data. *Impact @ Griffith Sciences.* Retrieved from http://app.griffith.edu.au/sciencesimpact/deep-learning-big-data/

Scott, A. (2012) Personalizing Medicine with Clinical Pharmacogenetics. National Institute of Health, 13(12).

Sebastiani, F. (2002). Machine learning in automated text categorization. *ACM Computing Surveys, 34*(1), 1–47. doi:10.1145/505282.505283

Seethalakshmi, P., & Vengataasalam, S. (2014). Application of Rough Set Approach in Dengue Diagnosis. *Applied Mathematical Sciences, 8*(127), 6313–6324.

Seiler, M., Huang, C. C., Szalma, S., & Bhanot, G. (2010). Consensus Cluster: A software tool for unsupervised cluster discovery in numerical data. *OMICS: A Journal of Integrative Biology, 14*(1), 109–113. doi:10.1089/omi.2009.0083 PMID:20141333

Seising, R. (2004). A history of medical diagnosis using fuzzy relations. *Proc. of the Conf. on Fuzziness.* Retrieved from http://www.mnh.si.edu

Senthilkumaran, N., & Rajesh, R. (2009). A Study on Rough Set Theory for Medical Image Segmentation. *International Journal of Recent Trends in Engineering, 2*(2), 236–238.

Shah, S.C., & Kusiak, A.(2004). Data Mining and Genetic Algorithm Based Gene Selection. *Artificial Intelligence in Medicine, 31*, 183-196.

Shahzadi, N., Atta-ur-Rahman & A. Shaheen. (2011). Semantic Network based Semantic Search of Religious Repository. *International Journal of Computer Applications, 36*(9), pp. 1-5.

Shahzadi, N., Atta-ur-rahman, A.-, & Jamil Sawar, M. (2012). Semantic Network based Classifier of Holy Quran. *International Journal of Computers and Applications, 39*(5), 43–47. doi:10.5120/4820-7069

Shannon, P., Markiel, A., Ozier, O., Baliga, N. S., Wang, J. T., Ramage, D., . . . Ideker, T. (2003). Cytoscape: a software environment for integrated models of biomolecular interaction networks. *Genome Res, 13*(11), 2498-2504. doi: 10.1101/gr.1239303

Shen, X., & Chen, J., Wang, Zhi., & Sun, Y. (2006). Grid Scan: A Simple and Effective Approach for Coverage Issue in Wireless Sensor Networks. *Proceedings of theIEEE International Communications Conference* (Vol. 8, pp. 3480-3484). doi:10.1109/ICC.2006.255611

Shi, W. (2005). *Principles of modeling uncertainties in spatial data and analysis, Science. CRC Press.* Taylor & Francis.

Shmulevich, I., Dougherty, E. R., Kim, S., & Zhang, W. (2002). Probabilistic Boolean networks: A rule-based uncertainty model for gene regulatory networks. *Bioinformatics (Oxford, England), 18*(2), 261–274. doi:10.1093/bioinformatics/18.2.261 PMID:11847074

Shoemaker, B. A., & Panchenko, A. R. (2007). Deciphering protein-protein interactions. Part I. Experimental techniques and databases. *PLoS Comput Biol, 3*(3), e42. doi:10.1371/journal.pcbi.0030042

Shokri, M., Tizhoosh, H. R., & Kamel, M. (2006).Opposition-based Q (λ) algorithm.*Proceedings of the IEEE World Congr. Comput. Intell.*, Vancouver,BC, Canada (pp. 646–653).

Sirbu, A., Ruskin, H. J., & Crane, M. (2010). Comparison of evolutionary algorithms in gene regulatory network model inference. *BMC Bioinformatics*, *11*(1), 59. doi:10.1186/1471-2105-11-59 PMID:20105328

Skrabanek, L., Saini, H. K., Bader, G. D., & Enright, A. J. (2008). Computational prediction of protein-protein interactions. *Molecular Biotechnology*, *38*(1), 1–17. doi:10.1007/s12033-007-0069-2 PMID:18095187

Slezak, D. (2000). Various approaches to reasoning with frequency-based decision reducts: a survey. In L. Polkowski, S. Tsumoto, & T. Y. Lin (Eds.), *Rough Sets in Soft Computing and Knowledge Discovery: New Developments*. Physica Verlag.

Slowinski, K., Slowinski, R., & Stefanowski, J. (1988). Rough sets approach to analysis of data from peritoneal lavage in acute pancreatic. *International Journal of Medical Informatics*. PMID:3054367

Smith, C. (2014). Social Media's New Big Data Frontiers -- Artificial Intelligence, Deep Learning, And Predictive *Marketing*. *Business Insider.com*. Retrieved from: http://www.businessinsider.com.au/social-medias-new-big-data-frontiers-artificial-intelligence-deep-learning-and-predictive-marketing-2014-2

Smith, S. (1983).Flexible learning of problem solving heuristics through adaptive search. *Proceedings of the Eighth Intl. Joint Conference on Artificial Intelligence*, Karlsruche, Germany (pp. 422-425). William Kaufmann

Smith, G. P. (1985). Filamentous fusion phage: Novel expression vectors that display cloned antigens on the virion surface. *Science*, *228*(4705), 1315–1317. doi:10.1126/science.4001944 PMID:4001944

Smyth, G. (2004). Statistical applications in genetics and molecular biology. Linear models and empirical Bayes methods for assessing differential expression in microarray experiments.

Snel, B., Lehmann, G., Bork, P., & Huynen, M. A. (2000). STRING: A web-server to retrieve and display the repeatedly occurring neighbourhood of a gene. *Nucleic Acids Research*, *28*(18), 3442–3444. doi:10.1093/nar/28.18.3442 PMID:10982861

Song, C., & Kulldorff, M. (2003). Power evaluation of disease clustering tests. *International Journal of Health Geographics*, *2*(1), 9. doi:10.1186/1476-072X-2-9 PMID:14687424

Soubra, D. (2012). The 3Vs that define Big Data. *Data Science Central.com*.http://www.datasciencecentral.com/forum/topics/the-3vs-that-define-big-data

Sowa, J.F., & Borgida, A. (1991). Principles of Semantic Networks: Explorations in the Representation of Knowledge.

Squassina, A., Manchia, M., Manolopoulos, V. G., Artac, M., Lappa-Manakou, C., Karkabouna, S., & Patrinos, G.P. et al. (2010). Realities, and Expectations of Pharmacogenomics and Personalized Medicine: Impact of translating Genetic knowledge into Clinical Practice. *Future Medicine*, *11*(8), 1149–1167. PMID:20712531

Sridevi T. & Murugan A. (2012): Rough set theory based attribute reduction for breast cancer Diagnosis. Indian J. Innovations Dev., 1(5), 309 – 313.

Srimani, P. K. a& Manjula, S. K. (2014). Knowledge Discovery in Medical Data by using Rough Set Rule Induction Algorithms. *Indian Journal of Science and Technology*, *7*(7), 905–915.

Srimani, P. K., & Koti, M. S. (2011). The Impact of Rough Set Approach on Medical Diagnosis for Cost Effective Feature Selection. *International Journal of Current Research*, *3*(12), 175–178.

Srimani, P. K., & Koti, M. S. (2014). Rough set (RS) approach for optimal rule generation in medical data. *International Journal of Conceptions on Computing and Information Technology*, *2*(2), 9–13.

Srinivas, N., & Deb, K. (1995). Multi objective function optimization using non dominated sorting genetic algorithms. *Evolutionary Computation, 2*(3), 221248.

Stark, C., Breitkreutz, B. J., Chatr-Aryamontri, A., Boucher, L., Oughtred, R., Livstone, M. S., . . . Tyers, M. (2011). The BioGRID Interaction Database: 2011 update. *Nucleic Acids Res, 39*(Database issue), D698-704. doi: 10.1093/nar/gkq1116

Stark, C., Breitkreutz, B. J., Reguly, T., Boucher, L., Breitkreutz, A., & Tyers, M. (2006). BioGRID: a general repository for interaction datasets. *Nucleic Acids Res, 34*(Database issue), D535-539. doi:10.1093/nar/gkj109

Stears, R. L., Martinsky, T., & Schena, M. (2003). Trends in microarray analysis. *Nature Medicine, 9*(1), 140–145. doi:10.1038/nm0103-140 PMID:12514728

Stefanini, L. (2008). A generalization of Hukuhara difference for interval and fuzzy arithmetic. In D. Dubois, M. A. Lubiano, H. Prade, M. A. Gil, P. Grzegorzewski, & O. Hryniewicz (Eds.), *Soft Methods for Handling Variability and Imprecision, in: Series on Advances in Soft Computing, 48*. doi:10.1007/978-3-540-85027-4_25

Stefanini, L., & Bede, B. (2009). Generalized Hukuhara differentiability of interval-valued functions and interval differential equations. *Nonlinear Analysis, 71*(3-4), 1311–1328. doi:10.1016/j.na.2008.12.005

Storn, R., & K. Price, K. (1995). Differential Evolution - a Simple and Efficient Adaptive Scheme for Global Optimization over Continuous Spaces (Technical Report TR-95-012). ICSI.

Storn, R. (1999). System Design by Constraint Adaptation and Differential Evolution. *IEEE Transactions on Evolutionary Computation, 3*(1), 22–34.

Su, C. T., Yang, C., Hsu, K., & Chiu, W. (2006). Data mining for the diagnosis of type II diabetes from three-dimensional body surface anthropometrical scanning data. *Computers & Mathematics with Applications (Oxford, England), 51*(6–7), 1075–1092. doi:10.1016/j.camwa.2005.08.034

Sun, Y., Feng, G., & Cao, J. (2010). A new approach to dynamic fuzzy modelling of genetic regulatory networks. *IEEE Transactions on NanoBioscience, 9*(4), 263–272.

Surade, S., & Blundell, T. L. (2012). Structural biology and drug discovery of difficult targets: the limits of ligandability. *Chem Biol, 19*(1), 42-50. doi: 10.1016/j.chembiol.2011.12.013

Swain, M. T., Mandel, J. J., & Dubitzky, W. (2010). Comparative study of three commonly used continuous deterministic methods for modelling gene regulation networks. *BMC Bioinformatics, 11*(1), 459. doi:10.1186/1471-2105-11-459 PMID:20840745

Swarm Intelligence. (2006). Particle Swarm Optimization. Retrieved from www.swarmintelligence.org

Swiniarski, R. W., Lim, H. J., Shin, Y. H., & Skowron, A. (2006). Independent component analysis, principal component analysis and rough set in hybrid mammogram classification. *Proceedings of theInternational Conference on Image Processing, Computer Vision, and Pattern Recognition* (pp. 640–645).

Swiniarski, R., & Skowron, A. (2003). Rough set methods in feature selection and recognition. *Pattern Recognition Letters, 24*(6), 833–849. doi:10.1016/S0167-8655(02)00196-4

Syahir, A., Usui, K., Tomizaki, K., Kajikawa, K. & Mihara, H. (2015). Label and Label-Free Detection Techniques for Protein Microarrays. *Microarrays journal,*4, 228-244.

Szewczy, K. R., Osterweil, E., Polastre, J., & Hamilton, A. (2004). Habitat monitoring with sensor networks. *Communications of the ACM, 47*(6), 34–44. doi:10.1145/990680.990704

Szilagyi, A., Grimm, V., Arakaki, A. K., & Skolnick, J. (2005). Prediction of physical protein-protein interactions. *Phys Biol, 2*(2), S1-16. doi:10.1088/1478-3975/2/2/S01

Szkola, A., Linares, E. M., Worbs, S., Dorner, B. G., Dietrich, R., Martlbauer, E., & Seidel, M. et al. (2014). Rapid and simultaneous detection of ricin, staphylococcal enterotoxin B and saxitoxin by chemiluminescence-based microarray immunoassay. *Analyst (London), 139*(22), 5885–5892. doi:10.1039/C4AN00345D PMID:25237676

Takeda, K., & Onodera, T. (2013). Artificial Intelligence: Learning Through Interactions and Big Data. IBM Redbooks Point-of-View publication. Retrieved from http://www.redbooks.ibm.com/abstracts/redp4974.html?Open

Tamames, J., Casari, G., Ouzounis, C., & Valencia, A. (1997). Conserved clusters of functionally related genes in two bacterial genomes. *Journal of Molecular Evolution, 44*(1), 66–73. doi:10.1007/PL00006122 PMID:9010137

Tanford, C. (1962). Contribution of hydrophobic interactions to the stability of the globular conformation of proteins. *Journal of the American Chemical Society, 84*(22), 42404274. doi:10.1021/ja00881a009

Tan, W. (2010). Unified tuning of PID load frequency controller for power systems via IMC. *IEEE Transactions on Power Systems, 25*(1), 341–350. doi:10.1109/TPWRS.2009.2036463

Tapaswini, S., & Chakraverty, S. (2013). Numerical Solution of Fuzzy Arbitrary Order Predator-Prey Equations, Appl. *Applications of Mathematics, 8*(2), 647–672.

Tatusov, R. L., Koonin, E. V., & Lipman, D. J. (1997). A genomic perspective on protein families. *Science, 278*(5338), 631–637. doi:10.1126/science.278.5338.631 PMID:9381173

Teyra, J., Doms, A., Schroeder, M., & Pisabarro, M. T. (2006). SCOWLP: a web-based database for detailed characterization and visualization of protein interfaces. *BMC Bioinformatics, 7*, 104. doi:10.1186/1471-2105-7-104

Teyra, J., Paszkowski-Rogacz, M., Anders, G., & Pisabarro, M. T. (2008). SCOWLP classification: structural comparison and analysis of protein binding regions. *BMC Bioinformatics, 9*, 9. doi: 10.1186/1471-2105-9-9

Teyra, J., Samsonov, S. A., Schreiber, S., & Pisabarro, M. T. (2011). SCOWLP update: 3D classification of protein-protein, -peptide, -saccharide and -nucleic acid interactions, and structure-based binding inferences across folds. *BMC Bioinformatics, 12*, 398. doi: 10.1186/1471-2105-12-398

Thangavel, K., Bagyamani, J., & Rathipriya, R. (2011). Novel Hybrid PSO-SA Model for Biclustering of Expression Data. *Proceedings of theInternational Conference on Communication Technology and System Design* (pp. 1048 – 1055).

Thangavel, K., & Pethalakshmi, A. (2006). Feature selection for medical database using rough system. *International Journal of Artificial Intelligence and Machine Learning, 6*(1), 11–17.

The Daily Neuron. (n. d.). Intelligence. Retrieved from http://thedailyneuron.com/intelligence/

The University of Utah. (n. d.). Retrieved from www.learn.genetics.utah.edu

Thomas, A., & Thibault, H. (2010). Robust biomarker identification for cancer diagnosis with ensemble feature selection methods. *Bioinformatics (Oxford, England), 26*(3), 392–398. doi:10.1093/bioinformatics/btp630 PMID:19942583

Tian, T., & Burrage, K. (2003). Stochastic neural network models for gene regulatory networks. Proceedings of the 2003 congress on Evolutionary computation CEC '03. (Vol. 1, pp. 162-169). doi:10.1109/CEC.2003.1299570

Tizhoosh, H.R., & Ventesca, M.M. (2008). Oppositional Concepts. In Computational Intelligence. Springer.

Tizhoosh, H. R. (2005). Opposition-based learning: A new scheme for machine intelligence.*Proceedings. Int. Conf. Comput. Intell. Modeling Control and Autom.*, Vienna(Vol. 1, pp. 695–701).

Tolouti, S. J., & Ahmadi, M. B. (2010). Fuzzy Laplace Transform on Two Order Derivative and Solving Fuzzy Two Order Differential Equation. *Int. J. Industrial Mathematics, 2*(4), 279–293.

Tomasz, K. (2012). Hepatitis disease diagnosis using Rough Set- modification of the preprocessing algorithm. Proceedings of the*ICTIC 12* (pp. 47–50).

Traut, R. R., Casiano, C., & Zecherle, N. (1989). Crosslinking of protein subunits and ligands by the introduction of disulphide bonds. In T. E. Creighton (Ed.), *Protein function: a practical approach* (pp. 101–133). Oxford: IRL Press.

Tripathy, B. K., & Mittal, D. (2015b): Efficiency Analysis of Kernel Functions in Uncertainty Based C-Means Algorithms. *Presentation at the International Conference on Advances in Computing, Communications and Informatics*, Kochi.

Tripathy, B. K., Tripathy, A., & Govindarajulu, K. (2015a). On PRIFCM Algorithm for Data Clustering, Image Segmentation and Comparative Analysis. *Presentation at the IACC conference*, Bangalore (pp. 12 -13).

Tripathy, B.K., Tripathy, A. & Govindarajulu, K. (2014b). Possibilistic rough fuzzy C-means algorithm in data clustering and image segmentation. *Proceedings of the IEEE ICCIC2014* (pp. 981-986).

Tripathy, B.K., Tripathy, A., Govindarajulu, K. & Bhargav, R. (2014a). On kernel Based rough Intuitionistic Fuzzy C-means algorithm and a comparative analysis. *Smart innovation systems and technologies, 27*, 349-359.

Tripathy, B. K., Acharjya, D. P., & Cynthia, V. (2011). A Framework for Intelligent Medical Diagnosis Using Rough Set With Formal Concept Analysis. *International Journal of Artificial Intelligence & Applications, 2*(2), 45–66. doi:10.5121/ijaia.2011.2204

Tripathy, B. K., & Govindarajulu, K. (2013). Data mining a kidney failure data set using Rough Sets. *International Journal of Electronics and Computer Science Engineering, 2*(3), 949–954.

Tsumoto, S. & Tanaka, H. (1996). Automated Discovery of Medical Expert System Rules from Clinical Databases based on Rough Sets. *Data Mining Applications, 1996*, 63-69.

Tsumoto, S. (1999). Discovery of Knowledge about Drug Side Effects in Clinical Databases based on Rough Set Model. AAAI Technical Report SS-99-01. Retrieved from www.aaai.org

Tsumoto, S. (2004). Mining diagnostic rules from clinical databases using rough sets and medical diagnostic model. *Information Sciences, 162*(2), 65–80. doi:10.1016/j.ins.2004.03.002

Tuncbag, N., Gursoy, A., Nussinov, R., & Keskin, O. (2011). Predicting protein-protein interactions on a proteome scale by matching evolutionary and structural similarities at interfaces using PRISM. *Nat Protoc, 6*(9), 1341-1354. doi: 10.1038/nprot.2011.367

Tusher, V. G., Tibshirani, R., & Chu, G. (2001). Significance analysis of microarrays applied to the ionizing radiation response. *Proceedings of the National Academy of Sciences of the United States of America, 98*(9), 5116–5121. doi:10.1073/pnas.091062498 PMID:11309499

Tyson, J. J., Csikasz-Nagy, A., & Novak, B. (2002). The dynamics of cell cycle regulation. *BioEssays, 24*(12), 1095–1109. doi:10.1002/bies.10191 PMID:12447975

U.S. Food and Drug Administration. (2013). Paving the way for Personalized Medicine.

Ulegtekin, N., Alkoy, S., Seker, D. Z., & Goksel, C. (2007). Use of GIS in Epidemiology: A case study in Istanbul. *International Journal of Environmental Science & Health, 41*(9), 2013–2026.

UniProt: a hub for protein information. (2015). *Nucleic Acids Res, 43*(Database issue), D204-212. doi:10.1093/nar/gku989

Ursem, R. K., & Vadstrup, P. (2003, December 8-12). Parameter identification of induction motors using differential evolution. *Proceedings of the 2003 Congress onEvolutionaryComputation CEC2003*, Canberra (pp. 790-796).

Ursem, R. K., & Vadstrup, P. (2004). Parameter identification of induction motors using stochastic optimization algorithm. *Applied Soft Computing, 4*(1), 49–64.

Usman, A., & Divakar, B. P. (2012). Simulation study of load frequency control of single and two area systems. *Proceedings of theIEEE Global Humanitarian Technology Conference* (pp. 214-219). doi:10.1109/GHTC.2012.38

Vainshtein, Y., Sanchez, M., Brazma, A., Hentze, M. W., Dandekar, T., & Muckenthaler, M. U. (2010). The Iron Chip evaluation package: A package of pemodules for robust analysis of custom microarrays. *BMC Bioinformatics, 11*(1), 112. doi:10.1186/1471-2105-11-112 PMID:20193060

Vaishali, P.K. & Vinayababu, A. (2011). Application of Microarray Technology and Soft-computing in Cancer Biology: A Review. *International Journal of Biometrics and Bioinformatics, 5*(4).

Valencia, A., & Pazos, F. (2002). Computational methods for the prediction of protein interactions. *Curr Opin Struct Biol, 12*(3), 368-373.

Valencia, A., & Pazos, F. (2003). Prediction of protein-protein interactions from evolutionary information. *Methods of Biochemical Analysis, 44*, 411–426. PMID:12647397

van Rijmenam, M. (2014). Is Artificial Intelligence About To Change Doing Business Forever? Retrieved from http://www.bigdata-startups.com/artificial-intelligence-change-business-forever/

Van't Veer, L. J., & Bernards, R. (2008). Enabling personalized cancer medicine through analysis of gene-expression patterns. *Nature, 452*(7187), 564–570. doi:10.1038/nature06915 PMID:18385730

Venema, L. (2007). Applied physics: Weight inside. *Nature, 7*, 446, 994.

Vimaladevi, M. & Kalaavathi, B. (2014). Cancer Classification using Hybrid Fast Particle Swarm Optimization with Back-propagation Neural Network, *International Journal of computer and communication technology, 3*(11).

Vincent, Y., Bernard, C., & Kockara, S. (n. d.). Extraction of Protein Sequence Motifs Information by Bi-Clustering Algorithm.

Vinterbo, S., & Øhrn, A. (2000). Minimal Approximate Hitting Sets and Rule Templates. *International Journal of Approximate Reasoning, 25*(2), 123–143. doi:10.1016/S0888-613X(00)00051-7

Vohradskffy, J. (2001). Neural network model of gene expression. *The FASEB Journal, 15*(3), 846-854.

Vora. (2013). A Survey on K-mean Clustering and Particle Swarm Optimization. *International Journal of Science and Modern Engineering, 1*(3), 24-26.

Voss, M. S., & Feng, X. (2002).A New Methodology For Emergent System Identification Using Particle Swarm Optimization (PSO) And The Group Method Data Handling (GMDH).*Proceedings of the Genetic and Evolutionary Computation Conference* (pp. 1227-1232).

Walter, J. G., Kokpinar, O., Friehs, K., Stahl, F., & Scheper, T. (2008). Systematic investigation of optimal aptamer immobilization for protein-microarray applications. *Analytical Chemistry, 80*(19), 7372–7378. doi:10.1021/ac801081v PMID:18729475

Wang, F., Pan, D., & Ding, J. (2008). A new approach combined fuzzy clustering and bayesian networks for modeling gene regulatory networks. Proceedings of the international conference on Biomedical engineering and informatics BMEI '08 (Vol. 1, pp. 29-33). doi:10.1109/BMEI.2008.117

Wang, G., & Dunbrack, R. (2003). PISCES: a protein sequence culling server in Bioinformatics, 19(12), 1589-1591.

Wang, J. F. (2006). Spatial Dynamics of an epidemic of severe acute respiratory syndrome in an urban area. *Bulletin of the World Health Organization, 84*(12), 965–968. doi:10.2471/BLT.06.030247 PMID:17242832

Wang, L. X. (1997). *A Course in Fuzzy Systems and Controls*. Prentice Hall Publications.

Wang, S. L., Wang, X. Z., & Shi, W. Z. (2001). Developing and Testing Geo-Spatial. *Information Science, 4*(1), 68–76.

Wang, W., Chua, K. C., & Srinivasan, V. (2008). Coverage in Hybrid Mobile Sensor Networks. *IEEE Transactions on Mobile Computing, 7*(11), 1374–1387. doi:10.1109/TMC.2008.68

Wassaf, D., Kuang, G., Kopacz, K., Wu, Q.-L., Nguyen, Q., Toews, M., & Sexton, D. J. et al. (2006). High-throughput affinity ranking of antibodies using surface plasmon resonance microarrays. *Analytical Biochemistry, 351*(2), 241–253. doi:10.1016/j.ab.2006.01.043 PMID:16510109

Weaver, D. C., Workman, C. T., & Stormo, G. D. (1999). Modeling regulatory networks with weight matrices. In Pacific symposium on biocomputing (Vol. 4, pp. 112-123).

Wei, G., Liu, D., & Liang, C. (2004). Charting gene regulatory networks: Strategies, challenges and perspectives. *The Biochemical Journal, 381*(1), 1–12. doi:10.1042/BJ20040311 PMID:15080794

Wei, M. H., Cheng, C. H., Huang, C. S., & Chiang, P. C. (2001). Discovering medical quality of total hip arthroplasty by rough set classifier with imbalanced class, Quality & Quantity. *International Journal of Methodology, 47*(3), 1761–1779.

Whirl-Carrillo, M., McDonagh, E.M., Hebert, J.M., Gong, L., Sangkuhl, K., Thorn, C.F., Altman, R.B. & Klein, T.E. (2012) Pharmacogenomics knowledge for Personalised Medicine. *Clin. Pharmcol. Ther., 92*(4).

Whitley, D., Starkweather, T., & Fuquay, D. (1989).Scheduling problems and traveling salesmen: the genetic edge recombination operator.*Proceedings of the Third Intl. Conference on Genetic Algorithms*, Fairfax, VA (pp. 133-140). Morgan Kaufmann.

Widz, S., Revett, K., & Slezak, D. (2004): Application of rough set based dynamic parameter optimization to MRI segmentation. *Proceedings of the23rd International Conference of the North American Fuzzy Information Processing Society* (pp. 440–445). doi:10.1109/NAFIPS.2004.1336323

Wikipedia. (n. d.). Pharmacogenetics. Retrieved from http://en.wikipedia.org/wiki/pharmacogenetics

Wilson, C. G., & Arkin, M. R. (2011). Small-molecule inhibitors of IL-2/IL-2R: Lessons learned and applied. *Current Topics in Microbiology and Immunology, 348*, 25–59. doi:10.1007/82_2010_93 PMID:20703966

Wilson, D. S., & Nock, S. (2003). Recent developments in protein microarray, technology. *Angewandte Chemie International Edition in English, 42*(5), 494–500. doi:10.1002/anie.200390150 PMID:12569479

Winter, C., Henschel, A., Kim, W. K., & Schroeder, M. (2006). SCOPPI: a structural classification of protein-protein interfaces. *Nucleic Acids Res, 34*(Database issue), D310-314. doi:10.1093/nar/gkj099

Wojcik, Z. (1987). Rough approximation of shapes in pattern recognition. *Computer Vision Graphics and Image Processing, 40*(2), 228–249. doi:10.1016/S0734-189X(87)80117-2

Woolf, P. J., & Wang, Y. (2000). A fuzzy logic approach to analyzing gene expression data. *Physiological Genomics, 3*(1), 9–15. PMID:11015595

Wright, G. W., & Simon, R. M. (2003). A random variance model for detection of differential gene expression in small microarray experiments. *Bioinformatics (Oxford, England)*, *19*(18), 2448–2455. doi:10.1093/bioinformatics/btg345 PMID:14668230

Wu, J., & Li, H. (1999). On calculating connected dominating set for efficient routing in ad hoc wireless networks. *Proceedings of the Third International Workshop on Discrete Algorithms and Methods for Mobile Computing and Communications*. doi:10.1145/313239.313261

Wu, J., Dai, F., Gao, M., & Stojmenovic, I. (2002). On calculating power aware connected dominating sets for efficient routing in ad hoc wireless networks. *Journal of Communications and Networks.*, *4*(1), 59–70. doi:10.1109/JCN.2002.6596934

Xenarios, I., Rice, D. W., Salwinski, L., Baron, M. K., Marcotte, E. M., & Eisenberg, D. (2000). DIP: the database of interacting proteins. *Nucleic Acids Res, 28*(1), 289-291.

Xia, J. F., Han, K., & Huang, D. S. (2010). Sequence-based prediction of protein-protein interactions by means of rotation forest and autocorrelation descriptor. *Protein and Peptide Letters*, *17*(1), 137–145. doi:10.2174/092986610789909403 PMID:20214637

Xiao, X., Dow, E. R., Eberhart, R. C., Miled, Z. B., & Oppelt, R. J. (2003). Gene Clustering Using Self-Organizing Maps and Particle Swarm Optimization. *Proc. of the 17th International Symposium on Parallel and Distributed Processing (PDPS'03)*, Washington DC. doi:10.1109/IPDPS.2003.1213290

Xing, G., Wang, X., & Zhang, Y. LU, C., Pless, R., & Gill, C. (2005). Integrated coverage and connectivity configuration for energy conservation in sensor networks. ACM Transactions on Sensor Network (Vol. 1, pp. 36–72).

Xiong, H., Tan, P., & Kumar, V. (2003). mining strong affinity association pattern in datasets with skewed support distribution. *Proceedings of international third Conference on Data Mining*, pp. 387-394. doi:10.1109/ICDM.2003.1250944

Xu, C.-G., Liu, K.-H., & Huang, D.-S. (2009). The analysis of microarray datasets using a genetic programming. In Computational intelligence in bioinformatics and computational biology, 2009. CIBCB'09. IEEE symposium on (pp. 176-181). doi:10.1109/CIBCB.2009.4925725

Xu, D., & Li, F. (2010). Research and Application of CT Image Mining based on Rough Sets Theory and Association Rules. Proceedings of the 2010 3rd IEEE International Conference on Computer Science and Information Technology (ICCSIT) (pp. 392-394).

Xu, D. (2008). *Applications of fuzzy logic in bioinformatics* (Vol. 9). Imperial College Press.

Xu, R., Venayagamoorthy, G. K., & Wunsch, D. C. II. (2007a). Modeling of gene regulatory networks with hybrid differential evolution and particle swarm optimization. *Neural Networks*, *20*(8), 917–927. doi:10.1016/j.neunet.2007.07.002 PMID:17714912

Xu, R., Wunsch, I. I. D., & Frank, R. (2007b). Inference of genetic regulatory networks with recurrent neural network models using particle swarm optimization. *IEEE/ACM Transactions on Computational Biology and Bioinformatics*, *4*(4), 681–692. doi:10.1109/TCBB.2007.1057 PMID:17975278

Yan, J. (2013). Big Data, Bigger Opportunities. *Meritalk*. Retrieved from http://www.meritalk.com/pdfs/bdx/bdx-whitepaper-090413.pdf

Yang, X.-S., & Deb, S. (2009). Cuckoo search via levy flights. In Nature & biologically inspired computing, 2009. NABIC 2009. world congress on (pp. 210{214).

Yang, K., Cai, Z., Li, J., & Lin, G. (2006). A stable gene selection in microarray data analysis. *BMC Bioinformatics*, *7*(1), 228. doi:10.1186/1471-2105-7-228 PMID:16643657

Yang, P., Yang, Y. H., Zhou, B. B., & Zomaya, A. Y. (2010). A review of ensemble methods in bioinformatics. *Current Bioinformatics, 5*(4), 296–308. doi:10.2174/157489310794072508

Yang, Y., Yao, Q., Chen, Z., Xiang, J., William, F. E., Gibbs, R. A., & Chen, C. (2013). Genetic and molecular alterations in pancreatic cancer: Implications for personalized medicine. *Medical Science Monitor.* doi:10.12659/MSM.889636

Yan, Q. (2010). Immunoinformatics and systems biology methods for personalized medicine. *Methods in Molecular Biology (Clifton, N.J.), 662,* 203–220. doi:10.1007/978-1-60761-800-3_10 PMID:20824473

Yao, Y. Y. (1998). Relational Interpretations of Neighborhood Operators and Rough Set Approximation Operators. *Information Science, 111*(1-4), 239–259. doi:10.1016/S0020-0255(98)10006-3

Ye, F., Luo, H., Cheng, J., Lu, S., & Zhang, L. (2002). A two-tier data dissemination model for large-scale wireless sensor networks. *Proceedings of the 8th Annual International Conference on Mobile Computing and Networking*, Atlanta, Georgia, USA. doi:10.1145/570645.570664

Yongjun, P., Minghao, P., Kiejung, P., & Keun, H. R. (2012). An ensemble correlation-based gene selection algorithm for cancer classification with gene expression data, *Data and Text Mining. Bioinformatics (Oxford, England), 28*(24), 3306–3315. doi:10.1093/bioinformatics/bts602 PMID:23060613

Young, R. A., & Davis, R. W. (1983). Yeast RNA polymerase II genes: Isolation with antibody probes. *Science, 222*(4625), 778–782. doi:10.1126/science.6356359 PMID:6356359

Yu, L., & Liu, H. (2003). Feature selection for high-dimensional data: a fast correlation- based filter solution, Proc. *Proceedings of theTwentieth International Conference on Machine Learning* (pp. 856–863).

Yun, T., Hwang, T., Cha, K., & Yi, G. S. (2010). CLIC: Clustering analysis of large microarray datasets with Individual dimension-based clustering. *Nucleic Acids Research, 2010, 38.* PMID:20529873

Yu, X., Schneiderhan-Marra, N., & Joos, T. O. (2011). Protein microarrays and personalized medicine. *Annales de Biologie Clinique, 69,* 17–29. PMID:21463992

Zadeh, L. (2005). Toward a generalized theory of uncertainty (GTU) – an outline. *Information Sciences, 172*(1-2), 1–40. doi:10.1016/j.ins.2005.01.017

Zadeh, L. A. (1965). Fuzzy sets. *Information and Control, 8*(3), 338–353. doi:10.1016/S0019-9958(65)90241-X

Zadeh, L. A. (1996). Fuzzy logic= computing with words. *IEEE Transactions on Fuzzy Systems, 4*(2), 103–111.

Zahiri, J., Bozorgmehr, J. H., & Masoudi-Nejad, A. (2013). Computational Prediction of Protein-Protein Interaction Networks: Algo-rithms and Resources. *Curr Genomics, 14*(6), 397-414. doi:10.2174/1389202911314060004

Zajac, A., Song, D., Qian, W., & Zhukov, T. (2007). Protein microarrays and quantum dot probes for early cancer detection. *Colloids and Surfaces. B, Biointerfaces, 58*(2), 309–314. doi:10.1016/j.colsurfb.2007.02.019 PMID:17408931

Zang, Y. (2007). Load Frequency Control of Multiple-Area Power Systems [Master of Science in Electrical Engineering]. Tsinghua University.

Zanzoni, A., Montecchi-Palazzi, L., Quondam, M., Ausiello, G., Helmer-Citterich, M., & Cesareni, G. (2002). MINT: a Molecular INTeraction database. *FEBS Lett, 513*(1), 135-140.

Zarei, H., Kamyad, A. V., & Heydari, A. A. (2012). Fuzzy Modeling and Control of HIV Infection, Computational and Mathematical Methods in Medicine, Volume 2012, Article ID 893474, 17 pages.

Zhang, T.L, Ding, Y.S & Chou, K.C (2008). Prediction protein structural classes with pseudo-amino acid composition: approximate entropy and hydrophobicity pattern. *J. Theoretical Biology, 250*, 186-193.

Zhang, C.-X., & Zhang, J.-S. (2008). RotBoost: A technique for combining rotation forest and Adaboost. *Pattern Recognition Letters, 29*(10), 1524–1536. doi:10.1016/j.patrec.2008.03.006

Zhang, C.-X., & Zhang, J.-S. (2010). A variant of rotation forest for constructing ensemble classifiers. *Pattern Analysis & Applications, 13*(1), 59–77. doi:10.1007/s10044-009-0168-8

Zhang, H., & Hou, J. C. (2005). Maintaining Sensing Coverage and Connectivity in Large Sensor Networks. *Ad Hoc & Sensor Wireless Networks., 1*, 89–124.

Zhang, H., Wang, Y., Wang, L., Lin, Y., & Liu, P. (2013). A Hierarchical Diagnosis Model for Syndrome Prediction in TCM of Post-Hepatitic Cirrhosis. *International Journal of Integrative Medicine, 1*(24), 1–7.

Zhang, T. L., & Ding, Y. S. (2007). Using pseudo amino acid composition and binary tree support vector machines to predict protein structural classes. *Amino Acids, 33*(4), 623629. doi:10.1007/s00726-007-0496-1 PMID:17308864

Zhang, T., Ramakrishnan, R., & Livny, M. (1996). *BIRCH: An efficient data clustering method for very large database. Proceedings of ASM-SIGMOD international conference on management of data* (pp. 103–114). New York: ACM. doi:10.1145/233269.233324

Zhang, W. W. (2003). The use of gene-specific IgY antibodies for drug target discovery. *Drug Discovery Today, 8*(8), 364–371. doi:10.1016/S1359-6446(03)02655-2 PMID:12681940

Zhang, Y., Xuan, J., de los Reyes, B. G., Clarke, R., & Ressom, H. W. (2009). Reverse engineering module networks by pso-rnn hybrid modeling. *BMC Genomics, 10*(Suppl. 1), S15. doi:10.1186/1471-2164-10-S1-S15 PMID:19594874

Zhao, F., & Guibas, L. (2004). *Wireless Sensor Networks. An Information Processing Approach*. Morgan Kaufmann.

Zhaoa-Xing-Ming. (2005). A novel approach to extracting features from motif content and protein composition for protein sequence classification. Neural Networks, 2005, 1019–1028. PubMed PMID:16153801

Zhou, Z.-H., Chawla, N. V., Jin, Y., & Williams, G. J. (2014). *Big Data Opportunities and Challenges: Discussions from Data Analytics Perspectives*. IEEE Computational Intelligence Magazine, 9(4). 62-74.

Zhou, G. (1998). An intriguing controversy over protein structural class prediction. *Journal of Protein Chemistry, 17*(8), 729738. doi:10.1023/A:1020713915365 PMID:9988519

Zhou, X., Wang, X., Pal, R., Ivanov, I., Bittner, M., & Dougherty, E. R. (2004). A Bayesian connectivity-based approach to constructing probabilistic gene regulatory networks. *Bioinformatics (Oxford, England), 20*(17), 2918–2927. doi:10.1093/bioinformatics/bth318 PMID:15145802

Zhu, H., Domingues, F. S., Sommer, I., & Lengauer, T. (2006). NOXclass: prediction of protein-protein interaction types. *BMC Bioinformatics, 7*, 27. doi:10.1186/1471-2105-7-27

Zhu, X., Gerstein, M., & Snyder, M. (2007). Getting connected: analysis and principles of biological networks. *Genes Dev, 21*(9), 1010-1024. doi:10.1101/gad.1528707

Zikopoulous, P., Deroos, D., Parasuraman, K., Deutsch, T., Corrigan, D., & Giles, J. (2013). *Harness the Power of Big Data*. McGraw-Hill.

Zinovyev, A., Viara, E., Calzone, L., & Barillot, E. (2008). BiNoM: a Cytoscape plugin for manipulating and analyzing biological networks. *Bioinformatics, 24*(6), 876-877. doi:10.1093/bioinformatics/btm553

About the Contributors

Sujata Dash received her Ph.D. degree in Computational Modelling from Berhampur University, Orissa, India in 1995. She is an Associate Professor in P.G. Department of Computer Science & Application, North Orissa University, at Baripada, India. She has published more than 80 technical papers in international journals, conferences and book chapters of reputed publications. She has guided many scholars for their Ph.D degrees in computer science. She is associated with many professional bodies like the CSI, the ISTE, the OITS, the OMS, the IACSIT, the IMS and the IAENG. She is on the editorial board of several international journals and also a reviewer of many international journals. Her current research interests include Machine Learning, Distributed Data Mining, Bioinformatics, Intelligent Agent, Web Data Mining, Image Processing and Cloud Computing.

Bidyadhar Subudhi received a Bachelor's Degree in Electrical Engineering from the National Institute of Technology (NIT), Rourkela, India, Master of Technology in Control & Instrumentation from Indian Institute of Technology, Delhi in 1988 and 1994 respectively and PhD degree in Control System Engineering from Univ. of Sheffield in 2003. He was a postdoctoral research fellow in the Dept. of Electrical & Computer Engg., NUS, Singapore during May-Nov 2005. Currently, he is a professor in the Department of Electrical Engineering at NIT Rourkela and coordinator, centre of excellence on renewable energy systems. He is a Senior Member of the IEEE and a Fellow of the IET. His research interests include system identification & adaptive control, networked control systems, control of flexible and under water robots, estimation and filtering with application to power system and control of renewable energy systems.

* * *

Prathik A. is a Research Associate in the School of Information Technology and Engineering, VIT University in Vellore, Tamil Nadu. He received M.Tech in the field of Information Technology-Networking from VIT University, Vellore in the year 2015.He is currently completing a PhD at VIT University, Vellore, Tamil Nadu, India. His research interests include, Spatial Data Mining, communication networks, computation, operations research, circuit design, communication network addressing and data base management.

Sharmila Banu is working as an Assistant Professor (Senior) in the School of Computer Science & Engineering, VIT University Vellore since June 2009.

Sonika Bhatnagar completed her Ph.D. in Biophysics from A.I.I.M.S. and currently works as an Associate Professor of Biotechnology. Her research interests lie in the application of Computational and Structural Biology tools for gaining insights into Cardiovascular Disease and Bacterial Stress response with a long term focus on Drug target selection, Drug design and Repurposing.

Arun C. (born 17.10. 1985) studied Industrial biotechnology and Environmental science and technology at Anna University, Chennai. He obtained a grant during his post-graduation under a "Student project scheme" from the Tamil Nadu state council for science and technology. After that he worked as Environmental consultant in Environmental consulting organization (from Aug 2010 to June2011) and then he started his career as an Assistant professor in the Department of environmental engineering (from June 2011 to September 2012). He started his research in the field of biochemical engineering (from October 2012 to present).

Nilamadhab Dash has completed his M.Tech in Computer Science and Engineering from Biju Pattnaik University of Technology, Odisha in the year 2009. Currently, he is working as an Assistant Professor in the department of Information Technology of C. V. Raman College of Engineering. His research areas of interest include Soft Computing, Computational Intelligence, Data Mining and Image Processing. He has published more than twelve papers in reputed international journals and conferences.

Sushmita Ekka is a M.Tech student in the department of Electrical Engineering, NIT Rourkela. She has research interest on Power system operation & Control and Power quality.

Yasha Hasija (B.Tech, M.Tech, and Ph.D.) completed her Ph.D. at the Institute of Genomics and Integrative Biology, CSIR and University of Pune. She is currently working as an Assistant Professor and an Associate Head at Department of Biotechnology, Delhi Technological University (formerly the Delhi College of Engineering). She has published several papers in national and international journals of high repute, and has been awarded several prestigious awards, including the Department of Science and Technology Award for attending the meeting of Nobel Laureates and Students in Lindau in 2002; & Human Gene Nomenclature Award at the Human Genome Meeting-2010 held at Montpellier, France. She is the Project Investigator of several sponsored research projects from SERB, CSIR-OSDD, etc. She is also the Associate Editor of International Journal of Bioinformatics Research, the Executive Editor of the International Journal of Advanced Biotechnology and Bioinformatics (IJABB), and an Editorial Board Member of several international journals, including the International Journal of Biometrics and Bioinformatics (IJBB) and the Review of Bioinformatics and Biometrics (RBB). She has served as an invited expert and has delivered invited technical and memorial talks at several prestigious universities. She is an active researcher supervising M.Tech (Bioinformatics) and Ph.D. students at DTU. Her broad areas of research include genome informatics, genome annotation, microbial informatics, integration of genome-scale data for systems biology and personalized genomics.

Anuradha Jagadeesan is an Associate Professor in School of Computing Science and Engineering, VIT University in Vellore, Tamil Nadu. She has more than 11 years of teaching experience and received a Ph.D degree in Computer Science and Engineering. She has published technical papers in international journals/ proceedings of international conferences/ edited book chapters of reputed publications. Her current research interest includes Fuzzy sets and systems, Rough sets and knowledge engineering, Data Mining, Big Data Analytics, soft computing, and Medical Diagnosis.

Debashisha Jena received his PhD from NIT Rourkela in 2010. Now he is continuing as an Assistant Professor in the department of Electrical and Electronics Engineering at NITK, Surathkal.

Prabhat Kumar Mahanti is a Professor of Dept. of Applied Statistics (CSAS), University of New Brunswick Canada. He obtained his M.Sc. from IIT-Kharagpur, India, and Ph.D. from IIT-Bombay India. His research interests include software engineering, software metrics, reliability modelling, modelling and simulation, numerical algorithms, finite elements, mobile and soft computing, and verification of embedded software, neural computing, data analysis and multi-agent systems. He has more than 100 research papers and technical reports to his credit.

Rupa Mahanti is an Information Management consultant with Tata Consultancy Services Ltd specializing in Data Warehousing, Data Strategy, Data Quality Management and Big Data. She has more than 13 years of experience which includes research, teaching, and industry experience. She has cross-industry experience in finance, healthcare, telecom and utilities across the US, UK and Asia Pacific geographies. Her research interests center on data quality, software quality, Six Sigma, survey-based research, environmental management, software engineering education, and simulation and modeling. She is a reviewer with several international journals.

Babita Majhi completed her Ph.D. degree in 2009 from the National Institute of Technology Rourkela and Post Doctoral research work at the University of Sheffield, UK (Dec.2011-Dec. 2012) under a Boyscast Fellowship of DST, from the Govt. of India. She is presently working as an Assistant Professor in the department of Computer Science and Information Technology, Central University, Bilaspur, India. Prior to this position, she was working as an Assistant Professor in the CSIT department of ITER, Siksha 'O' Anusandhan University, Bhubaneswar, Odisha. She has guided 2 Ph.D. and 7 M.Tech. theses in the field of adaptive signal processing, computational finance and Soft-computing and has published 100 research papers in various referred International journals and conferences. She is a Member of IEEE. She received the prestigious BOYSCAST Fellowship of DST, Govt. of India for pursuing her postdoctoral work for the year 2010-11, the Kalpana Chawla award for best technical research on the 8th of March 2013 (International Womens' day) at Jayadev Bhawan, Odisha and the best Ph. D. thesis award from the IEEE NaBIC in 2009. Her research interests are: Adaptive Signal Processing, Soft Computing, Evolutionary Computing, Computational Finance, Distributed Signal Processing and Data Mining.

Brojo Kishore Mishra has completed his Ph.D in Computer Science from Berhampur University in the year 2012. Currently, he is working as an Associate Professor in the department of Information Technology of C. V. Raman College of Engineering, Bhubaneswar. Before joining this organization he worked as a Principal of the MITS Institute of Polytechnic, Rayagada. Now he is a State Student Coordinator (Odisha) for the Computer Society of India (CSI). He is a life member of the CSI, the ISTE and a member of the IAENG, the CSTA, the ACCS, and the UACEE professional societies. Also he also a Jury Coordination Committee Member of All IEEE Young Engineers' Humanitarian Challenge (AI-YEHUM 2015) project competition, organized by IEEE Region 10 (Asia pacific). His research interests include Data/Opinion Mining, Soft Computing, Big Data & Cloud Computing. He has published more than twenty papers published in reputed international journals and conferences.

Rachita Misra has completed her Ph.D (Digital Image Processing) - IIT Kharagpur in the year 1990. Currently she is working as a Professor and Head in the department of Information Technology of C. V. Raman College of Engineering. Her research areas of interest include Digital Image Processing, Data Mining, Soft Computing, Parallel Computing, Software Engineering and Project Management. She is a member of IEEE, ACM, PMI, Life member CSI, OITS, AISCA, IUPRAI and has published more than thirty papers in reputed international journals and conferences.

R. K. Mohanty is pursuing his MS (By Research) in computer science under the guidance of Dr. B.K. Tripathy. His area of research interest is in soft set theory and its applications in soft computing and decision making.

Sankar Prasad Mondal is a Teaching Assistant in the Department of Mathematics at the National Institute of Technology, Agartala, Tripura, India. He received M.Sc (Applied Mathematics) degree from Indian Institute of Engineering Science and Technology (Formally Bengal Engineering and Science University), Shibpur, West Bengal, India and Ph.D degree from Indian Institute of Engineering Science and Technology, Shibpur, West Bengal, India .His current research interest is in Fuzzy Differential Equation and its applications.

Selvakumar P. (born 1987) studied Biotechnology at Anna University, Chennai (India). From 2012 to 2015, he worked as an Assistant Professor in the Department of Biotechnology. He has four publications in various international journals. Since 2015, he is completing his research on enhancement of lipid synthesis through microbes.

Bishnupriya Panda is an assistant professor working in the department of computer science and engineering, S'O'A University Odisha. Prior to this, she was working as an Assistant Professor in CVRCE Bhubaneswar. She is a Gold Medalist recipient for her M.Tech degree and is currently pursuing her Ph.D. in Computer Science and Engineering at S'O'A University. She has wide horizon of research interest like soft computing, Evolutionary computing and Data mining.

Subhendu Kumar Pani is currently working as a Professor(Associate) of Orissa Engineering College, Bhubaneswar. During last 13 years of academic careers, he has actively been involved in Teaching, Research, Curriculum Development and Academic Administration. His specific research focus is in the areas of Data Mining, Web Mining, Soft and Evolutionary Computing, Software engineering. To date he has 75 research publications, out of which 30 papers are in reputed peer reviewed journals and the others have been presented in the conferences and have appeared in conference proceedings. He has also authored a Book in Data Mining. He is a regular reviewer of many international journals. He is a life, fellow and senior member of many professional societies.

Rojalina Priyadarshini has completed her M.Tech from SOA University in the year 2010. Currently, she is working as an Assistant Professor in the department of Information Technology of C. V. Raman College of Engineering and pursuing Ph.D. Her research areas of interest include Soft Computing, Computational Intelligence, Data Mining and Cloud Computing. She has published more than twelve papers in reputed international journals and conferences.

Rathipriya R is an Assistant Professor in the Dept. of Computer Science at Periyar University. Her research interest is Bio-Inspired Optimization techniques and its application on various domains like Web mining, Bioinformatics. Currently carrying out the research on Bio-inspired optimization techniques for Big Data applications.

Sooraj T.R. is pursuing his Ph.D. in computer science under the guidance of Dr. B.K. Tripathy. His area of research interest is soft set theory and it's applications in soft computing and decision making.

Sneha Rai is currently pursuing her Ph.D. degree. Her research work is in the area of Mining and Modeling of Protein Protein interactions in Hyperlipidemia. She has previously completed her M.Tech. Bioinformatics from Gautam Buddha University, U.P.

Gowri Rajasekaran is a Ph. D research Scholar. Department of Computer Science, Periyar University, Salem,Tamilnadu. Pursuing her full time research under guidance of Dr. R. Rathipriya, Assistant Professor, Periyar University. Her research interest is Bio-inspired Computing Techniques and Bioinformatics especially Protein.

Pravat Kumar Ray received his B.S. degree in electrical engineering from Indira Gandhi Institute of Technology Sarang, Odisha, India, in 2000, and his M.E. degree in electrical engineering from Bengal Engineering and Science University, Howrah, India, in 2003, and his Ph.D. degree in electrical engineering from National Institute of Technology (NIT) Rourkela, Rourkela, India, in 2011. He is currently an Assistant Professor with the Department of Electrical Engineering, NIT Rourkela. His research interests include system identification, signal processing, and soft computing applications to power system, estimation of signal, and systems.

Khalid Raza is currently working as an Assistant Professor at the Department of Computer Science, Jamia Millia Islamia (Central University), New Delhi, India. He obtained his Bachelors and Master's degree in Computer Applications, cleared UGC-NET-JRF conducted by University Grants Commissin (UGC), India and joined the Department of Computer Science in the year 2010. He completed his PhD in the area of Soft Computing and Computational Biology from Jamia Millia Islamia in 2014. He has contributed 1 book and over 20 research articles in refereed international journals, conference proceedings and as book chapters. He has received grants for two Govt. funded research projects and worked as the Principal Investigator. He is the recipient of the Indian Academy of Sciences Faculty Summer Research Fellowship. He is a reviewer of several international journals, member of several conference review committees. He is a member of the ACM, a Life Member of Computer Society of India (CSI) and the Soft Computing Research Society, a Regular Member of Machine Intelligence Research (MIR) Lab., and a Regular Member of Indian Science Congress Association. He has delivered several invited talks at conferences/workshops.

P. Sivashanmugam is working as a Professor and the Head of the Chemical department at the National Institute of Technology, Tiruchirapalli, India with 23 years of teaching and research experience. He is completing research in the area of process Engineering, Biotechnology, and Environmental Engineering. He has produced 8 Ph.Ds, guided 40 M.Tech thesis, published 60 papers in peer reviewed International Journals and 18 papers in peer reviewed national journals and 63 papers in international and national conference. He has written a book on Basics of Environmental Engineering. He has also had many R & D projects and MODROB projects.

Navneet Kaur Soni is currently working as Software Engineer in Accenture, India. She has completed a Bachelors of Technology in Biotechnology at Anand Engineering College, Agra in 2011 and then served as a Lecturer for the Axis Group of Colleges, Kanpur. She then went on to pursue a Masters of Technology in Bioinformatics from Delhi Technological University. She has one publication to her name. Her interest lies in computational biology and proteomics.

Nitin Thukral has a B.Tech Hons. (Biotechnology), and M.Tech (Bioinformatics).

Balakrushna Tripathy is a Senior Professor at SCSE, VIT University, Vellore, India. He has received fellowships from UGC, DST, SERC and DOE of Govt. of India. He has published more than 300 technical papers and has mentored 21 PhDs, 13 MPhils and 2 M.S (By research) under his supervision. Dr. Tripathy has published a textbook on Soft Computing and has edited two research volumes for IGI publications. He is a life-time and senior member of the IEEE, the ACM, the IRSS, the CSI and the IMS. He is an editorial board member/reviewer of more than 60 journals. His research interest includes fuzzy sets and systems, rough sets and knowledge engineering, data clustering, social network analysis, soft computing, granular computing, content based learning, neighbourhood systems, soft set theory and applications, multiset theory, list theory and multi-criteria decision making.

Atta ur Rahman is currently working at the Barani Institute of Information Technology (BIIT), PMAS Arid Agriculture University, Rawalpindi, Pakistan, as an Associate Professor & Deputy Director (R&D). He has been working with BIIT since February 2006 in different capacities like Lecturer, Assistant Professor, Associate Professor (in faculty) and as Assistant Director (Academics), Head Student Affairs and Deputy Director (administration). Dr. Atta has completed his BS degree in Computer Science from University of The Punjab, Lahore, Pakistan; MS degree in Electronic Engineering from International Islamic University, Islamabad, Pakistan and PhD degree in Electronic Engineering from ISRA University, Islamabad Campus, Islamabad, Pakistan in years 2004, 2008 and 2012, respectively. His research interests include, evolutionary computing, coding theory, adaptive communication, data mining and dynamic resource allocation.

Index

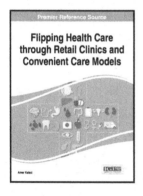

Printed in the United States
By Bookmasters